THE JAPAN JOURNALS

THE JAPAN JOURNALS
1947—2004

DONALD RICHIE

Edited by Leza Lowitz

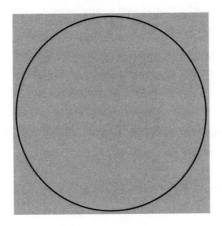

Stone Bridge Press • Berkeley, California

Published by
Stone Bridge Press
P.O. Box 8208
Berkeley, CA 94707
TEL 510-524-8732 • sbp@stonebridge.com • www.stonebridge.com

Portions of these journals were originally published in *Orient/West; Newsweek; Where Are the Victors?; Public People, Private People; The Japan Times; Tokyo Journal; Prairie Schooner; Winds; Asian Film; The New Yorker; Tokyo: A View of the City;* and the introduction to *The Crimson Gang of Asakusa* as well as *The Donald Richie Reader.*

The word order of Japanese names follows current usage, family name first.

All photographs supplied by the author.

Text © 2004 Donald Richie.

Front-cover photograph by Holloway Brown.

Cover and text design by Linda Ronan.

Printed in the United States of America.

2008 2007 2006 2005 2004   10 9 8 7 6 5 4 3 2 1

LIBRARY OF CONGRESS CATALOGING-IN-PUBLICATION DATA
Library of Congress Cataloging-in-Publication Data
  Richie, Donald, 1924–.
    The Japan journals 1947–2004 / Donald Richie; edited by Leza Lowitz.
      p. cm.
    ISBN 1-880656-91-4.
    1. Japan—Civilization—1945–. 2. Richie, Donald, 1924–. I. Lowitz, Leza. II. Title.
    DS822.5.R515 2004
    952.04'092--dc22

                                                          2004016239

Contents

Introduction

The Japan Journals is the chronicle of a person who has lived an extraordinary life. At the same time it is all that is left of a changing world seen from the chronicler's oblique angle—Japan from 1947 until now, more than half a century of incredible transformation. The evolution of Japan was one of the great spectacles of the century, and Donald Richie was there to see and describe it.

What he recapitulates in his journals is both more and less than the large spectacle. Richie was more attracted to the private than to the public. He sometimes mentions big events but more often it is the detail he describes. His emphasis is usually upon his reactions rather than the events themselves. The great spectacle, the encounter between East and West, begun decades before and continuing even now, is thus revealed by someone intent upon describing both it and the effect that it had through its various particularities.

*

Donald Richie was born in Lima, Ohio, on April 17, 1924. In the opening chapter of his unfinished memoir, *Watching Myself,* he remembers that he early wanted to leave. "Looking past the catalpa tree, over the syringa bushes, beyond the corner where the street ran straight south, past the park and into the future, I wanted to leave behind what I knew. What I wanted was what I didn't."

He wrote this long after he had left, indeed long after he had become a confirmed expatriate. There may thus be an amount of accounting-for in his choosing to remember exploration as a conditioning factor of childhood. At the same time, however, he actually did leave as soon as he could—he had turned eighteen, and had graduated from Lima Central High School.

As he was later to write in *The Inland Sea*, a voyage is also something of a flight. It was Lima he wanted to leave: home, family, friends— or a lack of all these. At the same time he wanted a future. Early, in 1931, seven years old, he had asked the local fortune-teller at the Allen Country Fair, a Madame Olga, if he was ever going to get out. She, as he tells it in the memoir, "looked down at me, wiped her rimless glasses, glanced at her crystal ball, and said: 'Yeah, you'll go far.'"

"Far . . . it sounded like what it was: a fast start, a take-off, and then a soaring up and out. I did not wonder why and I still don't. Even now when I know how it all turned out." What the seven-year-old Richie was experiencing is what all seven-year-olds experience, but few of them continue to plan their escape and when the chance comes actually accomplish it. Ten years later he was on the road, hitch-hiking straight south.

Richie reached New Orleans, a city that was not his goal. He had intended San Antonio, where he had a school friend, but his grasp of geography was weak and in any case the hitch-hiker is often subjected to the vagaries of his drivers. Once there he managed to get a number of jobs (soda jerk at Walgreen's lasted longest) and have a number of adventures (told in the unpublished sections of *Watching Myself*) and to savor all of the freedom of being somewhere completely different.

On his trip south he had seen how the "familiar Ohio ran into imagined Kentucky and spread into the unknown South, deep-dish black and opposite my pale North. Further off lay the blood-red Caribbean, so different from spit-colored Lake Erie." And further yet, "the whole world . . . deserts and jungles, pyramids and pagodas."

Richie was never to tire of travel. Greece, Morocco, Thailand were places he considered living. Though he eventually made his home in Tokyo (which still has several pagodas) he was always pleased to leave it. He became a permanent resident of Japan, but the road south continued all of his life.

His New Orleans summer over, Richie was saved from returning to Ohio by World War II, Pearl Harbor, and the draft. He was also spared the Army since he managed to enter the U.S. Maritime Service. There he got himself into the officer training program and by the end of 1942 was an ensign-purser/medical officer.

His various voyages—Algeria, Sicily, Italy, France, Scotland, China—are reflected in journals and in the unpublished "novels" he made of them: *Fifth Voyage* and *Seventh Voyage*. Once the war was over, in 1945, Richie continued to sail and it was not until 1946 that he once again—further resources gone—found himself threatened with a return to Lima.

By then, however, he had heard that the U.S. Civil Service was accepting applications for overseas appointments in the occupied countries of Germany and Japan. He applied and was accepted—as a typist, a skill acquired at Lima Central High. Though accomplished at the typewriter, Richie was not fond of his talent and shortly found himself more congenial employment at *The Pacific Stars and Stripes*. On January 1, 1947, he arrived in Tokyo.

*

This volume contains what remains of the journals that Donald Richie wrote in Japan. Much has been lost. Richie's journal-keeping was not methodical—an occurrence would demand to be chronicled and the impulse would last for several weeks or months, but the rest of the year might go unrecorded. Also, once written, some journal entries were carelessly filed and over the years vanished. At the same time Richie often reworked journal entries into his various books and then threw away the originals. It was, for example, pages from his earliest Japan journals that he used when, nearly forty-five years later, he wrote an account intended as the opening chapter for a memoir (later published as an essay in *The Donald Richie Reader*).

The extant diary segments often begin with an occurrence that Richie wanted to save—perhaps for eventual further use, but often also for its own sake since otherwise it would have been lost. Indeed, such threatening loss is one of the themes of the journals. At the same time, this method of journal-keeping cannot be said to faithfully reflect the shape of the author's life.

Yet it was Richie himself who decided that these pages were worth being published. As they piled up, he saw how, in an almost inadvertent manner, he had compiled an account of his time and his own position in it. He wanted his journals to be read and during the later years would make copies to send to his friends. I was one of these and found them so interesting that I wanted to read more. This led to his opening the files and sending me copies of what he found.

As I read through Richie's journals, that world of more than fifty years ago came alive for me, and I became convinced of the value of these pages. It was then that I asked for and received his permission to edit them, to present them as an entity. In so doing I have also provided when I could a context for them and included a number of them in the essay forms they sometimes took. I have also in this introduction sketched in some of the biographical details that Richie left out and have tried to draw some conclusions that Richie has not himself attempted.

Much of Richie's work is about self (see, for example, his books *The Inland Sea; Public People, Private People; The Honorable Visitors*), and this autobiographical impulse is certainly present in these pages. As always, the author is candid in the presentation—the only question is how truthful he is. Richie apparently tells few lies, but he does excise. The pages that follow have all been several times edited by their author and each revision has seen more excisions. One may judge what was left in, but one can only guess at what was left out.

One thing left out was duplication. Richie, like his friend James Merrill, decided that if he had given information in one book he would not repeat it in the next. Thus Richie is not in the Merrill memoir because the poet had already written about him. Similarly, if one is going to follow any kind of Richie biography it will be necessary to read not only the *Journals* but also *The Inland Sea, The Richie Reader, Public People, Private People*, and a number of interviews.

In any event, none of the original texts of these journals exist. In 1990, when Richie decided to collate what remained, he had them all retyped. The originals (hand-written for the travel diaries, typed for the rest) were then destroyed. It was this typed manuscript that he reworked over the following years. He also removed material and put it into different categories. The full version of the *Japan Journals* (twice as long as this one) is now with the rest of Richie's papers including all the other journals at the Howard Gotlieb Archival Research Center, Boston University.

*

What was Richie's purpose in these journals? Certainly, like anyone who keeps a journal, he wanted to intervene, to make lasting the ordinary perishable, to save experience. Among the reasons for saving it was that he would be otherwise bereft of it. Typical is the beginning of the journal entry for 18 December 1996: "I walk the windy streets of Shibuya, a territory completely given over to the young. Here they come in their hordes, driven by fashion and their glands. Let me describe them lest this motley show be lost forever."

There are other reasons for journal-keeping as well. Richie was, like any foreigner, restricted to the role of spectator. Even though he has lived most of his life in Japan he has never become a citizen, only a permanent resident. He pays full taxes but he cannot vote. And, given Japan's peculiar attitude toward foreigners, he has been powerless in many other ways as well.

As he writes in one entry (5 December 1999): "I may have rejected the U.S.A. where I was born, but I did not decide to be Japanese. That is an impossible decision, since the Japanese prevent it. Rather, I decided to decorate Limbo and become a citizen of this most attractive, intensely democratic republic." In any event, he says, quoting Rilke, "we are born, so to speak, provisionally, it doesn't matter where; it is only gradually that we compose, within ourselves, our true place of origin, so that we may be born there retrospectively."

There are many other reasons for keeping a journal, some more personal than others. "How do you write after you know that what you are writing will be read after you are dead?" he asks (26 September 1998). "Since you can no longer defend yourself, you begin early by protecting against any and all possible allegations. It is like planning the perfect suicide. You must think of just everything. Also, the need to make a pattern, any pattern, since it is the unpatterned that is to be avoided. And the drive for vindication, as if you had to prove your right to have lived."

The search for meaningful patterns in the chaos of raw life is certainly one of the themes of these journals. So is the hunt for absolution: proving one's right to have lived is a plea for acquittal, a request for exoneration. Perhaps this is common—maybe this why journals so often turn into confessions.

With Richie, both his strong liking and his continued regard for Japan was partially based, as he himself acknowledges in these pages, upon his own emotional direction—one proscribed and indeed illegal in the United States of his early years. To be attracted mainly to other men in a culture that does not allow it is reason enough for leaving. In Japan he discovered much that was not permitted, but that this was.

*

Richie's first fame came for his work on the Japanese cinema. With Joseph Anderson he wrote what is still regarded as the seminal study of Japanese film. Later he went on to write his well-regarded books on Kurosawa Akira and Ozu Yasujiro, as well as further histories of Japanese film itself. In addition he has written numerous essays on cinema, taught film at various universities, served on many film festival juries, and so on.

Whatever its other qualities, film demands observation. You sit in the dark and regard. Though one is aware of this one is also in the passive position of doing nothing but regarding it. A sane person does not try to enter the screen.

In addition to his maintaining this position of observation, it is fitting that Richie's life of looking should have been spent in places high up, from where the view is best. It began on the eighth floor of the "Hotel Continental" and is concluding on the eighth floor of his Ueno apartment over Shinobazu Pond. He is sitting looking out over Japan. And even when he descends, in 2004 as in 1947, and walks the land, he still retains this detachment.

Detachment is one of the qualities that makes Richie's observations so valuable. He can stand apart from himself and observe not only the context of his life but also its sensitive center—himself. This is something he learned how to do. He begins his life in these journals in 1947, when he is already twenty-three years old. His disinclination to examine his origins, his tacit denial of all hard wiring, his refusal of the burden of his history—all of these are already there, and one of his favorite formulas is a paraphrase of Jean-Paul Sartre: It is not important what life has done to you—what is important is what you do with what life has done to you.

This valuable ability is not so evident in the early pages of his journals. It grows as he learns. And since the majority of the entries were written in his late maturity and early old age, they offer a perspective that youth cannot. For example, he writes (16 August 2002): "But now I can see that I am getting older because there are waves of memory, a tide that wants to sweep me back to where I came from. This will not occur but I must experience its effects. I, who have spent my time meditating on difference, am now presented with 'similarity'—what I experienced then and what I remember now." Life, he elsewhere writes, "is a palindrome—as we entered, so backward we depart."

Richie has called himself a descriptive journalist and, in one sense, he is. In an entry for 27 September 1998 he writes: "I want to be the person who penned the best likeness. This is a possible ambition because for the last half century I have been in the best position to do so. Smilingly excluded here in Japan, politely stigmatized, I can from my angle attempt only objectivity since my subjective self will not fit into the space I am allotted. [. . . So,] how fortunate I am to occupy this niche with its lateral view. In America I would be denied this place. I would live on the flat surface of a plain. In Japan, from where I am sitting, the light falls just right—I can see the peaks and valleys, the crags and crevasses."

Part of the fascination of these journals lies in just this, their rich immediacy, their passion for detail, and their impartiality. Each page is like a scene from the past, brought alive again and illuminated by the writer's intelligence and by his concern. Not that the tableau is ever complete. We always seem to be examining a corner but in great detail. And with that we are aware of an attitude, a person, a style. We are being told something of great interest, something the writer was moved enough to record for posterity. It is these small moments that make up the "great spectacle" of life itself.

Leza Lowitz
Tokyo, Japan

THE JAPAN JOURNALS
1947—2004

The Japan Journals begins with an evocation of early morning in Tokyo, 1947, not long after Richie's first arrival. It is based on early journal entries. Other sections of this early journal have appeared elsewhere, for example as the opening to Richie's first novel, *Where Are the Victors?* (aka *This Scorching Earth*, 1955). The account of the destruction of Tokyo that follows this is taken from interviews and then given to one of the characters in the novel. For another memoir, *In Between*, Richie used pages about meeting a number of people. These are here reconstructed. There are also memoir re-workings of material that appears in different form in the *Donald Richie Reader* (2001).

WINTER 1947. Tokyo lies deep under a bank of clouds which move slowly out to sea as the sun climbs higher. Between the moving clouds are sections of the city: the raw gray of whole burned blocks spotted with the yellow of new-cut wood and the shining tile of recent roofs, the reds and browns of sections unburned, the dusty green of barely damaged parks, and the shallow blue of ornamental lakes. In the middle is the palace, moated and rectangular, gray outlined with green, the city stretching to the horizons all around it.

The smoke of early household hearths, of newly renovated factories, of the waiting, charcoal-burning taxis, rises and with it the freshness of late winter, the bitter yellow smoke of burning cedar shavings, the smell of breakfast: barley, sweet potato, roasted chestnuts. In the houses the bedding is folded into closets and tatami mats are swept.

Beneath the hanging pillars of the early rising smoke there is the morning rattling of night shutters thrust back into the narrow walls. Behind the banging of the shutters is the sound of wooden geta—the faint percussive sound of people walking—and the distant bronze boom of a temple bell. Jeeps explode into motion, and the tinny clang of the streetcars sound above the bleatings of the nearby fishing boats. Somewhere a phonograph is running down—Josephine Baker goes from contralto to baritone.

A distant radio militantly delivers the Japanese news of the day and a few MPs, still in pairs, roam the recently empty streets. A single woman, modest in bright red, knees together, maybe a geisha going home, hurries. Greer Garson luxuriates, her paper face half in the morning sun, and a man dressed like Charlie Chaplin, a placard on his shoulders, begins his daily advertising.

In the alleys, the empty pedicabs are lined up, and around the early alley fires the all-night drivers yawn and warm their hands while early farmers lead

Tokyo/Shinjuku, Winter, 1947.

their laden horses into the city. An empty Occupation bus, with "Dallas" stenciled on both sides, makes its customary stops—the PX, the Commissary, the Motor Pool—but no riders are in it. Occupation women with khaki skirts, out early, try unsuccessfully to hail a passing U.S. 8th Army jeep.

The rising sun is now caught by the blank windows of the taller buildings and casts reflections—the silver flash of spectacles, a passing gold tooth, the dead white of a mouth-mask. The food shops open and the spicy bitterness of pickled radish mingles with the sweet stench of fish, mingles with the scents of the passing nightsoil carrier, his oxen and his cart.

The rolled metal shutters of the smaller shops are still locked but before the open entrances of larger buildings MPs stand and wait, their white-gloved hands behind their backs, their white helmets above their white faces. They stand in front of most of the Occupation buildings—the gray Dai Ichi Building, the square Meiji Building, the pale Taisho Building, the squat Yusen. To the south rises the box-like Radio Tokyo and, in all directions, the billets of the Occupation itself, the American flag floating above them.

The clouds drift out to sea and the city lies under the winter sun. The pedicab drivers go home, and the wives serve the morning soup. The sun and smoke rise into the air and the radios shout into the sky, while the streetcars rattle and the auto horns honk, and the fishing boats cry, and the railroads fill up the city.

The account of the destruction of Tokyo that follows is taken from interviews and then given to one of the characters in Richie's novel *Where Are the Victors?*

He remembered the day. It was in a cool, sunny, unseasonably windy March [1945]. The children who had them still wore their furs. His two sisters, dressed alike in little fur hoods with cats' heads embroidered on them, were sent off to school, and his father went to work next door at his lumberyard.

It was the third day of a leave from the Army. He had a new lieutenant's uniform. His mother wanted him to stay near home and call on the neighbors. He wanted to walk around the city and show off his new uniform.

Their home was in Fukagawa, which was like no place else in Tokyo. The carpenters pulled their saws, and the logs floated in the canals. The factories blew smoke to the sky, and the dye from the chemical plants made the canals green as leaves. The Chinese ran restaurants and even the poor Koreans happily opened oysters all day long.

Some of Tokyo had already been bombed, but those few districts were far away, and the people in the rest of the city were not afraid. The radio said that the Americans dropped bombs indiscriminately and that there was no need to fear a mass attack as the radar would detect the intruders and give ample time for escape.

Just a year before Fukagawa had been bombed, but the damage had been slight. The bombs fell mostly into the countryside and people decided that the Americans were not very skilled in this important matter of bomb dropping. Fukagawa, in the suburbs, seemed as safe as Shinbashi, in the center.

[That evening] he heard the watchman at eleven when the call of the watch was interrupted by the air-raid sirens. Earlier in the afternoon, while at the movies, he had heard an alert, but the all clear had sounded immediately after.

Now he walked swiftly through Shinbashi Station and ran through the standing passengers, past the halted trains, to the top level of the station. He didn't really expect to see anything. He only wanted to be soldierly.

He arrived just in time to see the sudden flare of massed incendiary bombs. It was Fukagawa. The planes were apparently traveling at great speed. It was impossible to say how many there were but it seemed hundreds.

A great ring of fire was spreading. The planes were so low he couldn't see them and could tell where they had been only by the fires that sprang behind them. There was an enormous explosion, like August rockets on the Sumida River, and a great ball of fire fell back on the district. A chemical plant had been hit. Seconds later he felt the warm burst of air from the blast, miles away.

Later he heard that the planes had come in so low that they escaped the radar. The antiaircraft could do nothing against planes that near and that swift. The stiff March wind spread the flames and he later remembered thinking of the canals that cut through the section, and thought that people would at least find safety in the water. There would be water enough for everyone.

He didn't remember how long he stood on the top platform of Shinbashi Station and watched the destruction of Fukagawa, Honjo, Asakusa, Ueno. But he remembered wondering why they were so selective—why not the Ginza, why not Shinbashi, why not he himself? He later remembered walking up the deserted streets past the closed motion picture house where he had been that afternoon. It was near dawn when he reached the bridge across the Sumida, the last pink of the fires replaced by the first pink of dawn.

There he saw those coming from Fukagawa. Most had been burned. They carried scorched bedding on their backs, or trundled bicycles with possessions strapped to them. They walked slowly and did not look at him as they passed. He wondered where they were all going and stopped an old man who told him that everything had been burned, and that everyone had been killed.

He walked across the bridge and finally reached Fukagawa. He could not believe what he saw. There was nothing. Nothing but black and smoking ruins as far as he could see. He had never known that so much could be destroyed in one night.

On the street he found a bicycle that belonged to no one and on it he started toward his home. But nothing looked the same. There were no streets any more. In cleared places were piles of burned bodies, as though a family had huddled beneath a roof that had now vanished. They seemed very small and looked like charcoal.

He peddled slowly along what had been a street. Long lines of quiet, burned people, all looking the same, came toward him. He didn't know where to turn north to go to his father's lumberyard. Nothing was familiar. He leaned his bicycle against a smoking factory wall and looked toward where his home should have been but wasn't. The lines of the burned moved slowly by, and suddenly he began to cry.

After he had cried he looked at the people again and saw his younger brother coming toward him. They stood, looking at each other, amazed that such a thing could happen. His brother had spent the night at school because he had had to finish a war work project of some kind, and he had not heard about the raid until he woke up. Now he too had just arrived and didn't know where their home was either. So in the growing light they began walking.

Troops had been brought in and were clearing the streets, or where they supposed streets had been. They shifted the bodies with large hooks and loaded them, one after the other, onto trucks. Often the burned flesh pulled apart, making the work more difficult.

[The brothers] walked on, past mothers holding burned babies to their breasts, past little children, boys and girls, all dead, crouched together as though for warmth. Once they passed an air-raid shelter and looked in. It was full of bodies, many of them still smoldering.

The next bridge was destroyed, so they decided to separate. His brother would go north and he south. It was the first time they had used these terms with each other. Usually they spoke of up by the elementary school or down by the chemical plant. His brother started crying and walked away, rubbing his eyes. They were to meet at their uncle's house in Shinagawa.

He walked south to the factory sections. The chemical works had exploded and what little remained was too hot to get near. Some of the walls were standing, burned a bright green from the dye, the color of leaves. In a locomotive yard the engines were smoking, as though ready for a journey, the cars jammed together as in a railway accident.

There were some in the ruins still alive, burned or wounded. Those who couldn't walk were patiently waiting for help by the side of the tracks. There was no sound but the moaning of an old woman. It sounded like a lullaby.

He saw only two ambulances. They were full of wounded, lying there as though dead. Farther on, prisoners of war were clearing the smoking ruins. They wore red uniforms and carried blankets to remove the dead.

Eventually he recognized the Susaki district. Yesterday it had been a pleasure center, with sidewalk stalls, music, women peeping from behind latticework screens. Now there was nothing. The houses, like all the decorations, had been made only of wood and paper and had burned almost at once. Now no one moved. He turned back.

The small bridges across the canals had been burned. He had to stay on the large island connected to Nihonbashi by the bridge across the Sumida. He looked across the canals and saw people still alive on the little, smoking islands. They shouted and waved, but there was nothing he could do, so he went on. Some were swimming across to the large island. They had to push aside others who floated there, face down.

In a burned primary school he saw the bodies of children who had run there, to their teachers, for protection. Later he learned that there were two thousand dead children in that school alone. They lay face down on the scorched concrete floor, as though asleep. The kimono of some still smoked. The teachers to whom they had fled lay among them.

It was past noon when, suddenly very tired, he walked back across the bridge to Nihonbashi where he took a trolley to Shinagawa. It stopped continually. It was filled with wounded. Others, less wounded, hung from the roof and the sides. He could have arrived sooner by walking.

At his uncle's house he found his brother and, surprisingly, his uncle. The latter's arm was badly burned. He had come home that afternoon, walking the entire distance. He told them about their family. They had been sitting at the table, his sister and himself. The younger girls had already gone to bed and his brother-in-law was at Susaki.

The first planes bombed around Fukagawa, and then closed the circle, making it smaller and smaller. It was hard to escape because it happened so fast. Almost instantly there was fire on all sides.

By the time the air-raid sirens had begun they heard the explosions, and flames were leaping up in the distance. The planes wheeled over them and the circle of fire was much nearer. They got the girls up, but by the time they were dressed the fire was only a block away. They tried to escape from the lumberyard but the little bridge that led to the Tokyo road was burning. So they climbed into the canal in back of the house.

Bombs were constantly dropping and finally one of them hit the neighborhood. The heat was terrible. Even the logs in the canal began to smoke. They watched the fire spread, in just a few seconds, to the storehouses and across the entire island. His mother and sisters held onto a log and began to cry.

Their uncle found a pan and dipped water over their heads and shoulders. The little fur hoods with cats embroidered on them helped protect the children for a while, but when the fur began smoking, he tore off the hoods and poured water directly on their hair. The half of the log above water cracked in the heat but he kept on pouring.

There he had remained until early morning. Around one, the fire burning around them just as fiercely as before, he became very tired. He tried to get a better grip on the log but found his arm so burned that it stuck to the wood. He was not able both to hold up his sister and nieces and at the same time continue to pour water on them.

They were very quiet and, he was sure, unconscious. His arm was so tired that he too must have lost consciousness. The pain of his arm's slipping across the burning log woke him. The mother and two little girls were gone.

The next day he and his brother went again to Fukagawa. It was now filled with rescue workers. They found their canal and where their home had been. Everything was gone. Only the ground remained. They identified the house from its foundation stones. Near where the house had been they were removing bodies. He tried to find some of the neighbors but couldn't— everyone there was a stranger. No one knew where his father's workers were either. They had lived above the warehouse where the finished lumber had been stored.

Later he learned that thirty thousand people had been killed that night. Some said it was the unseasonable wind that had done the most damage. It spread the fire and heat. The explosions caused more wind until, about one in the morning, it blew through the flames at a mile a minute.

It was almost a week before the Emperor inspected the ruins. By this time the bodies had all been removed. Already the streets were being mapped and bright wooden bridges connected the islands. People said that the Army had delayed the Emperor's arrival. They didn't want him to see how terrible the fire had been. If he had, he would have stopped the war at once. But now, with a new week's fighting begun, he could do nothing about it. It was the fault of the Army.

For the rest of the summer his brother lived with his uncle and he himself was sent to Tachikawa Air Base. Then it was August and the war was over. When he saw Fukagawa again people were living there once more. The main business was still lumber. Before the fire there had been over two thousand lumber dealers, but now there were only a little over a hundred. There were no chemical plants but the dye works had opened and the canals were green again. The Chinese restaurants were thriving as usual and even small Korean centers had sprung up. But now their old occupation—opening oysters—had been taken over the Japanese. It was about the only way to make a living in Fukagawa.

*

From the window of my billet, Kyo-bashi looks like Hiroshima—the same holes where whole buildings once were, the same odd empty spaces in what once was solid street. Further off there are more buildings stand-ing, though separately, revealing that there was once something between.

At the Ginza crossing there are quite a few buildings standing. The Mitsukoshi Department Store, gutted, hit by a firebomb, even the window frames twisted by the heat. Across the street is the white stone Hattori Building, its clock tower with its cornices and pediments much as it had been.

There is not much else left: the ruins of the burned-out Kabuki-za, the round, red, drum-like Nichigeki, undamaged. At Yurakucho, on the edge of the Ginza, are a few office build-ings and the Tokyo Takarazuka Theater, now renamed the Ernie Pyle.

EIGHTH ARMY SIGNAL CORPS

Tokyo/Ginza, Winter, 1947.

Otherwise, block after block of rubble, stretching to the horizon. Wood-en buildings do not survive firestorms. Those that stand were made of stone or brick. Yet, already, among these ruins there is the yellow sheen of new wood. People are returning to the city.

*

I have some photos taken last year in the subway corridors of Ueno Station. There, sitting or lying on straw mats or the bare concrete, are some of the thousands of the hungry homeless. Men, women, a few children,

In one photo, they are being inspected by two bespectacled policemen wearing mouth masks. Many of the people are dirty, and all wear remnants of what they had owned during the war: cracked shoes, torn blouses, battered hats, buttonless shirts. But no one looks sad.

Everyone is smiling—everyone except the policemen, and maybe they are

STARS AND STRIPES

Ueno Subway Station, 1946.

as well beneath their masks. Smiling for the camera, making a good impression, best foot forward. Even in the depths of national poverty everyone remembers this.

Up above, on the plaza, around the statue of Saigo Takamori, there are many more, sitting on benches and embankments—all of them waiting. Waiting, it seemed, for this too to pass so that they can get on with their lives.

Many have been and gone. The pedestal of Saigo's statue is plastered with handwritten notices; I had someone look at the photo and read them to me. "Watanabe Noriko—Your Mother Waits Here Every Day from One to Five; Grandmother Kumagai—Shiro and Tetsuko Have Gone to Uncle Sato's in Aomori—Please Come; Suzuki Tetsuro—Your Father Is Sitting on the Staircase to the Left—If You See This Please Come."

The snows and rains have washed the older notices away and new ones are put up. They are like the votive messages left at shrines, invoking supernatural aid. Answered or not, they are left there until rained away or covered by notices of later misfortunes.

Though many entries were used in *Where Are the Victors?* (1956) and *Public People, Private People* (1987), a few unused pages remain. Among them are accounts of meeting the writer Kawabata Yasunari and the Zen scholar Suzuki Daisetz that are somewhat different from those in *Public People, Private People* and *Zen Inklings*. The continuations about Kawabata occur in their proper chronological places—9 January 1960 and 1 January 1973.

STARS AND STRIPES

Ueno Plaza, 1946.

EARLY SPRING 1947. The Sumida River, silver in the winter sun, glistened beneath us. We were on the roof of the Asakusa subway terminal tower, looking out over downtown Tokyo, still in ruins, still showing the conflagration of two years earlier, burned concrete black against the lemon yellow of new wood.

This had been the amusement quarter of Tokyo. Around the great temple of Kannon, now a blackened, empty square, had grown a warren of bars, theaters, archery stalls, circus tents, peep shows, places where the all-girl opera sang and kicked, where the tattooed gamblers met and bet, where trained dogs walked on hind legs, and Japan's fattest lady sat in state.

Now two years after all of this had gone up in flames, after so many of those who worked and played here had burned in the streets or boiled in the canals as the incendiary bombs fell and the B-29s thundered—now, the empty squares were again turning into lanes as tents, reed lean-tos, a few frame buildings began appearing. Girls in wedgies were sitting in front of new tearooms, but I saw no sign of the world's fattest lady. Perhaps she had bubbled away in the fire.

Was that what he was thinking?—I wondered, looking at the avian profile of the middle-aged man standing beside me, outlined against the pale winter sky.

I had no way of knowing. He spoke no English and I spoke no Japanese.

Kawabata Yasunari.

I did not know that Kawabata Yasunari was already famous and would become more famous yet. But I did know he was a writer because I had heard he had written about Asakusa and it was the place itself that interested me.

"Yumiko," I said, pointing to the silver river beneath us. This was the name of the heroine of the novel, *Asakusa Kurenaidan*, which Kawabata had written when he—twenty years before, then about the same age I was, and as enraptured of the place as I was now—walked the labyrinth and saw, as he later wrote, the jazz reviews, the kiss-dances, the exhibitions of the White Russian girls, and the passing Japanese flappers with their rolled stockings. Yumiko had confronted the gangster, crushed an arsenic pill between her teeth, and then kissed him full on the lips.

Perhaps he was thinking of this scene from his novel and of the lost Yumiko, tough, muscled, beautiful. Or, looking over that blackened landscape, under this huge white winter sky, he was perhaps feeling a great sorrow. All those lives lost in that blazing, roaring conflagration beneath.

Imagining a sadness that I assumed that I in his place would be feeling, I looked at that birdlike profile. It did not seem sad. Rather, Kawabata smiled, looked over the parapet and indicated the river.

This was where, I knew, the insolent Yumiko, having given the kiss of death to the older man (who, it transpired, was the lover of the local madwoman who, it turned out, was really our heroine's sister), leaped through the porthole of the waiting boat, and sped away just as the water police arrived.

I knew all this without knowing any Japanese because as a member of the Allied Occupation I had translators at my command and had ordered an English précis of the novel. Now, looking at the author leaning over the edge, as had Left-Handed Hiko as he spied the escaping Yumiko, I thought about Kawabata's love for Asakusa.

He had begun his book with the intention "to write a long and curious story set in Asakusa ... in which vulgar women predominate." It had perhaps been for him as it was for me, a place that allowed anonymity, freedom, where life flowed on no matter what, where you could pick up pleasure, and where small rooms with paper flowers were rented by the hour.

Did he, I wonder, find freedom in flesh, as I had learned to? It was here, on the roof of the terminal, that Oharu had permitted herself to be kissed— and more—by members of the gang and had thus earned herself the title of Bride of the Eiffel Tower. It was here that the Akaobi-kan, that group of red-sashed girls who in the daytime worked in respectable department stores, boasted about the bad things they did at night. Here that Umekichi disclosed that he had been raped at the age of six by a forty year-old woman.

I wondered at all of this but had no way of asking. And now, chilled by that great sky, we went down the steep stairs, companionable but inarticulate. I had given him an outing; he had given me his bird's eye view of Asakusa.

EARLY SUMMER 1947—KITA KAMAKURA. I stood before the great gate at Engakuji. The naked guardians grimaced, the carved eaves stretched above me, the roof soared and touched the pines. I was about to enter the abode of the Buddha, the world of Daruma, the land of Zen. I said the word softly to myself—the cicada-like drone of the syllable, the sudden halt of the consonant.

As I did a soft summer breeze struck the overhead pines. The needles rustled and from them fell a fragrance I had known as a child. Looking up, deep into that glittering green, I felt a memory surface, then turn and disappear before I could recognize it. But its passing brought a tear—just one, but real.

Then I was walking through the gate and into the temple, only an hour from Tokyo but already another world to me. In the silence I looked around— the main temple, the graveyard, what I took to be the zendo, a number of vegetable patches.

Around in back I found the small tiled-roof house. There I waited, letter and gifts in hand, waited for my teacher. I had read that the Zen adept waited all day—all night too, through rain, through snow. None of this, however, proved necessary, for the man I had come to see, who had not known I was

Suzuki Daisetz.

coming nor that he was my teacher, soon noticed the large foreigner standing in the cabbage patch and came out on the veranda.

Suzuki Daisetz was a small man with steel spectacles hooked behind his ears, long hairs in his eyebrows, several moles. He was in a rumpled kimono and he cocked his head to one side as he peered at the intruder. He looked like an older man just awakened, but to me he was the picture of Zen: the fuzzy eyebrows, the high forehead, the childlike gaze—my patriarch.

He read the letter of introduction from the wife of a colleague, deceased in New York. And he received my offerings—Ritz, Spam, Velveeta, all that the Army PX could contrive. These the patriarch bundled away and then returned with a cup of tepid cracked-wheat tea for me. And there I was, finally, sitting on a cane chair on the veranda of my teacher, inhaling the smell of the tea and the odor of temple—mildew, mice, old paper. Deeply I breathed in the scent of what I took to be sutras, moldering and holy. Now my learning would begin—I had found my *roshi*.

Only I had not. It was not that he refused to be my teacher but that he refused to be anyone's teacher. He was, he insisted, no matter the priestly resemblance, a layman. If anything he was a learner too.

This was told me in English accented by years in London. Still, he added, sounding like a British don, as a learner he had learned a lot. Yet, though he knew about mountain climbing he had never climbed Mount Sumeru.

He then waited for me to catch up. I knew that this was a fabled Buddhist peak, the scaled summit of which, I hazarded, meant *satori*. So this statement I took to mean that he had not himself yet reached what I fancied to be the terminal of Zen Buddhism.

One of the things he did know, however, he said, was that one did not climb mountains by merely looking at them. All too many people, he maintained, thought that Zen was some sort of mysticism, concerned with visions of the eternal and the like, that you simply sat and looked at it. This was not so.

Dr. Suzuki I later learned often defined things by what they were not. His remarks on Zen—gleaned by me over a series of Sunday afternoons, outside the pines sighing in the summer winds, inside the still smell of mice droppings—were entirely negative. The only positive description I received was that mountain climbing was hard work.

This was given with a glance in my direction. It had been ascertained that I never worked. Further, it was understood between us that I never would. Our bond, in that we had one, was that he did not either. Not if you defined work as *zazen*.

But that was what I had come for so he introduced me into the zendo and I had indeed sat for a time on my folded legs, my mind busy with what I had done that morning, what I would do later that afternoon, and wondering in what form my illumination would arrive.

This—my believing I was practicing *zazen*—went on for a time. The others, all Japanese, paid no attention to the interloper. They sat properly, eyes unfocused, backs straight, minds empty. They were on their way—traveling at great speed sitting completely still.

I, on the other hand, was shortly complaining that my legs hurt. Also I had questions, wanted descriptions and assurances. Consequently, after a short time, while others sat in the lotus position in the zendo, I sat comfortably on the sofa with Dr. Suzuki.

There he talked and I listened, hoping that learning would somehow rub off. In a way it did, because Dr. Suzuki eventually gave me an appetite for something he knew I could never eat.

Every Sunday I would appear with my crackers and cheeses, canned meats, peanut clusters—offerings from the PX for my *sensei*. These he would graciously receive and carry off to the larder. In return I would be given my cup of tea and a talk. It was always about Zen and I never understood a word. Or, rather, it was the words alone I understood—and sometimes the sentences, but never the paragraphs. Still, I was learning.

Other discourses I had heard were rational, logical, but Dr. Suzuki's were something else. The process seemed associative, one thought suggesting another, apparently at random. But, as one idea followed another, I saw the randomness was only apparent. Each was attached to the other by the linearity they formed.

And as I listened I understood that there were other means of structuring thought, ways of thinking different from those I had always known and believed unique.

This was really all I ever learned from my teacher but it was a lesson of the greatest importance. Dr. Suzuki never gave me satori in exchange for my Velveeta, but he gave me the priceless apprehension of other modes of thought.

He also initially gave me a koan—the one about Nansen's cat. This eminent Zen master saw two monks quarreling over the animal. He held it up and said that if they could give an answer the cat would be saved—otherwise not. Not knowing what to answer, there being no apparent question, they were silent and Nansen cut the cat in two. Later he told another priest about the incident. This person removed a sandal, placed it on his head, and walked off. Nansen then said that had he been there the cat would have been saved.

It is typical of my disposition that the first and only reaction was a concern for the unfortunate feline. And, of course, I too came nowhere near a reply since I did not comprehend that an enquiry was concerned.

Dr. Suzuki was patient. Either he saw something in me to interest him or he really needed the cheese and crackers. And so we continued until one early summer day with the cicadas screaming—*zen, zen, zen*—he smiled and said that I need not come again.

I understood his reasons but felt rejected. This he saw, stood up, and took a picture from the wall. It was a seated Kannon, black ink on white paper, framed in wicker, an oval picture of great beauty that I had often seen and admired.

It was also a genuine Hakuin. He told me to take it home with me and live with it for a while. He did not tell me why or for how long, but I understood that I would eventually return it to him.

The blow softened, I held Kannon on my lap all the way back to Tokyo. And as the train pulled from the Kita-Kamakura station I seemed to smell again the pines, and thought about that vanishing thought that had surfaced and disappeared. No longer feeling sorry for myself, clear-eyed, I patted the picture.

Some months later, already autumn, I was again on a train—a streetcar, rounding the corner at Ueno Park. Suddenly I again smelled the great pines of Kamakura. The scent, strong as the smell of the sea, swooped upon me, and the forgotten memory lay there basking. It was the smell of bath salts, pine-scented, that were put in the tub if I had been a good boy.

That then was why I felt so young, as though the world was just beginning, when I stood, single tear on cheek, in front of the great gate of Engakuji. I told my companion.

"How very fascinating," he said. Then, as he often did, he turned the experience into something of his own. "I often have had experiences like that," he said. "I am very close to my childhood. Though with me it is cinnamon toast."

And he brushed back his salt and pepper hair, cut in the loose and boyish fashion then favored by Englishmen of his age—not as old as my *sensei* but considerably older than I.

This was R. H. Blyth, a friend of Dr. Suzuki's, whom I had met at Engakuji where he had regarded my efforts on the sofa with a silent but apparent amusement.

"Bath salts, eh? Perhaps you thought that Zen would be a hot bath? More like a cold shower, eh, what? Not that I know much about it."

And he tossed his head as he usually did when he said this, always thus disassociating himself from the Zen that had appeared in the titles of several of his books. "No, no. Literature. I am all literature. Never knew anything about Zen. Fact is, you know, no one does."

When I would bring up some Buddhist matter, he would answer with an affectionate scorn, "Oh, that stuff. That's old Suzuki's department, scarcely mine. Give me Wordsworth any day."

Then he would quote something. He was a prodigious quoter, could go on for whole paragraphs, and never apparently make a mistake. Then, "What do you want to study that stuff for anyway?"

I told him that I didn't study, not really, just listened to Dr. Suzuki.

"Well, that's better," he said, as though mollified. Then, "There is nothing the matter with it, you understand. It's just that it's not for study." Then, "Suzuki's a great talker." This was presented as fact rather than opinion. We knew what that stuff was worth. It was worth a great deal. It was not worth all that much.

As I listened to Blyth, who was also a great talker, I sat back and appreciated the rationality, the logic. He usually expounded on Wordsworth or Blake or the haiku. And what he said seemed to me attractively vague after the rock-hard incomprehensibilities of Dr. Suzuki. And Blyth's concept of revelation was quite different from that of my *sensei*. It was not the result of time and hard work. Wordsworthian revelation could occur just about any time, any place.

"It could occur even in bed. Oh, yes, seriously. Suddenly. In bed."

Then he regarded me in an owlish manner and I remembered his having told me of a beautiful girl who was apparently a member of his large and attractively disordered household. I smiled, picturing him in a sudden state of satori, and at that moment my eyes opened, my smile faded, and I saw a connection—a real one, a bridge of living tissue between my faltering need for religion, my inclination for whatever I thought Zen was, and something I knew quite well: that inchoate bundle of needs, satisfactions and exhaustions which I called my sex life.

The pines of Ueno had long passed but now their fragrance returned. The bridge was there. Another means of thought had been revealed, and for the first time Zen seemed real to me.

Kannon was again sitting on my lap. I was returning her to Engakuji. The plum blossoms had passed, the cherry blossoms were budding, and it was raining. I had lived with Kannon for more than half a year, had derived comfort, pleasure, and pride—a Hakuin on my humble wall. Then, as is the way with pictures, or as is the way with me, I gradually forgot about it. Now, carefully wrapped, she rested on my knees. Going home.

Once there we sat in the now nostalgic odor of mice. Dr. Suzuki removed the wrapping, and held the picture at arm's length as though to renew acquaintance. Then back she went on the wall.

I thanked him for everything and he smiled. Then, as though offering a further gift, "Not at all, Mr. Richie. You are, you know, very much of this world, very much of this flesh."

He then smiled as though the smile were a way of shaking an understanding head at the ways of this world. And he was right about me. I nodded and as I admitted this to myself I understood—a kind of illumination it was—that I had no vocation and never would, not because anything was missing but because I would never summon up the necessary discipline. Not that it was impossible—nothing is impossible—merely that it was very unlikely.

I looked at Kannon, back on the wall and looking at home no matter what wall she was on, and at Dr. Suzuki, always a man in the present tense, and I thought of the slender but sturdy bridge that now connected me to my own reality.

Richie's billet was the Continental Hotel, originally the main office of Ajinomoto KK until the Occupation moved in. There he

roomed with Herschel Webb and Eugene Langston, who became Japanese scholars. For a memoir Richie reworked some of the 1947 journal entries that told how he met them.

SUMMER 1947. I was late for breakfast and all the tables in the basement dining room were taken, so I asked a man reading a book if I could sit with him. He looked up and smiled, but so politely and so briefly that I was not tempted to begin a conversation. Until I saw what he was reading—then we had lots to talk about.

The book was Djuna Barnes's *Nightwood* and the reader was named Gene Langston and though only a few years older than I, he had already met the author.

"What was she like?" I wanted to know.

"Well, let me see," he began—a reasoned response which I soon learned was typical of him. "A bit abrupt, dark, not given to smiling, at least not with me. She was lesbian, of course."

I marveled. Never had it occurred to me that authors might share attributes with their characters.

"Not that that is either here or there," he said, a smile already apologizing for an observation which might have been misinterpreted as criticism. He did not criticize, the smile said.

Then, learning that I too had read the book, he became more interested—for it was unlikely that two members of the Allied Occupation of Japan were both reading *Nightwood*.

He also became more confiding and said that the character he liked best so far was the doctor. All I remembered about the doctor was his saying that what he wanted in life was to cook some good man's potatoes. But perhaps my new acquaintance had not yet gotten that far in the book. In any event it was too early in our relationship for me to mention it.

Instead, I asked about his work. It was in ATIS, the translation section. Yes, he could read and write Japanese.

"And speak it too?" I wondered.

"*Mo chotto bata o motte kite kudasai,*" he politely asked the waiter, requesting that more butter be brought. The waiter, delighted to be spared English, smiled and further pats were produced.

I was impressed. I wanted to be able to speak too and couldn't. Then he looked at my breakfast and asked how I could eat it. It was the customary contintental fare: gelid egg, frigid toast. Then I saw that his was the only Japa-

Tokyo/Hibiya Crossing, Dai-Ichi Building, 1947.

nese breakfast in the room: rice with raw egg, miso soup, seaweed squares, and pickled plums. The butter had been thoughtfully ordered for me.

Thereafter, we always breakfasted together. He had read part of Proust, had braved a delinquency report to sneak into a Noh drama, believed that we should democratize the Japanese, and showed a healthy disrespect for authority.

"Shall we go see Jeanette?" he asked over a late breakfast. I was mystified. Jeanette who?

My wonder grew as we walked across to Ginza, past Yurakucho and—just in time—joined the throng in front of the Dai Ichi Building. I knew what was going to happen because the great local sight was neither Ginza nor Fuji, but an important event that occurred twice a day: once at lunchtime, once just before dinner.

An olive drab limousine pulled up to the curb. The MPs guarding the pillared façade directly across the moat from the Imperial Palace, smartly straightened. Snappy salutes were proffered and out from the portal sailed General Douglas MacArthur.

The performance was always the same. In the wings he had put on his famous hat, tilted it at the proper angle, adjusted his profile, and started off, this soldier whom some called with no irony at all "The New Emperor of Japan."

A number thought so. Today, a country mother held up her child, pointing out the famous sight to the infant's wondering eyes, an ex-soldier with one leg stood more sharply, and an old man gazed at the pavement in, perhaps, reverence.

And as the famous general sped past and stepped into his sedan, Gene turned to me and said: "There goes Jeanette."

The mysterious reference was later explained. Singing film-star Jeanette MacDonald, dressed as a page, had, in one of those movies of hers, navigated a staircase in Meyerbeer's *Les Huguenots*, in just such an assured, even pert fashion. Struck by the resemblance between the performances, Gene occasionally came to enjoy it.

"Also," he said, "you might say it is a kind of penance." He said this with a smile that was already half a question, a slight invitation to partake, and at the same time indifference if I did not.

I had somewhere read that identity requires the presence of someone by whom one is known—someone who knows who you are, often before you yourself do. Gene observed my enthusiasm, shared some of my dislikes, but always put some distance between himself and these. Though I was beginning to find him a possible model in my relations with this country, he did nothing to encourage me.

He believed in a kind of perfection yet excused everyone from attaining it—except himself. We were talking about *The New Yorker*, a publication excluded from both commissary and PX after it ran John Hersey's issue-long account of Hiroshima.

"It never contains a typographical error," he said.

I, believing in unavoidable sloppiness, said that this was impossible.

"Oh no, it's not," he said mildly. "It is quite possible. All that is necessary is that every error is caught. I admire the editor."

Perfection was possible, all one had to do was to take all possible care. I watched him doing so. When he practiced his calligraphy no mistake was made—the forming of the *kanji*, the width of the stroke, the pressure of the brush—everything was as it ought to be. Methodical, he built up, line upon line, his ideal world.

And yet he was never solemn and could smile at the foibles (Jeanette) he found around him. He was serious without being earnest, and I had never met anyone like him. Yet, he was not a very good model for me. Besides that he would not have wanted to be; he was ascetic, which I certainly wasn't.

Eugene Langston.

Austere—he was not making a statement with his Japanese breakfasts; he had a liking for the acerbic—he was rigorous with himself and even seemed to enjoy the forbidden. Once when I was dreading our next worming, he said, "Oh, no, think of it as purification."

"They have a right to live too," I said, surprising myself.

He gave me a look of deep approval, "So they do, so they do."

It was then that I thought of penance and hazarded that the worming might be some sort of atonement. But for what, I wondered. Hiroshima? Jeanette? Being Occupiers? And if so, why? I certainly felt none of the compunctions I sensed in him. Healthily opportunistic, I never questioned a single opportunity and Gene seemed to be questioning them all. He was not, however, usable. I could not model myself on him. But the deeper I knew him the more I admired him.

*

Through Gene I met his roommate. Tall, inquisitive eyes, intelligent nose—this was Herschel Webb. I admired him as well. Even though there still were signs around that sternly mandated "No Fraternization with the Indigenous Personnel," he had confounded the MPs and gone to the Noh drama.

"I saw *Funa Benkei,*" he said.

"What does that mean?" I asked.

"It means 'Benkei in the Boat,'" and it refers to one of the exploits of the strong bodyguard and friend of the rebel General Yoshitsune, as you will remember."

I remembered nothing of the sort but Herschel always gave one credit for more learning than one had.

"And now we must have *Denwa Benkei,*" he continued, not even smiling, and it was some time before I discovered that this means "Benkei on the Telephone."

Herschel could also sing all of Bach's forty-eight preludes and fugues, managing this through a series of mnemonic aids: "Oh, once there was a crocodile and he was sunning on the Nile." He could sing opera in English as well. A favorite was from *Il Trovatore*. It went: "Oh! Oh! They're burning her at the stake. Oh, how I quake. At the sight."

Much as I liked him, he was also no model for me. Despite all the fun he was deeply shy. Every day one had to thaw him out before he could begin to respond. Often he helped himself with whiskey. Once thawed he was a delight, but it took time,

Herschel Webb.

during which he was polite but reserved, gave short answers if any. When I mentioned this to Gene he nodded and then said that if one wore a lot of armor it took a long time to take it all off.

Sometimes I invited them out for weekends. Across the valley from Engakuji, the temple where Dr. Suzuki lived, was a guest house, empty, which I was told I could use. Square and spartan, it was two rooms, a kitchen, and a view over the Kamakura hills. It had no running water, no gas, and the toilet was an outhouse over a pit. Ideal—so different from the American comforts with which I grew up and which were being imported into the billet where I was presently living.

Trying to boil water for tea over a charcoal hibachi, trying to battle the bees that had taken lodging in the *benjo*, I felt that I was truly living. Back in Tokyo I was, somehow, merely existing.

We brought food from the PX, and camped out in the two rooms. Gene took at once to its austerity. Like me he believed that the spare was the authentic. When he discovered that the Engakuji library was next door and that he might use it, he was even more contented and would disappear into it for hours.

DONALD RICHIE

Holloway Brown.

Herschel approved of the austere more on aesthetic than on ethical grounds. Also he regretted the absence of ice for the afternoon martini, saying sadly that a warm martini was like a Manhattan with an olive. And, though fearful of the bees in the *benjo*, and refusing to use it unless absolutely necessary, he admired the view and would sit on the veranda and look at it for hours.

We also amused ourselves in various ways. Once we decided to make a musical comedy out of *Le Sacre du Printemps*, and put words to the melodies. Those for the opening bassoon solo went: "Oh, baby, see the moon. Oh, baby, see the moon. Way up high, so high. Oh, baby, see the moon."

Also, using the bedding—sleeved quilts—we put on a Noh drama. Gene was the *waki*, the character who always explains who he is and where he comes from: "I am an American scholar. I come from near Nihonbashi in Edo." Herschel was the orchestra, expertly simulating the whistling, pops and groans. I was the *shite*, the protagonist given to protean change. Most often I was a monster.

We talked about an opera based on Proust. Odette was a mezzo and would have many sforzando markings. Swann would be a typically French tenor: lots of vibrato and a tendency to bleat. A first act aria contained: "*O, seul, monotone*, all alone by my telephone."

We also cast a Warner Brothers' Proust. Odette was, naturally, Bette Davis, and Joseph Cotton was Swann, for want of better. Sydney Greenstreet was, of course, Charlus, but who could Jupien be? "Peter Lorre," said Herschel with a laugh that soon turned into a cough for he, like Proust, was asthmatic. He used to wheeze on the Ginza and later, after he had become a well-known Japanologist, he could visit the country no longer. "Oh, dear," he used to say, "I'm allergic to my specialty."

Evenings, the sun going behind us, flooding the roofs of Engakuji across the valley, we would grill our Spam on the hibachi, boil the wiener cocktail sausages, crunch the Ritz, guzzle the gin, and enjoy the luxury of our Japanese life.

EUGENE LANGSTON

Noh drama, with Herschel Webb, 1947.

Most of the other pages of this period have been previously used, particularly in *Where Are the Victors?* and in the unfinished memoir *In Between*. Here are some excerpts from the latter.

LATE SUMMER 1947. Wandering in the city after work, smelling camellia hair oil, dusty long unaired kimono, the passing night soil wagon with its patient ox, listening to the incomprehensible murmur of conversation around me, looking into eyes suddenly averted, I try to make sense of what I see.

In a way it already makes sense—Tokyo in ruins still reveals something known from Chicago, New York and, during the war, Naples, Marseilles: the look of a big city just anywhere. In another way, however, I begin to apprehend alternatives to things as I already know them.

The way the buildings stand—those that still do—in relation to each other; the way the rooms—those few I have seen—with their tatami matting, their interior stages for scrolls and flower arrangements, divide space: this is different. The politeness—for so I read it—of people who might not be starving but who clearly do not have enough to eat: this too is unlike. And the acceptance, the shrugs, the smiles, the willingness to continue, to begin again, to look on the bright side of things—I wonder how my hometown would have reacted to a near annihilation.

Another country, I am discovering, is another self. I am regarded as different, and so I become different—two people at once. I am a native of Ohio who really knew only the streets of little Lima, and I am also a foreigner who is coming to know the streets of Tokyo, largest city in the world. Consequently I can compare them, and since comparison is creation, I am able to learn about both.

Already I am as absolved as I will ever be from prejudices of class and caste. I cannot detect them here and no one here can detect them in me, since my foreignness is difference enough. So, I remain in a state of surprise, and this leads to heightened interest and hence perception. Like a child with a puzzle, I am forever putting pieces together and saying: Of course.

Or, *naruhodo*, since I am trying somehow to learn Japanese. And knowing a language does indeed create a different person since words determine facts. Here, however, I am still an intelligence-impaired person since I cannot communicate and have, like a child or an animal, to intuit from gestures, from intent, from expression.

Language will perhaps eventually free me from such elemental means of communication but at the same time ignorance is teaching me a lesson I would not otherwise have learned. While it is humiliating to ideas of self to be reduced to what one says—nothing at all if one does not know Japanese—it teaches that there are avenues other than speech.

I knew a little about this. In Italy or France during the war, sitting through foreign films without English titles, I did not learn much about the film but I learned a lot about filmmaking. How the director and his writer and cameraman had thought about time and space, the assumptions they had made, the suppositions they had built upon, their apparently unthinking inferences. Now again, in a very different country, I am again beginning to understand the film without comprehending the plot.

I look at the janitor's closet in the Kokubu Building where I work, see the box for shoes and otherwise the luxury of empty space; peer into the translator's desk drawer and notice that she has classified differently—all long things are in one place, all round things in another; gaze at the mat-floored room where the ex-president once sat, and perceive the *tokonoma*, the stage-like space where sat time itself, in the shape of a seasonal scroll and an oft-changed arrangement where the flowers were always fresh and always looked the same—both renewed by an ancient secretary whom the war had left untouched though it had carried the president away. Trying to read things like this is like learning Braille, as though another sense is involved, where sensing becomes something like grammar.

After only a month, I see that I risk ignorance if I remain typing away in what I scornfully call Little America. My job, nine-to-five in an office that could have been anywhere; my home life at the Continental Hotel, all Spam and powdered potatoes and lumpy pillows; my recreations, the PX, a cheap made-in-America bazaar, the allowed entertainments, movies with the GIs and bingo night at the American Club, occasionally special Occupier-night, one performance only, at the Kokusai Gekijo All-Girl Dance Theater—all of this begins to appear more and more unreal to me.

Unreal and unpleasant. Little America, try though it does to impart democracy and individualism, is also a territory where the Japanese are worried over, and are made objects of condescension. They are treated like blacks in the American south, or like the "natives" in Forster's *A Passage to India*, a work I recently read. Or worse. Our two GI drivers call our janitor a gook. I soon see I will experience nothing, learn nothing if I stay within these commodious and American folds.

Thus when I learn that we, the Occupiers, are regularly wormed, I am somehow pleased. Back in Ohio worming was for animals or what we still called "poor white trash." Here, however, our salads are cultivated with something called "night soil," a fertilizer composed of the excrement of the Occupied. We consequently get whatever they have.

This is indeed an Occupation—our American bowels a nurturing home to native Japanese fauna. No matter our own sense of superiority, our manifest efforts to recreate our own civilization in these far islands, we are every three months reminded that we are merely human after all. This we ascertain by glancing into the bowl and then hurriedly flushing it. Going to the toilet after having taken worm medicine is a great leveler.

While never looking forward to the doses, I welcome the effect. Not only am I then worm-free for another three months, but also I am sharing something with the Occupied. In a situation where our people call their people gooks and where we are forbidden to make their social acquaintance, where they are held to be morally as well as socially inferior to us and are thus in need of purging, their worms seem positively friendly.

I look about the office of the Allied Cultural Property Division where I work. Stay I must in body, since I am here to work, but SCAP has little control over my ambitions. Therefore I long to fraternize with the forbidden indigenous personnel. Indeed such aggressive and self-conscious segregation—Japanese and Americans, Occupied and Occupiers, Them and Us, Gooks and Gentry—make me want to flout such authority. Abrogating arrogant and useless rules is attractive in itself, but a further reason is that these orders are the glass against which I press my longing face, no less than do the Japanese when, alien in their own country, they gaze packed and flat-faced at solitary me in my Allied-Only car on the Tokyo trains.

*

The offices of the Allied Cultural Property Division have a weekly mimeographed bulletin and I know the person who compiles it. She tells me they are looking for "human-interest" material and I decide to fill this need. Having read Nitobe Inazo on Bushido, Ruth Benedict on toilet training, R. H. Blyth on the haiku, I now want to write something myself.

I have the means. I can type—indeed, I have often thought that I became a writer simply because I know how to typewrite. First comes technique, then style; no typing prowess and I would have turned into something else. My problem in Japan is where to begin—there is too much to write about. But here, however, was something specific—human-interest.

I find some. Just upstream from our building just off Nihonbashi is this other bridge, smaller and so far as I know, nameless. A man lives under it, among the girders. Having moved in after the war, he there remains. Grizzled, he is often seen perched in his watery home. So I go to see him, taking with me the unwilling office interpreter.

She had said we would be bothering him. No, I said, we would be interviewing him, trying to make it sound as though this would be no bother. He is a poor man, she had said. We couldn't pay him, I said, but we could give him something—maybe Spam, or cigarettes.

Cigarettes, she said, so we set out with pencil, pad, and a carton of Camels.

Our host, Iwasaki Kiyoshi, is appreciative of the cigarettes and loquacious in return. Shortly, our newsletter carries: "Man Under a Bridge—The Story of a Refugee from Ruin." This refugee "though clothed in rags, maintained a venerable dignity," as he told his uncomplicated story. "He answered questions courteously and simply but there was no hint of the obsequious in his manner."

There was plenty in mine. I had written about the amenities of his dwelling using such phrases from far Ohio as "snug as a bug in a rug," and observed that "the sight of the foreigner coming to visit apparently caused no alarm, though later he said he had at first thought that we were coming to take his home from him."

My completed work excites some interest among the office staff—this kind of "coverage" is still rare. Some think the Japanese still somehow enemies. My kind of condescension is new. Consequently, it also attracts the notice of the feature desk of the *Pacific Stars and Stripes*, the Occupation newspaper. Summoned thither I am told by the editor that he guesses I have gotten myself a new job. I have, he says, the human touch.

This I much doubt, and even if I do have it, do not believe that my GI readers will be interested. Nonetheless, I am assured that my piece has human-interest and that hu-

Richie's first feature in Stars and Stripes, *1947.*

man-interest fits in with the major aims of a democratic press. As such my man under the bridge qualifies and, consequently, so do I.

Eighth Army photographers are sent to capture Mr. Iwasaki in his watery lair and a rewritten version of my article becomes a cover story in the *Stars and Stripes Weekly* where it again excites some mild interest.

A year before it would have excited none—lots of people were living under bridges. But now they are few, there is creeping fraternization, and the Occupying stance is relaxing. The days of Japs and Gooks are numbered. We are now living with a fellow race. I have, despite or because of my patronization, indicated this. The newspaper authorizes my transfer, my grade is moved a step up, and I am feature writer and film reviewer.

Feeling guilty at having gotten so much from this penniless person, I take further cigarettes as well as a fifth of Four Roses to my benefactor under the bridge. He is, however, no longer there. My article has alerted the Japanese police, who have swiftly removed this unwelcome relic from the old days.

Having ruined the life of an affable old man, I find myself haunted by his ghost. In my new office at *Stars and Stripes* comes the shout: "Get Richie to do it. He's good at human-interest."

*

I, strangely, did not regard movies as human-interest stories. Perhaps because, as for so many of my generation—those who, like me, had profitably spent their youth in the dark—films had become sacerdotal, something so out-of-body that they were no longer quite human.

For me, as for so many, the movies were a preferable form of life. I knew nothing about films themselves—did not know how they were made, or why. And if I knew next to nothing about the movies of my own country, I knew nothing at all about Japanese films: did not understand the language, recognized neither stars nor directors, and knew little about Japan itself. From such beginnings knowledge of the Japanese cinema could only grow.

Though I was supposed to merely endure the latest Hollywood product in the comfort of the Signal Corps screening room, I defined my mission as otherwise. Coat collar turned up, eyes alert for the marauding MP, I bravely sneaked into Japanese motion pictures theaters all over the city, where I was forever getting sisters confused with wives and mistresses with mothers, and becoming lost in the labyrinths of the period film.

Dumbly I absorbed reel after reel, sitting in the summer heat of the Nikkatsu or the winter cold of the Hibiya Gekijo. Yet, in these uncomprehending viewings of one opaque picture after another, I was being aided by my ignorance. Undistracted by dialogue, undisturbed by story, I was able to attend to the intentions of the director, to notice his assumptions and to observe how he contrived his effects.

Though I understood little about cinema, I had seen a lot of it, and now I began to realize that space was used differently in Japanese films. There was a careful flatness, a reliance upon two dimensions which I knew from Japanese woodblock prints. And emptiness, I had already guessed, was distributed differently. Compositions seemed bottom-heavy, but then I realized that—as in the hanging scrolls I had seen—the empty space was there to define what was below: it had its own weight.

And there were also many fewer close-ups than I was accustomed to in American films. The camera seemed always further away from the actors—as though to show the space in between. A character was to be explained in long shot, his environment speaking for him. Sometimes I could not even make out his face, but I knew who he was by what surrounded him.

I also noticed the pace of the films of the period: slow, very slow. Time, lots of it—long scenes, long sequences—was necessary. Feelings flowed and flowered to what Ohio would have thought extravagant lengths. The screen was awash with undammed emotion. Yet, though allergic to the displays of

Joan Crawford and Bette Davis, I somehow did not mind the emotionality of women I later discovered to be Tanaka Kinuyo and Takamine Hideko.

Wondering why I so willingly wept along with them, I decided that the very fact that they were so far away, and crying for such a long time, compelled my moving nearer, and hence feeling more. So different from the big and demanding close-ups of Joan and Bette, their nostrils large enough to drive trucks into. Being apparently asked for nothing I gave more. And so, sitting there, smelling the rice sweat and the camellia pomade, I was learning my early lessons in Japanese art.

I wonder which films taught me. 1947—one could have been Ozu Yasujiro's *Record of a Tenement Gentleman*, released that May; another could have been Mizoguchi's *The Loves of Sumako* (with Tanaka Kinuyo), released that August. Whatever I saw, I have forgotten, if I ever knew. I later looked at both the Ozu and the Mizoguchi but not a memory budged. The first Japanese film scene that I could identify was one I recognized only because I had watched it being made.

*

I was taken to the Toho Studios not because of my new critical position, but because I had met with the composer Hayasaka Fumio. He was a pale, spectacled man who having heard that I had some recordings of new music, wanted to meet me. Regulations on fraternization with the indigenous personnel having been relaxed, I could ask him to my billet, and escort him up in the front elevator. In my room we heard the Berg *Violin Concerto*, newly recorded and inexplicably on sale in the PX. He sat silent, lost in the music, and when the Bach chorale appeared his eyes filled with tears.

Hayasaka responded by inviting me to Toho to watch being filmed a movie for which he was doing the score. Setting out early to avoid the MPs, late risers all, we stood bouncing in the suburban train as it bumped and rattled through the new, raw countryside west of Tokyo.

The Toho Studios, large white barns, were in the midst of muddy paddies. Inside, the big, muffled prewar camera clunked by on metal rails and the mike was held aloft on a bamboo pole. Both of these were aimed at a carefully ruined set of buildings, meticulously constructed, every brick out of place, in back a dirty gray cyclorama with miniature ruins on the nearby horizon.

A whole blasted neighborhood had been built around a scummy-surfaced sump on the banks of which were a few new plywood buildings, their fronts festooned with neon. In the sump itself floated carefully placed garbage, a single shoe, a cardboard box, and a child's lost doll. Yet what I was seeing was no different from what I had seen on my way there.

It had not occurred to me that film heightened reality. I had always thought of it as an alternate. Yet this—though different from Johnny Weissmuller's lost city or from Norma Shearer's Versailles—was still a movie set. Obviously so, yet, huge on the black and silver screen, it would look real.

There was the camera, there was the mike, and there were banks of lights. And there was the director, wearing a white floppy hat; there was someone I guessed was the star. He, in a loose Hawaii-shirt, a young actor with slicked back hair, was practicing menacing an older man with a beard and round-rimmed glasses.

The young man was supposed to walk along the sump toward the older man. This short scene was taken several times very swiftly, no stopping, apparently, for consideration. I wondered at the speed with which this reality was captured, having always thought that making films took an enormous amount of time.

And the noise. Shouting and clattering, things dropped. I had thought of the film studio as a kind of cathedral, filled with a hushed and reverent silence as the great arcs illuminated a famous profile. Instead, cacophony as one scene was finished and another was begun. It had never occurred to me before that movies were actually *made*.

For each of the walking scenes the doll in the sump had been repositioned. Now it sank. The director smiled, shook his head, waved his hand, and signaled for a break. Seeing Hayasaka he came over and I was introduced. Then the two actors came and I met them too. I could not speak Japanese and Hayasaka often mumbled, so I caught no names.

Later, Richie has elsewhere said, the composer took him to the Toho screening room to see the finished picture and he learned that the young man in the shirt was Mifune Toshiro; the man with the beard was Shimura Takeshi; the man in the floppy hat was Kurosawa Akira, and the film was *Drunken Angel*. Whenever he now sees this film and that sequence by the sump comes on, he looks to the right of the screen: "There I am, just a few feet off the edge, twenty-four years-old, watching a movie being made." Otherwise, from the period 1947 to 1949 the only journals remaining in their original state are those below. The first of these appears in a different version in *The Donald Richie Reader*.

16 OCTOBER 1948. This afternoon Meredith [Weatherby] and I went to a performance of Bugaku in Ueno Park. And this afternoon, watching Ono [Tadamaro] again dance, I felt that he had come to contain for me the beauty, grace, and dedication of Japan—as though he were an emblem of his country.

Meredith and I entered the small park behind the museum and came upon the small tent where the performers were already putting on their costumes, where the orchestra was already tuning or warming their instruments. I thought of the Heian period recaptured: the costumes of antiquity, the different flavor of everything Japanese. We passed the tent (for we could not stop and stare, so conscious were we of being foreigners—which attitude we conscientiously cultivated so as to be differentiated from other of our countrymen here); passed four little boys dressed in costumes of the eighth century court, with wings and little tails attached to them; passed the musicians already arranging their brocade and the dancers still taking off their street clothes; till we reached the red square lacquer platform with its copper railing and, before it, the empty seats for the audience.

Invitations apparently were given only to higher officers. Consular representatives were here, and Meredith saw many acquaintances. [Weatherby was at this time in the consular service. Later he was to create and head the publishing firm John Weatherhill, Inc.] The various missions were here as well, as were the more socially prominent in the Occupation. We were told that today was the elite party and tomorrow the plebeian. I had had no invitation at all to this one but found my press card acceptable.

Just before the musicians arrived Prince Takamatsu appeared—a tall thin man with a large nose and dark eyes. He never missed a social engagement—indeed, was probably not allowed to. Princess Takamatsu was less in the background than usual, wearing a pretty kimono and a smile, and they were soon surrounded by Allied friends.

Then the music began. "Celestial" is the word I always think of, and so it is since it does not seem of this world. The sound of the *sho*, that frail, dissonant noise floating into attending trees, disappearing into the clear blue sky; the curious double time, the apparently accidental syncopations, the stately stance of the music—surely this is celestial.

The dancing—maybe that is what makes the music celestial; the simple opening prelude, unchanged for a thousand years: the dancer with halberd, walking forward to kneel, then the slow turning of the head to the right until the profile shows against the sky, and the unexpected, mechanical quick

Ono Tadamaro performing Bugaku.

movement which brings the profile to the left.

Ono appeared only in the last dance, a famous one I'd seen once before, in which four men performed in the costumes of the eighth century, covered with brocades and stiff gauzes, hats of lacquered wire, halberds of lacquered wood, only their heads and hands visible. As each of the four entered the platform from among the trees and emerged into the sun, the same choreographic formula was repeated, like a fugue or, more exactly, a four-part canon, repeating each other's movements, a movement behind.

All four stood, each at a corner of the platform, and then began the dance—a war dance in which a stylized battle takes place. The two on the left precisely imitate those on the right. Swords are therefore held both toward and away from you at the same time and all movements are identical. The most beautiful moment comes when, the accompaniment of the music reaching that curious double beat, the dancers begin slowly moving around the inside of the square, each occupying, within two beats, the place left vacant by the man before him. The movement, the deliberate raising of the leg and bending of the foot and knee, the squat with hands on thighs as the dancers change position, the curious up and down motions as they bend their toes in their rounded lacquer boots. The prescribed, ritualistic movements of the hands, all in exact accord with the other. The studied expressionless faces and blank dark eyes which so ignore the three other dancers. The movements are like beautiful human machinery and the music soars to the sky.

The dance is finished and the dancers depart: all four describing a figure—one steps down, leaves three, steps down, leaves two, and finally Ono alone describes the figure. His back is to the audience but I still see his face. For, in this hour, he has embodied all that Japan holds for me.

Later I have Meredith take me to the tent, now shorn of its Heian associations: it is simply a garden tent where Japanese are replacing Western clothes, tying shoes, fixing worn neckties and putting back on black horn-rimmed spectacles. Ono is introduced to me. He is wearing a coat too small for him, a clean but worn white shirt, a dark necktie. In his lapel is one of the tiny red feathers which mean the wearer has contributed to the current Community Chest drive. He smiles, bows and then shakes hands.

Am I disappointed? Oh, no. How could I be disappointed with the Heian period? Meredith later said that Ono is not particularly attractive—and I suppose he's not. Without his costume he becomes ordinary and on the street I shouldn't notice him. But I have seen him wearing stiffened gauzes and salmon brocades, and I have seen his head surmounted with lacquered wire and the feathers from birds that ceased to live a thousand years ago. I have seen Japan in him.

17 OCTOBER 1948. Like so many of these autumn days, this one began in clouds and damp mists and, looking from the window at six this morning, it seemed the day would not be fit for picture-taking.

Later in the morning Al [Raynor, a friend in the same billet] and I went to Kanda to buy books. This was arranged, put off, rearranged, and again scheduled several times before we actually left. The reason for this was Al. Originally he had wanted to go into the country today, for he revels in great open spaces and likes to shake from his heels not only the dust of the city, but also every place where he is acquainted and knows his way about. He often says he would be perfectly content traveling always, but I doubt it. He is too fond of study (his translation of a Noh we have been polishing these last two weeks) and too fond of comfort too (his attachment to his room and habitual three helpings at meals) to ever be more than mildly fond of the movable life.

This morning he was looking for Noh books and I was looking for the one on masques that I saw last summer and have been looking for ever since. I didn't find it but did buy a 1922 number of *Broom* with half of Claudel's *Protée* translated in it, and the Sacheveral Sitwell book on southern baroque art I'd been wanting for some time. Also I got several copies of this month's *Europa* that has my article on Gide in it. While at the magazine stand I noticed a young student reading it and longed to declare myself the author. Also found an early Shakespeare Company edition of *Ulysses*, only the price was over two thousand yen and the proprietor knew its value. Al found a Noh picture book that pleased him.

It was now time to go again to the Bugaku. Al suddenly said he would rather go out in the country and was already regretting he had spent the time in Kanda. I began feeling sorry for myself, wondering what I should do if he wouldn't go; he doubtless feeling I was using him—as I was naturally—and resenting the fact that he wasn't out in the country. We drove for a long time in silence. He broke it once to ask me to stand up: we were going fast and I like to stand up in the roofless jeep when traveling fast, but I refused and he said no more for a time.

The silence continued and was then rent by his flatly stating in a tone of exclamation that he was going to the Bugaku and that we were going to stay all the way through, too—just as though I'd been disagreeing with him.

The crowd was much grander this afternoon, much smaller. When we arrived, about half an hour before the performance, the little tent was surrounded by Americans. Cameras were everywhere, from box cameras to big German models, from hand-wound motion picture cameras to large and expensive tripod battery-run affairs.

Ono appeared, this time in full costume, looking again like living Japanese history. He was polite, talked some with Al about the dance and then asked where we wanted to take the pictures. I drew him away from the crowd and posed him in the sunlight. Then, ashamed at being among the snappers, I took several pictures and had Al take my picture with him. Again, through Al, I asked Ono to visit me, and he, through Al, said that he would be pleased to. I told him that I would let him know the time and date. Exactly why I did that—why I invited him—I don't know but I knew I didn't want to lose what I had captured.

18 OCTOBER 1948. In the afternoon I willfully stay in the [*Stars and Stripes*] office working over a synopsis of the vampire cat of Urashima for the paper. In the evening—while Holloway [Brown, his current roommate] entertains a Mr. Gunji and his younger brother—the elder Gunji absurdly good looking, noisy, and as American as possible, while the younger Gunji, not at all good looking, is reserved to the point of being incomprehensible—I work with Al, editing his translation of Sumidagawa. I don't like the lines:

> By the shores of Horie
> High above the busy boatmen
> Always crying, always crying
> Are seen *miyako-dori*.

I recite this Longfellow-like to the tune of *Hiawatha*, which irritates the translator. He likes his original, arguing that, after all, it is a quoted poem. I, in turn, state that no Japanese poem ever sounded like that. After half an hour of wrangling we straighten it out; but now, neither is satisfied.

> By the shores of Horiegawa
> Always crying as they fly
> High above the busy boatmen
> Are seen *miyako-dori.*

Any translation from Japanese to English, certainly including my neglected *Asakusa Kurenaidan,* [the Kawabata novel] contains the difficulty of connotation. Every Japanese knows that *miyako-dori* are seagulls and are mentioned in a famous poem by Inahara, and are called the capital bird because they are, for some reason, never seen in the old capital. You can't say that in English and if you do the book is mostly footnotes. Al feels this is such a difficult point that we get no further on the subject.

19 OCTOBER 1948. Sho [Kajima Shozo] in to see me this morning, wanting nothing in particular, just to talk. Small, eyes so big they look round, he is the only Japanese I have met whose English is so good that we can carry on conversations about things that matter to us. Particularly matter to him. Anything foreign, as though he has been starved for so long that he cannot get enough.

Now we discuss the possibilities of translating Camus into Japanese, and how the intellectuals here now shun Sartre. Sho blames it on *Life* magazine, just now discovering existentialism and hence degrading its current reputation in Japan.

Sho understands the subtleties of this and can express them. In Japan, he tells me, everything is fashion and the opinion of others. This is not a good thing but it is so. Even Juliet Greco is no longer so popular now that *Life* has taken her up.

Conversely, I can talk about nothing Japanese since he is not interested and says he does not know. I ask him about brush painting. Doesn't know. Ask about the difference between *waka* and *tanka.* Doesn't know.

I am to write something for his magazine. I suggest something Japanese, and then I could learn something too. Oh, no, not that. He suggests André Gide, since I am reading the journals and since this author is now back in critical favor in Japan.

20 OCTOBER 1948. Late, a soldier, Irish, appears and stays for three hours. We talk mostly about him. He has a problem—which of the two sexes he likes better. He's had no actual experience with either and so the discussion is a bit academic.

But I like people who look one thing and think they are another. Irish looks like an ordinary GI but has what he thinks is this problem. I tell him that one needn't make the choice and point out that I have, at great personal inconvenience, put it off for a number of years by never calling myself one thing or another, and that I have consequently had a great deal of pleasure with all kinds of people. In his longing for security, however, Irish rushes to the grand and unnecessary generalization.

All the time, however, I think this talk might not be the real reason for his visit. He keeps saying that he has to go back to the barracks but makes no move to do so. I don't know whether to be flattered or annoyed. It is nothing to me, however, and so he eventually goes home after having heard my preferences. He hasn't "gone in" for the Japanese, he says, which puts rather a gulf between us, since I certainly have.

Later to bed with—instead—Gide's *The Immoralist*.

23 OCTOBER 1948. Al and I read through our translation of *Sumidagawa* for the final time and when it was finished we were each ready to leap at the other's throat. He took the tone a stern parent takes toward a naughty child when I lectured him on the habit of his overusing that most sensational of punctuation marks, the exclamation point—thus destroying its efficiency. Consequently, I slid into a hauteur that found me separating each syllable, affecting an English accent and behaving in a manner I considered exquisitely polite. I offered no more suggestions but had prepared many pretty phrases had it come to a head. It did not however. Gene came back, and later guests, so the day passed with no argument. I'm not sure this ill feeling affects him as much as it does me, but I think he dislikes it more. As the Noh play is finished, however, we'll have no more fights

Received the pictures taken of Ono today. The ones of him alone are nice and show his costume well, but I wish they were in color. The one of me with him is no good. I am standing in a strange attitude and even though you can't see them you can almost smell the aliens—colonels, majors and captains—surrounding me and being partially responsible for my stilted stance.

25 OCTOBER 1948. This afternoon I went for a luncheon engagement at the new subway hotel. I have no compunction about eating the fine food, all of it black market. The hotel people I eat with all went to Cornell before the war; all speak

good English. They are also charming to me, for I am going to honor
them with a page in *Stars and Stripes*,
the only American paper in Japan.

Later the *Stars and Stripes* soldier photographer came. Turned out
to be the one who I heard was gos-
siping about me. Not afraid of his
insinuations, for as he puts them
they are false, but I am curious to
know why he made them. Then he

MEREDITH WEATHERBY

With Ono Tadamaro.

said, "Seen Richie around lately?" He hadn't recognized me, and later when
he showed me his assignment slip my name was not there, instead, another
of the men on the paper. But, couldn't I have taken advantage of this happy
mistake? Apparently not, for I said, "I am Richie."

Bit my tongue the minute I said it, for I had had the chance to play a real
role. I can imagine the conversation that might have ensued had I been less
self-assured and more afraid. I would have intelligently drawn him further
and further out, cut off one by one his chances for denial. How cleverly I
would have turned the conversation to the suspicions themselves—he would
doubtless have readily repeated them. And as he gossiped on, I would have
had the rare opportunity of watching a man's mind innocently working before I, with a mighty pounce, brought him up short—thrown off my invisible
cloak—and witnessed him skidding to a panicked halt. But no. I spoiled it.
What is the good of admiring [Gide's] Lafcadio if I miss the chance to be
him?

26 OCTOBER 1948. Watanabe [Isamu], met at a construction site, comes over.
Gene, supposed to go out, has come back by this time and Al has arrived.
Watanabe brings along many interesting pictures, some of himself as a pilot
during the war, and also part of his WWII propaganda collection. The American is the most subtle, the German is not—it is completely obvious—the
British does nothing much and there is no Italian. I think that the American
was most successful because it illustrated Japanese poems and famous plays,
proverbs and sayings already in the mouths of every soldier. These are neces-
sarily so erudite that, as Watanabe said, all were astonished when they picked
them up after they'd been tossed from the plane. I had no idea that anything
that intelligent was going on

28 OCTOBER 1948. I'm more than halfway through the second volume of the Gide journals. What impresses me most is his ability to put down precisely what he means. In reading over this journal of my own I see the difference. Gide lives close with himself; I live at a distance from myself. I only imply what I mean; Gide states.

His theory of literary construction (lengthy incubation) bothers me because I feel that I should not agree, but it fits too well with my laziness for me to object too strenuously. He says that things must grow within one, that yesterday's blossom will wilt today and was therefore not worth the keeping, that the plant will prune itself and emerge, in time, effortlessly. But I remember another piece of advice—this from Bernard Shaw—which says that ideas are like ducks that fly by: you have to bag them at once for they'll never fly by again.

I've not sufficiently made up my mind about either method. Perhaps both should be used, determined by the subject, or the nature, of the material. My novel on Tokyo [*Where Are the Victors?*] should use the Shavian duck-shooting method because it must deal with historical facts. If I were going to write another kind of novel however, like one by Gide, then it would have to hibernate. Gide says one shouldn't force, yet he advocates daily writing.

How good to apply myself—yet I never do. What of the Tokyo novel? Daily I have thought of it. It stopped changing shape some time ago. I am counting on days and nights back in Ohio to put a quick end to this particular indecision.

29 OCTOBER 1948. Most of the morning rewriting a letter beginning: "Dear Jesus. Usually I write Santa but this year I thought I would write you." This is for the Christmas edition [of the *Pacific Stars and Stripes*]—for which, however, I've found some good Dürers, including a head of Christ by one of his pupils, that I must sandwich in somehow. The whole piece is preposterous in its stupidity. Worse, I could change it if I had the will. So much easier to obey orders and ask no questions. What could I do with it that would please me? Nothing.

In the evening I took Nomura [the room boy] to the ballet. Also along went Gene, Jimmy [Sekiguchi, Gene's friend], and Al. It was *Swan Lake*, done in what is understood as the Russian tradition. The dancers all wear big blonde wigs, the boys wear makeup, the girls in the corps de ballet smile—the dental display is blinding.

While all of us were making fun of it, Nomura was quietly enjoying it.

He was awed by the tinsel magnificence, appreciative of the efforts shown on the stage, and kind when obvious mistakes were made. In the end he laughed with us but it was plain that he enjoyed it and was but being polite. He was particularly taken with the dance of the little swans.

Later we all came back to the room. I typed Nomura a letter to the Suginami Police Station where they are holding clothes that I gave him—and which I said I did in the letter—but, oddly, they are not holding him.

Nice turn for the novel if I were to get picked up by the CID for giving the clothes to him. This in turn would reveal something, then more would be revealed and finally the novel would end for lack of characters still remaining in Japan, all having been sent back. Particularly ironic because Nomura is honest, I am honest, and we would be blamed and punished for something of which we were not guilty.

While we were writing the letter I saw a white figure behind me in the room and, at the same time, a sudden expression of dismay on the face of Nomura. Turning about I found myself faced with a lady of indeterminate age in a long white dress, with necklace and bracelets and wiry hair. Advancing into the room with heavy stride, she asked me, in a deep and familiar voice, if I knew where Bruce [Rogers] was. Then I recognized him. It was the sergeant acquaintance of Bruce's whom I'd seen only once before—in uniform.

The transformation was complete. Pancake make-up, lipstick, mascara, wig and a long skirt that he kept kicking. I asked him what he had underneath. He obligingly lifted his skirts and displayed panties and garter belt as well as silk hose. Then I asked about his breasts and felt them. They were cleverly made of cotton.

Nomura remained dismayed and I realized that he still thought it was an extremely forward woman and was growing afraid of her friendly mascara-fringed glances. I introduced them and, once Nomura had understood that this was a man, he became even more terrified.

Al meantime, having glimpsed the soldier in the elevator coming up, had gotten interested, thinking her a loose colored lady. He was all affability until he was introduced to the sergeant. He looked closely and his face went quite blank; smiling tightly he left.

Sarge, it being near Halloween, had gotten himself up, and all over Tokyo traveled with other soldier friends, going to the rough Club Ichiban, enjoying the feels the other soldiers gave him; went to the Dai Ichi Grill and passed as an interesting person of color. He was having a good time, getting away with it, and sat down in the big chair as he told us all about it.

Later Al and I had a conversation about why people did things like this. He thought it might be to solicit young men but I pointed out that, so far as I knew, that almost never happened. If it had it would have been better somehow because some definite purpose would have been served—but instead, to merely go about acting female could only result in a trip into the mirror.

30 OCTOBER 1948. To Hibiya Hall for the premiere of Hayasaka's piano concerto. He gave me two tickets, but I went alone. What a nice piece of music, particularly the rondo with a Chinese-sounding tune that always comes back, looking different each time. The concerto was sandwiched between William Schuman's *American Festival Overture* and Aaron Copland's *El Salon Mexico.* CIE [Civil Information and Education] pushes things American. At the same time, however, the Japanese have not heard much modern music since before the war. Here is an elegant and nourishing sandwich for them. A big audience, and a young one.

31 OCTOBER 1948. Not a cloud in the sky, all a brilliant blue and the air cool. There is a sharpness, an invigoration of the senses. Japan—mountains beautiful in the fog, forests in the rain—is even more beautiful when with such clearness every pebble is seen.

I notice again that nothing now is actually incongruous in Japan. Everything fits. The period may be a bastard one, like rococo, but everything is harmonious. Temple boys in full costumes on motor scooters and neon signs on the Kamakura Kannon are no more incongruous than is Fuji at sunset.

Al and I took advantage of the weather and drove out to the Emperor Taisho's tomb. When there is no reason for disagreeing we get along well, like today when we anticipated each other's words, laughed at the same things and made wide allowance for each other's whims. We do a number of things that put the trip in the category of an adventure. We drink beer and take pictures in a secluded glade of the mausoleum, shout to all the little children we see, and carry back to his house from the bottom of a hill he could never have climbed, a very old and very drunk gentleman. We arrived home late, half frozen.

1 NOVEMBER 1948. Saw Meredith briefly and asked about Ono. I had merely, it seems, desired to photograph him. Meredith says a meeting can be arranged now at anytime but I hang back. I have often noticed that it is quite sufficient for me to know that something is within my grasp for me to lose interest. When I know that something I want is possible, finally, after weeks of attention, I cease to want it. I don't thereby want it to go away, however. I don't want to lose ground, but I am satisfied that I can have it if I want it. Its immediacy and its availability both conspire to afford me more satisfaction than, possibly, the thing itself. All of this, of course, without one thought about the feelings of the object.

2 NOVEMBER 1948. The afternoon spent in gathering pictures for the Christmas Edition: "I want pictures of hungry babies—of poor starved mothers and hungry babies—of sick babies, poor families," says the editor. I search the morgue, our modest picture collection, and find none. Do not want to. Would if I could have believed that this would do starved mothers and hungry babes any good, but it won't.

I will always remember with pain last month when I had to go with the photographer and get pictures of butt sniping in Tokyo. I hated it from the first but it wasn't until later that I hated myself. I had to plant the cigarette—smoke it half way and then throw it down—in Ueno—and the hidden photographer would snap as the next person stooped to pick it up.

But none of this happened. I had to go under the arcades and implore an old woman to pick up the cigarette, to pose with it. She was frightened and wouldn't. A ring of people, wondering faces, surrounded me. Finally I had to stop a poor young boy. Showed him what I wanted him to do. Held him until the photographer was ready and them make him stop in the humiliating position while the picture was taken. I wanted to give him every cigarette I had, but the minute he felt my hand leave him he ran into the crowd, afraid probably I'd attempt to retake the cigarette he'd just picked up. Yes, I did that. Now, I would never do that again—I would quit first.

The unpublished *In Between* contains further scenes taken from the original *Journals*. These, below, now indicate a chronology that the journal remnants themselves do not.

Japan—I was continuing to learn about my new land by writing about it: bonsai, ikebana, Japanese dance, festivals—all in my rage for knowledge I inflicted on my GI readers. Here I am on the Kabuki, an Allied-only night when the Occupiers gathered at the Tokyo Theater, just up the street from the ruins of the Kabuki-za. "Japan's most refined art ... receives boost into former favor when wartime banned classic employs services of the two greatest Kabuki actors." (Don Richie, Staff Writer).

The banned classic was *Sesshu Gappo ga Tsuji* and the actors were Nakamura Kichiemon who impersonated old Gappo and Nakamura Baigyoku who played his young daughter, O-Tsuji. It was she who, married, had fallen in love with her stepson.

This had led to the play being banned a number of times including during WWII. Now, however, continues shameless Don Richie: "with the freedom brought by SCAP, the play has been revived for the first time in seven years."

Also, for the first time since the Occupation had begun, SCAP did not find it necessary to powder the seats and sets with DDT. The actors were thus spared—though earlier artists had made their entrances coughing and wheezing.

The Tokyo Theater, now officially bugless, was filled that evening—brass in the front, government issue and civilians in the rear—all attentive before culture as only Americans can be. Me too, seeing all this for the first time. Seeing it with emotions that, as the play progressed, slowly became mixed. Though I was much in favor of it because it was Japanese, because it had been banned, because I had a small part in publicizing it, I now became aware that I was also disapproving of it.

So long as I thought Tsuji loved the stripling, I nodded at true romance and sided against the adamant father. But when it turned out that she was merely some kind of Japanese Camille dying for the beloved's own unwitting good, I began to disapprove.

I still do. Warriors who cut off the heads of their young to spare those of the lord, mothers who stab daughters to save their betters social embarrassment—these continue to repel, and these are mainly what Kabuki seems to be about. At the same time I knew my feeling was foolish. It would make equal sense to take seriously the dramaturgy of Donizetti.

But disapproval was not all I felt. As an appreciative if baffled audience drifted out of the Tokyo Theater and into waiting sedans, jeeps, and buses, I (looking back at the striped curtain—deep green, terracotta, black, colors I had never before seen in this combination) remember thinking again of what I had seen.

Amid the feudal remains had stood something that made me believe in a kind of reality I had not known before, an impossible authenticity, a false actuality. For I had seen a seventy-three-year-old man turn into a nineteen-year-old woman.

As Baigyoku made his way along the *hanamichi*, dead white tabi gliding, white showing at the sleeves and hem of the black kimono, hands and face as white as the socks, I saw merely an old male dressed as a female.

With Stars and Stripes *staff, 1948.*

Then, as he continued, the shuffle became a delicate walk, the hands were not those of an old man clamped together but those of a young woman modestly folded, and by the time the actor had reached the stage proper, Baigyoku had become that young woman—all alone, frightened, brave.

Where I had come from such a spectacle would have been an impossibility. In Ohio old men do not turn into young girls. Yet I had seen this and, despite the moral imbecility of the plot, I believed it.

After the audience had left, after all the green military sedans and jeeps had moved off, after the big army bus filled with lower-rated civilians had gone, after the theater was dark, I loitered on, standing under the willows which then stood there, and looked at the lights of Higashi-Ginza reflected in the broad canal that then flowed there.

It is, I suppose, typical that I should remember all this and yet not recall that during this same summer a general strike had been planned, one that would have indicated a real protest—one further that was patterned upon those in the homeland, the U.S.A. Japanese were uniting to strike against abuses that were continuing from the war years. One might have thought that SCAP, so eager to root out feudal remnants, would have supported such a movement, but in fact MacArthur banned the strike before it had even begun.

Nor did I realize that this marked the beginning of a change in the aims of SCAP itself. Earlier the objective was not merely to get rid of Imperial Japan, nor to make certain that the Japanese never again waged war. A major ambition also was to rebuild Japan in the American image—Little America was seriously envisioned. Already a year and a half into the Occupation many Japanese had begun to believe in what they were being taught: individualism, group effort, unionized fronts, and democracy.

Yet now when these were for the first time attempted it was SCAP itself that prevented them—first by order and later by the threat of troops. Consequently many Japanese felt betrayed and Allied efforts began to be regarded with skepticism. Maybe the new model was not really any better than the old one.

I felt nothing because I noticed nothing, had no idea that the Occupation had changed direction, that its reforms were now seen as leftist, that the New Deal now read "Red." Japan was no longer the latest convert to American-style democracy—it had become a part of the Western defense system, a "bastion of freedom."

I must have read 1947 U.S. headlines: "Has the Job Been Bungled?"—meaning that the Occupying attitude had not until now noticed the Russian menace. I ought, being a part of it, to have heard about the Occupation taking a "reverse course" against the "excesses of democracy"; should have seen that by 1948 industrial complexes were being unofficially built up; but it was not until the 1949 purgings (now of communists rather than fascists) that I finally caught on.

In the spring of 1949 Richie left Japan and went to New York to go to Columbia University. There he continued his journal; a number of pages are extant. Among them is his account, written up after the event, of the first time he met the novelist Mishima Yukio.

EARLY WINTER 1952. Meredith [Weatherby], now at Harvard, called to ask me to look after a young Japanese author who had just arrived in New York and one of whose books he was translating. The book was *Confessions of a Mask,* and the author was Mishima Yukio.

Specifically, I was asked to show Mishima the city so that he could write about it for the *Asahi Shinbun,* whose "special correspondent" he had become, a position that allowed him to travel—otherwise difficult because the Allied

Occupation forces were still occupying his country and Japanese could leave it only if accredited.

His accounts of life abroad ("The Far-Sighted Traveler," "On Not Falling in Love with Paris") were published and later collected, but he saw much more than he wrote about. Indeed, his earliest use for me was to show him something other than the usual tourist sites.

I knew no Japanese then and his English was not yet as idiomatic as it later became. Nonetheless, we managed to communicate well enough for me to understand his wishes. He wanted to visit every Saint Sebastian hanging in New York, to see the Strauss *Salome* at the Met, and to experience a real gay bar. He gave as reason for this last that he was halfway through his next novel, *Forbidden Colors,* which contained scenes in several such locales, and he wished to compare, evaluate, and capture local color.

There were several such in Greenwich Village, I had heard, and so we set out and eventually located one called Mary's. There we sat over our drinks and watched middle-aged men talk like women. This was something neither of us had expected and it was not very interesting.

Nonetheless he gravely thanked me and on our next outing we hunted down Saint Sebastian. Though we did not find him, Mishima remained convinced that his saint was somehow hiding in the Metropolitan Museum, and so we searched wing after wing. In the bookstore he finally found a reproduction of the one by Guido Reni, a portrait he already knew intimately. This he purchased.

I remember the search, disappointing though it had been, because during it I was impressed both by Mishima's invariable courtesy—he had the finest social manners of anyone I had ever met—and by his conviction of the importance of what we were doing.

With Mishima one became objective, saw oneself dispassionately. It was he who created this heightened atmosphere because of an inner consistency upon which he insisted. To be with Mishima was to take part in a drama.

Perhaps consequently there was little spontaneity, a quality that he seemed both to distrust and to dislike, perhaps because it was inconsistent. And there was also little humor, for Mishima's mirth was always serious. But, as though in compensation, there was a sense of high intelligence, a feeling that one was engaged in something important—in short, a sense of theater.

A result of all this theater was a kind of formality. One always tried to be at one's best with Mishima—up to his level, as it were, attempt to emulate that ideal, which he himself represented, of being true to one's own self. This

Mishima Yukio, 1953.

is difficult if, like myself, you do not know who you are, and have to settle for some daily invention. Mishima, however, seemed to have no such doubts.

Next time we met I mentioned our fruitless Greenwich Village quest, ready to smile at the memory, but I discovered that he had already rendered it epic, me as Virgil to his Dante, both dangerously descending into the maelstrom of Sodom. It was no longer a simple single excursion into the pathetic Mary's, but a perilous quest somehow successfully accomplished. And, indeed, details would be, he told me, incorporated into the continuation of that serious and responsible study, *Forbidden Colors.*

A Saint Sebastian postcard, this depicting one by Il Sodoma, later arrived from Rome, and on the back Mishima wrote that Greece had filled him with "classical aspirations." I later learned that he had read Longus at the Parthenon and been given the idea of writing his own *Daphnis and Chloe.* This became *The Sound of Waves,* a novella he began once back in Japan, a country he would shortly return to, several years before me to be sure, but we would certainly often meet again. Most sincerely yours, Yukio.

In early 1954 Richie returned to Japan, began studying the lan-

guage, and supported himself by teaching at Waseda University, correcting correspondence for the newly formed Japan Air Lines and becoming film critic for the *Japan Times*.

26 APRIL 1954. I was hoping to get to review *Seven Samurai*—but the senior critic, the otherwise supportive Saisho Fumi, wanted it. I got, however, to go to the premiere today.

It was at the big Nichigeki, Toho's best house. Kurosawa had so gone over the budget that the company decided it must exploit the picture and this included a big star-filled gala premiere, but later someone told me the company would cut the picture for other local screenings. I was thus a member of that favored audience who got to see the complete picture—a single showing.

It is probably just as well that I was prevented from reviewing it. My Japanese is not nearly good enough to handle period language. I went to one of Daiei Studio's samurai films and was baffled by the many stately injunctions to go to the toilet. The toilet? asked the queried publicity person, incredulous. Yes, I quoted—*Benjo e mairo*. No, no, no, he said: Not *benjo* but (an old term for the palace court) *denjo*.

Even though I could not follow the language of *Seven Samurai*, it made little difference to my appreciation (as separate from my understanding) of the film. I have seen Alexander Dovzhenko now, and John Ford, and I was able to understand the accomplishment of Kurosawa and to recognize in that final reel one of the great feats of editing, and to see in the final scene one of cinema's great moral statements.

And there, as though in long shot on the Nichigeki stage, was Kurosawa, without the floppy hat, and my friend Hayasaka, ill I hear, standing solemn in his round horn-rimmed glasses, but still shyly smiling.

In Tokyo Richie was living in the home of Meredith Weatherby. This was a large farmhouse, a *minka*, that had been moved from the mountains of Okutama and re-erected in what was then the quiet residential district of Roppongi. The extant entries are largely about Mishima Yukio. This is because any others were used elsewhere, but these were collected for a projected book about the author, one never written.

5 MAY 1954. Meredith and I drive out to Jiyugaoka to watch Mishima take part in a local festival. He is already beside the portable shrine that he, with the others, will carry aloft, jostling the happy deity presumed inside. He is also already in costume, like the rest of the neighborhood youths—a short coat, a headband, straw sandals, no pants, just a tight loin cloth that hides the sex and cleaves the butt. Already the drums have begun their thumping and soon the neighborhood procession will begin. Yukio is only a year younger than I am—that makes him twenty-nine, but he looks nine at the most. Frail, with a narrow childish chest, he is right now grinning with excitement.

What so excites him, I wonder. If I had to run around naked in straw sandals bearing those beams until my shoulders ran blood, I would not be grinning with excitement. Then I see that all the boys are being matey with each other, that there is much good-natured joshing, and that there will be lots of touching when they push aloft the shrine. But it is not, I think, the tactile, that excites these groups; it is that what they are doing they are doing together.

Mishima, so solitary, so alone, so isolated—and this is what he always writes about—can for an hour or two be a part of society in which there are no individuals, only sets of arms and pairs of legs. What freedom he must feel. No wonder he grins.

The boys all squat down, take the great beams gratefully onto their shoulders, then stand, staggering, as the drums pound and the flute purls and this strange creature, part man, part god, begins its unsteady way down the road and Yukio grins and shouts as he passes.

1 JUNE 1954. Mishima came over this afternoon. Meredith is translating *The Sound of Waves* and Yukio's English has gotten so good that he can help. Later he often comes upstairs to where the silkworms were kept when this was a farmhouse, which is where I live.

As always, so polite that he is at the beginning distant, and yet always determined. This is because he has uses for us all. Yukio is not only a dramatist but also a practicing stage director. For the drama of his life, he has cast us in our various roles, those demanded by the rigor of the script. Each of us has his or her purpose—or else we would not have seen him at all.

Meredith is an important translator and so his relationship with Mishima is literary and concerned with the translations. I, however, am of no literary use and my role is more indeterminate. I am cast as a kind of confidante, and after he had studied the translation with Meredith downstairs he often relaxes upstairs.

Today he wanted to know more about Suetonius—was captivated by those suspicious accounts of Tiberius and Nero. I told him about Dio Cassius

Meredith Weatherby's home, 1954.

and together we looked into Heliogabalus, an emperor whose excesses interested him. Mishima today said that he felt separated from the things he really liked. He said he thought that some time in Rome under Tiberius would have been interesting—or maybe Diocletian—he was thinking of Sebastian. He toyed with the idea of reincarnation—not seriously, but as a kind of hopeful possibility, wondered if he hadn't been a Persian slave boy in an earlier life, or an indulgent emperor.

We also talked about Sanya, the working-class district of Japan where I sometimes go; about the bar run by Abe Sada, the woman who, having accidentally killed her lover, cut off his penis and carried it around with her until she was apprehended. Mishima has often told me how much he would like to go to the place—Hoshikikusui, Star Chrysanthemum Water is its name—and how he regrets he cannot.

Here the barrier is spatial, not temporal. He cannot go because of who he has already become. Thanks to the publicity he so courts, he would have been recognized. His reaction to fame is to both desire it and to deplore it. When we are out together and people recognize him he is uncomfortable. Though they do not directly approach—this is not the Japanese way—people do move

With Meredith Weatherby, 1953.

closer, and keep glancing, if not staring. He will then hail a taxi. Yet, at the same time he keeps on doing things—acting, singing, carrying on—that ensure just this troublesome kind of renown.

UNDATED, 1955. Today as we sat on my sofa and the late afternoon sun lay great horizontal rays across us, I again noticed Yukio's strong resemblance to the young André Gide: the same narrow temples, against which authors put a finger when having their pictures taken, the flat and virginal temples of the thinker, the face held like a book between those pale, flat bookends.

Also Gide-like the jaw line, long, lean, pushing the chin into an aggressive angle that seems to lead the face. These two create a strain, pull against each other—the jawbone, strong as that of a horse, leading against the restraint of the cloistered temples.

And the dichotomy continues: above, the eyes dark, even in mirth, the gaze of a divinity student; beneath, the mouth full, struggling to hold itself in. In Gide the mouth makes me think of a pomegranate; in Mishima, a flower. Not so much a rose as something more exotic—a hibiscus, perhaps.

This is a mouth that has tasted good things, but has learned not to smack its lips. It is an abstemious mouth, the kind that learns to nibble. Still, Mishima is not a French Protestant, but a Japanese with leanings toward folk-festival Shinto. The dichotomy is there, but different.

When I first met him again last year I was rereading Gide's *Journals* and had just finished the part where he, reading Stendhal's *Journals*, had come upon Napoleon's smile, ". . . in which the teeth are shown but the eyes do not smile." Mishima and Napoleon—not a bad comparison.

UNDATED, 1955. Yukio is a dandy, in the sense that Gide, like Baudelaire, was a dandy. There is nothing openly ostentatious about, say, his clothes. But if you look closely you will see that the cut is superior, that the material is the best. He's like those Tokugawa merchants who wore sober kimonos, the linings of which cost much more. For them it was governmental authority that denied display. For Mishima it is an even stricter self-denial.

A man is a dandy as a man is an epicure. With self so precious, dandyism becomes (the words are Baudelaire's) ". . . nothing but a form of gymnastics designed to fortify the will and discipline the spirit." But one may dandify the body as well as the wardrobe. Mishima tries to form himself into the image he desires, all fat, all excess melted away: spirit and body become one—a lean, hard mind in a lean, hard body.

A dandy, far from being the individual eccentric he is often thought to be, is really a strict conformist. He is beating the world at its own game. If the world says be neat, then he will astonish it by being immaculate. This is not because he himself thinks neatness a virtue. It is because the world thinks so, or says it does. To beat the world at its own game is to purposely display through excess.

But the dandy is no rebel, and no true reformer or renegade was ever a dandy. Maybe that is why society is so tolerant of dandies. They are not dangerous, since they too, in their own way, conform. This is because the dandy is not really concerned with the outside world. He is concerned only with the image he projects and—in turn—receives. Sometimes he creates a multiplicity of images through which he confounds, but only in order to dazzle himself.

There are, to be sure, intellectual dandies who push conventional ideas to extremes. This Mishima does not, cannot do. He reminds us of the dandies of an earlier time because he is so concerned with his mirror-like image of himself—stern with puritan eyes, and a full, rich mouth, often used for laughing since the eyes don't, can't laugh.

UNDATED, 1955. Mishima takes us out to a new restaurant he has discovered—French. Over the terrine he tells me that he is going to change his style, that he now admires Mori Ogai and is writing an essay on him. Mori's style is strong, sound, heavy, and will be quite different from the decorative style which Meredith assures me is Yukio's.

Meredith thinks he knows the reason for the change of style and later tells me. It is that Ishihara Shintaro and his brand new bestseller *Taiyo no Kisetsu* [Season of the Sun] have captured the attention of the young all over Japan—something that Yukio thought he had.

During dinner he talks about a topical novel—something to appeal to a wider audience—he is writing about the monk who burned down the Golden Pavilion. It will presumably be in the strong, sound, heavy style. It is now almost finished, he says, and adds that and he is going to celebrate by doing something about his body. He says he is determined to begin boxing lessons at the Nihon University Boxing Club.

During this dinner I realize that I am witnessing part of an ongoing process—the continual transformation of Yukio's life, his constant redoing of himself. And behind the still-frail framework I see the bulky inspiration It is still Omi, the early beloved, the older classmate in *Confessions of a Mask*. When I come back home I look up the passage, in Meredith's translation: "Because of him I began to love strength, an impression of overflowing blood, ignorance, rough gestures, careless speech and the savage melancholy inherent in flesh not tainted in any way with intellect."

In addition to his Tokyo journals, Richie also kept travel diaries. The first covers an extended 1954–55 visit to the Kansai beginning with a day-long trip that the bullet train now accomplishes in three hours. Following this there were trips to Sado and to Kyushu. As in his wartime journals, he was evolving a form that could accommodate both what he saw and how he felt. These culminated in his best-known work, *The Inland Sea* (1971).

27 DECEMBER 1954. I buy a pot of barley tea from my window, and as the train slides out of Tokyo Station I look down at the familiar scenes from above. This is where I have many times walked, but now I am riding. I sip my tea and quietly enjoy the thought of travel.

From my moving window I watch a man climb a smokestack, both man and chimney black against the blue of this winter sky. Children play New Year's games along the streets, and workers on the far tracks chant as their hammers simultaneously stop in midair, then crash down.

Sunlight, and Tokyo's winter colors: blue, white, black, gray. I look out at the passing city, so crossed with wires—telegraph, telephone, streetcar—that it looks like an etching.

From Yokohama the country begins—abruptly. You leave the station and you are in the fields. Buildings change, too. The roofs become thatch, and under these architecture becomes visible.

And with the farmhouses, hills and forests—forests one would not dream of in Tokyo—not a hill without its thick crest of trees. Not that the hand of man is invisible. These fields are decorated—there is neither a valley nor a hill without its advertisement. Everywhere, singers loud in the landscape. But for me, illiterate, they are welcome bits of color in the dun vocabulary of winter. Japan is particularly beautiful for those of us who cannot read.

At Ofuna, to contrast with all the beauty, there is the concrete Kannon, molded by some prewar millionaire. Enormous as it is, however, it is not pretentious. There is indeed something winning about its colossal plainness. One can become fond of the tasteless as one can of bad manners. The Ofuna Kannon, like public urination, seems to speak of some natural state beyond good taste.

Lots of people in the ugly station. People are my preferred scenery. Their presence for me informs the landscape. I know that under the thatched roof or the concrete ceiling is someone I would want to know. But we start—the platform is snatched away.

The mountains are so near. The long black, snow-covered hills close about us. Then, from behind, sliding out suddenly, is Fuji, an apparition, an impossible white. This mountain never looks real because it never looks natural. The shape is so perfect it could not but be artificial. Easy to believe it was thought sacred, even now when it is thought not—except by foreigners.

Suddenly, the sea—a blinding silver in the sun. The land drops, fields patched as in a quilt, roll down to the rocks. And, opposite, Fuji steps out like a tenor, flank forward, head in the clouds. Below, touches of color, mandarin oranges ripening on their trees. Semi-tropical, Izu at hand, the warm black current coursing along beside the tracks. Just an hour from Tokyo and I am buying from my window iced tangerines, five of them like orange snowballs.

History begins outside this Kanto Plain I am leaving. There is still room for it here. Our train track parallels the old highway, the Tokaido. I can see it swaying, closer and further, as it wobbles around our straight track, always recognizable by the double rows of cryptomeria that border it. Suddenly it turns and we do not, and I see in instant perspective the twin lanes of trees, the white road in-between. From the window of my express I am seeing what Hiroshige saw.

Odawara, a city hemmed between sea and mountain, a city trying to be as modern as Tokyo. But it cannot. History lies too heavily upon the land and Fuji rears above it like an ancestor. Odawara's shiny new electrical plant hasn't a chance.

Atami, blinding in the sun, has more successfully escaped, perhaps because the Tokaido goes elsewhere. A pleasure resort, a toy city of terraced hotels, clinging to cliffs and marching down to the flat sea. Great favorite with honeymooners—hot springs, a few lonely looking palms, strangers in a strange land. It is a nowhere city, with frivolous strings of lanterns and flags decorating the empty daytime streets.

Behind the mountains climb up and hide a stern Fuji, hanging high, invisible but felt. I look at the city below turning like a carousel as the train goes round the last curve before the tunnel, and I finish my final tangerine.

Mishima, close to cloud-covered Fuji, which still hangs above the landscape, defining it. I look at the people from my window. They seem to feel the weight. The open look of Tokyo, the pragmatic set of the mouth, the inquiring eye—there is little of this. These are the faces of those who live on the Fuji plain. Pale, eyes wary, mouths cautious, as though expecting the mountain to fall upon them. Fuji, now invisible, hangs there above the lion-colored hills.

Numazu, and we leave behind the mountains. I write this in the dining car, and at the next table are a group of Japanese ex-soldiers. One still has his cropped hair, after all these years. He also has the wary eyes of the district. He seems to know the country, covertly points out sights to the others as they pass. To me, too, it seems unfamiliar. I have not seen this land for seven years; saw it last from the window of the Allied Car in the occupied days.

Above are the hills leading back to Atami and ocean. I remember best a view of Numazu, the bay, the sea, and Fuji, spread out before me like an illuminated map, a view I remember from near a decade ago now—seen from those very hills, through the windshield of an Army jeep.

Just then the clouds shift and Fuji emerges, huge, dwarfing the towns and villages spread upward on its apron. As I write, the crown slowly parts the clouds. Now it is free, an impossibly perfect cone, floating upon the clouds, some great triangle escaped from geometry itself. At the top, snow in the crevasses, making it look old, wrinkled, the way that Hokusai shows it. But he only had a piece of paper and Fuji has an entire hemisphere. It is huge. The absurd perfection seen from a distance has vanished. Something this large can only be dangerous.

The train turns and Fuji looms then drops behind. Ahead the black hills part and I see distant icy peaks, like a row of teeth: the Japan Alps, the spine of the island itself.

At Shimizu, brilliant sun, the radishes hung to dry in the trees look like tropical fruit. Here are the real tropics. Atami is merely Florida—Shimizu is South America. The sea extends along one side, a curving bay. The water looks warm enough to swim in, and in Tokyo this morning it was freezing.

Shizuoka, one tall building, Venetian rococo it seems, and right beside it a Shinto shrine, all ancient lacquer. In the station, electric clocks painted apple green and in front of them men sweeping the floors wearing twelfth-century hats. No one finds this novel or charming or incongruous except me.

In the passing freight car, lumber from the mountains, great shaggy logs covered with thick bark and thin snow. A party boards, very drunk, and begins singing folk songs in steady voices while Fuji, now demoted to a hill, solemnly waves at us as we round a bend. In front of it a single red advertising balloon hangs like a long-stemmed cherry—all that is left of Shizuoka.

Bentenjima, halfway to Kyoto. I stopped overnight many years ago but now recognize nothing, nor does the train, which rushes by without looking. But it is a pretty town—a country village by the sea or a seaside hamlet in the fields. The ocean has invaded the town on one side, and a mountain river presses against it on the other. Caught between the two, little Bentenjima makes the best of it.

I go to the end of the car and stand hanging out of the doorway as the wind rushes past and the town dwindles. Even on the smallest railways where I came from in America, you can't do this. You're too well taken care of. You can't even open the train windows any more. But not here. Life is cheap. Anyone who wishes may lean from the doorway of the moving train. Those who care to fall out may do so.

Back in my seat I eat the grass-green caramels I bought at Hamamatsu, bought mainly to enjoy the illicit delights of buying through an open window. They taste like the sickly waxen taffy I chewed when very young. Japan is the land where all penny-candy should come from.

Much colder now as we leave the sea and turn to the mountains. No more citron, only piles of lemon-colored rice straw and the light green of the radish tops against the brown soil—these are country colors. And at Ozaki a country train boy in the platform house across the track is drinking tea, staring straight head, does not see me, and seems to be thinking. Absurdly, I want him to see me. The train jerks. He does not.

Travel in Japan gives a sense of accomplishment. I have just looked at my map and discovered that if I had gone in a line straight west of Tokyo I would now be far out in the Japan Sea, having crossed the entire island.

Yet Japan does not seem small. It is a full-sized country, larger than England. Its earlier reputation of being tiny, dainty, delicate, comes from imagination alone. Japan is a big country but one that does not lie down on you, like America or Australia. It is the right size for human habitation.

Nagoya, more barley tea from the window, but the pot is different. No longer is it the squat Kanto shape but now, already, the graceful and impractical spouted pot from the Kansai. Even the embossed logos are different—here a little fan. Kanto and Kansai are much more different than just East and West. I look out of the window and see passing me the tiled roofs of the city—itself a pottery center. They are blacker and heavier-seeming than those of Tokyo. Here Osaka is already felt.

Owari-Ichinomiya—late afternoon sun, the browns become reddish, the greens deepen into black, and the playing children in the passing shrine cast long shadows behind them like capes. The silhouette of the train and its smoke races along the bank, then suddenly rears and rolls—a terrible wreck—as the bank turns to a wall, a station, a crossing. In the distance, russet mountains, the houses all black, still too early for the supper lights.

Gifu, a mountain of stained wood, black tiled roofs and barred windows. Directly beyond it are miniature mountains, arranged in the steep, impossible shapes of mountains in Chinese scrolls. The late afternoon sun turns the water red, then black. I look for cormorants on the oily evening river, but see none.

Across the aisle a middle-aged pair are entertaining each other. From the window he has endlessly bought beer, chocolate, rice cakes, tangerines, gumdrops. These he feeds her. They laugh too much, are having too good a time to be married. When he gets up—the toilet doubtless—I glance up and she stares boldly back. They are enjoying themselves.

Sekigahara—a plain where a barrier stands, you might translate it. Here is where Ieyasu fought—and won. It is much colder, the glass pane frosts, and the train is traveling more slowly, as though winded. We are on a high plateau with round, snow-covered mountains on either side. The dim sun still reaches the clouds and they turn a cold pink. But down here in the high valley it is dark and the houses are lighted.

A fine, light snow is falling and the window is cold. I pass a small boy playing with his dog in the snow. Then we enter a short tunnel. Two minutes later I see another boy playing with his dog in the snow. The two boys will never meet, nor will the dogs—a whole mountain lies between them.

It grows darker and the pines are black. The pink clouds have faded to gray, like dying embers. The smoke from the engine turns white as spume and catches in the limbs of the black pines. In the distance, lights. It is suppertime all over the land and families are gathering. As we chug by I try to look into the passing houses to glimpse the families illuminated, caught forever with ladle in the pot, spoon in the soup.

Now it is dark, and yet, in the faint light from the dying sky I see one old man. He is still working in a snowy field, turning the soil. The work is finished but for this small corner. This is what the old man has done while I have been traveling from Tokyo.

Then Maibara, now quite dark, the station lighted. There is a winter feeling to this early darkness, and I have the taste of cinders in my mouth and the air is chill. Somewhere before long, Lake Biwa, but we will not see it.

Kyoto. Here it has been raining, and I sit in the Nara train waiting for it to leave. Kyoto is black and silent under the heavy sky. Few people about. I look at those who are. It is difficult to describe the Kansai face, but I think its difference lies in its shape. There is a fullness, a roundness which in Kyoto is called full-moon beauty in both men and women. In men too, perhaps a slightly lighter complexion, slightly thinner features, something in the curve of the cheek. The young man across the aisle from me, for example. Were this Tokyo I would still guess Kyoto.

And behind him sit the couple from the Tokyo train. It is quiet enough now that I can overhear. She is saying that it is too bad it was so dark going through Hachiman for she was unable to make anything of it. She also is calling him *sensei*. This is an important clue but at the same time a confusing one. Is he really her teacher? Is she actually his student? Or is it simply being used in an honorary sense—in which case he can be anything at all. She raises her arm a bit coquettishly for a student and her kimono sleeve falls back. I gaze into her armpit but she doesn't look back.

Now a friend of the boy across the way has come and they are talking and I realize that I cannot understand one word of what is being said. A girl joins them and that makes things a bit more comprehensible. She is talking about her *sueta* [sweater], otherwise it is all thick, heavy Kansai accent. I wonder if

I will be able to understand anything down here. They, thanks to radio and movies, will be able to understand me.

In what other country, I wonder, could eight hours of travel make this much difference? If I traveled eight more I would reach Kyushu, where even a Japanese from somewhere else is linguistically lost?

Nara—the mistress of the inn is busy making me feel at home. I can understand her, but then she is, as she tells me, from Shizuoka. We like to talk in Shizuoka, she says. Says she is happy she can understand me.

She goes to see about the bath and I look around. A large celadon rabbit in the alcove, and the scroll is a Nara scene. The same thing is outside the window, the famous pond. No celluloid kewpie in the alcove, I am happy to see. And not only for aesthetic reasons. Celluloid kewpies mean a certain kind of half-baked, hopefully-Western way of thinking that repulses romantic me.

In the bath more conversation, this about what I am going to have for supper. The real purpose of the talk is her perfectly natural desire to see a naked foreigner. This desire is divorced from any erotic intent. She is merely curious. Satisfied, we agree that I am to have sashimi and tempura. She says she is happy at the choice.

Back in the room, there she is again. This time with a modest request. She wants to know how to say *kutsu o nuide kudasai* in English. I tell her: please take off your shoes. Says she is happy. This is to be used on foreigners who would otherwise walk her mats in their footwear. We are a troublesome lot, it is true. As I left the bath I noticed that the maid ran in at once to ascertain that I had not, indeed, used the soap in it.

The mistress herself serves my supper and then sits to watch me eat it, talking the while. She assumes that I know more Japanese than I do and I consequently understand less and less. Fortunately, however, she knows little English—merely one phrase that, oddly, is: I am happy.

28 DECEMBER 1954. At a way station in the forests above Kasuga Shrine. From where I sit, the path, mossy even in winter, disappears around a bend, lost among the great trees of these park-like woods. The pines shut out the winter sun but the forest floor is dappled. It is yet early and, hanging in the higher branches, the morning mist still rises. It is cold and my breath too rises to the rafters of this deserted hut in which I sit.

I have just left Kasuga Shrine itself, vermilion in the early morning sun, the priests moving, dim and white, through the dark and polished corridors. It is an open shrine, more like a pavilion in the woods, and its colors are red and white against the evergreen of the trees and the blue of the morning winter sky.

Below, in the park, the deer wander through the groves. Their coats are shaggy because it is winter and their horns are short because they are cut in the fall. They look at me with their Asiatic eyes and are not afraid. Then one turns, flicks his tail, and they bound over the frosted moss to disappear into the furthest fringe of the forest.

An old woman with a tray came by offering cakes to feed the deer. They hear her and return, looking expectantly at me. Now, high in the forest, I can see them still, wandering below, but the old woman has gone. The sun shines but it is not warm. There is a silence broken only by the cry of a winter bird.

By a pond near the Shosoin. The birds call and the deer bark, and the stagnant pond lies brown and mottled, reflecting the great roof of the Daibutsuden. The sun has gone and a cold wind ruffles the surface. The upside-down temple shudders.

Kofukuji. Across a narrow reflecting pond is the five-storied pagoda. As I gaze up at it I hear two women behind me talking. One is saying that it is not really the best, not that old. I look it up in my guidebook and, sure enough, it is a reconstruction. But then what isn't—the original was ninth century. Then I read more carefully. This recent copy was made about fifty years before America was discovered.

Having descended into town, I drink coffee in a small shop made hideous with advertisements of something in CinemaScope. Nara the city is banal; Nara, the ancient capital, the park, is—well—sublime. And sitting here sipping my mocha, I suddenly understand why.

Nature—nature roams the park, and the works of man have either vanished or exist but in fragments. Like the deer, nature does as it will, and the shrines above are where it rests. And this modern and stifling little coffee shop is only fifteen minutes by foot from the depths of the forest where I was this morning.

Later, I meet some Tokyo students feeding the deer and ask if they know of a cheap inn. They suggest theirs, very near the park and very cheap. So now I have moved from the most expensive place in Nara to the least. The other was a thousand five hundred yen a night with two meals. This one is four hundred with one.

The tatami is dusty, the windows leak cold air, and no one brings me tea, but I like it better. My new landlady regards me with such suspicion that she leaves me entirely alone. I did not again see the talkative mistress from my prior inn but I imagine she is not happy at the loss of a customer. The taxi driver who carried me and my bag from one domicile to the other was astonished. The economic shift I had made was enormous and the only thing that would have surprised him more would have been if it had been in the opposite direction.

The new landlady has just brought tea, after all. She is still suspicious but now more curious. She keeps turning her head to one side as she regards me—like one of the deer. Now I sit in a restaurant near the station having wandered about trying to find the office of the *Yamato Times*. Taking many a wrong turning I have consequently seen most of the city.

Nara is smaller than I thought. It took about an hour to walk around it. Once off the main avenues the streets turn narrow and the houses hang over the traffic. Like a lot of Kansai, the place looks more like China than anything in Tokyo does. If I look down one of these cluttered black perspectives and smell the charcoal burning, I can be back in Shanghai in the winter.

These streets keep leading me back to the lake and park. I come across a small pagoda, three stories, unpretentious, a dusty red. I admire it. For so large a building it seems to weigh little. The structure is apparent and the space under and around the eaves balances that of the bulk. I stay and admire until the deer find me. So I buy them some cakes. Trying these myself I wonder at their enthusiasm. No taste at all—dry, hard, empty.

Having written this, I look up and see a student sitting at the next table. His name, I am to learn, is Tani Hiroaki, and he is kind enough to help me find the *Yamato Times*. Big, boisterous, very polite, he stays with me while I talk with the editor who gives me, in addition to his time, a map of the city, and expresses a polite interest in my newspaper, the *Japan Times*, in the distant capital. After that Tani has to go home but we are to meet again this evening.

Rest of the afternoon spent trying find a place to go to the toilet. This is always a problem in Japan and even if a place is found it never has any paper. The Japanese wisely carry their own. Since I do not, I tramped the streets and finally retreated to my inn, where I hoped they had some.

They didn't, so I had to ask for some. At once the serving girl set up a merry noise. The spectacle of a foreigner in a Japanese toilet is a happy one and it is even better to be informed of it in advance. My simple request brought gurgles of delight. Of course her pleasure had a point. The Japanese toilet is supposed difficult for Westerns to manage. Strange that these people who willingly relinquish traditional underwear and phallic worship should cling to their toilets. Even now I can hear the maids chattering of the event. I have made their day interesting, memorable, and worthwhile.

29 DECEMBER 1954. Late in the morning. We overslept and Tani is now down washing. The breakfast is on the table and as I wait for him I write, this page cold against my hand.

Last night he took me on a tour of the brothels of Nara. They are nothing like what Tokyo offers. Rather, they are low, black, Naniwa-style, with wide front entrances, like brightly lighted stables. And, on either side of the gate-like door, two old women huddled over braziers and called out to the passersby. Just inside, as though on stage, sit the girls, some in kimono, some in dresses. They read, talk, and warm themselves. The customers step into the entryway and stare at them. It is like a waxworks, a *tableau vivant*. Except that the girls talk, make jokes, and stare back.

I ask Tani where they come from and he says probably from the country. In one place he asks and she says she is from Tokyo. He tells me that they all say they are from Tokyo. We look a lot, then go out and have more sake.

He is now returned from the bath and we eat breakfast—miso soup, seaweed, egg to put on the rice, pickles, and tea. Sometimes I have trouble with the Japanese breakfast—want my coffee, my toast, my jam. With the smiling Tani opposite me I happily slurp my soup.

He was born and raised in Nara but now goes to school in Tokyo. Is home for the holidays. His hair and eyebrows are very black and his teeth are very white; his hands are chapped and red, knuckles are big and flat. He is a member of the boxing team at university. Is just twenty-one.

We are in the train but still at the station—Nara Station, which seeks, outside at any rate, to suggest ninth-century architecture. Inside, however, it is all done in Ordinary Railway Station—tiles, fluorescent light, benches. Tani wants to know what I am writing. I do not know how to say journal. So I say Jean-Jacques Rousseau. Since he receives the enormous smattering that all Japanese students get, he nods and is now convinced I am writing my confessions. Which, in a way, I suppose I am. Ah, the bells are ringing and the orange and candy sellers gather around the windows. We are off for Horyuji.

Horyuji. We walk through the paddies for almost half an hour before seeing it—a walled compound, half hidden in pine, the pagoda bristling above the trees. Just as we mount the steps leading to the great gate the sun appears for the first time today.

The Kondo is a square, intricately wrought building, dragons flying at all

With Tani Hiroaki. Nara, 1954.

angles, the inner eaves supported by patient lions. The building is square and flat as a Quaker meeting hall, and inside stand the statues, dimly gleaming, as though testifying.

Outside the compound we sit and smoke. Tani has just gone over to examine one of the trees that flank the court. It is a shell, hollowed out by the years until it looks like a large ebony carving. The sky is visible through its holes and yet it lives—from the top green leaves appear. Tani has asked the local photographer its name. He doesn't know. So he asks him to take our pictures.

We visit the Daihozoden, a museum turned into a church by the offerings left in front of the art works. An idea we might well emulate. I would leave mine in front of Vermeer, Chardin.

Then, around a corner, I come upon the Kudara Kannon, whose picture I have often seen. But photographs have not prepared me for the effect. It is frightening—the cry of a large bird or the sudden appearance of a giant nursemaid. The face is feathered with verdigris—and she is eight feet tall and from Korea. Also she is a thousand years old.

Walking along we come across the Yumendo, the octagonal building I have often seen. It was in a volume of the *Book of Knowledge* that I gazed at as a child. It is also on the reverse side of the thousand yen bill. We stand, Tani, the priest in charge, and me, just such a bill in hand, and solemnly compare. See, it is just the same.

Tani is full of questions. Is that kind of wood expensive? How much did that gilt cost? He properly pays no attention to the beauty of the work, only its value. Others also ask questions. An elderly couple turns to one another. "It is very old," says one. "Maybe one hundred years," ventures the other. "No," says the priest, "more like a thousand." "Oh," they say, "*very* old."

30 DECEMBER 1954. A brilliant day and we slept until ten. After breakfast, however, the sun retired and so I wrote postcards and Tani read movie magazines, just as if we were waiting for its reappearance.

I suddenly realize how happy I am—it is an instant assurance, but when I try to grasp it, it slips to one side, eludes me. It seems to me that I ask little to be so happy, yet this kind of conscious happiness is so rare that I remember all the times when it has occurred. This is now one of them. Ah, see, the clouds are parting. Tani looks out of the window and up at the sky, his neck strong in the weak light.

Todaiji—looking like a section of some celestial city, but sharing with the rest of Nara the pleasing appearance of a capital in ruins. Inside the hall, big as a stadium, we see the famous Daibutsu himself. There is something theatrical about him. I am reminded of backstage at the opera, during, perhaps, *Lakmé*. This is because everything is so huge. The statue looms like a holy King Kong. And behind, the rows of statues make the place even more theater-like. They are the patient audience to all this absurd grandeur.

In so secular an atmosphere the crowd makes no effort to hush itself. A tourist party, laughter echoing back and forth, attempts to push a small and reluctant child through a hole in one of the pillars. "No, no, go on now," says an adult in Tokyo dialect, "One time through means good luck forever."

Nigatsudo—up on the side of the mountain, the roof of the Daibutsu a colossal tent below. Around it the rest of Nara, clear and sharp as in a photograph. This pavilion of the second month is not kept up. It is dirty and dusty and the neighborhood children play familiarly at the front gate. From here the stairs start and climb the hill behind to the great veranda that encircles the temple proper.

We sit there and look at the view, the big pagoda by the distant pond standing like a pine, the fertile vale of old Yamato stretching to the mountains on the horizon—and Tani makes a sketch of what he sees while I write in this journal until the wind chills the fingers and I can no longer hold the pen.

We stop, cold, in a warm open shop and eat *warabi mochi*, a hot and grainy concoction, made of *yuba* powder and sugar and probably much else. Tani discovers that the shop is built around a live pine tree and runs outside to observe the effect.

Back at the inn we wait for the bath to be free, both of us lying on the floor by the brazier and talking about the war. He was about ten at the time. It was terrible, he says. You couldn't get any candy or anything. Then he tells me about some war hero he particularly admired but I don't know any military history, and so we give up.

31 DECEMBER 1954. Tonight we walk the lanes of Kyoto, and I am once again struck by the difference from Tokyo. It is just as busy, just as full of neon and pachinko, yet not at all the same. Perhaps it is that the neon is attached to an ancient façade and that the pachinko is next to an eighteenth-century dwelling. It is the feeling of the old still alive in this city that makes it different. And today the women and children are already in kimono, that traditional dress.

I wander about without my map, trusting to memory, but soon become lost. We sit in the courtyard of a temple I may once have been in and watch the children fly their kites, sharp against the cold winter sky. One kite is caught against the telephone wires and the wind beats it to death. Later, on the other side of town, we are in a coffee shop and it is quietly raining—as it always seems to be here. The streets are full and I look at the people but see no other foreigners.

Later, near Yasuka Shrine, the streets are so full I walk in the gutter. *Maiko* and geisha are out, parading on the edge of the Gion. Maybe Japan looked like this fifty years ago. Here people turn to look at me. They seem surprised when I smile.

A small boy with his parents sits drinking hot orange juice and staring at me, turning away when I look, but always swiveling back. Friendly and shy, he drinks with both hands. On his head is a baseball cap with a large M on it. Now he lifts the glass, trying to get at the sugar at the bottom with his little pink tongue. The *geta* on the foot of a sleeping little girl is nudged by a tired parent, and I hear the little bell inside it.

1 JANUARY 1955. Excitedly awakened by the maids who insist upon our coming down to the big room for breakfast—the ceremonial first meal of the first day. We are given *otose*, very sweet herb-filled sake, then charred fish, lotus roots, preserved beans, frozen tofu, lots more sake. Before we are fully awake we are drunk.

Ceremony often takes the place of civility here. Politeness, in my sense, is sometimes missing. Instead, we are given to understand that an honor is being done us. Here we are treated to food and flattery but we are not the objects, we are the side-benefits.

This is not so with Tani at the train station, however. He must go home—his parents doubtless wondering just where he has been these past few days. Our ceremony of departure is personal. We ourselves are the reason for our formality. He bows, I bow, we shake hands. We will meet again, in Tokyo, often, always. And he stands soberly, black in his student uniform as the train pulls out, looking until I disappear.

My coach is almost empty. Only a man and his son, and a soldier. My room for the night shakes, comes alive, and I look back over black Kyoto and there is the moon rising.

The friendship with Tani Hiroaki was to continue through the lives of the two men. (Those wishing to read a fuller version of the meeting and to learn what followed are referred to the "Hiroyasu Yano" section of *Public People, Private People*, 1987.)

2 MAY 1955. On the steamer from Niigata to Sado Island, Tani and I lie on the tatami in the big, second-class salon. We have just been given tea and the ship is already rolling. Overhead the loudspeakers are pouring out recorded folksongs from fabled Sado, and the decks are full. So is the tatami; I had my feet on someone's open book.

We left Tokyo yesterday noon, for no reason other than that we wanted to, and in six hours had crossed the island, gone over the still snow-covered mountains, and gently descended to the plains by the Sea of Japan.

Ah, the motion of the boat has already lulled Tani to sleep.

*

At Aikawa. Sado is much larger than I had thought. The bus trip across it took almost two hours. And it has high, snowy mountains, too—as well as streams and lakes. Not much like an island except that you can see the sea more often.

Tani is impressed by its resemblance to his part of the country, near Nara, and accents on the bus indicate that, indeed, almost everything came from Kansai. I look from the window of the bus and recognize the architecture, and the shape of the fields—like the fields of Kyoto.

Sado is still pleasingly primitive, however, and considering its fame, is still not touristy. The towns remind me of Calabrian villages—they are that plainly, that casually put together. Ryotsu, where we landed, could have been a village on the Adriatic.

We are now in an inn on the other side of the island, drinking tea and eating cakes the like of which I have not seen before. Brown and bitter. My audience sits and looks. The hotel maids find my white skin and round eyes so different they cannot bring themselves to leave. They keep staring at me and then at the cakes. Probably expect me to rub them into my hair.

A long walk, both of us in *geta*, and at the end we reach a small park beside the sea. There are bridges and a hill and a toy temple, desolate and swept by a strong, steady wind from the Sea of Japan. I see that the bushes, even the trees, have learned over the years to lean away from it. It must always blow.

We rent a boat and Tani rows me far off to the pebbly shore, where a single, enormous rock hangs suspended between two cliffs. We were going to explore, but the boat drifts off and we catch it just in time.

After supper we go to the local theater to see a dance program—the famed Sado Okesa. Though this is famous as a women's dance, all eight dancers tonight are boys. They wear girls' kimono and red ribbons, but this is their single concession to femininity. They are probably carpenter apprentices or fishermen, and they dance like it—rough, male. This unison dance is full of high steps, the kimono opening as the dancer turns. But instead of the rounded calves of fisher maids, we see the muscular thighs of the local boys. Japan is casual about gender. This is the dance the men know too, and so they perform it for the benefit of their neighbors and whatever visitors the town might be having.

Performance over, I congratulate the boys in their women's straw hats and pretty ribbons. They are flushed and friendly, but not very used to foreigners. The children, for example, do not shout out *haro*, as they do in Kyoto, or simply pay no attention as they now do in Tokyo. Rather, they look, mouth open, then turn away, suddenly shy. This is true of many of the adults, too. No one seems to stare and yet, when you look back, the gazes are still sliding away.

Much later. Tani is asleep on his stomach, half on the *futon*, half not. He breathes quietly, regularly, his profile sharp against the shoji, shadowless in the night light.

3 MAY 1955. A boat ride to Senkakuwan, a large and rocky bay with an island at the further end and a hanging bridge famous for some reason or other. We

left the boat and went up a steep path to the plateau from where we can see the whole coast.

Tani has already seen the place. It is famous as the location for some movie. Here, he tells me, is where Michiko stood and wept. Why? I asked. Because she had yet again missed her lover. And they almost met on that bridge back there. Then I remembered the film, *Kimi no Na wa [What Is Your Name?]*, in which the two followed each other all over Japan, always missing by inches.

After a long and seemingly perilous bus ride we have come to Ogi, on the southern side of the island. It is a pleasant fishing village, more prosperous-looking than most, and split into two by a large cliff. We take the top floor, a single room, of an enormous, rambling old inn. From here the wind shakes the windows and we can see miles out to sea.

Later we get a rowboat and go out into the bay, heading for a small shrine on the opposite shore, past little islands that hold large sea caves. We row into one and push our way up a dim channel to a dark beach where the rocks and sands are black.

The light from the distant opening is bright, but the cave is like night and reflections as though from the moon are cast across its ceiling. We beach the boat and look for interesting stones. Tani finds so many that we cannot carry them all, though we fill all our pockets

When we leave the sun has gone and wind come up. We row with it, and just as we reach the hotel the rain begins. Now the windows are rattling and there is the smell of brine in the room. The electric light flickers and Tani sits across from me, looking at what I write, wondering if it is about him, but not asking.

4 MAY 1955. The weather has now cleared and Tani has gone to the harbor while I, having slipped on the rocks in my *geta* this morning, stay in. We had rented a motorboat and gone to a pair of small islands off the coast, Yajima and Kyojima. These little islands, each only a couple hundred yards across, rise straight from the sea, and hold some tiny peaks, upon one of which Nichiren is supposed to have sat for a month or so. Clumping about in my *geta*, carrying my paper umbrella, I was thinking about the predicament of the foreigner—ridiculous if he does not adapt, amusing if he does—when I slipped and banged my foot.

Now, laying down my pen, I look out over the bay and there is Tani now, tiny in the distance, black in his school uniform, paddling along in a small, perfectly round boat, unable to make any progress at all. I regard him for a time as he struggles and then wish I had gone with him so that we could have enjoyed the predicament together.

5 MAY 1955. Boy's Day, paper carp flying from the roofs indicating the number of male children within—some have up to five. We take a bus to Akadomari and get a room directly on the sea. Here people do stare, so I must seem truly odd. The girl at the inn tells me that no foreigners have come for five years. I believe it. I am followed about the streets by processions of small boys who perhaps think that I am part of their celebration. When I turn to show my fangs, however, they scatter.

Tani and I leave the hotel to walk along the beach and a whole group is lying in ambush, but one look at my horrid face and they flee. All except one, who falls down. I stand over him and say that foreigners find nothing more delicious than a child. The others, coming back to rescue him, stand in a line, and I turn and ask which among them tasted best. They look wide-eyed, and then the older and more sophisticated begin to smile. By this time, however, the fallen boy under my feet has scrambled away in terror.

We walk along the seaside so far as the shrine, high up on a cliff, surrounded by cedar. It is so still at the top, that I can hear the whisper of the surf far below and the cry of the distant sea bird. In every Japanese village there is such a place—clean and quiet, where anyone may come.

Akadomari is a poor village, like many on Sado. Here the poverty hidden in the towns is displayed. The main street is unpaved, the houses are old, and the plaster is cracked. Children play in the dust and munch stalks of burdock. I do not see any of those candy stores beloved of the big town young.

As the maid puts down our *futon* she tells me that I have been the main entertainment this boy's festival, that the children are talking of nothing else. She also adds politely that she herself is so excited she does not know what to do. All this is Kansai-accented language, which she is not at all surprised to see that I understand. Indeed, no one is surprised that I speak Japanese. In the cities one is being forever complimented, as though learning the language of the country you live in is some kind of feat. Not here. Here we are so strange in ourselves that an added bit of oddness—knowing the language, for example—is as nothing by comparison.

In the bath sliced iris stems are floating, filling the surface. Tani and I sit in this prehistoric lake, and I am a mighty brontosaurus, head breaking the surface. He says he is a baby brontosaurus and lies on his back to allow the smaller head to rise. I ask him if the iris, so much a part of Boy's Day, is truly invigorating. He says he thinks so.

6 MAY 1955. Waiting for the steamer back to Honshu we walk about, look at the souvenirs, eat when not hungry, drink when not thirsty, all those things one does when waiting. There are boats to rent and Tani is wild to row again, but after all we have now drunk and eaten we decide not to. Instead we get a haircut for me.

The steamer is crowded and we can barely find room. Children everywhere, boys mainly. Perhaps returning from their holiday. Perhaps going for a holiday. On the island, as in the rest of rural Japan nowadays, lots of kids and oldsters, lots of girls too, but few young men. They have all gone to the city to work. Not many will return.

In the train, waiting for it to start back to Tokyo. The station loudspeaker is playing Poulenc. In what other country, I wonder, would they play *Les Biches* as departure music? No other country. In Japan, however, the music is merely Western, of no particular cut or shape. Like Guy Lombardo, Bach, and "Jingle Bells," it is appropriate, particularly for departure, adding its modish, festive, Western tone.

Tani sits across from me, his feet in my lap. He is sleeping, indeed is usually sleeping when I write in this journal. He is tired but happy because this trip has taken him to the ends of the earth, the great edge of the empire. But now he has awakened and is looking at me writing. I shall stop, for soon we will start.

17 SEPTEMBER 1955. Fukuoka from the air looks like Cleveland; on the ground it looks like Pittsburgh—but a Pittsburgh that something has happened to. Fukuoka is one of the few Japanese cities that still looks as though it has been destroyed. And now the reconstruction chokes the streets and tosses its waste to the skies. Along with this, a lack of friendliness. My questions are answered politely but shortly, my inquiries with a firm courtesy and nothing more. Then I notice that there are still lots of jeeps and young male foreigners on the streets. The U.S. Army is still here, years after the end of the Occupation. I understand this aloofness.

Karatsu—one of those seaside towns that seem always out of season. Just enough of the festive—strings of lanterns, plastic maple leaves—to lend an air of sustained melancholy. A few lights glimmer; there is a distant phonograph, a faraway laugh, and the sound of *amado* being slid shut. It is all very sad. I amble through the darkened streets and finally sit down in front of the bus terminal, where two men are already sitting. I remark that it is a sad town. Yes, they agree. Karatsu is a sad and lonely town. They are both carpenters, and both have had enough to drink, to become melancholy but still coherent. "If you really want to have fun," says one of them, "there is some place to go, though, a really nice place—Fukuoka."

18 SEPTEMBER 1955. Early morning at the Karatsu station, the clouds hang low over the far mountains then fall like cascades down the slopes, a part still clinging to the pines at the top. It begins to rain and the mountains are gone, their places taken by ink washes, only a dim outline remaining, impossible to see which is mountain, which cloud.

Near me on the station platform sit two older women, two girls, and a baby. Every once in a while one of the girls turns to the baby and says *o-me-me,* and the child, obedient, opens wide its little eyes and turns them high into its little head. The girls shriek with delight and the baby, having performed its single trick, screams as well. Finally, the older women must shake their fingers in order to continue their own interrupted conversation. Then one of the girls says *o-me-me,* and it starts all over again. The baby crows, claps its hands, and the girls lean against each other in their delight.

Kubata—a small, gray square surrounded by small, frame buildings. It rains, and inside, the station steams. Then the train shudders, begins to steam as well, and the trip to Nagasaki begins. We click and patter along an oyster gray sea, with high cliffs and houses at preposterous angles, leaning out toward the small islands that dot the bay, all decorated with small, fragile-looking pines. Around a bend slides Mount Unzen, the meadows in front foreshortened by the black and steaming mass behind. Staring at all these sights hitherto unseen, I buy a *bento* and recognize everything in it, except something that looks like orange peel and tastes like fish.

Nagasaki, a true southern city, with parasols, shirtsleeves, palms, and a bright, dusty atmosphere. The downtown is hidden away in the alleys and is difficult to find. It reminds me of a Chinese city, with its labyrinth of lanes and its shops that open out into your lap. In all my wanderings here, however, I have not been able to find a cheap hotel.

Determined to economize later, I now sit high above a formal-looking garden, gazing at the distant hills and drinking a sweet tea I have never tasted before. Made of flowers, it seems. And the sunny afternoon is so quiet, morning rains all gone, that I can hear the crickets below me.

In the evening I walk about the back streets of the city. In general, I am disregarded. Foreigners have been here before. Some even came and dropped an atom bomb on the city. I feel more of an outsider here than I ever do in Shinjuku or Asakusa. Yet, Nagasaki at night is much like those two pleasure quarters—everything is given over to the appetites.

I go to Maruyama, the prostitute section. It is large and very logically laid out. Like Washington, D.C., it has main avenues, circles, spoked streets, and an apparent assumption that it will last forever. As in the Kansai, the girls sit in large and brightly lighted *genkan,* as though on stages. Dressed in the brightest kimono, each assumes a mannequin-like pose, fan in hand, head turned back or shoulder raised, an erotic neckline showing. Two old women on either side of the doorway attempt to direct the traffic, and occasionally the girls themselves cry out in shrill, birdlike voices.

A few English words are tried out on me as I pass (Hey, you), but when I stop and step into one of the brilliantly lighted entryways, all twittering stops. After I offer polite phrases in Japanese (*Konban wa. Ikaga desu ka?*), there is silence, and then, suddenly, laughter. This is not derision, but a sort of surprise, a kind of friendliness that seeks to put me at my ease. Two come forward, smiling through their makeup, ready to maneuver me upstairs. Such, however, does not occur. Rather, we stand there and talk about various things—about how nice Nagasaki is; how I ought to have gone to Karatsu only for the festival, for it is then lively enough for anyone; that in Kumamoto I should try the horse—delicious. Then, a young girl in a red kimono asks, "And what is Tokyo like?"

And the way in which she asks it, that half-hidden tone of longing, that self-deprecating shake of the head as though Tokyo has been often thought of, but—it is so far away, so expensive—always given up on. The two old ladies suddenly bark, and I suddenly see her life as she sees it. Then, with a show of vivacity, she asks, "And the Ginza? I was there once." And the spell is broken. I am on the outside again, looking in.

Past midnight, I stop and talk to the young doorman at a cabaret called The Florida. "Don't bother," he says, looking at me looking inside the paneled door. "We're closing up anyway." So, I invite him to come with me and have a drink. He hangs up his epauletted coat, and we drink beer and eat cheese in a small bar at the edge of Shinbashi, the night district. His name is Sakaguchi, and he is from the farm, and after graduating high school this was all in the way of a job he could manage. He then says his generation is truly unfortunate. I ask why. He says that those now over thirty at least knew the war, knew what life was like before it, and though much poorer now, at least they knew what they could do because they had done it. His generation, however, was different. It had never had the opportunity of doing anything, and so does not know what it can do and, he added, never will. All of this is said with no self-pity. He is sorry for his generation, not for himself.

19 SEPTEMBER 1955. The bus ride from Isohara to Shimabara, through Unzen Park, filled with forested mountain slopes and stately hotels with steam coming from the roofs like smoke. Here was the great prewar spa, where people from Shanghai and Hong Kong came to take the waters, to ride, to play golf, and to dance until dawn. It seems no longer so elegant. I see tour buses in front of the façades, like buggies at the Ritz. And here around the corner comes the tour group: office workers, keeping step, singing at the top of their lungs, safe in their crocodile.

Shimabara, down by the sea, is not elegant at all. It is all business, all crisscrossed with narrow lanes and with no direct approach to the bay. Nets are carried through the streets; fishermen in their boots walk along the streetcar tracks, and for supper I eat a prawn as big as a small dog. This is where the last Christians held out after Hideyoshi went after them, but you would never know it.

20 SEPTEMBER 1955. On the boat to Kumamoto. The sea is a lake and the ship seems hardly to move at all. Only the passing fishing boats show that we glide through the heavy water with a kind of imperative energy, as though we must move like an airplane or else we will drop like a rock to the bottom. Away from the shore the sea turns light green, celadon under the first light of the clouded sun.

I sit on the third class deck and wish for breakfast, while around me, those wiser drink cold sake from teacups. They are now well through the bottle and are singing. It is *Saraba Raburu,* but in place of that lost Pacific port they have substituted Matsubara, which means some extra syllables to cope with. At the end of the first line they still have a mouthful, and turn to look at each other. Then they repeat it. They, indeed, never get further than this first line.

A further complication is that the ship's loudspeakers have decided to regale us with Stephen Foster. This, I feel, is no accident. Indeed, I believe that the majesty of Unzen looming over us, with its crags and peaks, is thought well-augmented by these homemade strains from far away. Soon the native singers themselves are all nodding their heads over Jeanie with the light brown hair, while the sublime mountain recedes.

Kumamoto—the bombings still visible a decade later. Vacant lots in the middle of the city, cleaned up, but empty, naked looking. Indications of the Occupation as well—signs to the Ordinance Dump, a shirt maker's sign in English, a jeep or two on the streets but driven by Japanese, perhaps sold to them by departing Occupiers. The conductor on the streetcar I took into town from the port was filled with understanding, a sure sign that he is used to the lost, the strayed, the foreign.

This is the only place in Kyushu where I know anyone—the family of a friend in Tokyo. I find the house and they, having been forewarned, are expecting to see me. My loneliness lifts like a cloud when they take me into the family. Watermelon is produced, the son is spoken of, and a soft *futon* is provided.

21 SEPTEMBER 1955. The younger brother of a friend shows me the ruins of Kumamoto Castle and describes the siege of a century ago in a vocabulary I cannot possibly understand. Then we go to the museum. Since he is keen on history, he acts out some of the historical exploits, waving his arms, jumping up into the ramparts. I ask how Saigo died, hoping for a *harakiri*, but he tells me that he expired in Kagoshima, and that is out of his province.

In the afternoon I take the express to that city, and pass many fishing villages, each so beautiful with its coves and crags and little seaside shrine that I want to stop and stay forever. But the train goes so fast that by the time I have managed to read the first syllable of its name, flashing by on the platform sign, the entire place has been yanked from view, never to be seen again.

Viewed from the city of Kagoshima, the volcano of Sakurajima seems as big as Vesuvius, and the city huddles around its skirts like a smaller Napoli. Here I encounter the famed and feared Kagoshima-*ben,* a dialect so fierce that those from other parts of Japan are intimidated when they hear it. Still, I am understood when I ask a question, and I can understand the answer. Then I realize that those addressed are resorting to *hyojungo,* standard Tokyo dialect. I realize this after I have talked to some children who are ready enough to talk, but who know no *hyojungo.*

Later, a young man in a *yukata* takes me to a bar where we sit in a large room, drink, beer, and look at four girls. One of them, fat little face and lustrous large eyes, sings a song apparently daring, but all lost on me. The *yukata*-clad youngster laughs uproariously. His mood changes, however, when the bill is produced. Parting, poorer, I am walking back to the inn when I am stopped by a young taxi driver who wants to talk. Since there are no customers, we drive up into the hills and park, and in the dark look at the city laid out in its Neapolitan splendor beneath us. Afterward he drives me back.

22 SEPTEMBER 1955. The taxi driver was supposed to call for me at noon but does not, so I walk into town. It is easy to meet people here, but difficult to keep anything going for very long. Perhaps it is because here, unlike Tokyo, people do not want anything from me—or, better put, I have nothing to give anyone. Different from the cities where people want to learn English. Here, no one has any interest in English. What would they do with it? So I am deprived of one of my attractions and feel a bit poorer, as though a stranger with no coins of the realm jingling in my pocket.

23 SEPTEMBER 1955. A crowded train ride through the mountains and I stand most of the way. Get off at a small town on the sea named Shibushi. I go swimming and the children come and talk. They speak right out, in their native *ben*, as though there is no other. A few of the older, having been to school, know Tokyo dialect. They act as interpreters—Japanese to Japanese. Jabber-jabber, says the smaller boy. "How old are you?" translates the larger. "I am thirty," I answer. Jabber-jabber, translates the older to the younger, who shakes his head.

Late in the afternoon, passing the station, I see a youth I remembered speaking with on the streets of Kagoshima last night. He had taken the noon train to, he thought, Miyazaki, but it had stopped here. What to do? No more trains till morning. Guessed he would have to spend another night on the streets. So I bring him back to my inn.

Modern-minded type. Has been to Tokyo, learned just enough to rub off some of his country innocence, but by no means all: "Yeah, just tell the bartender you're twenty-one, and it's OK." "How old are you?" I ask. "Eighteen," he says, ducking his head in a rustic manner. All country children are asked how old they are. All of them duck their heads when they answer.

"With girls you got to be tough. I got these dark glasses. They work sometimes." I ask if that means that he takes advantage of the young ladies. "You bet," he says with a city grin. "They're just a bunch of country broads anyway." I pull out my dark glasses and put them on. He laughs nervously, very much a country youth.

He is going to Tokyo tomorrow. Is excited at the prospect. Can hardly wait to get back to Kabukicho—"that's in Shinjuku, you know, a really swell place," he says in his rustic accent.

24 SEPTEMBER 1955. Nakayama, for that is his name, wanting to catch the early morning train to Shinjuku, let himself out of the inn. I slept until nine, then walked along the beach and looked at the single island, distant in the bay. The children form processions behind me wherever I go, and occasionally mimic me when I have difficulty with my *geta*. A young man, burned black by the sun and wearing only a pair of pajama-like *suteteko* trousers, comes by and I ask him about the island. It is a deserted island though tourists sometimes go there in the summer. Then, since I apparently look longing, he offers to take me out in his boat.

It is a large boat with nets piled in it and green glass floats shining in the sun, and is powered by a small motor that makes tiny gray smoke rings in the still summer air. When we reach the wide sea there are small waves, though the bay is flat, and the boat bobs and dips until we reach the island with its pink cliffs and deep blue trees. There, in water so clear that the bottom is sharp at twenty feet, we swim and try to dive for that red stone just under me. I cannot get down even halfway, but the young man says he can go four times his own height. Once he tried five times, but that hurt his ears. "There, you see," he says—holding up the red stone.

He takes good care of me, as though he has been entrusted with some large and probably breakable object. He warns me away from the brightly colored jelly fish, informs me when a large wave is coming in, and tells me not to step on a spiny sea urchin so large it looks like a mine.

Later we dry in the sun and I learn that he is twenty-three, and has left little Shibushi only once, and that was to go up the coast and fetch a boat back home. We talk about Tokyo and he asks which is best: Asakusa or Ueno. And so he echoes the poet of more than a century past who asked: *Asakusa ka? Ueno ka?*

Dried, beginning to burn, we go up and lie in the shade of a palm. I had noticed that his *suteteko*, being thick cotton, are still damp from the swim, and so I suggest he take them off and hang them on a branch to dry. He does so.

*

Later, in the afternoon, I take a train around the coast and eventually reach Miyazaki, where I board a rattling bus down to Aoshima, a drop-shaped island appended to that rough coast. It is made of diagonally stratified rock base—shelves along the sea, looking like steps set sidewise and leading nowhere. The bus girl obligingly informs us that they are called the devil's washboard. In between are other formations, bigger, rounder, browner. I am suddenly reminded of something—but what? It is round and brown and very nice indeed. What could it be? Then I remember. Yes, chocolate pudding, drying out.

It is near sunset when we reach Aoshima, windy but not cold. It is like an atoll, with palm trees and white sand. It looks man-made, a vacationland to be called something like Tropical Paradise. But it is apparently natural, just a bit of Samoa that somehow floated north. I stay at the big white hotel across the causeway and eat a local fish.

In the evening I go for a walk and am joined by one of the cooks, whose name is Yamanaka, who strolls with me along the darkened beach and says it is lonely there. He sings one of the local songs, which sounds lonely indeed. Then he wants me to sing a lonely song. Stephen Foster, he says. What he really wants is "Jeanie with the Light Brown Hair." Though I cannot remember the words, I do know, I discover, all of "Camptown Races," which I render. He thanks me, but says it did not sound very lonely.

Later we shop in the empty tourist arcades and buy some beautiful and indecent objects—cups you turn over to discover a coupled couple, an articulated vagina disguised as a shell, and a sake cup with a mushroom-shaped penis attached. One is to suck the sake from the mushroom head.

25 SEPTEMBER 1955. In the morning Yamanaka, having made breakfast, accompanies me across the long white bridge to the island itself. It is covered with tropical foliage, but one cannot get into it, I discover. One walks around the perimeter—all of us, since it is Sunday and the buses have come. Yamanaka buys me a towel, as he noticed I had forgotten mine in Kagoshima. I give him one of my articulated vaginas. Then he puts me on the bus for Miyazaki.

Miyazaki is noted for its clean, wide streets. There is, it turns out, just one of them, and it stretches—clean and wide—for miles and miles, and I finally find the place along its inordinate length where the express bus to Beppu stops.

Beppu—lots of small, squat and sickly looking palms, many frame, stucco buildings, and miles of neon. Like Atami. Lots of folks strolling around in *yukata* with nothing at all to do.

26 SEPTEMBER 1955. In the morning Beppu looks less garish, but also less attractive. It looks, in the new light, like a town with a hangover. The wandering revelers in *yukata* are now back in their clothes, serious, responsible, paying bills. I sit and sip coffee at a shop by the sea, and over me Rachmaninoff rains. When I look out I see the steamer coming in from Osaka, right on time. It will dock precisely when it is supposed to.

The boat is crowded with school children, all leaving Beppu for the first excursion of the year—all the way to exotic Kansai. Yes, I have been there, I say when asked. I saw Kyoto live. No, the Golden Pavilion is not made of real gold (this in answer to a first-year student), but it looks like it. No, I do not know how much a geisha costs (this in answer to a high school junior)—his chances of acquiring one are, in any event, slight.

The ship sails through the afternoon sea, a white scroll of foam at its prow. By morning Osaka will be outside my waiting porthole and my Kyushu trip will be over.

> In 1956 Richie published *Where Are the Victors?* and in 1958 appeared (in Japanese translation only) his first book on film, *Eiga Geijutsu no Kakumei* (The Cinematographic View). He had also met Joseph Anderson, and the two of them began the research that would result in *The Japanese Film: Art and Industry* (1959).
>
> Writing in the *Japan Times* and appearing in magazines abroad, Richie began to be known outside Japan and consequently met interested visitors. Although he apparently kept some journals during this time, these were mainly about film matters and were used in later books and articles. He did, however, keep notes about the visitors. These pages were to make up a volume to be called *The Sociable Lions*. Some of them were later incorporated into *The Honorable Visitors* (1994). Below are some that were not.

TRUMAN CAPOTE, 1955. His trip got off to a bad start. He had not known that a visa was necessary. Consequently he was refused at the Tokyo airport, had to return to Guam, wait there until the visa was issued, and only then was allowed into Japan.

Cecil Beaton and I went to pick him up. Truman had originally come with Cecil, who had known all about necessary visas and had acquired one. Consequently he had already been here three days. "It is so nice here, Truman," he said. "You will like it."

"I doubt that very much," he said, "this country is very chintzy about its visas." Truman had already lost three days of a two-week stay. He now glared about the airport. "All I can say is that you certainly wouldn't know they'd lost the war."

"One of the things the matter is that no one here is taller than Truman," said Cecil next day. "He needs someone taller than he is." We were waiting for the American author. I was taking them sightseeing. "It tends to keep him in line. Otherwise, it is fine. All the chairs fit him. Even the toilets."

Truman, when he appeared, did not, however, think it fine. Complained. The water tasted funny. Was I absolutely certain that it was all right to drink it? I was? Well, I'd better be. It was all on my head—his subsequent illness, death, who knew what?

On the Ginza, Truman talked about New York and Paris. In the Hama Detached Palace grounds, about Fontainebleau and the Villa d'Este. On the boat up the Sumida, about friends in far places that neither Cecil nor I knew, and, in Asakusa, about his wretched publisher.

But then he suddenly turned, peered about at the lanterns, the distant temple, and the cherry blossoms. "Why," he said with some surprise, "it is a veritable fairy-land." The appreciation lasted for a time and he bought an imitation geisha wig. "Oh, no, not for me, my dear. For fun!"

On the way back to the Imperial he entertained us with stories. All were grisly. An especial favorite of his, he told us, was the one about a mother and son. They were like pals, went everyplace together. Then one day, out on the pier of some Long Island estate, people saw them feeding the birds. The gulls collected in great flocks. She was waving her umbrella in presumed greeting. Investigators later found them there, their eyes picked out, faces almost unrecognizable. They had indeed been "feeding the birds."

"You know, he told me that story in London last year, and again on the flight over," said Cecil later, shaking his head. "It seems to have some meaning for him."

"Anti-pally-mothers," I said.

"Or sons," said he.

"At any rate, it is pro-bird." Then, "You said that one of the things the matter was that no one was taller than he is. What are the other things?"

"Oh, no," said Cecil kindly, mouth pursed with concern, "You are not to take him so seriously. He is like that, you know."

"He is?"

"Why, yes, of course," said Cecil smiling, as though disclosing before me one of the facts of life. "You wait. After we have gone out of an evening he will much improve."

So we went out of an evening. Cecil enjoyed himself and was seemingly pleased with the results. Truman wasn't. He was rude, sent the boy back, spat out, "Little pussy cats!" and went off to bed alone.

One of the things the matter, as Cecil would have said, was that Truman had nothing to do. He had come over because Cecil was coming. At the last moment he got the *New Yorker* to finance the trip by suggesting he interview Marlon Brando, now on film location near Kyoto but at present too busy to see him.

Cecil on the other hand was so busy that he had little time for Truman. His trip was financed by *Vogue* and he was supposed to be photographing Japanese high society. Since Japan has no high society except for a few potted royals and the sedate wives of robber barons he was busy indeed—searching everywhere. Consequently Truman was much alone, a state which did not agree with him.

"Hello," he drawled into the receiver. "It's me again. Bet you think I don't do anything but telephone. But I am so bored. I cannot tell you how bored I am. So I just called up to have a chat. . . ."

I told him I would like to chat but that I couldn't right then.

"Oh, really?" Disbelief followed by resentment. "Well, in that case . . ." Then, anxious at being once more alone, "Still, just a minute or two is all right. Right? You know what Barbara Hutton said last time when I was there?" I did not know what she had said but I soon learned.

What I did not understand about Truman was how anyone could go to a new country, any country, and pay so little attention to it. He was supposed to be some sort of reporter, at least he was reporting for his magazine, but he stayed entirely in the Imperial, ate there, slept there. And, he never asked a question.

"But he's always like that," said Cecil, wondering at my complaint. "You really do not know him very well, do you?"

"No," I said.

Several days later I was to take Truman out shopping. I phoned up from the lobby. "I am not going," said the small, petulant voice. Asked why not, he sighed and with the air of beginning a long story said, "Well, I was washing my hair . . ."

Then he stopped. "My neck. It's my neck." I said that the Imperial had a stable of masseurs. "I would not let them touch me," said Truman virtuously. "But you may come up," he added.

Instead, I persuaded him to come down. We sat in the coffee shop. Truman was cross, tired, and bored—he looked ten years old, and acted it. "I don't see why you came here anyway," I finally said.

He looked at me, wonderingly. "Why to do Brando, of course."

"Not to see Japan?"

"Why no," he said, as though mystified that anyone should think anything so unlikely. Then he looked at me severely. "Look, I have seen Japan. And I may just as well tell you that I do not like a country that has little cocks."

"I beg your pardon?" I said.

"Little cocks, little cocks!" he repeated irritably, his high tight voice carrying through the coffee shop. "This country has little cocks. Not a single tenpenny among them!"

"A what?"

"A tenpenny!" he said then, seeing that I did not understand the expression; and pleased, as always, to be explaining, his expression softened, a slight smile appeared, and—now that it was much too late—he lowered his voice.

"A tenpenny? Why that's what we call them down South. You see, you get it there and you lay it on a table or something and if you can line up ten pennies in a row on its back, then it's called a tenpenny. Understand?"

I understood. Pleased, Truman then told me again what Barbara Hutton had said, went on to other topics of equal interest, and was in good temper when we said goodbye.

The mood did not, apparently, last. When the interview with Brando came out in the *New Yorker* I saw that black bile had returned and that the actor was being made to pay for all that Japan, or perhaps Truman himself, wasn't. Yet, a note from Cecil seemed to indicate otherwise. "Saw Truman at a party. Charming as usual. So full of Japan. Told most wonderful stories of Asakusa, of Kyoto. Made it all so real. Says he is thinking of doing a book."

SACHEVERELL SITWELL, 1958. We were talking about Japan. Or, rather, he was. I was not saying much because I could not understand what he was saying. Never having heard a true upper-class English accent, I could make nothing of the long-drawn vowels, the swallowed syllables, and the sudden spurts and equally sudden stops. Words appeared here and there—"geisha," "cunning carp," "little paper triangles," "Mount Fuji"—but I, not comprehending their context, could extract no meaning.

That I could not understand did not deter him. He sat with his head thrown back, his nose high, and his eyes half closed, and delivered what I thought were probably his opinions. Nonetheless I was disappointed. I had admired his writings and wanted very much to know what he thought of Japan. He seemed to be thinking a lot, he was talking so much.

Seeing my predicament, his wife kindly took me to one side while he talked on at the others. Since she was Canadian I had less difficulty with her accent.

"Sir Sacheverell seems very interested in Japan," I said.

"Knows it. Backward and forward. Studied it for years."

"Probably a book will be appearing then."

"Oh, undoubtedly."

Then in order to demonstrate that I in turn knew something about him I began to talk about his book on southern baroque art. At the same time I marveled that she, who spoke English so well, could apparently understand everything that he said.

She turned and smiled, aware that she was interpreting. "He is speaking of those cunning ivory cages into which singing summer insects are placed to cry away the dwindling day." I was struck with the sentence and wondered whether it was hers or was, perhaps, a literal translation.

In order to interest her I told her about two *kirigirisu*, a kind of katydid, I once had. Perhaps she would tell Sir Sacheverell and it would amuse him. I had, I told her, forgotten to give them their daily slice of cucumber and when I came home I thought them gone. The cage was empty. Or, it appeared empty. Actually, it was not. There in the corner were the two heads in a pool of green slime, still gnawing at each other's necks.

But my story did not interest her. At least she did not translate it. He was still talking to the others, all of whom apparently understood him. I caught "marvelous brocades" and "cunning little match boxes." Lady Sitwell's interest was, after my little story, turning elsewhere and so, in a perhaps ill-advised attempt to divert it again to myself, I again started talking about her husband's books.

In so doing I said that I liked his essay on romantic ruins and particularly liked his pages on Hubert Robert.

"Who?" she asked suddenly, sharply.

"Hubert Robert," I repeated, innocently, pronouncing the name as though the French painter had been an Englishman—or, perhaps, an American.

"Who could that be? Did he ever write about anyone named . . . Oh, I see. Oh, this is just too precious. Sachy, Sachy, you simply must hear this."

Sachy stopped in mid-rumble, turning an unfriendly eye upon her. "I know, I know," she said, having apparently been warned not to interrupt, but all the same certain that this time it was quite worth it.

"This is simply too exquisite. Do you know what this gentleman just said to me? He was speaking of *Hubert Robert*. Yes, goggle you well may. You see, he obviously has seen the name written—in something of yours. And so, oh, it is so darling, he speaks of *Hubert Robert*."

Seeing the look on her husband's face, she filled in. "It is of course Hubert Robert he means," she said giving the name its proper French pronunciation. "But isn't that too dear?"

He smacked his lips and allowed that it was, then turned and resumed the monologue. I too turned, and went and sat down in the next room.

Later, not so much later, his book came out. *The Bridge of the Brocade Sash* was its name. It was about cunning little matchboxes (a whole chapter on them) and ornamental carp and grand geisha. It was also about the Japanese character. He observed that often the Japanese are given to unintentional rudeness when the foreigner gets something wrong about their culture, mispronounces a word, for example. And that confronted with a new culture that they cannot understand (the English, for example), they make many a laughable gaffe.

ROMOLA NIJINSKY, 1958. Big fur hat, swathed to the neck, jeweled fingers, and a pleasantly carnivorous expression. She looked like a witch, but a familiar one, the one perhaps from *Hansel und Gretel*.

Her friend with whom she was traveling, was a very tall, manly, German photographer and big game hunter. She was playing Hansel to Romola's witch. No Gretels in sight, but they were looking. "Every day," she said. "We go to Takarazuka, we sit in front, we look, we watch. *Ach*, how lovely. Romola, she never get tired and so near, just across from hotel here. Yesterday one smiled. Today we go and smile again, perhaps we meet."

"Yes, but so difficult to meet in Japan," said Romola.

"Certainly easier than elsewhere," I said.

"Ah, but you have the tongue," said her friend.

"I beg your pardon?"

"You speak Japanese."

"Oh."

Then Romola suddenly, as was her way, began speaking of the past. "Ah, Ravel. Charming, you know. Too charming. A little man, small. But what you call a fashion plate. Oo-la-la, such clothings. I wild with jealous. But too charming. And cold. My late husband thought so too."

This perhaps prompted further memories, "One man my late husband hate. Stravinsky! My late husband, he trust him, work with him, *Le Sacre du Printemps*, then monster goes writes horrid things in *Figaro*, *Le Matin*, I no longer know. He never forgive. And me too. Never forgive."

"Then, years after, I hear Stravinsky ill in Azores. Is dying. Pneumonia.

Me and Cocteau put together our heads and I send telegram. I will sue for millions. Igor and money! He read, he gasp—Roberto Craft and Vera come but too late. He die. He no die, *hélas*, not pneumonia, only cold."

"Now you go home," said the friend, towering over me, gray eyes, gray hair, gray teeth. "Today Takarazuka has performance. We go. We smile."

So they went and they smiled, and somehow they also got backstage and at last met the one who had, perhaps, smiled at them. Then they left Tokyo and I did not hear the sequel until the following year when Romola returned.

"*Ach*," she said, "it was hell. Los Angeles. But better now. Idiot Ed Sullivan, he want stupid 'Dance Around the World' so I go round and round the world. Very pleasant for me. I come see Harumi."

Harumi was the Takarazuka girl. She sang and danced. She was also one of those who played girls. I was shown a picture. Very pretty she was too, too pretty to play a boy. She was in the starched organdy and picture hat that the Takarazuka girl-girls always wear. The boy-girls on the other hand wear flowing ties and sideburns.

Romola, with the help of one of Ed Sullivan's helpers, had sent Harumi a letter in Japanese. An answer arrived. Then, also from Ed Sullivan's office, Romola began a series of long distance telephone calls to Japan.

Since neither could understand the other's language, the conversation was a series of sighs and giggles, the operator expertly switching these noises about. Eventually, curious, she was brought in to interpret. The foreign lady wanted to visit. Well, the Japanese girl guessed that that was probably all right. And the kind white person wanted to bring a gift. Well, the Japanese person had never owned a silver fox stole. "Stole?" said Romola, "Hah, I want bring mink—a cape." So she went again to Ed Sullivan.

She showed the article to me the day before she made the presentation. Very handsome. Romola herself was also very handsome. The witch had vanished and she was magically transformed into an attractive matron with a smart Paris hat, a single gold ring on a slender finger.

Then again I did not see her for a time. A year later came a crackly call from Riga. "Riga? Oh, idiot 'Dance Around the World.' Harumi, she no write. She ill? She angry?" The anger, it appeared was perhaps due to Romola's refusing to send a present to a favorite aunt. Romola had already sent gifts to mother, father, brothers, sisters and a single uncle and felt that the family might go on and on. "Family, family—uncles, aunts, cousins. It is like Russia."

Again in Tokyo (idiot "Dance Around the World"), she had me to tea.

How were things with Harumi, I wanted to know. "Not good," she said. "Expense is OK but a lot." She began counting on her fingers. "Adults' Day, then Children's Day, then Emperor's Birthday, then *her* birthday, then . . ."

"And a present for each?" I asked.

"Oh, but you should see her dear little face, it light up when she get present."

"I can imagine."

There was a silence, then a sigh, then, "You tell me. How do you do it?"

"How do I do what?"

"Not you. How does one do it? In this country. With these people. It is so difficult. I no understand."

"You mean . . ."

She nodded sadly.

"You've been putting out for the Emperor's birthday and all and haven't even . . ."

"One embrace. After the cape. That is all."

"Romola, you are very slow," I said. "At your age . . ."

"My age. That is the problem." She looked at me, her eyes bleak. "When my age and then love comes you must not hurt it, you must shelter it," and she folded her hands as though they contained a bird. "It is precious. It is all that I have." Then, recovering some animation, "How they do it, Japanese girls?"

"Well, I don't know . . . fingers maybe?"

"No, that I know. The occasion, I mean."

"Maybe you ought to be firm."

"She says she want go to Paris . . ."

"That's it, Romola. You take her to Paris, you lock her up at the Ritz or somewhere, and you have your way."

"But what will she think?"

"Romola! She is in the Takarazuka. This will come as no surprise to her. All the girls must know about it after the first week."

"Yes," said Romola with sudden scorn, "The big ones, who play men, with hats." Then as sometimes happened, the past clouded the present. "Ah, Debussy. Such a nice man, so warm. Nice eyes. And all the last pretty things written standing at the mantelpiece. Yes, no sitting down. Cancer. Behind. Oh, no, no," she wagged a mischievous finger, "Not what you think. Not at all. No, *hélas*, bicycle accident when small." Then, "My late husband like Debussy, but Debussy no like my late husband's *Jeux*. So sad."

I heard nothing further. Then a friend called to my attention a small news item. One Takaoka Harumi, deported from France where she had been living. Had run up massive bills at Le Printemps and others of the *grands magazins*. Curious, I tried to discover where Romola was. I called Ed Sullivan's Tokyo representative and was hung up on once my business was known.

Months later a friend told me that he had seen Romola at a spa in Austria. She was there for treatment. Arthritis. Said she was wearing black, looked like a spider. She had again transformed back into a witch. And she was wearing a veil, they said. And when asked if someone were dead, she answered that, yes, someone was.

PHILIP JOHNSON, 1958. We were at the Sanbo-in, near Kyoto. Reconstruction was going on. The pagoda had been newly painted—orange, white, and green.

"Now that I like," said Philip Johnson. Someone demurred. "Not at all," he continued, "This is the way they were and this is the way they should be. That is why Nikko is better than Nara. They keep it up." Then, after a glance at the guidebook, "But, where is it?" Where was what? "Why, the geometrical sand garden, of course—the one with the circles. Tells all about it right here." A strong finger jabbed the guidebook.

Johnson then forged ahead, tall, strong profile, like the figurehead on a Yankee clipper, cleaving his way through whatever separated him from where he wanted to be. "We'll find it," he said, shortly, then, "Trust to them"—they were two young Buddhist acolytes we had brought along—"and we'd never find it. Don't know your own culture too well, eh?" he said, turning to the acolytes who knew no English but who now laughed politely at what they took to be a jest.

"Yes, here's where the corridor bends," he said, consulting the map in the guidebook, "but where are those damn gardens then?" He strode on, leading, peering left and right, now more American bald eagle than clipper. "Philip," said someone, "Remember to check your guidebook after you've run something down. If you don't put a big check mark there you might forget you've seen it." Philip nodded vigorously, striding on, then brandished the book and said, "Oh, yes, yes. I always check it."

"He'll love these gardens if he finds them," said one of his friends. "They have no people in them, you see. And we'll have some quiet. The only time he has remained silent for more than two minutes was at that inhuman Ryoanji the other day. For a full five minutes he said absolutely nothing. It was heaven."

"Now where in the hell are they," asked Johnson, forging ahead.

Hideyoshi's garden spread before us. "Oh, lovely," said someone, but Johnson complained after a swift glance. "Doesn't have any sand circles in it."

"It was a pleasure garden . . ." someone began.

"Do be quiet," said someone else, "that's enough to turn him against it . . . pleasure, people!"

I had been told about a row he had had once. New building, all completed, and then an argument about there being no drinking fountain outside the auditorium. "No, no, no," he is supposed to have said, "drinking fountains are hideous, they would spoil the line." "But people have to drink," he was reminded. "No, they don't," was the reply.

And I remembered that in Tokyo he and I had talked about people. I had asked what kind he liked. "Oh, any kind. But, here, in Japan, well—I rather want to be like Madame Butterfly, but in reverse. I want people to like me, and then be terribly disappointed when I leave, to feel miserable, and never quite get over it." I asked him if he also wanted them to kill themselves. "Heavens, no. What a bother."

"Philip can't help it," said someone, the one who had spoken of the pleasure garden. "He's just like that."

"Now, God damn it," said Philip. "Just where the hell does it think it is." He turned a corner. There it was, circles and ovals of gravel.

"Lovely," he said.

I asked one of the acolytes what the gravel meant, why it was in that shape. The acolyte told me that it was because this garden had been used for drinking parties. The guests sat there, on those little islands of greenery outlined by the gravel. That was why some of them were in the shape of gourds. That was because they used to drink sake from gourds. I explained all this.

"Drinking parties?" said Philip Johnson. His tone indicated surprised displeasure. "You mean that people actually sat there?"

"Lots of them," I said, "And drank sake too."

He shook his head. It was really too much for him, the way people behaved, even back in the seventeenth century. Then he turned, garden forgotten. "Come on," he said. "We've had it." And again he strode back through the corridors.

"Philip," called someone, "don't forget to check your guidebook."

LINCOLN KIRSTEIN, 1958. He looks very Western in Japan, the large nose, the black eyebrows, and the big body—a seagoing New England prophet. At the same time a natural, massive gentleness. He is here in Japan even more, as though his large feet might stomp holes in the tatami. Tall, he apologetically curls under lintels. Heavy, he tries out floors with a smile of trepidation.

His is the gentleness of very strong people, those who do not need to exhibit their strength. The clumsiness is also that of the big—particularly here in the land of the nominally small.

Hands too big for any practical purpose, head too large for easy thoughts. Lincoln in his own home decides to move the big chair and does so with one hand, holding it aloft. He could, one thinks, have as easily moved the bed. But Lincoln in Japan in the print shop trying to turn over the pictures with his thick fingers; Lincoln trying to leaf through a book, the pages jamming; Lincoln trying to pay the bills, the money refusing to separate, the thousand yen bills sticking together in the mighty grasp, fingers ineffectively shuffling—it is like watching Moses trying to pick up the tab.

Lincoln and money. Here he turns very Japanese. It is there for use but is not somehow quite right. Old-fashioned Japanese wrap it in white paper in order to be able to handle it. Perhaps he ought to try that. Certainly, he thinks of money as the Japanese do. It is for use. Its only value is in its buying potential. It is for the present and perhaps the future.

In the same way both Lincoln and the Japanese regard people. These are also a kind of currency. A man is worth what he does. Lincoln upon hearing a new name asks, "What does he do?" Almost never, "What has he done?" Much more often, "What does he want to do?" He invests in people—as do the Japanese, and just as freely, just as openly. People are currency. They pay dividends. Both Lincoln and the Japanese pay high dividends too. The resulting relationship is one of nature's happiest—symbiosis.

Flesh may dazzle, wit may seduce, but not for long. Infatuation over in a matter of minutes, Lincoln wants to know, "Now, what is it that you can do best?" He wants to know because then, to protect his investment, he will put you on the proper road, help you achieve your potential. Often in his own country Lincoln is misunderstood. They do not comprehend that there are rewards for accomplishment but that there is no sympathy for failure.

Japan understands well. This most pragmatic of people do not count hopes or intentions as accomplishments. A man is what he does. After his death, he is what he has done.

Consequently Lincoln in Japan for the first time meets a nation that feels as he does, a whole people whose values are his own. Since such values are,

With Lincoln Kirstein. Nara, 1958.

eventually, about power, Lincoln soon learns to use it in a very effective and quite Japanese fashion.

When he wanted the Kabuki to go to New York and could not get the proper cooperation from its sponsors, the mighty Shochiku entertainment combine, he deliberately went up to the man in charge of the troupe at a formal function and gave him the longest, lowest, coldest, most venomous bow that this Japanese could ever have seen a foreigner give. Such a show of submissive despicability could not go unanswered. It led to a series of meetings the outcome of which was that, Lincoln getting his way, the Kabuki went to New York.

Once Lincoln woke from a sound sleep and sprang up to say, "Oh, a vision." He had seen Tokugawa-period Japan as a system of closed *fusuma*. One opened and there was the shogun himself. But then the doors behind him opened and there was the real shogun manipulating the first like a Bunraku puppet. But then the doors opened behind him, and there was the really real shogun. But then those doors behind him opened and on and on. He was going to tell Balanchine about this. It would be the basis of a new ballet.

It was not, but the grasp shown of the structure of power and responsibility in Japan remained. The Kabuki, the Bugaku, the Gagaku, anything that Lincoln had liked and thought worth seeing, were all eventually pried loose and sent over. People too, talented people, sculptors, designers, all were one after the other sent back to the land Lincoln came from.

They gained much from the experience and, from Lincoln's point of view, they had paid off their investment. They had been successes. He had helped. Trouble he might have sorting out the bills to pay for the dinner but he had no difficulty at all in manipulating all of the powerful sources that would eventually pay for everything and make the potential into a reality.

And what happens when the potential had become a reality, when it had happened, when it was done, when it was over? Why then, in the most natural manner possible Japan loses its interest. Lincoln too. It had been done, why look backward? Everything, everyone, must pay his, her, its own way. After it had done, so it gets dropped.

Dropped. The massive fingers loosen; the colossus turns its head, attention elsewhere. The fingers open and down you go, away from the multiplicity of opportunity, away from the infinite possibilities of life with Lincoln.

And then, so Japanese of him, Lincoln's, "Oh, no, you don't want to know him. A horror of the first order. An utter and complete shit." Or, if the retained memory remains a good one, a smile and, "Oh, absolutely, unbelievably monstrous." But these are only token attentions to the past. In actuality Lincoln lives in the fluid and promising future. The present is there only in order to lead to promise.

This being precisely the way that Japan as a nation also thinks, I—firmly dropped myself—waited with interest to see which of the titans, Lincoln vs. Japan, would first get rid of the other.

Of course, it was Lincoln. He won. He dropped Japan before Japan was ready to drop him. He found that it had really little of interest. It was actually, he discovered, a very provincial little place. Funny in its way but dowdy, tawdry actually. Now that he had plundered it, there was not, he seemed to say, very much there. Balanchine was advised not to come. The ballet, misunderstood its first time in Japan, was not to give these people a second chance.

How Japanese of Lincoln. They too, having taken what they wanted from other countries, always despise the rest. When they have what they want, they bad-mouth. And what could be more natural? The Japanese and the Lincolns of this world are the true realists.

So, the Japanese would have dropped Lincoln and his demands after a time had not Lincoln first dropped Japan. But, had they been wise, they would somehow have held onto him. He would have made the most remarkable ambassador Japan had ever had. He was, for one thing, one of the few foreigners who instinctively understood. And he was, for another, just as pragmatic as they are. Life is, after all, for use.

ANGUS WILSON, 1959. An animated manner, a vivacious tongue, a high-pitched voice: "And so there I was, my dear, in the midst of one of our famous fogs, could see nothing whatsoever, and became quite lost. Stumbling into trees I eventually collided with a gentleman and I said that I begged his pardon but could he direct me out of the park, and he said, 'I believe it is over in that direction, but these fogs often lift quite suddenly and once it has I will take the pleasure of guiding you out myself, madame,' and the fog did lift just then and there we were face to face, two middle-aged gentlemen confronting each other."

Like many of his jokes, this one was against himself and he relished the telling, the high voice modulated itself into a melisma and with a dying fall into "confronting each other." Then, the yelp. There was always a little yelp at the end, as though there were a canine inside enjoying the tale.

He curled up in the chair, tucked his feet under, and extended a paw for his tea. There was indeed something doggy about him, something to do with the gray mane, the docile but guarded eyes, the bulldog expression. But not all was canine; there was something more.

As I gazed I saw that Angus was the Mad Hatter, without the hat. The same nose down which he looked, the same mouth, the same eyes. He looked like the Tenniel illustration, and he spoke as the Hatter would have. "Years in the British Museum, years, I assure you. Imagine—books, handing books to elderly parties for years. Then putting them *back*. And all during this time, some modest writing about people I did not much like. Much? Well, what is much? And those books. Those years. Oh, dear."

He leaned forward. "You see, success came so late, so very late, that it was natural that I am regarded as an upstart." He glanced around the lobby of International House as narrowly as his wide, round, Anglo-Saxon eyes would permit. "And the jealousies, my dear, the jealousies."

"To be sure, I *do* have a poison pen. Oh, you would be shocked to learn the number of people nightly praying that I do not *do* their portraits. This, however, is not what I do best, merely what I do *most*. I am, you see, a very good mimic."

Then the stories, one after the other, unrolling, narrative ribbons festooning. A moment of repose, of silence, then another spasm, another story. But the stories after a time stopped. "You know, my dear, I am not actually like this at all. As you may have already guessed, I am a moralist." And he turned to look at me with his large, round, gray, humorless eyes. "I am not in the Waugh line at all. Actually, I am Dickens. I am preparing a book on him at this very moment."

I had earlier seen signs of moral earnestness. He had irritated Stephen Spender by springing to his feet at the PEN conference and—at the conclusion of a speech by the older poet—saying, voice waving like a tiny pennant: "We of the *younger* generation of British intellectuals would seek to differ . . ."

Later, speaking of Spender. "You see, he feels—feels mind you—that he has been passed over, become even something of a relic. Oh, I understand because the same horrid machinery has made me feel the upstart. Oh, yes, I can quite assure you that I am *made* to feel the parvenu."

Then he looked out of the window and said, "Oh, we have this wonderfully remote place. And right in the middle is this entire Chinese room that came with the house. It is sort of bad Chippendale, unbelievably hideous, and I breakfast there mornings."

"Tony has said time and again that we should raze it but I am adamant when I wish to be. I also managed some delicious drapes, very French, very old, shepherds and things on them, and amid all the red lacquer and teak the effect is simply unbelievable."

"Tony dislikes these too, I believe. Oh, dear Tony, what do you suppose he is doing now? Heavens but I shall be happy to be home."

Such serious moments were, however, few. Mostly Angus was almost excessively entertaining. "You see, I am quite good at this sort of thing. Quite amusing, good for picnics, much better than the ants." And another part of the repertoire would spout—but the only story I remember is the one about the fog.

And at night, exhausted by his day, he always took his medication. "Triple the dose while I am abroad—always." He composed himself on his *futon* . "Don't mind me," were his last words. "When I fall asleep everything falls in. I think the tongue gets swallowed, and the sinuses do something horrid—the entire palate collapses, you see. It will begin in just a second or two. Well, good night, dear."

It began almost at once: a stern, nineteenth-century sound, iron on iron, Mad Hatter turned Mr. Murdstone, interrupted by barks and yips and growls. Lying awake I realized toward morning that it was also very deep, very strong, very male.

ALBERTO MORAVIA, 1959. "You must show us the real Japan, said Stephen [Spender], looking about the hotel lobby—the French windows, the Italian floors, the American cash register. "Yes, you must guide us," said Angus. "We will positively penetrate those cunning paper doors."

Already we were calling each other by our first names, indicating the relief that was felt that the PEN Conference was over, that they were no longer obliged to be Mr. Spender, distinguished British poet, and Mr. Wilson, eminent British novelist. Relief—and the prospect of leaving disappointingly modern Tokyo and discovering what Stephen called "the real Japan."

"No," said Alberto Moravia, who was joining us only because he did not want to be left behind. "Tokyo is real. Tokyo is real Japan."

I agreed. Not, however, for his reasons. These I had already discovered, having noticed him at the celebrated temple looking at the attractive young lady guide, at the famous view regarding the excursioning schoolgirls, and at the holy shrine delighting in and then disappointed by the flapping skirts of the priests. Further, I had been pressed into interpreting for him with a young lady who worked as a cashier and was not averse to foreigners, particularly if they had written *Woman of Rome*.

The Italian author had taken us both to the Queen Bee Night Club where he had scotch, she had crème de violette, and I had a coke.

"Ask her if she honors me with a dance."

"Would you honor him with a dance?"

"Yes."

Once back, he said, "She is a good dancer. You tell her."

"You are a good dancer."

"But you haven't danced with me," she said.

"No, that's what he said."

"That you haven't danced with me?" she asked.

"No, no. That you are a good dancer."

"What she say? What she say?"

Despite my interpreting, Moravia was successful in his aims. I received his gratitude. "You are my only help," he said, holding me with his dark gaze, his warm Italian smile. She received a crocodile bag.

Having discovered the real Japan, Moravia now wanted to stay in Tokyo. The other two, having not as yet discovered it, had no such reasons for remaining.

In a bar, late, with the poet, I said, "Stephen, don't you think we could go now? Which one do you want?"

He gazed benevolently first on the left, then on the right. "Oh, it is so difficult to choose. I really don't know. The problem is, you see, if you take one, then the other feels so terribly left out. And that would be unkind." Being unkind called for the strongest censure.

But it was late and I was tired. "No, it wouldn't. People who hang out in places like this are quite accustomed to being left out."

"Oh, but it is so nice to sit here, choice unmade, but pregnant as it were."

"You could take both," I suggested.

"To that hotel?" He smiled at my absurdity. "Besides, it is so pleasant here, so—well—cuddly, don't you think?" And he smiled, gripped hard, and closed his eyes.

With Tokunaga Osamu, Stephen Spender, Alberto Moravia, Angus Wilson. Koya-san, 1959.

So I said, "Of course we're keeping the help up. They want to close. It does seem a bit unkind." Instantly he was standing. "Oh, how perfectly dreadful. Why didn't you tell me?" Shortly we left and he took neither.

With Angus the question of choice never even arose. He peered about in the gloom and said, "We have places like this back home. Why are they always so dark? Don't tell me. I know. Same reason we keep the lights low in the house. Wrinkles, my dear. Wrinkles." Then, eyes on the dim ceiling, "Oh, home. Would I were there. Dear Tony, what do you suppose he is doing now?"

With Stephen irresolute and Angus nostalgic, there was nothing to keep them in the capital. They were ready to be diverted by authenticity, and be quit of the summer heat of Tokyo. And the following evening we were in the coolness of Koya-san, holy mountain, which I had decided was the real Japan—dozens of temples, some with pagodas, lots of paper doors, a whole cemetery.

Their reaction to the real Japan was not, however, happy.

With Angus Wilson, Alberto Moravia, Tokunaga Osamu, Stephen Spender. Kyoto, 1959.

"Are we supposed to sleep *there*?" asked Stephen in dismay, looking at the thin *futon* spread on the hard tatami. "Are we supposed to eat *that*?" asked Angus with disgust, looking at the frozen tofu. "We take a bath in *that*?" asked Moravia in disbelief, staring at the bubbling cannibal pot, the *goemonburo* in which he was supposed to immerse himself. And when my literary trio saw the real Japanese toilet, an enameled chasm, they turned away without a word.

They did not like the noted cemetery either. "Grey wouldn't have made much of this," sniffed Angus. "Oh, I don't know," said Stephen. "The lowing herd winds slowly o'er the lea," he observed, looking at the other tourists.

He was attempting to keep up our spirits. This was necessary since Moravia was unhappy. After the inedible dinner, the impossible bath, a night of insomnia on the dreaded mats, and the terrors of the toilet, he had after the hideous breakfast turned and snapped at the other two writers.

"*Agh*, so easy for you! So fortunate homosexuals. You run down beach, you find simple fisher lad, you come back radiant. But, *agh*, we heterosexuals. The hope, the failure. So difficult."

"What beach?" asked Stephen.

"There, there," said Angus soothingly. "He is missing his cashier."

I looked sympathetically at the sufferer. Here we were in the real Japan and his manhood was steadily accumulating. And not, apparently, only that.

He was not hungry, pushed away his tofu, his color was bad. "I am ill," he said.

He looked ill. To cheer him up I told him that women were now admitted to Mount Koya, though they hadn't used to be. But even the later sight of two sturdy females in climbing boots just outside our paper windows did not rouse him.

Feeling responsible I managed to discover the nature of the complaint, went to the drugstore, and bought some medicine, the kind marked strong. But he would not take it. Already he was breathing on his chopsticks, then polishing them, inquiring into the nature of the local water then dismissing news of its safety with a wave of the hand. Now he refused the medicine.

With Angus Wilson, Stephen Spender. Shirahama, 1959.

"If you don't take the medicine you won't get well," I said, guide turned doctor. "And part of your trouble is that you aren't drinking enough water." But to this he only shook a gloomy head. "Idiot—water make me *more* ill."

Eventually lack of water, food, medicine, proper toilet facilities, and female companionship rendered the Italian writer prostrate—he lay on his side, panting. Angus and Stephen exchanged worried glances and went shopping. I called the doctor.

The local practitioner was not certain that he wanted to treat a foreigner, particularly one with this complaint. But I persisted, spoke warmly of *Woman of Rome*, and he reluctantly agreed. So there Moravia was, on his side again, and the doctor was applying a clyster.

"Agh. Tell him he hurts."

"He says you hurt."

The doctor said he was sorry but that usually people performed this operation on themselves. Otherwise it was practiced only in hospital or upon the unconscious. And would I please help. "Here, hold this."

But the author of *Woman of Rome* did not like my helping. He turned his dark gaze upon me. He did not like my being there. He did not, in fact, like me. Here I had dragged him into the wilderness, had made him ill, and was now enjoying his degradation.

"Tell him to relax."

"The doctor said you are to relax."

"You shut up!"

Despite the patient, the operation was a success and when the two British authors returned from their expedition—Stephen had bought some attractive Buddhist prayer beads, Angus had, however, found nothing Tony would have liked—the Italian novelist was sitting up on a number of stacked cushions, drinking tea.

"Well," said Angus, "I see that at least one of us has—er—penetrated— ha-ha—the real Japan."

After that I took them down the mountain to Shirahama, a resort town, where they had canned orange juice, innersprings, expensive steaks, and sit-down toilets.

They were much happier than they had been in the real Japan. Even Moravia brightened up and told long stories about women in Rome. Told to Stephen and Angus, however, not to me. Not only did he tell me no stories, he also did not speak to me—ever again. And when we returned to Tokyo he apparently found someone else to interpret for his love affairs and his illnesses alike.

One by one the unlikely trio left the country and I would have heard nothing further had I not met Stephen later. He was remembering our search for the real Japan.

"Such a good guide too. Even procured a bit, I believe."

"No, he found the cashier all by himself."

"Well, at least you provided the enema. And, oh, how tiresome Angus was, going on about *penetrating*.

Then, reminded, "Did you know that Moravia is writing about his stay here?" Long pause while Stephen looked at the French windows, the Italian floors. "Anyway, one story is about this dreadful American in Tokyo whose only pleasure is in forcing unprincipled women on famous and unwary visitors." His pink laugh tinkled. Then he remembered to look sad and said, "But it *is* a bit unkind, isn't it?"

STEPHEN SPENDER, 1959. "Yeats and the Noh—terribly interesting that. But, don't you think, actually, that it is rather the case of his having found the perfect receptacle for his thought, rather than the other way around, if you what I mean. What I really mean is that for him Hawk's Well did not exist, as it were, on any definite level. Of course, he may well have thought it did, but it was, I sometimes think, a thing which was seized upon, quite outside any considerations of worth (and I must admit that I do sometimes think considerations of meaning as well) of the object itself. At any rate, so it has seemed to me. Don't you think?"

Don't you think? A phrase that hung over his talk, a demand for confirmation, a cry for understanding. Also a courtesy, opening the door and standing aside. A question completely satisfied with a simple yes.

No, on the other hand, would bring concern, the pupils suddenly focused. One had become very small, something to be searched for until the poet's head with its mane, a corolla, would turn away, as though in consternation.

One consequently rarely said no. One wanted, rather, to emulate. To imitate this exquisite show of hesitation among shadings, to share a politeness, to cultivate a humbleness.

"Yes, right? Oh, one is quite afraid to move. Particularly in this mannered land. It is so easy to wound. So difficult not to. Still, if one stood very still, one might, perhaps, not, just might not injure. Don't you think?"

Consideration for others continued. In the taxi, going to yet another literary gathering, I asked, "But if you hate them so much why go? It can only be punishing for you."

"But, don't you see? It will not be punishing for *them*. And they have invited me. They want me." This graciously acknowledged failure. The smile implying that failure occurred, that nothing but failure occurred, yet one must somehow keep on trying.

His attempts were constant. Involved conversations with graduate students solemn about Firbank, Babylonian dialogues with professors during which Henry James grew gradually opaque and then slowly disappeared.

In the taxi going back I said, "Such verbalizing."

"Yes," he said, then, "but if I did not trust words, just what would I trust?" Then, the smile, "Oh, I know. It *is* ghastly, isn't it." Then, "Still . . ." and the qualifying statement.

On the other hand, yes, if one thinks about the matter, still, I wonder . . . he was conciliatory to the degree that the Japanese, unused to this prized quality in foreigners, were invariably charmed.

He could be provoked but the retort was then delivered in a manner that rendered it unnoticed. One tiresome literature student's effusions on Lawrence Houseman brought forth: "Quite, but one must not forget the other Lawrence—Lawrence Hope."

When I mentioned this he said, "One of the things you must understand about me is that I refuse to hurt."

"That must be difficult."

"Quite."

"Even Beverly Nichols?

"If you knew him you would not say that."

"You would say worse."

"You are very unkind." This strong term of censure was accompanied by a quick look: I had become small, difficult to discern.

Such failures of communication—his with me—were acknowledged by a show of sadness. He was thus reminded that he had just seen Moravia in Rome. "Terribly sad it was. We were having a drink, sitting in a cafe and he was upset about something and said that all he ever seemed to do was to sit in cafes and have drinks with utterly boring people."

"Now, naturally, I knew he didn't mean it, did not mean *me*, but I felt sorry for him, so sorry, terribly saddened, that after an interval, I excused myself. I left."

"I had nowhere else to go. I am not really that fond of Rome, actually. Yet I felt I must leave him. And you know he seemed actually distressed. And surprised. But then I could hardly have stayed on now, could I have. I mean, it would have been *inconsiderate* of me."

"And so I walked away, and I am not all that fond of Rome, you know, and I looked back and there he was sitting, all alone, and it is so terribly, profoundly, well, sad, if you see what I mean. Don't you think?"

The awareness of others. He was in a few days particularly aware of someone named [Tokunaga] Osamu. "Human relations are dreadfully difficult." This was said pensively, eyes on an invisible horizon. "But," and the gaze refocused, "dreadfully important, too, don't you think?"

Later, "But you see, what makes it so difficult is that I *am* in love, I suppose. I *do* care, you see. And it *is* hopeless. Oh, I know all of this, don't you see. But I will not be unkind. I refuse. I will not raise false hopes."

"But you have already raised hopes and these, as you point out, can be nothing but false."

"Oh, you don't really think so, do you? How utterly ghastly."

"Stephen," I said, having had enough of this. "Someone once told me you had love affairs in all the great capitals of the world and after each, weeping bitter tears, you left them behind to run out in front of the airplane as you soared away." Then I added, "He was very unkind."

"Not at all. He was perfectly correct. It does happen."

"And that the reason you attend all these conferences in Rangoon and Riga is to . . ."

"No, that it not true," he said. "I can see why your mysterious informant would so believe but he is incorrect. I attend these deadly conferences because I want to help; I want to influence a bit; I want to do what I can."

"Through congresses of intellectuals?"

"Precisely."

I looked at him standing there, his white mane glowing, brave, the poet on the battlefield.

"But," he said, "what am I to do about Osamu?"

"Don't do anything," I said, but I saw his dilemma. He was a man walking on eggs and complaining that he was crushing them. "Stephen," I said warmly, "You ought to stay in Japan. It was made for you."

"Do be serious. What am I to do? I refuse to hurt."

The blazing blue eyes, the halo of hair, the long neck rising from the open collar. And now I saw the resemblance so clear that I was surprised I had been blind to it—the poet Shelley.

W. SOMERSET MAUGHAM, 1959. A very old man, neck corded, skin leathery and wrinkled, a nose like a beak, sunken eyes that seemed to be gazing at the distant past. He has already outlived nearly everyone—born a year before Ravel, five years older than Klee, eight when Joyce was born.

"There we are," he says, having managed the stretch of parquet in his slippers, settled into a chair, handling himself with care the way that old men do, knowing they are breakable. "There, we h-h-have c-c-come b-b-back."

The stutter is initially surprising. He is so very old, and stuttering is an affliction of the young. Even more adolescent seeming is that he has apparently never accustomed himself to it. It still retains, after all these decades, the power to disturb. He remains embarrassed by it.

He turns away when he speaks. "I suppose you two are off to paint the town red," he says, stuttering.

His secretary turns to me, "He always says that. I am allowed out once every three weeks. It is always the same. I am forever painting towns red."

"Alan," says Maugham, "Don't mumble. You know perfectly well that I am hard of hearing. And yet you mumble."

"It is because you are hard of hearing, that I mumble," says Alan in a louder voice, "I was saying something I did not want you to hear. That is why I mumbled."

Maugham snorts, offended I thought but, it appears, amused. "There," he says, "You hear that?" And he snorts, a chuckle deeply hidden, almost inaudible, sunken amid the years.

"Does he dislike being alone?" I ask, lowering my voice, wondering if third-person references were usual.

"Loathes it, hates it. Either stays up until I come back to berate me, or takes double his usual dose and goes straight off, to punish me."

"Not very entertaining, I must say," says Maugham, "you two mumbling away there." But he is not irritated. When I look at him he is gazing at the opposite wall as though he had not spoken at all.

The telephone rings. This he has heard, looks apprehensive.

Alan reappears, "It was *Life*, wanted your impressions of Japan, said you could name your own price."

"Refuse," said Maugham, and his mouth shuts like a beak.

"I already have," says Alan.

"My impressions of Japan," he then says. "I don't have any, shut up here like this. Oh, I was here once before though. So young. I walked in the park. Some good-looking people, some awful policemen. But Japan was even then too neat for me. I like places with a bit of mess, you see." He sighs. "And now it is quite horrid. They will never leave one alone. I do believe that that young lady is still outside the door. Do look, Alan. Are you certain she has actually gone? Well, she was there. For hours. Waiting, dumbly. An autograph did not satisfy her. She wanted to talk about souls, it appeared. Though she was not, I believe, Christian and it is they, I believe, who have the monopoly in that commodity." Again the hidden chuckle, the snort of amusement, like a sigh, or a snore.

I say that he is indeed famous in Japan. Perhaps more famous than Shakespeare.

"It would be disarming, I dare say, for me to appear surprised at that information but, actually, my publishers keep me well informed. As they ought, given the amount they make off me." The telephone rings.

Alan returns. "Do you think the Emperor would ring him up?"

I say that I doubt it.

"Then I must have got it wrong. Someone official, however."

"Refuse," says Maugham, perhaps misunderstanding.

Conversation is difficult. Alan keeps fidgeting yet makes no attempt to leave. Maugham continues to look at the wall. Then, as though speaking to it, "I was here before, years ago. No," as though in answer to a question, "I wrote nothing about the country. It was all so long ago. I don't remember it really. Well, yes, the Imperial Hotel here. And the park across the street. I used to walk there. But nothing else. Change, change. Heavens. Neither of you were born back then." And the chuckle, but perhaps it is not a meaningful sound, perhaps something to do with his impediment, or perhaps digestion.

Conversation probably would in any event have been difficult. I had been told there were two topics not to be even brushed against. Sex and death. He was too far from one and too near the other. Their absence indeed limits talk.

Yet, during dinner at the grill, he himself seems to skirt them. He lays down his salad fork and addressing no one, or everyone in the restaurant, he says, "So strange. I have, you know, this neighbor at Cap Ferrat."

"Jean Cocteau," supplies Alan.

"And I don't know if you have seen them but in his youth he did a number of drawings, sailors mostly, sleeping mostly. And now he has in his old age done this chapel there. And in it he has drawn angels. There they are—angels, needing only wings and halos. But as you look you see—why, it is those sailors again, the very ones. And here they are, probably all dead by now, and he has made them angels—as they were, you see. The very ones." Silence, then, "He is getting old." Then, for the first time, he laughs.

Finally Alan says, "Well, we ought to be cracking."

"What did you say?" asks Maugham.

"That we should be going."

"Oh, really," he says and slowly rises from his chair. Polite, gentlemanly, he holds out his long, wide hand. "You have been so very kind," he says. Then he turns to Alan and holds out his hand until he recognizes him. Snatching it back, he says, "And you are not to be late. Do you hear. Not. Late." Then, again turning to me, he chuckles, and waves a long, old finger. "You take care of him, but don't let him stay out too late. He likes to do that you see, from time to time, stay out late at night."

We walk to the door. I turn and watch him slowly settle himself into his chair again, arranging his legs with his hands. His head nods. He seems to be chuckling to himself. But his gaze is fixed, unseeing.

Still, he hears our leaving. As the door is closing I hear him call in a voice surprisingly strong, "G-g-good n-n-night."

IGOR STRAVINSKY, 1959. At the Kabuki he sat very still, his glasses reflecting the light from the stage, behind them his eyes alert, his hands folded in front of him, the rings on his fingers shining in the dark. With his small, compact body, his large, sleek head, and his big folded hands he looked like a cat—a cat intently staring, a cat about to jump.

We were seeing *Kanjincho* and Benkei was beating Yoshitsune. Stravinsky sat in his seat as though poised for a leap, and then one finger loosened itself from the others and began to tap.

As the play ended, the clappers sounding, and the great striped curtain pulled across the stage, the cat pounced. "Oh, I had no idea it was like this. I had no idea." He beamed, looking from his wife, Vera, to Robert Craft. "Oh, the rhythm, the rhythm was fantastic. Fantastic. And, oh, the tempo." He turned to me suddenly, "They are not the same, you know, rhythm and tempo."

In the interval he continued, "I do not understand. I conduct *Petrouchka* here and they are all right, good rhythm. But, tempo? No, no idea. And yet here! Ouf! Fantastic, incredible."

"And the way they sang!" said Craft. Stravinsky nodded enthusiastically, "That is the way to sing Renaissance madrigals. In fact that is the way they originally sang them. No bel canto. Straight from the throat."

"And the colors," said Vera. "Oh, the colors!"

"Oh, we must hear more, more, more," said Stravinsky, leaning forward in his chair.

Unfailingly curious, Stravinsky. In Kanda, looking at books and prints, "What is that? What are they doing? What does that mean?" He looked with quick, appraising glances, as though he could thus extract meaning. "Ah, look at that. See, look at this." As soon as he learned something he explained it at once (over again) to Robert and Vera.

He was shown some *shunga* prints. There was silence and then, "What is that?" Then, "Ah, so?" Then, "But the Japanese they are not really so large." I said I thought they were probably not. When he found that reality was not reflected he abruptly lost interest. "OK, perhaps. Because *not* sexy. More like medical drawings. But inaccurate."

He wanted to know where the prices were. They were on the back. "Look, each of the dirty pictures cost so much. And the others are much cheaper. You would think it the other way around. More dirty, more cheap."

He shortly discovered the very cheap, a pile at one of the tables. This he turned completely over and riffled through the prints until he had located the two least expensive, both scenes of the Russo-Japanese war. These he bought.

Among the books, attempting to decide between four early European travel books and an expensive four-volume encyclopedia in Russian, he suddenly pounced.

"Ah-hah," he cried, clutching a copy of his own *Poetique Musicale* in Japanese, the title alone in French. "This is it, yes, this is it, the culprit book. There, it says so here, in English, shameless David-sha. Famous. I know all about this. Not one cent. They never paid me one cent. They paid nothing. Villain David-sha. And we could do nothing. Nothing."

I explained that David Publishing had gone bankrupt and that was perhaps the reason they had not paid. "Oh, no. They would not have. They would have taken. Here, this I will buy. How much, how much? They ought to *give* it to me."

Economy, an unwillingness to waste—heard in the music, seen in the man. I told him about the singing insects of Japan, sold in small bamboo cages in July and August. "Oh, I will come in July and August, again." One of them, I mentioned, sang only two notes. "Two notes," he said, as though in reverence. "Imagine. Two notes." Then, "How wonderful, a long piece in two notes. Long, very long." Then, remembering, "Oh, I wrote a piece about one of them, but it was short, and it used many more than two notes."

With this reference to the *Three Japanese Lyrics* he next wondered why the Japanese did not make more of this work. I told him that the Japanese tend to regard things Westerners do using their materials as, well, quaint. He nodded soberly. "That is Russian of them. Very Russian."

Later Craft told me of another example of Russian economy. Stravinsky was writing away, the *Movements for Piano and Orchestra,* and turned suddenly and asked how much the commission had been. Told, he looked at the manuscript page, then added a few notes, drew the double bar at the end, and signed it.

At the geisha party, the same unfailing curiosity as at the Kabuki, the Noh, the print shop, the concert. "What is she doing, what does it mean? I see." Then, hands in lap, legs folded under him Japanese-style, he listened to the samisen and watched the dance.

Afterward he was very affable as, I had noticed, he often was with women. Much kissing of hands, then holding on to them. "I am old now," he had said the day before, indicating a passing girl, "But she is truly lovely." Then, after a time, indicating another, "Now that, that is the way to stand." Later yet, at the coffee shop, looking at the waitress, "That is a lovely face, a noble face, a true mask."

The geisha gather round, they know perfectly well who he is; they all know *Haru no Saiten*. "How do you say that?" one of them wondered. "*The Rite of Spring*." I said. "No, no," she said, frowning, "in French." Whether she would have then produced it for the pleasure of the master I do not know. They were obviously much taken with his manners.

Extreme politeness, always standing when introduced, always last out of the door, always bowing. And hand kissing. The geisha were enchanted. I remembered that Marian Korn, often his hostess in Tokyo, had said, "I knew he was great, knew the music, but I didn't know how great. It takes a very, very great man to be sure enough of himself to behave so exquisitely with women."

Party over, time to go home, with the geisha insisting as was their duty, that it go on, that the guests stay. Stravinsky smiled, blew kisses. "No, I am old. I go. But you, Robert, you stay." He had seen that Robert, much enjoying himself, wanted to stay.

"No," said Vera, "Robert must come back with us."

"*Ce n'est pas important*," said Stravinsky, turning away.

"*Pas du toute*," said Vera, contradicting.

They then went into Russian. Robert stood between them. He had been somewhat like a confidant, a family friend, a secretary, but he was now plainly the son, and his parents were having a small and quiet argument about him.

It was time now, to leave, leave Japan, and Stravinsky was hosting a splendid lunch at the Imperial. All sorts of delicacies, everything done perfectly, very expensive. Like everyone leaving, he had already left—his mind was back home in California. "My books, oh, but I have missed my books." He was thinking also of the airplane. He spread his arms like a small eagle, holding them out at either side, looked down at his plate. "This is the way I want airplane to fly. Strong." Then he flapped his arms and rolled his head. "I do not want airplane to fly this way. Not strong, frightening."

He turned, smiled, reached for the whiskey. "Like milk to me," he said with his cat's grin. "Blood too thick. This is my medicine." He beamed. "Doctor's orders!"

After we had eaten, drunk, talked, and it was time to go to the airport, Vera seeing to last-minute packing, Robert assisting—Stravinsky folded his hands, looked at his napkin, then looked up at me, curious, appraising.

As he had the day before when he signed my copy of the full score of

DONALD RICHIE

With Igor Stravinsky, Marian Korn. Tokyo/Mejiro, 1959.

Threni, then stopped midway through, looked up, alert, and said, "You did buy this copy, didn't you?"

Now he looked up again, intelligence manifest, and said, "You tell me. Gagaku—do I have it right?" A single finger unfolded and began to beat out the opening rhythm, from very slow to very fast, an unbroken tempo of beats, consistently accelerating—a Japanese concept of time, one unknown to the West.

He did it perfectly.

RUDOLF ARNHEIM, 1960. A boxer's face, and a gentleness found often in those so strong that appearing weak is of no concern. Slow, large, graceful, the kind of man who can pick up a kitten without frightening it.

After dinner he talks about Russia, about Eisenstein. "I only met him once. Only once was I allowed to talk with the great man. Didn't understand a word he said, though he spoke perfect German. He was leaning on a mantelpiece, holding forth—his theories. What a mixed-up man."

I mentioned that the Russian director had wanted to come to Japan, almost had. "Oh, yes," said Arnheim, "and what a good thing he didn't. He would have gotten it wrong too." Then, "Now, Dziga Vertov. He was tru-

YATO TAMOTSU

Mary Evans (Richie), 1958.

ly amazing. He lived in the house of this most respectable married couple, friends of mine. "And he used to bring in his little friends to live with him, and the couple would say, 'Dziga, you cannot do this, this is not to be done.' And he would say, 'No, in Russia, this is physical *kultur*, physical *kultur*.'"

"And the last time I saw him he was going back to Russia, this was all in German, you understand. And naturally he had bought everything you were not supposed to buy in capitalistic countries. When I came in he had dozens of silk shirts, all new, lying on the floor. The first thing he said was, 'Are your shoes dirty?' When I said they probably were, he said, 'Good. Now you will please step on my shirts.' So I walked back and forth on them and eventually they were dirty enough that he could get them into Russia as laundry."

He then began talking about beauty, female beauty. He had noticed it all around—the Japanese eyes, the Japanese hair, the Japanese skin. "But, you know, it is an abstract beauty for me because I have no associations. Oh, some glimpses of woodblock prints, things like that, but that is scarcely enough. And beauty, beauty you can understand and feel, that is almost entirely association.

"Take Garbo, for example. That beauty is the kind we call perfect, and what we mean by it is it is both inviolate and inviolable. It is odd that we should think first of destruction when presented with perfection, but we do. She is really the Pre-Raphaelite beauty brought up to date, a prime romantic beauty.

"We put her in a shrine, we worship her. Do you know that story of Kästner's about the beautiful girl who complained about it—men wanting to put her in a niche, never touching her? Which means, of course, that Garbo's beauty appeals most strongly to those who feel safe only when she is enshrined, endistanced, made inhuman."

"That's what I mean by an associative appreciation of beauty. We all know this Garbo-type of beauty. We all agree upon it. Look at Mary there." He indicated the writer Mary Evans, tall, beautiful, now backlit by the bridge lamp.

He talked on—I was listening to intelligence, inquiring, comparing. It is rare that intelligence speaks. With Arnheim one saw behind the talk, glimpsed the intelligence, outlining, isolating, and defining the pool of the mind.

Not many journals were kept during the late 1950s. The pages below, on Mishima, stand by themselves.

UNDATED, 1958. I am to meet Mishima at the Korakuen Gym for a workout in the late afternoon. Soon, much out of shape, I am sore, but I like the gym. The bodies are nice, but that isn't it. Actually, a gym is rather like a butcher-shop—lots of good meat, but all this display does not whet the appetite.

No, I like the gym because it is warm and friendly and everyone is doing the same thing and everyone is in a way, well, humble. No one is vainglorious of his body. That is saved for outside. The gym is the workshop. The worst body and the best are after all bodies and in that, they are alike. The best remembers when it was bad, and the worst can look forward to being better.

Tonight is crowded but Yukio is not yet here. He usually guides my efforts and originally got me accepted. I have often watched him work over the top half of his body and neglect the lower. Muscled torso on spindly legs. I am just as bad. Without him there to push I don't even use all the machines. Just as well. Ache from those I do. The thirties are not the twenties. But thirty-four is no time to sit back and give up. I like the way that physical exercise makes me feel. I can see why Mishima so much enjoys it.

"Where's your pal?" ask my bench-pressing partners. Since Mishima originally brought me I am now regarded as a part of him. He is popular at the Korakuen Gym. This is because he doesn't give himself airs. He is not a famous author, singer, boxer, actor. He is just one of the boys—all of them pulling together, all of them working on the buffing of the body, the building of that domicile which will more fittingly house them.

Yet he keeps his distance and this they also appreciate. After all the straining and grunting, sweat coursing, it is customary to hit the bath, a large tiled tub filled with very hot water, built to contain dozens. This I always look forward to—not only the healing heat and the soothing lustrations, but all those big, beefy bodies with you in the soup.

Not for Mishima, however. For him a solitary shower, front decently turned, towel in place, then back into the jockey shorts, the invariable tan slacks, the black jumper, the gold chain around the neck. Then the comradely wave, the quick smile, and the body-builder author vanishes until the next time. Not me. I hang around, loll in the tub, and talk about dumbbell techniques with friendly flat-nosed fellows twice my size.

I am today thinking of leaving when he finally appears, full of apologies. He is naturally sorry to have kept someone waiting, but he is even sorrier that he is the kind of person who, if he isn't careful, appears less than courteous. Consequently we sit down and he has to tell me the reason. He was rereading *Shiosai* [The Sound of Waves], and despite everything Greece meant to him, he is not satisfied with this novel based on Longus' late Greek romance. What he had done was too artificial. It was, he said, Greece in the style of the Trianon at Versailles. Too late to do much about that, but he was attempting to. Hence his tardiness.

Since the reason had been the most serious one he could think of—work—I was to accept this and forgive his lateness. When I did so he gave me a smile and asked how I was coming with the weights. He then went on to show me what he could do. Much more than myself, and I watched as he pushed and sweated and the muscles grew and the mass expanded.

UNDATED, 1958. Party at Meredith's. Even as I enter the gate I can hear Mishima's laugh, that great, ugly laugh of his—one that it is said his grandmother taught him. It is a part of his heavy buffoonery. When such protection seems necessary, he turns himself into a harlequin, a zany, is weightily paradoxical, and makes outrageous statements.

He clowns about the things closest to him. Like killing himself. The reason that none of us ever take this seriously is his endless chatter about it. It disarms us. It is intended to.

Much of Yukio's considerable charm is that when it suits his purposes he pretends not to take serious things seriously. In this he is like that historical personage he much admires—Yuranosuke in the seventh act of the *Kanadehon Chushingura*.

Here the leader of the now masterless forty-seven samurai pretends to give himself to dissipation and frivolity. In actuality, this is a sham, a cover for his plans for revenge. It is as though both he and Mishima are involved in similar projects.

Laughter continues until late. Not too late, however. Yukio is always home by midnight. Then the serious part of life begins—writing. No laughter then.

UNDATED, 1958. A man is what he wears (a woman too), projecting a desired image. Whether we think about the effect or not, we create it. It is our costume and expresses our intentions. Look at Mishima, that casual wardrobe—the leather jacket, the medallion on its thin gold chain, the boots, the tight trousers, and the wide belt. These create a cutout figure, an outline, and a recognizable icon. We can trace its lineage. From Hemingway to Brando and beyond, this image presumes virility.

No less for the bike people than for Yukio, this icon is magical. But it originally meant that civility was courted, was sought for. It did not presume that it had been already attained. That this image is even now seen as clone-gear in Village ghettos indicates that the search has not ended .

The leather-look, of which Yukio's is a modified version, is, I think, about a super-virility that can exist only for the wearer and for those who share his dream. Like all icons, this one can never be tested—it is ideal. The icon designates the deity and eventually becomes it.

UNDATED, 1959. Yukio and his deities. Saint Sebastian, for example. This popular sufferer—drawn, painted, sculpted, poeticized, turned into music—has, like most, a double aspect. One can be him, or one can regard him. If the former, then one is the saint; if the latter, then one of the archers.

Mishima, despite his draped and ecclesiastical posings for photographers, would say he was really one of the archers. Yet, unlike them, he knows that a single look from Sebastian will scatter them all. The sadist cannot stand that blow from the eyes of the other. He is so occupied in turning that body into a thing for his pleasure that he leaves himself open to invasion from that very body. It need only reassert its individuality to remove all of his pleasure. Sadism as a means of communication is doomed to failure because communication creates empathy, and this devastates the sadistic impulse.

He talks a lot about sadism, Mishima does, resting after having been translated or photographed. He is as interested (as have been some of his models—Barbey d'Aurevilly, Swinburne, Wilde, Gide) in "evil." Perhaps he confuses the two. Yet this interest confines itself. Like Baudelaire, who found in *diablerie* an extension of bourgeois interests, so Mishima retains the sadistic pose because it continues the cult of the self that is so important to him.

It doesn't go very far. Yukio is not what the books call a practicing sadist. Instead he is a practicing author, and his life like any other involves placation and compromise. These were qualities not unknown to Saint Sebastian himself, slumped there, pumped full of arrows. But those who think they are lined up, bow ready, just one of the soldiers, are really already tied to the post. Sadism is an illusion born from the needs of its opposite. We are all of us masochists, no matter how much leather we wear.

UNDATED, 1958. A party at the Mishima's new house. It is all concrete, somewhat Spanish-looking with its whiteness, its tiles. Yukio calls it his "anti-Zen house," and I have heard others describe it as "Montgomery Ward Colonial."

There is a large naked man in the forecourt, a copy of, I think, the Apollo Belvedere, and there is a grotto lined with Delft-blue tiles. Inside, the house is light, airy, spacious—and a little strange.

A staircase suddenly descends directly into what would be the drawing room, but it leads nowhere—just up to a high little door with a balcony around it. It is from this staircase that Mishima descends upon his guests, having revealed himself first on the little balcony. In another part of the house is a big, wide set of stairs to the second floor, and this is what the family and servants use.

We guests are served drinks—big choice, scotch, any cocktail you can think of, sherry—and amuse ourselves until the descent of the host. No sign of his wife. Probably in the kitchen being wifely. When he takes her out he is completely solicitous but in the house she turns into a more Japanese spouse.

We hear his laugh above us, and then he is among us, making sure that glasses are filled, a word for everyone, complete charm as he circles among us, addressing remarks mainly in English. This is because the guests are mainly foreigners or Japanese who have lived abroad. One of the reasons is certainly that few foreigners speak Japanese and few Japanese speak foreign languages. Another, however, is that Mishima likes to control an audience. Perhaps he acts differently in front of an all-Japanese party.

In front of us he is charisma itself—fascinating (he explains the philosophy of the Japanese sword), sincere (he admits to doubts about this same philosophy), amusing (he invites a minor ambassador to immolate himself on the carpet), and self-deprecating (tells how clumsy he is, finds difficulty in returning sword to sheath). All of the time being the most considerate of hosts.

The food is very good—fish, steak, fruit—and well served by, I think, hired caterers. No sign of Yoko, however, until the very end when, like a chef, she is brought on. We all sit around and drink chartreuse and Grand Marnier for a time. Typical of Yukio and the enormous divisions he cultivates in himself—house all Western but in

Mishima Yukio, 1958.

side ruled by Japanese customs regarding wives; outside, liberal, egalitarian, solicitous; inside, a Japanese husband.

At the same time, however, signs of concessions. Last week when we lunched he asked me not to send him any more St. Sebastian postcards from my various travels, a habit I have gotten into. The reason is that Yoko has asked that I stop.

There are also from this period several descriptive essays that Richie made from diaries, apparently intending them to be a part of some autobiographical work. One of these is about the marriage of his friend Tani Hiroaki.

1958—NAGATORO. I sat all dressed up and looked at the happy couple, while the spring smell of muddy water filled the room. Outside the brown river ran, and Tani stood straight in his new black suit, white gloves in hand, tie crooked. At his side sat the bride in kimono, sleeves trailing on the floor, a white headpiece hiding the jealous horns that brides traditionally wear.

A flash, a cloud, a smell, and there they stood on the photographic plate forever. The local artisan, pursing his lips to indicate optimism, placed the cap back on the lens and we all applauded, while the bride put two fingers into her tight obi and shifted the fan that took the place of the dagger brides once carried to use against themselves if dishonored.

Back at the inn, in a large, low room, cushions had been arranged for the wedding party, small, low tables in front of each, and at the far end a dais for the couple. Outside the low windows the river flowed, rich and muddy in the early spring.

There now sat Tani, enthroned with his bride, and here sat I, first in the row that held his party, all men, all about his own age. They had politely ignored me until it was learned that I could, after a fashion, speak. They then dropped their solemn shyness and wanted to know how I had come to meet their friend.

Prepared, I lied about school, English class, and promising pupil. This explanation was so expected that it was at once accepted and the muscular young man in a white three-piece next to me tried out a few modest English phrases.

The river murmured, the spring smell of fresh water filled the room, and the bride entered, elaborately careful of skirts and sleeves, while Tani gripped his gloves and looked straight ahead as the assembled women broke into a little patter of applause.

These were all of the bride's party, older, in sober kimono, her mother beaming. She was why we were in this country inn on the banks of the Arakawa in far Chichibu, the low mountains just outside the window. Her daughter had to be married in her homeland.

So city boy Tani had had to transport his party, all members of the same construction gang, and myself, into the deep country. On the way his friends pointed out the horses and pigs to each other and one, upon arrival, had gotten too near a bull, which snorted and sent him scampering down the lane.

Now wary of the country, they sat formally, their legs under them, and looked about as the applause died and bride seated herself on the dais by her new husband.

She was really just as citified as he, had been working a Shinjuku bar frequented by members of this small gang to which Tani now belonged. It was the construction boss who had served as go-between. He was interested in the bar she tended. And she wanted marriage, needing some stability in her fluid life. As for Tani, he found her pretty, didn't have a steady girlfriend, and as the latest member had to listen to advice from the boss.

Sake was poured, even before the first speech. Local sake, and lots of beer, and a big, brown bottle of whisky for me. Tani smiled, tie still crooked, and indicated that I should relax, stretch my legs out. This I did and his gang friends, all uncomfortable sitting on their calves, spread out as well, pointed out a passing dog, slurped their sake, and turned to look down at the muddy flow,

The bride smiled down upon them. She included even me. Originally I had been a threat—the foreign friend. When I first went with Tani to the bar where she worked, her manner had been coolly professional, a chilly hostess doing her duty. Later, however, she warmed. Maybe I was a good influence after all—keeping him away from all those awful other women.

Now the speeches began—long and stilted, about her virtue or his, older people mumbling about future promise. Then, cups and glasses filled, more toasts. And food—country food: boiled radish and salted river fish, burdock, miso baked on eggplant, and pickled fiddler fern.

Speeches again, but now short and funny, as though having observed the sublimity of marriage we might now allow ourselves its foibles. As a foreigner—and foreigners are famous for being funny—I was first.

Prepared and knowing what was expected, I spoke of the groom's doomed efforts to learn my language, made affectionate fun, skillfully suggested an apparent stupidity, and ended by blaming myself for all lack of progress.

Laughter, applause, and for me a reward from Tani, now sitting crosslegged in his new suit, a glance of connivance, and a short smile from the bride, and from my three-piece neighbor a solemn paw and a level and approving gaze.

More toasts, more speeches. One old woman with loose teeth spoke loudly of the joys of the marriage bed. The room roared, the member with the perm spilled beer on himself, and the bride, virgin for a day, covered herself with confusion. Everyone was getting drunk.

Me too. I looked at the handsome Tani, lolling up there with his bride, useless white gloves still firmly in fist, and felt sorry for myself. You are losing your friend, I thought, and a tear actually appeared.

The ceiling gently rotated, the river rose, and the smell of spring and mud ran over the mats, while the creamy three-piece pounded me on the back, brimming cup in hand. I drank, handed it back, filled it up, watched him drain it, and then back it came.

This went on for a while—minutes, hours—then it was time to dance. The old women wove among their cushions, the men slapped their country thighs in time, while the boys shuffled and twisted, the bride clapped and shrieked, and Tani grinned, tie askew.

Pulled to my feet, I stood between the young man in the white three-piece and his permed friend. We were to dance, a special dance from their native place—far and fabled Kyushu. I attempted to sit down. My new acquaintance leaned over and pulled me up again, reassuring in a warm whisper that it was real easy.

So it was. While his friend knelt, banged the glasses and sang, he advanced upon me, holding a large empty sake bottle between his legs. I was to hold tight to the folded cushion between my own legs and receive the bottle. We were then to move in an illustrative manner while his friend sang, veins showing, and then back off and begin all over again.

Here he came, sake bottle up, and I was ready with my folded cushion. Bottle erect between his tight thighs, he put both arms around me and humped as the old women screamed and the men shouted with laughter.

This went on until my groom fell down, bottle rolling, and I, the bride, opened my legs and let the pummeled cushion drop. The floor vibrated with the applause and the passing river rippled. Looking at the groom on his dais, I received a smile. This was a wedding, it seemed to say, what did I expect?

Wedding? I think I thought—no: divorce! Eyes full I turned and staggered up onto the dais where I leaned against him, reached out and slowly, carefully, straightened his tie. Slight discomfort from my groom, a ripple of real annoyance from the bride, still in her hood to hide the horns, and then three-piece tackled me, pulled me back, and lay on me as he poured beer down my throat.

The river ran, the sake flowed, the smell of spring mud lay over me as I lolled on the mats, a foot in my face. Then the boats arrived.

At Nagatoro you went boating, that was why you had come, and so a trip was planned, no matter the condition of the boaters. One old woman got her white stockings all dirty when she missed the stern; one old man missed the boat entirely.

Pushed or pulled, the others boarded and the boat swayed. Tani and his smiling bride were in the prow where we would see them, while the rest of the guests gripped the gunwales. I was next to the boy with the perm. His three-piece friend was nowhere in sight, and I gazed about as though seeing for the first time the bright blue sky of early afternoon, the rich clay-brown of the passing river.

Farmland glided past, a curious cow, and we were in the gorge, where the river splashed and the big rock walls slid by, where the bride, pretending fear, clung to her new husband, and one old farmer in braces got sick in the frothing tide.

On and on, the boatman plied his single oar in the wake of the bumping boat, until a pool was reached and we were pulled to one side while he pointed into the depths and told us that here lurked the fabled carp, one traditionally friendly to such brave endeavors as marriage.

Turning I saw that my three-piece neighbor had reappeared. Now he was standing up, pulling off his three pieces and then, only in his own creamy skin, jumped into the chocolate river.

I wanted to save him—a new friend already imperiled—but the permed pal had already pulled off his own clothes and joined him in the muddy stream where they snorted and sported like muscled porpoises, while Tani laughed and the bride, face to his shoulder, hid her gaze from the naughty nudity.

All eyes, I stared down at the naked boys. One floated on his back, chest and loins surfacing, and the other, all buttocks, dove into the depths. Then they gamboled around the boat as the old women shrieked, the men sang, and the boatman beamed.

Back on shore with the afternoon sun low, the two swimmers, though now more modest in long cotton kimono, did not seem much more sober. They and their friends rolled about and told the bride what awaited her, as the sun declined and the shadows lengthened, long and cool, across the mats. The distant rush of the waters, more sake, more beer, more whiskey—and, quite suddenly, sleep.

I awoke in a different room, my pants off but still in my tie and shirt, lying on a mat, a coverlet over me. The ceiling swam in the upper gloom and the river murmured as though asleep itself and it was dark night.

In the dim light from the corridor I saw that several bodies were in the room with me—bundles of sleep, an arm or a leg sticking out here and there. The smell of spring mud lay rich and fleshy across us.

And an arm fell heavily on me while someone asked in a husky whisper if it was really true that I taught English. It was the creamy swimmer, now piece-less and under the same coverlet. I said I had never taught English in my life. Then what had I taught Tani he wanted to know in his low, urgent, drunken whisper. "I'd like to learn," he said, "I'm a good learner."

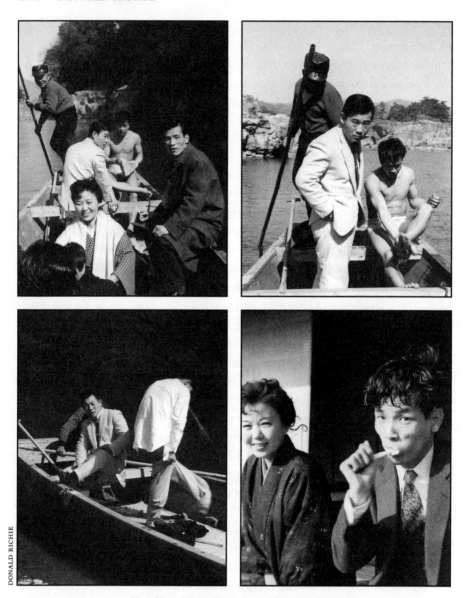

Tani Hiroaki's wedding party. Nagatoro, 1958.

And I thought about my friend Tani, under this very roof with his pretty bride, his necktie now off. The odor of mud, of flesh, lay heavy in the dark and I thought about weddings and daggers at the waist, took a deep breath of the soil-scented night and turned to face the Kyushu friend.

In the morning I was wakened by the sound of water, a vision of a vast cool blue lake, and a terrible thirst. Pushing off my sprawled and sleeping partner I staggered to the bathroom, enveloped now by the country smell of urine, and drank heavily from the faucet.

The door opened. There was Tani, fresh from the bath. He wanted to know if I had a hangover. Well, he wasn't surprised, not after all I had drunk. Not him though—bad thing about getting married was you couldn't drink, had to sit there watch everyone else make fools of themselves. Liked my dance, incidentally.

"How was yours?" I wanted to know.

"Come on. I was tired. Besides, I've done it enough with Machiko already." Then, "Hope you behaved yourself."

"Certainly did."

The sound of running water, the river—like the sound of someone taking a leak." Oh, shit," I said. "Forgot my toothbrush."

"Here," he said, and as he often had before, lent me his.

I was bent over the basin brushing when Machiko appeared, a summer kimono gathered about her. She smiled, said good morning, and I rinsed off her husband's toothbrush and gave it back to him.

She kept on smiling—he was hers now, shared toothbrushes mattered little. And I thought of the picture and the two of them preserved in the flesh on the photographic plate and their never changing.

But now in the bright morning light reflected off the surface of the uncoiling river, amid the smell of mud and piss and the gentle odor of miso soup warming in the kitchen, we three stood there, our flesh firm, filled with future promise.

From 1960 on, Richie began to keep a fuller record of his life. From now on, the journals have an existence in their own right. Consequently they take the shape of Richie's life.

He had come to live in a land as far from Ohio as he could get, and it was becoming his home. Indications of the freedom he found in Japan have already been noted in these pages, but now he began to be aware of an irony. He was free not because he was no longer compelled to "join," but because he was not allowed to. This was because he was foreign. If he had been Japanese he would have been forced to join. It would have been worse than Ohio. With a growing appreciation of this came an attitude toward self that was quite different from that in, say, the journal entries of 1948.

It took the form of an awareness of his singular position in Japanese society, and with it a growing interest in communicating, dramatizing it. An early expression is found in *The Inland Sea*, but before that, in these journal pages, there are indications. Richie once said that he had thought he was a window, but he turned out to be a bridge. In the meantime he continued to live the life he was just beginning to record in the journals. Since he made little money from any of his books, he continued to support himself doing things—teaching, reviewing, editing—that were not central to the way he saw himself. Though he had a number of avocations—painting, composing, stage and film directing—he really saw himself as a writer, a "creative" writer rather than a critic. He once said that if the house were on fire he would neglect *Kurosawa* and *Ozu* in order to save *The Inland Sea* and *Public People, Private People*. He was also moving about the city, trying out different neighborhoods. In 1957 Richie had lived in a house in Shimo-ochiai, near Mejiro Station, and in 1959 he lived in a small house on the hill above Otsuka in the north of Tokyo. Here he met Zushiden Tsukasa, a Kyushu student going to Chuo University, and they lived together for a time. In 1961 Richie married Mary Evans and they lived in a small house near Roppongi. In 1971 Richie would buy an apartment in Tsukiji, then sell it and move to Yanaka (1980), eventually settling in Ueno (1996).

5 JANUARY 1960. I dream of an experience I had thought forgotten: I am again on the beach at Chiba, and it is the day of the dead, before dawn. I cannot sleep, and wander out onto the beach, looking upward at the summer stars. At my feet is a boy curled up in a hole in the sand and sound asleep. I look further and find the beach is full of sleeping boys, all children. Like animals in their burrows, two and three to a hole, they are curled sleeping. Then I remember that today is the day the dead return. The children are waiting for the dawn, when their dead come from the sea.

I awake and it is dawn: the whole experience, precisely as it was, I see with hallucinatory brilliance. It does not fade, but stays with me all day long. It asks me to use it, to do something with it, not to lose it, now that it has made the immense distance back to me.

In the evening Erik [Klestadt] comes over. He is feeling depressed; feels so wretched that there is something gallant about his consenting to remain the person I know, and to reassure me through various ways of speaking, ways of holding himself, that it is indeed he.

Not sympathetic, I say that such depression is the price he has to pay, that he has made a choice and this is one of the consequences. For Eric is a brilliant linguist who does not use his talents; he is a first-rate critic who never criticizes; possessing extraordinary sensitivity, he allows it to prey on him and never once himself preys on it. He, who can sit down and read a Japanese paper or magazine as though it were English or German, who possesses the ability further to fully comprehend what is left out as well as put in, makes no uses of this gift. He works daily in an office selling scrap metal.

"Oh, you make it sound so easy," he says. "And perhaps it is easy for you, but something is lacking in me." He is going to explain, but then that is too difficult. He merely says, "I am terribly lazy."

I look at him and realize how very much I like him, how much I want to save him. I see him as a swimmer in the unruly surf, sinking, sinking, yet refusing to call for help; smiling with exhausted reassurance, as yet another wave topples. I want to gallop into the raging sea and pull him out; and I would try, but that he would probably pull back and refuse. I tell him this, and he smiles and says, "Well, at least I don't think I would be strong enough to pull you under as well."

6 JANUARY 1960. Zushiden [Tsukasa] makes supper and afterward we sit in the electric kotatsu and eat mikan, and he talks about Kagoshima from where he has just returned: tells me that even in winter he used to go barefoot when he was a schoolboy; that they had no gas and still used charcoal; that even now in the single motion-picture theater the crowd applauds when the film begins, and applauds all the credits as well; and that they also clap when the plot takes a turn to their liking.

He also tells me about various early amorous adventures. The first little girl with whom he played doctor (she was patient; he, doctor; she had to have an operation) he saw again just this month at home. "And did you play doctor?" I asked. "No," he said, "it was all very proper," and he did a parody of the way in which he greeted her: important in his Tokyo student uniform, the slight nod, the slight smile, and dignity about all. Then he broke down laughing at himself.

Zushiden is only twenty but knows himself better than do many grown men, including this one. He is proud of his body, but only for what it will do for him; says he thinks he is not too smart but knows that he's not dumb.

Zushiden Tsukasa. Mejiro, 1960.

Won't study, though—is interested in the team and the school; stays home here most of the time and reads sports newspapers; willing and obliging, and one of the least selfish people I know, perhaps because one of the least ambitious.

Yet this will change; I have seen it change, and in only five years people just as open and as at peace as Zushiden transformed into insecure, scheming, harassed Japanese adults. Perhaps it is the curse of the city; perhaps the mark of society; perhaps merely another form of the adaptation that I am admiring.

7 JANUARY 1960. A cold day. Hurrying home after the public bath, steam rising from my hair, I notice girls sitting in the open shops, boys lounging by open upstairs windows. It is quite true that heating is not needed in this country. Even people who have it do not use it. The hands, the face, become red and chapped. When someone is really cold he doesn't dance around, his whole body chilled; rather, he pats his cheeks, wrings his fingers. Then (and what a graceful gesture that is) one hand is extended over the charcoal in the hibachi. In the bath, however, with what abandon do the washers douse themselves with scalding water before they plunge into the boiling.

9 JANUARY 1960. At the PEN meeting, the sun reflecting off the Sukiyabashi Canal just outside the big French windows, I am introduced to a bird-like, white-haired man.

"Oh, but we know each other," he said to the man who was introducing us. "We spent a very cold afternoon together some ten years or so ago. I caught a cold. Was in bed for a week."

Kawabata Yasunari looked at me, kindly, inquisitively, and released my hand, "I imagine he doesn't even remember me."

"But I do," I said.

"He speaks," said the writer, surprised. Then, to the other man, "There we were, stuck up there, the old subway tower in Asakusa, and I was wondering what to do about him. He was so terribly enthusiastic and kept pointing things out. And we couldn't talk."

"Tell me," I said, a decade-old curiosity returning, "What were you thinking of that day on the roof when we were looking out over Asakusa?"

"I don't remember."

"But how did you feel about Asakusa all burned. You were seeing it for the first time since the war was over."

"Oh, that. I don't know. Surprise maybe. Sadness probably."

He had gotten over Asakusa. Had he gotten over it when we stood there in that cold glare? I wasn't over it, even yet, doubted I ever would be. For me Asakusa had spread to cover the city, the country, maybe even the world.

"And you, did you ever translate *Asakusa Kurenaidan*?" he asked.

"I never learned to read."

"Well, at least you learned to speak. We can talk, finally."

And he smiled, his white head birdlike against the flowing glare of the slow canal and the distant clamor of the Tokyo traffic.

But we never did. And now people were pushing, wanting to speak with the famous novelist. We had already had our talk. And whenever we thereafter met Kawabata would cock his head on one side and look at me quizzically, humorously, as though we had had something in common.

13 JANUARY 1960. My last day of teaching. Making out the final term marks, I half-heartedly attempt to feel something, anything, about my leaving Waseda [University] for good. Nothing comes. I try again; this time something does: Suddenly I realize how tired I am of it all, with what lack of interest I face my classes. All of which makes me realize what a poor teacher I probably am, that—for my students' sake if not my own—I should have stopped before.

Yet, this is not true. I am liked, liked for the wrong reasons perhaps, liked because of the show, but the show was there because I wanted to entertain them into learning. And this has been good. I have proof—the letter that came last June after I had stopped two weeks early because I did not feel I could go on, and which I will in part copy here because I want to keep it:

> We will all miss you, Mr. Richie! You really brighten our school
> life. As you may know most of our classes are boring, dry and
> some even meaningless. We are fed up with old-typed school-
> ing, such as studying the English language in Japanese, which is
> really meaningless and even harmful, I think. For that, perhaps
> the bad tradition in English education in this country is respon-

sible. But your class is different; it is interesting, enjoyable, and lively. In fact, your class is one of the few classes we enjoy and like to attend. But we don't want to ruin your health, and hope you will have a good time this summer and look forward to seeing you in September, and may I ask you to please put up with us once again.

And then it is signed by a young man who sits in the front row and about whom I know little else—Yabuki Keiji.

16 JANUARY 1960. Zushiden here. He makes supper. We sit in the *kotatsu*; he drinks whiskey and I drink *awamori*. We talk. I realize that I have a home and a family. The electric fire warms our feet; the alcohol warms our bodies. After supper, warm, we sit and talk. It gets later. Then it is time for the warm bed and warm bodies.

17 JANUARY 1960. A brilliant day, Fuji hanging over the city, Shinjuku small against its base, everything foreshortened and minutely clear as though seen through a telephoto lens. Meredith and I drive out into the country to see Holloway.

I have glimpses of two domestic households: Meredith and [Yato] Tamotsu have a joking relationship, bunkies, pals, supported by affection, by regard, by need; jocular rough talk to each other; laughed insults; rather matey—a domestic arrangement.

Holloway and [Kamata] Michio have another kind: no jokes to speak of, constant support. I think of bookends, of pairs (plaid sox, plaid tie), of dressalikes. The two make such warmth that the bad cold world is kept out. So shielded and sheltered that the one's opinion is asked before the other makes up his mind.

Wonder what my household looks like. But which one? Well, right now, with Zushiden. It is roommates. People who go their own ways but attend the same classes. We don't have a social life together. We have a personal life. This family is more like a boarding house.

18 JANUARY 1960. In the evening I enjoy another glimpse of domesticity, this sanctioned by marriage. Frank and Marian [Korn]—married long enough to have three almost grown kids. Hence perhaps Marian's: "Oh, no, you are very stupid. You are utterly wrong. You just don't know." On the other hand: "Oh, you are so very clever," followed at once by "I'm just a stupid woman. Oh, yes. I am, I am," even when no one contradicts her.

Frank is determined common sense itself when around his wife. Occasionally public caresses to which Marian lends herself like a petted cat. She holds on to a person as though trying to remember the contours, as though attempting to convince herself that it is all real. Marian, charming figure, charming dimple, turning serious: something of Madame Verdurin there; Frank, something of Basin: a refined, reflective, and self-abnegating cruelty.

With Marian Korn, 1960.

Marian on Stravinsky and Craft: "Well, I know who I am putting my money on. The old one, he's had it; but the young one now he's coming right up. I imagine that in ten years or so, he will be it—the old one has had it." Of any composer she doesn't like (Webern before [Heuwell] Tircuit put her straight): "He doesn't know what he is doing!" Folk-wisdom—her mother must have said the same thing about some clumsy neighbor farmer.

Frank is, on the other hand, slightly above the arts, patronizes them: in his canon only Bruckner, Mahler, and Beethoven ("Jews every one of them," a joke) and an I-know-what-I-like attitude.

Both Frank and Marian are now very tired, they are falling apart, they are asleep. I look at my final family, for here I have a place too. Perhaps it was my open unavailability that first interested Marian, perhaps it was Frank's philandering. At any rate the unlikely happened and I found her doing to me what I do to others. This, I think she thought was the way to my heart. I could never be what Marian wanted me to be—bold, impetuous, headlong. I could not rape. I could only be raped. Thus our small passion petered out and we remained friends.

Now I watch my slumbering hosts, so like a father and mother, and remembered my attempts to confess my philandering to Frank—whom I found just as attractive as I did Marian. And his alacrity at avoiding these confessions. These he did not want to hear. About my boyfriends he was complaisant but not about my girlfriends, at least not this particular one.

20 JANUARY 1960. Sick from the dentist and Mary [Evans] tall, wide-eyed, flaxen-hair down to the shoulders, comes over to take care of me. She brings me a bottle of kirsch and curls up on the bed while we talk. Beautiful, strange, something like a tall bird—perhaps a heron. Extraordinary eyes: very wide, large, Egyptian; with those eyes and the El Greco figure I think of Burne-Jones—she is his *demoiselle elue*. Swann would have thought of Botticelli.

25 JANUARY 1960. Had Daiei show me *Hiroshima, Mon Amour.* It received bad treatment in Japan—Daiei, committed, put it on the bottom half of a double bill and showed it only in the suburbs.

Its destruction of chronology is impressive. Particularly I liked the feeling of intimacy achieved by two actors and a camera; and the hallucinatory final scenes of an apparently completely empty, moonlit Hiroshima. Wonderful passage where Okada Eiji raises his head in the nightclub and looks around, and we know that it is day.

Took Edward Seidensticker with me and afterward we decide what was wrong. He didn't like it as much as I did. First, why Hiroshima? The use of that particular city seems to equate the atrocity with the simple shearing of the heroine, it makes a false connection—unless Renais perhaps wanted two symbols of war: the dead city, the near-dead girl in the basement. All other slips are because Renais knew nothing of the Japanese and made people do unlikely things.

Okada [male lead in the film] is, to be sure, a Western-type, and much may be excused (the fact, for example, that he and the girl ever got together at all), but I cannot imagine a Japanese man allowing intimacies in public like that, and the face-slapping scene is nonsense; what Japanese would do that? Would do it to a Japanese woman all right, but not a foreign one. When she goes back to the coffee shop or whatever it was, the *noren* curtain was still up. Renais didn't know that *noren* are always taken in. Rather ludicrous series of slips in the station scenes. Sound track carried Japanese platform announcements for three in the afternoon when the scenes are set for two in the morning. Only truly Japanese scene is where Okada reaches impolitely across the face of the old lady to offer a cigarette—*that* he would have done. Meaningless final scene: "You are Nevers, I am Hiroshima." Ed is probably right in saying that the final scene is, after all, why they had to use Hiroshima. "Can you imagine his having to say: 'You are Nevers, I am Fukuoka?'"

Haven't seen Ed since his trip to Europe. Still both barbed and gentle—reminds of one of those smooth, ivory objects, which when properly pushed produce a small but sharp blade for opening letters, paring nails, cleaning ears and the like. Almost deceptively mild-appearing given his sharp tongue, which cuts. I stick my own out and together we reduce a number of mutual acquaintances to ribbons. As always with him I feel that I am being effusive and that he is being evasive; I always talk too much, he never talks enough. He does not talk in any connected manner: always comments thrown out to which one responds as ducks to bread. For that reason I always find it difficult to remember anything we have said.

26 JANUARY 1960. Dick Brown [friend, met in 1955] comes over and we drink hot buttered rum after hot buttered rum, becoming more loquacious the while. We talk about existentialism, how we originally became interested. It was through the Walter Kaufmann book [*Existentialism: From Dostoevsky to Sartre*]. Dick says, "It was like someone turning on the light or opening the door. I had always thought that philosophy was the history of epistemology, never even guessed it could be equated with anything I really cared for—with me, for example."

I remember, too, the feeling, after I had read Kaufmann's introduction. The liberty of realizing that I am responsible for everything that I am, and have been, and will be. It is no one's fault but my own, and I have chosen. No matter how mixed up I have later gotten in Sartre and Heidegger and Jaspers, that has remained, with its hard-mindedness, its lack of sentimentality, its rock-like weight, and its cold comfort.

Dick has been thinking about it and has come up with a definition, which he has devised for himself:

> Applied existentialism is the creation of the self into something
> (true and good and beautiful) by the ability to act on the basis
> of decision (commitment) that such-and-such is true, without
> the certainty that it is true.

29 JANUARY 1960. Have coffee with Watanabe [Miyako] studying the Kabuki here at the Kabuki-za—has been doing it for eight or so years now. Tells me that the role of the guardian barrier-keeper in *Kanjincho* was originally not a starring role, and that Togashi was simply played by one of the minor actors. But then a famous actor started starring in it and hence it grew; but the script couldn't be changed and so began the various ambiguities that now plague the actor. Does Togashi know the scroll is empty, and if so when? Does he commit suicide afterward, and if so how to show it? She says Kabuki is full of things like this.

30 JANUARY 1960. Today the day I am to have my front teeth sawed off, Mary comes over to stay with me. Brings the new Noh record that she recorded, flowers, honey from Hokkaido, and cakes. We sit upstairs and picnic and she tells me about Cape Breton which she loved.

Something very young about Mary, and one forgets how tall she is: She seems to shrink; she is Alice herself. Brings along an 1896 English guide for German tourists. Scene in the Stage Coach; Scene at the Promenade: ("Oh, and how long have you been ill?" "Since I last had the pleasure of seeing you at my uncle's"); and On the Ferry: ("Oh, the wind is beginning to rise." "Oh, watch out." "Oh—the gentleman and the beefsteak")—we read these dialogues to each other and roll about with laughter.

When the time comes I go and have my teeth sawed off. It doesn't hurt.

5 MARCH 1960. With Meredith [Weatherby] and Nagare [Masayuki] down to the Izu Peninsula to stay in a hotel that Nagare admires. A bright sunny day, growing warmer as the train travels south. In just two hours from Tokyo we are riding through orchards of blossoming plum and peach. One can understand much about Japan by traveling through it. In the evenings in the mountains one sees that the woodprint artists were not being creative when they merely outlined a far mountain in white and left the inside bare, the mountains really look like that. And the formalized blossom pattern one finds is nature itself: each tree looking as though the blossoms had been tied on by hand.

Almost hot in Mishima where we changed trains. Fuji above us, invisible in the clouds. A slow, pleasant, dusty train journey to Shuzenji, ravages of the typhoon last spring still visible. Then a longish taxi ride straight into the mountains, then the hotel. Much *japonais moderne* with floor fabrics used on the ceiling and the like, but the one building Nagare had liked (middle Tokugawa period) is rustic and pleasant. There we had a fine supper of fresh Ise lobster, sliced raw tuna, pickled sea urchins and bean sprouts, a clear mountain-lake-like soup, and—the main course—a wild boar stew, all washed down with sake and followed by fresh mandarin oranges, picked that day.

Later, while I work on my novel [*Companions of the Holiday*, 1968] Nagare and Meredith talk and drink, and I hear a touching conversation. He is telling Nagare that he is thinking of enlarging his garage and adding a room above it, asking if Nagare doesn't want it as a workshop, pointing out that Nagare is now really a well-known sculptor, what with the pieces Mrs. Rockefeller bought, and the Museum of Modern Art purchase, and the coming show he is having at Asia House. Instead of traveling constantly from one seashore to the other, instead of working here, there, and everywhere, wouldn't he like a place to settle down? And Nagare says no.

The contrast is complete. Meredith is secure (his big house, his bank account) and instead of creating, he collects. To be sure he designs beautiful books, but that isn't so important as writing them. Nagare, on the other hand, has never stopped moving, and he is moving still. He hears about some kind of stones on the Sea of Japan and he goes there and lives in a hut and looks at them; in Tokyo he changes his hotels (always cheap though he has become wealthy) every night; he doesn't even have a place to stay in Kyoto, but just keeps moving around. He knows precisely what he wants to do and he cares little for comfort or the other things that money can buy. Nagare nicely and kindly, because, though tough as the stone he works on, he is nice and kind, refuses and Meredith looks into his scotch.

10 MARCH 1960. Go to my neighborhood bath (Zushiden still off at training camp with the wrestling team and I don't like bathing alone anymore) and stay a long time. I am very fond of it; it is the nearest thing to church, to the barber's, to a family.

They are all more or less alike, these baths, one to every neighborhood, there must be thousands in Tokyo: a large barn-like building, tall chimney attached that begins smoking about two in the afternoon and continues to midnight; big entryway with places for shoes, and a tile painting—mine is a crane, symbol of longevity. Inside, the building is divided into four equal-sized rooms. The back two (the baths) have a half-wall between; the front two have a partition with a booth for the girl in charge so she can survey both sides (men's and women's) at the same time. The clothes are left in large baskets. Pay the money to the girl—sixteen yen; shampoo or a razor are five yen each; usually carry your own soap and towel.

Most of the bathers hold their towels in front of them when they go in; a habitual gesture; you see the same gesture in fully dressed men when they are cold; they cover their genitals. Originally I thought it was because of the girls working around but it is not. They pay no attention to the men or the men to them. This is the country of the time and place for everything and the bath is not the place for sex.

Foreigners are told that they must wash outside the big tile baths, using the taps and little wooden buckets, and then get in. Well, maybe foreigners do but the Japanese certainly don't. On cold nights, like tonight, they climb in all dirty and let the communal water soak it off. At best the tap rinse is a mere token: feet, hands, balls maybe, but not often.

Everyone says the Japanese aren't dirty, that they are in fact clean. Well, I suppose they are cleaner than many, but no Japanese that I know bathes because he likes it. He bathes to get warm usually (once out and covered up the body heat remains, for the water is scalding) and he bathes to meet his friends. But not, I think, to get any cleaner than anyone else. Certainly not many bathe completely. Most men don't skin back and wash; and I have been told that women think it is immodest to get soap up inside. Once the bath is over, too, the dirty underwear goes right back on.

But it is nice in the bath and that is quite enough. You sit back and scald. It is relaxing. Perhaps that is why, in the bath and turning lobster-red, Japanese will say things they would otherwise not. Perhaps this is why one can always hear neighborhood gossip in the bath.

One sits back in water, which doesn't feel as dirty as it is only because it is so hot, looks at the picture (all bath houses have one, a giant mural against the back wall, sometimes Western-type scenes—castle and sailboat and deer, sometimes a Chinese palace, nothing Japanese in sight, all oil on tin and mildew), reads the advertisements (Love Beauty Salon, Suzuki's Expert TV Repair, Fame Barber Shop), and listens to the gossip.

Today I learn that that nice Mrs. Watanabe (down the street) doesn't know that that nice Mr. Watanabe (seen him on the street—glasses and a wen) is keeping a girl young enough to be his daughter. Also learn that the eldest Hamada boy (much given to body building, has a bulging neck) is going to be the death of his parents, plays around with girls, and him so careful of his body too. Then someone says that if he had Mrs. Watanabe around he'd keep *two* girls; another, that with parents like that he wonders the Hamada boy hasn't run away years ago.

Maybe if I hadn't been there I too would have had a defender the day my grocer turned to a neighbor and said, "And that foreigner, the one with all the hair; you know he never pulls down the blinds . . . well, the other night . . ." but just then he saw me bending forward with interest. I wanted to find out what had happened just the other night but he sank deeper into the hot water until just his eyes showed.

Once out of the tub then everyone washes (my soap at present is Chlorophyll Cow) using a sponge and a kind of pumice stone on the hands and feet. My towel has naked ladies on it, which is always good for a conversation or two.

In the bath the attitude toward sex is representative. No people have it more firmly in place. They are a bit puritanical sometimes, and a number of prudes exist, but there is no people less prurient. What they *are* prurient about is money. Some Japanese treat money as we treat sex. But, as for sex—well, there are no young bloods trying to peak over the partition.

14 MARCH 1960. Mary comes over and we talk about Atsumori. [In the *Heike Monogatari* he is the beautiful Taira youth unwillingly killed in battle by the Minamoto warrior Kumagai.] She sees Kumagai's dilemma as an existential one. He has involved himself in battle, has committed himself to it, and then is confronted (in Atsumori himself) with something he appreciates, likes, and wants to live. Yet his committed business is killing, not letting live. He is caught.

Atsumori, actually, is much more ready to play the game than he. He knows he is caught, knows that he chose, knows the rules, and is willing to die. He is quite ready to sacrifice what he is, his being, his personality. Kumagai's problem is that he has recognized the originality, the individuality of this other person and, once having recognized this, once having removed the blinders that make killing possible, can no longer want to kill.

Mary thinks that this idea is at the root of much Japanese drama—the Kabuki *giri-ninjo*, for example. I think of doing the Atsumori-Kumagai incident as an existential episode, as a novel, a short novel. Just two characters, the army rushing about in the distance, sea, sand, shore, pines, but each detail dwelt upon. Do it in the style of Robbe-Grillet, but make it more interesting. Make it a slow-motion study—one hundred pages to tell thirty minutes. And behind the story, a full existential exposition: man makes himself, man chooses. [These thoughts later turned into a film script, and eventually became the historical novel *Memoirs of the Warrior Kumagai*.]

15 MARCH 1960. Zushiden comes home after ten days gone for wrestling team spring sessions, brown with the sun, smelling and tasting of the sea. We go out and drink in the neighborhood bars, filled even on weekdays with that frenetic gaiety which is Japan—tipsy bargirls, indifferent hugs on the dance floors, the face of beauty glimpsed in the distance, the toilet door ajar, the friendly bartenders—all weary to the eyes. Then we come home and go to bed.

16 MARCH 1960. Marian took the Israeli General Moshe Dayan to the Kabuki, and I assisted. He appears taller than he is, balding, riveting all with his single eye; the other is covered with a patch, the chord of which cuts across his bare head like the string of a garrote. Around the covered eye the face is wrenched; the nose has been pushed to one side so that it slants diagonally across the face; beneath the patch one can see the edges of the hole. He looks like a Malraux hero.

His hands are enormous. Large, strong, flexible hands which, when folded, attract the eye as the face of others attracts. Large curved nails that seem to have once been pulled out and then let to grow back in. Speaks a soft, hesitant English. I heard him say a few words of Hebrew—his voice changes, and goes down. His English (as with most people's second languages) is pitched higher.

He has just returned from Izu and needs a cup of tea. We go to the Imperial, and he talks about his collecting. He digs for things, and describes to me a Phoenician glass vase, a large one, that he has found. "It is not difficult, but one must know where to dig to find. I know some bulldozer people, and they, too, tell me when they discover something I would like. Most is too new, Greek and Roman you know. But occasionally nice, older, things are found."

He turns graciously to Marian, indicates the tea, and says, "You saved my life," then continues, "But it is ever so much more difficult to save life than to take it, just the other day . . ." and I listen harder, but Marian begins babbling about the relative merits of coffee and tea, and the rest is lost.

At the Kabuki Marian enthuses, but not too successfully. The general says, "I will not say that I liked it—it is too foreign. Still, it was interesting to have seen." He is dropping with weariness, and his single eye is red, like some Biblical god of war. I leave them. They will have their problems. Marian has scheduled a great, elegant, expensive, seafood dinner with geisha. The General may like the geisha, but he has confided that he cannot abide even to look at seafood.

17 MARCH 1960. Went to Marian's, and she tells me about the disaster of the night before. Frank took an instant dislike to Dayan; the feeling was apparently mutual, and Marian spend the evening dancing with the general (who, it turns out, didn't eat a bite at the all-seafood dinner), but who was most attentive, and while waltzing managed an erection that quite frightened her—she said it almost wasn't human. I said that just looking at the thumbs I had guessed. She said she had had no idea. Said at first she thought it was his leg.

Marian is admirable, I don't know anyone more honest about herself.

She condemns others, but she also condemns herself; and she is harder on herself than she is on anyone else. Also has a knack of going directly to the core of a subject. At the same time, she also cultivates a kind of flightiness, plus a great deal of talking to hear herself.

Silly remark today: I'd put on the Vaughan Williams *Wasps* because I wanted to hear the march. "I didn't know Williams was communist," she said. "He wasn't," I said. "Must have been," she said. "Only communists can write marches like that." Wise remark today: talking about geisha and how they fawn over men and act seductive and pout. "This is," she says, "the most primitive form of love-making."

With Marian Korn, Frank Korn, Heuwell Tircuit, 1960.

18 MARCH 1960. Marian's *soirée-musicale*: house packed, servants threading their ways about, almost a hundred guests. Tokyo's nearest equivalent to the parties at the Princess de Guermantes'—not that tony but near it. Tokyo has no society (except for distant royalty and the dowdy wives of the ruling families; one was present last night—fat Mrs. Tokugawa, done up in a green kimono, like an expecting caterpillar), but it has its pretensions.

Marian quite wonderful at these functions; does whatever she wants all day long, doesn't worry, doesn't plan, knowing that it will go or it won't, not really caring. Frank really caring much more, hiding this with laughter and cynicism but unable to quite hide the strain. Marian in her element like a fish finally back in water—flirting, kissing, carrying on, all meaningless to her, and consequently she is good at it.

Music was Couperin, *un souper du roi,* then the Webern violin pieces (played twice); then the Ravel *Duo,* the best thing on the program. Food included ham, chicken, pheasant, aspic, Czech pancakes, Stilton, lots of chafing dish affairs only one of which I could identify, and a big almond cake with mounds of whipped cream for dessert.

Guests enjoying themselves. General agreement during dinner not to mention Webern. Lots of conversation, bright, animated, each sentence ending with, "don't you think so, now?" I talked most of the time with Takemitsu [Toru].

Small, frail, big head, tiny body, enormous talent; is very pleased that the Chicago Symphony is doing something of his. Had the relative bravery (in avant-garde Japan) to side with me last year in finding Stravinsky's *Firebird* still magnificent.

24 MARCH 1960. Go with Gene [Langston] to Niigata, all the way across Japan, from one ocean to another in six hours and through three climates. Tokyo is rainy and warm, the Japan Alps have deep snow, and the plains on the other side are as cold as November, the Siberian winds sweeping across them.

I haven't really spoken with Gene since his return. We sit quite companionably and have nothing to say at first; then bit by bit we remember, things come back; we end the journey jabbering. No one is less changed by the years than Gene. I notice a slightly awkward stoop and it makes me think of age, then I realize that Gene has always had this stoop. A laugh, slightly nervous, strikes me as a bit odd until I recognize it as that of fifteen years ago.

At the station is his friend and, for me, Ito [Sadao], whom I've not seen all year. He is a farm boy—sent to school in Tokyo, turned bad, brought back home, now works on the farm, and will all of his life. Wants to hear all the news from Ginza; follows Tokyo life on the TV and knows a number of things about it that I don't.

On the bus going to the hot springs resort we pass houses like his. Stones to keep the roof on during the windy winter, an open front, barricaded in the winter, a cavernous interior with the single unblinking eye of the television set (everyone in Japan seems to have one now) staring out, half obscured by the heads of gazing children. That and the radio and, for the grown ups, alcohol and making babies—that is all there is. Ito gets into Niigata on weekends sometimes, has a drink at a bar, and has to catch the last bus (7:30 P.M.) home. Perhaps consequentially seems pleased at my visit.

We drive for hours and finally, at the foothills of the northern Alps find a small collection of hotels, and a hot spring, steam escaping. We take baths and drink sake, play games and talk, and I am happy. Happy with Gene, happy with Ito—all of me satisfied.

25 MARCH 1960. In the train, going back to Tokyo, I write in my journal: The voluptuousness of another's body, the joys of the fingers, the skin, the lips, the tongue. I burrow into the body, as though I will wear it, like another skin; I want to lose myself entirely in this other or else to make it completely mine.

It is only during this that I know I am real; I am naked, vulnerable, and the fact that I exist and the knowledge that I do for one blessed hour coincide. And yet I gain this only through losing myself, through attempting to sink into the body of another. The adoration of the body has its reasons, and like all true adorations its end is a kind of annihilation that becomes a realization.

Kissing his armpits, his chest, his stomach (not his lips for Ito, a good boy who is fond of me and who humors me, does not approve of our kissing; that is what men and women do, and though he would much prefer a woman, there are never any when I happen to be around and I am better than nothing), I draw nearer and nearer the very totem of my desire; I no longer stand aside and regard myself because I am myself, and I cannot then consider anything degraded or degrading which so naturally follows my desires and through which I become so free. A sense, too, of possession, and of power. Almost unaware of giving pleasure, then, so completely am I absorbed in receiving it.

The feel of skin, the odor of heat, tasting all the varied textures of the body; the exploration in the dark continues. I am burning like a candle—and even during the frenzy itself, this flame burns unwavering.

The tension, the tightening, known and memorized, yet forever new: then the pinnacle, the sudden relief, the body falling into pieces, the candle extinguished—I have been returned, and what might have been called lust might now be called compassion, for a wave of tenderness falls upon me, lifts me, holds me, returns me to shore. I was gone, vanished, merged—for all of five minutes.

Little by little the room comes back, the cool body, now only that, rests beside me. Now everything is normal. I too am normal. I begin thinking in the past and in the future again after my moment in the present. Must pull the covers up or he will be cold; must turn out the light. But he is asleep already, flat on his back, and it is time for me to sleep too.

13 APRIL 1960. I go to the dress rehearsal of Mishima's *Salome*, his adaptation of the Wilde play, given a lavish production by the Bungakuza at Toyoko Hall in Shibuya.

The writer turned director has not found a lot to change but much to emphasize. The attraction between the sentinel and the page is rendered more noticeable, and Salome's kissing of the severed head of Jokannan is much prolonged. Also the platter that holds the head is filled with something very like blood, which is then encouraged to cascade out and onto the stage. Kishida Kyoko will be soaked during every performance.

After the rehearsal everyone stood around and talked. Mishima said that he had wanted to play Jokannan himself but that he felt he had done enough acting for a time. Just a month before, he had completed a film role, the gangster Takeo in Masumura Yasuzo's *Afraid to Die* (Kazekara Yaro). Not only had he acted, but he also wrote the lyrics for its theme song, which he had now just finished recording commercially for King Records. So he had occupied the limelight quite long enough, and it was good to get back to literature.

I did not ask if he considered the Wilde literature because he obviously did. So I said that it was good to see something non-political, referring to the question of the new U.S.-Japan Security Pact, which is being strenuously debated. Oh, no, he said, Salome was political as well, in her own way. She stood against authority. Well, maybe, but if so in the same mottled way that Mishima does himself.

SUMMER 1961. Mishima called me up and asked me to dinner at a new place he had found just across the street from the Tokyo Onsen, a place I went to but he could not because of his fame and his new respectability: a second child is about to be born. This time, however, he did not want to know what went on there. Instead he wanted, strangely, to talk about literature, usually the one thing we never talk about. Even more oddly, about Ernest Hemingway, a writer whom he had disliked to a marked degree, either because of, or in spite of, similarities.

Both are conscious stylists, both are romantics, both are given to macho posturing, and both are subscribers to obsolete codes. It turned out, however, that it was not the author's work that Mishima wanted to talk about. It was the American's recent suicide.

He might still dislike the man as a writer, Mishima said, but he had come to admire the man himself. It was the suicide that had earned his new regard, and the resolute manner in which it had been accomplished. The rifle in the mouth, the trigger pulled—with the big toe he had heard. Was that correct?

And as we ate and talked I again wondered why it was that, like Hemingway's, Mishima's best work is found in the stories and not in the novels. Hemingway's novels are as flaccid as his stories are terse. Mishima's novels are as verbose as his stories are laconic.

Maybe this is because in the short story an author is under no compulsion to "make" character. Ten pages is too short a span to fully characterize, but it is just right for the telling observation. Here both authors may sketch from life in their best impressionistic styles. And here both they and we are spared the hours of sheer toil with which "characters" are compulsively constructed.

Also, Mishima is the kind of writer who prefers to tell rather than to show. The major points of any Mishima work are always related by the author, not by the characters. Here I will look up an example: "Kagawa felt an immense irritation at seeing what should have been a simple, unclouded decision to leave Jiro prey in this way to a moment's clever calculations." Kagawa shows us nothing because Mishima tells us everything.

Now, however, he is showing me something, though. He shakes his head. He is demonstrating thoughtful approval. He is thinking of the gun in the mouth, the toe on the trigger. He is still savoring Hemingway's suicide. Then he asks if it was just one shot.

I did not know but thought one shot had probably been sufficient. He smiled and went back to his food and I knew that the complacency that had been shown was for me and not for Hemingway. It was not that Yukio particularly cared for my opinion but that I happened to be the only available audience to witness Mishima on Hemingway's suicide. He was gauging his performance—something he so often does nowadays. And, since he does it, one notices and begins to doubt its authenticity. Then he changed the subject, asked what Tokyo Onsen had been like.

> **Richie wrote no more journals for four years. During that time he traveled, and finished or began a number of books: _The Land and People of Japan_ (1961), _Japanese Movies_ (1961), editions of the letters from Japan of Henry Adams and Rudyard Kipling, and the translation of six Kabuki plays with Watanabe Miyako. He also made a number of films—_War Games_ (1962), _Life_ (1962), _Atami Blues_ (1962)— and began going to foreign festivals and arranging retrospectives of Japanese films: in Cannes, Venice, Berlin. In addition, he married Mary Evans in 1961—they would divorce in 1965.**

20 DECEMBER 1964. Thought for the day: "Love is what occurs when you become aware of the emptiness of your own life." No, that is not precise. The "when" should be "if" and the "emptiness" should be "meaninglessness."

The search for paradise, the turning over of lumps of fool's gold, this fatal and noble assurance of meaning. As though meaning were something one just discovered, when the only meaning is the kind one makes. That is the kind one eventually agrees to find.

I make forms; I make patterns, as though they were ammunition in this continual war against meaninglessness. Form from chaos. But now I wonder about chaos. I think that it has been maligned. Is not chaos what I should be living with rather than form? I have proved to myself that I cannot tolerate continual form. But could I tolerate chaos? No, I think not.

23 DECEMBER 1964. One of those days. I run off the track. I can see, when I look back, the plodding footprints in the desert behind me. Just where do I think I am going? Here I am a novelist who writes few novels, a critic who usually can't even criticize himself, a husband who prefers sleeping with men. Yet, somehow all those unwritten novels were supposed to appear; my criticism was to strike every target; and marriage was to save me. But no, not at all—and marriage is killing me.

The reluctance to find oneself—the evasions. And the burden of it. No wonder I wanted someone to share it. But one does not drop one's history any more than does the plodding turtle drop its shell.

But now, standing under the high glare of noon in the desert, I can sight the sun and guess where I am. Heading south, I would think. And there behind me lead my footprints, stretching from the cold north. And I feel a stir, life a fresh breeze in this airless waste. It is a twinge of interest. This is curious—what I am doing, standing here. I look around with opened eyes and I feel as though I had found a piece of amber in this desert. I am turning its smooth surface over and over, between my fingers. Strange stuff, amber. It makes electricity.

24 DECEMBER 1964. A party here with Ted [Wilkes] and Eric [Klestadt] and Dick [Brown], Mary and myself, ending up by playing with that infernal book of Prince Leopold of Lowenstein and William Gerhardi, which no matter how you turn it always comes up with the right answers. Here is its truth about me:

> In normal conditions people like you are none too well able to
> cope, but conditions may arise when they thrive and possibly im-
> print the mark of their personality on an entire age. It is difficult
> to see how you could ever form a true relationship in love. To be
> able to love means accepting and acknowledging the fact that the
> other person is a separate entity, a different and wholly individual

unit, and not what we want or imagine. This act of recognition is very difficult for people like you who, after the manner of a nation at war, have substituted the contact of fighting for the more civilized contact based on mutual respect. And like a nation at war, you see the "other side" in the light of your own distorted projection. You might be fascinated and attracted by those figments of your imagination; you might indeed "fall in love" easily and often. But the disenchantment would follow swiftly, for all the time you are in fact dealing with counterfeit emotions.

I still can't see how Lowenstein and Gerhardi do it. It is knowledge parceled out, with all allowances made for the unfairness of parcels, but the contents are useful. The above description describes me now. What they cannot account for is change and any criteria other than their own. They are interested in a person's living well with his surroundings. But there are other criteria.

Yet, how close the description comes to me—and how it describes my life with Mary. I am impossible to live with and I know it. This is true, right now, but I am coming slowly out of the maze of myself, and I see the light. I will have lost her, that is true, but then I have lost so much. On the other hand, I have gained too, burning people alive like this, and Mary is merely the most charred.

27 DECEMBER 1964. Dinner with Hani Susumu and his wife Hidari Sachiko. He just back from Africa and a new film; she fresh from film prizes, including the Berlin. I see them separately quite often. Together not often at all.

Theirs seems a very companionate marriage. Only occasionally do I see that Susumu wonders at his being married, only occasionally that Sachiko wonders why she is not with a man who would sweep her off her feet. Like Mary, she wants both and neither. Women do not want men as men want women. Men really want a woman they can turn off and on like a faucet. Women want in men a faucet that is never turned off tight and is always liable to dribble and spray. I think that women more than anything else want to be surprised.

Sachiko is venturesome. The kind of girl that when young would have done almost anything on a dare. I think of our meeting, some ten years ago, before either of us was married. How stupid I was, how naive. I know enough now to recognize the look that was in the beautiful Sachiko's eyes. I didn't then. The look is no longer there—I'm an old friend of her husband's and that is that.

If I were a woman this would be fertile ground into which I would sow.

Being a man I am confused by thoughts of friendship, ties, appearances, and such. What I like and loathe about women is that they never are—they merely give lip service to this morality that men really believe in.

30 DECEMBER 1964. Over to see Dick [Brown]. He mixes a martini. He drinks because when he is plastered it doesn't hurt so much to live. It is a local anesthetic against existence, against acknowledgement of emptiness.

"My only problem is sheerly technical," he says; "I want to make an arrangement of some kind where I can have it in the quantity I want when I want it. If I want it now, then I can have it now." That is a logical wish, not a person alive that doesn't want just that. But what if you do it? What then? It is never enough. It can't be, because it is the fire screen against the stray sparks of living. That is its function. It defends. So, when you realize your ambitions you work against yourself, and you find that the hot flames of life are nibbling at the ankles instead of just the toasty toes.

But Dick won't ever get enough. He will instead say that there isn't that much in the whole world. He'll have to say it. He won't *let* himself get enough. At the same time, he cunningly arranges that he gets less and less. He knows, deep down, what would happen if lots and lots continued. He would have to criticize the commodity itself. He cannot afford to do that, and so he somehow or other manages to get less and less.

This makes him very unhappy, naturally. And this is what a neurosis is—this collision between mutually incompatible wishes. I don't think that masochism has anything to do with it. He is like the diabetic whose main reason for existing is his sweet tooth.

31 DECEMBER 1964. Tani comes up from Osaka for the holidays. We have ten years of memories we don't bother to mention; a number of assumptions we decline to talk about; I listen to him and he listens to me; there is no competition, and that is a blessed state.

Further, I admire him. For two reasons. The first is that he carved his own empire, and it must have been like carving one out of basalt, and at the end of two years was a rich man. The other is that he borrowed a sum of money from me years ago and has now returned all of it.

We eat chicken à la Kiev and drink Neucastle and talk about the Aztecs and the Lost Continent of Mu and the Sargasso Sea—he envies my having actually seen the latter. It is this, perhaps, that made it possible for him in two years to become rich, and legally too—the kind of mind that finds the Lost Continent of Mu exciting.

I remember ten years ago this month. It was in Nara and he was a student in his black uniform and he came back and we stayed at my hotel and in the morning drank *ozoni*. He has not changed—his character was formed some time before this, maybe when he was a poor little boy on some farm far in the mountains.

1 JANUARY 1965. Am rewriting *Man on Fire* [an unpublished novel]. It was almost a year ago that I wrote it; it is strange to me now, leading a life of its own. Rewriting is a creative act. As I type I keep pushing the novel further away from me, trying to create that distance in which it can breathe.

Mary is also working on her writing in the next room, New Year's Day though it is. My idea of domestic bliss is two people doing their work in separate rooms, aware of each other's distant company. I don't know that it is hers as well, but she thinks as highly of work as I do and we are never closer than when we are working separately.

2 JANUARY 1965. Mary tells me that when I try to impress I lose my natural manners, I revert to my Ohio accent; I do not act according to what I know now but what I thought I knew then. So, tonight, guests here, I try not to impress; I listen rather than talk. Apparently it sits well upon me. Apparently this is me.

But also I miss something. I miss the bad manners; I miss the thrust. I want to be attractive, I want to be liked, and so I will keep on trying. Something new will come out. Right now, however, I feel that something is missing.

3 JANUARY 1965. An endless Sunday. All Sundays are endless. It was on Sundays that my mother and father always had their exhibitions, put on their displays for the children, for the neighbors. Now that I am married I find an all too natural disposition for pain on Sunday.

I think of Gide and his Emmanuelle. The parallel is not precise. I do not have Gide's rigor; Mary does not have Emmanuelle's selfishness. A closer parallel might be with Lincoln [Kirstein] and Fidelma [Cadmus Kirstein]. But, no—theirs is more the André-Emmanuelle relationship. Mary and I are different.

Poor Mary. She married someone she loved and then she never saw him again. I am quite different with her. It is wrong of me, and yet it is wrong of her too. It takes two to fight—even though (alas) we never fight.

This is our last Sunday. We have had about two hundred of them. More, because some of the weekdays were Sundays, too. Now that she is

With Mary Richie, 1963.

going, she allows herself criticism, complaint. At once the air clears. Why didn't she before? Why didn't I?

4 JANUARY 1965. I keep turning my marriage over and over in my hands, looking at it, trying to see what shape it is, pushing things here and there: why didn't it work? What went wrong with the mechanism? It is a certainly a very odd shape—corners where one doesn't expect them, hidden drawers, concealed buttons.

Mary does the same. But she handles it differently. She asks it questions. What does it want? That is the question she asks it most often. Silly question. As though it could answer. So there, with our hands full, we part.

She left today. Now she is gone. She had tears in her eyes, I in mine. Oh, what is it, what is it? We cannot live with each other; we cannot live without each other.

Now I have returned to the house. It is a different place now. Quiet. I like it—so still, all mine. I call her name. Silence. Sadness at this but pleasure, too. These qualities are not antithetical. Maybe all emotions must be double, like this. Love and hate? This is what all couples must feel, must learn to live with if they are to stay together. We couldn't.

7 JANUARY 1965. I find Mary's journal—accidentally left behind, just like in a Japanese novel. Entries beginning as late as November—after our wedding anniversary.

> That I should brood because he was angry with me for being late, that I should be depressed all throughout dinner remembering similar incidents. Why is he always angry with me before others for lateness or other lapses? To seem to dominate, to disassociate himself from me? To express, as he dares not, as I dare not privately, a resentment?

I (blamed? scolded? can't make it out) him for triumph-
ing in trivial accomplishments (the two-minute film, the great
journey he was starting). Of course I was severe and very harsh
and unfeeling, so that when he blew his nose in bed I thought
maybe he was crying and I felt regret. I harden my heart against
him so easily. Why? Blaming him. Disassociating myself, I
guess, as he has himself.

Then this morning he wanted me to kiss him goodbye and
I kissed him only on the cheek, and again at the door he wanted
to be kissed, and again I kissed only his cheek. And when he
had gone I cried, and felt lonely and unwanted and ugly.

Then she draws a shrewd portrait of me:

Donald, I must admit he is intelligent, quick, gifted by nature,
and very affectionate, but ruined as a boy and so afraid of affection, easily unsure, so amused by the trivial, or is it that only the
topical and prankish seems to him "interesting"—he wants to
see authority flouted because authority threatens him, wanting
so to be loved, and is so afraid of love, a boyish loving, a suspicious, retrospective (destructive?) side—severe with himself
and yet unable to go forward, very liberal in theory, in practice
needs an unchanging child's world, which, like a growing child,
he must (flaunt?) and escape often; home must be rigid order,
emotion all in place. Thus he can say that I can have other men,
but at any such talk he turns hypochondriac. For me this order
without warmth and passion and support, is terribly hard. I am
a threat to him; I won't keep my place.

An honest picture, well observed, a good likeness, but there is one thing
left out. She thinks that this me exists apart from her. She does not know that
it is she who built this me. I tell her it is OK to go with men (as though she
needed me to tell her that), and when she does I become childish and get ill.
Well, so be it. What she wants is either a firmly permissive yes or an equally
strict no. Of course, it is because she doesn't really want things that way. She
wants a lover as a husband, and a husband as a lover, and I just wonder if she'll
ever find that. Isn't her problem with me her problem with life?

She knows this: "To accept that one might be loved, that makes me feel
so vulnerable. I am so afraid of admitting my vulnerability, so I give love as

an attack. To feel fulfilled in loving what is less than one, to love what is more than one, would this be unpleasant?"

No, it would not be. And in fact, that *is* love—not this evenly matched boxing match. After all, we are very much alike although she would never admit to being afraid of love, as I do. She is terrified of it and the above is the closest I have ever seen her coming to admit it. We are twins. That is why our marriage won't work.

She wanted to know what went wrong. I don't know but I do have some historical anecdotes, some little tableaux from our mutual past that indicate to me several of the turnings on the wrong way:

First, the honeymoon. I prattled on and she knew it would not work. But what kept her silent—until recently—and what kept her at it? Simply: I'm not going to let him win in this, I'm not going to let this get me down; I'm going to see it through. A dandy way to begin a marriage.

Next, the famous day she caught me trying to take Zushiden away on a trip and leaving her behind. She knew before I went. But again her pride kept her silent—until I returned. She hadn't been long in finding out that I was very unsure, as she notes, of my love life with boys. She turned it into a game that we two could make fun of.

Then, sex itself, or the lack of it. What she says of my fears, of my terrors, this is quite true. But she didn't want to rape me. She didn't want me that way. She never saw that that was the only way—at first. After that I might have proceeded on my own steam.

I'm a type who must be raped in order to get it up. That, at least, is my slender heterosexual history—LaVerne, chanteuse in New Orleans, then my female philosophy teacher at school, then others, then Marian—strong women all, they knew what they wanted, saw it, took it: and I lay back. Whether she liked it or not, Mary I thought knew this, but now I wonder.

Still, she knew part of my sexual history almost as well as I did. She knew what was likely to have an effect and what not. She must have remembered my trust when on our honeymoon in Athens. I was confident that somehow Perikles [Stamous] would help and we would be loving friends all three—or even in Tokyo, when I wanted Zushiden right in there.

I look at myself incredulously. Did I really expect her to understand? Yes, because she proposed to me only after she had heard all the details. But I forgot that to merely know about something is very different from having to learn it, again and again, day after day, having to live with it. This was her lot with me.

8 JANUARY 1965. [Nakano] Yuji comes to stay for a few days before going to Osaka. Delighted to find himself in novel surroundings, he shows what a good boy he is by doing the dishes while we are still eating off them.

A real proletariat barbarian. Cannot bring him to a necktie, cannot make him hang up his clothes— no, he folds them and wrinkles them

Nakano Yuji, 1965.

because he has always folded and wrinkled. Cannot make him use soap and hot water on the dishes because he has never had soap or hot water. Finds his ideal of luxury when he discovers that I have liquor in the house. Imagine that, a whole bottle right in the kitchen; and he always thought people only went out to drink.

9 JANUARY 1965. Yuji has been so battered, so bruised by life. First reform school at sixteen; then life in Sanya and selling his blood to make a living; then selling his spirit to Soka Gakkai (and taking it back)—and yet all of this having his face rubbed into the grime of life's backside has not ruined him. He tries, continues to try, though he has so far seen only failure. He picks himself up, starts all over again. "I'm not smart," he says. This is true. "I'm bad," he adds. This is not.

I fear that at the last moment his new job in Osaka will just seem too good to be true, or that he will doubt, or that he will disappear. I will breathe more easily when he is put onto the train. [Richie had gotten his friend Tani to give Nakano a construction job.]

10 JANUARY 1965. I breathe more easily. Took him down and put him on the super-express with his suitcase, so small, weighing so little, all he owns in the world packed into one square foot. He waves, is pulled from sight.

I will miss him. My doctor [Anne Kaemmerer; Richie had been in analysis, off and on, for several years], upon hearing of my satisfaction at having finally found him a job, says that it must mean I am ready finally to help (though for years I always said that I was helping, yet never once succeeded in getting anyone a job)—well, that's so, I guess.

11 JANUARY 1965. Dr. K. also says, "What I have never been able to understand about you is your ambitions, your goals, what you want to do, what you want to be—how strong they are and where they are leading you; whether they are indeed you, or whether they are indeed not."

I answer that this is the process of living, isn't it? That I will find this out as I live it. Yes, that is so, but how much then of this do I already know and how much is hidden from me?

12 JANUARY 1965. To supper at Meredith's. I have known him for over fifteen years now and have watched him change. Tall, courtly in the Texas manner, he collected prints, traditional Japanese carpenter's tools, and cultivated a gentrified air—vests, a dog, eventually a cane which was not needed. He knew Japanese, had translated a Noh play already, and would go on to translate Mishima, and found a publishing house, Weatherhill.

He also was a fine stylist and was concerned about mine. Much of what I acquired I learned from him. Once he gave me a double present—two books, which indicated his breadth, one he was recommending to me: Fowler's *The King's English* and Doughty's *Arabia Deserta*.

I also remember when he would race taxi drivers—eyes glowing, rage itself—if they cut in front of him. I remember when he became furious when a subservient person used the simple *anata* with him, not giving him he thought his due of dignity. I remember when life with him was impossible because he always thought that one ought to know what he wanted. There were these moral laws which he observed and which you ought to too, only you never knew what they were.

But now (he is ten years older than I, he is fifty) he is more at rest. [Yato] Tamotsu always calls him *kimi*—much more familiar than the resented *anata*—and he makes jokes about himself. Ten years ago, compulsion ceased. He says it is because he thought about it and decided. Well, that is one way; that is the cleanest, and in many ways the best—if it is possible.

1 MARCH 1965. Up at six. Then, not sleepy, I look at these journals, read pages here and there, from twenty years back, fifteen, ten years back.

I always seemed to be doing something I didn't want to do; I always seemed to be worrying that what I was doing was right. I wonder why I didn't enjoy myself; I wonder why I thought something had to be "right."

Then I remember a recent lunch with Karl Deutsch and we were talking about the Buddhist idea of repeating the sinful action endlessly. He mentioned that some Christian hells were also shown as compulsion, that the true punishment *is* compulsion.

It is true. Compulsion is hell. Old ideas rerun to tatters. The new relationship, the deeper relationship, the new coupling of ideas—that is life; that is to be alive and human.

I am reading the Sartre autobiography [*The Words*], which much moves me. I wish I had written it. Perhaps I will.

APRIL 1965. Some time ago Mishima called up and said he had a question. It was about Richard Wagner. He wanted a recording of *Tristan und Isolde*, but one without any voices. Was such a thing possible? He had heard of recordings of non-vocal excerpts from the *Ring* and there was, of course, the *Liebestod* of Isolde, but he needed something longer.

I told him about the "symphonic synthesis" that Leopold Stokowski had made years ago with the Philadelphia Orchestra. It should contain the half-hour of music that he required. Curious, I asked what it was for and he said it was still a secret but would let me know in time.

Today he asked me to the Daiei film studio. There, in a set built to look like a Noh stage, was Mishima in a prewar army uniform, his hat pulled low over his forehead, pretending to commit harakiri. This was the final rehearsal of the final scene.

The movie, *The Rite of Love and Death*, based on his short story *Patriotism*, was already more than half completed and this was the second day of filming. A container of pig intestines stood ready, and after rehearsal these were packaged inside Mishima's trousers. When the sword seemed to enter the author's abdomen it would actually cut into the plastic sack containing the guts. These would then ooze realistically down into Mishima's lap.

This climax was filmed without mishap and Mishima, laughing, making light of the accomplishment, was cleaned up and prepared for facial close-ups. In between he told me that the mixing in of the music was going to take place at the Aoi Studios next week and that I must be there, since I was the "musical director."

UNDATED, 1965. Someone on the staff had finally located a copy of the old 78-rpm Stokowski recording, and it was this that was to be the soundtrack for the film. As befit my position as "musical director" I was seated next to Mishima, and so together we watched this first merging of image and sound.

Slowly, as ritualistic as the Noh itself, the film unfolded, black and white, sparse as the calligraphy—Mishima's own—that scrolled across the screen at the beginning. At the same time, the *Tristan* prelude began its slow ascent.

And the two kept pace. As the drama increased, the music tightened, climaxing in the harakiri scene.

Climaxing in another sense as well. I had not remembered how sensuous, how sexual the music was. The tentative sliding gestures, motifs half articulated, rising higher and higher, then seeming to lose all control as the climax approached, fragments tossed, repeated, tempo increasing, flooding into final ecstasy—just as the pig guts were loosened and flooded the crotch of the director. Wagner thus illustrated the identity of sex and death, an idea that consumed both composer and writer/director.

This experience is strong. There was silence in the screening room after it was over and the lights came on. Mishima had tears in his eyes. He too had been impressed. And he both showed and excused this with a typical reaction. Turning to me he said, humbly and sincerely, "Thank you for having made this picture beautiful." Giving credit where none was due, transferring his own emotion into gratitude, he then turned with a smile to the others and shook his head as though to say that it wasn't half bad.

WINTER 1967. Today, back in my old room for the afternoon, from my old window overlooking the garden I watch [Yato] Tamotsu taking pictures of Yukio in the snow. The photographer is bundled up with scarf and sweater; the author is naked except for a white loincloth. He also brandishes a sword and tries various poses.

All these gestures illustrate some samurai extreme. Kneeling, sword in hand, he is expressing dedication. On his back in a drift, he is still valiantly defending himself. Or, already dead, he sprawls in the snow, the sword still gripped—a samurai faithful to the end.

These photos are designed to show the author as a man of action, one unconcerned with discomfort (lying naked in the snow) and pain (the coming *coup de grâce*), a man of sheer sensation who even in these extremes does not forget the dedication of the warrior.

Yukio rolled about and Tamotsu snapped while I looked down on them and remembered myself as a child playing in the snow. We used to lie on our backs and move our arms to make snow angels. Mishima, however, was tracing something more serious.

And then I remembered Omi—the black footprints the narrator follows until he discovers the big schoolboy tracing his name—O–M–I—in the snow. The narrator is still wearing the woolen gloves of boyhood, but Omi has grown-up gloves. These he thrusts into his face.

YATO TAMOTSU

Mishima Yukio. Roppongi, 1967.

Later I look up the passage. "I dodged. A raw carnal feeling blazed up within me, branding my cheeks. I felt myself staring at him with crystal-clear eyes. . . . From that time on I was in love with Omi."

WINTER 1970. I'm to write something about Mishima's suicide for the *Japan Times* but I don't know what to say. The paper is waiting for its copy, for what they hope will be a human-interest story, but I have no idea how even to begin it.

I suppose I should again recall the day, now a couple of weeks ago, when he and his faithful followers took captive a general, held him to ensure that the troops gathered would listen to the author addressing them, exhorting them: "Rise with us, and for righteousness and honor, die with us." But they didn't listen, they jeered—so Mishima shouted, "Long live the Emperor!" three times, then retreated and committed *harakiri* with a short sword, slitting open his abdomen. His assistant, young Morita Masakatsu, long sword aloft, charged with the duty of ending the agony by cutting off the head, made two chops, which failed to accomplish this. One of the larger cadets then took the sword and concluded the process. Morita knelt and, as was his duty, pushed his dagger into his belly, and was himself promptly beheaded. The theatricality of this sort of death, as melodramatic as the plots of any of Mishima's plays, was a necessary piece in the life so spectacularly terminated. That is what I thought when I learned of Mishima's suicide. There was no surprise. He had so often spoken of suicide before he committed it that I was more or less used to the possibility. He talked more about it because we had met much more often.

All of Mishima's friends had seen more of him than usual. He phoned more, wrote more notes to us, paid more attention. When he and I met we gossiped much less. Instead he talked about writers and writing. I said that he ought to run for office. He made a face. "A writer cannot be like a politician. Look at Ishihara Shintaro. He is neither. All a writer can do is show something."

As Mishima more and more became the man he wanted to become, he more and more saw himself—as an artist must, I suppose—as an exemplar, a model. I refused to take seriously signs of this awareness. I made fun of his private army, the Tatenokai. I called it Mishima's Boy Scouts. He did not object to this, merely wanted to know what was the matter with Boy Scouts.

"With these few Boy Scouts," he said, "I have at least a core of order." I asked if he could possibly mean civic order and he solemnly nodded. "You are impossible," I remember saying. "You are more imperial than the Emperor." I said this as a joke but he did not smile. "So I am," he said.

And so he proved. The Emperor did not kill himself, which is what Mishima did. He truly hated the rationalizing, pragmatic, conciliatory ways that had become those of his country. "Japan," I remember his saying, last summer, "Japan is gone, vanished, disappeared."

"But surely," I said, "the real Japan must still exist someplace or other if you look around for it." He shook his head.

"Is there no way to save it?" I wondered. "No," he said, "there is nothing left to save."

When I learned of his suicide that is what I first remembered—that he already knew that there was nothing more to save. His may have been a political statement, an aesthetic statement, but it was also a despairing personal statement.

I also thought of Saigo Takamori. The last time I saw Mishima, several weeks before his death, he took us—Meredith, Tamotsu, and myself—to dinner at The Crescent, a restaurant he liked and where he would have his last supper with the Tatenokai. We spoke of many things, but Mishima returned again and again to Saigo, the final suicide, and the faithful friend who dispatched him before killing himself. Saigo had seen, he said, that the revolution had failed. He had thought he was reestablishing stern and ancient virtues, but he now saw this new government delivered over to accommodating bureaucrats.

I remember that he spoke at length of the beauty of Saigo's actions—that gesture when all had failed, when there was no more hope. "Saigo," I remember his saying, "was the last true samurai." But as he said this he knew, I now see, that it was he, himself, who would be the last.

In this Mishima was intensely romantic. His death was indeed so romantic that its seriousness alone saves it from melodrama. But, as Mishima might have asked, what is the matter with melodrama? It too is a form of drama, and drama is life. And it is true that a real romantic is he who compares things as they are with things as they ought to be and then has the strength of character to live by those standards which he himself finds better.

When he also has the strength to die by them we no longer know what to say. We have no words for such an event. Those crazy enough to say he was insane merely show us that their vocabulary cannot encompass such an extraordinary act.

And such a logical one. Now that the fact is accomplished it suddenly strikes everyone as inevitable. One could trace a pattern, invisible until the moment of death, which began on the first pages of the *Confessions*, which made *Patriotism* prophetic, each new work adding its weight, incising this inescapable pattern seen in his recent single Kabuki, in the Noh plays, in the various dramas and psychodramas of the later works, extending right onto the balcony of the headquarters of the Self-Defense Forces. Mishima's suicide, then, was the final stone in the arch of his life.

And so it must be viewed. It was a single, personal, creative act. It did not mean a resurgence of militarism, a reversion to wartime ideals, or anything of the sort because—and this Mishima must have known so well that the jeering of the soldiers he was addressing could not have surprised him—his suicide was entirely ritual. It had few connections with and little meaning for contemporary Japan. And it was just this that created the consternation that accompanied the shock of his death, and the means through which it had been crafted.

I remember asking him what he was to do after he had finished this very long novel he was working on. "I don't know," he said. "I think I have said everything I can." He was silent, then said, "This novel I am finishing now is hard work. I don't know how it is going to end. I have no idea. I don't know how to do it."

Upon my saying nothing, he continued, "And it is strange, but I am afraid to end this book." I had been surprised to hear Mishima, he who was always so sure of everything, speak of unsureness. Now I was amazed because I had never once heard Mishima speak of fear.

"What are you afraid of?" I asked, adding, "After all, it is just ending a long book." And Mishima then said something I have since thought of: "Yes, I know, but I'm afraid and I don't really know why." Was it a clue? Was I intended, after the fact, to remember the fear, just as I was to recollect that, no, it was Mishima who was the last samurai? I knew I was an actor in the drama of Mishima's life, not one of the main ones—even occasionally comic relief—but still a person who could be relied upon to ponder the meaning of the remains. Was this yet further manipulation by this master director?

Or was it more a glimpse of what lay behind the mask and its various confessions? I now think it was. I want to think that a very human moment through which I saw, perfectly clearly, the honest, and very private man who had always been there, at the heart of this courageous life that he had created.

The last thing that Mishima wrote was a note, left on his desk. It read: "Human life is limited, but I would like to live forever." And so, I suppose, he does.

The above entry, with some earlier entries, is a fuller version of the essay on Mishima based on these journals and published in both the *Japan Times* and in *Partial Views*. What follows is, again, a long period for which there are no continued journals. During this time Richie wrote *The Japanese Movie* (1965), *The Films of Akira Kurosawa* (1965), *The Erotic Gods* (1966), *Companions of the Holiday* (1968), *The Inland Sea* (1971), the book on George Stevens, and the translations of *Rashomon*, *Ikiru*, and *Seven Samurai*. He also made a number of films: *Dead Youth* (1967), *Nozoki Monogatari* (1967), *Boy with Cat* (1967), *Five Filosphical Fables* (1967), *A Doll* (1968), *Khajuraho* (1968), and *Cybele* (1968). He directed Marlowe's *Edward II* (1968) and wrote and directed his *Three Modern Kyogen* (1969). He also began painting, later studying under his friend Maurice Grosser. Also, from May 1969 to April 1972, he was Curator of Film at the New York Museum of Modern Art. During one of his summers in Japan, he met Mizushima Fumio, who would become another life-long friend.

1 JANUARY 1973. I think of Kawabata. The translation of *The House of the Sleeping Beauties* appeared, and I saw that Kawabata had been as true to his vision of Asakusa as I had been to mine. Yumiko, or her daughter, was now in this strange house in Kamakura where old men could find their youth in these sleeping girls, in that firm and dormant flesh.

And then, one day last year, a quarter of a century after he and I had stood on the Asakusa tower and thought of Yumiko, I saw his face flashed onto the television screen. The avian profile flew past—noted author dead, a suicide.

I did not believe it. Dead, yes, but not a suicide. How could anyone who so loved life, flesh, Asakusa, kill himself? No, it was an accident. The bathroom. The body had been found there, the water running. He had been going to take a bath. He had used the gas hose as a support. He pulled it loose, was overcome. This I wanted to believe. I could hear the water running and I remembered the silver of the Sumida and the muddy bronze of the Sukiyabashi Canal.

But in time I too have come to believe that this was suicide. The gas-filled arsenic kiss had been chosen. Naked, free, Kawabata had stepped into the water just as Yumiko had slipped into the boat.

24 SEPTEMBER 1973. Went to Kamakura to the exhibition there. I've taken that hour-long ride so often over the years to see Suzuki Daisetz, loaded with PX Ritz crackers and Kraft cheeses, to go sit at Engakuji. Here already are Hodogaya, Ofuna; they have much changed, and what used to be valleys filled with groves and paddies are now valleys filled with parking lots and bowling alleys. Only Kita-Kamakura is unchanged because the cliffs come so near the line that nothing can be built.

Kamakura was always seedy. Now that the double row of cherries leading to the Hachiman Shrine is accompanied by a quadruple line of traffic, it isn't all that much worse. The main change is that, like all famous places in Japan, it has become self-conscious. There are lots of fake rustic shops selling *kamakura-bori* at inflated prices, and there has been apparently some attempt to make the place into an artists' colony, or at least an artistic colony.

Streets full of little stores selling Modigliani reproductions, little coffee shops done in that rough-hewn Swiss chalet style for which little girls have such fondness, little boutiques with "Madame Aki" or "L'Etoile" on the window. The Great Buddha is up the street and round the corner. I don't go. Have never liked it. From the first it looked like a big incense burner to me.

I do go for a bit along the street leading to it, however. A quarter of a century ago I was wandering here and found a record store where I saw a single disc—the old Bernac recording of Ravel's *Sainte*. I came from Tokyo two or three times to try to persuade the owner to sell it me. It was the only record in the shop he would not sell, and he had no machine on which I could hear it. I had to wait twenty years to hear that song, and I have still never heard Bernac sing it. I search for the shop. It is no longer there. Now there is the Grande Passion Fruits Parlour; next door, a small and ratty restaurant with a single sign in the window: "A Nice Dish—Japanese Sukiyaki"; on the other side a Honda motorcycle store with young aficionados tuning up their machines, and Madame Kazuko's "Salon de Mode."

Went to the museum to see the Odilon Redon show. I spent some time over the 1910 *Char d'Apollon* but the other viewers liked the flowers better and enormous clumps gathered about the asters and poppies. As always, the Japanese viewer is surprisingly knowledgeable. "You know," I heard a longhaired student tell his girlfriend, "He has something of Gustave Moreau in him." "Who?" she asked, and was enlightened.

Space empty in front of *Bouddha à sa Jeunesse*. The Japanese don't really like it when they find Asia in Western hands. The Van Gogh copy of Hiroshige is all right because it is only a copy, and a bad one at that. But anyone showing any real understanding, or anyone making any use of creative imagination (*The Youth of Buddha*), embarrasses.

25 SEPTEMBER 1973. Eric [Klestadt] and I talk of why we found Japan attractive, restricting ourselves to its emotional aspects. We both agreed that the ease and the general lack of complication appealed to us, that the impossibility of what is grandly called "a real relationship" is refreshing, and that the general lack of consequence is winning. He adds that it is also because we find Asiatics attractive. I add that it is because we still, in our deepest, dankest, darkest hearts regard them as an inferior folk. He—Jewish, refugee from the Nazis—is shocked for a second. But only for a second. We know very well that it is the Japanese who think us foreigners the truly inferior folk.

28 SEPTEMBER 1973. [Mizushima] Fumio's younger brother died early in the morning—twenty-one years old, stomach cancer, six months in the hospital, until shortly before the end he believed, as he had been told, that it was ulcers and that he would recover.

The wake is far out in Tsurumi, near Yokohama, a place rented for the evening: a plain room, the doors removed, with one end banked in chrysanthemums, an altar, a picture of the deceased, and the coffin hidden beneath the flowers. The family in a semicircle, a table on the left with refreshments for the guests. It is like a stage—such serious rituals as marriages, baptisms, and deaths resemble theater.

This drama is simply staged because Fumio's family is poor and most of the money has already been used up on hospital and doctors' bills. The food is rice balls; the drink is cider or orange juice. Usually sake is served but Fumio's mother is Christian, as was her dead son, and so there is none. Also, though the service looks Buddhist there is no incense. The offering to the dead is the single cut white chrysanthemum that one places on a tray before the altar.

I sign my name in the death-book and offer my envelope on which is my name and a condolence message. Inside is another envelope containing money, the amount (a Japanese touch) plainly written. I give these to Miss Shibuya [Yasuko], Fumio's long-time girlfriend, a pretty twenty-three-year-old with the wry and smiling deprecation of girls who have been born in the country and brought to the big city. He will marry her. Already he lives with her on the days he doesn't live with me, and they have been cohabiting since he was eighteen. I liked her from the first, and she liked me. We have much in common—Fumio.

Having practiced and asked advice, I know what to do. From the entry-way I make a low bow to the family. Fumio bows in return. He is dressed up. The first time I have ever seen him in suit and tie. And on his sleeve a band of crepe held in place by a safety pin. He introduces me to his mother whom I am meeting for the first time. We bow and I look at this strong woman who, deserted by her husband when Fumio was a child, managed to bring up, educate, feed, and dress eight children. More, managed to give them a good, sound morality, and a proper degree of pride.

Then the eldest son, Nobuo, is introduced, a big man, sorry they can offer me no sake, apologetic to the other guests because there is no incense, "but he was Christian, you see." I know him only as the Soka Gakkai brother and have heard of his earlier efforts to convert Fumio—efforts which came to nothing because Fumio is neither Buddhist nor Christian nor Shinto nor Soka Gakkai. He is nothing—like me.

Then the other brothers. The one I already know, Ritsuro, the truckdriver brother, has been crying. He bows very low and we both remain crouched on the tatami for a time. Then the youngest, the one I know as the newspaper-delivery-boy brother. He has cried the most and his face is puffy.

But now the time for crying is over because a wake, even after such a young death as this, is a dignified occasion. This family has been more than touched by death, they have lived with it daily for over half a year. But now tears and hope and resignation have all been put aside. The atmosphere is helpful and warm. The smell of life continuing is as strong as the scent of the chrysanthemums.

I bow to the bier, put a flower on the lacquer stand, and then fold my hands as though in prayer. The picture of the dead boy is a school picture from several years before—probably the only picture of him they had. It has been blown up large, and this small picture had consequently faded and blurred. The boy looks lost, as though already a ghost. Then I bow again and, ritual over, am invited to the table to drink and to talk with the others.

From the conversation, I learn that Fumio, in accounting for me in his life, has invented several stories. Unfortunately they have been varied, told to different people, and now all the people are in one room together and all meeting me. I learn that I am an English teacher and also a drama teacher; that I am at the same time somehow high in the Christian church, and simultaneously deeply interested in Buddhism; that I am still married but my wife cannot leave America; that I am also a widower with two children, also that my two children are quite dead—auto accident. Fumio has been lavish with his accounting and now sits uncomfortably and listens to all of it. I acquit myself well and agree to all the accounts, offering connecting links when one or the other becomes too unlikely.

Only Miss Shibuya knows the truth. I told Fumio to go see *Sunday, Bloody Sunday* because it was our story—his, hers and mine. He didn't go, but repeated what I had said to a classmate who *had* seen the film and thereafter gave Fumio strange looks and a wide berth.

I do not stay, but drink a glass of juice and then begin the farewell bows. How well the Japanese live with death, and consequently life. There was no hypocrisy in this simple ceremony I have taken part in: neither the hypocrisy of exaggerated respect, nor that of unnatural solemnity; there was no talk of a better life he had gone to; no talk of well, seeing as how he was so sick perhaps it was better so, etc. No such talk at all and—consequently—compassion.

2 OCTOBER 1973. Fumio came over after school to stay the night. Told me how his brother died. On the day of his death he told his mother to call the family, all eight children, and to call all of his friends. They tried to dissuade him but, for the first time, he gave orders and would tolerate no refusal. Distant friends who pleaded off with a cold were sternly ordered (brothers telephoning, sisters telegraphing) to appear. By evening everyone was on his or her way to the hospital. They started coming in about six in the evening, and kept on coming until midnight. He said farewell to each, held their hands, thanked them for their gifts, all of which he remembered, begged pardon for dying. They could only tell him not to die, to struggle on—as Japanese do when one is ill. But his mother understood. She said, no, he had struggled enough, he need struggle no longer. He, who had been ashamed of his wasted body, now pulled off the covers to expose his legs. This much I have struggled he said, showing them—this much. About midnight the friends left. He had thanked each one. Then, and only then, his death agony began. His eyes remained open, and the strain of the day had made the muscles so stiff that after he was dead they could not close the eyes. He looked at the ceiling, and his breath became more labored. The doctor said he could still hear. His mother talked to him and tears formed in his almost lifeless eyes, forever locked, never again to move. The family pressed around. If you can hear, just nod your head, he was told. He slowly nodded and the collected tears ran down his cheeks.

Here Fumio, who was telling me all this, also began to cry. After his brother was dead, the doctor said he had never known a case of stomach cancer so painless. Then they found the diary, a diary he had kept and hidden when the family came. It spoke of the pain, of its texture, of what it was like; it was a description of pain. And yet he did not scream or shout. At the most he would close his eyes and say, in a small voice, that it hurt. In the same way, he only once, the day before dying, told Fumio that he was afraid. In the face of pain and in the face of fear to behave as he did makes the tragedy, in a way, worse: a boy capable of doing this would have been a splendid man. In another way, however, he vindicated his death.

3 OCTOBER 1973. Fumio slept until noon, exhausted. But we spoke no more of his brother; instead we talked of Fumio and what he would do today, this year, the rest of his life. How close I have come to him, and how close he has come to me.

While he slept I worked on a new painting—my largest so far. It is of acrobats exercising, but it is the composition, a square within a square, which interests me—making the bodies fit and yet remain natural. The brain is stilled, for a time. It is my fingers that paint, not my head.

For this moment, I am whole.

4 OCTOBER 1973. With Fujikawa Gyo, who has not been in Japan for thirty years. I imagined her shocked by the change. Not at all. It has changed so much that she recognizes nothing at all and, in any event, "I've changed too

in thirty years, believe you me." Lived all these years in New York. Unmarried, and with that restrained and meticulous independence that unmarried women have; a children's illustrator and so all children everywhere are hers. We speak mainly English because her Japanese is good as far as it goes but doesn't go very far. She still, however, speaks with the pure, prewar Tokyo accent, now almost disappeared, a language free from Osaka vulgarisms, though it had some of its own.

After eating, a walk on the Ginza. That has a Thirties sound to it, walking on the Ginza. Gyo says that in 1930 Tokyo was "the kind of city you stroll in. Everyone strolled and there were willows everywhere and you could hire a car or take a small taxi for longer excursions, but usually you strolled. "We, the young ladies of the period, strolled into the Imperial Hotel, the old one, though it was new then, and that is where we fashionable young things had our tea."

We had earlier been to a photographic exhibition at Wako, forty-five years of Ginza—scenes in 1935, then in 1945, all ruined, and now in 1973, unrecognizable. I talked with the photographer and asked him where the smart matrons of 1935 met and had their éclairs and coffee. History always supplies the names of politicians, but equally important things such as which restaurant was fashionable at a period are never recorded. On the Ginza itself, he told me, the truly fashionable went to the Shiseido (still standing but no longer smart), but that the climbers and those not quite in went to the Columbin (which I remembered, now torn down)—I find information like this fascinating because it brings the past so very close to me. Later Gyo went on to again walk the Ginza (dodging the taxis, the drunks, the crowds of people still piling into the subways) but I came home.

Again a period of five years, during which, apparently, no journals were kept—or, if kept, not saved. Richie's impetus for diary writing was not an everyday accounting, such as the habit that his friend Edward Seidensticker shared with one of Richie's models, André Gide. Rather, something would occur that the author wished to save. He would put it down so it wouldn't be lost, starting an interest in this sporadic journal, and he would continue with further entries—always spaced further and further apart—until the series stopped.

Deciding what to record from his life seemed to depend upon what the experience reflected. Perhaps something of Japan that was passing, something of himself he felt changing. He sought to make

some form of his life in Japan and to achieve some kind of balance. As these journals progress, a definite shape is to be perceived and he, perceiving it, added to and reinforced it.

In his final editing of these journals he took care to choose themes whose progress he could follow: Kawabata, the Bugaku, Tani, Gide, the Kudara Kannon, Takemitsu, Seidensticker, Zushiden, Mizushima, among others. The story is that of a man who is remembering and ordering so that he can understand the shape he is creating. It is not surprising that Richie much admired the autobiographical writings of Nabokov (*Speak, Memory*) and Sartre (*The Words*), which had successfully attempted the same thing. Ian Buruma's words are fitting: "Richie has found his home in Japan. He has turned this home into art."

During this time Richie published *Ozu* (1974), directed a program of four verse plays by Eliot, Cummings, Yeats, and Stein, and for Ito Teiji wrote (under that author's name—a commission) *The Gardens of Japan* (1973). He also scripted and directed the documentary *Akira Kurosawa*, and with Eric Klestadt translated the Ozu/Noda script for *Tokyo Story* (1977).

5 MAY 1978. With Lynn [Levy-Matsuoka] to sketch the sumo wrestlers. Met her on the other side of the river in Ryogoku, center of the city in the eighteenth century, now all warehouses. The sumo stadium is still there, however, and so are the stables of the wrestlers.

It is a small world of its own, and a closed one. We are admitted by six-foot apprentices in stiff loincloths, and then sit on the dais and watch the practice. This consists of one young wrestler after another trying to push the head wrestler, an enormous man, from the earthen ring. He does not budge—then slaps them to one side and they roll to the ground. One after another they take their turn. The man stands there like a mountain.

Lynn sketches—her strong line holding the bulging form, suggesting the latent force. When practice is over all the wrestlers go to take a bath, and we are invited upstairs to watch them and then eat with them. A large tatami room, their washing drying at the windows, a long low table, and a big kitchen, since they eat a lot. The younger wrestlers already busy, grating *daikon*, slicing squid and cabbage, their enormous fingers awkwardly holding knives and chopsticks—all still in their stiff loincloths as they stand, sit, or squat. It is like a boys' school, or like a barracks.

It is also like a stable. The men are so enormous that they are like animals—fat animals, with slabs and rolls of meat and wide, vacant faces. And they behave with the silent deference of beasts, swinging their heads. I am bid to eat with syllables and lowered eyes and an awkward hand. In contrast, the *oyabun*, a seated mountain, is at ease and it is I who defer to him and use my most polite language, sitting properly all through the meal on my aching calves.

Theirs is a world of order—the old order where differences in station are never questioned. Without a word, he holds out his rice bowl and a young wrestler hurries forward, eyes averted, to take it. The older man leans on an elbow, his strength, his visible power, making him appear arrogant. As he eats, another young wrestler squats and massages his thigh. In the corner of the kitchen, two more young wrestlers whisper, hug each other, and giggle. He pays no attention, shaking his head as though a fly is bothering him—a very intelligent bull. All of this Lynn captures with her pencil, this whole Genroku world she is so in love with, this living remnant of old Edo.

6 MAY 1978. To the Israeli Embassy. The wife of the ambassador is dancing. In kimono she flutters to some haiku that Ted [Wilkes] reads, as he has read at such entertainments for years. The flutist accompanies with something by Fukushima. Marian [Korn] is thinking of the days when she had *soirées-musicales*, and when Fukushima was a young composer she was taking up. She turns to me and says quite audibly, "That *is* our Fukushima, isn't it?" She is still Madame Verdurin.

It is, in other ways as well, Proust's last party. I am introduced to a venerable Japanese with a white walrus moustache. It turns out to be young Mr. Hasegawa, once so dashing with his camera, who used to take pictures of such artistic gatherings for the local newspaper.

The Israeli dancer is now Spanish, Ted is reciting Lorca, the flute is playing Ibert. Sheelagh [Lebowitz, née Cluny] with whom I came, whispers, "One does not know *where* to look." She is Oriane de Guermantes, with her Rolls, her amusing comments, her forthright way, and her aura of awful boredom.

The ambassador's wife is now doing the Bible. Arise, ye daughters of Zion. This she does very well, her cropped and birdlike head impressive, like an Assyrian relief. Movements precise, practiced. She is professional. I think of Rachel performing in the homes of the great. Except that in this society Rachel herself is great. Lots of Barons de Charlus around, all now stout and discreet, as they eye the young Japanese waiters.

Marian, eyes shining, remembers when we did *Façade* at her house and Sheelagh in another part of the room turns and says to a wall, "Lilly and Daisy, silly and lazy." "Oh, we must do it all again," says Marian, just like a girl with gray hair. "We should never have stopped. Donald you must help again." But Donald—Marcel for a day—is feeling old.

7 MAY 1978. Dinner at Kuroyanagi Tetsuko's. Her apartment has a real Marie Laurencin, and in the bedroom an enormous portrait of herself done by a local artist in the Laurencin manner. Lots of Dresden around, kitchen full of unworkable gadgets, gilt picture frames in the bathroom, and a bottle of Chanel for those using it.

"I have the tastes of a little girl," she says, noticing my looking about. "A virgin, of good family." Then she laughs—not at all taken in by herself. At the same time, however, she is not really laughing. She loves her role. She is roguish. Little her fixing a big meal for us. Can she? Assisted by a stolid assistant who does everything, she squats on the floor ("This place is so *tiny* . . ."), as she grinds the coffee.

The party is for Oida Yoshi, the actor, who is putting together a new show to take to Europe. Among the guests is Hira Mikijiro, matinee idol, who is talking about "my Hamlet." He is careful to use the rough and masculine *ore no* for the "my" thus hopefully countering any vanity or affectation. It is not successful because he cannot resist bridling, smiling, throwing back his head. His will be a strange Hamlet. He has just played Euripides' *Medea* in drag. It was a big success. Whole busloads of women's organizations came. They love this kind of entertainment. It is cultural but daring.

I look at the two actors. Yoshi, hair short, is like an old-style Japanese carpenter plunked down in this Frenchified drawing room. Hira is all poses, hands carefully arranged, as phony as the furniture. And Tetsuko, playing at being little-girl hostess ("Oh, do sit on the floor!"), but not really fooling herself. Conversation lags and she takes over. She is not a television star for nothing.

Tells a long funny story about a local impersonator who went for a sex change operation in Morocco. ". . . and he was on the second floor and on the third was the maternity ward. It was awful. Women screaming and breaching on the third, men screaming and—well, what would you call it?—on the second. And apparently the resulting hole must be the size, or width at least, of the organ removed, so men well-endowed come out with something like this"—she held up her hands. "Unusable, one would think."

With Aratama Michio, Kawakita Kashiko.   *With Mori Iwao, Noguchi Hisamitsu, Matsue*
Tokyo International House, 1978.   *Yoichi, Kurosawa Akira, 1978.*

This is soberly listened to by two muscle-bound young men in neck-ties. They are two of the *chanbara* boys from Yoshi's troupe who have gotten dressed up and are being awed by the famous people and the Chanel in the bathroom. They sit on chairs, away from the "family" group on the floor that Tetsuko has arranged. No attempt is made to include them. Nor would they want to be included. They sit with their whiskey-waters in hand and must be urged to eat. They are the audience. Tetsuko loves an audience. It is her undoing. She is an actress of great delicacy and real feeling, but she is also dependent upon instant gratification. TV answers this need. Instant playback, instant feedback. She does it well, but it is only TV. I speak about her roles on stage, in film. "Oh, *those*," she says.

9 MAY 1978. Party for the publication of the Japanese edition of the Ozu book. I was given a corsage of red roses to wear, such being the custom. Forty people came; food, drink, speeches; it lasted three hours, from six to nine.

Madame Kawakita [Kashiko], in a mauve kimono as always, spoke about me and Japanese movies. Lots of other speeches—testimonials to Ozu and to me. Shinoda [Masahiro], standing stiff like a schoolboy, rubbing his boyish head, now gray. Gosho [Heinosuke], the oldest of the directors, hand in sling (car door), talked about the old days. He was the only one who got to call Ozu, Ozu-*kun*. And Ryu Chishu, who did something splendid. In the middle of the party he announced that he was going to again sing—thirty years later—the *hayashi* that he did in Ozu's *Record of a Tenement Gentleman*. And he did.

At the end I made a short speech. Ozu never much liked parties but he liked to drink and he liked to talk. We'd all drunk and talked—we'd made just the kind of party that Ozu would have liked.

With Oshima Nagisa, Gosho Heinosuke,
1978.

With Ryu Chishu, 1978.

10 MAY 1978. Oda Mayumi to lunch. She is getting back to woodcuts and silk screens after a bout with oils. Oils give one too many chances, too much opportunity, too many ways to correct: she prefers a medium where she cannot make a mistake. More big women? Oh, yes, many more. I ask if her original influence came from *otsue*, which her pictures seem to me to resemble. Not at all. She was influenced by kimono designs, both the design of the kimono and the design the woman makes in wearing one.

The Zen *roshi* from California, Richard Baker, also at lunch and much taken with her—keeps asking questions, trying to define her. I know that temptation. Mayumi is not easy to define. She is so natural that one thinks she must have some secret. But she has none. She is as natural as the tree in the garden that she stops to admire. I cannot imagine her having any doubts. She sees connections in everything—the tree and the rock, the picture and the pattern of the shadows. Richard much taken because Zen is in the connection business.

Mayumi has made and brought a pie. She did not want the pie to be sweet and so she made it, not sour, but non-sweet. I have never seen a pie that looked so much like a pie and yet had so much difference about it. It crumbled at once, like a fragile work of art, dissolved into crumbs, and it did not taste like a pie at all. It had all the appearance of itself, and yet it was something else. Just like her.

She was also taken with Richard and they went off to her yoga lesson together. He is very like that. If there is food he eats, if not he fasts; will drink if there is something to drink, otherwise not. I see an affinity between them.

12 MAY 1978. To see the rough cut of John Nathan's new film about Katsu

Shintaro. Katsu created Zatoichi, the blind swordsman, and to that extent became him. John's picture is about these two—creator and created. Which is which? As always, John shows and never says. Katsu at work, Katsu drunk, Katsu and his children and wife. Bit by bit, like a mosaic, the pattern is revealed. At the end, the coda after credits, Katsu is driving and singing along with Zatoichi's son. The fusion is complete.

Curious effect. To show (and not tell) is to reveal. And to be dispassionate is in film (somehow) to disapprove. Katsu is never put down, but the film ends by questioning all of his values. Cinema seems so real (its only virtue and at the same time its prime limitation), that it demands some kind of ordering. The director (a subtle one, like John) imposes order, but only from the inside. The result is something cool and—though this can be unintended—critical. This fat little man, Katsu, held together by an ego that consumes all those around him, not very talented himself, he is consumed as well. An hour with him reveals everything—the hollow space behind the films he makes, the absence of anything and anyone when Zatoichi is not there. It is we, the watchers, who put all of this together.

One strange scene: Katsu being interviewed by a fatuous young fan magazine reporter. Did not want to be. John apparently insisted. Result is that John is in scene, sitting beside him. One silly question follows another. John sits silent as Katsu expostulates. He rubs his chin, and glances warily at the camera; John does too. The effect is that the director is questioning the validity of the film fan. Another effect is that he is putting down Katsu for going through with this. Actually, however, he tells me, these actions were only intended to convey to the idiot cameraman that he ought to tighten in to Katsu and take John out of the frame. No matter this intention, what is on film is richly ambivalent.

Had hoped Mayumi [Oda, Nathan's wife] might be there. She wasn't—home watching the kids, I suppose. Another girl was—Belgian, beautiful. I would have stayed longer and talked about the film, but it became apparent that John (compulsive as ever) really wanted to put the make on her. (At noon? At the Aoi Studio?) She was intelligent about the film. It is sad she said, but only because life is.

15 MAY 1978. Sunday, Ian [Buruma] over early with two tattooed men. The rest of the morning and early afternoon spent photographing them for our book [*The Japanese Tattoo*, 1979]. Asami Tadashi, thirty, has an Oniwaka on a carp on his back, cherry-blossoms on his shoulders, and on the sides of

his chest the strong boy, Kintaro. Obara Tsutomu, twenty-eight, a su-shiya, has a fierce Fudomyoo on his back, an Oniwaka (again) and Go-ban Tadanobu on chest, with Setaka Doji and Kongara Doji crouched on his thighs. Both came in elegant and subdued kimono, under which they wore white underwear, under which were white fundoshi. These all they eventually removed, and they stood in the garden, or in the bamboo grove, or by the *rokka*, while Ian snapped away with three different cameras. Both men were polite, but not reserved. Proud of their decorations and quite willing to have them admired. I, in turn, admire them. They both know how to tie obi in

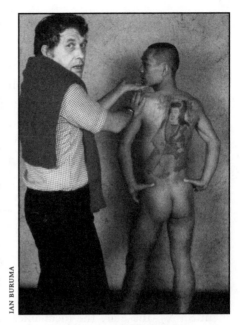

IAN BURUMA

With Asami Tadashi, 1978.

the old Edo style and they move as naturally in 1778 as in 1978. For them history is a part of their environment. But I doubt they think of it. Both were born after World War II, when the last of old Japan disappeared, and yet here they are, embodying it. In the West we would find such people pedantic and affected—which they would be. Not here—they are simple, unaffected; they simply are what they are.

I asked the reasons for their choice of tattoos. Did it mean that they wanted to be like the images chosen (carp is strong, perseveres), or because they thought they already were? Neither. Obara chose a seated Fudo because one of the men with whom he works has a standing Fudo and he wanted to match. Asami liked the looks of Oniwaka and knew that this figure was a celebrated one—and that his tattoo-master drew it particularly well. Both chose carp because it is a watery creature and traditionally such were always included—creatures such as fish and dragons—since the tattoo began with the Edo firemen who were professionally always in need of water. Also, they are both cooks, and this is a watery business traditionally. Another reason, though they did not give this one, is that both are *mizushobai*, those professions which, like the river, flow and change . . . water work. Both know Edo history; both are gentle and manly (a combination rare I think in other countries), and both have the politeness of absolutely natural people. They are each of a single piece. A tattoo must, in a way, put a person together.

16 MAY 1978. To see [Kobayashi] Toshiko in Cocteau's *Le Bel Indifferent*, the play written for Piaf. Toshiko can't sing, but she can dance, so the heroine becomes a hoofer and opens with a solo production number. Toshiko is in her mid-forties. She ought to be showing us a dancer in decline. But the theater is filled with her female fans. Toshiko must not be allowed to grow old. So, signs of age are overlooked—by everyone, including Toshiko. Given the play, how poignant her age would have been had she used it, but she did not. Actually, tonight's play was to have been my own *Gendai Sekidera Komachi* and not the Cocteau, but Toshiko was afraid of it. An hour of her alone on the stage in a Noh? Playing the ghost of a stripper? What would her fans think? This was better. So she's also had an open rehearsal of the Cocteau for the fans, and they voted not to let Toshiko, our Toshiko, kill herself, as demanded by the text.

20 MAY 1978. To an exhibition of the *karakuri ningyo* at Matsuya [Department Store]. These are the mechanical dolls of (mainly) the Edo and Meiji periods—automata, small as a mouse, large as a child, either string-pulled or clockwork, which so delighted the Japanese then as (looking at the faces at the show) now.

A magician three feet tall who snaps open his fan, turns around, and in a flash has transformed himself into a box; a bald baby acolyte who holds a tray—when you put a cup of tea on it he races across the *tatami* to the guest and, after the guest has taken the cup, turns around and races back; little Momotaro making rattling sounds while inside his peach and then, as the fruit splits, steps out; an acrobat with hinged arms and legs, who throws himself through the air, catching onto supports in the most lifelike manner; a Chinese gentleman walking. This one I work myself by pulling ropes: as you pull he puts one foot before the other, swings his arms, and turns his smiling face.

The smiles. All the dolls smile, their enamel faces wreathed, their black eyes (some inset with glass) wrinkled with laughter. Nothing wistful or sad, as is usually seen in high-class dolls; nor haughty, nor martial, as is seen in the seasonal dolls, such as those for Girls' and Boys' Days. Simple good nature: the state of happiness. Most of the dolls are "Chinese," that being the fashion during at least this part of the Edo period. Cute things Chinese were always conceived reassuringly small by the Japanese: little boys, tiny dogs, baby "lions," etc. All in bright primary colors. A love for the infantile, imposed upon that sprawling and dangerously mature continent.

I watch a young woman work a smiling Chinese girl who writes (with a magic marker). And can she write English? "Yes, she can," the woman answers. And then the Chinese doll draws a cat's face and under it writes C-A-T. "She is very skillful," I say. "Well, she tries," answers the young woman.

I remember the collection of automata in Paris, Marie Antoinette's collection, I think. Much more austere. Those two great silver acrobats that circled with the precision of Descartes. And the child Mozart at a rococo instrument, little hands doing a minuet, little face pensive, sensing death. These dolls were dead and we knew it, and we marveled as we might have at visible ghosts. The Japanese dolls are alive, and we marvel at them as we might at humans.

21 MAY 1978. To the Sanja Matsuri in Asakusa, that annual spring festival that for a day returns Tokyo to its rural ancestry. Bands of men (and nowadays girls) carry the mighty *omikoshi* on their shoulders, pressed against each other, wearing festival clothes from earlier times, shoulders and cheeks against the wood and the gilt, feet moving together as though each had become part of a centipede, lurching together, chanting, shouting, each caught, finally, gratefully, in the grip of something larger, bouncing the happy god aloft in his portable shrine. And for every person participating, one thousand who had come to see. By two in the afternoon the press was such that one could not move. *Nakama doshi* in every street, all by the god in his darkness, swaying in his shrine. An exciting, exhausting sight.

Ian and I go to take pictures of tattooed men—floats with the fully tattooed standing aloft, swaying; decorated men naked but for a *fundoshi*, straining and heaving under the crawling shrine; older men with belts and kimonos open, just a glimpse of rare old tattooing, leading the holy procession through the streets. A small, handsome, middle-aged man, strong legs, a paunch, cloth-strip around loins, cloth strip around head. Up the left arm swims a carp, down the right arm glides a carp, just that, and a scattering of cherry blossoms. Perspiring tattoos—Kannon weeping, Kintaro sweating with exertion, Fudo glistening in his painted fire as though covered with fresh blood.

Foreigners are always encouraged at this *matsuri*. Japanese are here so fully enmeshed in each other that they can drop the national xenophobia. They become Elizabethan, filled with gusto and cheer. I always feel like an early emissary—perhaps fifteenth century, probably Portuguese. People very friendly. The only time I have ever been touched, handled by the Japanese— by unknown Japanese, at any rate—is at festivals where a comradely hand is expected. A glimpse of history—more, a view of the Japanese as they might have been before the Tokugawa cookie-cutter descended. A haze of fellow feeling and good-cheer. Up to a point. Promising conversations cut short by the magic call of the shrine and its god, and all those waiting compatriots.

23 MAY 1978. Autograph signing for the Japanese translation of the Ozu book. I gave an introduction to *Tokyo Story*, recounting how Ozu hated just this kind of introduction. Explanation is always unnecessary. If you use your eyes and your ears properly you will understand; if you do not, no amount of explanation will inform you. The reason is that Ozu is interested in showing, not explaining. He implies; you infer. He builds his half of the bridge; you build yours. Each having made some effort, a real communication becomes possible. No effort, no communication.

This, I realize, is the only kind of art I admire. Jane Austen, Ivy Compton-Burnett, Henry Green. In the movies Ozu, Bresson, sometimes Tarkovsky, and less often Antonioni; lots of examples from painting because pictures cannot explain, and from music—in this sense the most mute of all the arts.

Then we sat and watched the film.

28 MAY 1978. Sunday—with Earle [Ernst] and Meredith to the *nomi no ichiba*, the Sunday flea market. There, spread on the plaza, is apparently all that is left of old Japan—battered remnants from the Tokugawa, from Meiji, from Taisho and early Showa; war medals from the long dead; an old doll, face cracked; bad prints, lots of late blue and white; some early Mickey Mouse shards from middle Showa—it is as though there had been a prewar explosion and this is the debris.

Like that, except for the prices. Tens of thousands of yen now for old sword guards. Ten years ago the price would have been mere hundreds. The inflation of scarcity, and the boom in history. Lots of customers, mainly young Japanese, picking through the ruins of their traditional culture. And not even recognizing it. It is a sale of "foreign" objects.

I watch two girls turning a flint lighter from Meiji this way and that, completely unable to decide what it is. A rather good Tokugawa tea caddy (priced at the equivalent of nearly a thousand dollars) is right next to a piece of 1930s beaded glass. A young couple talks about them and, oddly, decides that the glass is older. Watching the people milling as though in some nomad's open market, seeing the hunched figures of the seated sellers, I think of people in ruins, scavenging, and I remember the street stalls along the Ginza in 1947.

Earle observes all this as well, but is by nature more sanguine than I.

Change, he says, is inevitable and should therefore be embraced. "We must live with change, therefore must accept it." I say that we should not, since change is always for the worse. He says this is not so, that a hundred years ago half of the older folks around now would never have had a chance to get that old. That in any event, all are now living better. I say that all are living higher, but it hasn't made them any happier. "Oh, well, if you are going to go on like that," he says. And he is right, of course.

Next to us a girl picks up some nicely cut Tokugawa kimono stencils, quite small. "Go on," urges her friend, "Buy some. You can use them as coasters."

1 AUGUST 1978. Zushiden on the telephone. *Chotto hanashitai koto ga aru.* Sinking heart. Why? One ought to be happy to see an old friend after all these years. The trouble is both his language and my experience. "Have something to talk over with you," all too often means a request—almost invariably for money. Japanese *amaeru* at work after all these years?

Meet in Roppongi. Zushiden is now long-married, three little girls, and a manager at Kokusai Jidosha. A student at Chuo, captain of the wrestling team, he lived with me when he was twenty, for over a year—just before I got married. Mary, who could somehow tolerate all my other friends, could never stand him because he meant so much to me.

So there he stands in Roppongi, still looking much like himself. All the lines sharper now, once square shoulders sloping, a small and modest pot, a habit of keeping his mouth half open—an old man's expression.

What he wants turns out to be (so often the case) just the opposite of what I had expected. Has so much money now that he wants advice on how to use it. Has a brave new idea. He will quit Kokusai Jidosha and use the money to open a store (sports goods maybe) or a Japanese-style *nomiya.* "After all, I'm thirty-six now and what fun do I get out of life? My most fun is playing with my kids. And that is all right. But it's not enough." So he will throw away his security, use his money to make something. And as Zushi talks he becomes animated, his eyes shine, he closes his mouth and his smile is the smile of a twenty year-old again. Hope, curiosity, interest, these have kept him young.

I ask him, what had been his ambition when he was young. "Oh, you remember me, I never had one. I just wanted to be a salaried worker. Well I am one now. I'm a manager and I'll never go any higher, but I've got my dream. I'm a late bloomer." We talk for over an hour. And at the end Zushi is going to do something. It is like just before a wrestling match when he was young. He is determined.

2 AUGUST 1978. To Zakone—Fumio's bar, and mine too, until he pays back the money I lent him to get it started. Small, nine *tsubo*, a four-story walk-up, but right in the middle of Shinjuku.

Bars in Japan have their own clientele as soon as they open their doors. People do not wander in off the street in Japan. They are introduced and the place becomes a home away from home. It has shelves of bottles with patron's names on them. It is cheaper this way, to buy a whole bottle.

People bring people, friends bring friends—and little by little the bar makes money. Fumio decided everything ought to cost the same—five hundred yen—be it whiskey or beer or coke or a plate of cheese and crackers. He figures he has to make forty thousand yen a night to break even. He has been doing better than that in the two months he has been open now. He made a million net last month.

He is very good at *mizushobai*, the service industry. The customer is always agreed with, yet for a bar person to be a mere yes-man is no good. One must gauge the degree of resistance necessary. Not that the Japanese customer is all that demanding. He too is constrained by good manners. And not that Fumio did not always have this art of pleasing.

How did he learn it? Well—impoverished background, father disappeared, mother left to raise eight children all by herself on nothing at all. She worked on the roads to get money to support her family—still does. The boys started work at seven or eight—milk boys, then newspaper boys, then on into other jobs. Always wore hand-me-downs. Fumio, being second from last, got them when they were just barely wearable. Don't know what his younger brother did.

I watched him last night being the host and behaving with a tact and a friendliness, a naturalness and a self-respect which is really only possible here—this miracle of the *mizushobai*.

4 AUGUST 1978. To the *ueki-ichi* at Shinobazu in Ueno. The wide, shallow pond, dark with leaves, filled with large pink lotuses, each tightly closed into a big bud. Night, the shore outlined with red and blue lanterns proclaiming the name of their donor—Kirin Beer. Under them the stalls: all kinds of bonsai—one perfect miniature red maple selling for a thousand dollars; rocks, big and little; fish stalls with many kinds of goldfish swimming, specially bred, enormous heads like bulldogs or long fins like the tails of sacred roosters; the insect stalls with little cages holding a bell bug or a katydid, larger cages with struggling stag beetles in them; shaved ice sellers, glazed squid stands, makers of spun sugar, crystallized cakes of brown sugar, or fruit in ice on sticks; fried soba, glass animals, quilted beasts, fireworks, the minnow game with hooks that bend, and paper nets that dissolve.

Japan in the summer is always more Japanese, and never more so that at this fair. Families in summer *yukata*, clacking along on *geta*, gang boys hawking in cummerbunds and shorts; old gentlemen shuffling about in *sutetetako* and underwear tops, carrying fans; girls back from the bath with wet hair sleeked back, towels in hands. This is what Japan once looked like. Summer brings it back again.

And old attitudes as well. A sudden interest in nature. Exclamations at the size of the lotus buds. And a much slower tempo. No one striding, everyone strolling. And with it, the old politeness. People standing to one side for each other. Nor are they self-conscious in their "native" dress. This is because these few summer weeks are still the proper time for it. They get out the *yukata* every year. Usually there is dancing as well, but last night was too early. The tower is ready, and the drums are there, but the dancing circle is empty. People wander around it but no one even attempts to dance. It is not yet the time or the place. They look at the budded lotus, pink and heavy. These will open at dawn.

During this period Richie was suffering a good deal from a herniated disc. Finally, he was operated on and spent two months in hospital and convalescence. After that he traveled more than ever. He and Mizushima Fumio had been to many islands in the Okinawa chain before; now they went to the Gilberts, to the Marianas, to Palau, to Phuket, to Bali, and in 1979, traveled around the United States. On such trips Richie rarely kept a diary. Also, between illness and traveling, he wrote nothing except *The Japanese Tattoo*.

9 JANUARY 1979. To the *machiai* where Francis Ford Coppola is staying. He is giving a big party—Neapolitan food he cooked himself, served by geisha. At the last minute he went out and bought a recording of *Madama Butterfly* to symbolize this meeting of Italy and Japan, while the geisha served spaghetti with chopsticks and tried to make us drink the wine out of sake cups. Francis himself worked all day in the kitchen with the maids, all of whom got red and tipsy from trying the Chianti. One of them kept getting unbalanced by the

With Francis Coppola, Kawakita Kazuko, Tom Luddy. Tokyo/Yurakucho, 1979.

big bow of her obi and sitting down suddenly. Francis in messy but complete command.

Oshima Nagisa in a new purple silk shirt. Takemitsu Toru supposed to go to the hospital next day for a checkup and told to eat·and drink nothing after eight in the evening. One in the morning found him stiff with brandy. Event of the evening was Katsu Shintaro and his entourage.

I have not met Katsu for years, though he is fairly inescapable on TV and in films. Now that he is chosen for the lead in the new Kurosawa film [*Kagemusha*] and has successfully escaped the drug charge (opium, of all exotic things), he is ebullient again.

He also rather takes over a party. Endless stream of talk. Tells me about funny experiences in Las Vegas. Girl asks him if he likes love "French fashion." Has no idea what she means. She at once goes down on him. It tickles. He does not know how to say it tickles in English. Has to, finally, content himself with telling her that he does not like chewing gum. Also, another girl, while making love asks if he is "ready." Not knowing she means ready to come, and misunderstanding the word, he hears "lady" instead of "ready." "No, I not lady," he says indignantly, "I gentleman," etc.

Also plays the samisen—then a duet with Francis who taps one samisen with his chopsticks while Katsu improvises on the other. Everyone says it is very beautiful. The geisha hear this and after that refuse to play themselves. They would be too humiliated. It was at this point that they turned into waitresses. Probably the most expensive waitresses Francis will ever hire.

Francis now drunk as well, and expansively enjoying himself at his own party. Singing Puccini (joined by Takemitsu) and dishing out the food and pouring out the wine. All the Japanese under this sunny influence become themselves almost

With Katsu Shintaro, unidentified girl, 1979.

Italian. Everything gets more and more messy, legs stretched out. Katsu pulls up his kimono (is wearing loose jockey shorts) and walks on the table, very skillfully, not upsetting a thing.

Then more of his entourage come in—the Toei gangster contingent. That surly little man so popular now as a *yakuza* comedian, I forget his name. All smiles and hard little eyes. And Hagiwara Kenichi, the young heartthrob, not looking very well—jeans and T-shirt, the ugly look having hit Japan ten years late.

Slowly the party polarizes. Oshima, quite used to being made much of, sits at one side of the table, and Katsu and his crowd at the other. These two know each other (everyone knows each other in the Japanese entertainment world) but, as becomes increasingly clear, do not really like each other. Nor is there any reason they should. I cannot imagine two men further apart. Katsu with his Osaka ways, his rightist thug buddies and his smarmy bonhomie; Oshima with his cultured Kyoto background, his liberal political views, his shyness, and his effeminacy—the latter strongly outlined now against Katsu's macho posing.

Oshima holds his own very well in a situation like this. Always attacks. Soon the air is blue. Francis, oblivious of everything, had his arm about a somewhat apprehensive Kawakita Kazuko. Bested, Katsu turns into a lonely little boy and talks to his pals. And to me, since I am on his side of the table. I know he hates John Nathan's film about him, and I try to tell him why it is good. This is difficult because the reason it is good is that it shows him to be a lonely little boy.

Katsu sulks. No one is paying attention to him. The Toei contingent is bored. There are no fights. Hagiwara is bored too, but then that is his state. So they decide to leave. Katsu very consciously gracious. Comes and shakes each hand, including Oshima's, held limp in front of him. Nothing remains from the polarization. Gap is closed in very Japanese style, by being ignored.

All of us, all old friends now that the intruders have left, go down to Francis's room—the party was in the banquet room—and get more smashed. Francis puts on old favorites and Takemitsu does exquisite ocarina improvisations on "Don't Get Around Much Any More" etc. Oshima gets the giggles. Francis tries to hug Kazuko some more. I have my arms around Non-chan [Nogami Teruyo]. We try to get into the *kotatsu* and, failing this, try to guess whose feet are whose. I get a large foot in my lap. Turns out to be Francis's who takes it away when he finds out into whose lap he has fallen.

I remember some scraps of conversation. I tell Takemitsu what Robert Craft told me, what Igor Stravinsky said about Olivier Messiaen's being "an enormous crucifix made of sugar." Francis talks about his new movie and Brando being something called "The Talking Head." Kazuko remembers when we first met—at Cannes, and she was seventeen. I suddenly remember too—a very pretty, very shy girl against the blue bay. Everyone is remembering. Toru remembers that we met in front of Wako in 1948, which I had forgotten. Francis now on floor, arms around Kazuko. I tell him about her husband. "Why is everyone always *taken?* Isn't there anyone who is not already taken? This is the story of my life."

Somehow I get home, alone, at two in the morning. Successful party.

10 JANUARY 1979. Strange about the feeling of concern—seems made mainly of worry. Like today. Fumio said he would come by in the early morning after the bar was closed. He didn't, but then sometimes he does not do what he says he will. Still, ten years of leaning on him has resulted in his only rarely not doing what he says he will, so I wondered when he did not appear, to wake me up and climb into bed just as I climbed out to begin my day. In the evening I phoned the bar. At seven, just when it is supposed to open. No answer. What had happened? And worry pounced.

Bar had never not opened before. Once they forgot to take the money out of the pay phone, which meant it got too heavy and incoming calls could not come in. But that wouldn't have happened again. Then, let's see, he had been having trouble with this snotty helper, Akira, and was going to fire him. Maybe dangerous Akira had done something dreadful. Or maybe it was the

DONALD RICHIE

Mizushima Fumio.

gangsters. They dropped in from time to time, and Fumio had kept them in line. Until now. Or, maybe, January being a very dry month, there had been a great fire which had swept through the place and Fumio's mother was trying unsuccessfully to reach me to let me know that her poor child, terribly scarred by flames, at this very moment lay dead in some temple awaiting the further fire of cremation.

And I was off. Terrible worry. I, who resist the terrors of possession and jealousy, am easy prey to common concern. When I face the unknown, my only thought is to get to know it. Otherwise it gnaws and I am unable to think of anything else. So off I went to Shinjuku, to the bar, imagining the worst all the time.

Now what kind of self-indulgence is this? Is fear a wish? Am I frightening myself for fun? Anyway the bar was open, just. And Fumio was there. He had been late because he had fired Akira. Reason for his not coming in the morning was that he was exhausted, had fallen asleep after the bar closed. Had called me when he woke up but I was already out. Very simple. And over this I had had my crisis, my mad rushing through the subway passages, my pounding heart, my flight to Shinjuku. I let him know none of this, just said I had wondered a little, thought I would drop in, had been passing by.

No wonder the ancients called love a fever.

11 JANUARY 1979. Took Francis to dinner and then to the Zakone. He talked about a film he wants to make here. Part of the idea comes from Goethe—people are like chemicals: elective affinities. Part of it comes from the pattern of his own life, which will determine the pattern of the film. Part of it is a metaphor suggested by both Goethe and his life—one person and another, one country and another, one civilization and another. He wants to stretch the film across time and across space—the two countries, the various generations. Right now he is living here, and experiencing what he will later create.

Big and bearded, large gentle eyes, full mouth. Francis does not give the impression of hiding behind his beard as so many bearded men do—as though they are in camouflage, peering through hedges. The beard seems as much a part of him as his big hands and feet. Very gentle, like many large men. Particularly here, where everyone acts small.

Decides he really likes small women best. All of his women—there have been numbers—have been small. He likes narrow waists and large hips and sound legs. Breasts are not so interesting. The waist is that part where, if women were insects, he would pick them up. Fairly compulsive about women. Not, he says, about sex, but certainly, he says, about women.

Has a life full of complications, beginning with his wife and all the other women he attracts. I can see the attraction. Not handsome, and this reassures women; very gentle, also reassuring. Very (apparently) sincere and straightforward. This too is found appealing. He must be irresistible.

Then we go on to the Cradle, the new literary bar, where he has already captivated the woman who runs it. We talk about Kurosawa. The thing that surprises Francis is that it became obvious at once that Kurosawa does not know what he has done, does not know what he is doing, nor what he will do—and does not know how he does it. Very true—Kurosawa, the un-self-examined person. Francis, on the other hand, is very much aware of himself—painfully so. He knows that too much knowledge paralyzes. He knows one must go on despite knowing. All of this would not be understandable to Kurosawa.

At the beginning of the following year, 1980, Mizushima Fumio married Shibuya Yasuko. Richie traveled in Europe and North Africa, and in the autumn moved to the old section of Tokyo, the quarter of Yanaka. Here he wrote the short pieces that would become _Zen Inklings_ (1982) and also began a study of contemporary

Japanese culture that resulted in a number of essays, many of them included in the collections *A Lateral View* (1987), *Partial Views* (1995), and *The Image Factory* (2003). He neglected his journals. There is only one entry for 1980, and he did not again begin until the fall of 1981. From then until 1988 the journals were kept only sporadically.

15 JANUARY 1980. Fumio formal, Yasuko in lace and veil, their respective mothers in kimono, we all stood in line waiting to enter the chapel. At the head stood a small man in a black suit. Fumio's eldest brother found me back in the line, brought me forward, and put me in the small man's place. The man stared at me, then looked away and left the line. We marched into the chapel and I was put in the first pew, next to Fumio's mother. After the ceremony pictures were taken and I was again seated next to her. This is the traditional seat for the father, and when I was called upon to give the first speech the master of these ceremonies said that I had been as close to the groom as a true parent. Heads were turned, gazes curious—a foreigner in the place of honor. Later during the reception I was once more placed next to Fumio's mother and acted as her husband. While we were sitting there the small man again appeared again, stood in front of me, made a deep bow, introduced himself as Fumio's father, said that he had long heard of me, had known of how I had helped his son, was most grateful, and that I must give his regards and congratulations to the happy couple. I stood up, responded, but his wife looked straight ahead, giving him not even a glance.

I offered him a drink and then we stood there. This was the famous missing father. He who had left wife and family and disappeared. Alone and poor, the mother had raised her children herself. Ten years before, when I met Fumio, and shortly his family, there had been no talk of the father. And now, having somehow gotten word, here he was. Fumio had not seen him since he was three years old.

The father, after all still a husband, began paying attention to his wife—offering her a drink, or some food. She only inclined her head, did not answer or look at him. Then, reception over, the wedding party had to line up while the mothers received flowers from their new son and their new daughter and Fumio made a speech.

He told how he had known Yasuko for over twenty years, how poor his family had been, how he had had no father, that is, until he had met me. But he was fortunate because his real father was dead. And as he said this he

Mizushima Fumio's wedding. With Mizushima's mother (front row, 3rd from left) and Mizushima's father (2nd row, 4th from left), 1980.

looked straight at him and heads turned to follow his gaze, because there, in the corner, alone, stood his real father.

Then the reception line was again formed, me once more by Fumio's mother, once more the husband, and the departing guests were thanked. The real father was not among them; perhaps he had stayed behind. When the guests left I too went home. I had been father for the ceremony but I was not a member of the family. Later I heard the father had been seen crying by the service exit.

15 MARCH 1980. We meet at the Imperial. Joseph Losey is standing there, very tall, very battered looking. "Someplace where I can sit down," he says in his soft voice. He is just in, just off the plane. As we walk across the lobby of the hotel he looks about and says, "Everything looks like an airport now." We go to the bar, which looks like a VIP lounge.

This is his first time in Japan. "Not that I am going to see much of it. Casting is going to take most of the time. Shooting, the rest. And we must hurry, because," he adds mysteriously, "the trout spawning season is almost over." Then, "No, no, I don't travel for pleasure, not any more. Just for work. And every place is an airport lobby."

I ask about the Proust, not having seen him since it fell through. "I really don't know. We were coming along and suddenly the money was no longer there. Been pulled out." He shook his head at the gravity of it all. "Vodka," he said, very carefully to the kimonoed waitress who, like an airline hostess, hovered beside us.

Thinks maybe it was just as well. He had wanted an all French cast ("It is really the only way—one of the reasons the Visconti would have been so bad . . . Helmut Berger?"), and the moneyman hadn't. Sipping his vodka he remembers trouble he has had with actors.

"No, Laughton was no trouble. He was too eager for the role. But he was terrified. Why? Working with me, of course. Oh, he would certainly have testified against me, if he had had to. He wasn't an American citizen. He was truly frightened of McCarthy and his committee. So he was frightened of me and my friends." He motioned toward us the kimonoed stewardess. "Another vodka," he said, very distinctly.

Losey shows what he has been through. He looks like a Roman statue left out in the rain. His features seem to have run into one another. His nose is now rounded in a way such suggests that it was not always. His ears are long. And the corrosion has been interior as well. He seems frail, large as he is. He handles himself carefully.

Promising stage and screen director, catastrophe, and exile. A new career, equally brilliant, perhaps. But now something tired. Legacy, perhaps, of years of worry, frustration, anger. Has, in consequence, made himself soft, gentle. He sits there in the Imperial, and I sense a quality. It is patience.

"How I would like to just travel, sometime," he said. "As a boy I always wanted to see Japan. Now I am in Japan but I am not seeing it. I would like to give myself to it. You could guide me. Nara, Kyoto, people, adventures. But, no," he smiled his agreeably crooked smile, "I am here for the trout spawning season. I will see only Japanese trout. What? Oh, it is called *La Truite*, something by Boris Vian. It's been on the books for years now. We finally just got funding, as we call it."

He looked at the lobby. "What interests, and appalls me is how much the world has now come to look the same. The death of diversity—that ought to be a major theme. We could be sitting anywhere. Los Angeles."

"But Tokyo doesn't act like Los Angeles," I said.

"Not yet," he said, and then, turning to the girl in what was no longer her national dress, he said very slowly and carefully, "One more vodka, please."

19 SEPTEMBER 1981. To Iwasaki Akira's funeral, a cloudy day that turned to rain. Held at a Nichiren temple way out in Ikegami. Very high church. Chanting, bells, gongs, lots of incense, and most of the two hours the congregation *seiza*, sitting on their feet.

Iwasaki was a political figure; his work was almost entirely in film. Considered radical, perhaps communist, in prewar and wartime Japan. This resulted in his being imprisoned and tortured by the Japanese *kenpeitai*. They beat his face badly, and he carried these scars for the rest of his life. After the war, of course, these became scars of honor—he was one of the very few Japanese who had stood, for whatever reason, against the militarists. Active in leftist film (along with Yamamoto Satsuo, Kamei Fumio, the younger Shindo Kaneto, and Imai Tadashi) he probably kept up communist affiliations in some form to the end.

In some form, because Iwasaki was not doctrinaire and was probably too liberal for the Japanese Communist Party. He, for example, was the first Japanese critic to find reason in *Rashomon* when everyone else was finding horrid nihilism. He was, if a communist, a very old-fashioned one, the kind that now embarrasses Moscow, the sort of communist who believes in the rights of the little people and making a new and better world.

Iwasaki managed to be kind and helpful without ever compromising himself. He never, unlike almost everyone else, aligned himself with power or postwar big business. And there he lies today, his photograph showing a smiling, scarred, eternally optimistic man.

He helped me as few others did. Though I shared none of his political views, this seemed to make no difference to him. He knew I did not like the so-called socially conscious films of Imai and the rest, and that made no difference either.

At the funeral, however, no Imai, no Kamei, no Shindo. I sat with Sato Tadao and his wife, Hisako (she helped by telling me during which sections of the ceremony I could get off my numbed feet). Yamamoto was there, however, and was the first to pay respects—in a touching speech addressed directly to the deceased. Called him *kimi*, remembered their work together, and at the end gave *sayonara* its original connotation of permanent parting. Outside, offering incense (I was inside), were members of the orthodox film community, all the company representatives, and Oshima Nagisa, a dissident like Iwasaki.

The assembled company was highly respectable, rather rightish, and I wondered at the vagaries of life that this political man should be buried in such non-political company. But that was fitting. Life was always more important than politics and he never thought them to be identical.

Incense, flowers, the hearse, and it was over in the rain.

28 SEPTEMBER 1981. At the round bar of the Zakone, Robert Wilson looks at the girls opposite him. His regard, serious behind glasses, is heavy. It assesses.

He is tall, thin, an appearance as ordinary as his name, made more so by carefully unexceptional suit and tie. Eyes set close together as though always focused on something just in front of him. He is also silent. There is no talk, no attempt at presentation. He is there like the bar stool is there. Silence is pronounced. But one can break it with a question.

"Japan? It is very new. New to me. Though I know the Noh. That sounds like a joke." Then, "Japanese movement. I like Japanese movement." Measured speech, the talk of a man who is slowly describing what he is seeing, accurately. The accuracy is important. A man who is trying to tell what he sees.

He talks about Delphine Seyrig and the way she walks in the new Duras film. She walks in a way he finds seductively beautiful. He attempts to explain, then to show. His large hand is her body and two massive fingers her legs. The fingers walk slowly across the surface of the bar. Then they crumble. No, that is not it.

Silence. He suddenly stops and it is as though a door has closed. He looks straight ahead, self-absorbed.

Occasionally, a question of his own suddenly appears. How did I come to Japan? I tell him. Interest appears. A certain kind. Here is something he might be able to use. After I had concluded the account there was no response. He now has the information.

But mention of the Noh started a thought. It now appeared like a bubble rising on the surface. *Parsifal*. All underwater, a lake, then an iceberg floats to the center of the stage, and from it Amphortas takes an Egyptian box, and from that an ivory cask, and there is Parsifal sitting with his back to the audience, because he is us, you see, because he does not understand, and when he says he does not, then the audience knows just what he means.

A passage is described. The eyes regard me; the finger is raised. "As soft as this," and the finger strokes my cheek. "No," he says, correcting himself, "that is too aggressive. Like this," and the finger strokes my cheek even more softly.

The girls are covertly gazing at the two foreigners, one of them stroking the other's cheek. One giggles. He turns to look but the sight does not register. He is still seeing *Parsifal*.

Wagner—very right for someone as tall and serious as he is. The short, curvy, giggling girls are miles from this. He stands on his iceberg and stares, thinking.

Then, this train of thought having moved us to the unexpected terminal of Pierre Cardin, I am told how Wilson himself delayed a performance at L'Espace for two successive nights, making the suffering dress designer appear twice before his elegant audience to tell them that the Wilson work they had been about to see was not quite ready.

Perhaps the slowness of the Noh has occasioned this information. But what, I wondered, could have been his purpose in telling me? With most, the motivation would be apparent. Look at me: I am this important; see what I can do. Not with Robert Wilson. The story was told with no pride, no smiles. It was just something interesting that had happened. Then silence.

If he lived in Japan this masterful silence would be his most prized quality. Japanese from all walks of life would come to observe it. It is thought that nothing befits a person like silence; nothing speaks more strongly of character. And the monumental silence of Wilson—so unlike the ordinary quiet patches in an ordinary foreigner—would shortly become an object of national admiration.

And how much, I wondered, was learned from the Japanese—from the Kagura, from the Noh. Slowness, silence—and when he does talk the need for an example (the walking fingers, the finger on my cheek), as though words could not be trusted even when (especially when) used.

The two girls closely regarded our silence. They had never seen any foreigners like this before. They cannot understand that we were, right now, the more Japanese.

29 SEPTEMBER 1981. With Kurosawa to see a special showing arranged for him of Fellini's *La Citta della Donna*—without subtitles. Thus I could understand it no better than he could, but was spared because he turned down explanations. "Gets in the way of watching the picture," he said. We sat side by side, and I wondered what he was thinking of it—this most disciplined of directors watching two and a half hours by the most self-indulgent.

Afterward I asked him if he liked Fellini. "Well, I've seen almost everything," he said, not answering the question. But why then had he wanted to see this new film? "Well, it's this way. I'm going to Sorrento to pick up the Donatello Prize and Fellini is supposed to give it to me. Then we have to talk about something. So I thought I should see his new picture."

Later, I went to the JAL party, a big buffet at the Otani. The special guest to lead the toast was Takamine Hideko. I had not seen her for years. She is now older—it shows in the shape of her face, the sharpness of her features.

Old, and in the manner of Japanese women, angular. And, as old ladies are supposed to, she has developed a whole new set of public mannerisms: argumentative, forthright, and no-nonsense.

She also cultivates that slight awkwardness that Japan finds winning in its aging famous, as though she is surprised at the fuss made about her. Her pre-toast speech was about how she lost her wedding ring down a JAL plane toilet and how kind the staff was in getting it back. Just the proper sort of story—down-to-earth, no-nonsense. She has grown to fit her role. Later, I talk with her, wanting to ask her about Naruse. "Oh, Naruse," laughing heartily, "What a long memory you have."

Later, at home, I started remembering her in Naruse's *Flowing*, and in Yamamoto's *Horses*, when she was still a child. Then I remembered that Kurosawa was assistant director on that latter film. And then I recalled the story that he had fallen in love with her, that he had wanted to marry her, that nothing came of this, and that he was not loved back. Now he is seventy-one and she must be in her sixties, and I had seen them both in the same day and they had not seen each other.

7 OCTOBER 1981. To see Professor Doctor Takemi Taro, President of the Japan Medical Association. Not ill. I am editing his book. Had been warned that he was touchy, egotistical to a degree, and purposely difficult.

I am ushered into large room. Burl paneling, expensive exotic birds stuffed in cases, a picture of Fuji by a famous academic. And, on one wall, a fat little man in full dress with the order of something or other, one hand on a globe—a globe of the world. The door opened and the fat little man came in—a one-man procession.

His book is a series of diatribes against the government, against the insurance companies. I had been told that he poses as a philanthropist. But upon listening, I discover that he *is* one. He has "the health of the nation" as his major concern. As I listen to him hold forth he seems less ugly, and less short as well.

His arrogance, I find, is caused by his determination that everyone be healthy and his scorn is for those who would compromise this noble aim. When the interview is over I look again at the silly painting on the wall. It no longer resembles the man sitting in front of me—dedicated, selfless, and in his way quite handsome.

13 OCTOBER 1981. Dinner with Richard Storry. Now frail, had a heart attack earlier, and just a few days ago suffered something that may have been another. He is now living, I should think, with full knowledge of his own mortality. Yet, as always, so gracious, so interested, so amusing, so just, and so affectionate.

And so British. Only *they* have, I think, become so advanced that they may take an amused attitude toward themselves as a nation. To think of Storry is to think of civilization, of a culture so serious it need not take itself seriously.

I ask for some information, if he has any, about the origin of the idea of *kata* in Japan, where it came from. No information is forthcoming but, instead (and certainly almost equally useful), encouragement, interest, expression of approval, and interest about the work I am planning.

His disinterested encouragement—so different from the ordinary academic, particularly in Japanese studies, this willingness to help, to be of assistance. Tempered with the most enchanting waspishness about academic members. But these are always nameless, though very much there. Names are given only to those who are smart and interesting.

It always surprises me to see goodness. I never believe in it until, like last night, it is sitting in front of me. And goodness is always dying.

14 OCTOBER 1981. In Mukojima Park, dusk. A group of men gathered. Heads turned as I passed. One of them, a fat man of fifty or so, smiled. When I came around the park again they were still sitting and talking. One of them called to me and I went over. They were talking about a certain theater in Asakusa, the hole in the toilet wall of which had unfortunately been boarded over.

"You don't remember me," said the fat man. "It was thirty-five years ago, in another park. In Hibiya Park right after the war. You were very nice to me. You gave me a pair of sunglasses and took me to eat at Peter's." He was right, I did not remember him, and searching those fat features in the growing dusk detected nothing at all familiar. "Oh I've changed, I have. But not you. I recognized you at once. You foreigners, you never change."

I cannot imagine ever having taken this fat man anyplace, but I remember Peter's, a certain restaurant back when there were few of them, near the park and something, for its period, of a rendezvous. Mishima used to go there, during that same period. It is in *Forbidden Colors*.

"Time, time," said the fat man and smiled at me.

During the following year Richie suffered a heart attack, which resulted in his stopping smoking. He also began to receive awards (the first Kawakita Foundation Award was given to him), and he

traveled. In 1983 he went on a world tour with Mizushima, who was having second thoughts about his marriage, though he had become a father. Richie's journals continued to be composed not so much as a daily record of occurrences as a reaction to those things that he wanted to preserve—for example, the meeting with Marguerite Yourcenar below, a longer account than that which he published in *The Honorable Visitors.*

16 OCTOBER 1982. Dinner with Marguerite Yourcenar. She is with her companion, Jerry Wilson, sitting there in her coat and scarf in the big, cold downstairs room at the French Embassy Residence. The scarf, of loosely woven wool, is the same color as her intensely blue eyes. It is these extraordinary eyes, which though now hooded with age, give this elderly woman the look of youth. They and the mind behind them, which is, as I discovered, as agile, inquiring, amused as that of an adolescent girl.

We talk of her work, she with complete detachment. "I am translating a play by Jimmy Baldwin. He is a good friend," she says in her accented English. I mention her earlier translations of Negro spirituals. "Oh, yes, and that is not all. Now I am beginning to translate blues and soul. I am interested in this, and amusing it is to try to translate precisely." Here she gives her young companion a glance that was both an affirmation and an acknowledgement, and I realize that he is interested in blacks.

She smiles. A strong, round face, wrinkled as a winter apple. A peasant face, Breton, Flemish, like the faces of Brueghel. Nothing of the aristocrat in her appearance. Firm, round body. But the youthfulness of her expression, the adolescent clarity of her eyes, they are from something earlier: an illuminated book of hours, *Aucassin and Nicolette.*

I ask about work not yet translated, and happen to mention *La Nouvelle Eurydice.* "Oh, no, not that. What a bad book. You see I had had some success with *Alexis,* my first book. So I thought that the second should be larger, grander. It was a great mistake. It will not be translated, nor brought back into print." I ask if there are other of her own works that she thought badly of. "Only one. My little book on Pindar. So bad, so inflated." What then is her favorite, if she has one. She thinks and then says, "It is difficult, but I do think probably *The Abyss.*" From then we speak of her biography. "I am supposed to be writing the third and last volume. But here in Japan of course, I am not working at all." When would it end? "Oh, around 1930 just after I started to write. After the death of my father."

When she speaks of death I notice now, and later when she speaks of the death of her companion, Grace Frick, that she looks through and past me. Those extraordinary eyes, distant. Later, following what train of thought I do not know, she again speaks of death. "I shall not kill myself. Not like Hadrian. Oh, he did not kill himself, to be sure. But he often thought of it." Again her eyes sought the distance. Had she too thought of it? This I do not ask.

I take them to dinner at the Chugoku Honten, which can be trusted to feed you well. Since neither she nor her companion eats red meat, we have abalone, sweet and sour fish, Peking style chicken, and green vegetables in cream, ending with fresh litchi and drinking Chinese wine the while.

Jerry Wilson is around thirty. Open, American face with reddish hair cut very short, a small gold ring in one pierced ear. His French is fluent, with a heavy American accent. Where did they meet I ask. "Well, let me see, it was several years ago. He came with a television team that was doing something with me and we discovered that we had much in common." Period.

He sometimes lives with her and always travels with her. Last year they went to Egypt together and now are on this Asiatic tour. The conversation turns to Mishima, about whom she has written a book, and then to homosexuality.

They had been to the Kabuki and had heard that there was a place where the young *onnagata* gather to relax. I tell them that there might be such a place, but that it is unvisitable. Instead there are, of course, *onnagata*-like places where I could take them, places where the young men are more feminine than any female. This, she said, she would like to see, and so in several weeks this is where I shall take them.

Much as I want to know more about Madame Yourcenar's long interest in homosexuality ("Alexis," Hadrian, Cavafy, Baldwin, and Mishima), I ask no more. She had been described to me as taking the interest of a "scholarly amateur" in the subject, and so it seems to be. Her interest is detached and exists for itself, offering no further information about herself. It is an interest, I would imagine, rather like Colette's. And for many of the same reasons.

I ask her if I could ask her a very personal question, and she smiled and said that of course I could. So I ask a question I have long wanted to. What were her influences; who had formed her; what had she read that had made her style? She thinks and then says, "You must understand that when I was young I read everything. I read until there was no more to read. I devoured. And I retained. Therefore the influence upon me, a very strong one, is the influence of everyone. This is not a satisfactory reply I know, but it is the only one I am capable of making. Shakespeare, Pindar, Basho, all the novelists—everyone made me." Pressed, she said, "Maybe most the Greek poets. Maybe it was them I most loved. That being so, maybe it was they who most formed me."

We then talk of other things. I ask her if her admission into the Academie Française was time-consuming. Mr. Wilson laughs. "No," he says, "she never goes." She turns to me and smiles. "It is, you see, a club for elderly gentlemen and so I felt I ought not attend and they feel, I should think, relieved that I do not." I ask if they pay her anything. "Not a penny. To be sure, the more assiduous" (she appears to regard the word and smiles, as though it is one new to her), "become caretakers in old houses or curators of collections and thus get an apartment free, but otherwise there are no material rewards." "Only spiritual ones," says Wilson and they both smile.

After jasmine tea, we leave. She turns and I help her into her wool coat. From the rear she is a shapeless old peasant woman. She turns and I give her her handbag and she thanks me with a glance from those marvelous eyes. She is now a proud, sure, serene adolescent.

18 OCTOBER 1982. At the conference Isamu Noguchi, for the first time since I have known him, talked about himself. To be sure, he usually talks about his opinions, beliefs, etc., usually at length. But here he spoke of what it felt like to be him—Japanese ancestry, born an American, back to Japan before the war, back to America, his work, then back to Japan after the war, then back and forth, back and forth. He spoke about what he discovered in Japan and in himself, talked about stone and rock.

Noguchi himself has become rock-like. He is veined and seamed and sits very still. As his outside has grown this patina, so his inside, his opinions, views, have softened, mellowed. It used to be that Noguchi's ideas were the most adamantine thing about him. Abrasive. You could cut yourself on them. Not now. The rock speaks softly.

Later, the long day over, we have coffee and talk of the Stravinsky/ Balanchine *Orpheus*, for which he did costumes and sets. He complains that in doing everything over for its revival he had to make everything larger. It was designed for the small City Center and not the large Lincoln Center. "It is really a chamber work. That is how I saw it, too, with my little rocks. Now those little rocks are enormous so that they will be visible in all that space. A great mistake. Scale is one of the most important of all things and we violated our

With Edwin Reischauer, Isamu Noguchi. Hakone, 1982.

scale. No. I violated it. Balanchine and Stravinsky kept things the same. Mine was the part that had to give. I regret it."

19 OCTOBER 1982. Lunch with Edwin Reischauer. He talks about the Great Kanto Earthquake, which he remembers. Wasn't in Tokyo but in Karuizawa. Nonetheless, the shock was so great that it knocked over chimneys and killed one person there—crushed under a roof.

What he remembers well is the massacre of the Koreans, which began at once, only hours after the earthquake. They, the minority, were being held responsible, not for the earthquake, but for the terror and despair of the Japanese themselves. Ridiculous charges: poisoning wells and the like.

He remembers a child, a girl, deaf, and consequently unable to speak. The crowd confronted her. She could not tell them that she was Japanese. They tore her to pieces. Whether she was Japanese or not is not the point, of course. A child was murdered.

Reischauer simply tells the story. He makes no apology, makes no attempt to account for what happened. Takes for granted that this is what the Japanese do—or did. Does not say so. No moral reflections at all. He knows his people very well. He knows and he accepts. So do I.

25 OCTOBER 1982. A curious dream. I was at a party at someone's house. The style was art deco and I knew that it had been made in the 1930s. Also, as I gradually became aware, this *was* the 1930s. The others were all men and we were sitting around drinking. I was speaking with Ravel. It took me some time to recognize this because he looked nothing like his pictures.

I also realized that I knew what was going to happen and he did not. It became very important to determine precisely in what year all this was occurring so that I would know how much time he had left. But he was charmingly vague. Pleased that I knew so much about his work, that I loved *L'Enfant et les Sortilèges* ("We must be the only ones, no one else knows of it"). Finally, I learned that it was about 1934 and I realized that the charming man in front of me would be dead in three years.

So I told him about his last composition. He was very interested since he had not yet started to write it. I told him about the film Gaumont was making on Don Quixote and the music they would commission. "For Panzera," said Ravel. "No, Chaliapin," said I. "Oh, dear," said Ravel. "That's all right," I said warmly, "You will not win the commission. Ibert will. But your work, called *Don Quichotte et Dulcinée*, will become much the more famous." "Well," said Ravel, "that's something at any rate." I did not tell him about the auto accident, the brain damage, the inability to compose, the operation, and the death.

Or perhaps I did. I was feeling the awful pathos of knowing what was going to happen, the inability to stop it, the touching innocence of the victim. Dreams mean something we are told. What does my role as messenger from the future mean? Anything?—Or is the brain at sleep really an idle computer amusing itself by punching at random?

28 OCTOBER 1982. Dinner with Marguerite Yourcenar and Jerry Wilson, all of us taken out by Eric Klestadt—to eat at the very elegant Kicho, then for coffee at the equally elegant Nishi no Ki.

Madame Yourcenar at one point speaks of herself. Her mother, who died when she was young, was Flemish. Her father, who died in the 1930s, was able to read her first book, *Alexis*, in manuscript. He was a great reader. Books were all over the house and Madame Yourcenar began reading very early.

"What did your father do?" "Nothing at all. Nothing." "But how did you live." "Land, tenant farming." "Did that devolve down on you?" "On neither myself nor my older half brother. My father lived gloriously. He lived right *through* it."

Jerry tells me she is seventy-nine. That, I think, is quite old, but years are apparently light upon her. She speaks of catching cold easily. "Fortunately, I caught my cold in the most beautiful place—Matsushima." And Jerry says that sometimes she forgets. Which she probably does, but part of the fond way in which he says this has to do with their relationship as much as with her forgetfulness.

She is fortunate she has him. He is devoted. Always ready with the wraps. Helping her, smoothing the way. They have that mutual look that certain married couples have. What is hers is his, his, hers, the look seems to say. They both turn to answer the same question.

During the conversation I learn that she is claustrophobic and once had a bad attack of asthma in the Paris metro. I describe my being caught in the same metro and experiencing the pangs of the same affliction. We smile and nod. Something in common.

She is very interested in Eric and his background: German Jew, fled, came to Japan. She also knows how to be the perfect guest. I admire this. Adaptability. I would imagine that she has a long experience as guest, being gracious with host. I do not know how she would be as hostess. Perhaps not so good. I can imagine her becoming tired of her guests very easily.

But now it is midnight, time to move on to the transvestite bar, which will have to serve as the place where the *onnagata* meet.

5 DECEMBER 1982. Invited to dinner by Madame Yourcenar and Jerry, just the three of us, at the Takanawa—sole for her, abalone for him, steak for me.

I watch her and Jerry together. It is like grandmother and grandson. It is also not like that at all. They are as much themselves with each other as though they have been married for years. At the same time, however, he is also there for her convenience. (In the bar for pre-dinner drinks, Madame went ahead. Usually it is he. This time he followed her, large among the little tables, and said, with a smile, "Where she goes, I follow." Said this with affection and good will.) At other times she is as permissive as a mother. Jerry did not like the Noh and, carried away, he turned it into a little act. He also, without knowing, turned himself into the very image of his Arkansas mother not liking the Noh. He used words ("land's sake") appropriate for her. This unconscious imitation apparently pleased Madame. She also offered further reasons for finding the Noh boring. But since she had not actually found it so, this was done with some playfulness, yet with no hidden acknowledgment to me that we were at this point seeing through Jerry. On the contrary, it was like a mother reveling in her child's foolishness.

Later, talk about Mishima. Madame astonished me with the pronouncement that his wife could not have much loved him, since she survived him. I asked if she were indeed that romantic, that she thought a great love could not survive a death. "Oh, yes," she said, cheerfully, "I'm just that romantic."

"But, you," I said, "survived and lived to write *Les Feux*." She looked at me as though trying to guess how much I knew. Since I knew nothing, this did not take long. She said, "Yes, it was a difficult time but it could not compare." Consequently, I learned nothing about this particular crisis of the soul she had undergone, and of which I had only vaguely heard.

She wondered if Mishima's wife knew, then said, "Of course she did but she did not want to believe, did not want to know." Said that sometimes the person himself did not want to know. Mentioned Henry James as an example. I told her I had heard that Leon Edel had kept back letters from James to Hugh Walpole that proved what the biographer did not want to believe. "Yes," agreed Madame, "because otherwise much of James's *The Pupil*, would not be understandable. Madame Mishima, like Edel, was merely trying to hide, not wanting to admit."

Not wanting to admit was also treated as just as normal, as was the homosexual impulse itself, however. Everything is normal in Madame Yourcenar's world; hence everything is understandable. It is not that she is Olympian, as has been said, but that she is so absolutely accepting.

She did, however, find Japan the most difficult country she had ever been in. The simplest things defeated them. They went out to buy pencils and returned, defeated, no pencils. I wondered how this could be and then realized that her world is entirely one of language and she has no language for this country. Some kind of converse, this is what she expects, and this is what she misses here. Not that it is not here. It is that it is not open to her. No Japanese language, and the Japanese themselves not often making the intuitive leap one finds admirable in Mediterranean countries. Blank incomprehension or evasion is what she is met with. This intrigues and puzzles. Of a consequence the two of them go mainly to the theater. Jerry simply "adores" the Kabuki and so this is what they have seen. Some forty hours of Kabuki since arrival—both because of interest and because it is, oddly, a place of refuge from Japan itself for them.

Looking at her I was suddenly struck by a resemblance I did not before see in her similarity to Colette. Not that they are both women, not that they are both androgynous, but rather their interest in detail, their fascination in how something is done, their acceptance of the natural world and their celebration of it—a combination of interest and awe. I watched her eating her sole with interest and concern, watched the way she savored a chopstickful, crumbling it with her lips.

What was it in this gesture? Something I have seen in Flemish paintings. Then a phrase, not a particularly good one but a descriptive one occurred: She is a patrician peasant. The lips are those in Brueghel, the eyes are those in the *Livre des Heures*. Feet squat on the ground she soars to an enormous height, her eyes (those eyes—she shares them with Simone Signoret) looking into the far distance. Is that the reason for her charm?—that she manages to encompass a dichotomy, closes it, and consequently appears so whole.

The evening was over. She picked up the tiny pot of living *plumeria* I brought her, and held it as though warming it in her rough hands. She was not tired, but she would be. I took my leave. She and Jerry looked after me as I departed, the two of them there, a woman who likes strange and beautiful sons and had none, a young man who likes old and wise mothers and had none.

10 DECEMBER 1982. I learn today that Herschel [Webb] is dead. And my first thought is that this is impossible because he was so young. But then I remembered that that was thirty-five years ago. Afterward he went to teach at Columbia and became a scholar and a full professor. I was here; he there, and we rarely met. And now he is dead. I had heard that, as I remembered, he retained his taste for martinis but I did not know to what extent until now. The Herschel I remember, though, was not a teacher; he was more like a student, an endlessly inventive one. And as I remembered him today I heard from somewhere the opening bassoon solo from *Sacre* and Herschel singing along, "Oh, baby, see the moon . . ."

12 DECEMBER 1982. I go to Kamakura. I sit in the train and look out of the window as Herschel and I had thirty-five years ago when we went down to spend the weekend at Dr. Suzuki's house. But I will get off at Kita-Kamakura today only to take a taxi to the museum.

Today is the last day of the Italian show and it has three Morandis I want to see again. One is particularly fine, all made of a single color, a reddish gray, against which the objects stand, their own contours often of the same color so that line becomes invisible. A work from 1928 to 1929, done with the paint oily, lots of brush marks, all invisible from three feet back.

Walking down from the Hachiman I notice a small print shop into which I had not gone for years. Go in. A small pile of original prints, all of them overpriced. And then, at the bottom, a beautiful Toyokuni. A tattooed man being ferried across a river on the shoulders of porters. Obviously just the middle section of a triptych, but quite splendid nonetheless. Done mainly in blue and red. Red for the tattoos, blue for the rest, with that Delft-like shading from very light to very dark. I admire, put it regretfully to one side, then notice the price. It is only fifty dollars. Upon asking why I am told that, though a first impression, it has watermarks on one side and, being part of a three-unit panel, is not complete. I do not argue—a Toyokuni this superior belongs in a museum. Nonetheless, it is now here in my house.

Suddenly I remember a dream I had last night. It was a continuation of something that really happened two years ago. What really happened was that Francis Coppola called me up, was in a bar across the street, come on over. There was Toru Takemitsu, a good friend, and Richard Brautigan, whom I had been avoiding. He knew this, had been told, and so now refused to shake hands, glowered, then turned to Coppola, and with that whine of his said, "But, Francis, you *know* you are making masterpieces, you know that, don't you, man?" I talked with Francis and Toru and then went home. Wondered after just why I had been called out. Because they were all drunk? Or was Francis staging one of his scenes? Never found out, but that was what happened. Now the event had a continuation in my dream last night. Continuation: I punch Brautigan and lay him out.

13 DECEMBER 1982. Did not sleep well last night. Do not sleep well unless I am alone or with someone I know well. Did not know well the soundly sleeping Hisashi, having only met him an hour before as he was dozing in a Steve McQueen all-nighter. Sturdy, rural, from Tohoku, twenty, in for a Saturday night in the city, not caring at all what happened to him so long as something did. Now, satisfied with his new experience, he sleeps with the audible sighs of farm youth everywhere.

In the morning he admires my paintings. Talks about their space (*kukan*), knows what he is talking about. Most Japanese know about art, and all can draw maps and carry tunes—and dance. He shows me some of the steps for the local Tohoku *matsuri*, thumping big-footed in his underwear. It is as though we have known each other for years—the gift for instant intimacy that the rural young still have. Later, went to have breakfast at the Park where I taught him the intricacies of eggs benedict.

7 JANUARY 1983. Sogetsu-ryu ikebana, the Hilton, the Pearl Room—chandeliers made of ropes of pearls—big party, mostly women, most in kimono, much display of good manners, lots of food including seven different kinds of cake, and lots of money spent, but then Sogetsu has it—the most affluent of all the flower-arrangement schools, thousands of pupils all over the world, and leading all the rest when it comes to paying taxes.

Iemoto Teshigahara Hiroshi, now grand in *hakama*, white-maned and patriarchal, makes the opening speech. And I remember when he was still a schoolboy, wanting to make movies, and getting to—the money coming from old Sofu, his dad, who had founded the lucrative school. Then Sofu died and Hiroshi's elder sister took over, but then she died and (Japanese arts schools having lineage, just like royalty) the position of *iemoto* devolved upon Hiroshi. He hated it, knew nothing about flowers, but the pressure of the school was stronger.

That was three years ago. Now he has become what was wanted—the head of the school. He handles himself well, has been a great success. The ladies love him. He speaks in respectful tones of his father while his mother, her hair now a light violet, sits and beams.

He has done a perhaps typical but nonetheless I suppose admirable thing. Since he could not change his circumstances, he changed himself. Knows all about flowers and the other materials (cellophane, plastic, egg-crates) avant-garde Sogetsu makes use of, left off his tweeds and suedes, and is now usually in kimono.

At the same time I wonder just how much this cost the director of *Woman in the Dunes*. My Western self says that he sold out. But my Eastern self wonders if what he did does not indicate a higher wisdom. We are so prone to think any accommodation a surrender. Hiroshi has chosen continuation. If the cost has been great, he seems—standing there, leonine, grand, a master—already to have discounted it.

7 JUNE 1983. Rereading *The Immoralist*. First read it nearly forty years ago. Sitting in Hibiya Park, as Michel sat in the park at Biskra. How old was I then—twenty-four? Proper age for reading this book. I am no longer at the proper age but I am curious. This book much influenced me. What is it like now; what am I like now?

How little I remembered of it. Almost nothing. And how I had colored what I had remembered. One's memory of a book is never accurate. It is a memory of the impression the book made. The impression now is much different. Michel I once found admirable. Now I find him pathological. Not in his immorality, of course. Rather, in his symptoms.

I suppose it is because I recognize them. I am impressed now rather by the truthfulness of Gide's observations about his travels with his wife, the compensatory neuroticism of the husband. The urge to rush from one place to the other, as though a new goal will be somehow better because it is new. I recognize this, having experienced it twenty years ago with my own new wife.

Do I now experience this because Michel so influenced me forty years ago? I wonder. Probably not. I was attracted to Michel because I was of the temperament to experience what he did. It was thus not Michel's rebellion that attracted me, but his feeling of guilt. This I seem to have recognized.

It is this that leads one to feel so responsible for another, to use them for this purpose, then to dislike them for it, and then to feel guilty for the dislike. How vulgar—because it has nothing to do with them. It has only to do with self.

And perhaps *that* is the true immorality of Michel—of all of us. This use of others for one's own dramatic purposes. As though one would not exist otherwise.

And I sense the chill that comes when one suspects nonexistence—the flight that follows, the rationalizations, and the panic terror. Gide, however, makes very little of this. Did he know what he was describing? Perhaps not. To him, Michel is still a hero.

8 JUNE 1983. Lunch with Richard Brautigan, one that came about in a curious fashion. I had seen him at a Parco opening and went up and asked why he had refused to shake my hand when he was here before. He was confused, remembered, said it was all a misunderstanding, as it indeed must have been; then last week he sent me a letter, very small writing on hotel stationery: "It is always very pleasant to clear up misunderstandings and I admire your courage to come up to me when last we met to talk it over and have it done with." Then he asked me to have a drink with him, and that turned into lunch.

Denim and corduroy, granny glasses, wispy red hair, uneven red mustache. Bright blue eyes, the moustache concealing an affable mouth. The aging hippy persona is there but is mostly due to the clothes: the studied appearance of the unlearned, does not know foreign languages, careful mispronunciations. Part of it is a pose, I think: the American anti-intellectual, Mark Twain, *Innocents Abroad*. But not all.

He talks about himself, which is perhaps to be expected, given our manner of meeting. He is not precisely attempting to justify himself, but is giving me a lot of information. Among the things spoken of is how different the public persona, created by "the media," is from the real self.

Speaks of Norman Mailer, apparently a close friend. Finds him generous, sweet, understanding, warm—all things different indeed from the public persona. From there we speak of ways in which the persona may be used. It is of use in getting people to go to bed with you. In fact, fame-fucking is a known result.

He has had much experience. Further, he prefers his partners young. His persona is very reassuring. He is filled with earth-wisdom and, as one of the original hippies, is by definition kind and understanding, things that female children, males as well, find attractive. He is at present with a young girl, "young enough to be my daughter."

We drink sangria, growing more mellow with each sip, and eat an excellent Spanish bouillabaisse. We talk about Francis, we mention the very bar where we first met and where the affront occurred. But we do not speak of it, being much too well bred to do so. I find his air of the faux-naïf very refreshing but I still do not know how faux it is. Perhaps it isn't. What he finds in me I don't know—we speak little about me.

17 JUNE 1983. Dinner with Paul Schrader, in Tokyo for the Mishima movie that he will direct. Talks about difficulties with Mishima Yoko and her efforts to make her dead husband into something more fitting. We talk about Yukio. "That is undoubtedly him. And that is just what I can't put into the movie, damn it. Not that we can't, you know. We have not signed anything away. We want to make our kind of movie, not hers."

I say that Mishima himself would probably have sided with Paul; that he would not, I think, have approved of the amount of censorship that Yoko is exercising. He was enough of an exhibitionist to want to project a little of the truth at least—to tantalize his audience, if nothing else.

Paul still has his engaging stutter, still has his charm, his bent smile, the sudden crinkling of the eyes. These he somehow kept in Hollywood. Or maybe has them back now that he is here. Talks of how he is going to structure his film: Mishima in real life, then Mishima as a boy, then Mishima as one of the characters in his various novels. These three will have a kind of conversation, and somehow in the interchange he hopes that something like the real author will appear—and that Yoko will not notice.

He is going to have his production man over; it is going to be all studio; it will be completely professional, all designed. I do not say that this is not the proper work for a Bresson scholar. But Paul never became Bresson and I suppose there is no reason why he should have. One need not become what one admires.

I see that Paul bites his nails now. Why do I find this engaging? Sign of weakness? No, a sign of something else, something more human. Paul presents such a reasoned and optimistic self that one welcomes something as human and doubtful as nail biting. Cutting him down to size? No, I don't think so. Rather, something one recognizes, sees as authentic.

18 JUNE 1983. Lunch with Francis [Coppola]. He is here to convince Mishima Yoko that a film on her late husband is a good idea—that the writer, director, and he himself, all are working for the proper picture. The difference lies in the interpretation. She wants the whitened sepulcher she has been daubing away at these last years. They want a commercial film that tells a bit of the truth. Consequently Francis is properly cynical, or as cynical as he ever gets.

"Is it true," he wonders aloud, "that a director is only as good as his last few films? Is it really like a ball game? Three strikes and you're out?" From anyone else, given Francis' recent experiences, this would certainly sound like irony. But when he asks this, his eyes gentle, his large and infantile mouth questioning, one detects no cynicism. Just the kind of wonder that such a thing might, perhaps, after all, be possible.

Francis is very childlike. Having put on weight again, he is like a fat little boy, and he has all the gentleness and sudden wildness that one associates with youngsters. A bearded baby, he is given to quick enthusiasms, flights of fancy, and a kind of weighty wit—irresistible because, like a child, Francis does not take himself seriously.

All of his recent bad luck, so much of it brought down by himself, seems not to have affected him. As though it happened to a person named Francis Coppola, someone sitting right there, but not actually, somehow, the same.

He talks about a South American place he has bought—El Getaway, he calls it. It is really very convenient. "Only a couple of hours from Miami in your plane, got its own airstrip, and it has lakes and waterfalls and the ancient ruins right there on the property. The sea? Oh, it's close. In a plane we can get there in a couple of minutes, about fifteen of them. Otherwise, it is days of hacking the jungle, of course. We could build this landing strip on the beach. Probably will."

Probably will. He is like a little boy, living entirely in his imagination with the difference, the great difference, that what Francis imagines always comes true. Both the good and the bad. He will get his airstrip and his planes. But he also got a great disaster, his studio—all because of his imaginatively walking too near the edge.

Hope—that is what it is. And with hope, certainty. Success, failure, but some certainty. And if the latter, then it, too, has its uses. Francis may be up or may be down, but Francis survives. He survives as a child survives. He believes—irony yes, cynicism no. He believes in Francis but, more important, he believes in the world, and still finds it quite wonderful.

8 AUGUST 1983. Taken to dinner by Mifune Toshiro at an elegant Akasaka *ryotei*—fancy food, geisha dances, lively girls to sit beside you and pour. The occasion was the entertainment of Nancy Dowd and John Dark who are here to do her film, *R&R*, and I had suggested Mifune Productions and introduced Toshiro. Hence my being included.

Mifune is older, has lost some of his hair. His shape has changed but his eyes are the same. And his smile—that wonderful smile, seen so little in the films: charming, genuine, disarming.

The smile is little seen because it does not fit his solemn machismo screen persona. It does not suit it because it is boyish. And it is the boyishness of Mifune, now well over sixty, which so charms. That and his almost adolescent-seeming self-deprecation. Whether this is genuine or not, I do not know. But I do see that he makes very little use of it. He has nothing to gain from it but more charm, and he is already exuding that. No, I think Mifune has an enchantingly poor opinion of himself.

Certainly the pattern of his life is that of a man who doubts himself. The period with Kurosawa in which he allowed himself to be molded, then the number of failures which followed: as director, as husband, as businessman, and even as actor, since left to himself he plays roles like that in *Shogun*. Mifune always strikes me as ready for failure but attempting, gamely, to avoid it.

He is charming at the party. Nancy is quite swept away, not only with him, but also with her first glimpse at high-powered Japanese entertaining—the food, the drink, and the concern. The kimonoed young lady and I have a perfectly proper conversation about underwear, what is worn under the kimono. She wears no panties, as is common nowadays. It ruins the line of the kimono. So she does not—except, she reminds me, once a month, then smiles charmingly. Mifune, it turns out always wore something like BVD's under everything, armor and all. The geisha dancer wears only a sheath of cloth under her kimono. Hers is red because she is an entertainer. The other girls' were pink or, if older, white. Nancy rolls her eyes deliriously when I translate all of this.

Mifune is much at home in this milieu. I have long thought that he might be a bit prudish. Perhaps he is. Here, however, such talk is not considered anything but proper. It has the right light touch. One is not interested and not uninterested, and this is proper. Mifune has learned to be very good at this. And he never goes too far.

With Mifune Toshiro, 1983.

Then he makes a speech, a charming one. I am the peg on which he hangs it: our long acquaintanceship, and now my introducing these splendid people. His poor attempts at entertainment and, he hopes, their understanding. . . .

Actually, Mifune Productions would very much like the business and promises to do well. But not a word of that. Fortunately John and Nancy already know how Japan works, and they are now capable of appreciating nuances and subtleties that would have left them blind in London and L.A. Then John makes just the proper speech, almost committing himself, but not quite. Then Nancy talks, properly, to the point. Then I, as is my role, bow and thank and indicate that the happy evening is over.

How well the Japanese do this. The sordid necessaries of heavy financial encounters turn butterfly-like during these light and so personal-seeming encounters. And the sincerity is quite there—so far as it goes. It is this that so completely undoes the West.

I wonder how many parties like this Mifune has a week. More than a few, I would imagine. If he tires of them there is no indication. There he is, boyish as always, smiling as broadly as he did decades ago. Only occasionally, when he thinks no one is looking, or when he forgets, does the smile relax; he will look someplace, the corner of the room perhaps, and there is the inward gaze of a man looking into himself, seeing nothing outside. Of what is he thinking then, I wonder. Of himself? Of life?

Then, with that smile he turns, sake bottle in hand, to pour you another drink, to clown his way through a story, to listen with absolute intentness to whatever it is that you are saying.

Mifune the good guy, the straight arrow. It is all real, it is all there. It is all on the surface, too. Is there anything more than surface? Well, that is not a question profitably to be asked in Japan, where the ostensible is always the real, where there is nothing more.

And yet. Inside are the bandit, the samurai, the shogun, the gambler, the shoe magnate, and Red Beard himself. How can so consummate an actor be only this? But there I have my answer. By being this, he is a consummate actor.

14 AUGUST 1983. The Fukagawa Tomioka Hachiman Festival, held every three years: an enormously long procession of *omikoshi*, the large cross-beamed floats carried on the shoulders of the participants, in the center the ornate house of the god, bells, the golden phoenix atop. Fifty of these floats, each supported by a hundred near-naked men—fifty under the beams chanting and dancing, the other fifty waiting to take their turn, dancing alongside. Each float is from a different section of Fukagawa, and so the half-kimonos, originally worn but shortly discarded, carry the quarter's name and its *mon* of a distinctive color. In fifty years, Fukagawa, completely destroyed by firebombs in 1945, has been rebuilt. Fifty floats, each with at least a hundred men—five thousand, and five times that number lining the streets, watching.

A spectacular festival—its size, the number of people involved, that it is so uninhibited, and that so much flesh is so casually displayed. Also, that it is held in the heat of summer, on a day traditionally the hottest. Hence the shed clothing, the sweat, the reddened, sun-tinged flesh.

Hence also the water. It has for hundreds of years been customary for the houses along the way to have buckets of water, or hoses, or water pumps—all ready for the passing shoulder-carried, hundred-legged floats. Streams of water curl into the air, water flung hangs before it descends. From all sides, all at once, continually—water descending. The nearly naked men are drenched.

Most are wearing only a tucked-in loincloth. Their drenched hair begins to steam in the sun; water runs down arms and legs, puddles, and evaporates. The humidity around the floats rises as the water turns to steam. The loincloths, white cotton, turn transparent as the water courses. The god appears.

Fertility is what this festival, like most, is about. The jostled god in his dark little box atop the float is a fertility god, and he thinks only of procreation and the things that allow it: heat, water, and movement.

The men wear their nakedness as though it were a costume. No one jokes or laughs, and no one stares as the loincloths turn transparent and the jostling dance continues.

This spectacle is deeply erotic because it is not concerned with actualities, but with possibilities. Like the blossom hidden in the bud, eroticism lies always in the future. These small and visible gods are not, after all, standing erect. They are merely there, made visible by the magic of the festival—fertility promised.

With rhythmic shouts, one float after another sways down between the lines of spectators. The procession takes two hours to pass. Two hours of naked thighs and barely masked loins, pounding buttocks, strained shoulders, and faces turned skyward, chanting the rhythmic cry of the *matsuri*. A spectacle—something from Japan's past, and something with us yet.

27 AUGUST 1983. Tonight I went again to Sumida Park. There is a grove on a hill, a still lake, paths that wind and rejoin. It is dark; a few street lamps cast pools and the stars are bright beyond the tracery of leaves.

The dark park, night—and I again relive my oldest dream. It occurred, several times it now seems, over half a century later. I was very young—six maybe. A park, perhaps, or a woods, and it was dark, late, and I was there alone. And from the shadows walked a man. I remember the man's strong face, half in the shadow, and the soft touch of his hard hand. And the look he gave me in the half-light, loving, protective, when he told me not to fear, that he would take care of me. I turned in my dream and buried my face, and his chest was hard against my cheek. Then I woke up.

But did I? Here I am again in the dark in a park, and I am now near sixty. The intervening years have seen many dark parks and, living my dream, many hard men. Each I have pressed my head against.

I am looking for the original, for the man in the dream, you will say. Well, yes. But when you have found him hundreds of times and still go on looking, for what then are you searching? If you have not found him by now, you never will. Or, conversely, if you find him every day, you may be certain that he does exist only in dreams.

What was it he said? Yes, that he would take care of me, look after me, that I would no longer be alone. Though I am sixty now, no longer six, they—he—are still the same age, twenty-something. They, the inhabitants of the dream, have not aged—the same strong face, the same hard hands.

Sometimes I, an adult, have turned these strong men again into boys, and it is I who have looked after them, taken care of them. But in the dark I am again the child, and it is they who are adult. What could it all mean? Anything? Nothing? No, if only because things cause other things, there is probably a meaning—but it is not one with which I am concerned as I watch the shadows in the darkened park.

Each new man—he is the answer. It is he whom I first saw over half a century now past. It never is, to be sure, but I am always there waiting. I surmise my reason. I am entertaining—yes, that is the word—entertaining hope. Something that affirming, that health-giving. I stand in the dark, calm, assured, faithful, hoping.

25 NOVEMBER 1983. Dinner with Paul Schrader and Mary Beth Hurt. He is having some difficulties. Yoko, Mishima's widow, has had second thoughts now that she has signed the contract and taken the money. For some time she has been cleaning up after her husband—suppressing his film *Yukoku*, [Patriotism], cutting off his ex-friends, denying things—in order to make him into the man she thinks he ought to have been. Now she sees that Paul wants to make a film about Mishima as he was. Very tempestuous luncheon the other day—tears, I understand.

The main problem is Mishima's homosexuality. She, who should know it best, is now denying it. Paul wants to include a part of it since he could not well leave it out. Tears, because their daughter somehow got hold of a copy of the script and was instantly devastated. The reason was not the strength of the script, but that the daughter had been uneducated as to just what her father was like. A slight reference in script to a gay bar. Stunned daughter. The son several years ago read the masturbation scene in his father's *Confessions of a Mask*. Trauma. Was Dad really like that?

I doubt this is true. Impossible to tell how much accuracy remains in all this, because it comes strained through the mother's rendition, then Francis's, then Paul's. Also, because Yoko is so playing her role. Still, it is probably true that she has kept the kids in ignorance. Part of her plan—perhaps part of her revenge as well. I remember her as a neglected bride. She had to live with the monster. It is now that she has her way, and in so doing chooses to geld him.

It comes as no surprise to learn that Yoko particularly did not want Paul to see me. I know too much. Also, I am not on her side because I have been known to criticize the illustrious and now sainted author. Last time I saw her she smiled and said that I was just not to be trusted. That is perfectly true. But I knew Mishima as well, and I want to have no part in what she is doing to him now that he is helplessly dead.

2 MARCH 1984. The opening of the Isamu Noguchi show at the Sogetsu Kaikan, in the indoor terraced stone garden that he himself designed for the building. Isamu there, brown, leathery, now nearly eighty, dressed in his Santa Fe best—big silver turquoise-studded belt. Though Japanese, he is very American, having been educated there, having lived there most of his life. He looks like Georgia O'Keefe now.

He has also gone into multiples—which is very American of him. The new work (hot-dipped galvanized steel) comes in editions, of eighteen or twenty-six. At the show was one of each, all twenty-six of them. One is encouraged to buy, or will be. The prices are not listed at the opening, however. Soft sell.

The pieces themselves are very Noguchi. They look as if made of silver cardboard, and fit into each other—their various parts have slits, like packing cases. The forms are "free," kidney-shaped. A slight flavor of the *Orpheus* props. I cannot imagine anyone wanting one.

Here in the antiseptic Sogetsu interior—done by Tange, all of whose interiors are like the insides of iceboxes with the lights left on—they seem unimpressive. Perhaps in a garden, a real one, they would fare better.

But then Isamu has always talked better art than he made. He is inspiring to listen to, particularly when he starts on Japanese garden aesthetics. But then from all this comes the work, which is sort of preschool. And now we have these multi-copy prefab kindergarten objects.

Isamu very much in his element at the party. Lots of famous people. Teshigara Hiroshi, lion-maned and sleek, melts into background discreetly taking pictures, determined that this is Isamu's show and he will not, absolutely will not intrude. That clown Okamoto Taro, whom some perhaps still regard as an artist, here but subdued—though certainly not from modesty and a desire to defer to Isamu. Maybe he is still feeling the death of Miro, the man from whom he took his style. Kamekura the designer, some TV and screen folk, and a few favored foreigners. Not the beautiful people—they go to Issey Miyake's—but the in-people. And there are no models, though there are two white American *shakuhachi* players.

12 AUGUST 1984. With Eric to the last performance of the final annual obon exhibition of Japanese folk festivals, held at the grounds of the Meiji Shrine. About ten thousand attended and five thousand, it seemed, performed.

Other countries may show their festivals en masse like this—I remember a Moroccan *festiva* in Marrakesh, and a Yugoslavian showing at Dubrovnik of dances from all its provinces—but only in Japan would these be uncommercialized, by amateurs, by people from the provinces themselves. And only, I think, in Japan, with such vigor and enthusiasm.

Things I remember from this final evening: The platform in the center suddenly invaded by dozens of young men in breechclouts waving enormous ship's flags, followed by a hundred or so young women in fishing wear, surrounded then by others in sea-blue kimono, and the drums and flutes and bells and voices doing the wonderful *Tairyo Bushi*. Then, at the last verse, those circling about suddenly produce long strips of blue cloth that are waved to simulate the sea.

Eight enormous floats from Shikoku, each fifty feet in height, held aloft and moved about by masses of young men from the island's provinces. A mock fight, like galleons on a sea of people, and an obeisance to the audience, like a herd of trained elephants.

A huge illuminated portable shrine from Akita that, held aloft by dozens beneath, floated like an apparition across the crowds, the lights inside illuminating every tracery.

Fireworks, enormous ones, from Hyogo, each *held* by a young man, a row of them clasping these roman candles like kegs. The fire sprayed past their faces and drowned them in a burning rain. They stood there, rows of them, like fiery caryatids.

A giant lion from Kobe: The head fifteen feet high, the cloth body manipulated by one hundred fifty men inside with long poles, pulled by a hundred more outside—a lion circus tent.

The Nebuta from Aomori: First a phalanx of dozens of drums, held in threes and pounded at the same time. Then a group of dancers, all girls. Then the big drums, on wheels, each hammered by five strong men. Then young men in loincloths, leaping and capering. Then the mighty illuminated float, fifty feet high, a hundred across, illuminated from the inside—a giant samurai, sword aloft. And following this, the people from Aomori all dancing and leaping. All of this began at five-thirty as the sun was setting, and ended at nine-thirty as the full moon was rising. A marvelous spectacle, and the last. It now simply costs too much. The committee has had to give it up.

13 AUGUST 1984. Thinking of visual spectacles today, the great ones I have seen. To be sure the Grand Canyon and Ryoanji are both visual spectacles and I have seen them both, but that is not what I mean. I mean man-made ones. Let me see:

When the curtain opened on the first night of Tudor's *Romeo*

The Kyogen Monkey-Skin Quiver, *Nomura Troupe. Last row center: Lincoln Kirstein, Meredith Weatherby, Richie.*

and Juliet and the Met audience saw the Berman set against that great blue cyclorama, that gasp of surprise and pleasure. Then Sir Thomas Beecham raised his baton and the Delius began.

In the Kabuki *Ibaraki*, a charming little dance for the page, all nautical references (pulling the oars, riding the waves) with the precision of nineteenth-century clockwork. Then, three comic dancers in the interlude—Edo street trash in the middle of fifteenth-century Kyoto. In the coda a wonderfully dance-like turn on the samisen, and the gliding exit of the three, legs up high, feet slapping, real high-stepping in a perfect parody of charm.

When the curtain of the second part of the first visit of the Beijing Circus to Tokyo (in the early sixties) went up and revealed a *second* curtain made entirely of jugglers standing on shoulders, filling the proscenium—all the hands and some of the legs juggling something.

A performance of the Nomura family of the Kyogen *Utsu-bozaru* (The Monkey-Skin Quiver), in which the monkey was played by a small child and the ensemble was of a perfection to draw tears.

The Great Black Current Tank at the Okinawa Exposition, where on either side, towering glass walls held the entire black current, simulated, with all of the fish, real, that are in it: shoals of tuna, fleets of dolphin, and armadas of whales, all circling, the ocean towering above.

A performance of *Hageromo* in Kanazawa, home of Noh, where the heavenly princess was a masked ninety-year-old man, whose every movement, every gesture, was that of a young, virginal, heavenly creature.

In the movies, lots: like the flight of the arrows in *Henry V* and its inspiration, the battle on the ice in *Alexander Nevsky;* the close-ups of the animals in *Au hazard, Balthazar;* Falconetti's face in *Jeanne;* the first glimpse backward over the length of Skull Island where we can see the distant great gate in *King Kong.*

Again a gap in the journals, this one four years—apparently no journals were compiled during this time. Much else, however, was written: *Viewing Film, A Taste of Japan, Tokyo Nights, Introducing Tokyo,* **and** *Public People, Private People.*

16 MAY 1988. Met Shulamith [Rubinfein] and Ed [Seidensticker] in front of the statue of Saigo at Ueno, and we went and ate blanched chicken *toriwasa* and pheasant *donburi*—though this was probably chicken as well. We are three legs of our four-legged Jane Austen Society (the fourth leg, Sheelagh [Cluny] is always now in London or Canada). After, we walked down Ameyokocho and Shulemith innocently asks what this place name means.

"It means 'Sweet American,' that's what it means," said Ed. "*Ame* is the contraction and it is homonymous with *ame*, the candy. The idea is that the Americans gave candy away after the war." "Oh, how sweet," said Shulamith with that girlish giggle she sometimes has. "Not at all," said Ed. "It is not a proper term. It is derogatory. It is like our calling them Jap for them to call us Ame."

This leads to other things and at the end of the meal we have not talked much about Jane. Later, over coffee, I wonder (to myself) just which of the characters we have come to resemble: Ed is Mr. Woodhouse with teeth; I fancy myself the witty and heartless Mr. Bennett; Shulamith, well, some-one very nice—maybe Elizabeth, grown older and minus Darcy; Sheelagh is Fanny's brother—hardly ever here.

23 MAY 1988. Reading Raymond Carver. Never had before. Liking him but suspicious of this. The stories are so laconic that I suspect formula. Have not, however, actually detected any. Certainly, I admire the brevity. As always, suc-cessful art inspires. I too want to write such stories, and think of a theme.

A man has a happy relationship based, on his part, on a natural passivity, and this continues on until another person starts a relationship with him. Passivity continues to the exclusion of the first person. Am obviously think-ing of me and the sergeant [Kiyota Kazuaki]. A naturally boyish youngest son's passivity allowed for a relationship that was not natural to him. Yet he drew from it things that sustained him—regard and knowledge. But then he was married, something his passivity also allowed—an arranged marriage that others wanted. And she is perfectly good, his wife. And his passivity extends. He neglects me. Despite knowledge missing, he takes the easy path, stays home. So what I had congratulated myself on discovering, his passiv-ity, becomes at the end something unwelcome. Told this way it doesn't seem much of a story, but the shape is nice. I turn it this way and that, admiring its symmetry. I think, however, I will have the story told by a woman. Will make the homo into non-marriage, make the non-homo into marriage. Can allow myself a bit of sentiment that way. [It became the short story "Ar-rangements."]

25 MAY 1988. Itami Juzo, famous director son of a famous director father. "Cut!" shouts Itami into his lapel mike, after the eighth take of the final scene of the second part of *A Taxing Woman* [*Marusa no Onna*]. He is wearing his black Chinese shirt, his slippers, his red scarf, his black fedora—emblems as necessary to image as is the constant cigarette, the continual cups of coffee, the hard candy he nibbles during shooting.

The script assistant confirms that this final scene consisted of six rehears-als and eight takes. "The first," says Itami, "was probably all right but I wanted to take one more to make sure and ended up doing eight. But that last one was all right too, I think." She agrees.

"Wasn't very economical though, was it?" he asks. Then, to me, "Money, money. So I work fast. This picture only took me fifty-four days. You save a lot of money that way."

Making money, that's one reason for making films. And saving money.

With Itami Juzo (in hat), 1988.

"That's the reason I star my wife in all my films. Want all the profits to stay in the family."

Making money is important. After all, Itami had had to mortgage everything he owned to make his first picture, *The Funeral.* He said, "I read that I would even have mortgaged my wife, had the banks wanted her."

The picture was successful, however, made money, and so he decided to become a full-time director. He hadn't always wanted to, however. He'd been an industrial illustrator, an essayist, a translator, a talk-show host, and an actor. It was only when he turned fifty that he became a director—like his father.

Itami Mansaku was one of Japan's most respected prewar directors, an innovative man who helped turn the Japanese period film into the humanistic expression that it for a short period became. In this he inspired an entire generation of postwar directors—Kurosawa Akira, Kobayashi Masaki, Uchida Tomu. He universalized the specifically Japanese, and in doing so he created films that were art.

He died when his son, Juzo, was thirteen. Left fatherless, raised by a mother of whom he later said "had no ability to bring up children," he moved from one profession to another. "I think I am about twenty years behind my generation," he somewhere wrote.

Becoming a director like his father brought him up to date. Though well known as an essayist and an actor, he was suddenly the film maker who had revived the movies in Japan. One of the first things he did with his newly earned money was to restore one of his father's films, the 1936 *Kakita Akanashi*.

Then he began consolidating his profession—making plans, making money. You had to make the audience want to come to the theater if you were going to show a profit. Making gentle fun of them, as in *The Funeral* and *Tampopo,* was one way.

This is because, as he explained, the viewer needs a surrogate; just as a child needs someone from outside the family to fully mature. What it needs is someone to dispute the family view and show another opinion.

He crunches a piece of hard candy. And this time, he says, in reference to the film he is now completing, the tax people don't get the money. This is because the hero, the wily leader of one of Japan's many new religions, has had all his illegal gold cast into Buddhist altar implements. The final scene shows him in his crypt, taunting the impotent tax officials.

"And all in just fifty-four days," he says. He can work so fast because of his system. While other directors are roaming the set and peering through the viewfinder, Itami sits quietly in the director's chair and looks into a television monitor, giving instructions through his lapel mike. This way, he says, he stays out of everyone's way and still, since the television camera looks directly through the camera's lens, can see everything the cameraman can. Handy, too, on a small set.

I peer inside. The gold-filled crypt is very small. The camera hung inside can be rotated. Inside too were the two actors—the hero and his pregnant girlfriend, and the cameraman—outside was the director. The scene on the small monitor was properly claustrophobic as the same actions were performed eight times.

Mikuni Rentaro, the head of the cult, had gleefully whipped off the covers, laughing maniacally, and displayed the gold. The pregnant girlfriend had reacted. Four times he flubbed his lines and once the camera ran out of film.

Itami did not lose his temper, nor even raise his voice. He crunched more candy. Smiling he turned me and said, "Stress." The reference was to when we had worked together on the English subtitles for *The Funeral* and he had first learned the meaning of the word—from me.

He had questioned every line of my work. And though he knows English, I know it better. "Now here you wrote 'for,'" he said, "but that is a preposition and prepositions are tricky. Wouldn't it be better if you had written 'to'? That's another preposition." All of this was in Japanese since, no matter how well he might think he knows English, he never uses it with a foreigner. The reference to stress was my outraged reaction to this.

The scripter shook her head. She thought he was referring to himself, and Itami was never stressed. Not at all like Kurosawa, or that monument to impatience, Mizoguchi Kenji. Nor much like his father.

26 SEPTEMBER 1988. Rain, more, again. This month has had one day of sunshine. The rest range from sprinkles to downpours. The Japanese, always prone to speak of the weather, usually with approval, are perturbed—and suspicious. Did we do this? We, with our exhausts, our chemicals, our hair spray? This, coupled with the discomfort. Walls sweating in the subway, niter in the passages, hot wet winds. We perspire under our umbrellas, and moths fly out of the closet. I find cockroaches in my sitting room. Usually only a few in the kitchen. A lady on the subway begins to complain even to me, ". . . and the backs fell, positively fell, right off my books." "And my piano is coming unglued," said a wet lady across the way. It is sure catastrophe when strangers start speaking to each other.

28 SEPTEMBER 1988. I always work on my own things in the morning, labor at making a living in the afternoon, and meet people or play in the evening. Day after day after day. Never get tired of it because each day is different, though the timings are about the same. Awake at seven, coffee, newspaper. Then shower and at work at desk by nine or before: right now it is the Oxford book on Japanese film. By noon, tired of this and lunch, in or out. Then making a living. Go to International House or go to Sogetsu, or go see films to do subtitles for, or go to the library to research an article. This can go on to six. Then I meet my friends, or go about looking for new ones. Usually home by eleven. Always in bed by twelve. Today was no different from other days.

29 SEPTEMBER 1988. Party. I am recognized. "Oh, aren't you . . . ?" "Yes, I am and who are you?" "Oh, no . . ." and then, "I just heard your lecture . . ." or, "I saw your picture in the paper . . ." or, "I saw your photo on the book jacket . . ." Why do none of these encounters ever turn into anything? I am ready. If people know who I am and come up and talk, they already know something about me. I like fame if this is what it is.

But, I would not like it if it got as large and dangerous as I saw it with poor Mishima, who used to have to cross streets to avoid crowds, or Kuroyanagi [Tetsuko], who gets quite nervous as people surround her on the street, smiling, well intentioned, but big, surrounding bodies nonetheless. I would not like that. But a few people here and there. . . .

Yet, they always leave me. I never leave them. I suppose they do not want to presume. I wish they would. We would have lots to talk about. Me.

I OCTOBER 1988. No, Japan has changed. What I thought never would—one of the reasons for spending my old age here—is gone, never to return. This is the possibility of meeting a stranger and making a friend. Right there, right then. Forever. Oh, meeting strangers is possible enough. Indeed all friends are initially strangers. But it is no longer possible to enter into that sudden intimacy that was once so much a part of the charm. The reason is that the attitude toward me, toward any foreigner, has changed.

It is because we are not needed any more. No one has any *use* for us. They do not see trips abroad in our eyes. These trips are something they can themselves afford. And there are so many of us. We have become common. And since Japan is rich now and the other countries are not, they need not imitate us.

I am speaking of my regretting imperialism, I know. I ought to rejoice that Japan is no longer subject to it, but I do not want to. It was too much fun being treated as someone quite special. And one no longer is. A foreign friend in speaking of this says, "Why, we might as well be living at home." I smile because it is amusing. Not he, he takes it seriously. Then looks for reasons. It is because he is getting old. Or it is because of fear of AIDS, which, of course, comes from foreign lands. But, it is not that. It is that the Japanese have outgrown us.

2 OCTOBER 1988. Sunday, a soft rain, but cooler now. Shinjuku, the streets shining, reflected umbrellas: pink, mauve, chartreuse—people in for the day. Country Japanese are fond of untoward colors. I see a boy with geranium-colored trousers. Day-tripping workmen often wear purple cummerbunds. Against the gray rainy cityscape these subtle colors shine and shimmer.

At Isetan I watch the quiet crowds. How well dressed everyone is now. More, how stylish. Not just the spikes and slashes of the young. Everyone else displays a kind of good taste—solid materials, well cut—the kind of taste you see in the Edo street scenes of Hokusai. Solid, plain, well-cut kimonos. Splashes of color here and there. And, I notice, as in the Hokusai, no faces. Is this because Japanese in crowds have never have had any? No, it is because in crowds we all have a kind of "faceless" expression. The face is there but it is not expressed. This is something Hokusai knew. One sees Japanese faces only when people are alone or where they are somewhere where they know each other.

3 OCTOBER 1988. A good long time now. He lies there in the center of the city, dying. Very old, very strong. Whoever would have thought that that skinny old man would be such a laster? And last he does, day after day—his doctors pumping blood into him as fast as it leaks out.

Hirohito has not a secret left. We not only know all about the rectal discharges, we even know their temperatures. An avid audience of about one hundred million people take in the enormous amount of information the media churns out—important TV broadcasts are interrupted to give us the latest non-news.

There are in addition hundreds who kneel in the drizzle in front of the gates of the Imperial Palace. They will probably catch their deaths themselves. And thousands who line up with umbrellas to sign the condolence books. I look at the line of colored umbrellas, which I see from the Press Club twenty floors high: a distant rainbow-tinted caterpillar in the drizzle.

There is some criticism of all this coverage. No private citizen, no other person, would be given it. And does this not mean some suspicious reversion to prewar thoughts? The Emperor is not a god. Why is he now treated as one? Right-wing militarism on its way back? Some think so. Leftist students are giving speeches at Ochanomizu Station. They warn of this. They do not want the right to overcome. They want the left to overcome.

I think the reason for this distasteful and massive public display of a single death is that for anyone over forty, the Emperor's life is bound up with their own. One mourns for lost youth as well. Another is that many Japanese always do the same thing at the same time, and it is an unusual person who will stand out against one of these mass movements.

Yet there are many such unusual people now. Not one person to whom I talk about the dying Emperor thinks proper the massive attention paid. Nor is anyone, including many of my contemporaries, upset by the coming death. Many make jokes. However, my friends are not arch-traditionalists or else they would not be my friends, so this probably proves little.

It suits many purposes, this crisis. The Diet uses it as excuse not to work. Major companies use it as excuse to avoid doing things they do not want to. Chiyonofuji, traditional sumo star, cancels a party out of deference. Itsuki Hiroshi, singer, cancels a wedding—but he is of Korean ancestry and so probably thought it safer to. Lots of cancellations. No fireworks here, no garden party there. I talked with someone on the phone who wanted me to write an article, and I said yes, but then she said, "Well, we haven't quite decided, there is this unfortunate Emperor thing." So even magazines are thinking what to print. Nothing too inflammatory, nothing too frivolous, nothing too foreign.

Me, I think this kind of mindlessness is as deplorable as it is human. I dislike any kind of joining—the Catholic Church, the Soka Gakkai, the Communist Party, or kneeling and praying for HIH. In my ideal world no one would pledge allegiance to anything.

I also notice a certain attitude. People sigh a lot. It is as though the Emperor is showing a lack of tact, of good taste, in being so long about it. Nonetheless I dread the days after the death. Certainly full national mourning—all for this frail, limited, stubborn little man. On the other hand I too can get a cheap thrill out of it. The longest reign in recorded history is about to end.

4 OCTOBER 1988. Walking down the street to International House—that annual odor. I remember the first time, many years ago. Since the street runs along a schoolyard I thought that bulging cesspools had overflowed, not stopping to consider that cesspools are long gone from central Tokyo. Then I noticed the squashed yellow splotches—crushed ginkgo nuts, and overhead a great yellow leafed ginkgo tree. I make a kind of haiku:

> *Oh the smell of shit.*
> *Ah, autumn is once more here.*

Why should the fruit smell of excrement? If it were spring and the blossoms smelled that way I could understand. It would attract the bugs and fertilize the tree. But in deep autumn there are no bugs about. And in the spring the smell of the blossoms is that of semen. What kind of tree is this?—semen in the spring, shit in the fall.

I remember the first time I was aware of the springtime smell. It was 1947 and I was in the courtyard of Engakuji in Kita-Kamakura, with Gene Langston, and we were spending the night at Dr. Suzuki's guest house, and Gene suddenly stopped, his nostrils twitching: "Amazing—it smells just like semen." And so it did.

5 OCTOBER 1988. Someone—who, Balzac?—said a man's character is to be disclosed by his library. Very well, let's see. In mine: the complete Jane Austen in the Folger Edition; all three novels of Lewis Carroll; all the poetry and a biography of Cavafy; all the short works of Kafka but none of the novels; some Henri Michaux, including *A Barbarian in Asia*; *Jules and Jim*; everything of Nagai Kafu in English; lots of Colette; historical fiction of Ibuse; short works of Naoya Shiga; Cocteau, all of the novels; everything in English of Borges; Sartre's biographical writings; Isherwood's *Berlin Stories*; collected Auden; collected Dylan Thomas stories; complete novels of Henry Green; lots of Marguerite Yourcenar (everything in English); lots of Susan Sontag; complete poems and prose of Elizabeth Bishop; *Sleepless Nights* of Elizabeth Hardwick; everything of Jimmy Merrill, etc. And that is only the fiction-poetry part.

There is a section given over to books on Japan including all my reference works. And a whole stack of film books, including my own. Space is a problem. I have to get rid of things. Recently exiled the Bible and the complete Shakespeare—on the shelves for decades and never read. But not thrown out. I am too sentimental (and superstitious) for that. Both from my mother—one (the Bible), nearly half a century ago. I keep them on a shelf with other discards. Not the shelf in the entryway however. Those discards are for people to pick up and carry home.

16 OCTOBER 1988. Sunday. To the Kabuki with Eric. Some modern trash, and two classical dances. One of them is *Yasuna* with Baiko. Though a "national treasure," Baiko still looks like a lady searching for a golf ball. In the other, *Sagimusume*, Jakuemon, his face often under the knife, looks odd but then he is supposed to be someone half a bird. But the hoyden way he carries on is not nearly elegant enough for this dance.

The interesting play was *Moritsuna Jinya*, the single act surviving of a much, much longer work and now a "Kabuki classic." As I watched its reprehensible story of a man quite cheerfully sacrificing his little boy, killing him because of loyalty to the lord, I was again struck by how wonderfully acted it all was. Takao as Moritsuna was immaculate. When he identified the (wrong) severed head he went through the canon of twelve emotions. And it was all there. It was like a great violinist. The violinist is only doing Paganini to be sure. And I realized that one of the most moving and touching things about Kabuki is that this talent is lovingly squandered on junk.

There is, however, a difference. Even Verdi and a clutch of fine singers cannot make one sympathize with poor Gilda. But at the Kabuki there were sniffles as the little boy spilled his guts and kept right on piping (children's Kabuki lines are all on one note—like the oboe sounding its A, for hours) and took as long to die as Camille. But people believed, for a time at any rate. I didn't, but I too was moved, though in a different way. This presentation of emotions (rather than the representation of them) was moving as a fine carpenter or master stone carver at work is moving. I am moved by the artistry of how the thing is done, not by the thing itself.

18 OCTOBER 1988. Gave a talk at the Press Club. Talked about "Being a Foreigner" and was listened to by a hundred or so of different nationalities and a few races. Many Japanese. I have talked in public for so many years now that I can tell what people will take and what not, what they will laugh at, what they will shake their heads over, or nod at. And, finally, I know how to be evangelical. Christ lost a good witness when he lost me.

But do I believe any of what I say? I do at the time, I know that. It seems such a good idea. But in the early morning hours when I wake, wake with such doubts that it awakens me, then I do not believe any of it. My heart beats like something trying to get out, and I am certain of nothing. Yet just hours before, there I was, certain of everything.

19 OCTOBER 1988. Sitting here all wired up. Electrodes various places on my chest, wires running into a tape recorder I must carry on a strap over my shoulder, complete with a special large switch on a separate wire that I must push to punctuate the tape when I "feel funny"—doctor's term, *chotto okashiku nareba*. Have not felt funny once. Having the machine on has obviously inhibited the unruly organ. Actually, the only time it ever really acted up was five years ago, when it leaped for hours like a frantic fish—a frantic frozen fish, for my chest was as though filled with crushed ice. This I thought, is angina pectoris. And so it was—my first and so far last. Still, routine tests have located something *okashii* going on. Hence the wire-job. Had it five years ago and felt funny wearing it, everyone stared so. Now, half a decade of handbags, shoulder bags, earphones, and straps have intervened. I walk about today and no one notices, except an acquaintance at the porno where I had gone to stimulate the organ. And he says, "Hey, what a cute litte tape walkman you got there. . . ."

> **From now on Richie no longer used his journals as sources for other works and became more interested in them for themselves. They began to have a purpose all of their own. One of the reasons was that he was himself experiencing life in a more intense way—time was passing; friends were dying. The evanescence of which he had often spoken was now apparent. He thus wanted more than ever to leave some account of what things (including himself) had been**

like. This led both to a closer observance of the world outside, and to a deeper, more frank investigation of himself and his motives.

12 MAY 1989. To see Bando Tamasaburo at the Embujo in an Ariyoshi adaptation, *Furu Amerika ni Sode wa Nurasaji*. It is Shinpa, but a comedy: Osono works in a Yokohama brothel: it is 1861 so the girls are divided between those for Japanese and those for foreigners, and one of the "Japanese" is claimed by a foreigner—so she kills herself. This at least is the story put out. People praised, anti-foreign *ronin* come to marvel; Osono becomes something of a priestess in this new cult but eventually goes too far and the entire edifice collapses.

Tamasaburo plays Osono in a cool, big sister manner, half tough *mizusho-bai* mama, half whore with a heart of gold. A performance, always hovering on the edge of camp, never falling over. Playing the cynical "priestess," he is at his best, in complete control until he comically loses it and must then retreat into "femininity." He knowingly impersonates that male invention and does it so well that he shows only those seams he wants to show.

Afterward I am taken backstage to call. He is in his mauve dressing gown, looking strangely Nell Gwyn—it is the decollete. All makeup off, he also has a scrubbed, very young look about him. "It isn't really Shinpa, you know. I don't think you'd like Shinpa—too weepy. This is a comedy." Talking on about Shinpa, with which he alternates Kabuki, he spoke of Izumi Kyoka and wondered why the West was not more familiar with him. I said it was true, they only knew *Taki no Shiraito* thanks to Mizoguchi, and *Demon Pond* thanks to Tamasaburo. "Well, they ought to know more. Look, people know Tanizaki and Kawabata. Why not Izumi." Why not indeed, we all wondered.

Tamasaburo is, like many actors, concerned to make an impression of seriousness. He wants to talk about ideas, as though to prove he is capable of them. At the same time it is impossible for him to hide a frivolous charm. This showed in a small contretemps at the beginning.

He had asked about my small role in Teshigahara's film *Rikyu*, of which he had heard. Then, with no transition, asked, "First time?" I, not unnaturally, thought we were speaking about me. "And not very good," I said. At which he gave a high, infectious laugh, and looked at me with apparent amusement. Then I realized that he meant was it my first time at Shinpa. Straightened out, the conversation continued but I had had a glimpse into the charm of an actor whose instant reaction was to disarm with laughter.

I sat on the fake Louis XVI petit point until the conversation stopped for a second and then, before it began again, stood up and thanked him. That is the way to behave in the green room. Otherwise the host becomes one's captive. Then, for the first time, he became effeminate, the good hostess seeing off her guests. Life is made of such roles—most men are male at hello and their mothers at goodbye.

14 MAY 1989. Go to get a haircut. My barbershop, the Ogawa in Shinjuku's "My City," is expensive enough that it is grand. Boys in attendance to bring things and take them away at a gesture from the head barber. Barbers calling each other *sensei*, flourishing with hot towels, or in convergence over a difficult head of hair.

While my *sensei* snipped and combed and I faced the large mirror and watched the goings on behind me, I was reminded me of the Utamaro, an even more expensive bath cum brothel in Kawasaki in the old days. One was met there too and bowed at, and the girls were forever having conferences, and probably calling each other *sensei*.

It was most striking, this similarity, when the new customer was brought in. Here at the Ogawa there was the same subservient leading gesture, the same fuss getting the patron seated, the same airs and graces with towels and scents. And the same expression. The girls had no choice over whom they got, and one saw a wry smile or an almost invisible shrug. Looking in the mirror too, I now saw the same thing. A barber made a small moué while escorting in a thug with an unkempt *punchi pama*, that permanent wave so notoriously difficult and time-consuming to set.

16 MAY 1989. Dinner with Brad Leithauser. We talk about Elizabeth Bishop, under whom he studied, and Elizabeth Hardwicke, whom he knows and whom I would like to know. ("She sort of takes you over of an evening, you know, hands on shoulders. Once my mother was along, and so I had two of them and infantilized at once.") And Robert Lowell. ("Knew him only when he was practicing to be old. 'Could any of you young people help me find a taxi?' sort of thing. And they told me what kind of commanding lion he had been and I could not put the two together.")

Leithauser now lives in Iceland. When he was in Japan he went to the Oki Islands. He likes that elemental landscape. It shows in his poetry. Strong lines, and few. Like that poem about looking down from a plane on one course at a ship he had once taken on another. I tell him about Marguerite Yourcenar. We both like to talk about people. Something we share with James Merrill, who is a friend of both of ours and, indeed, the reason we have met. We talk about reviews. He talks about how the bad ones he gets are crushing.

I wait for indication that he has read mine of his first novel. This does not come. I realize that he had not read it. Shall I tell him about it, send him a copy? Absolutely not. If he doesn't know, that is good. And I know me. Now that I know him, I would not have written the way I did, even though the novel didn't seem very good.

17 MAY 1989. Went to see Imamura's *Black Rain* again. This time, knowing what would happen, remembering the power, I am relatively unswayed and can pay attention to the construction. Before, immersed in the story I did not realize just how many doors are opened and shut, just how many windows are peered through. The interior architecture encloses and delineates this film. As in Ozu, the fact that domestic architecture confines also serve to shape these people. How free is the great outside, the paddy—and the big fish jumping. Perhaps a symbol, but more a big happy fish. No doors and windows for him. And the sick girl forgets herself in wonder at this great jumping fish. This is what art is made of, I think—a concern for parallels and balance, enclosure and freedom—contrast, opposites, but not many. Just two or three, enough to make a container to hold the strongest of emotions.

18 MAY 1989. Lectured the Harvard students on Japanese film aesthetics at International House. As always (I do this every year), they trouped in looking positively post-atomic, with tangled hair and Arab slipovers and Chinese blankets. And as always, they shortly revealed themselves as open, intelligent, interested, and imaginative—perfect students, at least perfect for me. I felt every word was landing on ready loam.

Also, as always, I feel phony. Not in what I say, that is solid enough, but in the little affectations of a populist egalitarianism that I display. I find myself using the colloquial, making depreciative asides, and demolishing popular agreed-upon demolition sites. Either they are too young to detect this act of mine, or else they are too polite to mention it. On the other hand, if I did not do this what would I do?

20 MAY 1989. Took John Ashbery and his friend David Kermani to see the Edo Shiryokan. Noticed that Ashbery shuffled and, since I knew he drank, thought it might be drink. We passed a toilet and he wanted to use it. A block later another toilet, which he used. On the way back he asked me if I thought there might be a toilet somewhere. I said yes, up the street. Then David said that perhaps that gas station over there had one. They did. John used it and then, alone with his friend, I learned why.

Almost eight years ago Ashbery contracted some rare and strange infection that polluted, if that is the word, the spinal fluid. As the toxic levels rose, his legs became paralyzed, then his hands. The lungs were stilled, and next the heart. Unconscious, he was taken to a hospital and pronounced deceased. Turned over, an autopsy was begun. Thinking he was dead they took little care, but opened up his spine to have a look. Then it was noticed that he was alive. So he was sewed up and the doctor said he was living, but would always be a vegetable.

Yet, several weeks later he was sitting up, then eating, then talking, and now walking about on a Japan tour reading his poems. However, there has been an amount of neural damage. Hence the shuffle. He wears special pads in his trousers just in case, but has become adept and rarely needs them.

Walking along I look at him. That fine beaked profile, those large intelligent eyes. Back from the grave by, apparently, iron will power. I find this admirable. And his continuing with his life, his ignoring this, his getting on with his work.

23 MAY 1989. Awakened from sleep, three in the morning, by the cries of fire engines, as they rounded my corner and ran screaming into the maze of wooden houses that is Yanaka where I live. I raised the blind and looked out. There in the middle distance was a tree of flame, shooting into the air, capped with black swirling smoke.

Flowers of Edo, what such fires used to be called—a blossom of growing crimson on the deep gray of the nocturnal city. And I felt a deep dread at the awfulness of that devouring element. Far away as it was—it took me ten minutes to walk there the following morning—and safe as I was, still I felt the cold of an unreasoning fear.

In the morning I found where the fire had been. Just off the road, back in a warren. Four houses, each very close to the other. Just charred supports now, the whole front of one burned to a crisp, like a deformed face. Inside, one whole room exposed. And there was the bookcase. And all the books were carbonized.

Over it all the desolate smell of burned wood and wet ash. Puddles still on the ground from the firemen's rain. These pretty wooden houses are the reason I live in Yanaka, old Edo, and I have often looked at them from my windows. But also I knew last night that I am somewhat safer living in this ugly, modern, tiled and more or less fireproof apartment.

26 MAY 1989. I go to see Gene Langston in the hospital. Still in a bad way.

Hole in his throat, trouble breathing, unable to eat, bone-thin. Today, however, though still thin, still with hole, still on respirator, he is better I am told.

I try to imagine it. In a country hospital, on his back, unable to read, fighting every inch of the way—toward what? Not to health—simply fighting to reach some level where he may continue to live. He is alert (no brain damage from the time he was shut down for hours) and—sign of health, perhaps—extremely impatient. Since he is weak, he is brusque. Nurse came in with her invariable thermometer and for the first time in all our years together I saw Gene rude to the help. He ignored her.

How good that made me feel. As though health is burgeoning in him, making him selfish. He must offer all of his energy to simply getting one thing done now. He has no time for niceties. And he knows it and he does not apologize for it. Also he is finally being fed—a nose tube. And he does seem less thin than he was. He wants to renew his International House membership. He has made up his mind. He wants to live.

29 MAY 1989. Roppongi is taking itself seriously: it is all "now" with post-modern architecture (the buildings chromed, mirrored, looking like big cigarette lighters or enormous lipsticks) and mottoes: "High Town Roppongi" is the slogan embossed on the overhead at the crossing. The veneer stops short, looks tacky. A striving for Trad but Mod. Traditional is on the sign of the Red Lobster. Established in 1988, it says. Modern is everywhere else. Particularly the people. Lots of dark glasses on the boys, and wet-looking clothes and hanging-bangs haircuts. A touch of punk but not much—a few pink locks, a few Mohawks.

The foreigners are all models. Pale eyes, disdainful lips. Forever chattering with each other. Both sexes fashionably androgynous. Cow-like, they wander around in designer finery and get together and have bread fights in respectable restaurants. The cops are very heavy on the place (nascent drug scene). I remember when Roppongi was a crossing for streetcars and that was about it.

31 MAY 1989. International House lecture by Don Hardy. Lots of people including a tattoo *sensei* from Yokohama. (No disclosure after the talk: both were ready, but it did not work out that way, such things taking calculated spontaneity.) Lots of women. But then women are much more at ease with their bodies than men are. Men drive theirs like reluctant beasts. Women lie down with theirs.

Good talk, lots of slides. Later, private room at the Chinese restaurant where Frank [Korn] had taken us. Chizuko [Korn] had seen nothing like this, was frankly curious. Don stood by the remains of beef and oyster sauce with his shirt off, shorts pulled down, hand over privates, while we gazed at his Benten and Kannon. Both women (the other was Chris [Blasdel]'s wife, Mika) plainly wanted to touch, but did not. The call of the flesh is strong. That of painted flesh doubly so, because it is a double vision: the picture and the skin on which it lies. The eye is not enough for the tattoo.

5 JUNE 1989. Met with Ed Seidensticker at the foot (feet?) of Saigo in Ueno. He was unwell and looked it. Bright red. It was the climb he said. Must sit down. After a while turned dead white. Then, slowly, he regained a more human coloring. I, always the busybody, began diagnosing—told him he was too fat, which is true but no one wants to hear that. I suggested exercise or less eating or (pause) *drinking*. This doubly unwished since he has such problems staying on the wagon. So we were, thanks to both of us, ready for a squabble.

He began on the Japanese, "these people," guessing that I would not like him to do so. And so, feeling outspoken, I told him that he really hated himself, not these people, and that he should acknowledge the depths of his self-loathing. This initially drew silence—as it would. Then he turned to me and solemnly said, "We must never again speak of this if we are to remain friends."

The expected attack came later when he had gotten over the jolt. "Actually, you know, Donald, you are the deluded one. You will not allow yourself to be furious with these people. Yet, you know at heart you are." By this time, however, the hurt was mastered and he was smiling. "Oh, dear," he complained merrily, "we have nothing more to talk about."

After the meal he wanted to go right home and did so. "But you know," he said upon parting. "We do not really disagree. Not *really* really." I at once agreed. And as we walked along he, encouraged, even had a few things to say about "these people" before we parted.

6 JUNE 1989. Big JAL party at the Imperial. How old everyone looks. I see a man there every year, and each year he has so aged that this string of parties seems in retrospect Jaques's ages of mankind—soon sans teeth, sans everything. Me too I suppose. I dress "young" however. My blue summer coat, navy Countess Mara shirt, pale blue spotted Hermes tie—a natty sight. Tom Chapman said, "My god, Donald, you look like something out of a fifties road company of *Guys and Dolls*." This pleased me more than not.

Ed there. He turned to our acquaintances and said, "Oh, Donald says the most awful things about one. We are quarreling." Then gave me a big smile.

25 JUNE 1989. Dinner at the Korns'. [Marian Korn had died, 24 February 1987, and Frank had remarried.] Talk turns to underwear and the playboy from Hokkaido opposite me informs that in kendo neither underwear nor support of any sort is ever used. The swordsmen are nude and hanging under their indigo trappings. At further questions from Chizuko [Korn] it transpires that the *kendoka* achieves erection during the moment before strike. Playboy demonstrates (to a point) by raising his hands as though a sword, frowning, puffing out his cheeks. "Does this not get in the way of the match?" someone wonders. "No, not at all. The point of the sword and the point of the penis are in alignment." "What happens then?" asked Tami, a very pretty girl whose profession I have not as yet ascertained. "Why," says our informant, "at the moment of striking, the metaphorical blood streams from the enemy and the literal blood retreats from the engorged organ." The men at table are inclined to take this as literally true and to find it somehow complimentary. The women on the other hand find it unlikely and scoff. Observes one, "With no underwear, it is liable to come right out of the kendo gear altogether." "Yes, so it does, so it does," the Hokkaido playboy cries. Bursts of merriment.

26 JUNE 1989. Dinner with Zushiden. He is forty-nine now—and it has been nearly thirty years since he and I were together in Otsuka. He's still a big, good-looking boy from Kagoshima.

He married early and then had various problems. He, handsome, widely admired, married a woman who would have nothing to do with him. She kept putting him off. Said he was too big. She could never, etc. Finally he went to a doctor who, in the Japanese manner, advised determination. Determination is nothing that the good-natured Zushi could easily summon, but he tried. And tried again and again.

Three children were the result. But now another problem. The first one has turned out bad. Like a cuckoo chick in the swallow's nest. Where could she have come from? Wild, glue-sniffing, promiscuous, insubordinate—still living at home, now twenty and not speaking to her parents.

However, just recently something nice happened to him. A long time ago when in high school he had this girlfriend he really liked. He was her first, and she his. Then he came to Tokyo, to university, and she married and went to LA and had kids, got divorced, got married again, became a widow, got married again—and looked up Zushi in the current high school graduate directory (Japan keeps these things up to date) and called him.

Then she came to see him. "And it was as though all those years had never existed," he said, as though in awe. "I didn't recognize her but she somehow recognized me. And we had dinner and it was just like always, and so we went to a hotel." Pause. "And guess what hotel we went to—the Urashima!"

And that great boyish laugh of his. [The hotel was named after Urashima Taro, a folk figure who, like Rip Van Winkle, came back from a period of enchantment and found himself old and everything changed.] Day after tomorrow he is going to Kagoshima and will again meet her. They will walk where they walked hand in hand three decades ago. I said it was like an English movie. "No," he said, "it's like a Japanese movie."

29 JUNE 1989. I go to see the Teshigahara *Rikyu*, the rough-cut version, no music yet. Very pretty—but on this viewing my major interest was

With Teshigahara Hiroshi on the set of Rikyu, *1989.*

myself. There I am in my surplice, my hat, my mustache—the head of the Portuguese mission. Astonishing resemblance to my paternal grandfather. Paternal grandfather in drag. How old I look, how awful—all the usual reactions to self suddenly revealed.

But what else I notice is that the editing has resulted in a credible performance. I am a stupid church father, but well intentioned. Just what the director wanted, I guess. Certainly my idea of playing a cynical worldly Jesuit is not apparent. Instead, an old child, silly but pleasant. A nice, understated comic performance that I did not know I was giving. [The entire scene is given in the "Hitomu Yamazaki" section of *Public People, Private People*.] And again, how strange the gulf between what you feel and what you are—what you show and what others see.

30 JUNE 1989. Showed *The Izu Dancer* at the International House, the Gosho

1933 silent version. Weak film, contrived, stupid added plot about a gold mine, travesty of the Kawabata novel. But in back of all of this—how astonishingly beautiful the Izu peninsula was half a century ago. Something then rarely noticed. I took it for granted in the forties and fifties, when it was still beautiful. It certainly isn't now. And so I gazed at this scratched, faded, black and white image and saw Eden.

4 JULY 1989. Murray Sayles called. Wanted permission to give my number to the *London Tatler*. What on earth for? "Well, they are doing a series on people who know everyone, in each city as it were, you know." No, I did not know. "Oh, you know. Like Harold Acton in Florence. And so I told them that you are their man in Tokyo."

Me? The Harold Acton of Tokyo? The way one must appear from the outside! Murray sees me as this. I look like this. Maybe I *am* this. But I never thought so before. And I never felt so until now, this very moment. The Harold Acton of Tokyo. Not a bad ring to it.

12 JULY 1989. Dentist. He took out the root, stump and all (prying, with something like a can opener), and it hurt. Home, aching, took a nap, then woke up and did not want to stay in. Pain better, and I felt I needed some recompense. Hunting around would have taken energy better spent in convalescing, and finding something would have been, given the great bloody hole in my lower jaw, both unhygienic and unaesthetic. So I decided on a cheap, dumb movie.

With unerring taste I chose *Indiana Jones and the Last Crusade*. It is energetic to no end, active to no result, and divertingly brainless. What with novelty all long gone, it is tired replay. Now no reference (the Comics, the Movies) seems real any longer. It is a walk-through, a staged rerun. Watching it is like being locked in with an over-active kid. The picture starts with Boy Scouts and never ages. It can't, for it is the creation of the two richest adolescents in the world: Lucas and Spielberg. They are very active in acting out their concerns. Again, a thing about fathers. That is where the love story is, too. Women, we cannot trust, any of 'em, ever. And sure enough the blonde is lost down a crack in the earth. But done with no knowing irony. One feels that Steve/George truly believe. The Power is With Them.

Not here so much. The film has just opened and the theater is half empty. It is not that young Japanese (all on dates) are above this. It is perhaps not brainless enough to draw. At any rate, not new enough. After all, their mothers probably went (on a date) to see the first of them, the mighty *Jaws*.

For me, just the thing. I was anesthetized for two hours, deafened by the

Richard Strauss score that fits the Nazi antics so well and makes me wonder if they are still villains. One wonders further when Harrison Ford is forced to say: "Oh, Nazis, I just *hate* those guys." Formerly this statement of dislike would not have been necessary. It could have been taken for granted. But now the Nazi are like the Comanche. You say you hate them, but you love to watch the scalping. Much set up by the viewing, came home, slept like a child.

18 AUGUST 1989. Chizuko Korn's birthday. Very lively, with everyone working quite hard, in the manner of successful Japanese parties. Much badinage about the centerpiece, a structure of chestnuts. From talk of these (*kuri*) to talk of squirrels (*risu*) and then the putting of them together—*kuri to risu*, which is, of course, Japanese for clitoris.

Wordplay is always popular at parties, and this was an enormous hit. The language is so proper that any hint of impropriety (even a medical term, Latin strained through English) is welcome. Also, most of the women had been in the *mizushobai* or are else emancipated enough to imitate it. Biggest hit was the stout Lio, hair slicked back, in a pin-stripe suit with white shirt and necktie. She threw back her head and chortled while her friend, older but more frilly, tittered at the other end of table.

Later Mr. Soda, the playboy from Hokkaido, kept telling us how sumo wrestlers force their testicles back into their bodies before their bouts. Then he insisted upon standing up and (through his trousers) demonstrating their probable route.

On June 4, 1988, Richie met Choi Dae-Yung in Seoul. It was a friendship that has remained to this day.

21 AUGUST 1989. I am here at my desk typing away when I get an early morning phone call from [Choi] Dae-Yung in Korea. Sounds in the same room. He actually was until last week, having spent two weeks with me here. Full of his plans—one more year as soccer coach, then a sports store. Is near thirty now, must be thinking of the future. His English is better, a year ago there was none.

But I wish it were much better still. His ghost is in the room with me, and all we have is words. I think of Proust's muses of the switchboard. We no longer have switchboard girls; we have microchips. But still there is this medium, this curtain of ether. Communicating with the dead must be something like the telephone.

Also striking is the coincidence of the call. I was just now writing about him, writing Earle Ernest, who is curious about someone who has come to mean so much to me. "You asked about Dae-Yung," I write:

> What he did before me and besides soccer? Well, he was born twenty-nine years ago in Pusan and had an ordinary childhood until he was ten, when his mother died. His father remarried and in three years was dead himself. He had married unwisely, because the new wife took everything and turned the orphaned Dae-Yung out on the streets. There he made a kind of living— paperboy, milk-boy, and ice-boy—until an uncle took pity and brought him into his home and sent him to school.
>
> Dae-Yung worked hard in school, particularly at sports for which he had an aptitude, one so strong that by the time he was sixteen he was school soccer star, and by eighteen was voted best high school player in all South Korea. After his military training he went to university and was star of the team. He was on TV; his picture was on sports magazine covers.
>
> Then another setback. Playing a game with Australia, he was hit in the back by a ball and injured. This led to a series of operations. He spent his twenty-second and twenty-third years on his back in a cast looking at the ceiling. His stepmother visited him once, to ask for money. Finally recovered, he was too old to be a soccer star, and though exercise brought back his strength, it could not bring back time lost. When he was twenty-six he was offered a coaching post in a small mountainside high school. This he took, and this is where he is now. During all of this time he, in the manner of sportsmen, devoted himself to his sport and nothing else. He had had a girlfriend for a time, and he had had sex with her when he was eighteen or so. Also like most Korean young men, he went to the whorehouses, where he found that his staying power made him popular.
>
> He was also popular with his teammates and with older men, several of whom made passes. These he rejected, but some persevered. This had the result of making Dae-Yung secretive about his private life, his real address, his telephone number, etc. Then came me.
>
> Due to the several mistimed and misinformed occurrences

Choi Dae-Yung, 1989.

that marked our meeting, I accidentally overwhelmed him. I also demonstrated that someone could like him, could even love him, and yet not threaten him. This was, apparently, the first time for him to experience this. So he found a place for me. I filled a need. I became the long-missing parent, and he has begun to address me as though I indeed were. It has been over two years since we first met.

Dae-Yung now shakes his head and says he has the kind of looks that women do not like and that men do. This is probably true. He says we fit well, a good combination. And so we do. He also says he wants us to always be together. And so we may. And all of his history is merely what I have been told. I have no proof of any of it. I write an address said to be his uncle's and the mail is given him; I have no phone number; I have never met one friend of his; I have no reason for believing him other than his word, his character, and the complete consistency of his history in all of its varied tellings to me. I complained once. And he nodded and looked sad and said he knew, but I must believe him, because it is true. So I will believe him. I keep remembering Psyche and Eros, and how it ended.

22 AUGUST 1989. Invitational premiere at Sogetsu Kaikan of *Rikyu*. [Teshigahara] Hiroshi made a speech about cultural history; Mikuni [Rentaro], now all hirsute (head, mustache, beard) after months of shave-pated Rikyu, talked about cultural history; Yamazaki [Tsutomu], granny glasses, all crooked from a recent bout with Richard III, talked about cultural history.

Audience was *tout* Tokyo. This meant a spattering of royalty—one prince, one princess, the cultural ones—and lots of "media personalities." No government people—these are never out unless the event is in a communist capital, or Washington, D.C.

Issey Miyake looking cast in copper, all red-brown skin and wire-stiff hair. Has not aged a wrinkle in twenty years. Asakura Setsu talking about the new production of *Tosca* she is doing, and about Ninagawa Yukio with whom she had a fight and out on whom she walked. Is pleased he has lost much luster. So he has, without her sets. Takemitsu Toru told me how he got that grand endless chord to accompany Rikyu in the boat: synthesizers, organs, and lots of celli. Akiyama Kuniharu and his wife, [Takahashi] Aki—who has now done the complete piano Satie. I remember him as a pale, slim youth. Now he is mustached, fattish, red. He has kept his enthusiasm, however. Inside of him sits the youngster who thirty years ago, on this very ground, pushed and pulled the Sogetsu film program into shape.

Many people I do not know. Women in modish hats with brilliant eyeliner smiles. Lots of men in Issey shirts and unruly hair. Rather strange buffet: sake in bamboo containers and little things on bamboo skewers. But then bamboo is Hiroshi's material. He has made it his own—as in the last scene of this movie.

Invested head of the Sogetsu school, starting from the shadow of his father, Hiroshi not only stepped out, he also has made it even stronger than his father did. He heads that enormous school, which must be something like heading the Pentagon, makes sure it makes money, and makes certain it does not look silly.

And for his premiere he can command the fashionable world of this capital. I remember ten years ago when he was very unhappy, having to give up film, pottery, himself. Now he is secure—no, serene. He can leave the bureaucracy long enough to make a film, and that is something.

24 AUGUST 1989. A walk with Eric along the new esplanade made on both sides of the Sumida River. The river laps right up to the steps. Both of us agree that the city fathers have, in this instance, spent our money wisely.

But how different everything is. Not just the steps and the esplanade. I have been in Tokyo off and on for over forty years now (and Eric for longer) and we have seen the city change. It has become larger and taller and—strangely—cleaner, or at any rate less cluttered. But the former clutter was human. In this new post-modern capital of planned cityscapes, the lack of clutter is in-human.

We look at the complex of towers rising from the Mukojima end of Azuma Bridge: a public housing construction, the multi-story Asahi Beer Building (shaped like a glass of that beverage, with the froth made of glass hexagonals and flashing lights), a disco on the top and an

With Eric Klestadt in Matsue.

enormous, black granite beer hall with a with a great Miro-like flame-shaped excrescence on the roof. With that in the neighborhood, the neighborhood has to change.

Eric had walked through Asakusa to meet me at Kaminarimon and complains at the extent of the gentrification. All artificial old-Japan now. One can tell by the number of girls dressed in cute camping clothes who time-travel. They run down from Harajuku to see olde Nippon. All of these painfully renovated *yakitoriya* and noodle shops must be losing money. In the evening no one is there. Everyone is back in Harajuku. The new Asakusa is an empty, barren place, expensively masquerading as what it once was.

25 AUGUST 1989. [Numata] Makiyo over for dinner. He is twenty-eight now— I met him five years ago. Has not much changed though his circumstances certainly have. If I were to have to choose a spokesman and paradigm for his age, it would be Makiyo. He is quintessential.

After only a bit more than a year he has made himself a company, one with branches in Kyushu and L.A., employs a number of people, is making a very good profit (took his whole family for a stay in Hawaii this summer), and hopes to continue to go straight up.

This is because he has that ability to do only one thing at a time and to do

DONALD RICHIE

Numata Makiyo.

it as hard as he can. When I met him it was soccer. After that it was English. And now it is real estate. There is nothing else to his life other than the reigning subject, and all of his considerable energy is devoted solely to it.

If you want something badly enough you can do anything. I have suspected this for a time and Makiyo proves it. The problem is wanting something, anything, badly enough.

Of course it is America he is buying large chunks of, and it is Japan that he is "developing." In a way he has joined the other side—but then he never left it. And he is candid, boyish, decent, fair.

He brings me his wedding pictures—I wanted them to add to his three volumes in my photo collection. Add and conclude it turns out. Just right—the last two pages will hold all the new pictures.

28 AUGUST 1989. Early morning, waking. Why is this the lowest point of the day? Many apparently wake up depressed. Byron writes about awakening to the dumps. Why must the mind wake up to worry something, like a dog worries a bone, first thing? Is it that we wake up sane and screaming and that then comforting lies and customs return to us our living shroud? Or is it that we wake up inchoate beasts, and that sanity then comes with coffee and crumpet to make us ourselves? A friend of mine wakes up to suicide every morning, he says. I believe him. I wake up questioning life in a manner as profound as I ever get.

29 AUGUST 1989. Took a walk along the Sumida and there sitting on a bench in a new cap was Morikawa. We were equally surprised. Over two years ago we had said goodbye in Asakusa and he was off to a new job in Nagasaki where he was born. He is in *Public People, Private People* (under his own family name), and though I left lots out (including his real first name) the picture is substantially him.

One of the details I left out was that I financed the trip south so that he could get a good job. I mention this suppressed information now because upon seeing me he took off the new cap, stood up, bowed, and said, as family members do upon their return: *Tadaima*.

He was mindful that I had provided the train ticket and might be thinking that he ought have stayed where I helped put him. When he was assured that I did not, in fact, think this, he then explained. He had really gone there. But after two years in the capital he just couldn't take small town life any more. And after having learned to laze around in the big city, the nine-to-five construction job he was stuck in (diversions were TV, manga, and the attentions of a bar girl whom he really did not like all that much) seemed impossible. So he talked with his dad who said, well you got to do what you want to, and that is fine if you don't hurt anyone doing it, and so he came back. Just three days ago. He had lazed around the big city; been surprised at all the changes (most of all, the higher prices), and just yesterday landed himself a job.

He remains cheerful, optimistic, not changed a bit. Then he said he was a little hard up. And since he did not mean money, I was happy to oblige.

30 AUGUST 1989. Went in the back of Shinjuku Station, east side, and there were the pushers busy with their wares—uppers and downers and stimulant drugs. They would be serving out heroin if they could, but they can't. Busy shifting supplies from one coin locker to another. I know some of them by sight now—ill-favored, rat-like faces. Then, in the corridor, I saw a couple of plainclothes cops. They were busy walking a youth toward a box. I followed. Inside the police box in front of the station they pushed him in, and in the back room, with all the doors open, began cuffing the lad about the head.

I stood and watched. Since I was foreign and hence uncomprehending, I was not driven away. In the same way, the pushers had worked right in front of me. The boy was cuffed in that offhand, exasperated big brother way that Japanese cops cultivate. I am sure he deserved it, had done something wrong.

At the same time, just in back of the station the criminals were unloading their drugs, and those thugs deserved the cuffing more than did the naughty boy.

After I had stared my fill I got on the subway and came home.

1 SEPTEMBER 1989. Morikawa was early, so was I. He was sitting there on the bench, still in his new cap and beside him a bag with his belongings in it. Tokyo had not proved welcoming. "Just two years and everything is changed." What had changed in particular was the method of hiring laborers. It has been consolidated. This means that, as in any kind of local distribution, so many middlemen have stepped in that no one makes much money. As a commodity, labor—like any product—has been ratified, which means that companies no longer use expensive labor brokers. They prefer to organize their own laboring forces. "So you either belong or you don't." And someone new from down country doesn't. Further problem is the number of foreign workers in Japan—Chinese, Thais, Filipinos. They are made to do the worst jobs for the worst pay. Any unconnected Japanese must now start on that level. "Lots of middle-aged Koreans too—with no jobs." What to do? "Well, tomorrow morning I am going to get up early and go to the labor union. I am not going to be fussy." And as for tonight: "Well, I thought maybe you could put me up."

I did—the Asakusa hotel, clean rooms, air-con, TV, a little window to slip the money in, no questions asked. Lying on the futon we talked about Kyushu and then he said, "But no matter what, I learned one real lesson there. I am a city boy. I got to come back here. Back to Tokyo."

After a while it was midnight, time for me to go home. We talked about how to meet again. He did not know where he was going to be, but would probably go to the country to work and get some money together before he returned to Tokyo. We finally settled on a method which does not seem likely but which somehow always works. We agreed to meet on that bench some Saturday night around eight in the evening after New Year's.

6 SEPTEMBER 1989. In the subway, no smoking allowed, I spot a smoker. When this occurs I am like a game dog at sight of a pheasant. Go, stare, and would bark if I dared. If the smoker snarls, however, I back off, tail between legs.

What is this? Am I so conservative that I wish everyone to obey all notices? Or, am I now so convinced that I am more Catholic than the Pope? It is a warm, full-blooded feeling as I go and pounce upon the prey and indicate my displeasure. But why? Even as I do this, I wonder. Something deeper?

Like racism? Like misanthropy? Like being psychotic? The reward is that I feel righteous. How ridiculous.

8 SEPTEMBER 1989. Called a *flaneur* in print. Looked it up. "Witty, insouciant, man of the world." Like that very much. Also, "not serious." Like that even better. It is like being a dandy without having to pay tailoring bills. An element of pose and nothing, such as earnestness, to mar the effect. Also, though this the dictionary does not say, someone who sees through appearances and who refuses to abide by the dull rules. Have no idea if all of this was intended by the writer [Arturo Silva] but I like the fit of it.

9 SEPTEMBER 1989. Out in the afternoon with Richard Avedon. Brought over by Canon for what purpose he knows not. I take him to the Edo reconstruction in Fukagawa, since he likes small and enclosed worlds, then to see the few real Edo buildings left in Asakusa.

He talks about how he felt, still feels, at exclusion in the photography field. He remembers the years when he was considered not serious by the establishment because he worked for magazines and did advertising features. This at a time when Steiglitz had done photos for Cunard. But that was forgotten.

Photographers on the West Coast would have nothing to do with flashy Easterners. "They liked their rocks, their integrity." And it continues, he says, which is why MoMA [New York Museum of Modern Art] has nothing of his. Talks of John Szarkowski [MoMA's Director of Photography] and his limitations. I listen and remember John, seeming to pursue some Calvinist ideal of photography. I remember what an unhappy man he seemed.

"But it hurt. It still hurts." And Avedon still feels excluded. I look at him, a very open man, always interested, and perhaps consequently always vulnerable. He has enormous charm as well. I understand part of it now. He seems really interested in the person he is talking with. Royalty sometimes cultivates this naturalness, this interest, and a very few of the wealthy (Mrs. [Babe] Paley) have acquired it as well. With Avedon it seems innate.

10 SEPTEMBER 1989. Took Richard Avedon and Norma Stevens to the DX Gekijo sex theater. When we went in a serious middle-aged man was earnestly sucking the breast of the girl on the stage, stroking her vagina the while. When he attempted to move downward, however, she, following some choreography of her own, moved up until he found himself facing her rump, which he then in somewhat perplexed fashion began to lick. She kept turning and he kept trying to catch up. It was like a pas de deux in which only one of the two knows the steps

It was amusing but no one smiled, because in this temple no one ever smiles. Then we looked at two girls who simulated lesbian passion, and watched another satisfy herself, or appear to, with a small device. And then we watched other customers play counting-out games and climbing onto the stage. One young man with a large member excited some interest, and his coupling technique was more uninhibited than most. But he was also a long-timer. After the others had somehow or other finished he still continued. Finally the girl told him to get off, which he did; still unfulfilled, he struggled to get his large hard cock back into his pants, then went and sat miserable in the corner.

Dick and Norma were astonished by this, as most foreigners are. The experience offers no handles; it is so smooth and featureless, so practiced, so benign—it is the last thing that the Christians and the Jews expect from sex. When I took Susan [Sontag] she said it all: "Well, I guess it is sexy but it is about as erotic as a cake bake-off." Richard thought of kindergarten; Norma thought of a day-care center. They also thought it very "sad"—which is a common reaction from liberal Americans. This tells more, however, about their assumptions than it does about the Japanese DX theater. They found it sad. I found it matter-of-fact. But then I think that Americans believe that being matter-of-fact about sex is sad. One must make it special: either celestial or infernal.

21 OCTOBER 1989. Gene Langston is very ill again, not expected to live; his trials—sufferings emphysema, with asthma, with his various pneumonias— seem about to end.

Today I went out to his hospital. The new nurse did not know me but bowed deeply. A bad sign. Before, the busy nurses waved a hand or indicated the room with their chin. This was a full, hands-folded bow.

Gene has much changed in the past month. He can no longer be fed because he can retain nothing. Can be given no more chemicals because they too now seep away. Consequently he is starving to death.

There is a generic similarity among such unfortunate people. I thought of pictures I have seen from Bergen-Belsen or Auschwitz, where people were systematically starved. Gene's starvation results in the same expression. The skull is visible, the skin taut, the eyes seeming larger. When I came in his eyes turned. He tried to smile but his skin was stretched too tight. He is alert, his eyes show this. They also show that he knows. He is lying and watching himself dissolve. He cannot talk because of his tracheotomy but his eyes speak for him.

I began to cry and he shook his head in gentle reproof, which I remembered from many other times during the more than forty years we have been friends. Then we talked, or I did. I told him we all know, we all wanted to do something, we all can't. He nodded and mouthed: Thank you.

When I left he looked at me again. And raised his hand to wave goodbye, that open-fingered gesture, hand moving sidewise, which

With Oba Masatoshi, Yodogawa Nagaharu, Yanagimachi Mitsuo, Kakeo Yoshio, 1989.

had always been his. But the strength did not last. His hand fell.

28 OCTOBER 1989. Kawakita Kazuko had a party for Hou Hsiao-hsien at her new house. Non-chan [Nogami Teruyo] was there and we talked about Kurosawa's next film. "Oh, it is late, as usual," she said. Not only because of Martin Scorsese, however, who was a month late himself. (He plays Van Gogh in what sounds a very peculiar picture [*Dreams*].) "Warners wanted it about now. They'll get it late winter. Opening at Cannes, they want. We'll see."

Yanagimachi Mitsuo there too, back from Hong Kong. "It was extremely difficult," he said about making his new film [*Shadow of China*] there. I had heard of some of it. Plans to shoot in Peking around beginning of June for example. Also heard about script problems, producer problems, John Lone problems. He did not speak of these, however, just kept shaking his head. "Well, it is finished now, the shooting. I am editing it now." Now he wants to make a nice "easy" film right here in Japan.

Said some of his problems were caused by the way Japan is perceived now. Seen as economic threat and this affects everyone, particularly Americans, particularly West Coast Americans. "I'm no threat," he says. "Yet being Japanese gets in my way all the time."

At that point Hou came over with his hands in his pockets, singing. He was imitating one of the characters in Yanagimachi's *Fire Festival.* Then he stopped and asked in his new English, "You name song?" And Yanagimachi had completely forgotten it. He turned red, stuttered.

31 OCTOBER 1989. At midnight Teshigahara Hiroshi called. People have told him *Rikyu* is too long. Wants to cut. Where? My opinion is asked because I am, after all, foreign, and it was abroad that his film was thought too long. I told him I thought the whole pre-credit sequence should go, that it was distracting, and poorly done. Silence at the end of the line. The *iemoto* of the Sogetsu School is not used to being told that he is capable, like everyone else, of sometimes doing poor work. Then he said he would think about it. Other foreigners have told me that they thought it a coffee table film, but this I did not tell him.

2 NOVEMBER 1989. At Frank's, sitting on the sofa with his sister Eva, a stout and highly opinionated person who often takes exception to whatever one is saying. She has stayed, visiting for two months. Frank and Chizuko are being very good to her. The toll is apparent. Anyway, I was on the sofa with her, and she turned to me and, talking about her various ills, said, "Well, one good thing. It is almost over. I do not think I would have the strength to do it again." At first I thought she was talking about the trip and then realized that she was speaking of her life. "I sometimes think of that," she said with a smile. "It will be nice, having everything finished. Having had lived." I looked at her, aware that I was being given a glimpse deep, very deep, into another human being who has fears and hopes the same as I, and who was facing these with more openness and bravery that I do.

7 NOVEMBER 1989. Trying to get my reentry permit since I will be going to Hawaii shortly. The Otemachi office is now impassable, with hundreds of Asians trying to extend visas and dozens of Japanese immigration officials trying to obstruct them. Hearing of the new, small office at Hakozaki, I went.

Too late. The *yakuza* have discovered it. Parties of Filipinas escorted by men in pinstripes. The girls chatter and show their curves. The Japanese gents bow low to the immigration officials who stamp away. If the girls want to make money, and the guys want to make money off the girls, that is fine. But what renders the scene comical is that officially Japan is shaking its warning finger, deploring what it so openly allows. And what renders the scene irritating is that I must wait until beauty is served. Still, it only takes an hour and a half. In Otemachi it would have taken three—merely to pay my fee (¥6,000 a time, which is why these reentry permits are needed) and get my passport stamped.

In the evening I go to see a selection of the earliest films of the brothers Lumière. These magical pictures show the world a century ago. And they are real. This is something only my generation can have seen—the living past. It is a truthful, reliable, actual picture. (Cataloging less so. The one called Tokyo Street Scene is not Tokyo. It is someplace in China.) I watch the baby being fed. That child, if alive, is ninety now. And during the entrance of the king of Sweden, a guard turns to look suspiciously at us, at the small, square black box whirring away. Little did that long dead soldier know that he was actually peering into the future—that a hundred years later, I would be peering back at *him*.

11 NOVEMBER 1989. Took some shirts to the laundry. Laundryman looked up, mock severe, head cocked, "I saw you!" he said accusingly. Instant guilt. What, where, with whom? Then I saw his sly smile. It was followed by the information: "I saw *Rikyu*." Ah, he'd seen me in the films. "Hai, hai. *Yoku gambatta*." In English this does not come out too well: "You did your best." It seems to leave something unexpressed. Not in Japanese, however. In Japanese it is highly appropriate. I say the proper thing: "*Yah, daikon datta yo*," which might be rendered as: "Naw, I was a real ham." Small flurry of denial. Then a question rather un-Japanese: "*Omoshirokatta?*" "Was it fun?"

17 DECEMBER 1989. The memorial gathering for Eugene Langston. White lilies, a rather severe picture of Gene in a black turtleneck, looking out at us. A few dozen of us, all elderly, all properly lining the walls, as though waiting our turns. Kamikawa in charge, that strange man with whose life Gene's was so entwined and who is now heir.

Half heir. I do not recognize the other half it has been so long. Bald, owlish, thick glasses—it is Burton Watson with whom I went to university and seen rarely since. "Gene must have wanted me to have his books," he says, surprised. "You will get considerably more than that," I tell him, since he gets half the assets. He shakes his head. Does not understand why. Nor do I, but I know that Gene always approved of Burt. He liked his perfect translations, his care, his getting everything right. Just as did Gene himself.

The doctor who presided over the long, painful, protracted death stands up and for half an hour gives us a painful day by day account of the dissolution. A part of the reason for this lack of tact is ordinary insensitivity, an inability to feel for anyone else. But a part is to ward off criticism (after all the patient died in his care) by showing how good he was.

After that, some pieties from Kamikawa—so mealy-mouthed, impossible to imagine him as the fierce kamikaze pilot he once was. Then other voices from the past. I come last. I at least talk about Gene as a friend, and as a fellow human.

Afterward approached by several. People I thought I had never seen, yet here and there, a certain inflection, a way of blinking, a stance, I seem to recognize under these years. Then, swimming to the surface would come: a pretty girl, flirtatious on a summer day in 1947; a good-looking boy with a wide country smile from 1948; a studious young man with slick black hair—now bald. These were all aged members of the Tokyo University English Speaking Society whom I last met more than forty years before.

And time has been no more kind to me—the extent of the ravage was indicated by my being so often assured that I have not changed at all.

18 DECEMBER 1989. Finally got to hear the main Kurt Weill work I had not—the comic opera, *The Czar Gets His Photograph Taken*. What heavy music for what slight entertainment! But I think the same about the Hindemith *Hind und Zuruk*. But when the couple puts on the tango record and sing over it, the work comes quite leanly alive. I think of the fat *Fedorah*, where the Chopin is magically sung to.

I wonder if I will ever get to hear and see those things I want to. I want to hear Rieti's *Noah's Ark*. I want to see Bresson's *Le Diable Probablement*. I remember when I was ten and my passion was to hear *Petrouchka*, about which I had only read. But in those days there was no FM, no classical music on the radio at all, and records were not to be found in my small and isolated township. Then, finally, Stokowski made a recording of the whole score, on 78s, and I worked a month (washing windows) to save money to buy it. I ordered it, got it, carried it home, waited until my father was out, my mother busy, my baby sister quiet—and put it on. What did I think? I no longer remember. I was hearing a kind of sound that was new to me, though it was now in the late 1930s. I remember later being able to make nothing of the sound, the timbre, of *L'Histoire d'un Soldat*. It sounded scratchy, unfinished, to me. (And, I later read that the sound of Brahms sounded "raw" and "unfinished" to his contemporaries.) *Petrouchka*, however I took to at once, I remember, and played the records bare.

20 DECEMBER 1989. Took Anthony Thwaite out for dinner. We have known each other since the fifties when he was here, young, shockheaded, and filled even then with that charming self-denial, that ability to "see through" himself, which is truly the first line of attack. He has never lost it. In fact, he has honed it. He never takes himself seriously in public, and nothing else but, I would imagine, in private.

We talk of much, of the old days, of [Dennis]Enright here, of [Edmund] Blunden, of poor dead Nigel [Sayers]. Also of his old nemesis James Kirkup, who quoted Anthony as saying something damaging about the Japanese, which he never said. Lawyers alerted. Flustered Kirkup cannot find letter he says he quoted from. Kirkup now in Andorra, where he has created the James Kirkup Commemorative Museum. I imagine him sitting there, waiting for pilgrims. Given the Japanese, a few will actually come. I do not know him. Met him once and experienced chemical aversion. "Chemical aversion, interesting term," says Anthony, busy with his salmon. "There probably is *just* such a thing. After all, there are affinities, elective or otherwise."

21 DECEMBER 1989. Alice Waters to dinner. How do you take Chez Panisse to dinner? No use spending money on second-rate European. I take her to my Ueno "Edo" place. Cheap, good, and odd. She picked at her toriwasa. Too strong? Too strange? Her husband spurned his. The pheasant on rice went better. Later I took them to the last phallic stone in Tokyo, on the Ueno island. This impressed, as did the ruined lotus lake. Alice still her same gentle, opinionated, charming self. She is like the girl next door who has made good.

26 DECEMBER 1989. Cut a big slice of ham from the box of meats sent me this year, as every year, by Hashima Kunio who keeps remembering that fifteen years ago I got him to America to school, and off the rap for knocking up a fifteen-year-old student at the school where he was athletic instructor. Then steeped two slices of cornbread from the corner bakery in whipped egg and milk. Fried both. Topped this with butter and the Maine maple syrup that Marguerite Yourcenar sent me. I still have a bit of it left, years now after her death. She sent it me because I had given her a large loaf of bread when I first went to see her. I had no idea she so missed bread and had not actually intended to give her the loaf. But she saw it, wanted it, got it, and never forgot. Eating my concoction, French toast with ham, I remember the past. Madame Yourcenar with her Breton blue eyes and Kunio, still a boy, with dirty fingernails and a sly smile.

30 DECEMBER 1989. On the Ginza. Many tourists, mostly American it seems. Seems from their clothes. If the Japanese dress up, the Americans dress down. Such a variety of tracksuits, sweat shirts, overalls, jeans, lumberjack shirts, stocking caps. And all of these are city people, of course, professionals, mon-eyed or else they would not be here. The false sartorial egalitarianism of the Americans. Jeans on those who never turned a day of manual labor. Was it Veblen who spoke of the affectation for the proletariat as one of the signs of decadence? And by comparison how dressed up and polished the Japanese look. How fifties.

I JANUARY 1990. I was sound asleep when the New Year was ushered in. Did not even hear the bells. Yet I seem to remember this New Year. In *Things to Come* it was the Year of the Wandering Sickness. People in 1990 tottered around until they dropped dead. In the real 1990 we have AIDS. The coming era, the twenty-first century, is all togas and towers and totalitarianism.

I go to see Patrick [Lovell] and [Yoshihara] Akira for the traditional breakfast of New Year's food. Together we go to the Benten shrine at Ueno and I make a prayer for Dae-Yung. Benten ought to like that. She was always a sucker for a handsome face. Then go to the phallic stone on the little island, the last from old Edo. Here my prayer is more fervent and more personal. I also put a hundred yen coin on the stone urethra opening. Then take it away. If I don't someone else will.

New Year's Day in Tokyo. Even now it takes me back. The streets are empty; seats in the subway; people stroll. And people smile, too, and look at each other. There are fewer Walkmen stuffed in ears, not so many manga opened on the lap. And little of the blind indifference that Tokyo now usually exhibits.

9 FEBRUARY 1990. Dinner with Makiyo. He was once a young Kyushu office worker who hated his job. Now he is president of Ace Corporation, a Tokyo land-sale company with branches in Seattle, L.A., and Beppu, which is where he is from. He hires his father and brothers, makes a great deal of money, and every day is interesting. Next month he is going to fly me down and back, and put me up at a grand hotel in Beppu so I can see the operation and meet the family again.

18 FEBRUARY 1990. The last day before Election Day. Very noisy. Japanese incumbents have only one way of soliciting votes—sound trucks. Numbers roam the streets, shouting. This begins two weeks earlier and continues daily, the pitch becoming higher and higher.

Today, they are hysterical, gabbling into their microphones, panting, rac-ing, and sobbing. This is because they must attempt to indicate, through voice alone, the extent of their striving and hence the depth of their determination.

"I am Suzuki Taro. Suzuki Taro. Remember my name. Suzuki Taro. I am doing my best, my level best. Suzuki Taro, Suzuki Taro." Over and over, the accent now agonized, so that we may visualize the tearful but determined gaze, the straining but valiant heart, and the gasping but dedicated breath.

The degree of mimesis is extraordinary. If other countries ran their elections this way there would be general laughter because the effect is to the Western ear so false. In Japan, however, the intention is the deed. Though everyone knows this is play-acting of a most amateur order, it is nonetheless accepted as a sign for what it stands for and is hence (Japanese connection) the thing itself.

19 FEBRUARY 1990. The outcome of all the noise is that the Liberal Democratic Party (which is neither liberal nor democratic) again captures its majority, and the opposition, divided as always, falters. Japan has declared its priorities. It prefers the convenient, the known—it spurns opportunity for change and a danger of instability. Stability: This the Japanese want more than anything else. Here any surprise is an unpleasant one. And the highly unpopular LDP sales tax is now to be engraved in stone.

24 FEBRUARY 1990. Lunch with Tom Wolfe, who is here to work up a novel. It has some Japanese in it, and he has come to see some Japanese. Tallish, wide forehead, gray eyes, and much sartorial splendor. He mentions this. "I guess I am old-fashioned," he says in reference to his Edwardian vest, his watch chain, and his wide-brimmed hat. But it is also a way of dress that alerts people. I had taken him to the Press Club, not the brightest or liveliest place, and everyone recognized him at once and several came sidling up.

He is also interested, understanding, curious. Says very little about himself unless one asks. Wants to learn. Is here for that reason. Is particularly interested in what happens to art here, how it turns into money. Tells me about the changed art scene in New York. The days of elegant galleries are over. Instead, one goes to the auction houses. So popular are they that room after room has merely a TV in it and an agent who transmits the bids. Talks also of parties held where the host invites friends to "observe" as he bids, higher and higher. "Of course, he must acquire or else there is no point to the event. Consequently a number of bankrupts."

Took him to Tokyo City Office, where they were polite and awed, and even honest when he asked if there were ethnic problems in Tokyo. (Yes, of two varieties: one, the resident Korean/Chinese minorities; two, the influx

With Tom Wolfe.

of Southeast Asian illegal workers.) Afterward I filled him in on the details of each.

25 FEBRUARY 1990. Lunch and dinner with Sarah [Gilles]. She has been working by day for *Vogue* and with the [Rolling] Stones at night. Mick [Jagger] wears a scarf around his lower face when outside. A cold? No, no. So long as one doesn't see the mouth he is not recognizable. Also, ah, these working class boys, so refreshing. Mick fucks anything standing still. Does this happen to Sarah? I wonder, then decide no because she is one of them, one of the boys. Not interested in girls, however, her own boyfriend probably squirreled away somewhere; she is a member of this late-twentieth-century version of *Our Gang*.

Interested in abstract fucking, I tell her how Paul Getty's then-wife led me to the top of the Moroccan palace and opened the grille, and we looked down on what she identified as Mick's bare bum as he pumped away at someone whom I later recognized by her hair ribbon. Inspired, Sarah and I decide to go to the fabled DX Gekijo.

What a disappointment. It has been completely redone. Now the girls merely come out and do their dance, then their dildos, then each other, and finally clean the patrons' hands with towelettes, and then loll and let themselves be fondled, during which they *talk*.

Imagine these sex goddesses—for so they once appeared—now descending and showing bad teeth in the guttural accents of Gunma. There was also a new and most unwelcome type—the hoyden. She did an eccentric naked dance, with splits, then came back and had a talk show. Also carried a small rubber hammer with which to hit playfully the heads of those customers who were rubbing her too hard or in the wrong direction.

The old air of mystery, of primitive religion, the innocent spectacle of customers shedding trousers and engaging in the sacred act of love—all this is gone. Customers no longer climb up. Instead, they stick in a finger or two and are admonished with rubber hammers. The worst is that the image of the goddess is gone. That of the kindergarten teacher, the indulgent mother, never far away, is now brazenly laid bare.

There is also a nasty undercurrent. In the front row are some Chinese—tourists or students or workers. Not much Japanese was spoken among them. Ms. Hoyden made a lot of this. Sly insults in the tongue her guests do not know. Undercover snickering from the audience. Man next to me, jovially, "Oh, these Chinese. They just don't understand." Don't understand what? asks the suspicious foreigner. "Well, our ways, we Japanese." Even when currying cunt, it is still we Japanese against all.

However, Ms. Hoyden got her comeuppance. Flushed with her success she took on Sarah. "Oh, I want that lovely white lady to take a picture of my pussy," she said, brandishing her Polaroid. I said no. She turned on me, "Even though you speak Japanese and all, you got to let the lady speak for herself. Nice little white lady." "Nice little white lady is not lesbian," I crisply averred. Loud laughter from the crowd, pouts from hoyden.

Then her big mistake: she harangued the crowd. Accused us of being stingy in not taking picture of pussy (five hundred yen the crack), and did so with no placating humor. Crowd grew cool, cold, and then sullen. Too late she sensed the turn against her. Beating a naked retreat she one last time turned to face us. "Why don't you just all go home." Ironic applause. I had to apologize to Sarah. Yet another aspect of old Japan vanished.

1 MAY 1990. In the evening at the U.S. Ambassador's residence, the reception for Martha Graham. She is ninety-six now, and we had expected her to be wheeled in like the cake, but the Armacosts always do things well: There she was, in another room, enthroned on a teak chair, and we were allowed in several at a time, like pilgrims.

She looked very Chinese—perhaps the chair suggested that. But Ming—late Ming. Her hair was pulled back tightly and she wore jewelry, like the idol she was. And, she looked lacquered, a living effigy. Cordial, smiling occasionally, and then, often, that terrible lost look that very old people have, like an aged child who has forgot its way. Then a graceful and unselfconscious recovery, and she was nodding and smiling. Then again, that awful lost gaze.

I heard the press conference was like that. Periods of lucidity, periods of blankness. Talk with an acquaintance about Copland, nearly that age himself now and even worse off. Some days there, some not; some days remembers everything, some days nothing. Not Alzheimer's—that rarely permits these merciless retreats to sanity. No, just old age, and the dimming of the brain.

KAWAKITA ZAIDAN

With Kurosawa Akira.   *With Oshima Nagisa.*

And I first saw them both when they were half this age. New York, the forties. *Appalachian Spring.* She had danced and he was in the audience. Smiling, bowing, hand in hand, the two of them. I did not know Aaron then, but I still remember him best smiling from the stage.

The notables lined up. A few of the American ladies attempt a curtsy. I did not join the line. The ambassador gave a speech. "Martha Graham: if America had a living national treasure, she would be it." Yes, that is what she would be, staring straight ahead, stiff in her chair, her jade earrings barely moving—a living national treasure.

23 MAY 1990. Party for Kurosawa—eighty now and just returned from the Cannes festival. Prolonged applause upon his smiling entrance. Like royalty. But then he has always been *tenno* [emperor]. The difference is only in the new affability. This is stressed in the various speeches. Fat old Yodogawa Nagaharu, TV film fan, kept exclaiming, "And there I was back in the old days, I wrote all the ads for *Sugata Sanshiro*; so maybe thanks to me, Kurosawa is what he is today, ha-ha. But seriously now, what I want to remark upon is the difference. . . ."

A great difference. In many ways. Kurosawa, who so rightly scorned the Japan Academy Awards for years, now takes money from Lucas and lets *Dreams* be "presented by" Spielberg, now goes to the Hollywood Academy Awards, now allows Warner's send him to Cannes. However, such thoughts as these do not intrude. Instead, Oshima makes an emotional speech and says, "Thank you, thank you, Mr. Kurosawa," he who only a decade ago was saying coldly that Kurosawa was what was the matter with Japanese cinema. Best speech was Ryu Chishu's. He must be near ninety. He stood there, now much older than when he impersonated himself in *Tokyo Story,* and said, "I don't really know what to say. Congratulations anyway. I'll step down now. Thanks anyway."

24 MAY 1990. In the park, stopped to talk to the resident prostitute. Pageboy, sensible shoes. When in spirits, given to wisecracks. "*Haro daringu,*" in English. Followed in Japanese by, "Real empty tonight. I only did two." "But that is good, isn't it?" I ask. Shake of the pageboy, one hand reassuring the breasts. "Good? No, three or four is average." "What was the most?" "Ten!" "Ten in one night?" "Between the hours of 7 and 11. Ten!" "You were busy." "I was just flying around." Laughter. Then, "Not so hot tonight. One in the bushes, one in the ladies' john. No sense taking that kind to a nice hotel."

I decided to ask something I had been curious about. "Do they know? Your customers?" "About half and half," was the candid reply. "Those that don't always get excited and feel my tits. Those that know half the time want to suck my cock or get fucked. You'd be surprised. Last week the straightest, butchest, gang-boy type you ever saw. Muscles, tattoos. And we get in the bushes and he drops his pants and bends over. Wanted it up the ass." "Did you oblige?" "Sure—he couldn't help it, probably got used to it in prison."

"Do you ever mix the two and try to fuck the one that thinks you're a lady?" Laughter, then, "All the time, all the time. It's a problem." Seeing I was ready for further details, "I don't get fucked you know, too dangerous, and I don't suck cock either." "What do you do then?" I wondered, thinking this a singularly untalented male prostitute.

In answer he swung his handbag and said, "Want to see my cunt?" I said I did, and he produced an object made of rubber. Then he demonstrated, hiked up his skirt, put it between his panty-hosed legs. "Feels just like a cunt," he said. "And I'm quick about it, have it right down there in no time. They never know." "It doesn't look much like a cunt," I said. "Not supposed to. No one ever sees it. No, no don't touch it, it's still full of cum from those two guys." "Don't you wash it out?" I asked. "No, that would ruin it. They would know it was rubber. But with all the cum squashing round inside it feels like cunt. They think they got me all wet, think they got me excited, big ego trip." "Big trip to the hospital," I say, "What if the first guy is sick, then the second dips his cock in all that gunk and he gets sick, too?"

"No, no," he said, "I am OK, I never get sick." "I'm not talking about you, I'm talking about your customers." "AIDS, huh?" "Yes, something like that." "Well, I just don't know," he said. "If I wash it they'll catch on. But once it is nice and squishy. . . ." "I just mentioned it," I said, "as a matter of possible interest to the health department."

Laughter, then, seriously, "In Japan, it's only the rich people who have AIDS; they never come down here to Ueno. You got to have money to go abroad and catch it." We talked for a bit more, and then he saw a likely businessman, portly, interested. Eventually they walked into the darkness, she with her dirty cunt secure in her handbag.

5 JUNE 1990. To dinner with Louis Harris of polling fame. Taking my advice in New York, he came and talked with Tsutsumi Seiji of department store fame, hoping to get funding for Jimmy Merrill's movie. It was at Jimmy's place in New York that I first thought of this avenue. And Lou, with his customary directness, picked up the idea at once and came brandishing it. Seiji had meant to give him twenty minutes and, probably, the time of day. Instead, he sat, stunned in his own office, while Lou outlined.

Harris is extraordinary. I have never met anyone so completely certain. There is none of that doubt of self that one so finds, particularly, in Americans, especially in New York. And even those gestures in that direction ("at least, that is what I think" etc.) are merely social.

His wife sits by, stunned not by him, but by jet lag. "I'm sleepy all the time." Not him. I cannot imagine him sleepy. Right now he only sips Chinese dumpling soup. "They have ruined my digestion," he says, speaking of the Japanese and the schedule arranged for him. But one does not believe it. Nothing will ever ruin any single part of him.

Napoleon must have been like this. So utterly sure, so completely certain, that he carried all before him. Seiji must have been overcome. It is not the charm, which is considerable, but the certainty. So rare, so valuable, so irresistible in our rationalized times.

6 JUNE 1990. Evening, explaining Ueno and low life in general to a foreign film producer who has asked for a few lessons. Having told him where to go and watched him enter, I fell into the hands of a *hentai fufu*. The male half moved into the dark near the pond, then, making sure I was looking, lifted his companion's skirt like a stage curtain, to show me she had no panties, nor had she shaved. Then he dragged out his equipment and she descended upon him, looking me straight in the eye the while. I do not know what I was supposed to make of this, but realized that I was an object, a third party, a witness. So I smiled and she smiled back, difficult though that was. Then I stretched forth a hand to assist her. Instantly he was buckled up again, and with a "time to

move on, time to move on," he shepherded her around the shores of the pond, she looking back (longingly I thought) from time to time. This is what they do, pairs like this—inflame innocents like myself, then "move on" when things look promising. That is why they are called hentai fufu, "a perverted pair."

8 JUNE 1990. Spent the morning writing about the *burakumin* (reviewing *Hashi ga Nai Kawa*), the proscribed caste, even now in this bigoted land; its creation yet another ploy to control the lives of the citizenry that continues to this day. Perhaps continues now even stronger, in that the citizenry has been persuaded to surrender itself, to exercise self-criticism, to implant the watchful eye within the bosom.

Lunch with Emiko Ohnuki-Tierney, anthropologist and also something of an expert on the *burakumin*, since her book, *Monkey as Mirror*, connects all these strands of historical Japan. She tells me that the publisher of the proposed translation said he would love to do it but with all these *burakumin* references he really couldn't. Now if she could just take them all out. . . . I tell her that when my *Inland Sea* was translated the publishers (TBS-Brittanica) cut out all references not only to *burakumin*, but also to lepers.

She left Japan early, opened her eyes, and has never again shut them. "And you?" she asks. "You are me in reverse. How does it come about? How does it continue?" It continues, of course, because I am not Japanese and hence not subject to any of these insular customs. I am not expected to conform, indeed am encouraged not to. "I would not stay here, not even for five minutes, if I were Japanese," I tell her. "But I am not. And that is all the difference. Plus, that I am a chronic non-joiner and early burst into tears at the prospect of the Boy Scouts." She nods. She understands.

9 JUNE 1990. With Jonathan Rauch, whom I take out to an Edo dinner and then to assorted glimpses of Ueno low life. He says, and I agree, that revisionism (let alone "Japan-bashing") is not the proper term for what is occurring. It is simply that a group of journalistic scholars are describing Japan for the first time. And, I say, doing so for the first time without reference to the Japanese model.

It is amazing that for so many years, so many scholars (Reischauer among them) have accepted the Japanese Version. I never have, and I have always tried to accurately describe the place. But I simply did (and do) not know enough—as much, for example, as Karel van Wolferen knows.

Jonathan, so young, so bright, says that he has yet to meet a Japanese any different from anyone where he came from—Phoenix. The institutions are peculiar, but then all institutions are peculiar. The explorer finding Japan "different" is, in a way, merely discovering the last standing wall of the once-imposing Nihonjinron edifice.

30 JUNE 1990. A Beethoven quartet a day. First I read d'Indy, and then Kerman. Then I listen to the quartet, with the score. Then I read Kerman again. So far I am most interested in Opus 95. In particular those two breathless chords, like some deathbed statement reconsidered.

Out at night enjoying the national mix. All sorts of different people. Homogeneous Japan—those who think they are homogeneous—feels threatened. On the bus coming back home there was a feisty little man with a toothpick and a domineering way with his wife. She was ordered to sit down, and then, himself standing, he looked around the bus. There was me and a Pakistani (probably), and two Filipinas, and perhaps a Chinese. And he turned to her and said in a loud voice, secure in his presumed insularity, "Nothing but damn foreigners these days." *(Saikin ya na, gaijin bakkashi da.)* I looked up from my Kerman and transfixed him with my alien and basilisk eye. He understood at once that he had been understood. He looked away. Then when the bus went around a corner, stole a glance. Horrors, the *gaijin* was still regarding him with a mute but ominous stare. He shifted his position, turned his back, snapped at his wife. When I got off the bus, I was pleased to see that he had chewed his toothpick into a pulp. Stress.

1 JULY 1990. Reading the short short stories of Colette, those that are all bunched together in the middle of the collected volume. I much admire this short-short form. These little netsuke are hard to carve, but worth it. Good for Colette too. When she gets long she often becomes winsome or jocular. She is best (as is everyone) when she is all bone and sinew. This short-short form saves the author from that authorial pose which, as I get older and older, makes me more and more sick. That ghastly attitude of looking on genially, smiling at a suffering world, the master puppeteer. Thackeray has it, James has it, even my worldly and discreet Colette at times. But not in these glorious stories. They make me want to write some myself.

2 JULY 1990. Busy day. Noon lecture, two hours, on Japanese culture for a group of adult academics from U.S.A.; proofing Kenneth Pyle's new article for the International House of Japan *Bulletin*; rewriting the library notes; then moderating Emiko Ohnuki-Tierney's talk on *Tampopo*.

Then I came home and found in my mailbox "The Best Radio Plays of

Paul Rhymer," that is, the best of *Vic and Sade*, the radio program that so delighted my childhood, which so formed me.

One of the joys of *Vic and Sade* was to stand to one side and learn to observe. Not criticize, observe. And to understand, and to accept. All of this was painless, of course. I thought they were "funny." And so they are, but they had the transcendental humor shared by Jane Austen and Ozu.

Made of very little, a handful of characters (usually three) in themselves a unit (family), in one setting (house), and this minimal means permitted the depths of fellow feeling which this series occasioned. I never wanted to meet Vic or Sade or Rush. At the same time they were not "examples." Rather, it was through them that great truths were viewed—beauty became truth.

In bed I read and read. Rhymer's dialogue is as crisp today as it was fifty years ago. His ability to reveal without stating is marvelous. He is pre-Pinter Pinter. I cannot think of anyone else writing this well on stage and screen, radio being dead.

But as I laughed my eyes filled with tears. It was not nostalgia. I remembered none of these scripts. It was delight, certainly, at the rightness, the sureness of the performance. But it was more. Then I recognized it.

It was love. That infantile, all encompassing love that as a child I gave to Laurel and Hardy. It was fellow feeling extended until I loved them for being so human, so much like me. I love Vic and Sade as I love the people in Ozu's *Tokyo Story* because I understand them. I do not want to leave them, and last night could not close the book. I awoke this morning, book still open, light still on.

4 JULY 1990. In the late morning I go to the American Embassy for the Fourth of July Reception. Great, joyous crush with, oddly, Chinese food. One woman in a red-white-and-blue straw hat. Otherwise, decent attire.

And there was Edward G. Seidensticker. "First time I am invited in years. Why, why, why?" "I think they wanted to look cultural this year," I said. "Oh, you are such a cynic," said Ed. Then, "What I really don't know is why they invited you. Me, I can understand. I, sir, am a patriot. You are No Such Thing."

Then I circulated through that great cool house, and outside in the garden saxophones were straining and people came up and said, "I bet you don't remember me," and they were absolutely right. Lots of military. So many chest decorations one could not tell the American officers from the Soviet.

Hours later, about eleven that night, I was walking home around Shinobazu Pond and there I beheld a familiar figure shuffling toward me. Yes,

Edward G. Seidensticker. "All is well with the world," I said. "We meet on familiar ground." He stood, swaying, before me. "Dr. Livingston, I presume." I told him I knew where he had been—to Asakusa. "Right again, sir." And drinking. "A man may drink," he said in the flat tones of Dr. Johnson.

Then, "Why do you suppose I was invited? I cannot imagine it. Oh, I was once on the list. Then I was removed. And now, lo, I am back on it again. Who does these things? Who makes up his mind about my destiny in this fashion?" "God?" I suggested. "Less levity," he said severely, then, "Yours is even more of a mystery. Why would they invite you? Me, yes, for I must admit that I find the Fourth still Glorious. Yes, you may smile in that superior fashion of yours. But I am not ashamed. Glorious!" And tears actually appeared in his eyes. Then, "But you wouldn't know about this, you old cynic, you. Well, off to home, which is probably not where *you* are going. *I* am. To write up my diary, sir."

5 JULY 1990. Though America yammers and Japan stealthily buys up the world, there is very little visible of this new war. Perhaps because war is made by governments and not by people. Very visible it is in Washington—I read Ian [Buruma] on this. Another new book names names: the Japan lobbyists—visible even in Tokyo as Japan tries to slam shut the door to protect itself while at the same time menacing everyone else. Oddly no one has said the obvious. America does not have to buy Japanese. No one is forcing it to.

7 JULY 1990. Eric, required to listen to yet one more of my tales of conquest, said, "But you seem to have deserted Japan in favor of the Third World." I thought about that and have now decided that it was not that I deserted Japan, but that Japan deserted the Third World.

Me, I have been faithful to that locality. It was the Third World in Japan that so appealed to lubricious me, and now that Japan is more First World than even the U.S.A., the appeal is no longer there. That makes me that figure of fun, the garden-variety colonial imperialistic predator.

8 JULY 1990. There are no articles in the Japanese language, and the lack of a definite article truly circumscribes. One cannot say "the dog," one must say "this dog" or "that dog" or "that dog over there." But the genus dog, that which makes something of a symbol of itself ("the dog is the most widespread of canines") is not possible. Symbolic thought (man's triumph it is said) is not triumphant in Japan. I cannot imagine Plato thriving here, with all his absolutes ("Truth," "Beauty"), but Aristotle thrives because he describes. Maybe

this is why Japan is so backward (by comparison) in some areas: philosophy, and diagnosis. And perhaps why it is so forward in others. After all, symbolic thought, logical progression, abstract ideas—these are not all of life, either.

9 JULY 1990. A cultural collision—Japan versus U.S.—escalates. And yet the antagonists so resemble each other. Japan is an unguided missile. No one is in the control room. When you get the people all pointed in the same direction there is no stopping them. Where is the brake? It is not included in this model. And the U.S.—it cannot even get everyone going in the same direction. People in the control booth, but no one minding the store. Minding the till, however. Both problems are colossal. The U.S., ailing, unable to stop its violent and criminal twitching, unable to care for itself, drooling and weeping. And Japan, locked inside of itself, nose at the windows, gasping for breath, unable to stop its violent impetus, and unable to get out.

Today a taxi driver turned around and said, "Well, I hope you people keep bashing us. That is the only way we are ever going to get any reform in this country."

A pronounced lack of fellow feeling (except for this sole taxi driver)—that is the harshest and truest thing one can say about the Japanese. In the West too a great lack of that quality, but it nevertheless exists. Here, all too often, the different is seen as inhuman. And even if some feel otherwise they are too cowardly to show it. But how the Americans respond to a show of fellow feeling. They open like flowers turning toward the sun, warming their cold and brittle petals.

25 JULY 1990. Continuing hot weather. And since no rainy season has occurred, continued fears of water shortage. Tokyo not at its best in such emergencies. Discomfort turns people in upon themselves. They close all the doors and windows, as it were. A train or subway car is filled with complete blanks. This fragile city breaks down upon any provocation. A light snowfall and traffic snarls; a small earthquake and all the trains halt; a typhoon warning and the buses stop running. This is a city designed to work only under optimum conditions, just like the country, and, in a way, just like the people.

In the evening I stroll around Shinobazu. The summer festival is going on. Stalls with plants, and stones, and whole trees. Lots of water. Caged insects, pottery you can paint and bake. This is usually when the city turns "Japanese" again—fans and *yukata* and *geta,* and an amount of flesh. Not this year. Just a few young girls, self-conscious (and uncomfortable) in summer kimono. There is less and less of this kind of tradition every year.

17 AUGUST 1990. In any event, all other concerns eclipsed in the press by Iraq. What timing. Just when the U.S.A. had lost its evil empire, the USSR, and badly needed a new one. Had tried Japan on for size but something was lacking. This one has everything: military threat, innocent hostages, rape of stewardesses, looting, a lone ten year-old-girl at peril, and behind it all greed, greed, greed. And, of course, the Threat is Real.

Of a consequence Japan is backed off the front page; carping is forgotten. As another consequence President Bush is off the domestic hook and balancing on the foreign one. The biggest relief for him must be the new and "vital" role for the military establishment, which must have thought it was going to lose a lot of money due to the collapse of the USSR. Now they will get more money than ever and Bully Boy can meet Bully Boy. Just like in a real war.

26 AUGUST 1990. To Kawakita Kazuko's, a party for Jim Jarmusch. Takemitsu Toru there as well. I ask him for a school to which to give the Donald Richie Commemorative Collection of Stringed Chamber Music. He shakes his head. Tells me that he had wanted to give his score collection to the Toho Music School. And they refused. "Just no more space in Japan," says Toru.

2 SEPTEMBER 1990. Learned a very interesting idiomatic difference. It came about this way: I was getting a cold drink at the machine, and a young *tobi-shoku* in *tabi* and cummerbund flashed a broad, white smile and said, in Japanese, "I'm not Japanese, either." Well, the big, dazzling smile directed at a complete unknown had already indicated that.

He was Korean, from Pusan, and was working high on one of the scaffoldings of the buildings going up around here. Now he was off for the day and thought he would go sit in the park, enjoying what cool the twilight would offer. While this was not issued as an invitation, I took it as such and joined him.

Strong, young (twenty-five, he told me), and with that courtly politeness of the Koreans among strangers. Handsome, blunt, very Korean features; big, hard Korean body, sitting there in the dusk with his legs open. Much taken, I held up my end of the conversation until it was practically perpendicular. But this was also necessary, because his Japanese was not all that good. Mine is much better, and so I kept trying different words until I hit upon one he knew.

He was, I learned, bumming around Asia. He would go to a country broke, work, get some money, and go on. He did not know where he would go next or for how long he would be in Japan. Had been in Indonesia, Taiwan,

With Jim Jarmusch, 1990.

Thailand, and the Philippines. Always somehow made out. Smiled at this. Big, wide, smile. I could see why he always made out.

Then, seeing my interest in him, he interpreted it in the simplest possible way and decided I wanted to hear about the girls in all these foreign places. He certainly knew a lot about them, including the two, yes, two, whom he had simultaneously enjoyed (friends of friends, no, no money, never), or the one who had enjoyed him just the evening before. Oh, just to think of them made his *chinchin okoru.*

Here came the interesting idiomatic difference: When we have erections, we sometimes say we "are ready." The Japanese usually say they "are hard." But the Koreans say something different. Dae-Yung speaks of his *chinchin* standing up by saying in English, "It is angry, very angry." And here was the Korean *tobi* saying the same thing in Japanese, since *okoru* means to become angry. How interesting. I wonder if this linguistic fact has ever before been noted by scholars. I tried to tell the *tobi* about this, but he could not understand. The spoken language not sufficing, I resorted to Braille.

Open, free, in that Korean way, he did not know if the *chinchin* could *okoru* at such short notice, but sure, why not, and besides he was tired after work, would like to rest a little. Well, to make a long story short (another idiom) *chinchin okoru*-cd, and then we went and had a big Korean meal with lots of *kimchee*.

Name was Lim Chun Sung and he was to leave the next day for Nagoya to work, but would be back on Thursday. We made a tentative date in the middle of the month, the 15th, but he didn't know where he would be here. At parting, with a big smile, as though it were a joke-gift, he taught me the Korean for *chinchin*—it is *chote*.

A most interesting linguistic finding. I had thought that Dae-Yung had made up the angry prick as a part of the pidgin through which we are sometimes forced to communicate. Not at all. It is a part of the Korean language itself. And how interesting that the Koreans have to get angry to make love.

15 SEPTEMBER 1990. Surprisingly (since I had not really expected it), Lim Chun Sung kept his promise and appeared, now in a summer sweater with the New York skyline on it, but the same *tobi* pants.

Over lunch (mainly beer), he told me something more about himself. He is a nomad all right, but this was because he had some trouble in Korea. Just what this consisted of I do not know—his Japanese is really bad. But, it had to do with clutching and slapping and shooting and stabbing and hanging, I guess. I guess, because these are the motions he went through, smiling that big, white, wide accepting Korean smile the while. Also, he was more curious about me. Where did I live, did I live alone, had I any friends? I wish it were possible to trust people, to take them home, to share things, but it is not. At least not people from the park in Ueno.

Later, coming home alone, I cut through the park and saw the young man I often see: crew cut, mid-twenties, nice looking, and somehow sad, also watchful as though waiting for something good to happen in his life. And over the months, I have talked with him. It was not girls he was waiting for, but it did not seem to be boys, either. And though he had some interest in talking about the *hentai fufu*, it was not voyeurism (which is all they offer), and the resident whore, even, did not know what he wanted though she had her own opinion: "*Homo da wa.*" So this evening I stopped to talk. Said his stomach was bothering him, gave a quick, apologetic smile, and looked vaguely about him. Just then a large man in a loose coat passed, and his eyes focused and he gave a short salute. And instantly the scales fell from my own eyes.

Of course. Why hadn't I thought of it myself? "You're fuzz!" (*Deka da!*)

I spontaneously cried. He instantly assumed that held-in poker face, which means that I am right, and made no attempt to deny anything. "That explains it all," I said. And so it does. He has no interest in these things other people in the park do, and the only thing he is waiting for is this criminal to walk into his life and get nabbed. "Awful for you," I said, "to have to perch here every night amid all the perverts and wait and spy and watch." But he said, smiling as though in apology, "It's not too bad."

What kind of criminal is he after? I wanted to know. Obviously no small fry. He is surrounded by these. Is it the Most Wanted Man or something like that? But, he merely showed his polite, closed face and did not answer. "But, I won't tell anyone," I said. "No you won't," he said, smiling. And I had gotten to know him so well, I'd thought, in the past months. You never know, do you? Things just never what they seem. Wow, isn't life surprising? etc. So I went my way and left him there, lonely looking, a cop on duty, all night long. Officer of the law, protector of the peace, no matter what the respectable prostitutes and pimps and perverts think.

1 OCTOBER 1990. In the evening to the opening concert of the week-long series commemorating Takemitsu's sixtieth birthday. He is in the lobby wearing black, but Issey Miyake black, with a little white (Hanae Mori?) butterfly. Smiling modestly, he always treats these great events of which he is the center as though he is just another guest.

Great event—the Emperor and Empress come. Due to some misunderstanding it was thought that I was diplomatic and so I am given a red ribbon and sit in the first row of the balcony, quite near the royals, separated only by a secret serviceman or two. Hence I can observe them.

They are gracious, as royalty is supposed to be. Certainly there is something Windsor in their waves but perhaps this is because there is only one way to wave. They are attentive during the music and appreciative after it. I wonder what they make of it—one hour and a half of Takemitsu's beautifully crafted, small sounds. As I listen I remember his once telling me, "Oh, I would give anything to be able to write a good 2/4 allegro." By the end of the concert I am feeling much the same.

5 OCTOBER 1990. After some months, ran into Hideki [last name unknown]— a cook who runs his own place in the suburbs, late twenties. Brought him home. He got into all this ten years or so ago. Has no particular feeling for it but it is now all he knows. Has a bad opinion of himself and is consequently hopeless with women, at any rate never met the several with whom this low

opinion would have assured affection. Has over the years stopped looking. Men are at least there.

Does everything but only, I feel, because he does not know what else to do. It apparently means little. Small excitement. He stands off and watches himself. Has casual if intimate affairs like with me, but his real friends would be as much strangers to all this as he originally was. He is like a soldier who has somehow strayed into the other camp and stayed because he does not know where else to go. Is pleased to come, is pleased to stay, is pleased to go—is not really pleased at all. But it represents, I guess, something better than nothing.

6 OCTOBER 1990. Haydn quartets—the delicious Opus 50. They are made up only of themselves. Like something perfectly tailored, not an inch left over, everything accounted for. And at the same time, a world of variety. I like art like that. That is why I like Jane Austen, why I like Henry Green, why I like Ozu, Bresson, and Tarkovsky. And why I do not like the big, inchoate people: Dickens, Liszt, and almost any other film directors one could name. Jonathan [Rauch] said, "You like Mendelssohn better than Beethoven." Right.

10 OCTOBER 1990. How Japan is changing. Now the rice market, the sacred rice market, is being opened. This commodity, which now costs seven times what it does elsewhere, will soon be as cheap (well, almost as cheap) as everywhere else. Not yet to be relinquished are all of those middle men who each take a bit off and thus drives up the price, all those distributors. But just as the small store is being eaten by the supermarket, shortly a successful single distributor will gobble up everyone in between. What will be slower to change is the reliance of the large concern on smaller subcontractors. It is these latter who have to work at a low price, with low paid labor. But so uneconomical is this (except for the large concern) that it cannot be expected to last.

16 OCTOBER 1990. With Frank [Korn] to the Mukai Gallery, where a small ceremony was to be held in honor of his giving a complete set of Marian's prints to the Machida City Museum of Graphic Arts. It was not a solemn occasion, what with the prints being counted, and the curators standing about and Frank pacing and me drinking tea. Still, I wished that Marian could have been there.

She was so ambitious for her art. And now a graphics museum requesting an edition of her work—how happy and proud she would have been. She often had shows at this gallery. I looked around, as I had so often at these various vernissages, but there was no Marian standing there, pleased, and smiling.

Frank took me to lunch and we talked about women. He maintained that he did not care what his women did so long as he did not know. As I well knew, remembering my strange and carnal affair with Marian, which lasted for years but occurred only a few times. I had felt worse and worse about Frank. I liked him better than I did Marian, but how do you let the cuckolded husband know this? We got drunk together once, in the wilds of Otsuka, and I remember almost pleading to let me tell him. Tears in my eyes, I wanted him to listen to my confession, all about his wife. And drunk as he was, with what skill he looped my confessions over my arm, turned me around, and sent me home. I never did get to apologize.

To change the subject I now asked him when his first time was. "Fourteen." In Vienna. "A business person?" "*Ach*, no. Wealthy housewife. She used to have her chauffeur wait in front of the school." "Did you do it in the Dusenberg?" "No, she would take me home. Have tea first. Maids in aprons, footmen." "Where was her husband?" "At work probably." Did this occur often? "Every day." "What a strong schoolboy." "Oh, no, each day a different school boy. I only got into the limousine once a week or so." What prewar Vienna must have been. . . .

17 OCTOBER 1990. I introduce a program of the films of Terayama Shuji at International House. When you look at these short pictures, you look into his mind. His mythology is there—beautiful, distant, wrong end of telescope, the past animated. And I remember him with his odd searching gaze, his rueful little boy smile, his sickly complexion—for the kidneys that killed him had gone bad in childhood. In the first film, the naval officer father takes off his pants, then his *fundoshi*, and staggers drunk and naked about the old farmhouse; and in the last, Terayama sits in his director's chair, back to camera, as the play of shadows is dismantled, and then gets up without a backward glance and leaves. And in an hour and a half I have encompassed a life.

19 OCTOBER 1990. John Haylock takes us out—Eric, Paul McCarthy, and me. We do not talk about sex but rather about religion and eventually about the saints. Paul tells of St. Agatha, depicted as having had her breasts sliced off and put before her on a plate. "Not a proper thing to discuss at table," said John peering down at his sautéed slices of eggplant.

I gave him Francis Partridge's new volume of diaries because some friends of his are in it. Duncan Grant, for example. This reminds John of the portrait that Grant did of him, left behind when the Turks invaded Cyprus. When he returned he found the flat a shambles, and there by the fireplace, crumpled, was the portrait. He unfolded it and found that some Turkish soldier had used it to wipe himself. Not, perhaps, a proper thing to discuss at table.

20 OCTOBER 1990. That sense of "them" and "us." The polarization; the breaking apart. It is stronger than ever. Visible everyplace. Though I can feel its attraction, I am one of the few, I think, who is aware—or at least aware and disapproving. I do not trust myself. I find myself thinking: them, them, them. How much is real; how much is "me"; how much is "them."

If it is true that "they" oscillate between open and closed, then they are going into a closed phase. The faces are closed; the minds are closed. At least the occasional opposite is no longer common: the open face, the open question, and the open smile.

Very well, the new bourgeoisie: timid, craven, yuppie. But how much now, I wonder, is it "us" as well—we spurned white lovers. Was it ever any different? Did I not experience the exceptions? And have not affluence and time made these exceptions fewer?

I do not know. But at least I question myself. This is not done by many foreigners here. They hate. It is there, on their faces, and in their books.

21 OCTOBER 1990. To see Martin Scorsese's *Goodfellas*. How luxurious to sit in a movie and from the first shot know that everything is going to be all right, that an intelligence is guiding, someone whose artistry, technique and morals you can trust.

And what a packed film it is. From the first, information is pouring in from different circuits. There are the visuals, smooth but fast, then there is the dialogue, which is broken, fragmentary, then the voice-over which is echoed by dialogue, and at the same time is not talking about the visuals, and then there is the constant music, hits of the day. And just as Robert de Niro ages and puts on his bi-focals, so the music changes from big band smooth to hard rock hard.

Wonderful shot: out of the taxi, into the back door of the Copacabana, down the stairs, through the kitchen, out onto the floor, the headwaiter, the table carried and laid, the floor show, our people watching, champagne poured. All in one fluid shot, and everything choreographed along the way.

It is intelligent and frantic, just like the director. I remember him here, all eyebrows and tics and malaise. And Isabel Rossellini (they were just married) trying to soothe him (it was in their fake Louis XV suite at the Tokyo Prince) and he was smiling and frowning at the same time. The film is just like him. Style is the man.

23 OCTOBER 1990. Big party hosted by Oshima Nagisa to celebrate thirty years of marriage. Also perhaps to raise money for the new film. [Tomiyama] Katsue and [Kawakita] Kazuko figured out that a free party always manages (like politicians' parties) to raise money. Usually nowadays when a person gives a party you are told how much it will cost you to go—equivalent of $100, $200. And so for a "free" celebratory party like this people usually get envelopes ready with $300 or $400 in them. Let me see, if there are 1,000 guests and each gives $300. . . .

At the event, the hall is so big and expensive (The Tokyo Prince Hotel), and the food so lavish (fresh lobster, boeuf Wellington, trout, mango, papaya) that it may have cost him that much. I bring a painting (one of my own) for them. Kazuko says, implying that I am getting off cheap, "Ah, you artists . . ." I ask what she brought. Flowers. "Ah, you florists . . ." I say.

Just everyone there. Everyone a generation later. I see lots of actors I have not seen since the days of Ozu—Tanaka Haruo, for example, now barely visible behind his age. Apparently I am also near unrecognizable. Approached by director Wakamatsu Koji, not seen for a time, with, "Wow, you got real old" (*Waa, sugoku toshi natchatta ne . . .*)—this from a fiftyish, wrinkled, salt-and-pepper oldster. I playfully pull one of his graying locks, but do not believe for a minute that his observation is without malice. I am, after all, the only one who has refused to take his cinematic effusions seriously.

He makes embarrassing soft-core psychodrama (or used to), and Noël Burch led the French into seeing great cinematic depths in *Violated Angels*. It occurs to no one that the reason for making it (nurses skinned alive) was non-cinematic. So, Koji was treated as though his junk meant something. And here he is a grand old man. If you last long enough just everyone becomes a grand old man. I am turning into one myself.

Then, a plump but well-preserved Yamamoto Fujiko gives a funny little speech—this long-stemmed Japanese beauty whom I will always remember in her single Ozu film, *Higanbana*. Shinoda Masahiro, all gray now but still very much the Boy Scout, asking just how I liked his *Days of Youth*, which I had not at all but can tell him I had recommended it to the Palm Springs Festival. Old Oba Hideo, he must be ninety now, gives the doddering toast, and the president of Toei the main speech. Not Shochiku? No. Shochiku, the

company who first sponsored Oshima and then fired him, is not even represented. A scandal, but an expected one.

I leave early and hence miss the unexpected scandal. Oshima had asked
novelist Nozaka Yoshiyuki to say a few words, then forgot that he had. Nozaka
waited around, drinking the while, and by the time that Oshima remembered,
was so smashed that he went to the podium, picked up the hand mike, and hit
his host over the head with it. The irate and no more sober Oshima responded
by brandishing the mike stand, and finally famous author and noted director
had to be parted by force.

25 NOVEMBER 1990. Interviewed for a provincial paper. During it I mention
that the Tokugawa period is not over, that self-imposed self-restraint, the acceptance of official guidance, the inability to stand out or stand up, and the
fearful cowardice the government fosters—all this is Tokugawa. Wide eyes
greet this. My interviewer has never once heard this opinion. Much intrigued.
Wonder what it will look like in the paper. Japan-bashing? Probably.

27 NOVEMBER 1990. To my old friend Marcel Grilli's wake. Since he was a
Catholic it is a long, tiresome, self-serving affair with the priest giving his
hype, saying such things as, "he experiences the greatest happiness who gives
himself unconditionally, entirely, to God." Service saved and made moving
by a talk from Peter Grilli, who remembered his parent with temperance and
consideration, and brought to the service the humanity it ought have had
from the beginning.

After all this Thanatos, a touch of Eros—I am taken by Eric to the most
expensive of the *urisen* bars. It used to be called The Herakles; now—times
being what they are—it is The Fitness Boy. Due to the rain and the fact that
it was Wednesday we had the place to ourselves, a number of bulging fitness
boys lounging about. When we arrived they took off their T-shirts. In other
professions you put *on* a shirt when customers come.

They sat around in their muscles, gratefully accepted drinks and smiled,
and horsed about with each other in boyish fashion. With a bit of encouragement they would have horsed about with us as well. I inquire as to the financial arrangements. Expensive—about five thousand or so for drinks, then five
thousand or so to take your choice off the premises, and then fifteen thousand
or so for the boy himself, who always expects about five thousand for tip. It all
comes up to three hundred dollars or so. "But," says my host judiciously, "you
must realize that girls nowadays cost twice this much."

A large projected TV image (takes up one whole wall) of young Japanese doing unspeakable things to each other. At the corner, a smaller TV set showing something different—Roger Moore in fact. I ask why. Well, the big one is for the guests, and the small one (James Bond at present) is to give the boys something to look at. The boys, well trained, drain their glasses. Time for another round. The cute one, nude to the waist, stands up humbly and thankfully to clink glasses with us. Humble muscles—the way to the homo heart.

2 JANUARY 1991. Last night a New Year's dream. Very vivid, beautiful, sad, mysterious. I am with Marguerite Yourcenar who is packing, getting ready to go. The train is waiting just beside the davenport, its smoke caught in the drapes. I am admiring her garden at the other end of the room. It is small, but climbs up the wall and is alive with lizards and salamanders, and water runs slowly down from the ceiling, and big snails fall heavily onto the moss beneath. I tell her she will hate to leave it. She says that she does not like leaving, but that it is necessary.

Then she gives me a large block of smoked glass. Holding it up I see, brown, dim, three men, as in a daguerreotype, one of whom is naked and shows a large, soft penis. They all shift back into the shadows, then out again. I understand that in their limited way they are alive. The entire effect is very beautiful, and I reluctantly hand it back to her. "Oh, no," says Madame, "it is for you. You may keep it." At once I am intensely, absurdly grateful. I cry, my voice breaks, and I make a small speech. I remember it still: "Oh, Madame," cry I, "you have given me everything. And now you have given me my death."

This was said with an insane sincerity, and such a gush of feeling that I woke up, the mysterious inhabited box in my hands as the dream began to fade. I know what it probably means but that is not important. Female approval of my looking at waving cocks may be what prompts that infant outburst, but what moves me is the beauty of it—the brownness of the miniature men, the broad whiteness of beautiful Madame, and my own emotion, surging, like a cut jugular, threatening to suffocate me with feeling.

3 JANUARY 1991. The annual party of Kawakita Kazuko and Shibata Hayato at their house—critic Kawarabata Tei, people from the Film Center and the Film Library Council, director Yanagimachi Mitsuo, and the dean of the TV film folk, old (eighty-two) Yodogawa Nagaharu.

And Osugi. He is half of an outrageous pair of twins. Pico is the other, but he has just lost an eye to cancer and is now more quiet. Osugi is not quiet. His screech cuts through any conversation, no matter how distant. And he is continually holding up his hands (a ring on each and every finger) for silence. However, he knows what he is doing.

He is a faggot giving an imitation of a faggot and being very good at it. And since he is a *Japanese* faggot, the bitchiness is soon seen as a pose and the malice as made up. He has become society's idea of a homosexual, and by being so has defanged the opposition.

Also, he has another and more traditional role. He is the *taikomochi*, the male geisha, a traditional figure, very necessary to the better parties. Being men, they can be much more outrageous than women are allowed to be. Camping it up is an ancient tradition in Japanese society.

Also, like the fool at the royal court, the *taikomochi* is allowed to tell the truth. This is what Osugi does. He is the only critic on TV who is outspoken. Everyone else is conciliatory, bowing to power. Not him. He openly called the new Kadokawa film a stupid little boy's epic, an infantile executive playing at toy soldiers. Many people listen, not to be amused by camp, but for information. He gets away with it because the accepted opinion is that no one would pay much attention to the opinions of a notorious fag. But everyone does.

I see that he and the venerable Yodogawa are now quite close. He calls the elder critic "father," and Yodogawa turns to me with a small smile and says, "Of course, I am really his mother." When they leave (hired car, ten-thirty sharp) people stand up, applaud, as at the end of a performance—which it was.

9 FEBRUARY 1991. With Peter Greenaway—interviewing him. I see it as a meeting, he, initially, as a duel. ". . . and I find the tube more noisy and bigger than . . . well, then, you," he says before we even begin. I recognize the ploy, having met many British. After charm is on the troubled greensward poured, he loses his suspicions, whatever they were, and becomes interested in himself. Literate, amusing, charming, and pensive, but always testing the way, every step. Maybe he has had bad interviews in the past. Or been interviewed mainly by the English. At first the information is heavy with quotations, Truffaut, Renoir, etc., as though to mine the field. Later it becomes more personal—he is seen playing tennis in the final shot of *Blowup*. Says that *The Draughtsman's Contract* ushered in the Thatcher era and that *The Cook, The Thief, His Wife, and Her Lover* ushered it out. Laughs. Is intensely concerned over impression made—he and his films alike.

11 FEBRUARY 1991. In the paper this morning that Inoue Yasushi died, in his eighties, pneumonia. Not unexpected, but sad. Sad because he was a writer who could imagine. He imagined the wastes of Dunhuang, the ruined Lou-lan, the various lives of the Emperor Goshirakawa, and the death of Confucius. These he reconstructed with the most scrupulous care, a base for his splendid conjurings. I have never found an arbitrary passage in his works, nor one that was not scrupulous in exposing his sources. It is rare to read a writer who retains the wonder of the past, who shows us the links between then and now, who treats the dead with respect. And now he is dead himself.

I remember him two years ago: I had arranged a showing of a film based on one of his works—*Dunhuang*. Though the film was a travesty of what he had written, he nonetheless courteously came and was introduced before the screening. He even stayed afterward to answer questions.

A tall old man, kindly and meticulous, a slow and smiling concern for just the right word, and—I thought—a sad gaze as he looked at the insensitive and corrupt version of his work. Or, maybe not. Maybe he knew that commercial cinema has its limitations, and no more resented this than he would have a child's version of one of his stories.

Perhaps his wisdom was deeper than his taste, deeper even than his ethics. Maybe he simply sat and understood. And I remember his style: plain, particular, always in work clothes, and containing a great strength. He made no appeal, but after you read him you understood and you remembered.

16 FEBRUARY 1991. Party with Francis Coppola and family—wife, daughter, and father. Francis much less up, much more on an even keel. Have never seen him with his father before. "Don't do that, Francis." "Oh, you always say that," says Francis. "Because you always do it," says father. Then, to no one, "Know how I named him? Looked out of the window and there was this Ford going by."

Daughter, only nineteen, is a forced bloom. I wonder if she was allowed any childhood. And now pushed into a movie role. Sweet. Unsure. Latches onto me in a nice kind of way. For protection. Looked around and decided I was the least threat. Also, I knew her before. Last time was when she was six. She does not remember but is told I am an Old Friend.

Later, the elder Coppola, Takemitsu, and I have long talk about music. Father talks. We listen. Tells about his lessons with Edgar Varese. "So poor he was. Used to meet him bringing back the garbage pail. Had to dump it himself." Also, "He had no system of teaching. None."

More stories, these about playing first flute under Toscanini. The Italian conductor shared the orchestra with Stokowski one season, and when it was

With Sofia Coppola.

With Carmen Coppola, Takemitsu Toru.

Toscanini's turn he would raise his baton, listen, then start screaming. "*Bruta, bruta,* that white hair freak he ruin my orchestra!" Coppola also indicates the difference between the two conductors. The Italian knew precisely what he wanted to do when he stepped on the podium. It was all worked out. The fake Russian, real Brit, knew nothing, waited for the orchestra to teach him—emoted, got inspired, etc.

And what is the most difficult flute passage in the orchestral repertoire? Is it the long exposed part in *Daphnis?* No, not at all, it is the last half of the scherzo from *A Midsummer Night's Dream,* when Mendelssohn makes the flute "hop, skip, jump and skitter right up to the top."

Takemitsu agreed, again, kind of, to do the score for the film they are making of my *Inland Sea.* We try to remember how long ago it was when we first met. Thirty years, thirty-five? He pats my cheek, "But you haven't changed at all."

No—he is the one who has not changed. Only grown. I heard the viola concerto on the radio the other day. That little boy could create such big, strange, wonderful sounds.

17 FEBRUARY 1991. Fumio in hospital, undiagnosed, danger of peritonitis. I find the hospital, go see him. He is lying curled up in bed looking much like he did twenty years ago when I would come back from work and wake him up. He is asleep and I look at him, needles in his arm, tubes everywhere, eyes closed, breathing deeply.

I weep, suddenly, unexpectedly. It is the sight of time recaptured, to be sure, but, more, it is worry and fear and the sudden possibility of his dying.

All of the physical affection I once felt returned, and I put my hand on his arm. Unlike twenty years ago, when he was still young, he now woke at once, his eyes opening, staring at me, knowing neither himself, nor me, then slowly intelligence returns. "Oh, Mr. Richie," he said, which is what he has always called me for two decades. We talk of the illness, what the doctor has said, how happy he is he changed hospitals, the good care they are taking of him. And we gradually return to being two adults.

There were no more journals for the spring and summer of 1991. The time was spent traveling, writing the *Japan Times* weekly literary column, all of the occasional pieces requested, and gathering material on early foreigners in Japan for what was to become *The Honorable Visitors*. His oldest foreign friend in Japan, Eric Klestadt, suffered a stroke.

21 SEPTEMBER 1991. Rain, a different kind of coolness, and something determined—autumn. Even a few days ago summer cicadas called—but in vain. Now they are silent—the only sound is the rain falling steadily, purposefully.

Fittingly elegiac sound for the continuation of this journal, sporadic as it is. But I want to continue it for a while because I do not want to see life going by unrecorded, no notice taken other than the living of it.

The early fall of 1991—the Soviets lie in ruins, Yugoslavia ruptures, China simmers, America whines, and selfish, natural, pragmatic Japan, uninhibited by any fellow feeling, opens wide its little mouth. Peaceful here, except for those who came seeking it. The Iranians silently starve in the park, the Pakistani have learned to batten off the others, the Chinese slyly rob each other, and the Japanese, stepping over the bodies, ignore all these frightened barbarians in their midst.

And Eric's stroke, his lying for six weeks now, unable to read or write, barely to speak, right arm and leg gone, buried alive. He who took such an interest in everything can now take interest in nothing. No books, no TV, no radio, no music. Nothing left.

His nurse tells me that he throws away all of his magazines, unopened and unread. Though I don't want them, trying to break through his apathy I tell him he should give them to me. He stares at me in that lopsided way that stroke sufferers have. I say, slowly, deliberately, that he is selfish. I say this because I want to reach him, to go beyond those little nods and noises that so insultingly seem to say that everything is all right. He opens his mouth and gets out a sentence: "I am selfish." He has to be. He is fighting for his sanity, locked up there with only the windows of his eyes to look out of.

I go every day and the nurses are chipper, the doctor is optimistic, and Eric lies there nodding and trying to smile. Trying to agree, no words coming. And I remember how adroit he was with language, and how proud of it, how dapper he was with words.

His mind remains clear. He knows what has happened to him.

27 DECEMBER 1991. Go with Chizuko to the private showing of Teshigahara's new film, *Basara: The Princess Go.* Director there, and star, Miyazawa Rie. Also the big TV star Beat Takeshi [Kitano], and the well-remembered boxer Akai Hidekazu, star of *Dotsuitarunen [Knockout].*

He has gotten a little beefy, but is still astonishing looking. Impressed, hence—not like me at all—I actually go and introduce myself, tell him about my titles for his film, about my taking it to San Francisco. At once, with an athletic grace, he is up and off the sofa and bowing. Delighted, has heard my name. Big, beefy hand proffered in acknowledgement of my Westerness. And, the most ingratiating smile. It is one I know from the films and the TV, and can identify. Most people in love with themselves have this captivating smile, one that illuminates inwardly and does not warm. One sees it a lot in sportsmen, particularly body builders. You sure see it in the captivating Akai. He in turn introduces the model turned actress.

Actually little Rie-chan and he have more in common than their presence here. They both posed for the same photographer. She, notoriously so. Shinoyama Kishin posed her in Santa Fe with no clothes, and the portfolio *Santa Fe,* at nearly $40 the copy, has sold, says the papers, five million. She is more famous now than the Prime Minister who shares her family name. But unbeknownst to her and to everyone else is that the famous photographer has also taken a portfolio of equally nude pictures of Akai.

Once this very long movie is over, everyone has to pee, and I find myself at the trough with Beat on one side of me and Akai on the other. Beat does not get a glance but my eyes still ache from trying to look down at Akai without turning my head. Glimpsed the private part. Blunt, heavy, Osaka-type.

Tell Chizuko, who smiles, then tells me of *her* bathroom adventure: Little Rie-chan was in tears in the lady's room. Why? I wondered. Doesn't know. I think it was the strain of seeing herself for the first time in her first major role. Today was her first viewing. She had not known what to expect. Since she is very good, these must have been tears of relief.

28 DECEMBER 1991. Cold night, chill wind. Came home early. Made own supper. Sausage from Frank, and French toast on which I put the Maine maple syrup, gift of Marguerite Yourcenar, and treasured in the back of the fridge. She sent it before she went to hospital, just after Jerry died. That was long ago. Now what remained was all lumpy from years in the cold. And it had changed. It had made its own mother, as we used to call what formed in vinegar. But it was sweet, like honey made from very old bees. I could spread it on the French toast. Which I did, and ate it. Mother Marguerite.

29 DECEMBER 1991. Thinking back over New York—Jonathan [Rauch], Chester [Biscardi], Tom [Wolfe], and Susan [Sontag]. They live in an element I do not. Theirs is the current of contemporary thought, and they swim—mostly against it—and grow sleek. I have no intellectual climate at all. I have no one with whom to speak of these concerns, no one to learn from, no one to teach. For fifty years I have lived alone in the library of my skull. Thus, I have learned to live with the immortals. But, I no longer live with people who think as I do. Consequently, I am out of touch with the climate of my times, except for what I can glean by reading the *New York Review of Books*, the *TLS*. Susan once asked me how I managed to keep up with things, presuming that I did. And I innocently answered: "*Newsweek*."

31 DECEMBER 1991. Dinner with Fumio. He is forty-two now and fat. But I still see the boy of twenty-two, slim. And his character has never changed. He is still honest, no cant at all. Tonight we remember the times were got drunk together: Tsugaru on New Year's, Ishigakijima, Amami Oshima, and (worst) Kurashiki, just before he got married. We were feeling awful and drinking made it worse.

Now he is divorced and I no longer feel awful at all, have not for years. He has his friends; I have mine. We are family now. He also has a hangover this evening. Party at his bar last night. Master has to drink or customers won't. He has to make them drink to make a living. So he has to get drunk. "Threw up three times on the way home, managed to get out of the taxi to do it." We eat Korean food. He perks up and by the time the *kimchee* is gone no longer looks bleary-eyed.

Now sixty-eight years old, Richie found ever-increasing interest in his journals. They became a way not only to salvage experience, but also to assess it. As his attitude changed, so did his tone. It became more intimate and more conversational. In addition to thinking of

his journals as a work in themselves and not merely a repository for future use, Richie felt he really had someone to talk to—the future readers whom he now acknowledged. The journals began to show a structure of their own. Richie was aware of this and was interested to see it emerging, unwilled as it were, from the chaos of everyday life.

21 JANUARY 1992. New Year's Day. I wander around. Look at the new buildings. The architecture now is the "kindergarten look"—buildings made of blocks, the cute made collossal. Is this, I wonder, the new rococo? Frivolity embodied by materials tortured into miracles of ingenuity.

22 JANUARY 1992. I behave in the Japanese manner. I refuse something, have to be urged, I say I am wrong when I am not. This brings smiles and nods. But I am not seen as behaving "like a Japanese." I am seen as behaving properly.

23 JANUARY 1992. A blond workman, long yellow strands straying from under the hard hat. Face that of elderly Japanese. The fashion last year was yellow streaks in the coiffeurs of the young. Now, in the manner of fashions, it has descended the social ladder. The proletariat has taken it up. It is the latest item in workman chic. Pierced ears are next.

26 JANUARY 1992. At the porno. Villain foiled in the middle, true love over somewhat later, and still the film has several reels to go. A divertissement-like coda consisting of pure fucking, no plot. Porno is constructed like the nineteenth-century ballet, like *Casse-noisette*. Story over at the end of the second act, the third is all dancing—Candyland.

28 JANUARY 1992. Dinner with Paul McCarthy. He tells me of being in Thailand and meeting an older professor at university there. Talk turned to Japanese literature and then to film, then to me. "Oh, yes," said the professor. "Donald Richie. Isn't she Donald Keene's wife?" Paul, surprised, said, that no, he was not. "But surely Rizzi is a woman's name, isn't it, and they have the same family name; I had always thought that they were related." Paul explained, but the professor was not convinced.

30 JANUARY 1992. Out with Leza [Lowitz] who now teaches at Disney. Told me a curious story about Mickey Mouse. Elsewhere he has four fingers. Apparently easier to draw that way. In Japan, however, four fingers is the common pejorative gesture for the *burakumin*, the proscribed class. Four fingers

With Leza Lowitz, 2002.

shown in derision refers to the four legs of a beast. With the Burakumin League now so litigious, they are taking no chances. In Japan the Mickey and Minnie logos are redrawn.

On the way back in the subway, I suddenly realized that being Japanese must be like being a teenager in an unusually repressive high school. Adolescents are always at the mercy of every fad—the sudden difference rendered identical in that everyone must at once evidence it; the single difference at once branding the person as hopelessly different. The truly different here in Japan are subject to all of the petty molestations common to high schools everywhere: banished, punished, and bullied.

Many Japanese are like high school students: unsure of self, settling for the group every time. And knowledge becomes knowing how to order the proper cherry coke at the single drugstore that is in fashion.

31 JANUARY 1992. The Donald Richie Commemorative Collection of Stringed Chamber Music continues to grow—now nine shelves of CDs, lots of LPs, and as many scores of the music as I can find. The catalogue is a dozen pages long now. I would never allow myself anything this expensive. Therefore it is going to a worthy cause, Tokushima University. Thus, I can enjoy it and not feel bad. It is really for someone else, all those anonymous, impoverished chamber music lovers I envision. It also means that I have to buy music I don't like—the Henze Quartets for example—since I have to be complete.

Today, however, I get something I do like: a Schnittke Trio. Got it in a small and specialized shop in Shibuya, where I had gone to practice the piano at the Kawaii showroom for my performance next week, accompanying *He Who Gets Slapped*. I have decided on a Schnittke-like score, dissident mazurkas intersperced with inane waltzes and galops, and lots of padding when Lon Chaney is working up his grand theory. But like everything else in Tokyo, the enormous Kawaii practice room complex is full. I can hear *Für Elise* tinkling in canon, and the "Moonlight" peddling away into the distance. Will return later.

1 FEBRUARY 1992. Woke up at six to a strange light. Usually still gray outside. Now it was white, a pure whiteness as though all my windows had shoji paper. I got up and looked out. All white. It had snowed during the night and now Tokyo was covered. I might have known it was snow as I lay in my warm futon and listened to the quiet. Snow blankets all sounds. I could have been in the distant mountains.

2 FEBRUARY 1992. There was a strong earthquake this morning at four. The jolts woke me and I scampered to the door to prop it open, for it is a metal door that would jam, and then would come the fire.

As I opened the door, there was the peaceful starry night scene, all the snow before me and then, another large jolt. As I watched, all the snow fell— off the roofs, off the trees, off the overhead wires—pulled down in a second by the shuddering ground.

It was like the transformation in the *danmari* in the Kabuki. Only there the dark curtain drops to reveal the light. Here the white dropped to reveal the black. I savored this wonderful spectacle and was glad to have been awakened to see it. Then back to bed, asleep in five minutes, not at all frightened—too entranced by the extraordinary sight.

3 FEBRUARY 1992. Letter from Darrell Davis, who writes that he finds me "... decidedly literary ... drawn to subtlety and completeness of characterization—of people, places, atmosphere—which seems to me a primarily literary pursuit. Is your continuing fascination with things Japanese a function of the incorrigible textuality of Japanese culture?" If so, this would explain, he thinks, "... the metaphorical direction your thinking about the culture seems to have taken—closer now to Barthes and to Burch."

Maybe. "Literature," I replied, "has been for me the screen through which I view the world. It began very young when I discovered the public library and realized that I could control my world though the word. Reading was one way. Writing was even better. But," I continued, "in Japan I never learned to read or write. Hence all signifiers and no signified, just like Barthes." And this means "control without being controlled."

I still believe this. When you learn *kanji* you enter into a great mind-set: Things have only one meaning from then on—the assigned one. My spoken Japanese is all right, but since I can't really read, it is still fluid, has not been defined by reading and writing, so I do not have to believe in it. My control is there, but only in English.

Darrell also says that he cannot imagine my feeling "at home" in Japan because, ". . . it is hard to imagine sustaining the kind of detachment necessary to write, the kind of reflective commentary you do when you're at home." Maybe, but then I find anyone who is "at home" in this universe a person seriously deluded. I would hate to be at home. But I do sometimes now think of myself as a bridge. But what kind? Suspension? Single span? Draw? Arch?

4 FEBRUARY 1992. Am snappy with the service. At Wendy's the waitress is not paying attention to me, stares at the ceiling, looks around, peers into the kitchen. But, I am her customer, he to whom she owes her very job. I am cold as ice when I finally capture her attention. My eyes speak stern volumes. My tone could freeze. She stares. Does not comprehend, but is hurt. I am mollified, having caused deserved pain. But I do not relent. I keep it up until my hamburger is in hand, change grabbed. Only then do I permit myself a moué and turn away.

Turn away to look at myself. Why did I do that? How could I behave that way? And then, there swims before me another pair of eyes, light blue, cold, outraged. My mother! When she is with the help or on the telephone talking to a reluctant tradesperson. My mother, ordering the service about. That was whom I turned into. I bite into my Wendy, pensive. I begin to believe in genes.

The anima. Am I still carrying her around with me? It is undignified for a man going on sixty-eight to still act like the worst in his mother. It is unnatural. Or is it? Maybe everyone does this and either does not notice or is too ashamed to admit it.

6 FEBRUARY 1992. Invective accelerating. The U.S. and Japan cannot say bad enough things about each other. Bad blood in the family of nations. Battling siblings. Easy enough to understand, though nonetheless deplorable. The U.S. slipping, lost its great supporting enemy in the collapse of the U.S.S.R. It needs another one, quick. Japan, slithering out of control, all cool heads hot in this drive to greed, displays an enormous insensitivity to others, and its own real concern for itself. America, angry, finds Japan an ingrate after all we did for it, and Japan, tired of being the idiot younger brother, makes remarks about the American lack of work ethic. All of this is easy to understand. What is not remarked upon is that the bickering is good for the economy of both countries. Just as wartime makes money, so do unfriendly relations. I don't think anyone really believes in this animosity except the stupid. But there are so many.

12 FEBRUARY 1992. A Ginza gentleman's club, the last one. It is immaculately prewar. The paneling is light oak and the floor is parquet. The style is late art deco, with Aztec lines and a Grand Rapids finish. The small windows are leaded in the Frank Lloyd Wright manner, lozenges of gray and yellow. I look at walls, and there it is—a reproduction of Maxfield Parrish's *Daybreak*, one androgynous ephebe leaning over another, against sun struck mountains out of *The Arabian Nights*—the same as that which hung over our Ohio piano and over which wandered my infant eyes, wondering at the immensity and beauty of the world.

13 FEBRUARY 1992. The sound of a temple bell. One does not hear the strike. Rather, the sound starts small and then rapidly builds, a soft explosion. The note is like some animal opening its mouth wide, the brazen roar afterward emerging.

14 FEBRUARY 1992. At the game center. Boy and girl playing Cop Killer, shooting electrical impulses at uniformed cartoon figures, who splatter or not. Two controls. He is shooting most of the cops, but she pulls her trigger now and again and remembers to smile when he turns to look at her. I see he has a package of chocolate on his lap. It is St. Valentine's Day. She has given him the chocolate, as is customary, and he has taken her to the only entertainment he knows anything about—video games. She stifles a yawn when he is not looking. But he rarely looks at her. He is interested in the game. Pow! Wow! Zap!

19 FEBRUARY 1992. Japan-bashing by America has begun to make slight ripples here. I find myself regarded on the train platform or in the subway car. Just regarded, assessed. I try to look European.

As this schism grows I am aware of other cracks. Ones I have myself climbed into. Smoking, for example. Since stopping I have become militant, a born-againer. I cannot "stand" to see people smoking where they "ought not." And so I march right up and tell them. And what a full, warm feeling I experience when I identify myself as a member of the "right" side. I feel for a moment almost a hate. It is warming, like a flame. This is what bashers must feel all the time—on either side. And they get hooked on their highs. Prejudice is addiction.

24 FEBRUARY 1992. The *shinchoge* is blooming in the cold. Spiked little blossoms of lavender and mauve, and giving the scent of summer right in the middle of winter. A lush, strong, tropical perfume—fleshy, like gardenia or magnolia—wafting from the small flowers, smelling of hot nights on these cold days.

Not a popular plant in Japan, however. The reason is that it was planted around latrines to temper the stench. The reputation lingers no matter how nice the smell. I had a plant in the house once. My cleaning lady's eyebrows arched. This was not done.

25 FEBRUARY 1992. Dinner with [Numata] Makiyo. Back here for dessert and coffee, he asked to see the pictures I had taken of him on our various trips—in Europe, in America, and him at university in Hawaii. He is now thirty and had, I thought, done well. He has his own company, has branches abroad, is married, and is taking care of his ailing parents. Success.

Recently, to be sure, with the collapse of Japan's inflated land prices I thought that as a developer he might be experiencing a slight recession. But I was not prepared for his suddenly telling me, in that earnest and schoolboy fashion of his, about a property in the desert outside Los Angeles that he has bought and is now making payments on.

Finally I understood that, in the oblique manner that has always been his, he was offering it as collateral. Collateral for what, and to whom? Well, to me. He needed a million yen before the end of the week.

This was surprising. I had not known things were so bad for him because he had never told me. I did not want the collateral, I said, but I would transfer the amount to his account tomorrow morning. One millon yen is a lot of money—eight thousand dollars. He promised to pay it all back by the end of June. Then I told him how surprised I was, and gently chided him for not letting me know the true state of his affairs. Gentle though I was, this push was enough.

He suddenly broke into tears—the first in the eight years of our friendship. The strong Makiyo cried like a man, choking back the sobs, face awash. Finally he said, "I wanted so much to succeed." I knew that was so. For as long as I have known him, it has been winning the marathon, and believing that if you throw yourself into it you will get it, whatever it is. "My Way" is his favorite song. And now, in front of me, the person who knows him best, he must admit failure. I told him what one tells people—the truth: One failure is not for a lifetime; everyone fails at something.

After a time the sobs stopped. He wiped his face and smiled ruefully at himself as though he were his own little brother. I gave him more Kleenex. He understood me, and my reasons. I could no longer continue to embarrass him by witnessing his tears—so in the most open and friendly fashion I told him to get out. Tomorrow I will go to the bank, and at the same time will now see my friend as an allegorical figure. Makiyo—Financially Over-Extended Japan.

26 FEBRUARY 1992. Coming back from visiting Eric in the hospital I pass again the small house atop an embankment: low tile roof, paper windows behind which a lamp is shining, bamboo fence, and a plum tree in blossom. The simplicity, the beauty, the comfort. When all houses looked like this, I did not notice. Now this is one of the few left.

In the neighborhood, two like it are already gone. In their places, correct concrete boxes with metal roofs and double-paned windows, and that Tinkertoy look called postmodern. I know why too. Back then, tile and bamboo and paper were least expensive and came in standardized units. Now concrete and plastic do.

In the subway coming home I observe the young. Eyes deep in *manga*, ears surrendered to Walkman. They try to insulate themselves. I see them making their bulky hamburger-fed bodies small, the girls particularly conscious of their size, trying to forget it by banding conspicuously together and talking "boy" language.

Boys are solitary, wear black, hide in the corners. Neither sex has any use for the elderly staring foreigner. Nor should they. He can do nothing for them. They need nothing from him. And I remember when just such a look of mine could bring a smile. Back then they were happy to have foreigners talk to them. Now the foreigners are happy if they can talk to the youngsters.

21 MARCH 1992. Reading Cyril Connolly. He says: "It is a mistake to expect good work from expatriates, for it is not what they do that matters but what they are not doing." For him expatriation is all about escape. "It gives them a breathing space in which to free themselves from commercialism, family ties, racial ties." OK, but expatriation is more than that. It is an embracing, a reaching out, a moving into as well as a moving away from. He seems to think so too—eventually.

Henry James, his example, ". . . was not an expatriate in so far as he repatriated himself as an Englishman." Yes, but there seems to be another position, which Connolly ignores. Mine. I am at home in Japan precisely because I am an alien body. I am no longer a member over there, and cannot become a member over here—this defines my perfectly satisfactory position. One does not *have* to be a member of something.

23 MARCH 1992. Fumio and Masudo come to Eric's long-empty house to help me. They move his books, some three thousand of them, from upstairs to down, so he can stagger in from the hospital and pick out those he wants to take with him to Melbourne. I will catalogue the pictures; we have already selected his clothes. And everything else must somehow to be gotten rid of. It is like the last reel of *Citizen Kane*—all of those belongings. But Kane was dead and Eric is not. He must sit here and look at the ruins himself.

He cannot but think of better times—of the day he bought that book, or the week he read it. Things still have voices. They will speak to him. I can see him struggling not to feel. Through the partial paralysis pain still reaches. I cannot bear to look.

24 MARCH 1992. The Kawakita Memorial Film Institute prize is given to [cinematographer] Miyagawa Kazuo, standing there on the podium, hands folded, smiling, eighty-four. I know his age because Madame Kawakita, sounding slightly scandalized, said, "Why he's just as old as I am." Mifune Toshiro, looking severe and sage, told me that *he* was seventy-two. Said it with an air of surprise and that kind of ironic seriousness that is so much a part of him and that has never appeared on the screen. Polite as always, he then remembered that some years ago he had promised to come to something or other I was organizing and then couldn't. I had forgotten all about it, but he hadn't.

Kurosawa, now eighty-one, told me about his new film. Does not have a proper title. "First time that ever happened." Doesn't like the working title, *Madadayo*, nor do I. I remind him that the phrase was used by Ozu in a film. He nods. One more count against it. Wanted to call it *Hide and Seek*, but Daiei doesn't like that. Shakes his head, smiles.

25 MARCH 1992. Perhaps more than an American high school, Japan is like an English public school. You are supposed to learn, excel, and win athletic distinctions—not for yourself, but for the house and for the country, for being Japanese. First on the field, all for the sake of your school. And then, the emptiness when you graduate.

31 MARCH 1992. Warm, sunny day, and the cherry blossoms are out. Ueno Park is covered with them, clouds of pink—like a Kano screen. The sakura are in full bloom. And how could a country which looks like this every year be anything but artificial?

More than usual this year, I also feel strongly what poets have called the "menace" of these blooms. There is a tradition that finds them sinister—madness in the blossoms, with long-haired and crazy maidens cavorting under burdened branches. Or, as Mishima used to say, in a sinister way quoting some minor master, homosexuality (*nanshoku*) is a "...wolf asleep under the blossoming *sakura*."

A reason for my ambivalence toward this year's blossom is that I remember Eric. One spring we were walking around Yanaka, and found in some temple courtyard a perfect *sakura* in full bloom. I have looked for it again and again in the labyrinth of that district, but never have found it. And now because Eric is mute and halt, and being carted off to Australia next Monday, I find cherry blossoms sinister.

1 APRIL 1992. Woken at six this morning by hovering helicopters battering the air above me. Peered out. High up, two of them, stationary. What could it be—disaster? riot? coup d'état? They hung around all morning, puttering in the sky, making an enormous racket. Finally I discovered what it was: the cherry blossoms. They were up there taking pictures for the press, showing the extent of the quiet blossoming, making life below hideous so that they could present tranquil beauty on the covers of rag and mag.

2 APRIL 1992. Thoughts on aging. It is not the thinning hair, the spreading wrinkles, the occasional misstep, or the misplaced word that bothers me. It is the creeping conservatism. I find myself agreeing with a majority opinion and am surprised to discover that emotionally I am with the masses, as I have not been since a child.

This seems to me craven. I grow afraid for self and even for property. The elderly, if they are not careful, turn bourgeois, anxious for their holdings. With this fear comes an inclination not only to be disagreeable, but also to collect injustices. All feelers out, I make up my mind about people in the street and idly criticize them—making it all up, of course.

When I am in temporary power, however, I am ruthless. How dreadful I could be if I did not watch myself. So cold, preemptory, for no reason but a chill center and fear for self. This is what growing old does, or does for me. It makes me afraid. I have never, all through my life, been far distant from that emotion, but now it moves closer, as close as it was in childhood. I must be vigilant and refuse it entry.

In the evening a party, sort of, for Eric. His expansive elder brother, Albert—carrying him off to the antipodes on Monday—was there, and the suave Sawada [Ichiro] in full kimono, and Frank and Chizuko. Only once did Eric look at me and slowly shake his head. The hopelessness of his awful life from now on. It was a moment of real communication. Then he returned to apathy.

4 APRIL 1992. The wedding of [Numata] Shinsaku, Makiyo's younger brother. It was held at the new Meguro Gajoen, a vast wedding palace, on the outside all chrome-period modern Japan. A fine example of the wedding industry.

The reception and dinner takes place in an enormous room, paneled in silk, chairs and tables faux Louis XV; hanging above all of this is lighting and sound equipment as in a recording studio: weddings as show biz.

Then the lights lower and John Williams is heard on the sound track; the spotlights flash on, and the voice of the compère asks us to give the couple a big hand as the portals open, and there stand the happy pair, he in *hakama*, she in wedding kimono, wig, and face painted white.

There are other touches of tradition. The compère chats throughout, in Japanese but the tone is that of Ralph Edwards telling you that *This Is Your Life*. Everything else is twenty-first century. No Wagner, no Mendelssohn, just *E.T.* And when the knife is inserted into the slit of the ten-foot high inedible plastic mock-up of a cake, a device is triggered that envelops both confection and couple in clouds of dry ice. The cut cake is wheeled off. At the end it will reappear, all wrapped, one piece for each guest. Or some cake will. It is always a different cake.

A toast next, champagne, then speeches from his side, speeches from hers, then a pause while the food is expertly dished about by the liveried waiters. The menu is "international"—Chinese/French with Japanese additions. Everyone holds back, as is proper until the sushi comes, and then something more basic than manners appears. In the scramble I end up with just one piece of squid because I was too polite.

The only foreigner there, I did not feel I ought to dive in like everyone else. For despite the international intentions, I was still something of an unknown quantity. People peered and then turned away. This was because they feared that I would utter something in a foreign tongue and embarrass them when they were not able to respond. Knowing this, I asked in Japanese a simple question about the printed menu ("What is that *kanji*?") and everyone was much relieved.

The couple returns—the groom in a white satin suit with a frilled shirt, looking like Xavier Cugat, and the bride in flamecolored silk with fan and tiara. I am at the mike because I am to lead off the lighter part of the festivities, supposed to dilute the seriousness of the prior speeches. So I begin by being skillfully insulting—talk about the groom's failed attempts to learn English, always a favorite topic. The crowd is receptive and pleased that I seem to understand my role. I am the Kyogen, an interlude during the Noh-like solemnities of this major Japanese ritual.

After me comes dessert (expensive melon, assorted petits fours) and more fun speeches about how awful the lovable pair is. Then songs and high jinks as the drinks (Chinese schnapps, hot sake, iced beer, whiskey, and sloe gin) take effect. My job done, I change tables, invited to the "family" table by Makiyo's parents, who are now relieved at having married off their last son. Makiyo's father is just like Makiyo will be when he is that age (two years younger than I am), and we share a cup or two while Makiyo looks benignly on at the getting-together of his two fathers.

I wondered if my loan might have paid a tiny fraction of this doubtless enormous bill. I said nothing. But Makiyo, with that way of his, understood, took me to one side, and let me know that the bride's side had paid for it all. And then I realized that poor Shinsaku had gone *yoshi*. This meant he had been adopted into his wife's family, was no longer on his own family register. It also meant that he was at the mercy of his in-laws. They wanted a child to continue the line and that was what he was there for—to make it.

I look at the groom, young, handsome, smiling, flushed with a drink or two, and wonder if he knows.

7 APRIL 1992. In the evening I give a dinner for Tani, my oldest friend, now fat and rich and with four children, each by a different mother. It is difficult to see under all that weight, all those years, the poor, bright boy I once loved.

I invited also Holloway and Michio. These three have not seen each other for three decades or so, when we all went to Nagano together, when Tani was still a student.

Now again we meet. They look at each other and observe the ravages of time, but before long they are remembering things and the years are falling away. "Remember that smoked trout? Remember when you told off the hotel lady because she wouldn't let Donald play the piano? Remember in the bath when Tani invented this soap with a picture of a naked lady in it, to make dirty students want to wash more?" The past flowed back and bathed us all.

And, too late, I remembered that alcohol and Tani do not agree. He became noisy in his company-president kind of way, opened his pants and pulled up his shirt to show off his scar, a stomach operation for ulcers—he had worried *that* much making his millions. Also, since this is the way men in his world act when together, he began joking about the host—complaining about me all of these years, said I never once bought him anything but a suit and he still had it, he took *that* good care of it. Also that Holloway and Michio are always together. This was a good thing. Me, I always had to have someone new. Not that the new ones are very much. Fumio runs a bar. Makiyo—well it takes someone smarter than him to be a good developer. And even a Korean—nice guy but a *Korean!*

All of this is tiresome and I parry it as best I can, realizing at the same time that he is still jealous without knowing it, and that also all those early years in my shadow (I had the money then, he didn't) made him resent me. It had never before come out because we had never been among old acquaintances with whom he could "joke" in this manner. Also he had never drunk this much with me before.

I know how he feels, but my idea of regard and of good manners is different from his. The ordinary Western idea of propriety is much more strict than the Japanese. I parry and turn pleasantly sarcastic so that my guests can have a good time. So they apparently do. At the end, Holloway says, quite innocently, "That Tani—still the life of the party. . . ."

11 MAY 1992. The elegiac thoughts occasioned by Dae-Yung's going back home to Korea always linger. Today I walk by the pond in the setting sun, and have in the warm spring air autumnal thoughts.

I remember walking by the little lake in Faurot Park in Lima some fifty years ago, wondering what to do with my life. Eighteen, soon out of high school, and all I had really decided was that I would not stay in a place where

I had to live only for how much money I could make, and what I could buy. This was how I saw materialistic wartime 1942 America.

And I did something about it. I left and eventually came to this poor, defeated island, where it was spirit that counted and not money because no one had any, and any money (what there was of it) was put in white paper before being paid over—that is how dirty it was. And it is here that I have remained, more or less happy.

And now, I look around. In fifty years it has changed: materialistic, peacetime Japan, 1992, where all that counts is how much you make, and what you can buy. I read *Main Street* and *Babbitt* back then and determined never to stay. It is now full circle: the Japanese are new-rich Babbits in the true American mold, and Tokyo is the new Main Street.

12 MAY 1992. In Japan, I interpret, assess an action, infer a meaning. Every day, every hour, every minute. Life here means never taking life for granted, never not noticing. For me alone I wonder? I do not see how a foreigner can live here and construct that shroud of inattention, which in the land from whence he came is his natural right and his natural tomb.

E. M. Forster used to say, ". . . only connect . . ." and it is with this live connection that the alert foreigner here lives. The electric current is turned on during all the waking hours: he or she is always occupied in noticing, evaluating, discovering, and concluding.

Maybe in another country the resemblances to where one came from would be strong enough that such continual regard would not be necessary and would not be rewarding. But Japan, which now so seems to resemble the worst of the land I came from, is actually so different that none of my habits protect, none of my prior assumptions are valid.

Denied, fortunate foreigner, the tepid if comfortable bath which is daily life back "home," he cannot sink back and let the music flow over, mindless, transparent; he must listen, score in hand.

I know the difference well. It is the difference between just going to a movie and living it for few hours, and going to the same film as a reviewer, taking notes, standing apart, criticizing, knowing that I must make an accounting of it. The former is the more comfortable; the latter is better.

I like this life of never being able to take my life for granted. The Japanese connect—in Forster's sense—less than any other people I know. Lafcadio Hearn once wrote Chamberlain about the nonspeculative quality of most Japanese—though he meant it as a compliment. And it is true that so many are so submerged in daily routines, so anesthetized by habit and agreed upon opinion, that they rarely stick their noses above the surface. When people observe that some Japanese have no fellow feeling, this it what they mean. Closed, boxed-in lives, taking just everything for granted. *Naruhodo*, the world.

Except those who do not. Fumio: always seeing the edge between the apparent and the real. And all the women I have known, kept alert by the lives they are forced to lead. Women are alive, vibrating, connecting. These are those I love and celebrate, and myself never take for granted.

13 MAY 1992. In the train I look at my fellow passengers. The public Japanese now has an indrawn look. Like an indrawn breath, it means caution, reserve, care, and fear. To be sure, anyone staring about at the rate I do would everywhere encounter this kind of retreat. Still, some people (young usually) behave that way with each other too. Gazes do not meet, but slide away, glances rolling over and out.

It did not used to be that way. People were openly curious, frankly stared, and if you smiled they did too. Not now. You smile and they turn away, fearful that this is prelude to some unwanted intimacy. I can hear their mothers indoctrinating them, over and over again. *Abunai* comes the matronly tone. What a loss. Is it always lost in First World countries? Like the U.S.A? Is it only to be found in the Third—like friendly Thailand? Is civilization really a plague? Is Rousseau right?

16 MAY 1992. Life in Japan, cut off, in exile. This is how other people see it. I am asked how I keep up with contemporary thought. I cannot seriously answer, never having thought of such a question. And I see why. Here, undisturbed by vagaries, I can regard what I think of as eternal. My world does not change—and the best, in Arnold's sense, is what I look at, listen to. Film for me is Bresson; art is Morandi. So I may be cut off, but I am always turned on.

19 MAY 1992. Went to the American Center Library to look up what they have on Jack Kerouac. A large, empty room filled with viewers and TV buzz and persons in frameless glasses, who look up and ask, "Who? Never heard of him. Will you please use our deck?" One pointed to a keyboard. I did not know how to use it. It was a computer of some sort. With ill grace and an unbelieving expression she pecked out after again asking, K/E/R/O/A/C. Pushed a button. Machine clicked. Nothing.

"We have nothing," she said. "You do not seem to have any books at all,"

I mildly remarked. "Would you care to see our magazine file?" "Can you really see it, or do you conjure that up too from buttons?" I asked, now revealing nastiness. She narrowed her eyes in irritation. "Are you truly a library?" I pursued. "Yes, we call ourselves a library," she said. "You are wrong," I said. "You are a database."

I do not know what a database is, but my chagrin and rage at finding out what had happened to what was once a perfectly good library was not immediately to be denied. Storming out was OK, but it still left me with my Kerouac problem. One which became even more complicated when I returned home and discovered that I had spelled the writer's name wrong. There is a U in Kerouac which I had left out. The computer, not being able to make allowances, could not find him, even if he was there, lying in the dark. Shall I go back? I think not.

22 MAY 1992. In the train going to Kyoto I meditate upon my former trips to the old capital. Almost half a century of them, from the eight hours of sleeping car at the beginning to the two and a half hours of bullet express right now. Over the years I have looked from the window. These used to open and the train stopped and I would buy local food and drink from farmer vendors. Now they are sealed shut, the vendors are gone, and in any event we stop only in Nagoya.

Just past Mishima is a culvert. Now it holds a bridge, pink, with a postmodern pergola on one side, part of a new golf course. But once, four decades ago, the train slowed down and I looked out of the open window and there in that small, wild gorge was a boy washing a horse in the stream. The animal was stamping in the water and the boy had taken off his clothes so he would not get them wet. The animal and the human, both naked, both beautiful and shining in the sun, and the train slowed down as though to show me this. I watched for the culvert this time. It is by in a flash, and I catch only the tiny trickle of water under the ridiculous pink bridge, but I remember and hold the vision of the boy and his horse.

Soon we are going past Fuji, soaring after the rains. And no one looks up from book or magazine, no, "Oh, look, Fuji!" Not even a child to crane a neck as this magnificent mountain moves majestically across the view. In all my trips before there has been someone, even if only a foreigner, to mark this passage with a bit of attention. Today, nothing. Fuji, like the bullet train itself, like Japan, like life itself has become a commonplace.

23 MAY 1992. Travel stirs. On the way back from Kyoto I thought of Tani and remembered his wedding, and with it came the smell of fresh water, the taste of sake, and into view slid the memory of his first wedding, in the country with his tough friends. It came in a shape like a small boat. All I needed do was to look up what I had written, and then the full memory sailed past.

25 MAY 1992. Rainy, clouds lined up, waiting turns, the drip of the broken gutter on the tin roof beneath my window. It plays its primitive tune over and over. The rain hangs like a curtain and a wet spider shelters under the ledge. Time to board the past and steam into the distance, to close my journal.

Closing and opening the journal became more frequent in these years—and there are many more relatively untouched pages. At the same time, completely untouched pages are probably fewer, since Richie had begun culling them in a different fashion. He told his editor that he thought their value was only in the picture of Japan they offered, and of himself looking at Japan. Consequently he began removing whole passages. These he kept separate. Thus, Richie's extant journals include several others in addition to this one. There are those written in New York (1949–53), the journals he kept while being analyzed, *The Persian Diaries* (devoted to the Iranians' plight in Tokyo), the *Journals—Exclusions*, and (a later addition) a file titled *Vita Sexualis*.

1 JULY 1992. In Ueno I see a middle-aged man, Japanese, clad only in his underpants and sandals. This seems to me sensible, one of the common forms of summer dress. He is, however, drunk—weaves, mumbles. He is also seen by a policeman, sweltering in his gray uniform, who stops him, says something, then pushes him. The nearly naked man strikes back, and two more police appear since their *koban* is right there, on the park corner.

Not so drunk as to ignore danger the man flees, and is pursued and stopped in the middle of the street, in front of a suddenly halted truck. There he is thrown to the ground, and the three cops pull his arms behind his back. But he seems the stronger, or at least the more assertive. He flings them off. By now a crowd has gathered—impassive citizens, jeering Iranians, and myself. The three police blow their whistles to summon help. Two patrol cars and ten policemen come. These struggle in the street, hats falling off, perspiring, trying to look authoritative, but unable to contain one smallish nude man. They produce a straight jacket, but do not know how to put it on while the man yells and lashes out. He hits one cop in the groin with his foot and the Iranians cheer while the cop rolls on the ground. Finally, however, force prevails. The culprit is trussed up, put into a body bag, the top (in this heat) is drawn shut, and he is lugged into the waiting patrol car. The Iranians ironically applaud. The Keystone Kops try to look fierce. And I wonder why they did this. The man was no menace. He was merely drunk and naked and going about his life. But he put up a good fight.

3 JULY 1992. Dinner with Makiyo. As I drag out more reluctant information from him, I find things much worse than I had thought. From its affluent height of several years back, his Ace Corporation has fallen low indeed. The bubble has burst. Anyone in the development business is out of a job. I now learn that he and his wife are camping out in their former apartment, staying rent-free until it is bought by someone else, and have already sold off their belongings. They just have their bedding and their clothes. The fine office is gone too. He now rents a corner of someone else's. We talk of his future. He is convinced he can make it, can get by, can return my money in another three months.

5 JULY 1992. Several encounters. At the hospital, getting my angina medicine, I have coffee at the single non-smoking table in the cafeteria. I asked the waiter for coffee, iced, no sugar. This they cannot do because, he says, they put sugar in when they make it. "And what do your diabetic patients do?" I ask. "They order iced tea," he says.

An older Japanese woman looks at me, seated opposite, and asks, "Do you have diabetes?" I say no and she laughs. Then we talk about the singularity of sugar in the hospital cafeteria at all, and smoking allowed at all tables but ours. She says to stop it you would need only one person to take responsibility. Just one. But, she concludes, you won't find this in Japan nowadays. I find that I remember Edmund Burke: "All that is necessary for the triumph of evil is that good men do nothing." This I attempt to translate. Much taken with it, she writes it down on her paper napkin.

Later, on the subway, there would be a seat if the man would only move over. He has half a seat on either side. I excuse myself politely but he does not budge. Then I see why. The seat is made of stripes of varied color. He is securely in one such. This he thinks is a seat. His seat. It is marked like a seat. If the others leave space and are sloppy that is their concern. Then when he is doing something properly, according to the rules, this foreigner comes in and asks him to move, threatening the symmetry of the universe.

This evening in the park, high school kids are raising a rumpus, setting off fireworks right next to the Kenei Kiyomizudera temple, which has big no-smoking, no-bonfire, no-naked-flame signs next to it. A man in his pajamas emerges followed by a lady in a housecoat. "Make them go away," she says. At first I think she means the idle, quiet Iranians lounging about, but she doesn't. Looks at me and I say, "Those kids?" "Yes." Then she says, "We called the patrol car half an hour ago. They never come." The final rocket and the whooping kids leave. Ten minutes later the lazy patrol car pulls up. "What's the commotion?" it wants to know. "What *was* the commotion," she corrects and then lectures the sheepish patrolmen. After they tip their caps and leave she comes back. "That's our tax money," she says pleasantly.

"Do you live in that house here, right here in the park?" I ask. "Yes, that's us." "I'm jealous," I say, "It must be wonderful to live here in the park." "No, it is not," she says. "One good thing though. These Iranians usually keep the noisy kids out."

18 JULY 1992. Shibuya, never my favorite part of the city, has now, like Roppongi or Harajuku, become positively irritating. This is because it is fatuous. Filled with the chinless young in their finery, it is all about people shopping and being seen. The goods are junk but expensive, the customers are teenaged, rich, and bored. The mothers and fathers of the Japan to come. Cannot find what I want amid all the fashion. I want a sensible desk.

29 AUGUST 1992. Tamasaburo invited me to his solo dance recital at the Saison Theater. Four dances, and an almost equal amount of time taken up by the three intermissions. Such waste of time is luxurious—like those glossy pages made up mainly of white margins, or those vacant nouvelle-cuisine plates containing one potato, seven peas, a bit of fish, and lots of porcelain.

The longer number is a new one, *The Princess Yang-Kuei-fei*, which was very Parco-style—since Parco-Seibu-Saison [department store chain] owns the theater: lots of beige on beige, with pair after pair of tan chiffon curtains which grandly open one set after another, like the picture window in a model home, but with rivulets of dry ice surging across the parquet. Hidden behind the last, barely visible under the layers, stands the princess herself. When revealed, Tamasaburo is all Chinese, with a porcelain white face and hands, peach at the edges, pink around the eyes.

I admire the way that he has incorporated Chinese dance into this Japanese syntax: the sudden stances, the accusing look, and the masculine turn of the neck that Chinese impersonators cultivate. He had observed this well: there was nothing simpering about this *Yang-Kuei-fei*.

Afterward I went to the dressing room. He was still in make-up, and seen up close rather alarming, all whitewash and red paint. I was reminded of the ruffled Velasquez at the Metropolitan Museum of Art in New York: From a distance that ruff is the finest tulle, one can even see the threads. Up close, it is Francis Bacon, all smeared whites, finger painting.

He was busy smearing lotion on himself, but wiped his hands, smiled, and handed me a big package. I responded with a wrapped, framed canvas. He was giving me photos of his former boxer friend, and I was giving him a picture I painted some years ago called *The Boxer and His Opponent*. One champ for another.

I left him scraping off the make-up and noticed that he wore his towel tight under his armpits, hiding his breasts, just as though he had any.

4 SEPTEMBER 1992. Big official party for the ASEAN Festival at the Hilton, paid for by the Tokyo City Government. At the Hilton because it is just next door to the city offices. Also because the food is good. A spread: smoked salmon, steak tartare, and beef Wellington.

There, drinking rather than eating, was Edward G. Seidensticker. He had just arrived. "Why is it," he wanted to know, "that when one is older the days seem to go by so much faster?" Then, to answer his own question, "It is because one is oneself so much slower." He is then whisked off by three city officials, and in turn their deep talk is interrupted by the entrance of the Awa Odori dancers, who snake about the room deafening us all with drums and bells.

When Ed returns, I lead him to the beef where, chewing, he asks, "Why is it that just when things get truly noisy, city officials always take one aside for deep discussions? This one was about whether Japan is a hand-society or a foot-society."

As the dancers cavorted among the tables, the pretty kimonoed girls in attendance produced *tenugui* and tried to place them around the guests' necks. This was to indicate that one should join the rout. A number did. I saw ambassadors waving their hands and smiling foolishly. Not us, however. Ed simply refused.

I took refuge with Robin Berrington, the American cultural attaché. "Foreigners like this," he said with a smile. "That, at least, is the general assumption." Then we remarked that everything had been especially Japanese this evening—including not one, but two *Fuji Musume,* and an exhibition of *mochi* pounding on top of that. It was perhaps an ethnic return for ethnic entertainment, since the other ASEAN people from Indonesia, Malaysia, etc., had brought all of their things over for the festival. But was it not also "something for our little brown brothers?" We remarked on the absence of little brown brothers at the festivity. Perhaps they were having another party, separate but equal. We are suspicious of governments digging into culture.

Going home through the heat I remark upon the number of fans in hands. In the subway I read in the evening paper that sales for hand fans is over double what it was last year. A new ethnic interest, I wonder. Or just the heat.

6 SEPTEMBER 1992. In the subway I see a young couple in each other's arms, willing victims to their glands. And I experience impatience with them. Then, realizing this, I begin to wonder why. I could just as logically experience pleasure at the sight. Why did I choose to condemn these two? Then, something in the position of his arm and her head made me realize that I was associating them with the use of cordless telephones in public places. My objections were not moralistic. They were ethical. They were based on the irritation that public flaunting and other ostentations always ought call forth and with me invariably do.

7 SEPTEMBER 1992. I am in the downstairs theater; the contortions I have already seen are continuing on the screen. The scene is where she, to taunt her husband, tangos with the other woman before beginning her short-term lesbian affair, a sequence I already know.

The tango is over and the band is playing the final reprise. I remember the scene because in back of the accordion player, a door suddenly opens. Some accident, probably, and on low budget soft-core you don't retake. I watched this door opening and wondered what was in the room next door, but it was too dark to see. Now I will watch the door opening again. But it does not. The accordionist smiles as always, fingers flying, and the door behind him remains shut. But I had seen it open. What has happened?

A dream. It means what it means, but what else does it say? I know about the attractions of a safe danger, and I know about the pull of power—to buy from people something with which they might not otherwise willingly part. But what is in the other room?

8 SEPTEMBER 1992. In the evening Tamasaburo over, bringing sushi for our supper. [A shorter version of this meeting occurs in *Public People, Private People.*] Wants to talk and so I learn a lot about his early life, about his feelings for his adopted father, about the replacements he has discovered since, and about how awful Utaemon is to just everyone, not just him. He also wants to listen. And so we have a real discussion about love and about life.

We talk about tastes. Since we share one, we wonder about this, what it means. He has accounted for it in his father feelings. Father-complex is the term he uses, there being such in Japanese. I say that being an *onnagata* anyway, it is not surprising that such masculinity is preferred. No, he says, the liking came first and being a female impersonator second.

I mentioned that our preferences do, however, imply not only some distaste for oneself but also the need for a degree of power. This is a new idea to him. His eyes widen. Power? "Yes," I say, "successfully seducing—all seduction is about power."

"But, I don't like gays," he says, considering, "not to sleep with certainly; they are too much like me." "Precisely," I say, "It is unnatural. Love is opposites, not similarities. Men and women are opposites, and in a way gays and straights are opposites too. But gays and gays . . . ?" "Unnatural," he says with a laugh.

18 SEPTEMBER 1992. Just back from Fukuoka, I miss Richard Howard and Anne Hollander, both of whom I wanted to see in Tokyo. They went to Kyoto by train as I flew over them on my way back to the capital. Talked to Howard on the phone. He is enjoying Japan and is much taken by the kindness but (lowering his voice) confesses also to being taken aback in that the Japanese do not know how to comport themselves as intellectuals.

This he discovered in his discourses here. Japanese on the panel did not discuss. They agreed and then, irrelevantly, gave their opinions. Nothing was built, nothing was concluded, and everything was at random. I agree, having noticed this often enough before, having heard Susan Sontag, another intellectual, complain of just this. How can I explain that there is another discourse other than the rational? How to tell them that logic is not the only structure. How to inform them that our dialectical narrative is not the sole one? So I do not attempt to. I merely say that they must not miss Ryoanji.

21 SEPTEMBER 1992. To Kodansha to supervise the translation of my long essay on Yokoo Tadanori. Again I see the difference between the two languages and the hopelessness of communicating. My best effects fall flat because they are conceived in English and I do not know enough about the connotations of Japanese to duplicate them.

Precisely, I do not know the specific gravity of their words and they do not know those of mine. Particularly difficult are those ideas for which there are no words. So the Japanese use ours. Thus my "irony" becomes *aironie*, and "style" becomes *sutairu*. Do the Japanese readers understand this? I am assured they do. I doubt it. If anything they understand something not intended. *Aironie* will end up known, but only as something quite different from 'irony.'

Editor is also apologetic. It seems that Yoko, Mishima's widow, is not going to allow two of Shinoyama's pictures in the Yokoo Tadanori essay, and she wants me to take out the part where I say her famous husband had no sense of humor. Actually I did not say that. I said he had no sense of irony, rather, that he had a sense of intrigue. He had no appreciation for humor, but had a great, braying laugh that stood in for it. He did, however, have a pointed sense of ridicule. But I am not, please, to say so. I agree. Yoko will be mollified. She has taken further aversion to me because, among other reasons, I did not like that camped-up, window-dressed version of the Noh plays she did, though I think Yukio would have. Also, anyone who knew her sainted husband as a living, breathing, practicing homosexual is anathema.

Working with the translator, I tell him that my reference to Issey Miyake and other dress designers is sarcastic. He understands. Suggests I call the celebrated couturier a *yofukuya*. I agree at once.

22 SEPTEMBER 1992. I notice a change in women's fashion; for once it is not ordained by the syndicate, but by women themselves. The ones I see are developing a new style. It consists of more expensive materials arranged in more expensive ways. Silks and velvets tucked and pleated, a torso swathed and looped. These things cost money and are commensurate with new economic strength. I recall that when the West was consolidating its financial position at the end of the last century, women's clothing turned into expensive upholstery, labor intensive.

There is something else as well: The women are turning into royalty. There are lots of inset embroideries, tassels and cords, and crowns stitched onto the material. This makes the women a bit overdressed as they buy eggs and tofu in the neighborhood supermarket. There is also a smart turn to the military look—epaulets, aide-de-camp ribbon effects. I do not find this sinister. It is a part of the look of new money. All of this seen only in middle-class women, all of them now dressed in a particularly recognizable form of bad taste: the overtly ostentatious. (The *covertly* ostentatious forms a different kind of bad taste, that which is called good.)

27 SEPTEMBER 1992. Sunset over Shinobazu. The sky an autumn orange, clean, clear; the buildings on the far side, already black as ash with lighted windows like embers; and on the darkened pond, the late lotus toss their leaves in the night breeze, showing green above, white below, like poplar trees when the north wind blows.

I think of passing time, of summer gone, but mostly I think of Magritte—that magical canvas of blue sky with nighttime buildings and a bright street light below. Art first, nature second. That is the natural order. Debussy did not look at waves; he looked at Hokusai.

Elegiac, I stand at the verge and watch the sunset slide into night. Never again, never again, I banally opine, and then again wonder idly if there is no way ever to hold onto the beautifully transient. No—one must instead celebrate the evanescence. That is the only way.

And I suddenly think of Roger Casement. That is what his diaries meant. With their lists of size, their correspondence of length and worth, he was in his way trying to stop time, to account for it, to turn these lads immortal. Of course, he never writes of they themselves, only mentions their single quality, but then *that* is the part he wished to preserve. And he did. There they stretch, anonymous, shadowed figures with floodlit groins. What I find unpleasant about Casement is that he also, with equal passion, put down how much he paid.

Me, I also want to snatch beauty whole from the mud of time. I want beauty, grace, and good will, to be recorded. That, and my own small part in arranging it.

1 OCTOBER 1992. Frank and Chizuko take me out for what he describes as a "bite." Ginza, back streets, elegant, restrained Kyoto-style façade. Inside all subdued colors, plain wood, the kind of place that even smells expensive.

It being autumn we started with a small tray of hors d'oeuvres, which contained a single piece of grilled sea eel on rice, a chestnut, half open, a quail egg disguised as a baby persimmon, a small purple fall potato, glutinous wheat paste in a maple leaf pattern, and pine needles made of soba, all held by a real maple leaf already turned. This kind of thing is cuisine-kitsch, and is dignified only by its expense.

Followed by fish, raw sole, yellowtail and bonito. After this, *dobinmushi*, an expensive Kyoto dish, a teapot filled with mushrooms—the excessively dear *matsutake*—shrimp, ginkgo nuts, white fish, and trefoil, all steeped. You pour out the soup into rustic sake cups and then dig into the pot.

Next, my favorite, *nasudengaku*, a young eggplant baked, then spread with two kinds of *miso,* then re-baked. Followed by duck, succulent pink slices in a sauce. Then, a perfectly toasted slab of rice ball with red miso soup and baby clams, pickles, and tea. Sake, whiskey, and beer as well, and the bill must have been hundreds of dollars. But that is what the best *kaiseki* cuisine has always been about—ostentation and the expensive freshness of things.

12 NOVEMBER 1992. I notice in the subway an advertisement for yet another revival of *A Chorus Line.* Why is this musical so popular here? It is revived more than any other. Then I realize that, of course, it is about a group—just like *The Forty-Seven Ronin.* It is a collective story and this is its enormous appeal to the Japanese. But only if it is done reverently, as *A Chorus Line* is indeed done. I remember the frowns I met when I suggested some years ago to a local dramatic group that I write a play to be called *The Forty-Eighth Ronin,* about the one who arrived late—overslept, alarm didn't go off, hangover or something. Complete disapproval.

14 NOVEMBER 1992. Last night woken at three by the *bosozoku,* boys on bikes who roam the neighborhood gunning their machines and making the night hideous for us honest folk. That is why they do it—to offend the good burghers.

These are blue-collar punks we are told, caught in dead-end jobs, and this is their moment of relief. They are Japan's modest answer to the skinheads. They were far from my apartment and did not really make enough noise to keep me awake, horrible as it must have been closer, but I was exercised that they would do it at all and so lay angry and sleepless.

Today the rightist trucks bore down on me, blaring, black, and decorated with blood-red Japanese flags. Inside sallow, crew cut punks sat smoking, most wearing dark glasses. The discommoded populace paid no attention, as always. I noticed that these trucks now carry posters of Mishima Yukio, their idol, it being close to the anniversary of his suicide. And I wonder how Mishima would have liked this apotheosis, firmly in the grip of these scrawny, chicken-breasted youths, pimply and white as mushrooms. Not much, I should think.

18 NOVEMBER 1992. My word processor turns on with a single chord. It is a minor chord. Today I suddenly recognize it. It is the chord which opens "Fêtes," the second of the Debussy *Nocturnes.* I do not have perfect pitch, but then maybe I do. I know it is the same chord. Know it in the same way that I can tell how many times the clock has struck, how many times the phone has rung, without counting them, and long after the events themselves.

Went to see the 1955 *Shin Heike Monogatari*. Went because it is about events only twenty-some years before my *Kumagai* takes place. Wanted to see what the world looked like back then and trusted Mizoguchi, his art director and his photographer. Therefore I remain undistracted by the silly story—it is based after all on that Yoshikawa Eiji novel, which is one of the anti-models for my own book.

Mizoguchi creates past life in a different way. In the opening crane shots of Kyoto, in the slow, swooping glide that settles finally on a single character, and when Kiyomori confronts his mother with questions of his parentage, Mizoguchi makes fine use of a simple pillar—having each on one side of it. The pillar is always a pillar, never a symbol, and yet it shows us something that nothing else could have.

19 NOVEMBER 1992. I awake at seven, make my first cup of coffee, and drink it with buttered and honeyed cornbread as I read the paper. Then, depending upon what is on FM, I take a shower. Today it is the "Archduke," so I do not delay the douche. Some days I do the laundry, but today it is raining and so I do as I usually do—write letters and tend to small tasks until nine.

This is when Frank calls. Every day. I encourage this. Living alone, I like something regular, a conversation with a close friend. And he needs me as part of his network. As one of his daughters remarked to me upon hearing of the morning call, "Oh, so you're part of the company, too."

After the call begins my work, on whatever I am doing. Right now it is *The Honorable Visitors*, and notes for *Kumagai*. Or sometimes I do my column for *The Japan Times*. This goes on until noon. Then I make lunch—soup, sandwich, salad—and then go out: to International House, to Sogetsu, to the paper, or to see a film to review for the *Herald-Tribune*—things to make money.

People seem to think that after forty-some books I could easily make my living from royalties. No, I would starve if I tried that. Five percent, or three—for my most popular book, two. In the evening, what is called social life. Tonight a late haircut, a quick burger, and ran into Jabu in the park.

This then is my day. How interesting if other diarists had thought to so spell out the prosaic, that which always gets lost. If only Gide had told what he had had for lunch. The future—at which all diaries are aimed—would be able to decipher the precious quotidian from such an account.

20 NOVEMBER 1992. Talked with Fumio about who survives from Mizoguchi films. Most do not. From his last, Wakao Ayako and Kyo Machiko. From the others, only Kyo. Then we talk about types, and I say that I, who for over half my life was only interested in Japanese, am surprised to find myself enlarged: Greeks, Turks, and Iranians. Fumio answers that it is because some Japanese are no good (*yokunai*) now. I ask why, wonder if it is all this money. No, he thinks that many are now simply not educated to be responsible, caring, or imaginative. They have no fellow feeling and so they are not attractive. He thinks it is the failure of their parents to properly teach them how to be human. Then, thinking of the decades, he said, "Did you know that in just three years I will be as old as you were when we first met?"

7 DECEMBER 1992. In the late evening, sleepless, walked around the pond. There sat ten drunk young women. Had been out at a year's end party. All in their early twenties, dressed up, lolling, smiling, but at the same time wary. Oh, a foreigner. Where did I come from? Canada? One had a boy friend from there once. A bad lot. Giggles. We were joined by a resident prostitute—the little one with frizzed hair.

"Hey, you're no girl," said the leader—even drunk they had a leader.

"No, I am not," said the skirted whore. "I am a hard-working husband and father." This is true. I have seen his kids when they drop by to get their allowance.

"But you got a wee-wee," said the drunkest.

"Yes, I have," he responded with dignity. He then told them how his lucrative act was accomplished—a *temanko*, a "hand-cunt"—and the girls all leaned forward, fascinated. He was also fascinated, since he is very fond of girls and once asked me all sorts of leading questions about a foreign lady friend whom I had taken for a park walk. Wanted to practice further perversion—troilism. Now, his audience before him, he dilated and became more animated than I had ever before seen him.

8 DECEMBER 1992. Go with [Kawakita] Kazuko to the Ginza Mikimoto to watch Francis [Coppola] as he deliberates between a large pearl pin and two pearl rings. For his mother, he says. I say that the brooch looks more motherly. "You don't know my mother," says Francis. "But mothers like brooches," says Kazuko and this apparently decides him.

10 DECEMBER 1992. To the wake of Atsuta Yushun, Ozu's cameraman. He survived by over thirty years the director who made him famous. And when people talked with him, they only wanted to talk about Ozu. I remember

With Alan Booth, 1990.

Wim Wenders going after him, pushing, probing, demanding, until the poor man burst into tears on camera, with Wim gloating through the view-finder.

Now here is all that is left—the remains hidden under the altar, the picture, smiling out of its frame. I remember watching him work. It was on the inn set for *Akibyori*. Ozu would indicate each set-up, look through the finder himself, and suggest. And Atsuta, attentive, a small smile on his face, would shift the camera. He liked working with Ozu. The small smile was approval.

II DECEMBER 1992. Alan Booth is now dying. Has about a month left, says Timothy [Harris]. Neglected tumor got through to the lymphatic system and thence everywhere else. Says Alan is in pain but tries to ignore it. Tries, says Tim, to punish his body for doing this to him. He has so believed in the power of the will that he has thought it would save his life. I think of Alan, feisty, charming, self-serving, his orphaned London life still towering behind him. And I think of spleen and black bile and *The Road to Sata*. Then I realize what I am doing: Trying to simplify, to create some false cause and effect, to find reason in the unreasonable. I watch myself doing this and do not condemn. It is fear that makes me do it—fear of the unknown, fear of the vulnerable self, as bile-filled as was ever Alan.

13 DECEMBER 1992. Walking through the high-priced shambles of Roppongi, I am suddenly aware of a feeling that I have seen it all before. In 1947. Why, I wonder, gazing about. Then I realize that I am looking at empty lots, lots of them, between the high-tech buildings. And this reminds me of the destruction of Tokyo—empty lots between the few buildings left standing. Except that now the empty places are all parking lots, land still too expensive to build on.

17 DECEMBER 1992. *PIA* [Magazine] party for young filmmakers. Oshima there in a kimono straight out of the Takarazuka All-Girl Opera. Yokoo Tadanori in black leather came up, very pleased, he said, with my essay about him. "You know me better than I do myself," he said appreciatively. "You know things about me that even I don't know." I nod. Probably so. For example, I bet he will now do something to distance himself from all of this official culture. After all, he is the big anti-establishment figure on the established jury.

Prizes are given. All the winners are about twenty, and how differently they behave from their elders. Only one or two take the trouble to appear embarrassed. Only one faked being overcome. Most chewed gum and stared at the audience and accepted the prize without a word or a bow. One young woman stood up and said she was very disappointed that she had only won the jury prize, when she had had her heart set on the grand prize. And sure enough, Yokoo, called upon to give the awards, stumbled over the pronunciation, pretended he could not read the characters, laughed, shook his head, scratched it, and behaved as I had expected.

11 MARCH 1993. Spent the day in the train, all the way to Kamogawa. Holloway has had more strokes and is in the hospital there. Found him cheerful, or making an effort to be, lying propped up in bed, surrounded by the mess of a country hospital. Small strokes in the frontal area of the cerebellum, caused by not getting enough blood to the vessels. The reason for that is age—he is seventy-two now—and also that he is so stout that he doesn't breathe deeply enough, and in addition his septum is closed, or something. They will ream it out or will make a hole in his throat. He looks mildly about as though not sensing his coming apart. Under all this I can still, in a smile or a glance, detect my friend of forty years ago. He also seems unaware that his friend, Michio, who has been with him for thirty of these years, is even more coming to pieces. Trembling hands, deep depression. It is hard for them to look at what is now staring at them.

I nap a bit in the train going back to Tokyo and wake up at Mobara. Why do I know this name? And then I remember. The village of Mobara was the turning point for the sea road to Kujikurihama, when back in 1947 we used to drive out in the jeep, Holloway and I, to the beach house, and I remember how he used to shout with pleasure and gun the motor as we raced across the fields to the open sea.

16 MARCH 1993. Call from Michio, Holloway's friend. Voice tight, control apparent. He cannot be helped by hospital. Nothing to be done. Brain will be permanently starved for oxygen. The doctor says he might die at any time, probably in his sleep. An apparent alternative is a stroke, which will leave him like Eric. "What will we do?" asks Michio. What is there to do, I wonder. They live far away, have no friends out there. "You are his only friend," says Michio. I do not say that they ought to have made more. I offer to help, but there is nothing I can do except go to see him.

Afternoon call from *Tokyo Shinbun*. A statement, please. On what? "Oh, you didn't know? Ryu Chishu died a few hours ago." Bladder cancer, aged eighty-eight. I tried to think of something to say. I saw him first as the young projectionist in *I Was Born, But*, then as the father in *Tokyo Story*, and all the roles in between and after. I remembered *There is a Father*, for in that picture he had a stroke and died on screen. I remembered him on his back on the tatami while his son tried to help him. And that was fifty years ago and now he is truly dead. The reporter at the end of the line was waiting. I said something about his honesty as an actor. "Ah, honesty," said the reporter, as though it were a new word.

Cold, a bitter wind, and my concrete square is chilled. I start the bath and go and sit in it. In my box of warmth I think of the coldness of the spring night. From the window I can see the stars through the steam.

18 MARCH 1993. To Kamakura for the wake of Ryu Chishu. In the station I learned that Ryu, always a gentleman, had arranged for buses to take us to the wake. Also, waiting there, were [Kawakita] Kazuko and Non-chan [Nogami Teruyo]. So we all went together. Small temple, outside klieg lights, cameras, like a nighttime set. Inside lots of efficient Shochiku people, the family kneeling, the body hidden behind banks of flowers, and a recent picture of him. They accepted no money, so I put mine back in my pocket and offered incense.

I remembered fifteen or twenty years ago when there was a party for the Ozu book and Ryu came and did the whole *hayashi* sequence from *Record of a Tenement Gentleman*. I now looked at his picture over the banks of chrysanthemums and remembered him smiling and singing as he banged the plates with his chopsticks.

"Oh, I remember that," said Kazuko. Nogami hadn't been there but had heard about it. Then, "I didn't much like Ryu's picture up over the casket." We all agreed that it made him look old and sick. To be sure he was eighty-eight and had bladder cancer, but this was not how we remembered him.

Nogami continued, recalling a conversation she had had with him a year or so back, when he was making the final sequence of *Dreams* with Kurosawa. The way to really please him, she said, was to remember how handsome he was in the Thirties, "I had seen *Asakusa no Hi* and he was really something in that, so I told him how good-looking he was and you should just have seen him shine all over, he was so pleased."

23 MARCH 1993. Kurosawa's eighty-third birthday party at the Tokyo Kaikan. Everyone there but Mifune—not that he was expected. Things have not been the same since *Red Beard*. And that was Kurosawa's last good film as well. He knows I think that—I have written it. Consequently he has become wary of me. I went over to congratulate him. He shook hands and then shook a mock severe finger. "Why weren't you here to make the titles for my new film? I was counting on you." I apologized. "So we got someone else," he said, "but he wasn't any good." Then he smiled. This is his way of being friendly. Kazuko was there and lots of people I know and talked to but whose names I have forgotten or never knew. Press got in free but friends and family had to pay ¥15,000 each. I was friends. Food was very good. I ate lots.

25 MARCH 1993. In trying to write my memoirs I am aware of a life design: Where I have chosen to live seems to have redressed the lack of it where I was born. Young, I feared dissent because in my family I saw too much of it, so I came to a land where dissent is hidden under manners, ritual, falsehoods. It became manageable. Back where I was born I decided to be a coward, and now I live in a land where cowardice is called common sense. When younger I feared competition so much that I would become physically ill during the gym period. Now I live in a land where I have no competition, no gym periods. To be sure, those around me have lots. Many Japanese suffer from terminal competition, but I am not Japanese. If I were I would never stay here—it is much worse than where I came from.

Richie wrote many short autobiographical pieces. These were to help him write a proper memoir. Among such attempts are *Family History*, *First Memoirs*, *In Between*, *Sections of a Child*, and *Watching Myself*. The proper memoir remained a project, however, though Richie regarded editing these journals as a promising first step.

29 MARCH 1993. In honor of my getting the Tokyo Culture Prize people give me money. What a nice custom this is. My dentist, Dr. Fujieda, gave me thirty thousand yen; [Kawakita] Kazuko gave me a silver spoon; [Teruyo] Nogami gave me a wallet, money inside; and this morning a limousine pulled up and I, all dressed up in my black suit with the pomegranate-colored tie Dae-Yung gave me, got in and was carried off to City Hall to be given (along with poet

TOKYO-TO

With Kuroyanagi Tetsuko.

Ooka Makoto and Miyagi Mariko of the handicapped children) my own Tokyo Metropolitan Cultural Award. Ushered in with lots of bowing, meeting with Mayor Suzuki, who seemed to be taking the proceedings seriously indeed. Then the photographs, the investiture, and official speeches. The other two each talked for ten minutes, but I talked for a merciful three. In the audience I could see my friends. There was Fumio, who had brought his camera. There was [Numata] Makiyo with his now quite pregnant wife.

There were Frank and Chizuko, he "resting his eyes" during all the speeches. And Kanaseki Hisao and Jean Silvestre and the Satos, Tadao and Hisako. It was like the last book of Dante or the end of a Fellini film, where you meet all your dead friends.

Speeches over, we were ushered into a hall, which had lots of food spread out, and were given flowers. Non-chan gave me roses from Kurosawa, and Hayashi [Kanako] a big bouquet from the Kawakitas, and Kuroyanagi Tetsuko came with an enormous bunch of hybrid tulips all with their thighs spread wide, a full-frontal genital display. She gave a little speech. We had been friends for a long time and though she knew the other two awardees well, still, it was to me (brandishing those pornographic flowers) she wanted to give this floral tribute.

Then lots of going from friend to friend, having pictures taken. I usually go onto automatic pilot during festivities this demanding and so do not remember everything. But in the limousine going home, with so many flowers that it was like being in a hearse, Fumio told me that I had behaved OK. Opened my presents—a gold lapel pin with the Tokyo crest (a ginkgo leaf) on it. The two million yen is already in the bank.

2 APRIL 1993. In the evening to Frank and Chizuko's. They had asked Fumio to come too. Good dinner, and they both put themselves out to be nice to him—Frank even restricting himself to speaking Japanese. I felt that two sides of my life were coming together, since these people are my best friends.

SEKI PHOTOS

With neighbors in Yanaka, 1993.

Earlier, at home, a telephone call, a wan voice. Holloway. Out of the hospital and back home. Strokes forgotten, now it is the esophagus and trouble eating. But the strokes have done their damage. He speaks very slowly, and when I change the subject he cannot follow me for a time. When I ask about Michio he says that he is just fine. Is he glad to be home? Yes, he is. The tone is close to Eric's now. It is like that of a good child, trying to conform, not to be exceptional lest he be punished.

3 APRIL 1993. The Sekis, who run the photo process shop on the way to the park, ask me to join the neighborhood group and go blossom viewing in Yanaka cemetery. With them is Mr. Kato, the district historian, and a lot of friends including the local veterinarian. Mrs. Seki has made much food, including oden and rice with eel—and for me, a congratulatory dish, sekihan, red-bean rice. Much is made of my prize—local boy makes good—and I receive a big bouquet and a Momotaro doll.

But for me the real prize is that I am accepted by my neighborhood. My winning the culture prize means something to those with whom I live, and the man from the Taito ward office leans over and talks about ways in which I can help Yanaka to keep its character. The reason I am so welcomed is, of course, because it is Yanaka—a small neighborhood that retains its past and is proud of it. One that also feels threatened by development and does not want to turn into a downtown Roppongi. It is perhaps felt that I have the ear of the mayor.

So we sit among the tombstones, and the blossoms stir above us like a canopy, and through its embroidered holes stares a large half-moon. The Seki's daughter sings, and their large dog dances, and the sushi shop owner tells me about the differences in *onnagata* tradition in the Kabuki. Playing the young girl he moves from the shoulders, playing the geisha he moves from the chest, but playing the courtesan he moves from the *back*.

Sake cups are raised, beer glasses clink, and I hold up my lemonade and wonder why I ever thought I was tired of cherry blossoms. Their ancient magic works, and we all look while a spring breeze ripples through the trees and a shower of petals remind us under the waning moon of the evanescence of all things, including Yanaka, including ourselves.

30 APRIL 1993. I am more and more able to detect a small but evident pattern in the carpet. My life seems to have been predicated upon not joining. So far as I can remember I have rejected the group, any group—the Boy Scouts, my family. Any kind of teamwork also makes me uncomfortable, any having to work with others—whether on shipboard during the war, during the Occupation of Japan, working in companies (Zokeisha)—all were unhappy times. I first thought this probably had to do with my fear of competition, but now I am not so sure. The reason is that with everyone rushing out of the closet and joining parties and making parades, I know that I would never join them. It is not competition but politics I dislike. I loathe nationalism in all forms, including the sexual. It is small, petty, self-serving, and dangerous. Then why did I come to live my life in the most conformist country on earth?

1 MAY 1993. What began as an obligatory outing became a moving moment. Willing to take Frank's aged sister off his hands for a bit, I agreed to escort her to the movies. So we went to see Mel Gibson in *Forever Young*. I never would have gone by myself, but thought she might like it, being so old, and at the worst I could nap. But I did not. From the first frame, I was struck by how much Gibson looks like my long lost, dead Uncle Kenneth, apple of my puberty-struck eye. And when he takes the little boy under his wing and teaches him how to fly the B-47, I was sitting straight in my seat, all quivering attention, while the sister slumbered, so palpable was the resemblence to my beloved relative's teaching me to ride a bike. The film brought it all back, my confused, desperate, turbulent adolescence, one which I have just now been trying to recapture in *A Divided View*, which is about me and my uncle. Mel Gibson looks so uncommonly like Uncle Kenny that I sat there awash.

Afterward, I asked the sister how she liked it. "Not at all, it was silly," she replied. And so, I suppose it was, but my eyes were wet.

4 MAY 1993. Was interviewed today for the *Yomiuri* by an interesting and straightforword twenty-five-year-old English girl named Naomi Coke. She had prepared herself well, and knew enough about me to understand how she wanted to shape me in the piece. And as we talked, I being as honest as I could, I noticed that she was opening herself more and more to me, and so I ended up knowing something about her as well. That is the only kind of interview that means anything—when you change places. We both agreed, without saying so, to leave out love.

11 MAY 1993. Dinner with Ed Seidensticker. We have Korean food and talk about literature. I tell him about Henry Green, whom he oddly does not know—though this author is in the direct line of those whom Ed most likes: Peacock to Compton-Burnett by way of Firbank. He tells me that once he was talking with the late Abe Kobo, who told him that he was fed up with everyone saying he was influenced by Kafka. It wasn't Kafka at all, he said. It was Lewis Carroll.

Then we remember "Janet" with pleasure and reverence. She used to show us her organ while riding the revolving stage at the DX Gekijo, and one day, having often noticed us there, she leaned over as she went by and said, "Isn't this the most boring thing you've ever seen?" We now observed a moment's silence for Janet and then Ed said, "She must be a grandmother now."

13 MAY 1993. Party for the Japan-American Friendship Commission. Ed Seidensticker comes, but this time he is off the wagon. Waves across the room, talks during Kenneth Pyle's opening address causing the turning of heads, grabs a highball as it whizzes past. Comes over and says, "Weren't you just charming last time. Wasn't I just charming. Weren't we just charming?" I ask him if he went home and put it all down in his journal. "You just bet I did." I tell him that I did, too. Change of expression. "You did?" Yes, and that I am going to write up this very conversation as well. "Oh?" Then to reassure him I tell him that he did not feature in the salacious sections, that he is only in the literary sections. "Well," he says, "in mine there are no literary sections. I do not write about things like that. But there are salacious sections. Oh, yes, salacious sections."

26 MAY 1993. In the subway. Japanese middle-aged man and an older women coming back from the MoMA exhibit in Ueno. He is carrying a sheaf of postcards, purchased there. She looks at the Gorky and shakes her head, then the Toulouse-Lautrec. "I rather liked that," she says. "Yes," he says, then holds up the Picasso. "No," she says. Just then the train slides into the station and against the window is an illuminated advertisement for the coming Louvre show—a Velasquez infanta. "Oh, I remember that—saw a postcard someplace." He frowned at her. "No, Mama—Paris."

30 MAY 1993. Go to the barber. In the hands of expensive Mr. Abe, I answer his various questions. This time he wants to know my status. I tell him I am a permanent resident. "Wouldn't citizenship have been easier than some exotic category like that?" So it would, but since no one would ever believe I was Japanese I decided not to be.

He laughed at this and said that if I were Korean or something then no one could tell. "Yes," I answered, "but they—being Japanese—would have found out." He smiled, then pursed his lips. That was very true what I had just said. And further than that, the Japanese had made a lot of trouble in Korea. Did I know about that? "Yes," I said. "The Japanese were terrible," he said shaking his head and bravely refusing to include himself. Just as I do when I complain about the Americans.

9 JUNE 1993. A fax. [Kawakita] Kazuko has died. A sudden stroke. Fifteen years younger than I am—healthy, smart, funny, a friend for thirty years. I think I have misheard, I think that the dead will come around the corner soon and explain it all away. This evening I dream we are once more looking at a movie together, Kazuko and I. It is *Zéro de Conduite*, a film we both love. And, when the boy turns a backward flip and the slow motion procession begins and the feathers fall like snow, I turn and she is crying.

17 JUNE 1993. I go to the stationery shop to get envelopes and am told that, being out of the country, I missed all the festivities for the royal wedding—the Crown Prince and his Princess. I say I am delighted to have done so, that it must have been terrible: crowds, and policemen everywhere. Seeing that she can now safely drop her social self, the stationery lady says, "Oh, it was awful. All those cops. Nothing else on the tube either. We finally had to rent *Raiders of the Lost Ark*—that was all they had left."

19 JUNE 1993. Some Japanese now openly say things they would not have before. At least they never said them to me before. Again, a taxi driver. "Well, what do you think of the place?" he asks. I say I like it but add that this might be because I am a foreigner and I might not like it so much if I were Japanese. "It's not because you're a foreigner," he says. "It's because you are a white foreigner. If you were Korean or from one of these places like Pakistan or Bangladesh you'd find that the Japanese are not nice and helpful. We got some kind of complex."

22 JUNE 1993. Makiyo to dinner and then back with me. Now a father. Little Maki, ten days old. I am shown a picture: small, red, like most babies are, but she has his nose. I give him the silver baby spoon I got for the child in Australia. Then, turning from the future, we talk of the past and remember the time we walked across London Bridge, and the time we ordered that awful saucisson on the Champs-Elysées, and the time he took the day-trip to Venice from Locarno, and the time he went to Zermatt and forgot to change trains and got back late and I was worried, and the time he went jogging in Detroit and all the houses looked alike and he could not find how to get back to my sister's and I sat there and worried some more.

The past is what you share. It is what holds friends together. It is congealed time, and one examines it and remembers it. It is like touching, like holding hands.

24 JUNE 1993. Kazuko's funeral at the big Nishihonganji in Tsukiji. It is a high Buddhist ceremony—Jodo, Pure Land. *Namu Amidabutsu*, chant the priests over and over again, always ending on a slow cadence, like late summer cicadas.

Next to me is Shirley Yamaguchi [Yoshiko], whom I have not seen for years. Now a beautiful elderly lady. I had not known she was so close to Kazuko, but we are sitting with the family. Then I remember that she is an old friend of her parents, and that she was in a number of the pictures that Kazuko's father made in China.

Speeches. Old Yodogawa Nagaharu, barely able to stand. Who would have thought that Kazuko would go before him? Then Oshima Nagisa's, during which his voice shook and he began to cry.

In the fashion of Japanese funerals, the speaker faces the urn and the large picture of the deceased, and directly addresses the dead. Kazuko was called *anata*, though living one is rarely called that. And is told what happened during her life—as though she was again a child, or already a spirit. This is appropriate. The priests have decided upon a posthumous name.

While others are speaking of their memories, I remember mine. Kazuko in

With Kawakita Kazuko, 1991.

Cannes in 1961 when she was eighteen or so and I was meeting her for the first time. She had come down from school to be with her parents. A shy girl, very beautiful. And she discovered that I loved Vigo as much as she did. Then Kazuko unhappy during her first marriage, to Itami Juzo, but bravely making the best of it—cooking for me when I went over, smiling at her impossible husband. And my working with her: making titles for *An Actor's Revenge* and her delight when we got it just right. And her laughter when we worked on the titles for *Okoge* together. And Kazuko in Hawaii just a year or two ago when we honored her parents at the film festival, and she and I took a long walk along the beach at Waikiki and we talked about what she wanted to do, what kind of films she wanted to bring in. And why not more Bresson? And just two weeks ago, when we had lunch and she said she was having trouble with one eye—something like double vision. Was that a sign of the stroke?

I did all my crying and then the ceremony was over and the priests again began, and their voices filled the room, and the soft bells and gongs and wavering chants sounded so like a departure that it was as though Kazuko was standing there before us and slowly disappearing forever.

After I had offered my incense and bowed to the family, I did not stay and have tea. I was crying again and so I walked out of the big incense-filled hall and stood on the corner and waited for Fumio, who had been further back in the line. I remembered the funeral of Ozu's cameraman and the funeral of Chishu Ryu, both of which Kazuko and I had gone to together. And I looked at the funeral announcement I had been given. And the salt and the single handkerchief. Just like the other two times. Always handkerchiefs. Why give handkerchiefs? To cry into?

Then Fumio came and we went and had coffee and talked about Kazuko. And wondered about her poor mother—Madame Kawakita—in the hospital, now near death herself, knowing that her daughter was already dead.

25 JUNE 1993. Introduced and showed Ozu's *Floating Weeds* at the International House. The film is like a still life. Everything is arranged, but arranged with such art that it becomes natural. We do not see the construction, yet we are aware of it: The touches of red in either corner of the frame, the pillars of the porch separating the quarreling couple, or the almost inaudible *obon* music (real, some temple down the way) just when the troupe is dying.

What I love about Ozu (and about still lifes), is that what is put before me is all there is, no hinting of depths below. And what is there is really there. More than look at it, we experience it. Peto's pipe; Ozu's red pot.

27 JUNE 1993. I look at my bookcases. Bulging. Something must go. But what? I look more closely. The shelves are lined with those I love. There is Morandi, all the books I have been able to find on him, almost one solid foot of them—his small, still, perfect world of bottles and paint. No I will not let him go. There is Jean Cocteau, sometimes irritating but always fresh, new, irrepressible. So full of himself that he makes you full of him. I have over two feet of him. I could let part of him go, but never the novels. No, I will keep him. Ah, there is Madame Yourcenar. Everything she wrote. Sententious, wise, a bit ponderous, but always honest. How could I ever let *Memoirs d'Hadrien* go? Or the woman who wrote it. No, she stays. Borges, all of him in English. My companion for years now. Am I not tired of him? In a way—his donnishness tires. But to throw out *Labyrinths*—and the man who wrote it? Never. Jane Austen? Of course not. She is part of me. What to do, then? Well, Shakespeare, whom I really do not much like. But it is only one volume and tossing him out would not save much space.

30 JUNE 1993. Rainy, deep monsoon season, and I take the two-hour express to the hospital in Kamogawa to see Holloway. Michio had told me that he is going fast now and I should not be too dismayed at how he looks.

But I am. Since he no longer eats, he has lost much weight, and he has that drawn look that Gene had before he died. Michio said he might be asleep, but he was awake and happy to see me. I am the first visitor they have had in the two weeks he has this time been in hospital.

He cannot leave it. The doctor says he thinks it will be about two weeks more. The cancer, of course, but it is slow and not yet painful. Rather, Holloway cannot eat. His hiatus hernia has narrowed his esophagus. There is nothing to be done. I suppose, like Gene, he is starving.

He does not seem uncomfortable, but he has no strength. He lies there in the bed, and his voice is very far away. He talks and I strain to catch what he is saying. "A doctor came in. Last Sunday. And—and he looked just like Dae-Yung."

Holloway smiles. Then the smile fades and it seems he is no longer there. His eyes are open but he is not looking at anything. I know that he knows—not that he has cancer (this he does not know), but that he is dying.

I stroke his hand and he puts his other hand on my shoulder, and I remember him forty-five years ago—that same hand.

1 JULY 1993. At NHK, being filmed. A documentary on the movie music of Takemitsu [Toru]. Peter [Grilli], just off camera range, asking the questions. I am no longer surprised that I can open my mouth and talk about anything—and that I never know what I am going to say until I hear myself saying it. I am still surprised, however, at how much—as I talk—I suddenly remember. There is Toru in his early twenties at the Sogetsu Kaikan, and as I speak I remember—not the other way around. He had on a tan corduroy coat, a way of tossing back his long hair. This I did not know until the words fell out of my mouth.

2 JULY 1993. A party at the U.S. Embassy to say goodbye to Ambassador [Richard] Armacost, (Ambassador [Walter] Mondale is coming), and to celebrate the glorious Fourth. To that end, ethnic food: potato salad, frankfurters, and hamburgers.

Ed Seidensticker there, talking about ambassadors. "Well," he says, "Mondale is coming. But he will not be better than Armacost. Armacost was very good indeed." So he was, I say, adding that he kept his balance. "Yes," says Ed, "whilst all around him were losing theirs. The Japanese did not like Armacost, I am happy to say," he says," but then an ambassador is not supposed to be popular. The Japanese divide them into 'good' and 'bad,' you know. The good ones were Reischauer and Mansfield. Not in my book. When they say 'good' the Japanese mean those who *agree* with them, that is all they mean." Then, "That Mansfield—he wasn't the American ambassador, he was the *Japanese* ambassador."

Later I talk with Kanaseki Kuniko, Hisao's wife—fine face, good bones, like a Mexican or an Eskimo. She asks me how many people I have had as lovers. I tell her that depends on how you define the term, but lots, if we are to be broad about it. Then I ask her if she was a virgin when she married Hisao. An entirely innocent question, to which she will not reply. So I guess I got my answer. Then Shiraishi Kazuko, the poet, came up in cerise and bangles. Our conversation was much to her taste. She is known for her black lovers, or was.

Now they are yellow. My figure is mentioned. She rolls up her eyes. "Oh, no, for me, never," she says modestly.

10 AUGUST 1993. The funeral of Madame Kawakita Kashiko. She died a month after Kazuko. I heard that after she had heard of the death of her daughter, she no longer ate.

The funeral, held in Aoyama, was enormous. Banks of purple flowers, her favorite color, reminding of the lavender and mauve she always wore; a very large color photograph of her, six priests (nuns, I believe), and all the attendants who make the rite run so smoothly in Japan.

Prayers, sutra readings, bells, drums—Jodo high church. Then, some speeches. The enormous picture, Madame Kawakita hanging like a Buddha herself, was addressed and spoken directly to.

Again, Shirley Yamaguchi, "Chinese" star of many a Japanese wartime film. A friend of Mr. Kawakita, I knew, but now, as she called the deceased "Mama," I realized that she was indeed a friend of the family and, as came out in her speech, had lived with them in Kamakura when they had returned from China after the war.

Tamasaburo, severe in a black kimono, also spoke. I had not known he was so close to Madame Kawakita nor, perhaps, was he, but she had encouraged him as a film director, and a Japanese funeral is a Japanese funeral. The deceased does not invite the speakers, the family does, and someone of the fame of Tamasaburo looks good.

Serge Silbermann, in from Paris, gave the "foreign" speech, and old Yodogawa gave the "family" one. Those who believe that Japanese never show their emotions in public should listen to one of these funeral orations. Yodogawa Nagaharu wept and kept pleading with Madame and Kazuko-chan to please meet together in paradise and be happy forever. Since he is of the age to think of such matters himself, he also asked them to tarry a bit until he joined them. This sort of thing is ordinary, and whether it goes down well or not it is tolerated and, indeed, customary.

During the service I looked at the big, glossy color photograph and remembered Madame Kawakita as I had last seen her. This was less than two weeks ago, when I went to her house in Kamakura for the *omiso*. That room where I had spent happy hours with her and her husband, with Kazuko; that room where we had sat with Satyajit Ray (dead now as well) and talked about Ozu. Now the room was unrecognizable, all gotten up in black and white drapes, with banks of flowers. And there she was, so fragile looking, and so small in her box.

With Kusakabe Kyushiro, Hashimoto Shinobu, Georges Sadoul, and Kawakita Kashiko.
Cannes, 1960.

We put flowers around her, and pictures of her husband and of Kazuko, as well as her favorite mauve shawl. Then the lid was shut and the coffin placed in a hearse, and we followed her to the crematorium in Zushi. Then, we waited while she was burned.

We talked, drank tea, [Sato] Hisako and I comforted each other, and then we were called back. The ashes were ready. Ashes they are called, but there is more to them that that. Cooling, as though on a large cookie tray, were Madame Kawakita's ribs, some of them, a section of the spinal column, a part of the pelvis, some of the cranium.

That sounds shocking now as I write, but it was not shocking then. We formed a double line, and two by two picked up the fragments with our chopsticks, and together lifted these into the waiting urn. I stared at all that remained of Madame Kawakita—this cooling mineral. We felt only that great, aimless sorrow that is so close to pity. And it is only now, later, that I fear that I did not respect her privacy, as though I had inadvertently spied upon her in some undignified position, viewing her naked remains like that.

Today, however, during the service, listening to the chants and the banging of the drums, I thought about her alive and about what I was losing through her death. As though my mind were a projector, I ran those memories I have of her.

Very early, the first—1948 or so—and she is young and beautiful, and I am twenty-four and sitting on the tatami in her old Kojimachi house, and she smiles because I am interested in films, and together we talk about Kurosawa because I have seen *Drunken Angel*. And perhaps she asks if I have ever heard of Ozu. I seem to think she did, but I no longer know.

But that memory brings up the next reel. She is taking me to Shochiku to the Ofuna Studios, to the open set of *An Autumn Afternoon*, and to meet Ozu, who drinks tea with us and seems amused at my reverent gaze since I indeed now know who he is. But before that (reels out of order), the party that she and her husband gave me when *The Japanese Film* came out, and I so enjoyed myself that I stayed and stayed, and finally Mr. Kawakita had to take me to the elevator and walk me right out onto the street so that the other guests could go home.

Another scene, with her in Cannes at the Mizoguchi Retrospective, and she is introducing me to the eighteen year-old Kazuko. And, another scene—we are in New York. She has come to see me at MoMA, and I take her to Paris Theater to see a film she wanted to see. What was it? I wonder. I do not remember. But I remember she liked

With Kawakita Kashiko and Satyajit Ray. Kamakura, 1960.

With Ozu Yasujiro, Kawakita Kashiko, and Noguchi Hisamatu. At the Shochiku Ofuna Studio, 1960.

With Takamine Hideko and Kawakita Kashiko.

it, and I remember her smile afterward when we went to have ice cream at Rumpelmayer's.

And I remember her instant acceptance, as though such occurred every day, when I finally got my courage up to ask her if she would be my sponsor when I applied for permanent residency in Japan. And she knew, which I did not, that it meant intrusive bureaucrats who would look, even, into her tax records.

One after another, the scenes of our friendship ran through my mind as I sat and looked at her up there, on the big screen as it were, and the soundtrack carried the farewell cadences of the sutras.

Then it was over. Outside the rain had begun. Very light, almost like a heavy mist. It descended in clouds as we, one by one, the hundreds of us, made our ways home.

11 AUGUST 1993. The most absurd urge upon coming home last night—to go out into the park, to lose myself in someone else, to forget about death in the fountain of life. Once I heard of a man who, on the evening of his beloved wife's funeral, went to the whorehouse. I understand why he wanted to. He was that afraid. Show me a promiscuous person and I will show you one who truly dreads death. I have had enough of death—Kazuko, her mother, and upon my return from Europe, the news that Holloway died when I was gone.

But now a brilliant post-typhoon sunny day, hot, damp—lizards appear, the water lilies pop open, bevies of butterflies, and the stones steam. After so much cold and rain it is suddenly festive, and clouds of amorous pigeons descend in their little pink spats, each with a dove-gray cravat.

16 AUGUST 1993. People are returning from the *obon* holidays and the streets are filling up again. This week they looked like those of any other big city; now they begin to look like Tokyo's—packed.

Having lived most of my life in the most crowded city in the world, I have become used to this constant physical proximity. Wherever I look the gaze is broken by people; in train and subway I am constantly brushed by others. One learns to ignore them, to see past them or through them. And when they get in the way, one politely endures them.

They are not regarded as people. There are too many of them. They are things. I read once that a wolf can tolerate the company of only fifty other wolves—after that he turns savage and attacks. With humans the number must be higher. Attacks occur, however, and will become more frequent as the earth fills up. And it will.

As humans become more and more common they become less and less valuable. The marketing of violence in entertainment is a symptom. Soon any sanctity of human life will be a memory. Even here.

Though Japan is still held together by its own brand of social glue, and what the neighbors think retains a power lost elsewhere, order is sagging. Rudeness is common now, as well as a growing disbelief in the feelings of others—particularly among the young. From a typical and isolated criminal (the young man who collected cartoon videos and eventually killed a number of little girls because they were "cute") one can learn nothing. He is an anomaly. But he is also a paradigm. And I can see him in the person who steps over one of the homeless without a glance, he who ignores the plight of the girl being harassed, she who pushes aside an old woman in taking a seat—all of which I have seen this week. I think of what rats do to each other when curious scientists keep five thousand in a container intended for five hundred.

17 AUGUST 1993. Party at Frank and Chizuko's for various birthdays, mainly hers and that of the Kabuki actor Jakuemon. There he is, dapper in a light cream summer suit, his tanned face beaming. He keeps himself tanned I am told because the failed face-lifts are less noticeable. They are still noticeable, but one forgets them because of the affability and good will that animates the man. And in full makeup on the stage as Fujimusume or, this fall he tells me, Sakurahime, he is an eighteen-year-old girl rather than an eighty-year-old man.

He is given a very good leather coat with fringes. This is a somewhat daring reference to the full leather drag into which he sometimes fits himself for walks through the bars of Shinjuku 2-chome. He is delighted, and keeps turning this way and that to make the fringes fly out.

Other guests include Chizuko's famous calligraphy teacher, who makes an enormous *kotobuki* on a huge piece of paper on the carpet and does not spill a drop; Mr. Soda—his birthday too—now at an age to be anxious for details of my prostate operation; the lady who owns the Perrier franchise with her girlfriend, and the artist Kaneko who, as usual, brings his tall, boyish chauffeur and then makes him sit in the corner and excludes him from the group photos.

Frank had asked me to mix, so I make conversation with everyone from the grand calligraphy *sensei* down to the little flower girls who help with the ikebana. I even politely include the chauffeur, but keep my congeniality distant, quite aware of Kaneko's staring, boring a hole in my head.

Wonderful food: whole salmon, brace of rabbit, sliced beef, champagne, chocolate cake, and mocha coffee. We all get boxes of Japanese cookies from the shop they are supposed to come from, the Toraya. Then all spill out into the street into waiting limousines or, in my case, the train.

29 AUGUST 1993. People show themselves. The carpenter used to indicate his calloused forefinger, a creation of the plane, and the newsboy had one shoulder lower than the other. Now the indications are less structural—not what you do but how you do it. I look at Chizuko and see traces of the *mizushobai*, that demimonde in which she spent a part of her life: a certain looseness, a certain professionalism, the ability to build and carry on what we used to call a kidding relationship.

I notice other signs in other people—for example, smoking homosexuals. In all countries they smoke their cigarettes at their fingertips. Everywhere, everyone—an indication certainly, but no indication that they know they are doing it. Wonder how it started. Wonder what it means.

5 SEPTEMBER 1993. Sunday—to Kamakura, Eishoji, for the internment of the remains of Madame Kawakita. There they are on the altar of this Jodo temple. While I have been living my life since last I saw them, there they have been sitting in their porcelain chamber, surmounted by their gold brocade cozy. Now the nuns chant and bang, and on a gilded shelf sits the black lacquer tablet with the posthumous name on it. Since she will, according to Buddhist belief, be starting a new life, she needs a new name after death. This one is made of elements of her old one—the first written is: Kita-en. A nun takes a wand and dips it in water, then draws one end over the name, anointing it. In front of her are numbers of wooden post-like objects, also containing the new name. These will be put at the grave.

Which is why we are gathered—for the installation of the remains. After the service all fifty-some of us start up the mountain. I had been there once before to see the grave of Mr. Kawakita, ten or more years ago. It is a small mountain but steep, and some of the company are the age of the Kawakitas, so it is a slow procession. Mr. Oba, the decent, harried, conscientious head of the Film Center; the Sato Tadaos, she walking second but really leading; the tall Takano Etsuko of Iwanami Hall, her hair in the eternal braids of the unmarried—and many others, all of us united because we were close to Madame Kawakita.

And now we are truly saying goodbye, for the remains of Madame Kawakita are being put into a small crypt under the family stone, and in its pantry-like recess I see the containers holding the ashes of both Nagamasa, her husband, and Kazuko, her daughter. The caretaker lowers Madame Kawakita into place, in the middle. The family united at last. And before the tomb is again closed, I see them sitting there, in a row, all three, a family scene. It is cozy, pleasant, and homely—and the cicadas sing away like a choir.

I turn and look from this mountaintop out over the forest spread beneath us under the Sunday afternoon sky, and remember when I last stood here— with Kazuko after we had put flowers on her father's grave and then turned and looked over this scene, beautiful enough for all eternity.

During this year Richie traveled more than ever; he received awards, and *The Honorable Visitors* was published. Also his journal became more full—this year's entries were the most complete yet. There are several reasons for this. A lot was happening, and he wanted to capture it. He was becoming more disciplined and was writing more. Also, he had few larger projects to take up his time, though he was doing research for *The Temples of Kyoto*.

20 JANUARY 1994. Reading a new grammar book. It tells me that there are at least seventeen forms one can use in Japanese to refer to self—all are first-person singular. They are also graded—one could probably stack them up from most respectful to least. Maybe that is why so few of them are actually used—the difficulties of juggling social status. I know enough not to say *boku* in reference to myself when I am speaking to a superior. And I almost never use *ore* (further down the scale), because I find it hard to condescend. The book tells me that women now use *watashi* rather than *atashi*, because it less hackneyed and because *watakushi* must be reserved for formal occasions. Also that *atakushi*, as opposed to *watakushi*, hints at cultivated elegance, rather than breeding. And that *jibun* reeks of discipline within some rigid system—that policemen tend to use this.

21 JANUARY 1994. The economic recession is making the poor more obvious. The tunnel between the Ueno Keisei and Japan Rail stations is now a place for derelicts, two between each column. They lie there all day long, bundled up in the cold, some of them reading newspapers, most sleeping. None beg—they all have a quiet self-sufficiency, returning stares from passersby with a neutral gaze. And I remember some forty years ago, when the Ueno tunnels were filled with the poor and the police helped rather than hindered. So much has happened in between—and so little.

30 JANUARY 1994. The worst cold weather since the threadbare days of the Occupation. Everyone complaining. The habit of putting up with things never did extend to the weather. No one complains about what he can do something about. I wear two pairs of socks and a blanket around the house—and I have the heat full on. What of those in the streets? The newspaper tells me that Japan now has ten thousand homeless, and then adds that in a country of over one hundred million this is "not bad." I look at those who are in this not-bad category: Old men trying to find cardboard to lay on during the raw night, one old woman who has found a futon and wears it like a coat, kneeling on a piece of carton outside a closed boutique that sells fake fur.

4 FEBRUARY 1994. To the opening of Alexandra Munroe's show, *Scream Against the Sky: Japanese Art after 1945,* at the Yokohama Museum of Art. I remembered much of this when it was new and I saw it in ateliers or small galleries. There was Noguchi's big haniwa called "War," and Kusama [Yayoi]'s silver dressing table made of erect cocks, Miki [Tomio]'s enormous aluminum ear and Shiraga [Kazuo]'s wild boar skin with red acrylic. And I remember standing by that boar skin decades ago with Porter McCray and his saying, "Well, really!"

Hijikata Tatsumi is given a whole dark little room to himself. In it are some artifacts from this father of Butoh, white hangings on which are projected the filmed records of performances, and for this opening only, five naked boy dancers, their heads covered with tied-up newspaper. Also, spotlighted on a pedestal: the golden penis with which Hijikata used to dance.

I turn to his widow, Ms. Motofuji, a large, commanding and self-possessed woman, and ask her if that is really a cast of Hijikata's cock. "Now, you would be just as good a judge of that as myself. Of course not. It belonged to some student of his. What was his name now? Something with *mura* in it." "Komura?" I guessed. "Yes, that's it. Works in a bank now. A *bucho*. You remembered him, how nice."

Now all of this art is up there on the walls—official, institutionalized, set into history, and looking much more handsome and much more important. Me too. I am the only white foreigner included in the show—(Nam June Paik is a yellow foreigner.) Two films of mine are there, *Boy with Cat* and *Five Filosphical Fables*. And I see now that I am a part of my times, something I had not noticed before.

II FEBRUARY 1994. Lunch with Ian [Buruma]. We talk about methods of composition. He says that he is like me—must have some kind of map, or blueprint, even if it is only a page long. Otherwise it seems arbitrary. And we agree that the arbitrary freezes. He tells me that Susan [Sontag] has a different method. She starts out just writing whatever occurs to her and fills pages. It is a great mess, she says, but then she carefully reads it and sees what she is trying to say. Then she begins cutting and underlining, and though it is hard work, eventually what she wants to say emerges.

12 MARCH 1994. Much going on about the liberalization of the rice market. American rice was bad enough, but at least it could be used for some non-traditional dishes, maybe. But, horrors, now Thai rice is on the market. And it is worse than useless. Already stones and twigs and bugs and dead mice have been found in it. "Found in it or put in it," said Takano Etsuko when we talked about it at last night's party. "But rice is Japan's roots."

She is right—it is emblematic of the country in a way that Mom's apple pie never was for the U.S.A.—even the Emperor used to have to muck about in the paddies for a brief demonstration. Now, in this morning's paper I see that what the press dignifies as "rice panic" has struck the populace: long lines of struggling housewives wild to get the "last" of Japan's real rice; grave fears that a "rice famine" will result. My country has nothing quite like this. What if a foreign franchise took over McDonald's—well, what if it did? No, the American behaves badly over other things—not food.

14 MARCH 1994. The world . . . After our late, liberal flirtation we are once more turning to the repressive right. Fundamentalism—that rush to the pre-destined terminal to don the blinders. I look at righteous Billy Graham, fist in the air, and at the righteous Iranians on their faces with their butts in the air, at the pious face on the Soka Gakkai as it buys up Shinanomachi. The embracing of the law, any law.

But during the very moment of my deep and warm dislike, a thought intrudes: this is, to be sure, merely a way of keeping people in line, but is it not also a viable alternative to their not being kept in line at all? And I turn the plate over and look at the back, and there I see what happens when the masses of the irresponsible are given liberal treatment. I quickly turn the plate back again since I do not want to see this, do not want to admit my own il-liberal thoughts. The majority of people need to be controlled because they are capable of destroying everything in their rush to greed. This is the fascist thought I harbor. And this I sit and ponder—on this St. Valentine's Day.

20 MARCH 1994. Newspapers today inform that the police have decided to do something about the indigent. They have dismantled the cardboard city that sheltered the homeless all along the tunneled road leading from Shinjuku Station out to the City Hall. They did it for the sake of the poor men who lived there, they said. It was no proper life. Now they will be housed some-where or other. There is a picture in the evening edition: Men looking on as their homes are folded away, as they are put into trucks.

25 MARCH 1994. Today the evening edition says that a group of homeless men have gotten together to sue the city government for destruction of their prop-erty. It seems that when their houses were taken away so were their belong-ings. Also, they themselves were simply taken to another part of the city and let loose. No proper housing is anywhere available—there is, in fact, no wel-fare system of any sort. Now the braver have gotten themselves an attorney. The American Way.

6 APRIL 1994. I go to NHK to see the film on Takemitsu. And there he is—both up on the screen and right there in the audience. He handles his fame with that gentle courtesy with which he treats everything. Later we talk about the new opera he is working on. I ask if it is going to have any fast passages. "It'd better," he says.

14 APRIL 1994. I am talking to one of the local whores when a largish form comes and stands beside us. It is Edward Seidensticker, swaying slightly and looking benevolently at our conversation. After she has left, he says, "I simply cannot talk to anyone I do not know. But you do; you thrive on it. You like to talk to strangers." I say that all are strangers until one has talked with them. He stops, thinks, sways, then says, "What I meant of course was in the better circles, not these," and he glances around the park.

Then, "But how do you go about it? How do you talk to them?" I answer, "I just say, 'hi, where you from?'" "You do?" "Or something like that. They are lonely too, you know." "Well, perhaps, but I could not bring myself to do that." Then—hollowly, "Hi, where you from?" Then, "No, no, no, no, no."

15 APRIL 1994. An early morning call from Tani in Osaka. Now sixty-one himself, he has remembered my coming birthday. "Thought you might be up, early as it is," he says. "We oldsters get up early." Talks about health. He now has half a stomach—ulcers. And his wife has liver problems. And his daughter, healthy enough, is twenty-nine and still lounges around the house and doesn't get married.

Financial health, however, is sound. "I never bought property—just bought and sold at once. So I wasn't caught." But he does have a lot of stock, which is just sitting there, not earning. At present he is spending much in drilling for hot water. Why? "Well, *onsen* water seems to help her pain, you see." It is typical of Tani that he does not send his ailing wife to a spa but brings one to her.

Then we speak of dead Holloway and he remembers the dinner of several years back and tells me (finally) what a good time he had. After that we wax nostalgic, and I find that he remembers that strange tree in the compound at Horyuji and the round boat on Sado Island. We look back over more than forty years, then we say goodbye, our friendship all mended.

17 APRIL 1994. Fumio took me out for a birthday dinner, Thai *shabu-shabu*. Had wanted to bring along a nineteen year-old, since he was now the age I was when he met me, and he was then just nineteen. Fumio has a fine sense of proportion. But he has a finer sense of balance, and knew that I really wanted just him at the dinner. Naturally, since we both also have a fine sense of the passage of time, we talked about the past. He remembers that it was July 1970, when we met. A quarter of a century: so soon, so fast. Then we smile at this banality.

But now into the nostalgic mode, we decide to walk (since we are in Roppongi anyway) down a road neither of us have taken for well over a decade, back to the old Weatherby house where I once lived and which, I had heard, had not yet been torn down. And as we turned that remembered corner off memory lane, there was its roof—a Meiji farmhouse brought to Tokyo by Meredith [Weatherby] and re-erected in the early fifties, then abandoned in 1980 or so. Abandoned because Meredith moved out and went to San Diego.

It was a lovely old building—beautiful because the structure was visible and one at once comprehended it, just as one understands a person who shows you who he or she is. This despite a certain *House Beautiful* air created by Meredith's turning doors into tables and *kotatsu* into whatnots, and filling all the space with "modern art." I kept my room plain. Just added bookshelves.

From my high window I could look out into the garden—at the single large tree, at the *sarusuberi* growing at a slant, at the pond. Up there Fumio and I used to lie and look out of the window and talk about the future. And now the future was at hand as we carefully slid open the stuck garden gate and, visitors from the future, walked through the dark garden, stumbling among the weeds and bumping against the *sarusuberi*, now grown so large that it crossed the path at head level. Over us the roof gaped, tile teeth missing, and there was dust on the doorknob, which for ten years had not turned. The pond was gone, bushes had billowed, and feral bamboo now waved above the ridge of the roof. We stood in the ruined garden. This was where Mishima had posed, miming his own death in the snow.

It was all dark. Yet peopled. There was one authentic ghost—[Yato] Tamotsu, who was exiled from the place by Meredith and died in his sleep in an apartment safely distant, for which Meredith had paid. Yet exiled though he was, Tamotsu had kept coming back. He still had a key. Meredith, in bed with his new friend, would awake in the night and there standing over him would be the black and baleful Tamotsu. Or the maids would find the exile asleep under the house, matches in his pocket. I too was concerned. I did not want the house burned down nor Meredith murdered in his sleep.

All dark. No—there in the back, a single bulb in what had been the maid's room. I knock. No answer. No one there, simply a precaution against intruders—like us. Put there by Mitsubishi Shoji, which owns the now expensive land on which the house is built. So expensive, indeed, that they cannot afford to tear the house down—that would clear the land and put it in a different, even more ruinous tax bracket. So, they will wait until it collapses and becomes a health menace, or until it is burned down in an accidental conflagration. Then they will bulldoze the garden and turn it all into a parking lot for a time—which also qualifies as a tax shelter. Then finally, years later, when Fumio and I come back from the past and peer up, there will be a skyscraper of steel and glass and marble, something from the twenty-first century, not the nineteenth.

18 APRIL 1994. The final Jane Austen Dinner—Shulamith took Ed and me to the restaurant at Tokyo Station. There, sitting by the big windows, we watched the trains coming in and out and ate our avocado mousse and pepper steak. It is like an old-fashioned English railway terminal—Victoria Station, end of the century. And so it was fitting that we were laying out Jane.

Not much talk about her, though—only about some dignified way to terminate our organization, which, since we had never told the mother society in England, was illegal anyway. Finally we simply raised our glasses (me, my water glass—after all, Jane did not drink, unlike Ed), and said goodbye.

And then Shulamith told us she would not be visiting again. She had been doing so to gather antiques for her modest California business, and there are no antiques anymore—the barrel has been scraped clean. So, no more reason to come, and no more money to come on. Ed and I both much cast down by this, since we are both very fond of her "Oh, but surely you will find a way," he said, a Christian, always hoping for the best despite his occasional curmudgeonly manner. "It really does not seem likely," said she, Jewish and consequently more realistically pessimistic, used to living with adversity. "Let's wait and see," say I, the atheist, the pragmatist .

Shulamith has some last advice. "Here is my plan: I want you two to write each other's autobiographies." Ed and I look at each other with concern. "I do not want to write his," said Ed, to which I add, "Me neither." Then, "We have already in a way. We both keep journals. Ed, are you going home to write this up?" "Yes, I am." "So, am I," I said, "So you see, Shulamith, your wish is already accomplished." "That is not what I meant," said Shulamith, as the smiling wraith of Jane Austen tarried above us.

20 APRIL 1994. Lunch with Makiyo, now much more sunny that things are looking up. The bubble burst and tossed him out, but now prosperity is just around the corner. He is, despite everything, ever hopeful. Not only did he take me to a good birthday lunch, and have a present for me, he also handed me an envelope with ¥100,000 in it. He is beginning to pay back the million. Even the gloom of the Yokoo Tadanori painting show we then went to see could not dim his spirits—he is as full of plans as he was five years ago. If there were any justice in this world he would be a millionaire.

22 APRIL 1994. Meeting of the board of the National Film Center. It was held in the boardroom of the Museum of Modern Art at Takebashi, a venue too small for all of us. Consequently, I was at one corner of the table. And next to me was Yamamoto Kikuo, that fine film scholar and translator, incidentally, of both my *Ozu* and *The Inland Sea*. Seeing me there, he said, "Oh, you are so big. You cannot fit there. Let's change places."

Seeing the foreigner as somehow huge, though I am certainly smaller than Oshima sitting at the other end of the table, is such a convention that it becomes tiresome. Yet I know enough to know what he means. Yamamoto wanted me to be comfortable as the only foreigner, and so he was using the size ploy so that I would feel all right about it. Consequently, I gratefully changed places rather than bridle (my first impulse) at perceived marginalization. Later we talked about his failing health. He told me about his operation and the state of his inner organs. And then, with that beautiful smile of his, he made a joke in English: "Yes, I have the liver of no return."

24 APRIL 1994. Demographic changes. Now on Sundays in Ueno, the plaza at the top of the stairs is filled with Chinese. They gather there as they do on a Sunday at the heights of the Summer Palace, talking, laughing, spitting out pistachio shells. Over them in bronze stands Saigo Takamori, stern nationalist. I wonder what he would think, he who was so committed to expelling the barbarians. I wonder what he thought forty years ago, when the same plaza held all those destitute and their pathetic advertisements for lost relatives.

21 MAY 1994. I am with Ozu at a long table, and we are facing a room full of journalists. The reason for this event is not apparent, but I feel privileged. I look at the light hair on Ozu's hands, the big thumbnails, and tell myself I must remember all of this. Together we are answering questions, and Ozu from time to time turns to me with a small smile inviting confidence or commiseration, I cannot tell which. In answer to something asked him, he says, "Oh, but that was a real scandal." Then turns to me and I say, "In contrast to now, which is a mere scandalette." This makes me laugh so hard that I wake up, but in the process I realize what the press conference is for. It is on the occasion of Ozu's return from the dead.

2 JUNE 1994. A swing around the new international red-light district, a modern Yoshiwara. This is an area near Shin Okubo, which is called Hyakunincho, the "Quarter of One Hundred People." Why I do not know, but it turns out that there are about a hundred people standing around on the street on a Saturday night. None are Japanese.

The whole neighborhood is Southeast Asian, and these girls are all from Thailand and Burma and Indonesia and Malaysia. They stand in various stages of undress—some in just tank tops and jeans, others in miniskirts. Some in native-looking slitsheaths. They smoke, chew gum, and engage in banter with possible customers. Again, no Japanese. The men are Indian, Pakistani, Afghan, and Iranian—the out-of-work work force for the city. Still, they must have some money or they would not come.

The Iranians play pocket-pool, the national sport, and occasionally a girl will pair off with one and they will go to a cheap hotel. (Not that cheap—least expensive I saw was $50 for an hour; more often it's $80.) I do not know what the girls get. One of the Iranians told me he thought they asked for $200 for a short time but rarely got it. It paid to haggle. I see no sign of the girls' keepers, but they are probably around.

I had seen a large bus pull up in front of one of those club-filled buildings in Kabukicho, and about two dozen women piled out. Prostitutes going to work. They filed in like kindergarten pupils. Herding them were hard-faced Japanese in suits, with punch-perms and probably fewer little fingers than ordinary. The girls seemed inured to their fate. Indeed, what can they do? The first thing that happens is that their passports are confiscated by the *yakuza;* the second is that they are burdened with debts they have to pay off. I heard that there are thousands of such women in the country, that every little town now has its bar with its dozen Thai girls to whom randy farmers swarm.

Now, walking along the street I see lots of blondes with full, rounded, white bodies. I stop and ask. Odessa. I wonder which is the worse health bet—Thai or Russian. We decide that Thai is, because AIDS has had such a head start there. I heard that half the women in the business in Bangkok have HIV. That means that perhaps half the girls I am looking at will die within five years or so, after having maybe infected a number of customers. Perhaps the Russians would be the better bet.

At that point, a good-looking Persian cruises by and stares at us. Whether he is business himself or simply recognizes us as distinguished amateurs, we decide against him as well. He has long been around, handsome and intent. I see that the authorities are alert to the problem. They have put up signs outside some of the hotels in both Japanese and English. The latter reads: Prohibit to Go Into with Foreign Ladies Who Are Waiting on the Road.

1 JULY 1994. I learn a new slang term. The *hotaruzoku*—the "firefly folk." These it turns out are husbands who, home from office in the evening, are banished into the darkened street to smoke.

3 JULY 1994. Go to Bunkamura to see the last day of the Sebastiao Salgado show—several dozen big photographs of workers from all over the world. Though there is no political focus, the political strength is great. Looking at child workers, one must consider the employers; watching Indian women sweating, one wonders about who hires them, pays them. Most explicit are spectacularly hideous shots of workers in some awful open mine in Brazil. There are so many, winding about the naked cliffs, climbing up the bamboo ladders, each with his own stone on his back, that I think of illustrations for Dante. It is that grand, that openly evil.

The young woman in back of me begins to laugh. For a second I am angry, and then realize that for some people (many of them Japanese) laughter is the only way they have of papering over an existence in which a rent has just occurred. In her comfortable life, such a thing as this monstrous Brazilian mine with its exhausted, naked workers should not occur.

Later I come upon a photo of two workers resting, Ukrainians, stark naked in a sauna. It is not just the nakedness. It is the context. Again I realize how much sexual attraction has to do with a presumed power—how sex is a way of bending to the will. These naked workers are defenseless against my gaze. This I understand and shake my head at myself—for what is the difference between the laughing girl and the lubricious me? But I buy a picture postcard of the Ukrainians nonetheless.

7 JULY 1994. I look at the summer fashions of the young. Those of the male are most curious. Big, heavy, leather-laced shoes have taken the place of last winter's big, heavy, laced track shoes. The shorts are of stout jersey, with great, wide leg openings and consequent panoramas of thigh. With this is worn a lettered tee-shirt—one with an algebraic formula, another in the Cyrillic alphabet, yet another, worn by a fresh-faced innocent, with "I Am a Pervert" on the back. Or, the outfit consists of a ragged dress shirt held together with safety pins and jeans that have been carefully ripped at the knees, suggesting some strenuous labor which has, in fact, not been undertaken. All of these soft-skinned kids are strangers to work. Their outfits cost money and came from Harajuku. They are affecting the proletariat.

This, says Veblen, occurs where money seeps far down, accompanied by a like decline in standards. Romans in full fashion dressing like Goths. All of this shabby finery looks strange in Ueno, however, where the fashionable young must compete with the real thing—bums with the knees of their pants honorably worn through, homeless old women actually needing to safety-pin shut their blouses.

27 JULY 1994. Ed [Seidensticker] had been having computer trouble and Patrick [Lovell] fixed it, so he has asked him out to dinner and me as well, since I was the go-between and since they really do not know each other except over the console.

Ed also is having hip trouble. He comes around the corner, walking slowly with a cane, his foot turned inward in that typical way. He still insists it is just a charley horse, and that it will go away, all he has to do is use it. I must tell him this is not so, but I will pick my time.

He takes us to the Ueno Indian place where we are waited on by lively Nepalese boys, and during mouthfuls speak of various things. I decide to tell him about his hip. But he has already come to the same conclusion: "I know, I know. A replacement." Then, "But not here, not here."

I looked, mystified, around the restaurant. "No, not *here*, silly," he said, "I meant Japan. Japanese doctors are just too, well, too virtuoso. They will reach in and hit a high C with the scalpel."

Then wiping up his *masala* with the last of his *nan*, he began wondering why his machine caused him so much trouble and Patrick, always thoughtful, was able to explain to both of us something of the mysterious nature of these word processors to which we have lent ourselves.

When time came to pay, Ed made some pleasantries about our sharing the bill but I managed to have it delivered to him and, since it was his invitation, he paid with good will.

28 JULY 1994. The twelfth Kawakita Award ceremony. It has been a dozen years since I stood there and got the first one and there was Madame Kawakita, smiling, and there was Kazuko making a winner's handshake. And now they are dead—today is also the anniversary of Madame Kawakita's death.

There was a picture of the three of them—father, mother, and daughter, taken just before his death. Under this picture, the empty stage and the voice of Marcel Guilaris. It was he who won this year's prize, but he is hospitalized, heart condition, and so he taped his message.

It was a subdued party. Yodogawa Nagaharu is now so bowed that to speak to him you have to bend double yourself. Also, he has stopped being affable. He is brusque with the boy who handles the mike. He is like a man who has just realized that this is an emergency. The emergency is death. He might not be here next year.

28 JULY 1994. I took Roger [Ebert] and his wife, Chaz, to lunch. They had been to Kyoto and Chaz, big, black, handsome, said that people looked a lot at her, as I imagine they did. And I hope with admiration.

Tells me she made many a mistake. At Ise Shrine she was invited to ask any question she wanted and so she, thinking of mystical Shinto, asked, "Will there be peace in our time?" The shrine head looked uncomfortable and then said, "Maybe you would like to ask something like how many priests there are here."

Roger has been reading *The Inland Sea* and is able to quote whole sections, which is gratifying to both of us. Any author likes this, and kind Roger loves to give pleasure.

After lunch they are going off to Sega Park to see virtual reality. He has a theory that it is really only good for games. That any movie using virtual reality would so work against the subjectivity of the film experience that it would not be satisfying at all. He believes that film demands a passive state, a suspended vision, which virtual reality rends.

30 JULY 1994. Out into this heat with Jonathan [Rauch]. Seven in the evening and still hot. Drag him to Hyakunincho to show off the latest demographic developments. Girls all wilted and running. Boys sweating and showing stains under arms and over crotch. Thai girl comes up and wants to know how to say how hot it is in Japanese. I tell her. She repeats it and then uses it, I notice, to begin other conversations. Beautiful Persian man with one of the girls. "Are you a customer or a pimp?" I ask. He smiles, "Neither, a friend." Turns out he lives with her. "Then you are a stud," I say. "No," he says, with that smile of his, "It's too hot." Jonathan and I both stand there, big spenders in the whore house but really far too shy to try anything with this resplendent, shining, dripping presence.

1 AUGUST 1994. To Karel van Wolferen's for dinner. Also there Ed, Ian [Buruma], and Gwen [Robinson]. Ed's leg is bad; he walks slowly, says it hurts.

With Roger Ebert, 1994.

Says he went to the doctor. I ask which doctor. Acupuncture doctor, he says. No wonder he doesn't get well.

A few drinks in him, however, and he livens up. Tells a joke: "Descartes walks into a bar and the bartender asks, 'Same as always?' And the French philosopher says, 'I don't think . . .' and vanishes." Cheered by the success of this sally he essays another. The three kings are bringing tribute but Melchior trips over the lintel of the stable and says, "Jesus Christ!" "Oh, Joseph," says Mary, turning to her husband, "That is a much nicer name than Irving."

Then we talk about North Korea. Ian and Gwen are going—as tourists. They have to get their visas in Beijing and then take the train. Twenty-four hours in this heat. Gwen says she is going to be a mistreated movie star, having heard of the predilections of the Dear Leader. Ian wonders what *he* will become. Ed wonders if they are going to get back at all.

4 AUGUST 1994. Dr. [Robert] Owen here for the AIDS conference in Yokohama. We stroll through the heat around the pond and he tells me the latest. He thinks no vaccine will be discovered, that eventually over the eons those who are left will become immune. We talk about safety. He tells me why it was that the homo population proved so prone. Not only were there the Owen Cells (named after their discoverer) dragging the poison in, but that so many in the New York and San Francisco bathhouse crowd were shooting up. He thinks that drug use in such venues was very high and much of it was intravenous. A real recipe. Otherwise, he still thinks that fellatio is small risk—but perhaps only in context of the big risk of buggery.

Owen is utterly out of whatever closet he may once have been in. Is resident Concerned Gay Medical Personnel, or some such. This being so, everything is devoted to the political aspect of homosexuality. And this means exclusivity. His is a polarized view. There are homos in the world and then there are heteros. Nothing else. A bipolar existence. Table d'hôte enforced. Either Lunch A or Lunch B. No à la carte.

All of his stories have a homo conclusion; all of his references are to the "gay community;" all conclusions point to a closed and intensely self-conscious group society. Part of the reason, of course, is that he is talking to me. But another part is that he has committed himself. And when you do this, you invest. Political preference takes over. You become a card-carrying Catholic, a card-carrying Communist, a card-carrying Cocksucker.

10 AUGUST 1994. I buy a cold drink from the machine. It says, in English, "Apple," then, in *kana*, Apuru, and there is a picture of the rosy-cheeked fruit. But nowhere at all does it say *ringo*, the Japanese word for apple. This is odd, I think, not to have the product named in the tongue of the realm. But not if the realm is Japan and the tongue Japanese—happens all the time.

I search for analogies. What if apple juice were known solely as *jus de pomme* in the U.S.A., what would that mean? Well, it would mean a new marketing device for apple juice, and it would presume a more moneyed and perhaps more literate audience, and it would very plainly say "new product." All of which it says in Japanese as well.

But I do not think there would be the assumption that *pomme* is a new English word, and that it has now fully entered the U.S. vocabulary. Though English-speakers appropriate (as do all other speakers), and such words as "chauffeur" are now English, there has not been the wholesale appropriation which Japan practices, often at the cost of understanding itself.

What about the poor farmers in far Tohoku, who do not yet know what an *apuru* is and are at this moment shaking their heads over the just-purchased can? Well, things happen fast. In no time at all the native tongue will have curled itself around the new word. Such appropriation of Japanese-English is, of course, not a new form of English, but a new form of Japanese.

18 AUGUST 1994. A Virtual Reality Parlour in Shinjuku. You put on the glove and helmet, and create this cartoon environment where everything is cardboard stiff and manga bright. I do not go in. I know what awaits. And besides, why should I, when the same thing is free on the streets of Shinjuku itself?

Tokyo as virtual reality. The architecture is comic book bulky; the streets are paper thin; and everything looks like a set for what it is. No glove, no helmet—Natural Virtual Reality.

19 AUGUST 1994. The August moon, round as a plate in the hot night sky. How many times have I gazed and remembered. It has become my memory dish, catching in its curved surface all of the icons of my past. The first time I remember looking and thinking was in 1942 at Newport News, after my mother had left and I was shipping out to Africa the following day. I walked on the beach and thought of the future. Now over fifty years later I walk in the park and think of the past.

I remember gazing at the moon in New Caledonia and turning slowly, and there was Dae –Yung , his profile silver, gazing as well. Tonight, wandering alone in Ueno, I turn but only to look in the darkened eternity of the rows of stone lanterns leading to the black temple of Benten.

19 NOVEMBER 1994. Big ruckus in Ueno. A rightist sound truck stops at the corner, and a black-shirted crew-cut youth begins his haranguing—something about Russia. Suddenly a fat little man from the crowd steps forward and in a surprisingly loud voice starts cursing. He tries to climb on the truck. And he stops the speech as the speaker climbs down and is joined by companions. They start shouting, but he shouts louder and with such energy that he backs them down. Then the police (ready for such an opportunity) arrive on the run.

They cannot touch the sound truckers, public nuisance though they are, but they can answer a complaint. Soon they have come between the screaming fat man and the furious rightists. In the end the fat man is led away and the sound truck crew is bid go elsewhere, which the youths meekly do. I see the fat man let go at the next corner.

And all the while, crowds of folks watching. No one does anything. Just as no one does anything about the haranguing rightists and their noise pollution. I don't do anything either. And I remember how disturbed Eric used to be at these noisy black-shirted rightist throngs—they reminded him so of Germany in the Hitler days. But here someone did something, for whatever reason—that gesticulating little fat man.

7 DECEMBER 1994. Day of Infamy. To celebrate the occasion, the U.S. Postal Service is going to issue a new stamp showing the Hiroshima atomic bomb explosion with a caption about how many lives it saved. Though Japan has long been rather proud of something similar—Pearl Harbor—it now reacts with resentment and shock. I too am taken aback by the effrontery of the U.S. Postal Service. It seeks to legitimatize—but it won't succeed.

10 DECEMBER 1994. Dinner at Karel van Wolferen's. We discuss Oe Kenzaburo and his Nobel Prize acceptance speech. Karel thinks that it is bad that a person who had done nothing political since the 1960s should stand up and parrot the "Socialist line" about the anti-war clause in the Constitution. Mr. Sharkey, the Irish Ambassador, thinks that Karel is too close to the subject, having studied political parties for years. We ought step back and see the speech in context. Then we would see what a brave and courageous person Oe is.

Karel then turned and said, "Donald here is always very quiet about such matters, what does he think?" I responded with, "Did you know that Oe is Itami Juzo's brother-in-law?" This created the desired diversion and Yasuda Hisako, the young lawyer sitting next to me, said that this explained it all. Oe had once told her that he had a relative by marriage who was handsome as a screen idol.

Karel was not to be dissuaded however, and so I said, "I think that Oe is a brave and honest person and that he has said what he believes about the government and its coercive ways; he has identified his own society, and in his own responsible actions has suggested the corrective." This, of course, ended the discussion and we went on to some excellent black goat cheese, some fruit, and a gingerbread "person" from Amsterdam whom we dismembered and ate.

13 DECEMBER 1994. Went to again see *Yukinojo Hengei* [An Actor's Revenge]— a melodramatic warhorse all caparisoned up with some of the slickest graphics in Japanese cinema and sent out to canter. The line between old-fashioned purport and contemporary intention creates a hovering irony, which never settles but provides a knowing atmosphere.

Whether Hasegawa Kazuo, playing the role for the second time, the first being the prewar Kinugasa version, knew this is unlikely. Big ham, he played his double role with his usual earnest dedication. But in the 1960s it was too late for a man dressed as a woman to make love to a woman without raising resonance. The fragile ironies of the picture sustain a spirit of fun that is neither satire nor camp. It is something else—a very subtle experience. One wonders also whether Ichikawa himself knew quite what he was doing.

I was there, on the set when the love scene was taken. Hasegawa, heavily made up, was embracing Wakao Ayako who was very businesslike about it. Neither seemed to think that what they were doing was in any way strange. Only I thought that. And perhaps Ichikawa. Maybe he did know what he was doing. I remember the eternal cigarette at a flippant angle, and an amused look when he turned away from the camera.

14 DECEMBER 1994. Teshigahara Hiroshi's Christmas party, the entrance to his big Ichigaya house all decorated with massive crossed bamboos—that material which has become his—a tunnel leading to an enormous downstairs atelier already filled when I arrived.

There was ex–Prime Minister Hosokawa, glass in hand; actress Matsunaga Rie in a boldly cut dress; I went to talk with Akiyama Kuniharu and his wife Takashashi Aki, the pianist. She was going to do a Paul Bowles disk, and so we talked about him and his music. I told her that he once told me that the theme for the final movement of the two-piano concerto was occasioned by a leaky roof—the sound of drops falling in an assortment of pans.

Takemitsu there as well, but I did not ask about the opera. I have asked about it enough, and each time the answer is a deep sigh. Then, tall, withered, elegant in black Hiroshi's ex-wife, Kobayashi Toshiko, whom I remember as a chubby stripper in the Kinoshita *Carmen* film. "Well, people say they want me to go back onto the stage, but what in?" I do not mention the play I once wrote for her—unperformed. Instead I suggest the Yvonne Bray role in *Les Parents Terribles.* "The Cocteau," she says as though remembering her childhood, "Yes, of course, we were too early in doing his plays—now is the time, don't you think?"

Another actress—Kishida Kyoko, whom I had first met when she was covered with blood in Mishima's *Salome,* then again met covered with sand in Hiroshi's *Woman in the Dunes.* Now the grand old lady of Japanese drama.

Kanaseki Hisao and Kuniko—in a pensive mood because they had gone to see *Pulp Fiction.* What had they expected, I wondered? "It wasn't the violence; it was the attitude." I told them it was just this brutal cool that had sold the tickets.

The journal entries now grow fuller. As Richie gets older, his life becomes more valuable the less there seems to be left of it. He was going to leave behind the record of half a century, so he was writing for posthumous readers. This is indicated by his interest in the

mechanics of journal keeping and his reading of the journals of others—not only those of Boswell, who remained a model for him, but of Saint-Simon, Pepys, the Goncourts, Waugh, Isherwood, and such contemporaries as John Cheever and Alan Bennett.

8 JANUARY 1995. Dae-Yung having gone back to Korea after our ten days together in Kyoto, I tell myself how happy I am to be alone again. But it isn't true. I miss him. So, after work, I go out and observe. The way to escape from one's inside is to look at the outside and attempt to describe it.

For example, with the New Year a new male fashion for the young has appeared. Before it was all hip-hop pants and the baseball cap worn backward. This is now all gone. The new look for the adolescent is to wear the stone-scrubbed designer jeans as low on the hips as possible. The belt cuts right along the pubic line. Along with this is a plethora of chains—key chains, wallet chains, chains around the waist and around the neck. Also, an amount of piercing—the newly fashionable face jewelry. I saw a boy whose ears were covered with rings—a small elephant as he jingled his way about. One with eyebrow rings. One with an inconvenient lip ring. How does he eat? No tit rings, I should think, and no cock rings either. If it is not on view, why have it? The other anomaly is that all of this metal is only on the males. Girls have earrings and that is that. As in certain species of grouse, it is the male who provides the display.

10 JANUARY 1995. In Ueno, dozens of people all in white snowsuits, and white bands around their heads to denote perseverance. They were stopping other people, turning from one group to another as though in some kind of feeding frenzy. Indeed, they reminded me of a flock or a school as they dipped and darted about. And as they approached they shouted out something that sounded like: *Saiko desu ka?* ("Aren't things just great?") At the same time they flourished a large board with paper and pencil attached. I stopped behind a middle-aged woman and her quarry, an old man with a briefcase. She was telling him all he had to do was pencil over the characters lightly printed on the page, sign his name and give his address, and everything would from then on be *saiko.* Such is the unquestioning, uncomplaining, uncomprehending nature of the populace that he did.

Now interested, I followed a few around and before long a youngish woman came up asking if I were *saiko,* and I saw that she was exhausted, as were they all, with their darting movements. Were they part of a new religion?

No, no, she shook her head, retreating. She had wanted to ask the questions, but was not prepared to supply the answers. Giving up on me at once she retreated and I, now quite interested, followed. Though she got away I managed to attract a fat young man, bulging out of his snowsuit and panting. In the face of my questions he produced a book from his backpack and brandished it. It had on its cover a picture of a man with charismatic eyebrows.

Finally I managed to be stopped by a young girl, her lips all chapped from questioning, who proved more forthcoming. No, it was not a religion. They were all *toku'n-chu*, which I suppose means *tokubetsu deshi*, or very special disciples. They were on the street doing their very best for their dear *sensei*. And who was this beloved teacher of theirs? Out came the man with the eyebrows. Fukunaga Sensei, of course. It was for him that they were all doing their best. Out there bringing *saiko* to everyone. And what did this bring to them, I wondered, doing all this work selling Sensei's book? Did he pay them? She looked at me with wonder. Oh, no. They were doing it because he had turned their lives around. Just look at her—and she licked her bleeding lips and blinked her exhausted eyes—all *saiko* now, thanks to Sensei.

Stopped next by a middle-aged man, I asked how many there were in the group. Oh, about a hundred right here he guessed, but many more elsewhere. Last night was Shinjuku, but as for tomorrow they had not yet received their instructions. I wondered if all those people who penciled in the sutra-like characters would next receive instructions through the mail and be pressed into the throng. This he did not know. So I asked why he did it—why he was rushing around accosting people, just to sell a book and to get names and addresses for what sounded to me a rather suspicious project. He did not attempt to explain, just looked at me with an expression that seemed to say it was past all comprehension, at least the kind of comprehension that I might bring to it.

Unsatisfied, I followed a few of the white-clad folk about and once when I was again accosted, in reply to *saiko*, I gave its antonym, *saitei*. But this caused such a pained expression, that I did not do it again. Indeed opportunities for being accosted were growing fewer. I thought that perhaps, like certain birds in flight, they had somehow communicated that something in the path was to be avoided, but it seemed that there were actually fewer. Then, suddenly, there were none. The flock had shifted and vanished and I was left on the pavement thinking that I had seen something like the medieval Pure Land adepts, or the Eijanaika dancers of the nineteenth century, or the beginnings of the brown and black shirts of our own time.

17 JANUARY 1995. Earthquake (7.2 on the Richter scale) in Kobe. I wake up at seven, turn on the radio, and hear all the details: it had occurred only half an hour before but already NHK had lots of information, including how many buildings collapsed, how many dead, how many injured. No panic, though an empty feeling when the announcer said, "Now we will hear from Kobe . . ."—and there was no answer. "Kobe, Kobe, are you there? Kobe, come in." No answer. Facts and figures hide the horror—silence reveals it.

The earthquake skipped over Tokyo where everyone was expecting it after the whole nest of earthquakes recently in the north. But nothing is safe in this quivering archipelago.

18 JANUARY 1995. For two hours the radio has been reading names, those of the missing in Kobe, Nishinomiya, and Osaka. One after the other, like a litany. It truly is. These people are dead. Yet the announcer, hopeful, reads on: "Will Minakami Jiro-san please contact Minakami Shizuko-san, she is worried about him."

More than 1,500 are dead and 1,000 are missing. A whole hospital collapsed; an elevated highway fell over with everyone on it; a bank caved in, fires broke out. In Kyoto, the Golden Pavilion cracked and several of the Kannons in the Sanjusangendo fell over. Most of those people killed were in their beds, since the earthquake came at 5:46 A.M.

I have not been able to reach Tani, who lives in Osaka. The operator says, over and over, that the lines are full, to please call again. I leave the radio on; the names continue, as though unscrolling. It does no good to listen, but I would be awful, somehow, not to.

19 JANUARY 1995. Got through to Tani. He is all right, though the house moved around a lot. He had gotten up early and he didn't know why. Then the earthquake, and he knew why. The death toll is much higher than originally thought. It will be over six thousand dead. Tokyo is very subdued. People on the streets, in the subway, have an inward look. Everyone is thinking the same thing.

21 FEBRUARY 1995. Just today, I am out of the hospital. Nearly a month in Jikei Daigaku Byoin, where I always go when I get sick. A cold turned into influenza, which turned into pneumonia. Now I know the cause: I have emphysema, asthma, and chronic bronchitis. This is just the trio that carried off Gene Langston—and my father as well. And, like the latter, I have angina pectoris, which makes conventional treatment of the lungs impossible. When my fa-

DONALD RICHIE

Robin Magowan, Octavio Ciano, Mizushima Fumio, Stephen Magowan, James Merrill, Numata Makiyo, Peter Hooten. Tokyo, 1986.

ther was in the hospital they didn't know this—he died at sixty-four. Now they know. I am saved at seventy. Conventional treatment was attempted but my heart went into spasm—I saw it on the machine; the pulse was so fast it looked like a video game. So, a long detour involving steroids. Got out after a month of intravenous antibiotics, with a one-third chance of within a month having to go back in again.

Friends gathered round, flowers, fruit, and phone calls. I finished *Temples of Kyoto* and wrote the second chapter of *Watching Myself*. So, the time was not entirely lost, but I had to cancel my tour of the U.S.A., on which I was supposed to be leaving day after tomorrow. And so first thing I did was call Jimmy [Merrill], for I was to fly first to Tucson to see him and then go on the Houston, Atlanta, Tampa, New York, and so on.

He sounded so well, so much better. He not only accepts his disease, but also he does something with it. He makes it a part of his life, though he knows that he will soon die. He asked about my angina, and then told me a joke about an elderly couple who are going to make love. The man becomes progressively disturbed the more she unveils. When she says that she ought also to tell him she has acute angina he says, "Well it better be. Nothing else is."

And a week later Jimmy is dead. His heart. I think of that fine intelligence—that mind that was Jimmy—inexorably blinking out, cell by cell, until at last he was no longer here.

I lay awake in the hospital and remembered being with him in Athens, and when we went to Persia together, and in Japan, and in New York, and in the Roman red dining room at Stonington. And turns of phrase, jokes, small admonitions—they returned all night long, a life unreeling before my closed eyes. And a few days later a book came to the hospital—from Jimmy, thinking to relieve the tedium of being ill.

22 FEBRUARY 1995. I call Tani on the phone. Turns out he had been calling me. We talk about his wife (liver cancer) and his daughter (dental school), and then the earthquake. He has had another fit of prophecy. I am not to be in Tokyo this August or September. That is when the big one is going to hit. "How do you know?" I ask. "Inspiration," he says. He was being driven to work in the Chrysler and it suddenly hit him. He at once told his chauffeur who, naturally, being his chauffeur, agreed with him.

I often think of Tani. His life has been so surprising. This poor but handsome twenty year-old student would eventually become, as he recently told me, the eighteenth richest man in Osaka. Now, on the phone, he suddenly remembers what he wanted to ask me. Did I know anyone at the Smithsonian Institution? Because they had a Japanese Zero fighter and he wanted to buy it. Where would he put it? I asked. "Oh, I'd build something," he said. I have to tell him that the Smithsonian is government-owned and not allowed to sell, even if it wanted to. He is very surprised, had thought everything was for sale in the U.S.A.

5 MARCH 1995. Went to the Edo-Tokyo Museum gallery to see the Tokyo Dai Senso Exhibition, a collection of things from 1940 to 1945. The pre-Pacific War period displayed old radios, umbrellas, children's games, and school uniforms—all lined up, like Assyrian remains. Then came the wartime things: army uniforms, piggy banks in the shape of cannon shells, and gas masks. Several films were being shown on monitors. One was American footage of the 1945 destruction of Tokyo. The B-59's took off; clouds parted, and there lay Tokyo. The bombs were off-loaded, plane after plane. Below the explosions blossomed, but the horror of Tokyo burning was not photographed—no pictures of Fukagawa on fire, people burned and boiled. Then came maps and photos to show how much had been destroyed, graphs and figures to show how many killed. The whole exhibit was neutral. And though the aerial photos showed the terrible destruction around the old sumo stadium (just where the Edo-Tokyo Museum now stands) no one looking seemed to have made the connection but me. But then most of the people viewing it were young. It was all history to them. But when I arrived in Japan, there were still ruins and barren fields. It is a part of my life.

21 MARCH 1995. Last night I found my answering machine had garbled my messages and so I did not know that Fumio had called, apparently in some alarm. He called again at six this morning and I learned that he was worried lest I had been on the subway yesterday. Passengers were attacked with sarin gas—six dead and dozens ill.

Everyone I talk to says it is the work of one of the new religions, the Aum Shinrikyo, which is run by a bearded man who calls himself Asahara Shoko. He is also suspected of having abducted a lawyer and his family. Also of having made off with a notary public whose sister was being pressured to give her land to the new religion.

22 MARCH 1995. The Sarin Attack. No one talks of anything else, TV and radio flooded with speculation. A part of the extraordinary attention is that the event itself is extraordinary: Safe Japan suddenly becomes a Death Trap. A part is due to the Japanese tendency to think in packs. There is always some sort of celebrated cause going on in the media. But part of it is the random suddenness, the calibrated cruelty, and the knowledge—for everyone knows—that this was done by the followers of a local führer. Just as during wartime ordinary people followed orders and committed every one of the atrocities one has heard of, so this postwar Japan has people in it who unthinkingly, blindly, do the same thing. This is enough to sober the entire nation.

27 MARCH 1995. An important day—I finally, after eighteen years of waiting, get to see Bresson's *Le Diable Probablement*. One of the reasons for my so wanting was that this was the only one of the director's pictures I had not seen. Another was that here was an unknown part of the work of a man I much admired, and from whom I had learned much. Yet another, the strongest perhaps, is that when you love someone, you want to learn everything, want to gaze long, want to become a part of the beloved vision.

From the lucid beginning, a newspaper clipping that tells the outcome of the picture so that the viewer will not be disturbed by story, to the laconic conclusion, action completed (but not in the way this viewer expected), I am in that reasoned world where there are no imposed moral values, just verities: a world that is black and white even when the film is in color. I am returned to this universe, beautiful in its severity, which is my true home.

The door opens (how many doors there are in Bresson, always for enter-ing—and how few windows, just one, *Une Femme Douce*, and that for jump-ing out of), and the camera—in its favorite position, gaze lowered—sees the knees, the thighs, part of the hand, of whoever enters. It turns to follow the figure and only then raises its lens, and by then the face is passed and we see but the back of the head. (A joke I remember: Bresson is finally being allowed to film the *Bible*. His producer has, following his instructions, built a great ark and assembled all the animals. Just before shooting, Bresson clamps the camera in his favorite position and says, "You realize, of course, that I am just going to photograph their hoofs.")

Again I see that admirable deletion of the inessential: On the bus, a crash, camera inside, focused on the door, thighs of the conductor, and then noth-ing at all while we listen to the noises of the accident (whatever it was), and its aftermath (whatever that is)—the camera focusing on the door of the bus alone. (I am reminded of the opening sequence of *Un Condamné à Mort s'est Echappé*, where the camera stays inside the car while the Gestapo are atro-ciously, but invisibly busy.)

And, again, here, the magic of Bresson's vision. At the end when the two men are going to the cemetery, the subway door opens and the station slowly glides past. Bresson's miracles are made of the mundane—as I do think all miracles are. The subway platform is utterly ordinary, but unscrolling like this, the camera unblinking, it is more magical than any magic carpet.

And the sudden shock of the ending—the film just stops. At the mo-ment of death. It has no reason to continue now that Charles is dead. And the death—here one minute (in the middle of a sentence), and gone the next. Whether this is the way real people die is not to the point—this is the way metaphysical death occurs. And so young. (Even younger—I later read an interview with this actor: He was fifteen when he made the film, something Bresson did not know.) And after the tape stopped and my viewing screen went black, I sat there in the dark for a time—moved, alive, refreshed, re-newed, restored.

And grateful. The Bresson was a gift. Dan Talbot, knowing I had been in hospital, knowing I wanted to see this film more than anything, sent me the cassette.

22 APRIL 1995. The Aum Effect continues. Though it would ordinarily be as difficult to enforce in Japan as anywhere else, concern is now such that the subway announcements asking patrons to leave nothing on the seats or overhead racks, not even newspapers and magazines, are fully obeyed. And there are no complaints about the trashcans all being removed, the coin lockers all closed, the rooms for baby care all shut.

The sarin attack is taken very seriously indeed. There are no jokes about it, sick or otherwise. No TV comic would attempt levity. At the same time, the media have turned it into an obsession. There is nothing else on the tube but culprit Asahara and his followers, nothing in the papers and magazines but that fat, stupid, self-satisfied face. Still, this is better than cynicism.

So serious is everyone that a small Yokohama "attack" is made much of, though no one was injured, let alone killed. It seems that someone with mace got loose in a station corridor. But this is something the press is only slowly admitting. I see in the evening paper that someone high up was eventually of the opinion that one or more Aum culprits could have done it. The rest was supplied by a people on the verge of hysteria—so unused to violence is this populace. Still, how much better this than complacency.

26 APRIL 1995. To Shinjuku to see the Maxfield Parrish show. Pictures lined up—the glaze still so brilliant that they looked illuminated from behind. I remember the artist's son giving the recipe for Maxfield Parrish blue: add emerald to cobalt. And there is *Daybreak*, that picture (pillars, androgynous creatures waking up, incredible mountain background) a reproduction of which used to hang over the piano when I was a child. Many times I stood on the precarious stool to look into those bright morning cliffs. I had never seen anything more beautiful. Now, again leaning forward, I examine those romantic mountains, glasses on, nose near canvas. They are just as magical as they were sixty years ago.

16 MAY 1995. The day after the Aum guru was brought to ground I had to get up and out early to go to the hospital, something I dislike since it means I hit the rush hour. But not that day. I got a seat, no people. The rush hour and no one was rushing—afraid to, frightened of an attack by the crazed followers. The media frenzy has taken its toll, made cowards of everyone. Except me. But then I do not have TV and only read the papers after it is all over.

I think that now whole populations, now seeing on TV things while they are actually happening, fail to use what reflective powers are left. If the naked actuality of an event is hanging there before them, they do not have to think about it. Reality resists interpretation.

17 MAY 1995. With Gwen [Robinson] to the *dohan kisa*, Kon. Among the potted plants much activity—people milling about, staring. I leaned over a booth back and watched a girl on her back with her legs open and a group of men bent over her crotch, intent. It looked like a medical inspection. In the next booth a man was standing looking about as though on a busy street corner while his girlfriend, or someone's girlfriend, sat in front of him and inexpertly sucked his cock.

When I came back to our booth, Gwen had been joined by a young man with a big smile, who already had his hand on her thigh. While he gently massaged, we talked. Married, one child, yes, a boy. Only his second time here—usually liked the one in Shinjuku better, a younger, more uninhibited crowd. Of course, there you are not allowed to walk around and stare as you are here.

He now had one hand on her thigh and one vigorously rubbing her breasts. "I hope you realize," said Gwen, "that I am enduring this only to further your anthropological interests." "Yes," I said, reached over and felt his cock—short, hard. "Your friend is very exciting," he said to me, with a smile, the kind of compliment men pay one another. Then he asked me if I had ever had a three-way—two men and a girl. I said that, yes, I had. So had he, he said. We were becoming mildly interested in each other when Gwen said she did not know how much more of this she could stand.

I sent him away, reclaimed my date, and asked why. She had meant the mauling of her breasts. "They know nothing of what might make a girl feel good," she said. "They learn this awful nipple pinching and breast rolling on the porno screen where they do it because that is the only visible thing they can do."

21 MAY 1955. The big day of the Sanja Matsuri in Asakusa, so I strolled through the neighborhood. This year the festival was much cut down. Government said the grand procession of all the *omikoshi* was too dangerous and would be stopped. Each just circled its own neighborhood. Creeping disciplines—in the late 1930s the processions were stopped entirely. If no one complains (and no one does) then governments do as they want. This year, with people afraid to congregate because of the insane guru, the police can protect them more effectively than ever. And, indeed, there were far fewer here than usual. I went to the north, now a ghetto for the tattooed. They made a fine show but the younger members are not able to sport many masterworks—the new tattoo style looks like manga and I saw lots of green!

23 MAY 1995. Ed [Seidensticker] takes Patrick [Lovell] and myself out to dinner—to thank the former for helping him with his computer, and the latter because three is better than two. We naturally speak of computers for a time, and of the Aum menace. It is difficult for Ed to speak well of the police, but I am appreciative of the way they plugged up all the holes before they smoked Aum out. "But they did it in a very suspicious manner," says Ed. "And they used illegal methods. Plainly illegal. This gives the police more authority than ever and there we go again."

I tell him that Phyllis Birnbaum was very disturbed about this aspect of the police's actions, that it reminded her much of the police in pre-Nazi Germany. "Precisely," says Ed. I then quote to him that lovely ditty (to be sung to the tune of "America, the Beautiful") that finds a place in his recently published novel:

> In *wabi* land, in *sabi* land
> One can yet find some peace.
> And quietly disturb it
> And enliven the police.

1 JUNE 1995. Susan [Sontag], Annie [Leibowitz], Ian [Buruma], and I went to the opening of the Araki [Nobuyoshi] photo show. Four walls of naked girls sporting their pubic air while being tied up, strapped down and otherwise held into place—a display little differing (except in size) from what is found in the pages of s/m albums. That, and the fact that it was public. It would not have been allowed five years ago.

This I tell Susan. "Progress?" she asks rhetorically, then, "How any woman could look at this and not feel angry I just don't know." Ian says, "Well, you know, it is really ritual display, nothing moral about it, just narcissistic." "Just!" says Susan. "Nothing moral!" says Susan. And Annie says, "Well, it makes me feel hungry."

Agreed, we go to Shin Okubo and before eating at the Shin Sekai, I take them on a tour of the Hyakunincho. But also taking tours are lots of cop cars, and they drive the girls off the street. I talk to one fleeing group. "Are the cops dangerous, I ask?" "Not really," says one—South American perhaps, in good Japanese—"but a royal pain in the ass *(mattaku mendokusai)*."

At the restaurant we eat fish and frog. Annie tells about when she was first in Japan, as a child, taken on the crowded subway: "And when we got off my dress was up to here!"—points to her ribs, indicating, I think, the press of the crowds. Susan says that when she comes to Japan she feels like a Eu-

With Susan Sontag, 1995.

ropean going to America. The new world, the twenty-first century, the burgeoning of the coming.

Later she tells me how much she liked my essay on Mishima. "Donald, as I have said a hundred times and will keep right on saying, you are truly smart—so much smarter than you usually write. You must stop not writing at your full potential."

So I must, but how do I begin to tell her of the difficulties? Or does everyone have these difficulties and not complain about them?—just go on and do it. It sounds like Getting in Touch with Your Inner Self—and in a way I suppose it is.

She once told me that I was far too conciliatory, and too much concerned with the impression I was making. The urge to please—is this what is doing me in? Once in New York, she told me I was just too nice. Am I still Pleasing Papa?

I know what she is saying. It is true. I know because I can compare this to how it feels when I am free. This is when I am describing something. Myself gets left out—only *it* is there: the object regarded, delineated, limned. All of my best writing is then. This is also what stops the memoirs. I don't have the "software" to move *me* into position. I still care about appearance, about self, about the process.

After the diced frogs (with ginger and chili) we decide against going back to view the whores. Annie gets up and pays the bill—she is getting a big per diem because of her show opening here. I tell her how I admire her recent portfolio of everyone involved in the Simpson court case, and ask how she is going to do all those official sports figures when she takes on the Atlanta Olympics, a new commission. "Same way," she says.

4 JUNE 1995. On the train going to Kamakura I look out of the window—Shinagawa, Kawasaki, Yokohama—and can still see the lineaments of fifty years ago. The present grows transparent, and I can see into my past.

This often occurs on the train, leaving behind habit and the blindness it brings. I can suddenly see again, and even glimpse that invisible bridge that connects me to the person I was. I need only walk across it, and I will again be in the past.

Then I return to my book, and after a time I begin to cry. Is it that I regret the past? Or, that I am going to Kamakura to attend Kazuko's memorial anniversary? No, it is the perfection of what I am reading—Nagai Kafu, a story called "Kunsho."

Looking straight at his postwar present Kafu saw the past, just as I had. And he saw it passing—the sprawled limbs of the girls, the big smile on the face of the man who brought the girls' lunches, the photograph never delivered, the past captured too late. It is so vulnerably beautiful, so helplessly true that tears come.

At Eihoji all of Kazuko's friends have gathered. We are now like a black-clad family. There is Oshima and his wife, Kawarabata the critic, Tomoyama in Issey Miyake black and Nike tennis shoes since she will climb the wet mountain (it is raining) to the Kawakita tomb, and the relatives, and the people from the Kawakita Foundation.

After the service comes the mountain climbing. I do not go, nor does Oshima. He says he cannot go because of his heart. Since that is my excuse as well, we are shortly in discussion of our problems. I only have angina, but he has something much grander, a kind of general collapse. His wife, who usually inserts her comments from time to time, says nothing and so I gather it is serious.

Nogami [Teruyo] stays behind too, though she says her heart is perfectly sound and she thus has no alibi. But, "I do not like the idea of climbing that hill in all this rain," she says, "and I am sure that Kazuko will forgive me." Later we are taken to a restaurant and eat Kamakura *kaiseki*—all sorts of dainties in bowls and boxes.

We begin talking about Chinese film directors—Nogami, Okajima [Hisashi] from the Film Center, and Toda [Natsuko] the film title translator, and myself—about one named Wong and one named Wang. "Oh, I know him," I say, "only he's Chinese-American." Then I tell them about the film he is considering making of Alan [Brown]'s novel, *Audrey Hepburn's Neck*—which I translate as *Odari Epuban no Kubi*. "Oh, how horrid," says Natsuko, "some kind of horror flick?" "No," I say, baffled, "a comedy." "A comedy!" marvels Non-chan, "What won't they do next?"

We finally get it straightened out. *Kubi* means a severed head, and not a neck as I had thought. "What you meant," says Hisashi, "is *unaji*—that is the proper word." So I say, "Oh, I got it, OK, *Odari Epuban no Unagi* (eel)." Cries, protestations, laughter.

10 JUNE 1995. At Ueno, by the steps going up to the plaza, stand two of the Aum girls. They are passing out a publication, which has photographs of their fat and bearded leader, and a message that says he is innocent and we must rally to his defense. No one does. Usually people take anything handed them on the street, but these crowds pass by the girls and their outstretched hands without even a glance. Everyone knows—except for the girls.

In their Aum white suits they do not seem aware of what is happening. They were told to go out and distribute their papers and like good girls this is what they do. One older man stops in front of one of them and I can see that he is giving her a lecture—his finger is wagging. She simply stands and nods, waiting for him to go away, so that she can get on with her job. She must know, must realize what her leader has done and what the sect now means, but of this she gives no sign. She simply waits, a good girl, and finally the older man moves on and she goes back to her distributing.

11 JUNE 1995. At Karel van Wolferen's for dinner. Ed [Seidensticker] is late. He was at the Jesuits for lunch. "Why?" asks Karel. "Why not?" counters Ed. I asked after their ethnic cuisine. He says it was American and that I should watch my tone—Ed is Catholic, though not, I believe, Jesuitical. He then suddenly observes that the Church in Japan is as full of bishops as a Chinese bed is of bedbugs. Why so many bishops, he wonders, why, why, why, and I understand that the Jesuits have been drinking as well as eating.

Then the Pope is brought up. Ian [Buruma] says the bishop of Nagasaki told him that the peace movement is really a big business. Karel says that is unlikely, that the Pope would never allow such a thing. Then the Pope is dismissed and an argument, surprisingly heated, begins as to the relative merits of Mozart and Beethoven. Ed is on the side of Wolfgang Amadeus and Karel on the side of Ludwig van.

"Admit, admit," cries Karel, "that the flute quartets are very minor." "Well," says Ed, drawing himself up, "as for that, just consider 'Für Elise,' sir." At which point the stew appears and more bottles are uncorked. Ian tells about students being lined up and made to shout: "Remember Nagasaki! No More War!" He imitates their Germanic stance and their strained voices. "It is just like the Hitler Jugend movement," he says.

Ed can usually be counted to bash away, but he is quiet this evening—

perhaps too much competition. Why is it, I wonder, that when expatriates in Japan get together they always do this—find fault. Do they do this in other countries? Oh, these Luxembourgians, these people! Now, Karel takes on the nation. "These people," he says, banging his bottle, "They cannot even have a debate!" It grows late, Ed is tired (he has also been the Noh) and so am I (I have a cold), and so we give our thanks and creep out.

27 JUNE 1995. Lunch with Ed [Seidensticker]. We talk about the kind of foreigner who takes to Japan. When expatriates get together they always talk about this, something not invariable in other places. Here, the country takes the place of the weather. Why, we wonder, should this residence so consume the foreign inhabitant? I mention the three classical stages: euphoria, disappointment, and indifference—the latter corresponding to the ordinary marriage.

Perhaps that is it, we decide. The hapless foreigner falls in love, and then falls out. "And you, Edward," I say, "never progressed past Stage Two." "And you, Donald," he says, "are stagnating in Stage Three. But then, why fall in love?"

We cast about for various reasons why. The difference? The "Orient?" The original imperialistic opportunity? I note that this initial flush of enthusiasm for the country is often accompanied by affection but not approval. It is more like a crush than true love. "Ah," says Ed sagely, "that would account for the fact that it does not last."

I then mention a puzzling fact—it seems that many of the foreign Japan specialists living here are homosexual. Ed looks out of the window at this—he does not really like to talk about the subject, though he makes a show of open tolerance. I bring it up because I see here a parallel—falling in love with Japan (Stage One) must be a danger for those of a deprived emotional background. Growing up in the U.S.A. of the 1930s and 1940s, romance denied, the early visitor to Japan found a beautiful, permissive folk.

"All very well," says Ed, "but in that case why didn't the Paris expatriates fall in love with France?" This question neither of us can answer.

28 JUNE 1995. To the American Embassy Residence—the Mondales are giving a reception for Martin and Mildred Friedman, good Wisconsins all. Had not been there since they have redecorated. The residence looked like something in old Saigon before. Now it looks like new Hong Kong—a bank.

Against this meretricious display, the sincerity of the Mondales stands out. He makes a charmingly self-deprecatory speech about having lost a lot of time in trying to get to be president; she talks about art, and believes in it. Later she and I talk about modern Japanese art. She thinks that the artist must have the last say—we are talking about a Japanese artist, Yanagi Yukinori, whose recent creations include national flags executed in colored sand, which are carefully invested with ant tunnels so that these industrious insects can deconstruct the symbols and thus create one world.

6 JULY 1995. Since the Aum-inspired catastrophes, Tokyo people are much more friendly to us foreigners. They will often go where we go and will, I notice, try to sit next to us in the train. This is because not being able to trust each other (anyone could be Aum), they trust us (no foreign members in any local Aum organizations). Since there were two more attempted "subway gas attacks" today (Kayabacho and Shinjuku), I notice coming home in the subway that there is some vying to get near me. One girl was successful, giving suspicious glances to fellow Japanese the while.

From Ueno I hailed a cab and got a hysterical driver. He had been driving around all day brooding about the gas attacks. "What is happening to us?" he wondered, rhetorically. "I just don't get it. No place is safe from these people any more. And who are these people? They don't come from outside. They are us. And they are smart folks too—scientists, even doctors. What is happening?"

It is *mappo,* I say, referring to the final age of Buddhist belief when the laws are dead. He turns briefly to stare and then says, "You know, I think you're right."

8 JULY 1995. Walking back through Ueno I am stopped time and again by young people who stand in my way and hold up solemn hands. These, I learn, are the Kannon folk. They want to pray for me. The Aum business has all the religious crazies crawling out. One bouncing young person had memorized his spiel in English. When he finished I told him in deadly accurate Japanese that it was impolite of him to approach a stranger in this manner; that religion was a private matter, that he was intruding and it was rude. That stopped him—his jaw dropped and I politely passed on, confident that I had ruined his proselytizing day.

Only a few minutes later a young woman stopped me. Palms already up, blessing begun. "Kids of Kannon I suppose," I said. She nodded confidently and so I started *my* spiel, the same one I had given the stunned young man. But she just said, "No, I don't think so," and continued blessing me. Irritated, I said, "Such intrusion as this into a private part of a person is like a rape." Such politically correct complaints would stop her, I thought. Not at all. "I don't think so," she said, continuing, and so I had to leave the field to her.

9 JULY 1995. I read in the newspaper that the Aum Shinrikyo people, funding cut off, have opened stores and are selling tee-shirts with his fat holiness on them, and that these stores are filled with the frivolous young, giggling and buying. I remember too that the thin-lipped young Aum spokesman is found "sexy" by a polled gaggle of girls, and one is quoted as saying that she might join if she could be sure of getting him.

Pondering this dangerous inanity, I suddenly see that the grotesque Aum cult is very much like the prewar Japanese government. One must join, one cannot resign, you will be killed if you do, also Armageddon is approaching and so we must prepare for it and, in fact, create it in order to show that it is upon us. And the majority in 1940 behaved just as does this frivolous minority in 1995. This tells nothing about the Japanese, of course, but it sure tells something about people.

15 JULY 1995. I go and stand by the underground entrance at Ueno, near the Okura theater, and watch the people. Two girls, both blondined and smoking cigarettes in flashy fashion, and laughing loud, horse-laughs. These are the young, out on the town, and flaunting it. Let one man make a pass, however, and it is weeping home to mother. Then there is the little punch-permed guy in the Ricci summer sweater who spends his time looking tough. And there is an elderly couple, she in a cotton dress, he in suspenders—country people in town for Saturday night. I look more closely. They could be the couple from *Tokyo Story*, lost in Ueno.

People-watching—when I was seven or so, my father and I would sit in the car on the public square in Lima, Ohio, and watch them walk past. I was excited by the variety, the shapes and sizes, the import of the walk, or the lack of it. From the open car window I looked wonderingly at the world—as I still do.

18 JULY 1995. I see in the papers that Stephen Spender has died—he was eighty-six. And I remember him still middle-aged, wild blue eyes, what we would now call big hair, very like Shelley. Like the earlier poet, too, his moral concern. Once he took offense at my frivolity. I forget what the charge was but I remember the words: "No, Donald, this is very serious. You are not to make light of serious things." Yes, I remember—it had to do with one of [Tokunaga] Osamu's sulks and my saying that this boyfriend of his was impossible. It was Osamu who later tried suicide in order to get Stephen's attention. Serious, indeed, except of course, Osamu failed, both in suicide and in getting attention. "Oh, dear," said Stephen after the fact, "I wonder if I did the right thing; I so often don't, you see." I can see him before the Great Gate of Heaven right now, wringing his hands and searching his motivations. This is somehow admirable.

19 JULY 1995. A farewell party for John Howes. Before it he wants to show me movies he took in 1946, on the boat that carried the both of us to Japan. There is the sea of half a century ago. And there is John himself, looking young and earnest—now he looks old and earnest. I was promised, but I did not appear. Maybe his brother had not sent that reel, he said.

Then pictures of Japan itself in 1947—bad lens, short attention span, Tokyo Central Station looking like some village whistle stop. A young girl in a cotton dress, smiling. A group of students in their beat-up caps. They wear an expression I had almost forgotten but which people used to have: fresh, hopeful, and (yes) innocent. And suddenly, a shrine, and as John's unskillful hands manipulate the machine, for a second, there in the corner stands Herschel [Webb] alive and well again, smiling after all these years dead.

At the party lots of important people, since John likes important people. And we all had to give speeches. I talked about the boat trip over. Ed [Seidensticker] gave a droll two minutes recounting how he had forgotten John's wife's maiden name. Afterward, since Ed doesn't like much to walk and since I had eaten too much and all the blood had drained to the stomach, we took a taxi all the way home. I told him my favorite limerick:

> There was a young lady named Tuck,
> Who had the most terrible luck.
> She went out in a punt,
> Fell over the front,
> And was bit in the leg by a duck.

And he told me his:

> I sat by the duchess at tea.
> She asked: Do you fart when you pee?
> I replied, with some wit:
> Do you belch when you shit?
> Which, I think, left the honors with me.

We agree that that last line is a masterpiece.

14 AUGUST 1995. Coming back on the late express, I saw that the black-clad, middle-aged man opposite was gazing intently. Then he turned to the man next to him and said something, then resumed his staring. This was all very benevolent, and so I smiled and nodded, at which he stood and came over, sat down beside me and took my hand, all unmindful of the stares around him and my own surprise. Then I looked more closely.

He was one of my old students—Waseda University, 1955. He, the man beside him, and several more on their side, all of them my former students, were coming back from the funeral of yet another of their number—one who had, they said, swam too far out and drowned. I thought the reference perhaps metaphorical but, no, he had gone to the beach with his family.

The man telling me this (his name was Saito I now remembered), said he had looked at me sitting there reading my book, and then he saw that I was making notes with my left hand, and that convinced him that here, sitting before him, was his old teacher—but looking so young, he quickly added. So we sat together and I watched these elderly men turn into boys as I removed layer after layer and again glimpsed those young, vanished faces. But try as I might I could not recall the face of the dead.

31 AUGUST 1995. In the evening out with Ed [Seidensticker] for no reason in particular—just to talk. He is pleased with my getting the Japan Foundation award, and I politely say that he got it first. "Oh, but that must have been a fluke. They should never have given it to me. Nor would the Japan Societies ever ask me to speak. You see, I am known as being critical of this country and they can never allow that. No, the award was a fluke."

To which I answer that I too am critical. He responds with, "Perhaps, but not as I am. I simply do not have as sunny a disposition as you do. And I could never stand there and say things I do not believe."

I look at my plate. He does not mean that I say things I do not believe and hence win awards. He is just thoughtless, and deaf to his own implications—though acute enough to those of others.

My thought is communicated. "Not," he says, "that I am saying that those who like this country are being insincere. That would be a foolish thing to say." I agree that it would be foolish.

2 SEPTEMBER 1995. Overnight, summer is done. This morning the air is clear and the sky is a deep blue. It is still hot, but the light is different. The hazy heat of full summer has vanished, and in the morning sun every distant roof is

clear, every antenna etched. This coup de saison occurs every year and I don't know how. Like all magic, it is suddenly there.

Walking past the National Science Museum in Ueno, I see that Natsume Soseki's brain is going to be on exhibition from the middle of the month. Preserved since his death in 1916 at age 50, it will now be for the first time viewed by the general public. To what end, I am not certain. His face, of course, graces the thousand yen bill, but what lay behind it has until now not been made visible. Still, the view, I am certain, will be educational.

9 SEPTEMBER 1995. Looking at the old people in the park—women and their grandchildren, a man painting—I notice that I am thinking about how nice they look. I wonder why and then remember something that Oida Yoshi told me years back when I asked why he liked only older men. He said, "But their lives are in their faces; their character is all there, built up line by line. How anyone could find those smooth, unformed faces of the young attractive I do not know."

11 SEPTEMBER 1995. Reading about the tribulations of Republican Senator Robert Packwood, I note that someone said, "Why didn't he just not keep a diary?" But I know why he thought he had to. He wanted to vindicate himself—to present himself as he wanted to be: big man in the Senate, wheeler-dealer, a way with the ladies, and maybe even President of the United States some happy day. Like all diary keepers, he wanted to present the basic pattern and be understood by it. It is ironic that it is this pattern that now relieves him of his senatorial duties, but this is a part of the pattern too.

One admits in order to be exonerated, and exonerated one is—Boswell, Pepys, Gide—if you are not in politics. But if you are, then never commit one private word to paper. Big Bob did nothing that would not be forgiven in anyone but a politician. He made muzzled little passes at women, and tried to get business friends to help him get jobs for his divorced wife—but he was also (as he says in his diary) powerful in the Senate. The competition got him. I think I understand him well—at least I recognize that need, known to all diarists, which fathers this compulsive urge to recreate, to explain.

13 SEPTEMBER 1995. She is quietly well-dressed: black, pearls, poised, a cigarette at her lips, a small smile, and a cup of coffee before her. He is in his baggy shorts and running shoes with his cap on backward, a chocolate parfait melting in front of him. Mother and child? No, a girl and a boy on a date.

26 SEPTEMBER 1995. Tokyo Film Festival Party at the Imperial. Oshima in full kimono. This he usually wears at international gatherings. It seems a statement, but what kind? He was leftist radical, and the kimono is (as a political sign) rightist radical.

Spoke with the Iranian directors. They were forthcoming about their troubles with their repressive government. Talking with them always reminds me of speaking with children who have despotic parents. They are all such good boys, and they are all treated so badly. Mifune used to attend gatherings like this, but there is no hope of seeing him now—he is in a home somewhere, memory gone, I hear.

2 OCTOBER 1995. They are everywhere, on every corner—young people, boys and girls, standing, hands outstretched, giving flyers to whoever will take them. Sometimes they are stuck into packages of tissue to make them more attractive. Usually they are naked, shamelessly advertising. This is an index of the economy. Nothing in this nation of merchants is selling. Stores are sitting with merchandise piled high, but no one is buying. Cash is in short supply and the great shopping boom—shopping instead of living—seems over. Even brand names sit glumly in their boxes. And there are not nearly enough jobs. Hence all these young hands, trying to reach you on street corners.

5 OCTOBER 1995. We got into our limousines and—a perk I earned by winning the Japan Foundation Prize—started for the Imperial Palace. Though the Hanzomon gate would have been nearer, we were taken in by the Sakashitamon, which is the one opposite Marunouchi. The reason was that we could thus see much more of the grounds.

This I much wanted to do. After fifty years of looking at the palace grounds from the public side of the moat, seeing the tops of the forest and the roofs of distant palaces I wanted to see for myself. Passing through police checkpoints and the outer gates, we were shortly inside the inner moat and passing through the park-like gardens of the Imperial Household (Kunaisho) Offices; then down what looked much like a country road, on either side of which were further walls, and behind them the virgin forest that is the heart of this land. I had heard that rabbits and foxes still lived here.

The cars pulled up under the porte-cochere of a large, recent building that looked like one of the grander wedding halls. It was the new palace—and chamberlains were waiting. Much bowing by everyone, and we were ushered into a series of rooms, all decorated in modified imperial style. This style was set in the Meiji period and is hence Victorian, with plush covered sofas, wainscoting, and coffered ceilings. Since this palace was built in 1993 and not

Greeting HIH Michiko and Akihito, 1995.

1893, however, there are no sofas and the plush has turned into brocade. Still, the imposing comfort of Windsor is there.

A chamberlain announced himself and then with great patience and kindness, explained how our audience would proceed. He had a piece of paper with circles drawn on it and arrows showing how everyone should move. My role was modest; I was second from the right and would simply bob back and forth. The president of the Japan Foundation had the most difficult role. He was choreographed to move forward, then to circle back, describing as he went an arc around the recipients about to be introduced, then he had to come full stop to our right. It was a complicated geometrical pattern—just like the Bugaku.

We then all lined up in a further room. This one owed more to Shinto than to Victoria. It was paneled with cedar and had hanging curtains, like in Ise, and though the furniture was Western—blonde wood holding gold brocade—it still looked ecclesiastical. Outside the wide windows stretched the gardens and beyond them the forest. It was like being in a lavish country estate far away from any city, though over one treetop I could see the staring eye of the Wacoal Building.

The chamberlains bustled about and I was struck by the resemblance of the palace and its staff to a really expensive *ryotei*, a Japanese restaurant which costs so much that absolutely nothing must go wrong. There were the same watchful glances, the same purposeful scurrying. Then someone of them solemnly said: "They are coming."

We all stood straight and in they walked, both smiling, the Emperor in a black suit and what looked like a school tie, the Empress in a cream-colored kimono with a matching obi. They took their places in front of us, just as the diagram had indicated, the president went through his steps, and then we looked at each other.

Good will was evident; both were half-smiling, and I realized that this too was part of the pattern. It was graciousness—they seemed so filled with good will that it verged on the solicitous. Aristocratic, the stance seemed to deliberately avoid condescension through this expression of concern. It was as though they were about to ask us if we really had enough money, or really felt all right.

They were also, however affable, grave. One did not, to be sure, expect laughter and tossed heads, but this gravity can resemble sadness. The graciousness was somehow funereal, like flowers slowly fading. And yet behind all this, I also saw something that looked like curiosity, and realized that we represented to them not only duty but, perhaps, diversion.

When my turn came the Emperor put out his hand and I shook it. This indicated that the reception would continue in a foreign manner and, sure enough, he congratulated me in English. Afterward, it being my turn to speak, I asked if there were any animals in the forest. Yes, he believed so. Some rabbits—yes, he had seen some rabbits.

He paused and I congratulated him on his new palace and noticed that you could still smell the cedar. He paused and then sniffed as though to ascertain this, then agreed. Following this, as was polite, he spoke of films. He was fond of Kurosawa and remembered seeing Ozu once when he had received an imperial award. Yes, *Tokyo Story*, he said, with something like relish.

The Emperor had been going up one side of our lines and the Empress had been coming down the other. Now they met, and with an adroitness one does not usually see off a dance floor, they pivoted around each other and she now stood before me.

Her husband had looked at me in that affable and detached manner I had before noticed only in the really wealthy, but her gaze was focused somewhere in front of me and slightly below, as though she were regarding my tie. Her voice was soft, modulated, and her English was good—better than his.

I congratulated her on her nice new house and she wanted to know where

I lived—exclaiming in a soft voice, and taking that affable, distant interest that, I have heard, is common to royals. "Ah, Shitamachi," she said, then, adroitly, like a good hostess, mindful of the guest's interests, "As in the films of Ozu."

Had she seen many? I wondered. "Well, *Tokyo Story* certainly," she said, then added that here at the palace they couldn't really see many films; what they saw was cassettes on television sets. They had a screening room at the Imperial Household office, but one didn't much go. So what they could get in the way of cassettes were mostly popular films or the classics." But I feel that I ought to—no, I want to—take an interest in younger directors and discover what they are doing." I told her about some younger directors and their films. "Oh, how I would like to see them," she said, and I promised to send her a list and some cassettes.

As we talked, I thought about her life. They were both sequestered here, and besides their duties there must have been little for them to do. Royalty is in this way held captive—displayed and then put back in the box. The temptation to escape must be strong. I remembered the princess in *Roman Holiday* and her escapade. But there was no escape for Michiko.

As she spoke I remembered pictures of her I had seen when she was young, tennis-playing. Now she was frail, gracious, tentative, and that steady gaze regarded my necktie. What a life, I thought, and resolved to send her all the cassettes I could find.

Later, talking to a chamberlain I mentioned what I had promised to do and wondered how to do it. What a good idea, just send them to me and I'll make sure she gets them. He gave me his card and I realized that the Imperial Palace had an address. It is: Imperial Palace, 1-1 Chiyoda, Chiyoda-ku, Tokyo 100.

We had been scheduled for thirty minutes, and sure enough their Imperial Highnesses were now back in their beginning positions and then, amid gracious smiles and bowing chamberlains, they glided from the room. Yes, glided—for their gait was also practiced.

The couple held the otherworldly aspect of royalty; they carried their sacerdotal roles in front of them, but behind these I saw the two people, and how heavy the roles were, and I saw the gentleness and sadness that goes with a resignation. I wondered if that soft glint of curiosity had been satisfied or whether we too had disappointed them.

After they had left there was a sudden lightness and we realized that we had been oppressed. Our departure was, consequently, less dignified than our entry, and we departed the palace in the best of spirits. The limousines rolled smoothly over the gravel and out into Tokyo, and I pondered over whether *Okaeri* would be a good film to send. It is about an unhappy wife who develops schizophrenia. And I remembered that when the Empress was recently attacked by the scurrilous media (she keeps the servants up after hours; she demands food at night; she is bossy . . .), she responded by turning mute—did not speak for weeks.

Our party was reunited that evening at a Yonbancho *ryotei*, quite expensive enough to behave just like the palace. As the elderly geisha-like waitresses wheeled expertly about on the tatami bringing us all sorts of *kaiseki* delicacies: red caviar on *udo*, egg-filled pregnant trout, one perfect *matsutake* mushroom—we caroused, lightheaded after our visit to the palace and all it had shown us.

Eventually, the cars were called and we all got to go home, after a most exhausting if interesting day. [A shorter version of these activities is included in *Public People, Private People*. The entire chapter is excluded, however, from the Japanese translation of the book.]

16 OCTOBER 1995. Letter from Ian [Buruma]. "Inspired by your description of Boswell's London diary, I instantly went to the London Library to borrow the book. It is, as you say, wonderful. The key to the success of these diaries is their ruthless honesty. Boswell hides very little: not his fear of impotence, not his moods of despair, and most important of all, not even his vanity. His boasts ring absolutely true. There is a boaster hidden in all of us, but only an innocent, or a rare writer would let that embarrassing braggart out of his cage. Perhaps it takes a kind of humility to be able to display one's vanity for all to see."

Also a kind of trust. After all, we all keep our journals for reasons beyond the ostensible. At the least, we wish to structure life, to make some sort of pattern. At the most we wish to forestall posthumous criticism, to redress supposed wrongs and (if we are the notorious autobiographer Frank Harris) to lie. Indeed to not lie requires a very real effort. The slippery nature of language assures that we will, of course, but the effort not to may make the accounting a bit more reliable.

My father used to keep a diary, I tell Ian. Every night at ten sharp, he would uncap his pen and open that green ledger, pages of which he had filled, dozens of volumes by the time he died. He recorded the temperature, and the barometric readings, which he had faithfully taken. Then the household news.

Donald to school. Jean scraped knee. And that was it. Jean and I used to laugh at this, but I would not laugh now because I know what he was doing—he was holding time at arm's length; he was finding a pattern; he was emblazoning a day. My own diaries are not that different from his.

Except they tell more; they are more like letters. I remember reading of the fuss that Gide made when he discovered that his unhappy wife had burned all of his early letters. "But they were my diaries, my very life!" cried the eminent author who, nevertheless, left behind five full volumes of journals—which he called his "major work." He was not writing for himself. But does one ever? Only, I think, when you really intend them as an *aide-mémoire*, and are going to mine them—they are then the quarry of the past.

18 OCTOBER 1995. A walk in Ueno Park, where I see that the workers are removing all the benches and putting in new ones. These are so much shorter that I stop a workman and ask if this is being done so that the homeless cannot sleep on them any more. He says that that perhaps is the reason and shakes his head, then adds, "But the couples on dates can still sit on them."

I wonder if this is a peculiarly Japanese way of solving a problem. You do not run off the homeless, nor help them get lodgings. Instead, you (at great expense) change the circumstances.

21 OCTOBER 1995. The trial of followers and leaders of the Aum cult has begun, and with it come further revelations. Since Asahara had prophesied Armageddon, he had to make it happen. Not only the subway gassing, but also germs spread by helicopter. But, fortunately, the followers were also inept—and the "success" of the subway gassings was mostly accidental. One welcome result of their trials is that the other cults keep off the streets. No more people wanting to pray over you; now, no more smiling folks asking if you are *genki*. Even the Soka Gakkai is getting perturbed. If the new law limiting religion goes into effect it will hurt their finances. Yet, every country needs such a law. If you can ban alcohol and nicotine, why can't you ban religion?

12 NOVEMBER 1995. Rummaging through old papers I come across Al Raynor's translation of the Noh *Atsumori*. I didn't know I had it. Looking at the careful pencil notes, I again see Al licking the point nearly fifty years ago before changing a word. I will send it back to him—his last letter was full of the troubles of his children and grandchildren and bad Blyth translations. This will cheer him up.

13 NOVEMBER 1995. I call Tani in Osaka, not having talked with him since his wife died. His daughter answers, her mouth full of supper. "Oh, Papa? He moved. Here's his number." I called the number and there is Papa. What happened? Why did he move? "Memories," he says. "That house was full of memories for me." And I think of him, so undemonstrative with his wife, so unfaithful, and now he misses her. I ask him to come see me in Tokyo. I will take him to dinner at the Press Club. He likes that. Tokyo high life. "No, I am too old," he says. "Tani-san," I say, "you are ten years younger than I am." "That's just what I mean." he says with that laugh I so well remember.

20 NOVEMBER 1995. A call from the Grand Chamberlain. Her Imperial Highness wishes to thank me for so kindly remembering and sending her the cassettes of the new films (*Okaeri* and *Maboroshi*) of which I spoke. She is looking forward to viewing them. My suspicious fears she would not get them nor be even told of their arrival are laid away—if he is telling the truth.

25 NOVEMBER 1995. Sawada Ichiro gave a party last night in honor of Mishima Yukio and Eric Klestadt, one now dead for twenty-five years, the other, one year. I think of them beyond the pale—Mishima probably knows his way around well. Hope that he has taken Eric under his arm and shown him about.

Guests were those who knew them and whom Ichiro still likes. Ishiguro Norio the designer, Japanese dance *iemoto* Umezu, Paul McCarthy, a man named Oikawa whom we refer to as the "Unagi King" since he runs a profitable chain of eel shops, and me. We naturally speak of the dead for a time.

I wonder if the regulations on Mishima are going to be lightened now that the widow is dead. No, not at all, says Norio. The daughter, now married and herself a mother, is maintaining the widowed line: only father as litterateur is allowed, not father as bodybuilder, much less anything else. And no showing of that movie [*Patriotism*], either.

At the same time, they have shut up the big house. The copy of the Apollo is dank in the deserted garden, that absurd staircase which went nowhere is even now more absurd with no Mishima, nor anyone else, to come down it. For a long time the widow kept everything as it was. The pen was still on the open notebook, says Norio. Now only darkness and the mice.

Where is the son? I wonder—that unhappy child. Norio tells me that he is a jeweler right here on the Ginza. We speak of the possibility of all of us going to look at him, and then decide that it would not be polite.

While we are appreciating Yukio for his own sake, two other memorial dinners are taking place. One, in Kudan, is a large one, vaguely political. The

ANZAI SHIGEO

With Christopher Blasdel.

other is somewhere else, very political indeed—Revere the Emperor. I doubt that Mishima would appreciate being taken up by rightist thugs.

7 DECEMBER 1995. Pearl Harbor Day, and not one newspaper mentions it. The ghost has been laid to rest by last year's anniversary, during which the media spoke of little else. As always, they overfed—now, upset tummy. No one wants to touch the wretched anniversary of the Day of Infamy.

In the evening Chris [Blasdel] and I go to Teshigahara's annual year's end party. [Kanaseki] Hisao appears, looking frazzled—chemotherapy, cancer. [Takemitsu] Toru, puffy, wearing a cap now that he is bald—chemotherapy, cancer. Akiyama Kuniharu there, all over his own cancer it seems. [Kobayashi] Toshiko very friendly, hugs, a hand on my aged rump. Thinks we ought to get together, "for old times sake." Oda Mayumi comes late, is pleased that her charity sale made lots of money for the cause of a nuclear-free environment. "And we stopped Monju," she says triumphantly, in reference to the accident at the nuclear power plant. At the raffle I win a lady's embroidered bag.

18 DECEMBER 1995. Noisome Roppongi now much subdued. No money. The employees of the various discos, clubs, and bars are on the street handing out advertisements, soliciting. Many are foreign. Big, jovial blacks from Senegal, Jamaica, and Alabama; pale, supercilious blonde models from Sweden and Minnesota; Middle-Eastern men in turbans; Mexicans in sombreros—all handing out flyers to the passing crowds.

A pretty girl with big eyes and a ponytail offers me one on which is printed: Club Pretty Girl, One Hour, Only ¥10,000 [$100], Including First Drink. "You people must be hurting bad," I say. "They've put you all out on the street." She smiles and says, "That's right, but you know what? I'd rather be out here catching cold on the street than in there getting felt up. And the pay's the same."

24 DECEMBER 1995. Cora [Rosevere] and I go to the Shoto Museum in Shibuya to see movies filmed in the Meiji period [1868–1912]. There are only two made by Japanese—one is the Kabuki *Momijigari* (1896), a famous one. The other is one I have never seen: a group of *oiran* [courtesans] doing their procession in a Japanese garden. This unlikely event is interrupted by a peddler with his pack, who gets in their way. They avoid him, and he is then attacked by a man dressed in a dog suit. Strange.

The rest, one long program—some thirty films, each about 30 seconds in length—are Japanese scenes photographed by whoever the Lumières sent over to do it. Geisha and swordsmen, lots of genre scenes (*La famille à souper*), but for me the most interesting were the street scenes. A Ginza corner (impossible a century later to determine just which), and anyone who happened by was immortalized. I particularly enjoyed a scene taken at Ueno (*Un parc japonais*)—in the foreground a young man drinks something from a bottle, has trouble, looks in at the neck, and laughs. What could he have found funny? The bigger joke is that all that is left of him now is that unconsidered act on that forgotten day?

Though Richie was working on the Lafcadio Hearn anthology, as well as on his newspaper column and numerous essays and articles, the journals continued to be his major creation. He kept adding to them, and at the same time began to prepare them for eventual publication. This meant cutting them—and putting the rejects into separate files. In this way Richie was shaping this long, accidental work—finding themes, motives, noting reoccurrences, and being careful to chronicle them in the life he was describing.

I JANUARY 1996. Dae-Yung and I went to Fumio's elder sister's house for New Year's with the whole Mizushima family—forty people in all. The celebration was held in a big country house in the far suburbs, over an hour from Tokyo, near the Hakone Mountains. Everyone was gathered at a long table on which were slabs of tuna, pots of hot oyster stew, trays of winter vegetables, and plates of pickles. People drank beer and *shochu* and sake and orange juice and Pocari Sweat.

All the brothers and sisters of the Mizushima family were there—and the long-missing father. I had not seen him since Fumio's wedding—now he is eighty-eight, a ruddy old gent with white hair. His daughters wanted to forgive him for running out on his wife and family forty years before, and now invite him to family events.

Though I had usurped his place at the wedding he is friendly, or has per-haps forgotten. The family has not, however. They address me, with smiles, as the alternate father, and remind the old man of the wedding, when he had to go and sit in the corner. He nods and smiles.

I find admirable the open way that Japanese often bring out what is hid-den. Though there is a lot of covering up in public, in private—like now—ev-erything is taken out and aired. "Remember when Mr. Richie here was the father and you were just a bad old man who kept getting in the way, remem-ber that?" the father is asked and he nods in pleased recollection.

More family members come, children and children's children. Then comes *otoshidama* time. This is the money given children at New Year's—it comes in pretty little envelopes. Since all the relatives give something to all the chil-dren, each one ends up with quite a bit. They usually bank it, or their parents do. Fumio surprises me by giving me an envelope, too. It contains ¥10,000 (\$100)—quite a lot. He surprises me even more by giving one to his father, a man to whom he has barely spoken for forty years. His father is astonished, gets on his knees, and bows.

Dae-Yung sits, looking at all this. No matter how badly he might (being a Korean) have been treated outside the sacred Japanese circle, once inside no discrimination is permitted and he is welcomed as warmly as they welcome each other. He is plied with food and drink, and when singing time comes he is given the microphone first and encouraged to sing one Korean song after the other. And he, an orphan who has never had a family, is moved by this. He is smiling, but his eyes are glistening and during a rendition one small tear rolls slowly down his cheek.

10 JANUARY 1996. On the street I see an acquaintance of some years standing. We always nod and sometimes talk. Usually he is looking around the theater, sidling up an aisle searching for someone to sit next to. Tonight he comes over, shaking his head. "Gone," he says, "absolutely no one. And it has been this for months now." I suggest the winter weather but he shakes his head bleakly. "No, they buy a tape, or rent it, and take it home and lock the door." His gesture—a clenched fist moving up and down—completes the thought. I sympathize and continue on my way home.

As I walk, I think about what he had said. He is right, of course—minis-trations such as his are no long needed. It is easier to do it yourself, and these self-centered youngsters are now typical in yet a larger sense. Brought up with little curiosity, and with a much-exaggerated idea of the dangers of their world, they are encouraged, boys and girls alike. Going into their rooms and shutting their doors is to be thought virtuous.

There they can study their brains out or beat themselves to death, the result is the same: a single person operating singly—no communication, no wish for, and eventually little ability for any contact.

I think of these solitaries and then look up into the evening sky where the e-mail courses and the internet surfs. Here, like modern sorcerers, fly the young, each alone, to type his or her way into what must pass as communication—but of a strange, limited kind: one where you must draw little faces with smiles or frowns to show what you feel—an analogue system of emotions, either yes or no, but nothing in between.

Here, it is said, a kind of dialogue takes place. But it takes place between two keyboards in two rooms in two cities or countries or continents. And the hands on those keyboards fabricate the person—he or she is arbitrarily created according to wishes or desires or compulsions of the moment: a protean creature, which can change into any self. It is not communication but imposture.

In a further sense as well—this is a universe of words, only words, and words are only agreed upon signals to denote a reality, not the reality itself. They are notoriously clumsy; they are coarse compared to the real. It is the real that is excised in this modern mode.

At the game center I stop to watch a young man standing in a simulator. Lights flash. He is wearing a helmet that hides his most recognizable part, his face. And a glove hides his hand. As I watch he seems to be fighting something. His weight shifts, the hand moves, the head dodges. It is probably a monster. His track shoes scuffle, he is perhaps running, like a dog asleep. I see a trickle of sweat run down his neck. He is perhaps afraid.

Alone he is indulging in the ultimate masturbation—that of person. He has voluntarily deserted the real for the fantasy, and pornography is one of the results when you do this. He is indulging in the pornography of fear, and his self is frozen in cybernetic attention.

A bell rings, the lights stop, he takes off the helmet. A young worker of some kind, he is smiling, the kind of weary smile the movies put on their actors when they want to indicate that a night of passion is over. He takes off his glove with what seems a practiced ease. He is back to himself.

But who is this? He has had an experience with no one, about nothing, and he is satisfied with this. If I, a real monster, were to walk up and spout flames of English, and put out a claw of companionship, he would be truly afraid and would turn his back upon the awful reality of me as he never does upon the comforting monstrousness of simulated reality.

I look and multiply this smiling young man by one hundred million. He is the future.

11 JANUARY 1996. At the International House, a reception for the visiting young artists, I give the toast and later am talking with Chris [Blasdel] who points out a short, bespectacled man and tells me that he is the leading *hichiriki* player in the Imperial Court orchestra, just as my friend Ono [Tadamaro], was the leading *sho* player—or had been. Did I know that he'd died last fall? Cancer.

Fifty years vanished and I again saw Ono as he was then, as he had been on that day in 1947, in his Bugaku costume and for me the very personification of the country. Since I never saw Ono again, he has remained always as he was then.

Chris, who knew him much later and studied under him, once asked how I could ever have been in love with him. I explained that I hadn't been, that I never knew the man, and had only seen him twice. It wasn't him with whom I was in love, but what I thought he embodied. I never made an effort to see Ono again, but I made many efforts to see the country within a single person.

Even now, when that kind of naturalness, that aesthetic sureness which I so admired is all but vanished, I still go around looking into tidal pools and turning over rocks, trying to find someone (preferably young, unformed, and handsome) who can stand for Japan. That I now find no such person does not discourage the search—it is, after all, its own end.

18 JANUARY 1996. After weeks of wondering how to do it, embarrassed city officials are going to move out of Shinjuku the homeless who camp out there in their cardboard city right along the tunnel that leads to the new city hall.

Now, however, the homeless have legal representation (moving them is against their human rights) and lots of "student" support. Still, I expect all of this will cave in under government pressure. The city has built homes for the homeless, camp-like structures in inconvenient places, which, say the homeless, will be closed in two months anyway.

Nothing is being done at all for the Ueno homeless (in contrast to the Shinjuku homeless), but then they are not organized, not embarrassing, just pitiful and tragic. A few evenings ago, standing by the edge of the pond, watching the ducks, I was approached by a woman I had seen often.

Her white hair is like thatch and she wears a blanket as though it were a cloak. She asks, oddly, if I have any cardboard. On these she will presumably sleep.

I did not, but she did not expect me to. Her question is to elicit money, and it is pathetic to see her trying to retain her dignity by asking for cardboard, knowing I have none. Pathetic though this is, I give nothing. She singles me out almost every time I go to the park. I did give her some money once but I do not now.

20 JANUARY 1996. I awake to white, dead light, and know it has been snowing. Also, the edge of the cold is different, sharper. Opening the window I watch the falling flakes, gray against the oyster sky. Maybe that was why I was dreaming about a hospital, an operating room, and the cold odor of chloroform.

Why are waking moments, the hopeful beginning of a new day, so often filled with death, I wonder. My doctor tells me heart attacks very often occur in the early morning hours—looking at me meaningfully the while. But my desolate wakings predate heart concerns.

I think they are always there, for everyone. We see plainest at the first, for man is the only animal stupid enough to know he is to die.

22 JANUARY 1996. Two middle-aged women are talking on the subway. While I cannot hear what they are saying, I watch their nodding heads, their narrow glances, their conspiratorial airs. This is so common—women as conspirators. One leans over to the other as though repeating something spiteful and the other grimly nods. Then the first begins to tell something funny and laughs a lot during the recitation. The other cracks not one smile. This is the way it always is with some middle-aged Japanese women when together—the talker always laughs, the listener, never.

I know why conversations take this form. It is because these women grew up powerless. Marginalized, their conversations are commiserations. Those narrowed eyes, the scandalized way of recounting, the lowered voices, the scornful agreements—this is something I remember seeing black women do when I was little, and effeminate homosexuals when I was older. Now the young Japanese women talk nothing like this. They are loud and often raucous, use man-talk and refuse to soften their voices in any pretense of gentility.

24 JANUARY 1996. Early this morning, six say the papers, the Tokyo police moved into Shinjuku Station and began evicting the homeless, those men who lived in their cardboard city in the sheltered tunnel leading to City Hall. Some two hundred homeless, some eight hundred police. It does not sound like a fair fight but, then, it was not supposed to be.

It was, however, a very Japanese one. It took years for the city fathers to act, and when they did they overacted. Yet those long months had not been wasted. The cops compiled complaints from nearby storeowners; they placated the public (what few needed it) with promises of a walkway, a people-mover, all the way from the train platforms to the very entryway of Governor Aoshima's offices.

One of the bereft shouted (according to the paper) that such an attack as this should never have been tolerated in a democratic society. True, but what could have led him to believe that this is a democratic society? There will be no complaints. The man on the street (one such, interviewed by one of the papers, said that the homeless stank) believes it all necessary, and that is enough for most to rationalize, as does the Governor, that "... the metropolitan government had no other choice than to mobilize the police."

I wonder how I feel about all of this. My leftover liberal reaction is to voice concern and pity. But only to voice it, not to do anything about it. Last night I was picking my way home through the homeless in Ueno Station, feeling bad about them but not feeling bad for them, not to the extent of giving out food or money, for example. Empty sentiment warmed me, but not them.

27 JANUARY 1996. The police are having trouble with the evacuees. Some eighty of the homeless remain in Shinjuku Station, making noises, vowing permanency and, according to several quotes from restaurateurs in the proximity, "making a stink." They are there also because they now have nowhere to go. The temporary shelter (complete with fence and moat) made for them can contain two hundred, but now contains less than half of that number. Nonetheless no more are being accepted because, you see, the deadline for entrance has run out. Also, since it was made for the Shinjuku sufferers, sufferers from other parts of the city cannot use it. Ten such hopefuls were rejected on the grounds that they had not lived at the Shinjuku eviction site.

In the meantime the government is attempting to steal some billions of yen from the taxpayers (about five thousand from each man, woman, and tax-paying child in the entire country) in order to bail out the criminal housing organizations whose generous loans the *yakuza* now refuse to pay back.

The Diet is stalled. Sleek Hashimoto, the new P.M., says that this is the only solution.

And continuing on is the three percent tax that so infuriated this patient public. Why do the people put up with it? Because they have no infrastructure through which to do anything else, that's why. There is no way for them to express indignation. Consequently we all pay three percent on everything; we will also pay off the delinquent and fraudulent loan organizations; and the homeless will be all swept under society's carpet.

2 FEBRUARY 1996. With some friends to the boy brothels of Shinjuku. The first is named Janny (Johnny). Some half-dozen boys are behind the bar and the master, one Mr. Manabu, sits at the table with us and explains his wares. They are all nineteen and they are all straight—two highly unlikely statements. The "system," as it is called, is that one makes one's choice, then pays for one's drinks (when I later paid for ours I found the amount equivalent to $35), then pays Mr. Manabu the sum of $170, one hundred of which is for the bedraggled boy when he returns after his two hours of passion in a hotel room, for which you will be soaked with another $60. Altogether it will cost about $300. We leave, but it is not the price which has deterred us, rather that the acned youths on display did not seem worth it.

The next place was called B-Flat—though B-Sharp might have been a better name. We were smartly ushered in, face towels flourished, orders taken, and information cannily offered. All were nineteen, all were straight, third from left was biggest, two on the end knew how to be sodomized, most could be brought to perform fellatio, straight though they might be, and the financial system was precisely the same—indicating some degree of cooperation among such establishments as these.

We ogled the merchandise and one of us foreigners wondered which one spoke English. None of them did, it transpired. "Oh, in that case . . . can't even talk to them." I also looked the boys over, but they naturally did not possess that appearance of innocence and lack of guile that so appeals to me. One of my friends, however, definitely liked the one on the left who, as a matter of fact, was already smiling back at him.

When I left, business talk was on, and I later learned that one was eventually selected but that the chosen lad could not only not be sodomized, he also could not even sodomize properly. In addition, though able to perform fellatio he did not do so with any degree of zest. Maybe the place really ought to be called B-Natural.

3 FEBRUARY 1996. Cold, winds from Siberia, no place for the homeless. They have disappeared from Ueno and the press is silent about Shinjuku. But the police are busy elsewhere. Now they are closing Harajuku. This was an area around the station and by the park that on Sundays was given over to the excesses of the young. There were bands and dancers and skateboarders and rock-n-rollers. It started some twenty years ago when the Takinokozoku, taking their name from a brand-shop, took to the Sunday streets, posturing and posing. Over the years the place has assumed the look of a benign counterculture—like the green plaza in front of Shinjuku Station in the sixties.

Law and order has long looked upon it with a cold eye. When the Iranians also gathered there to exchange their news and fry their kabobs, the cops found their reasons and moved in. Now they have moved on and destroyed the place by arguing that it is really only a "pedestrian paradise," one of a number throughout the city, and they are closing them all because they really do no good, they provide meeting places for undesirables, and they do not benefit the merchants in the area. I notice that the Ueno and Ginza paradises are still open on Sundays. Perhaps some paradises are more paradisiacal than others.

6 FEBRUARY 1996. Telephone call, voice at the other end, polite: "Mr. Richie?" And the years parted. It was Zushiden, after all this time. Just thought he would call me up. I was still around? I was OK? Yes, he was OK, too. No, no, was only fifty-six, not time to retire yet. We ought to get together.

So we ought. His voice was that of thirty years ago, and I remembered the house in Otsuka, and Zushi making the bath and us both in it, and our fight in a hotel room when I was married and we could meet only in such places, and his marriage when he proved too big for the bride, and the bad daughter.

"How is your bad daughter?" I asked. "Just the same," he said, "And she is still here, with us, unmarried, no one wants her. I don't blame them." And I said, "Oh, Zushiden, it is so good to hear your voice," for I had not known until that very moment how much I had missed hearing it.

10 FEBRUARY 1996. I dump Jane, after all these years, something I had never thought I would do. And I know why—it is Emma Thompson's fault, hers and the other "film versions," and their vulgarity. Not Jane Austen's fault, to be sure, but there had been signs that I would read no more.

We decorate ourselves with our books (besides initially enjoying them, learning from them, and feeling through them), and define who we are—they are our standard-bearers. I in this way went through Marcel [Proust], now Jane. And without any regret at all, except for where to find a home for my beloved discard.

One was at hand. Paul McCarthy, literate as he is, had never read Austen and so he received my Folger Society set of the novels and returned home well pleased.

17 FEBRUARY 1996. Gwen [Robinson] over for dinner—brought cod steaks and tollhouse cookies. I brought out the family album and showed pictures of my family, lying there like pressed flowers.

This must have occasioned my dream: I was showing Gwen around the hospital I called home; there was a stir, and a grand procession entered. Very excited, I dragged her over and sank on my knees in front of a large, black woman who was leading all the others—banners, trumpets, doves flying overhead. Adoringly, I grabbed the big, black hand, turning to explain that this woman had saved my life "after the operation." But the black hand was snatched away, and I looked up to see the white face and blue eyes of Madame Yourcenar looking reprovingly down. Guiltily I dropped the hand I had been about to kiss, reasoning that, of course Madame did not like displays of emotion. But then I suddenly realized the real reason. She had thought I had been about to kiss the ring and this would have blown her cover because she was really the Pope.

19 FEBRUARY 1996. I went to pay my taxes and the fat man to whose lot I fell glanced over my forms and told me I had taken far too many deductions and, anyway, where were my receipts? I told him that in decades of faithful tax-paying this question had never been asked. "I'm asking it now," said Mr. Takahashi, for such was his name.

Said it in English. From the first he was firm, rebuffing my attempts to speak his language—for I speak it much better than he spoke mine. He was, it seemed, spoiling for a fight. I should be pleased, I suppose, that the Japanese are no longer intimidated by a white face and a high-handed manner. And part of me is. But another part is not.

So I told him that it was customary to accept what the citizen said and then, if necessary, carry on an investigation. "They cost money," was the reply. "Well, you cost me money," I said. He considered this and then he said, "OK, only next year you bring receipts, yes?" "Yes." This was a very Japanese compromise, and I felt back on firm ground again—and got half a million yen refund.

20 FEBRUARY 1996. Zushiden is fifty-six now, graying, white in the eyebrows, heavier, the rounded shoulders of age. We sit at the Press Club and look at each other—it has been about six years since we last met. Then we fill each other in on who has died. Not so many on his side—but a fellow member of the Chuo Wrestling Team whom I remember as a tall, young student, dropped dead jogging just last month. The Team is going to have its reunion next month—at the Imperial Hotel, and it costs the equivalent of three hundred dollars each to attend. "I will go though. I am curious to see what all those old folks look like now." I tell him (speaking as his senior) that one of the best things about being old is that it is so interesting, finding out what finally happens to other people.

Over our fish (he cannot eat meat because of his stomach operation; I cannot eat it because of my arteries), we talk about finance. [Sato] Hisako has just told me that next month the banks are all going bust. "Even Dai-Ichi Kangyo?" I asked, referring to my bank, the largest in the world. "Oh, *especially* Dai-Ichi Kangyo."

Zushi says he doesn't doubt it. Japan has lived long all by itself, a single family. Now it cannot afford to. It has to live with other countries. It cannot protect just its own interests, this is now counter-productive . . . look at the economic mess. He himself keeps his money in stocks and bonds and the post office. Not that it makes any difference. If Dai-Ichi Kangyo goes, the whole country goes.

Talk turns again to the errant daughter, who has now reformed, has a job, joined something like AA for delinquents, and lives at home. "Twenty-six and not married," said Zushi. "Wish she would." I agree that that would be nice. "Nice for me," he says. "Get her out of the house." This leads to talk of women in general. He has a kind of girlfriend but she is in America. Just like me, I tell him. I have a kind of boyfriend but he is in Korea.

She was a college sweetheart. Did he know her when he was living with me? I wanted to know. "Let's see, I was a junior then, no, I met her when I was a senior." Then, with that big smile of his, "After I left you I graduated."

After hot apple pie and ice cream (bad for both stomach and arteries), I said goodbye until the next time and then came home where I had a message on my machine from Fumio—telling me that Takemitsu Toru died this afternoon.

21 FEBRUARY 1996. Chris and I went to the wake for Takemitsu this afternoon. It was held in a small hall, and they had not expected so many to attend.

When we got there the director was explaining to the family that he had thought only they would be there, that he was not prepared for the throngs, and that he hoped everything would be all right—by which I suppose he meant that he would not run out of incense or white chrysanthemums.

Toru was in a brocade box at the far end of the room, and on it was a color picture of him. I laid my white chrysanthemum in front of it and prayed. The box seemed so very small, like a child's coffin, and then I remembered that Toru was indeed small, but when he was alive with his bright eyes and his big smile one never noticed.

His widow and daughter were there, looking as though they had been hit. On the steps I talked to Yanagimachi Mitsuo—Toru had done a beautiful score for his *Fire Festival*—and upstairs was Shinoda Masahiro and Iwashita Shima. He was crying. Toru had often written for his films, and had himself created much of *Double Suicide*.

28 FEBRUARY 1996. I lunch with Gwen and we talk about an early division we both made—that between lover and friends. You could never fuck your friends, and you should not make friends with those you did fuck. We wonder how this came about.

She thinks that she got the idea due to the anonymous brutality of her first experience. He was a cocksure young surfer, and she was sure of nothing. "I didn't even know what was happening to me." She did not enjoy it or even guess that she was supposed to. No orgasms for her, perhaps consequently, despite constant experimentation, none until she was over twenty. What she sought to repeat was the anonymity of the first encounter, its astonishing force, and the fact that she knew that somehow she made it happen—she had this power.

We both agree that sex is about power, no matter how you cut it, and that the both of us are adept at losing the battle in order to win the war. We are also pleased that we have to a degree graduated: I love my friend, Dae-Yung, and she loves hers, Tim.

13 MARCH 1996. Dinner at Michishita Kyoko's—the other guests were Shiraishi Kazuko and Joan Mondale. Our hostess busied herself with glasses and dishes, and her female guests commented upon them—praising and finding pleasingly curious this and that, then turning gigglingly affirmative as women of a certain age often do together. It was nice for them, like playing house.

I, however, the only man, could not play. Further, the house cat, an ex-tom named Jack, having been raised with women, smelled me out, grew jealous,

DONALD RICHIE

With Shiraishi Kazuko, Joan and Walter Mondale, Michishita Kyoko, Jack, 1996

and attacked me under the table with his claws. Kyoko, more mother than wife, got under the table to get him out, and in so doing bumped about and knocked over a large vase of lilies, which landed on Jack, who with a howl was out of the room for the rest of the evening.

Excitement over, champagne drunk, sashimi downed, we could turn to interesting talk. Joan is reading the anonymous novel *Primary Colors* and is appalled by it. I say that I have never heard of a president so vilified as Clinton. "Yes," she says. "You know, Bush had a way with reporters. If they wrote something bad they were banned from the White House. Since they were on the White House beat they, as it were, lost their jobs. Very effective." I said that the Clintons should do something like that. "Can't," she said, smiling sweetly. "Only Republicans can do that."

Commotion in the hallway, Jack alarmed. It is Ambassador Mondale himself, not expected, who had come to see what it was all about. We'd finished the fish but he said he had eaten anyway and he began, in his patient and gentlemanly way, to find out about us. Me, he said, he felt he knew since he read me. Kazuko, however, he did not, and asked many a friendly question.

She, large, be-kohled, and sitting in her spotted fur, bloomed. Though I had often known her to be an assured and self-centered poet, I had never heard her so eloquent. Born in Vancouver, brought here at seven, she told what it felt like. There everything so brightly colored, here everything so gray—wartime Japan. "And they tried to make us believe that Americans, English, Canadians, were all devils, but I knew better. I had been there." At thirteen she worked in a factory and it was bombed on their single holiday. "Maybe that is why I became a poet," she said.

Then Michishita talks sensibly and feelingly about her growing up in far Sakhalin, and how her parents fled, and how many of her friends did not get away when the Russians arrived. "But, you know, all the governor's family, the police chief's, they got back to Japan at once. It's always that way. That's the reason for the vertical society, so that those on the top can get out easier."

We then talked of the local royals. Mondale had been presented and admired the choreography and was impressed when Michiko remembered meeting him in Belgium long before. We were all filled with admiration for the much-maligned Michiko, and I told my impressions. The ambassador shook his head and then said, in the most American manner, "I just don't see why the man doesn't protect his wife. He must certainly have the power to do so. Why doesn't he just say, 'lay off guys,' to those chamberlains?" I mentioned that much of the animosity had come from the empress-dowager. He nodded his head knowingly: "Mothers-in-law."

We move on to Reagan. "Absolutely out of it, now," he tells me, "though it is difficult to be sure—for so many year's that man's innocent ignorance and stupidity has served him so well. I remember someone's saying that the U.S. economy was in trouble. 'Well, yes,' said the President, 'but you know, it has to go down before it can go up.' Then that big Hollywood smile. And he got away with it."

I could imagine his feelings at seeing that fool in the White House. After all, he had almost gotten there himself. Now marginalized out here, he can do little but follow orders. This has not embittered him, however—he has grown nicely philosophical, if occasionally despairing. "Boy, do I have my plate full. That awful Okinawa [rape case] mess, and now China aiming at Taiwan, and I have to go to the Press Club and talk about it tomorrow and there is really nothing to do, though lots for someone to do. What are *you* going to do about it? I know, turn on the FM, get another cup of coffee, and write another book. Some people get all the breaks."

15 MARCH 1996. I just heard that Oshima has had a stroke. He was in the London airport waiting for a plane to Dublin. And I remembered our talking about his heart, his circulation. And I thought of him all alone and no longer himself. Later I learn that he was brought back and is now under rehabilitation—and I thought of Eric, buried alive by his illness. Later I tried to find where Oshima was, but was told that he wanted no visitors.

19 MARCH 1996. Chris tells me that Miss Michishita came up to him at a party and told him that when I was at her house I behaved in a shocking manner. "Jack got under the table and rolled around as he does and then he started pushing against Mr. Richie's legs. Oh, no. Jack is my cat, you see. And Mr. Richie, knowing that Jackie had been fixed, said, 'Oh, he's trying to get at my testicles.' Imagine! He used a word like that at my table!"

5 APRIL 1996. Dinner with Fumio. We go and see Kuroyanagi Tetsuko in the new Albee play [*Three Tall Women*]. Afterward we go and see her. She shows us all the wonderful makeup (skins, wrinkles, and gloves with liver spots and veins) to make her ninety-something in the first act. Tetsuko herself must be near sixty or over, and so this showing off of an extreme old age is something few actresses of that age would so revel in. But then Tetsuko is like that—terribly enthusiastic about real things.

They have cut the play. (The woman called A doesn't get to screw the groom, I don't know why.) But Fumio tells me that the translation is pleasingly colloquial and that Tetsuko lends her dryness, her humor, and makes the character both irritating and pleasing, which is perhaps something Albee intended.

7 APRIL 1996. Paul [McCarthy] and I lunch in Ueno and then go to the Central Asia exhibition—a collection of Buddhist art from the caves of Dunhuang and the archives of the Hermitage. We examine an eighth-century mandala showing not heaven but hell—a spectacular delineation of the temptations of the Buddha, including sexual details I have never before seen in early Asian art. One of the beasts has an erection, another has its hands in curious places, and, right in the middle, a creature has bent double and from its asshole pour flames, which lave the lotus upon which the Buddha sits—an infernal fart. "It looks like Bosch," says Paul.

9 APRIL 1996. Alex Kerr over for dinner. He is leaving tomorrow for Thailand, has had it with Japan. Feels the changes deeply and finds no compensatory factors. We discuss the reasons. These include wholesale despoliation—once the most beautiful of countries, Japan is now the ugliest. The return of Tokugawa totalitarianism, as evidenced in the male young, etc. All of which he has treated at length in his book [*Lost Japan*]. We do not mention that it is no longer easy to sleep with the younger population, but the air of easy romance has certainly dissipated. We talk about Japan the way it used to be. He says he has heard that men worked naked but that, of course, is sheer romantic wishing. I say, not at all, and show him my pictures of the Choshi fishermen at work, ca. 1947. He drops his bread into the *coq au vin* in surprise, examines the pictures with care.

We talk about what this means. I say that public nudity is read (by me) as public availability, and that we are rather like imperialists regretting the Raj. This he agrees to, though regretting the regretting, and I say that the problem is that Third World Japan became First World, and that that is why he is going to Third World Thailand, even though he's too late. We'll both end up in a Dayak long house and even there it will be too late. He agrees. He takes a long look at the naked fishermen, and we have chilled peaches with frozen yogurt and speak of other things.

15 APRIL 1996. Ed appeared with a large black eye, a scratched nose, and bruises on the upper lip. "No, no," he said at once. "I was perfectly sober." He has had balance problems before, and since his hip operation he is sometimes given to falling. "I fell against the wall." "Is that the wall near your home mentioned by Mori Ogai in *Wild Geese*?" I wanted to know. "The very same." "Well, you showed a fine literary sense then," I said, at which he smiled wanly.

Once seated with a bottle of beer, however, troubles were forgotten and we had a good talk. We discussed our affection for Gwen; we spoke of the decline in the quality of the Tokyo strip parlors, and paid brief but sincere tribute to our "Janet."

Then I admitted that I had given up Jane [Austen]. "It is like the moon," I explained. "It has been trodden upon by someone from Wapakoneta, Ohio." He was impressively restrained at this and said, "Well, so goes the world. About the moon, however, I know just how you feel."

16 APRIL 1996. To a party being given Beate Gordon upon publication of her memoir. She was here during the war, and after it was, despite her youth, entrusted with putting in the part about women into the postwar constitution because she was one of the few foreigners who understood Japanese. I knew her during the Occupation—a smart, slender, steady girl—and we have seen each other sometimes over the intervening half-century.

"And you stayed and I didn't," she said with that friendly directness that has always been hers. "And you know," she continued in the measured tone, which also was always hers, something a bit sententious but always for one's own good, "It is still a very good place to be. People tell me how changed it is, that they are leaving, and this too I can understand, but, still . . . How do you find it?"

I say that the whole world has changed but has retained its proportions. Japan, though reduced, is still best, at least for people like me.

She had been to see Empress Michiko that afternoon and wanted to compare impressions with me. Not much to compare. She had had the Empress all to herself with only a single lady-in-waiting, whom she already knew. Not a chamberlain in sight. Consequently Michiko was apparently much more herself, looked Beate in the eye as she spoke, laughed a lot, and had a good time.

"You only got half an hour, but *I* got an hour and a half," she said in her winningly arch way. "And at the end, she took me right to the foyer, right to the door, as a hostess ought."

8 MAY 1996. The Tokyo Broadcasting System has decided to cancel a news show because it had privately shown the finished program to the Aum people, who then went out and killed the lawyer who appeared on it. This had frightened TBS into not airing that program at all. The now-cancelled news show has nothing to do with the cancelled anti-Aum show, but it was felt something must be done, some gesture or other to placate public opinion. Public opinion will be placated. Justice by analogy.

The problem is not that Japanese behave this way. All people behave this way. The problem is that Japanese so often get away with it, are so rarely called to account. A symbolic placation appears and is accepted. As to why it happened in the first place it is, again, not because Japanese are prone to doing things like this. Everyone is. But few Japanese are prone to speaking up and denouncing. The reason is that they are afraid to. And the reason they are afraid is that such an individual would receive no support and much intimidation. He would also lose his job.

Yet more and more brave individuals are speaking out against this system, and losing jobs and friends and family in the process. They are truly brave, for the system is truly formidable.

10 MAY 1996. In the evening, in Ueno, I see two young girls loitering in front of the local porno, the Star-za. They are wearing the tartan skirts, dark sweaters, and thick ankle socks of a private school. I ask them if they like porno and they—one pretty, one not—say they don't. Then I ask if they are waiting for *kozukai*, spending money. This they say they are. How much? I ask. *Go-man yen*—that is, nearly five hundred dollars.

"For the both of you?" I ask. They nod. Still, it is a bit expensive, I say. "No," says the pretty one, "usually that is what just one high-school girl gets. You get two for the price of one."

At that point we were joined by a large and savvy Bengali, whom I often meet hanging around the place. "No short time," he says. "You spend the night. We go to my house." The girls confer and then the plain one says, "No penetration though."

"No penetration!" cries the Bengali. "What am I paying for?"

"Look," says the pretty one, "we have to get married sometime, we got to watch ourselves."

"What I get for my fifty thousand yen then?"

The pretty one smiles and delicately flicks her tongue.

"Oh," he says. Then he indicates me: "Better take him then, he likes to do that."

"Actually," I say, "this place around here is mainly homo."

"Homo!" cries the pretty one, then turns to her plain friend, "You picked the wrong place again." Then, "He's cute," politely indicating me. I smile and show my long, pink, foreign tongue, and they both laugh like the little girls they are.

We are then further joined by a well-dressed younger Japanese who is carrying a briefcase and following our conversation with interest. Also, a passing cop on the beat. The Bengali disappears as though by magic and I with a nod pass into the porno. When I look out again, the street is empty. I don't know what happened.

11 MAY 1996. I think about prostitution and wonder why anyone thinks it wrong. If the other person does not want to sell, well, maybe. But if she or he does, what's the problem? Yet these girls would be held up to shame in the hypocritical press, and my commerce will doubtless be so seen by an equally hypocritical posterity.

I feel about prostitution as Flaubert did. Let me quote the passage: "It may be a perverted taste, but I love prostitutition, and for itself, too, quite apart from its carnal aspects. My heart begins to pound every time I see one of those women in low-cut dresses walking under the lamplight in the rain, just as monks in their corded robes have always excited some deep, ascetic corner of my soul. The idea of prostitution is a meeting place of so many elements—lust, bitterness, complete absence of human contact, muscular frenzy, the clink of gold—that to peer into it deeply makes one reel. One learns so many things in a brothel, and feels such sadness, and dreams so longingly of love."

12 MAY 1996. In the evening I take my tape of Oshima's *Ai no Korida* [In the Realm of the Senses] over to Gwen's. She has a house full of people and serves Thai curry before we begin. I had not seen the film uncut since London well over ten years ago, and I am again moved by it.

It is so sad, and so honest. It properly equates love with fucking and fucking with love. Nakedness always gives you a choice: the chance to feel sexy or to feel sorry—you want to take on the unclothed body or you realize that we are all fragile, unprotected bipeds. Fucking too can inflame or douse. Oshima's great accomplishment is that it acknowledges sex as power, shows it in detail, and then exposes it in all of its hopelessness. Though his asocial lovers devote their lives to it, really try; he demonstrates that it is not enough—that nothing is enough.

Afterward I wonder why it was ever considered pornographic, that it could never turn one on. "Oh, I don't know about that," said Gwen, obviously much moved.

13 MAY 1996. I was talking with the taxi driver and he looked out of the window as we drove through Ueno Park and said, "You see that green? That's a real spring green. In the summer it will turn a lot darker—last year it got almost black—and that fresh feeling will be all gone. But this is the shade I really like, spring green." I looked out of the window and admired the light, fresh color. And I also admired the driver for liking it and I wondered in how many other countries I could have had this conversation with a taxi driver.

16 MAY 1996. Cold for May. I walk through the park to the station and notice that the north wind is blowing the leaves, turning them over. A lopsided haiku (four lines, five syllables each) occurs. I ought to save it, put in these pages a few months from now in its proper place, just as did the poets of yore. But I won't. Here it is:

> North winds turn the leaves.
> What had been July
> Becomes March again:
> Southern spring green.

23 MAY 1996. Alex [Kerr] came over I decided to make him accomplice to my desertion of a god. This deity, some kind of ur-Shinto folk god, has been sitting in his box ever since Frank cleaned house and gave him to me. He is hideous—a black hump, a small, narrow face, pursed mouth, and tiny eyes. Since I am superstitious I did not want simply to put him out with the garbage. So I decided to find him a new home and settled upon that little island, already filled with Shinto stones, off from the Benten Shrine in Shinobazu Pond. This is where stands that fine phallic stone, last of old Edo, before which I have performed many a rite. Not recently, however. All this year the gate to the island has been padlocked—too many young lovers, too many voyeurs. Today, in the late afternoon, however, we managed to crawl along the fence and get into the place. At the base of the phallic stone we reverently placed my ugly little deity, now among his own kind. As we climbed back over the fence I saw him grimacing happily into the setting sun.

1 JUNE 1996. The Dai-Ichi Bank does not collapse. Instead, it merges. Two sick banks get together and make a healthy bank. It is called by a new name, Mizuho. This is typical. Nothing ever fails in Japan. It merely changes its name. You can even sometimes use the old one and simply add *shin* (new). Recently a popular actor accidentally ran over a child. Feeling dreadful about it, he shaved his head and changed his given name.

8 JUNE 1996. A discussion, arranged by the people reviving my films, all taped and recorded. Two young directors were invited to come and talk with me—their unlikely names were Furusawa Binbun and Sono Shion. They were bright and funny and serious.

We talked about the sixties, which is to them something like the Gay Nineties used to be to me. Underground films, wow, what could they have been like? I tried to tell them what it was like thirty years ago when young people were trying to find out what the truth was, and were devising various ways to express or reflect it.

I told them about the excitement of a new Terayama play, or a Hani movie, or a Hijikata dance. I told them about Kara Juro and the antics of the Zero Jikken. They wagged their heads and wished they could have been alive then—an age of heroes.

I tell them that art is dissident—it undermines the status quo. That anything celebratory is not art. Art is by its nature critical. That is its moral dimension. This I believe. Back then Japan had a number of dissidents, those who disagreed, and who spoke out. Not now though. With a new generation bred not to think we only have that great accord of which Society is so fond. And yet without the dialectic of a social culture and a counter culture there is no art, underground or otherwise. Now official art is all there is. Artists, musicians, filmmakers, writers, are all social products. They have been subsumed into the social/financial structure of the country. Not just Japan either. The triumph of consensus.

They are respectful, are mindful that I am elder, but at the same time they are frank and honest. "I read your books," said Sono, "but I only thought I'd like to meet you when I learned you'd made a film about this guy who wants to jack off and his cat gets in the way. What a great idea."

10 JUNE 1996. I finally again finish *Kumagai*, after ten years of work on it. It has changed much. Originally it was a movie, a liebestodt about love and death, but that got a bit too perfumed even for me and so it turned into whatever I thought an anti-roman was, with pages of description and nothing much happening (the Battle of Ichinotani section still has part of this in it), and then slowly it became a fake diary of its hero, and then the hero himself turned fake and it turned out he did not kill Atsumori, the only reason the man is remembered at all. The book became his own feelings about this and his consenting, finally, to become his reputation.

Now what to do with it. I wish I had an agent—I could just send it off to him or her. But I can't. No agent has ever accepted me. You'd think they would. I'm now famous enough. But there are problems. First, I am perceived as about Japan, now a deeply irrelevant subject. Second, I am already placed—I am about film. What am I doing writing novels and the like? Publishers are New York folks who want a big, fast kill, and I am not that kind of author.

11 JUNE 1996. Rainy day. I awake from a dream of being lost in India, wallet gone. So I look into the gloom of morning and consider.

Life is a palindrome. As we entered, so we backward depart. I have now reached the correspondence of puberty. My juices are drying up and shortly the last drop will reflect the first spurt. Then I will continue on through the mirror image of being twelve, eight—then the legs will go and I will once more have trouble with stairways, and then I will crawl, and then I will lie down and squirm, and then I will end in something like that dark bed from which I came.

So one must prepare. I live in a third floor walk-up. The stairs now leave the heart pounding and will soon leave the lungs gasping. Just as I know I can now never see Tibet, so I learn that I must find a place with an elevator.

12 JUNE 1996. Coming home through the park I see that two of the homeless have found brooms and are carefully sweeping the plaza, the steps down to the water, and the paths. They are not paid for this. It is voluntary labor. Why, I wonder. Perhaps if they police their place the cops will let them stay undisturbed—but the cops do anyway. No, I think it is because working is all they know, and

View from Richie's balcony.

their enforced idleness is a terrible punishment for them. So they find brooms and in the middle of the night sweep. If they were given buckets and brushes they would scrub.

18 JUNE 1996. Lunch at my house with [Numata] Makiyo. He is going to help me apartment hunt. My lease is coming up in a month or so, and I know that sooner or later I must move.

We do not find much and then, passing the large apartment building at the southern end of Ueno Park, opposite Shinobazu Pond, I jokingly say that I have wanted to live there for ten years now. He looks and says, "There's an apartment listed, want to look?" We are taken to the eighth floor, let in, and there it is, from the balcony all of Shinobazu and Ueno hanging there before me like a mandala, with Benten right in the middle. "You got tears in your eyes," said Makiyo. And so I did.

"Well, if you feel that way, we got to get it for you," he said, and we went down and he went to work. Lots of proof of solvency needed, but I have that, and my official standing here, and my c.v., in two languages. The rent is a bit more than I am now spending, but I can afford it, for a time at any rate.

I am very excited by this move. All of the bother of moving is forgotten in my joy that I will be able to live the rest of my life in front of such beauty, just outside the window. As with a forthcoming journey, I am already there. I sit here, but I have already left.

21 JUNE 1996. I read that Kenzaburo Oe has said that the Japanese abroad, or in commerce with non-Japanese, tend to present self not as an individual but as "a Japanese." He criticizes this presentation of an agreed upon set of characteristics, a simulacrum offered as the real thing. And while it is true that other peoples do this ("as an American, I want to say that . . ."), they do so more openly (politicians, preachers), and they do not always get away with it.

Presenting self as American (or English or French or German) does not enjoy social approval. The reason is that one thus denies the individual. In Japan, however, one has been taught to deny the individual for over four hundred years. Consequently presentation of self as mere nationality is so rarely criticized that Oe's observation makes headlines.

As I read this I was listening to the NHK FM morning classical program. It is Beethoven's *Leonore* no. 3, Sinding's "Rustle of Spring," Webern's *Bagatelles*, Poldini's "Waltzing Doll," and the Brahms *Requiem.* I do not question the indigestible mixture—this is standard Japanese programming: All things foreign are equal. What I now notice, reflected from Oe's words, is that classical music is tokenized. There is an aquarium of works, which is kept in good order (including new and exotic varieties, such as Webern) and thus protects the listener from the unruly waves of Western music. This mismatch of a concert I am listening to consists of items taken from this tank. There are national sub-tanks as well. In the American the fish are: MacDowell piano pieces, *Billy the Kid*, *The Grand Canyon Suite*, Scott Joplin, *West Side Story*, and selected bits of Leroy Anderson. Nothing else. I have never heard a note of Elliot Carter on NHK.

1 JULY 96. Moving. My belongings lie about me. Most of the pictures I have already taken to the new place. The books are out of the shelves and lie on the floor. I feel like the hermit crab, all naked, looking for another shell.

How much the illusion of self is created by the domestic environment one constructs. One knows this only when it is dismantled. Then, all of my disciplines break down. My orderly days come apart, my hours, unaccounted for, slop over. I get sleepy in the morning and my various compulsions just give up.

In the new place I will build this new home, where everything has a place and is in it. Things will get thrown out; things will get dusted or washed. And I can really see, feel, my belongings. Oh, that book (on my shelves for fifteen years), I must read it. Oh, that beautiful little bronze (on my desk for an equal time), I must put it where I can see it. Soon, however, I will again settle into the grateful cradle of habit.

8 JULY 1996. A party for Sato Tadao upon the completion of his four-volume Japanese film history. There was Hidari Sachiko. She has aged elegantly, and tends to be grand. Looking at a somehow different-appearing Kurisaki Midori, she said, "She has had something done to her face. One of those things where they make new holes for the ears and pull everything up." I mention that the director of her latest film is there. "Where, where, I must snub him. He understood nothing about me. Nothing."

Oshima's wife [Koyama Akiko] is there with news that her husband is now in a wheelchair and is *genki,* if you can be that in a wheelchair. That he is going to be all right. The director of *Violated Angels,* Wakamatsu Koji, is there, now even more gray, even more affable. Since his old films were at the Haiyuza last week and my old ones are there this week, we talk of the brave days of 1965.

Adachi Masao's films are also being shown. He was a friend of the Red Army members, got implicated, left the country and has now for the last thirty years been in the Near East, unable to return. I remember him as a short, serious, handsome, bright actor (he was the police inspector in Oshima's *Death by Hanging*) and filmmaker. "He's gone all white," says Wakamatsu. I ask what he does there. Film? "Oh, no, well he works at what he can get. He speaks perfect Arabic now. Never got married." Does he want to come back? "It wouldn't do him any good. He never can. And he never did anything bad, you know." Wakamatsu goes all that distance, Damascus twice a year, just to see his old friend.

Obayashi Nobuhiko is the master of ceremonies and snares me into making a speech. I say whatever comes into my head, talk about the singular fact that one can trust Sato as a film critic, something rare in Japan; you always know he is speaking for himself and not for his old *sensei,* nor for some film company, nor for his country. No one listens—not to me, or to any of the other speakers. Once eating begins the ears are stopped. Me too. I aways put away large quantities of lobster and caviar and *uni* and roast beef and lamb and don't hear a word from anyone.

18 JULY 1996. Makiyo brought his wife and daughter over and I cooked. We had *coq au vin* and salad and ripe Camembert and a big chocolate cake for dessert. The little girl is three—very pretty, lively, and her father dotes on her. It is like being with a man very much in love with his dinner partner. His wife is more measured—after all, she is the one who must take care of the child.

Makiyo was himself like a child when I first met him fifteen years ago, but a very self-sufficient one. He had had to learn to be. [Numata Makiyo's story is given in *Public People, Private People.*] Friendly and open, he nonetheless hid his emotions and I never knew what he felt. Now, however, with his daughter, the feelings shine. He is in love.

Later we walk, just across the street, to the festival going on around Shinobazu. People in summer *yukata* looking at the plants for sale, at the watered stones shining in the dark, at the bell bugs and armored beetles for sale. The little girl and I decorate two pieces of bisque and have them baked, and then I give her the one that I made—a plate with black branches and small green fruit.

Before they left, Makiyo turned back and then reappeared with an enormous lantern plant, orange and green, for my new apartment.

24 JULY 1996. Gwen hosts a party for her eminent oldsters. There is Karel van Wolferen, eminent author, Edward Seidensticker, eminent translator, William Miller, eminent publisher, Stephen Shaw, eminent editor—and eminent me.

Fine food, lots to drink. The latter much softened up the party. Owlish Ed wandered in late, had gotten lost. "And I finally thought, if it isn't this place then it isn't anywhere, but it was." Stephen said, "Japan is doing quite badly at the Atlanta Olympics. Does one dare confess it makes one happy? Is one agreed with?" William said, "It doesn't make me happy at all, you beast." And Ed said, "It makes *me* happy, very, very happy." To which William replied, "I love Japan, and I don't care who knows it." To which Ed made reply, "Well, I don't and I don't care who knows it."

But before either could become too tiresome Gwen took away our plates, which had contained sea urchin penne, and brought in the bubbling Irish stew. Then Karel decided to treat us to the Dutch national anthem, in Dutch, following which Eithne [Jones] was forced to sing the Irish national anthem in Gaelic. Ed tried the German national anthem in German but forgot the words. "The words are not important anyway, the melody is sublime. That is because it's by Haydn. He wrote it for Austria but the Germans unkindly appropriated it." William decided we should make up anthems for those countries that did not have them, and attempted one for Zimbabwe but was shouted down.

Gwen looked at the ceiling and Eithne brought calm by reciting her Irish nun joke. The one where the head nun asked the novice her plans once out of the convent and fainted because she understood "Protestant" for "prostitute."

Here the conversation broke into small groups. Karel and Ed talked about Haydn, William and Eithne about Galway, and Stephen and I about our hearts. "Does it hurt right now?" he asked. No, it did not, I told him. "Mine does. It hurts right now." I pointed out that he had drunk almost a whole bottle himself and that this perhaps caused it. "Not at all, advanced medical opinion has it that alcohol, particularly wine, is *good* for the heart." I doubted

With Karel van Wolferen, Edward Seidensticker, Tim Young, Gwen Robinson, Stephen Shaw, William Miller, Eithne Jones, 1996.

that but William chimed in that he had read the same article, and finished his own bottle to prove it. Ed did not think so. He thought whiskey much better for the heart—though our hostess had wisely prepared none—and so they wrangled.

Gwen brought peace with a big ice cream cake and, since every last one of us loves a sweet, silence prevailed as we crunched and munched. I began talking with Tim [Young] who compensated for being left out (we were originally all *Gwen's* friends) by being a fine host and showing me big photos, which he had downloaded from the Tokyo University machine. One showed a just-exploded star, halo still intact. "That is what our sun will do," he told me, "but not right now. It is halfway through its life now. It is middle-aged."

"Who, who?" asked Ed. Then, "We're all middle-aged, every last one of us." William, five years younger, looked at him, "You are a somewhat mature middle-aged."

Tim showed me the other photo, something like tadpoles swimming, wakes behind them. It was a close up of the halo of the other picture. "Each one of these is much larger than our solar system, maybe even our universe. But the funny thing is that they are flying backward. You see that tail, like a comet? Well, that is the *front* of the object." I say that this means a change in our physics and he, an astrophysicist, nods.

After the cake, the cheese and the fresh cherries. (Ed: "Oh, what a treat to get real American cherries, the Japanese variety are pallid, tasteless, and outrageously expensive.") We all began examining our watches, wondered at the lateness of the hour, and one by one wandered out into the street.

11 AUGUST 1996. Sunday morning, very early. Yesterday I fell asleep at five in the afternoon and woke refreshed and ready for a new day at three-thirty in the morning. Since Shinobazu is now my front yard, I—never having seen it at this hour—decide to take a walk.

Dressed, I walk out into the still, cool dark and cross the street. The park is a negative of its daytime self—black water, gray closed lotus, dark trees among which a few white figures wander. One of them a late *okama*, the dyed one in the pants suit who is too shy to call out to possible customers. There are a few late young, coupled and huddled, waiting for the morning trains. But most of them are roused and ragged men—the homeless.

There are hundreds in the park, some still sleeping on the benches or on cardboard on the ground. So many, all lying about in abandoned attitudes. The roused ones wash at the drinking fountain and then I see a few have found brooms and already begun the day's work.

I walk to Ueno Station, the familiar street all now different, shutters down over all the shops. Even the electric cuckoo, leading the blind over the crossing, is silent. At the station I ask the two cops on duty when the station opens. Four, they say. Is there no all night coffee shop, I wonder? Oh, no, they say, surprised at the question, perhaps implying that a well-run society like this, no one at all on the streets at this early hour, would never need such.

Back in the park the sky has lightened and the black trees have turned gray. In the pond, glowing a faint pink, the closed lotus, surrounded by dark leaves. Above, the first crows cross, and soon their calls will grow to that morning cacophony that sometimes awakens me at five or six. Seeing and hearing them now is like attending the rehearsal of a performance I know well.

The pink lotuses glow and I turn to look at the closest. And there, this being Japan, are two photographers, lens extended, waiting to catch the moment of opening. We all wait and at just four-thirty I hear a plop, like a stroke on a finger drum, followed by the click of the shutter, and then—hanging for an instant in the air while the crows caw flying against the slowly lightning sky—the sweet and watery smell of the water lily.

15 AUGUST 1996. The end of World War II, fifty-one years ago today. I was on my way to China in a Liberty ship, happy it was over but unhappy that now I would to return to Ohio, since my country no longer needed to be defended against the foe. And now, fifty years later, I am in my tower, happy in the land of the former enemy, looking at the expanse of lotus below, pink as a funeral in the sunset.

A typhoon is on the way and I decide to descend and walk along the shore, enjoying the south wind. The sun has now gone and the sky is already that deep blue of autumn, against which sail enormous clouds so white that their reflected light makes it more morning than night.

The kingfisher is still there, motionless, right by the rail, waiting for fish, occasionally darting and showing a sliver of silver minnow before it swallows. In the daytime he sometimes attracts a small crowd, and I can see them below me, circled there, like curious town folk in Hokusai prints. Now, however, I am alone with the bird and then he too flies off.

Alone under the luminous sky, I think about my recent tic, which has a life of its own, then wonder if Debussy's portrait of Little Tic included the tic, then remember that Claude-Achille was a kleptomaniac and all his friends hid their silver when he came; then I thought of how something this common could somehow give rise to something so rare as the Saint Sebastian music, which made me think of Guido's painting, which made me think of Mishima, and thence to voluntary death.

I decided that I will not fight against the dying light. Only an egocentric like Dylan Thomas would do that. Even Stravinsky, who set the lyric and who was all ego himself, was too aware to fight against the dying light. We have an allotted time, and to hang around is as unseemly as staying on at the party even after the weary hostess has twice looked her watch and mentioned a heavy day tomorrow. The only problem is arranging the exit.

And I thought of the minnow. A flash of silver, a small movement—and then all gone. That is really all it is. A tiny spasm—man and minnow alike. Easeful death, another phrase from the poets. And I think of Jimmy [Merrill], bravely opening the closet and stepping into the eternal dark. And I think of Madame Yourcenar staring at the blackness with open eyes.

20 AUGUST 1996. I look at myself. In Japan I have lived my life in a state of consciousness. I look at everything, register it, and often judge it. I am aware of people on the street, the cracks in the pavement. Here too I have judgmental thoughts, but these are really for the purpose of shifting and sorting, putting things into categories, comparing.

I would have it no other way since, if extremes are to be considered, it is better than a life of unconsciousness, of blank eyes, deaf ears, dead brain. At the same time, I would sometimes like to relax this habitual and vigilant regard, would long to sink into oblivion, into the unselfconscious.

7 SEPTEMBER 1996. I look from my window and see that a small crowd has again gathered on the paved plaza in front of the southern reach of the pond. The kingfisher has again come and is fishing.

A large, handsome bird, he perches by the rail and intently searches the water for small fish. When he discovers one, there is a lizard-like stretch of the neck and a flash of silver in the beak as the fish goes down.

Various people watch, the late afternoon light casting their shadows black in back of them. Young couples giggle and pass on, salaried men clutch their briefcases and briefly stare, a housewife or two wave their parasols at the bird, and the many homeless who have nothing else to do come to watch.

To one of these the bird has become important. He is a mustached, heavy, middle-aged man in shorts who has appropriated the creature. He arrives with a bag of crusts and these he drops into the water in front of the bird to attract the fish. I can see him gesticulating as he explains. If I were near enough I could hear him expound.

The bird has become his occupation, since he has no other. Whenever it appears, so does he. As it sits, still as a snake, he moves about, tossing crusts, commenting upon its habits, explaining. A number of people listen for a time. They are learning something.

Then, for no reason, the kingfisher flies to the signboard that says not to fall in, and after it has surveyed the lotus for a while it takes flight. The mustached man, with no sign of disappointment, rather with the air of a man who has finished his work for the day, closes his bag of crumbs and likewise departs.

10 SEPTEMBER 1996. I come back late from teaching my course at Temple University, and find the back streets of Ueno awash with beautiful young women, all in the epaulets and monograms, brocades and miniskirts that signify the *mizushobai* service industry of the downtown. Usually the sight is hidden away in bars and clubs named You and Etoile and Hope, and costs an amount of money. Money is now not to be had, however, and so they have come outside, like exotic insects from under their rocks, and—much ill at ease in their indoor finery—stand in the open night air, hand out leaflets, and cajole.

They are joined by the homeless who are bedding down for the night, on cardboard in front of banks, or curled up in the little niche by the porno. A piquant combination: long tanned legs next to dirty shoes and sockless feet; much-brushed hair, stained fashionable mahogany or deep maple side by side with dirty, lank, infested strands; the smell of Chanel mingling with that of the rotgut that the homeless take to put themselves to sleep.

With Gwen Robinson, 1996.

19 SEPTEMBER 1996. Gwen and I go and see Ed, propped up in bed, covered with a blue blanket, getting solvent for the blood clots that have formed in the knee and are keeping him hospitalized. "These damn Japanese beds," were among his first words. "In America you just push a button, but here in the land of the Twenty-first Century, oh, no, you have to get out of bed and crank yourself up or down." I suggest he call a nurse. "Oh, I do, I do." I then say that, yes, and she comes and she smiles and she happily cranks his bed up or down and that I doubt this would invariably occur in the Land of the Free. We then go on and talk about his mysterious collapse in Sasebo and how long he must stay in hospital—two weeks.

Afterward Gwen and I go and have coffee. It being an old-fashioned place, we are then given tea. It is old-fashioned tea as well. *Konbucha.* "It tastes like cunt," I say. "I would not know," says Gwen, "but it smells like me if I'm not careful." "But it tastes good," I mollify. "Yes, some men quite like it. I have heard that some girls have been encouraged not to douche. It builds up." "Well," I counter, "some people like cock cheese." "Like feta, I have heard," she observes, then, "Always wanted to ask, how does it get made?" "Same way as cunt tea," I explain. "It is a real cheese too, fermented, everything." "One could toast it perhaps." "Perhaps, but it might be uncomfortable."

Finishing our repast we repaired to the street and linked arms and she said, "It is so good to talk with you. I know of no one else from whom I learn so much."

20 SEPTEMBER 1996. The level of public manners continues to fall in this once most polite of all lands. For example, the portable phone. People walking, driving, standing on corners, laughing, grimacing, shouting into their fists. "Just go away!" someone behind me shouts. "Get out! Never want to see you again!" Startled, I turn, but he is merely using the telephone.

Voices are now much louder and eating in public is epidemic. Not just the young, but also everyone now trails crumbs and mustard drippings from whatever fast food they are consuming.

Coming from where I do, I cannot criticize this, so I merely notice the difference. It is large. Still, public politeness was often based on fear of what others would think. It was, by definition, craven. So, mustard droppings and all, I am glad to see more personality. Except that now it is all the same personality—loud, brazen, and banal. There is nothing personal in the new persona. Before everyone was polite in the same way, now they are all impolite in the same way.

25 SEPTEMBER 1996. Paul [McCarthy], Gwen, and I go and see Ed—now much better, clots dissolved, and waiting in his new green pajamas for the rehabilitation man. Ed is anxious to get back to Hawaii. "I should not say this," and he makes a shocked face and puts two fingers to his lips, "but I trust American doctors so much more." I say that I would more trust a Japanese surgeon, but that I would more trust an American diagnostician. "Exactly," says Ed, as though I had agreed with him.

In the evening I walk around and inspect the damage done by furious Violet—that was the now-vanished typhoon's name. Now that the Americans have become convinced that fearful catastrophes are not invariably female, the next one will perhaps be named Vulcan.

A number of willow trees have had large parts torn off. Willow must be a soft wood. The cherries have fared better and the maples came out of it best of all. No one has come to clean up the damage, however. The dead willow clumps are like so many enormous heads of wilted cabbage. Probably there is a day for damage repair and they are waiting for the event.

Amid all this appropriately flailing willow, a madwoman. Barefooted, she stands in red slacks and a long green kimono-like coat, as she curses, apparently, the elements. When anyone gets close to her she begins to shriek in such a manner that very few come near. I too observe her from a distance. She is obviously homeless—dirty, no shoes, but did the madness unhouse her or was she rendered mad by loss of dwelling?

I hear the voice of sentimental posterity—why didn't you do anything? Well, what should I have done? Gotten shrieked at? I have given hamburg-

With Sam Jameson, Edward Seidensticker, Karel van Wolferen, Eithne Jones, 1996.

ers and rice balls to lots of the homeless and have talked with many and sent several off to the employment agency and given money to others. But this woman both moved and frightened me. I did not go near her.

10 OCTOBER 1996. A holiday, one of the prewar imperial ones now turned democratic. My cold is bad and I spend Green and Healthy Day in bed reading the manuscript of Karel's new book on what is wrong with Japan. What is wrong is that the citizens are still—post-Tokugawa though they be—too cowed to do much, even vote. His description is lucid and logical and, since it is intended for translation for a Japanese audience, will—I hope—make its mark.

11 OCTOBER 1996. A party for Ed's release—held in a drinking establishment near Karel's place in Mukojima. Here he comes, triumphant on his cane, leaning on the arm of Maki, Herb Passin's long-time girlfriend. Once sat down, he pulls up his trouser to show us his elegant service-weight stocking and the neat blue cast. We are all anxious to see what he orders after the long drought, and are all relieved that it is beer and beer alone.

Lots to eat, however—eggplant in miso and chicken wings and pork and vegetables—and the talk is about Japan, of course, but Ed utters nary a word on this subject except to agree with everyone. I do not know how it ends, however, after the beer has taken its toll. I am feeling lousy with my cold and leave early.

14 OCTOBER 1996. I look about me—in the park for example. Now that it is colder many poor homeless women have emerged. They sit all day by the pond and talk, keeping each other company, but they are homeless, and their shoes have holes. Also, in this cold, begging. A woman kneeling outside the Ueno Hirokoji subway stop with an empty soft drink can, its top open for coins in front of her. A man lying on his back suddenly raises one hand, makes the sign for money—thumb and forefinger forming a hole—then raises the other in Buddhist benediction.

And by Ueno station, something somehow tragic. A very old woman in rags kneeling, leaning forward. She is so bare that her dugs hang in the winter air. And I thought of her young, when this would have been immodest, and she would have blushed and hid. Now it is not immodest, it is monstrous. Equally monstrous, no one does anything to help her. Just as monstrous, neither do I.

23 OCTOBER 1996. The election is over and once again the Japanese people have chosen. Preferring stability to reform and predictability to improvement, they have agreed once more to let back in the Liberal Democratic Party, which is nothing like either of its adjectives suggests. Having escaped it two years ago, they welcome it back, forgetting all the scandals, all the graft, and all the incompetence.

It returned for two reasons. One is a new electoral formula that favors the reelection of incumbents. Two (says Tada Minoru, commentator) is that voters were influenced by public opinion polls that indicated that the LDP was likely to win. As for big winner, Hashimoto Ryutaro, Prime Minister, he said, "the reform proposals are too radical to be taken seriously."

There may be a third reason as well. Few voted. Thinking people, a minority here as elsewhere, feel that the bureaucratic machine is in charge anyway whoever wins, and it will see that nothing changes. Non-thinking people, in their frivolous, selfish, *eijanaika* mood, are not interested. They are too taken up with playing with their Nintendo machines, with karaoke, with their manga, and their Walkmen. These creations of the Education Ministry are the ideal citizens for a governing bureaucracy.

22 NOVEMBER 1996. Journal much neglected, Bali looming—soon Dae-Yung and I will be there. Travel, the continual sighting of the new—it has many advantages. Among them is that it saves self from self. I am not myself when I am somewhere else. I do not have to feel my familiar inner geography when I have the lay of the world to gaze upon. I remember Carlos Freer telling me that Madame Yourcenar, after Jerry's death, was frantic to travel. She kept suggesting places but she was over eighty and could not travel alone, though she did not want to be any longer with herself.

10 DECEMBER 1996. Lunch with Gwen at the Press Club where we were later joined by Karel [van Wolferen] who was on his way to see [ex–Prime Minister] Nakasone. He was going to ask him what he thinks of the recent breaking of the taboo about criticizing the Constitution. I told him how Eisenhower asked about this American-inspired document back in the 1950s: "What, you still got that worthless piece of paper around?" Karel pointed out of the window at the palace lying below us. "So long as we have him we are going to have taboos. They're a pain in the neck. They get in the way." I tell him that royalty cannot exist without taboos. "Just what I mean," he said.

Gwen brought up the subject of fetishism, not in regards to the royals but because we had been having a discussion about it. I said loose talk about politics was all right, but if we were to discuss something as important as fetishism we would have to define our terms. I then defined them: Fetishism is what erotically occurs when the part is taken for the whole. Karel's, says Gwen, is that pleasant little line just under the buttock where it smilingly joins the thigh. Her own was "bottoms, mens' bottoms." Then they asked mine and I had to say: "Everything." But this they would not accept. "If you fetishize everything you do not distinguish the part from the whole and we cannot accept this. It is a tautology."

11 DECEMBER 1996. Fumio came over to read me the translation of my *Honorable Visitors*, since I cannot read it myself. Over the years he has come to know the precise level of my Japanese. He knows what I am apt not to understand, reads a difficult passage and at once puts it into simpler language. I ask him if a portion includes the fact that it is ironic. No, he does not think so. This I will talk to the translator about. Not all languages are capable of the same things. This translation does not (cannot) render the nuances of my account of Jean Cocteau and Marcel Khill in Japan. All my meaning is between the lines. In the same fashion, Japanese poetry is too filled with connotations and meanings unwritten to be successfully translated.

15 DECEMBER 1996. I wander around and look at the girls in their Frankenstein boots and their elephant socks, and the boys under their variously colored thatch—blue is popular right now. I also listen to people talking on their cellular phones.

These focus all attention in the ears rather than, as is customary on the street, in the eyes. The users do not realize that they are spilling their lives into the ears of the passersby, and if they did they would not care.

I loiter near to hear what they are saying. They pay no attention. Besides, if they do notice, they see merely a foreigner, and foreigners are famous for not knowing the language. So I feel like Siegfried in the forest—understanding the language of the birds.

But this promiscuous telephoning can be dangerous. Last night's news told of a man using his phone on the platform as the express rushed by. He was so intent on what he was saying that he walked too close to the hurtling train, was drawn into it and sucked onto the tracks, where he made his final connection.

16 DECEMBER 1996. I go shopping at Ameyokocho, only a block from where I live, stretching for a long distance on either side of the tracks south of Ueno. It is indeed like a bazaar. I can see why all the Middle Easterners prefer it: right on the street, no doors or windows to bother with. Little caves, hundreds of them, filled with bargains, shopkeepers hovering. Wandering to the other side, I find a whole district I knew nothing about. It is given over to jewels—diamonds set in gold, silver, and—so it said—platinum.

I also find another store. This one is selling army surplus—from the East German Army. The prices are very low—a thick, woolen East German soldier's overcoat for the equivalent of five dollars. Nonetheless, few people were buying. The East German Army would look odd on the streets of Tokyo. There is one man, however, who has bought himself a whole outfit. He stands in front of a mirror—uniform, hat, coat, and boots. He looks the picture of an East German soldier, except that he still also looks like one of Tokyo's homeless—now a warm homeless though he is. I toy with a fur hat, but the East Germany Army insignia will not pull off and so I do not buy it.

18 DECEMBER 1996. I walk the windy streets of Shibuya, a territory completely given over to the young. Here they come in their hordes, driven by fashion. Let me describe them lest this motley show be lost forever.

Younger high school girls wear their plaid skirts and sweaters and their elephants socks, loose, baggy, white, which they say make their legs look thinner and often have to be held up with a kind of glue that is especially made and sold over the counter. They still sometimes wear old-fashioned braids, but their manners have been attuned to the times. Among themselves they use male language, mistaking this for a kind of emancipation.

Older girls often wear very short skirts coupled with built up boots, which reach the knee and thus offer an expanse of thigh. With this, a long overcoat unbuttoned so that the thighs may flash. Long hair dyed (chestnut, maple, mahogany) or streaked with peroxide or henna, and brown pancake make-up with silvered lip stick complete the ensemble.

It has a name. It is called *kogaru*—derived apparently from *kokosei garu* (high school girl), though the layered cut, the trimmed eyebrows, and the lipstick emulate the image of the older popular singer, Amuro Namie. Some of the girls show their navels in the summer, and often sport a ring in it.

Piercing is seen mainly in the boys. Those in high school wear eyebrow studs or lip studs as well as earrings. This with jeans (now firmly at the waist, since the groin-look is out of fashion), boots with thick soles, and lots of rings. Boys in Shibuya are more decorated than the girls are.

Along with this a new vocabulary. *Saiko* and *saitei* for best and worst are out. In is *choberiba* for very bad and *choberigu* for very good. I do not know the derivation of these. Another new word is *makudurama*, which can mean anything from a big sports event to a big rock concert to a big TV spectacular. Continuing into the new year is a teenage passion for *purikura*, photo stickers made in three minutes, showing you and your friend wearing funny hats, grinning, and making the V-sign, with which you can decorate your school locker or your letters, if you send any.

Back in Ueno, only twenty minutes on the subway, is another world. Here the young are more scarce and are not overly given to body piercing or wearing work clothes as a fashion indicator. Here such clothing is seen on the working young, but mainly on people older and poorer. Much less shopping going on. In the station, lines of old men—indigent, homeless, sitting on the pavement. I pass two in noisy conversation. One drunkenly tells the other, "I don't have a penny. (*Issen mo nai no yo*)," yet he must have had at least several to get this drunk.

During the fiftieth year of writing his journals, Richie, now seventy-three, is occasionally distracted by medical problems, but the clinical details of his illness are also there for their own sake; he chronicles old age much as others keep track of adolescence or the middle years. With two of the books on which he worked longest

(*Kumagai* and *A Divided View*) still unpublished, Richie spent his time writing essays and taking notes for a book on Tokyo, and for this journal.

6 JANUARY 1997. Everyone's first day back at work after the usual orgy of holidays—or at least the first day of attendance to indicate that work has begun. No one actually does any work. Everyone is going from office to office to give greetings and to mention work to come and their desire to be remembered in further enterprises.

Lots of bowing—people in the street, bending over for each other. I am bowed at, too, and bow back. This occurs at the International House, where I go to check the *Bulletin* before publication. The office staff bows. I stand up and bow. We tell each other that the New Year has begun (*Akemashite omedeto gozaimasu*) and that this year too we wish to be kindly remembered (*Kotoshi mo yoroshiku onegai itashimasu*).

Such occurs wherever one is known, however slightly. In the evening I drop into the porn theater (where they have a new policy—reduced priced tickets for the aged), and am so greeted by the women who work there taking tickets. Underpaid, worn down, having to spend their holiday in this dank place, they observe the custom and asked to be kindly remembered because the law of ritual is stronger than they are.

Once inside the darkened theater I see it is more full than usual and that the patrons are bunched at the back. Then I see why. Two long-haired young girls, maybe seventeen, all dressed up in long coats, are standing there surrounded by men in raincoats. Everyone is looking at the screen and paying careful attention to no one else.

They could stand thus all night, no one making a move, each so afraid of rebuff. I, for whom the rebuff holds no terrors, go and talk to the girls. They giggle and eventually inform me that they are from Saitama (very rural), in town for a day, and thought they ought to see the sights. I asked what they think of the local offering. "Very educational," says one as the woman on the screen writhes, orifices full.

The other men, emboldened, move closer, and so we three step into the lobby where the girls smoke and ask where I am from and giggle and I, having already seen this particular picture, tell them that an educational bit was coming up. The lady got to the screw the gentleman. How, they want to know. "With a dildo," I tell them. "Oh," they say, then, "Where?" "In the ass," I say. "Oh," they say.

Two of the men join us and we have a conversation until the ticket-taking women herd us back in. There we stand in a silent puddle, me firmly beside the prettiest one, the men stationed around us. But nothing happens. Nothing ever does. We could have stood all night and nothing would have happened. Eventually the girls tire of the spectacle, and with many an attractive smile and waggish wave they leave—back to Saitama, wiser.

One of the hovering men smiles and shakes his head. I say I thought at first they were *enjo kosei*—high school girls out for money. Oh, no, he knew from the first. Just a couple of kids having a good time in the big city. Then, in that spirit of disinterested learning one so often finds here, he enlightens me as to the literal meaning of the term. *Enjo kosei* translates as "assistance-oriented relationship."

12 JANUARY 1997. I read that an authority on psychology, one Tomita Takashi, has ascertained that the "territory area" of the Japanese is just forty-five centimeters, rather small compared to other nationalities. But so crowded are we in the cities that we have to make do. Thus, says Sensei, people send out signals that they are no threat, that they are behaving themselves. I wonder if I do that. Probably. I know I always dive for the neutral corner seat, if one is available, or at least the end of a row.

Another authority, this one named Saito Isamu, tells me that everyone does. We can, he says, let down our guard in this position, or at least only have to defend half of what we would were we in the middle. Dr. Saito goes on to tell me that men peeing always finish faster if the urinals on either side are taken. If there are no people, they dawdle. The most popular urinal is the one on the end. But do people idly dawdle? I have seen only dawdling with intent.

16 JANUARY 1997. Out with two women, both Americans, one blonde, one brunette, and after dinner we were wondering where to have coffee and I suggested the Shiro. But the fact that we were three might be a problem.

I asked one of the elderly and dignified transvestites who wait in the street and let themselves out to gentlemen who wish to go down those dank stairs but cannot without an at least nominal female.

"Oh, no," he said, "you can't get in with two women. Only allowed one. You ought to send them in as a pair and then take me along with you as another one."

Not wishing that, we all trouped down the dank stairs, where the waiter in charge said it was perfectly all right so long as we each ordered a cup of their pricey brew.

This agreed to, we penetrated the potted foliage and saw a gentleman in the distance being fellated. He saw us too, and positioned himself the better to show the ladies his small but rigid, spit-slicked prick. I pointed out this detail and many another to my interested wards, and we roamed about, cups in hand.

There was a man who had his date laid back like a cello, and was manipulating her with one hand. Sitting in rear was one of the men from outside, maturely pert in a cloche and fox fur. "How come you got in with two girls?" he said. "It's against the law." I told him everything was against the law, including himself.

A young couple came in. Both were good looking and, it turned out, well built. Her breasts once uncovered were beautiful and his member, pants once down to the knees, was ample. As she skillfully blew him I complimented him on his size. "Thank you," he said modestly. I then ran my hand over his bare bottom, at which point the member went limp and he sat down.

"He is such a party pooper," said the blonde of me. "Does it all the time." Thus admonished, I regarded the couple from a safer distance and watched his date skillfully repair my damage. When he was back in his stride I leaned over the back of their booth and said it was only fair that he practice cunnilingus upon her. He readily agreed and pulled down her panty hose. He was very skillful and reminded me of the octopus in the Hokusai print.

In the meantime my wards had also found something to look at. The two men right in front of them had their hands on their dates and were showing off their manual techniques. When they realized that they had an appreciative audience they scooted about to give the girls a better view.

"The younger one is more flashy," said one, "but the older one is much the better. He is a real master craftsman." "Like a traditional carpenter," said the other. "Yes, notice the concern, the care . . ."

We then talked about desire and wondered why it was that photographs could be pornographic (that is, exciting) but that this—the real thing—was, somehow, not. I suggested it was because it was not sordid, and mentioned that I did not find color porn exciting but got worked up over black and white. They did not know what to make of this, but one said that the real thing (like here) lacked the safe endistancing of the photo.

This led to talk of voyeurism, since we were practicing it, and exhibitionism, since the others were. I suggested that such oblique participation made an act the more authentic. It was like being a witness—in the religious sense, a witness to god. This I said was perhaps why one was not turned on.

"Who's not turned on?" they asked, eyes glued to the moving hands. I said that it was typical of the nature of the appeal that they would get turned on, if so they were, but merely by manipulation and not by the full fact of frontal sex.

Where, where? They wanted to know. I indicated the young couple's booth where she was on her back, legs in the air, and he was on top, trim butt bobbing. The girls spared it a glance but soon went back to the sliding, gliding, fingers—thus proving my point.

The master craftsman turned around, smiled, and said that it was getting late so that they would have to leave. They came all the way from Saitama. Twice a month. He thanked us and we thanked him. Then I paid for our expensive coffee and we too left.

17 JANUARY 1997. Observing me, an acquaintance says, in mock disbelief: "You're still at it." He is referring to my continuing search. His assumption is that once a certain age is reached the search stops. At seventy-two I am well over whatever that age is supposed to be, and am thus something of anomaly. Conventional wisdom has it that in the wisdom of one's years, one ceases to desire the object of the search.

But conventional wisdom is only that—conventional. It is never wise and indeed is often wrong. Existence is too vast for its petty confines, intended as these are for reassurance. Maybe in some age when humans, like animals, were urged mainly by their glands, interest ceased when glands stopped working. Not now. Glands are no longer even the half of it. Humans have complicated and enriched their existence. The search is internalized, psychologized, made central to this existence. Whether this is wise or not, it is what occurs.

And, it permits a kind of dialogue where there was hitherto none. It is a way to answer back to the demands of biology. The body says slow down, slack off, get ready to die. And the human spirit says fuck it. The search goes on because it is vital; it is life itself. To stop searching is to die. I admire the kind of *mono no aware* that permits acquiescence, but at the same time I resent such biological tyranny. In this sense I think that Kamo no Chomei (go along with life's little stream) and Dylan Thomas (go not willing into that cold night) are both right. I am right too.

25 JANUARY 1997. To Karel's for dinner. We talked mainly about food—talked so little about politics that Karel mentioned that we weren't. Long discussion about broccoli. Karel applauded President Bush for excoriating the unappetizing vegetable. I wondered at the wisdom of this, coming as it did from a leader who threw up at the banquet locally thrown in his honor. "Yes," reminded Eithne [Jones], "but he had the decency to warn people." American though that was, I pursued: he still spattered the Prime Minister's shoes.

Following this was a discussion as to where broccoli came from. Karel was certain it was that home of many abominations, America. Others thought differently. The proper volume of the *Encyclopedia Britannica* informed us: The Mediterranean was home to the unpopular vegetable.

The only political talk involved a remark I made disparaging patriotism. "No, no, we cannot have that," said Karel. "There is a difference: Patriotism is good; it is nationalism that is bad." I asked the difference. This was not forthcoming, but he added that it was good to support your country. I asked why, never having done so, and seeing little reason for attempting now.

31 JANUARY 1997. With Arturo [Silva] to the opening of the new photographic exhibition at the Yokohama Museum of Art. He is still thinking about the *festschriebe* for me. [This eventually became *The Donald Richie Reader.*] To this end, he has compiled a list of questions: Why did I get married; how do I reconcile the "emotionality of the journals with the cool person you present yourself as?" And then my "self-negating, voracious sexual appetite?" and, "Why did you never come out?"

This is going to be a strange kind of *festschriebe*. But, though I naturally think of Kinbote [the editor in Nabokov's *Pale Fire*], such questions might be interesting to try to answer. I will attempt the last one: Why did I never come out?—Let me count the ways.

First, because it never occurred to me to do so. Why should I so limit myself—and only for the sake of security within the ranks? True, I grew up when such disclosure would have been damaging, and it would not be that now. But I can also see almost no advantages. Just that of having refused plurality and the possibility of the pale comforts of a single-minded security—life finally rendered simple and sure amid the questionable charms of solidarity.

Second, an existential objection: When you name anything, you limit it; you slam the door on *becoming* and insist upon *being*. If a person comes out, he proclaims his belief that he is only one thing, has never been and could not ever be another. This is creepy.

Third, a political objection. A person who comes out chooses to predicate himself on his sexuality. And only on his sexuality. Whether he so intends or not, he has made a political statement. He is Homosexual; the world is not. And it is the world he has chosen to address by coming out. He has turned sexual preference into political preference. By insisting upon difference, he has condoned division.

But you are not socially responsible, says the critic. Of course not, I answer. Would a socially responsible person have chosen to spend his life outside his own society? I am not thinking of making life better for future queers, I say. I do not believe that life gets better for anyone. I believe it gets worse, and that in an increasingly overcrowded world more and more groups will splinter and battle, and what social comfort is left will be crowded out. Reforms are based on faith.

So, as I ponder why I never "came out," I realize how limited the question is. To come out means to have gone in and I never did. I have always been out—that is, have hidden nothing. The thing is, I have never advocated it, and it is concern at this that creates questions such as: "Why did you never come out?"

13 FEBRUARY 1997. I look from my window—a bright, cold day. In the distance, above the myriad concrete blocks of Tokyo, lie the blue folds of the Chichibu Mountains and beyond them a silver sliver, the snow on the distant Japan Alps. Nearer, the single finger of the Ikebukuro Sunshine Building, assorted business office spires I do not recognize, and, over the pond, the enormously ugly ex-Hotel Cosima. Having gone broke, it is now the Tokyo Sofitel.

Across the pond too, itself now brown and slate blue, the Benten temple, all white and red, with a green octagonal roof of its own. Passing by it, small figures, some walking, some on bikes, all bundled up. Two small bridges, the ducks brown smudges, the gulls white flying dots. Nearer, on this shore, the promenade.

There, by the water, sitting in the patch of sunlight, surrounded by shadows of tall buildings including my own, sit the old women. Every day from early morning, they come out in their coats and kerchiefs and spend the day. Unlike the ladies of the night they are not working—and they are all real women.

They have no work. And they have nowhere else to go. They sit and smoke. In warmer weather they were visited by equally aimless old men. At first I thought they were aged hookers. But, they are not; they are homeless. Everyday they have nowhere to go and so they come and sit companionably in the sun. I don't know where they go when it rains.

Lowering my gaze, I see on the other side of the toilet, hidden among the bushes, the old man who is there every day. He sits on a stone, bent almost double, and stays for hours. He too has no home. He does not move. The sun has long crept past him, but still he sits on his cardboard square. Blue cap, green coat. Hours he sits, face hidden in his upturned collar. He is dying.

Lower yet is the street. I bend over my balcony, and below me are cars and people walking. The world continuing.

16 FEBRUARY 1997. Doing proof on the [Lafcadio] Hearn book I am again struck that he, unlike [James Curtis] Hepburn, never learned Japanese, and yet that it is he rather than Hepburn who is credited with being the foreigner who most "understands" the place. Even if one uses the word in the Japanese sense ("understands" means "agrees with"), however, Hearn did not understand, nor did he attempt to. He attempted to describe, which is something quite different. Would knowing the language have gotten in the way? Possibly. Barthes would have thought so.

And then I think of myself, here fifty years to Hearn's fifteen, but almost equally illiterate. Very odd—and both of us utterly dependent upon language (our own) for our living. I cannot say that Barthes' beliefs apply to me. Though I distrust casual words, I still believe that the proper combination can preserve reality.

Why did I never learn to read and write? (I speak tolerably well—to be in Japan and not understand what is said to one would be intolerable.) But why, when I am otherwise so industrious, so lazy in learning the written tongue?

Ed [Seidensticker] (who knows the written tongue as do few others) thinks my ignorance a good thing. "I admire you, Donald," he once said. "You never learned to read. Believe me, if you had, you would not stay in this country for five minutes." Would, I wondered, the depths of mendacity displayed on the printed page drive me from my chosen land? Perhaps. Ignorance is also bliss.

I am not saying that I am better off illiterate, but that I can still manage, illiterate though I be. And, unlike Lafcadio Hearn, I do not attempt to hide this defect.

23 FEBRUARY 1997. It is now a year since Takemitsu died, and this afternoon his widow held a commemorative party at the Sogetsu Kaikan. Invited were people who had been close to him, people with whom he had lived and worked. Some music was played, and Kishida Kyoko read a poem he had written for her ten years before. A few speeches, the most interesting from his outspoken daughter, who said that there had been a lot of talk about the medication rather than the disease having killed Toru. She did not think so; the reason being that her father had worked closely with his doctors, had interested himself in his disease. Diseases actually, for in addition to cancer he had something call *kogenbyo*. (I have just looked up the word; the dictionary has nothing, probably I misheard it.) He knew what medication he was getting. Though this does not bar death by medicine, it makes it less likely.

The food we were served too had to do with the illness. As he lay in hospital, Toru could not eat. So he wrote imaginary menus for himself, and it was one of these we were served, food he would have wanted. There was deep-fried haddock and golden brown glazed chicken, spaghetti with squid, fried rice with duck, and some odd items—boiled cabbage with shaved *katsuobushi*. Since he did not get around to the pudding there were no desserts.

Oshima [Nagisa] was there, the first time I had seen him since his stroke. He was in a wheelchair but looked fit given what he has gone through. He took my hand with both of his, and his grip was strong. So was his smile, no sign of the lopsided grimace of the paralytic—like Eric. He created this all himself—has been in training for almost a year.

Ooka Makoto told me that this kind of exercise is very difficult. There is nothing to hold onto. It is like exercising in free fall. He himself knows about it. He had a stroke some years back. But much lighter, he said, nothing like Oshima's. Still, the battle to control the body, to retrain it, was not only difficult, it also seemed impossible. Had to start up once again—every day.

We talked about the Toru boom, the fact that you cannot turn on the radio without hearing something of his. I wonder if that is a good thing, such exposure. Ozawa Seiji says absolutely not, first because Toru would not have wanted it, second because they usually play his various pop arrangements and only them, and third because a listener backlash is bound to occur. He laughed, "Look what happened to Mozart."

I also heard from Non-chan [Nogami Teruyo] that Kurosawa is in a bad way. Broke his leg. Is now in bed. Sees no one, interested in nothing. We talk about Mifune. He perhaps, unlike Kurosawa, does not know what is happening to him. I learned that his wife took the child, upon whom he doted, and left when his Alzheimer's became apparent. At the same time, his first wife returned to take care of him, which was very traditional of her.

All this temporal talk was relieved by [Kanaseki] Kuniko who, though as bereaved as anyone, Hisao having died only eight months ago, said, "Well, so what. I think about it. And I think of my going next. And I think, why not? I've had a good time. I've had a good run for the money." And she smiled, that wide, happy smile of acceptance, which I so much admire in those strong enough to have it.

4 MARCH 1997. Spring slowly approaches, each day a little warmer, though still chilly. I take a stroll in the park and pause to look at the ground near Benten's island temple. It is rich, something pregnant.

The shallowness of Japan's geological history is seen in the richness of its soil. Here in these relatively recent islands, the earth has never been much walked on. It is still itself.

I remember India, where the earth has been trod upon for millenniums, so used by feet that it is as though baked, a smooth, claylike surface offering nothing to plants—turning back to stone. Not here. In Japan there is still renewal.

Walking on, circling the temple, crossing the bridges, taking the path leading around the lake, I think of renewal and that brings to mind the shrines of Ise. They are renewed every twenty years and are consequently always as they were. This has been going on since the seventh century (with one major interruption of over a hundred years when no one could afford to rebuild), and the last was in 1993, replacing the structures finished in 1973, which took the place of those built in 1953.

That is where I came in. I remember them because that 1953 was the year I returned to Japan and made my first visit there, and they were gleaming new, all white in the afternoon sun and still smelling of cypress. Then they grew old and gray and developed cracks and the reed roof turned to moss. After they were torn down the new structures were built (1973), but I do not remember those. The 1993 buildings, however, I saw a year or two later when Dae-Yung and I went to Ise. Still white, but no longer fragrant. Those in 2013 I will not see, but there is a strange kind of comfort in having accompanied the metamorphoses of Ise, and having observed—indeed, taken part in—this civilized reply to the demands of immortality.

5 MARCH 1997. At Kitazawa in Kanda I see the Isherwood diaries. For this forty-dollar book I pay the equivalent of seventy dollars, the usual mark up here on foreign books. But I want to read it. I am looking for models of journal presentation, and his seems to have all the apparatus. Also, I want to examine the binding. I did not know that over a thousand pages could be so sturdily bound (this is only the first volume), and I was thinking mine might be too long.

Finally, I wanted to read Christopher on himself. It was from him that I learned the presentation of the discrete self—learned it through the *Berlin Stories*. In his diaries I can expect something more unbuttoned, and I may yet learn something. Presentation of self is a kind of seduction of the reader, and though I can do without Christopher's soul searching, I am interested in his techniques.

I recognized him at once when we first met in 1957. We were so much alike. His admission of grave doubts about himself, his shrugging off of self, his half-appeal to one's better senses—all of this constituted charm and was intended to lure you close. For what reason? To be seduced if he found you likely, to be made a part of the procession if he did not. And behind it all something very real, something large and kind and a bit sentimental. Since I am much that way myself, I backed off a bit, though I too was in love with Herr Ishyvoo of the Berlin pieces and wanted to be him.

So, I turned into him. The first-person narrator in *The Inland Sea* would have been different without the example of *Goodbye to Berlin*. At the same time, though we saw something of each other over the years, we did not become close. I felt professional toward him. I had learned so much. So I asked his permission and dedicated *Tokyo Nights* to him. Now I am with him again reading these journals. How well he has captured his own tone. How painful the striving to be sincere, how apparent the failure.

7 MARCH 1997. To the bank: my investments are up for renewal. The efficient Ms. Yamaguchi tries to make sense of it all for me. And indeed it is not complicated, but whenever I am faced with large numbers I go blank, do not comprehend. My bank account is not that large, and so my failing has to do with something else.

This I began noticing when I was a child. Simply put, I cannot comprehend money, particularly when it is mine. I remember Lincoln [Kirstein] being all thumbs when it came to counting the bills. My head is like his fingers. It is something I willed early—not to interest myself in what interested my father most. I did not consider that he had to be interested, he had me and my sister to support. I simply and selfishly turned against it. Now I am paying for it. I write down all the sums because, though I carry in my memory all of the Köchel numbers of Mozart's pieces, I cannot remember how much money I have invested, and where.

8 MARCH 1997. Karel [van Wolferen] over for lunch. He had given me his new article to read, a piece about Japan's failure to come to terms with wartime facts, and the reasons for it. The rightist press refers to the masochistic leftist press (what there is left of it), and says enough of this. It is true that the left has tried to make political hay out of war crimes, as it has of Hiroshima and

Nagasaki. A result is that these atrocities are used as political ploys, and then the rightists say enough of this masochistic wallowing, when it is not that at all—it is political expediency.

I suggest that Karel make clearer that when the Japanese use *masohisimu* they do not mean our clinical masochism, and when the word is used in conjunction with comfort women and military brothels an odd image is formed. Also I think he ought temper his attack on Oe Kenzaburo, whom he holds aloft as a sniveling, self-proclaimed victim. But then Karel believes a nation ought to have an army, but not use it. When I tell him that this is a contradiction in terms, he shakes his head.

We go on to the horrid state of the Japanese young. They have no one to talk back too because no one is there. He wants to use their slavery to fashion as an indication of how controlled they are. After all, the hippy gear of thirty years ago was real counter-culture. But it now becomes fancy dress—punk and grunge fashion statements. Still, fashion statements are a kind of control, too.

13 MARCH 1997. Took Peter [Kubelka] around. He is interested in how the past lives on, so I took him to Yanaka. In the various small shops where we went he found a rustic basket from Iwate. "Oh, this I must have. It is five thousand years old." I said I doubted this. "No, really. This is how they made them—all over. Neolithic. Look. And still in use." Then I took him to Kappabashi, where he looked at modern kitchenware and tried to guess what certain unfamiliar instruments were for. He asked their names and wrote them down in his notebook. He also bought a bamboo grater.

Food is another interest. He liked his *toriwasa* and wanted the recipe. (Blanch chicken breasts, mix with *wasabi* and trefoil [*mitsuba*], sprinkle with strips of seaweed, and serve.) At Ameyokocho we spent an hour looking at edibles and asking the names of each, all of which went into the notebook. "Is that an eel too? If so, then, kindly ask what its name is. Yes, *unagi*, but what kind of *unagi*?"

At the *getamoniya* in Asakusa the notebook got a real workout. So did Peter when he discovered he could eat there. He ordered one pit viper, and one portion each of baby bees, pickled locust, and boiled silkworms. We watched as the owner cut off the head of the snake and then put it on the counter where it bit the surface for a time. The blood was drained into a shot glass and grape juice added. "Grape juice?" wondered Peter. "Surely that is not Japanese. Surely it is an importation."

He liked the marinated bees and the boiled silkworms. I tried one of the latter. It tasted, strangely, like mothballs. Did not like the bees. Too sweet. The rest of the snake was deep fried, bones and all, and served with cabbage and lemon. I tried a piece. Tough, no special taste.

"Not eating such things," said Peter, "is just imagination. Things like this are highly edible. Protein." My own imagination prevented my trying the locust, all legs and eyes, but I admired Peter for eating everything in his relentless pursuit of knowledge. To write everything down, to remember, to think and to savor—this is living.

The real treat, however, came in the *matsuriya* where he wanted to buy a *hyoshigi*, those pieces of wood that when clapped make a splendid stroke of sound. He bought two sets, shaman rattles, a musical rasp, two bells, and a small drum—paying the large bill with his credit card.

"What a fine day," he said with that round, friendly, accepting smile. "Thank you so much. Ah, my lovely basket, I must look at it again." And there on the street he unpacked his bag and admired his purchase.

14 MARCH 1997. Reading in the Isherwood diaries. Should one use one's diaries as vehicle for quandary? Christopher does this a lot, so does Gide—and others too . . . Rousseau. One should use journals for doubt, but as for muddle, I think not. It smells of hedging one's bets. For example, this domestic dilemma of Isherwood's.

"It is absolutely essential that this state of affairs" (living with the awful Bill Caskey) "shall *stop*." The question is how. Either he leaves Caskey or he doesn't. "Leaving Caskey—quite aside from being terribly painful—wouldn't really solve anything. Unless there were someone else to go to—which there isn't. . . . Therefore, we have to stay together."

It does not occur to him to live alone. He does not see that he is impossible to live with, does not understand that being alone does not mean being lonely. Since his pattern is to fight with his roommates, then to suffer, I am left to gather that it is the suffering that is necessary.

18 MARCH 1997. Cold, raining, and in the great tan pond below me are five slashes of white, like brush strokes—five heron fishing on this rainy day. They stay there the whole morning, occasionally taking a step or turning a head. And there, in the drizzle below me, sits the old man in the hat who seems to have grown there, like moss.

1 MAY 1997. Chris [Blasdel] takes me out to dinner—at the Nakano Tunisian restaurant. Afterward we have coffee at the Fugetsudo and talk about life after death. His idea is Rudolph Steiner's—that the physical body vanishes but others linger. The "astral body" lasts as long as do flowers on the bier, which is why they put flowers there. Others last longer. After that, everybody repairs to the stockpile and then gets recycled.

I tell him his idea is somewhat like that of Nils [Kreidner], now over for the last time before leaving to go back to school in Germany. We had talked about life after death. I said there is none: it is like turning off the light. He said there is, kind of. Not heaven and hell, of course. These are real, but we make them for ourselves, everyday, right here. No, we transmigrate, but the number of souls is finite. Eventually everybody gets to be everyone else . . . eventually. This is original—I have never heard this theory before.

As for my light bulb—instant nonexistence—even the most superstitious Japanese would agree. I wonder if this might not be because the individual is so much less stressed here, and hence so much less valued.

4 MAY 1997. Since I am now writing my introduction to the translation of *Asakusa Kurenaidan*, I once more go there, to Asakusa, to see if I can find any trace of what I once felt. Fifty years ago it was still alive, this great entertainment district. The merry-go-round was still there, and the movie theaters, the *yose*, even some remnants of the park. No longer. It has been gentrified, something which can occur only in a dead neighborhood. There is an amount of created nostalgia—statue of Enoken the Asakusa comedian, a new office building called the Denkikan, named after the first movie theater. The old theatrical district, the Rokko, is now gone. There is a sauna bath by that name and a new futuristic structure (Za Rokko), which houses cheesy little boutiques and fast junk food places. The only thing alive about the place is the Japan Racing Center, an enormous complex for people to go and place bets on distant horse races. The place is more insipid than depressing. I wander for an hour, but it is no longer Asakusa so I leave.

3 MAY 1997. Chizuko [Korn] here, alone, for a visit. I admire the way that she has adapted to life in New York—and life with Frank—neither at all easy. The carefully coiffed Chizuko, elegantly and expensively dressed, wafting the aroma of *mizushobai*, is gone. In place, a pleasant woman of fifty or so wearing a cotton shirt and granny glasses, with lots of big, loose, undyed hair. She is her age, has accepted it, and is perfectly natural with it.

We talk about their life in New York, just the two of them, with a few friends—like my ex-wife, Mary. She talks naturally about his children (against whom she was dagger-drawn when here), she even willingly talks about the dead Marion. Maybe it is having to take care of the eighty-three-year-old Frank that has made her so herself.

5 MAY 1997. Boys' Day, now called Childrens' Day (though girls are allowed to keep Girls' Day on March 3), the last of that chain of holidays optimistically dubbed Golden Week. Today people, exhausted by their idleness, confronted by masses of leisure choices, idle around the pond awaiting welcome work.

Bang-bang, loud, impatient, someone at the door, something that almost never happens in this well-guarded apartment. It is the police, a single, spectacled man with a large clipboard. He is checking the neighborhood he tells me. And I am—he peers at his papers—Mr. Donald. I explain that that is my first name and he makes an erasure. He then gives his speech. He is here to help me. I live alone it appears. (I have long learned that the cops know much more about me than I think they do—and the same for everyone else in the archipelago.) So if, for example, I one day find myself unable to move (he looks into my lined face) I need only call this number (handed over) and either he, Officer Kato, or one of his aides will come to rescue me. Then with a smart salute and a bow he is gone.

I hold my piece of paper with my lifeline telephone number on it and smile. How fortunate I am to live in this country, how very lucky I am to have come here forever, how grateful I am for this present on Boys' Day.

11 MAY 1997. To be political is to be engaged in administration, having an organized polity, taking a side in politics. Those who do have a stake in any outcome are attempting to create what they want. Disinterested politics is impossible. If one is political for gain it means one has faith in one's strength; if one is political for "the people," or any other such concept, one has faith in the object.

So many reasons for me to despise politics. It is self-serving; it is desire masquerading as good; at its worst it is rape, at its best it is seduction. Odd, since I do not resist any of this in its physical aspect (well, yes, rape), why do I so resist it in its ideological form? Why do I even think resistance possible? Politics is everything. I am playing politics even though I think I am not—pushing my agenda.

With such thoughts do I occupy my Sunday stroll. In Ueno Station I see coming toward me a limping, frowning old man. Then recognition—it is Edward Seidensticker. We stop. "What are you doing?" he asks. "My post-prandial," I say. "A likely story," says he, smiling broadly. "And yourself?" "Back from Maebara. Had to talk on a poet. Woke up at five this morning to think about what I could possibly say." "What did you possibly say?" "God knows." "Want to have a coffee?" I ask. "No," he says, "I am tired. I am going home." Upon parting he added, daringly, "Good hunting." "Tut-tut," say I, waving a finger. "Postprandial."

13 MAY 1997. At dinner Ed tells me that sumo is slipping. For the first time in a decade, seats have this week failed to sell out. Indeed, some four hundred, an unheard of number, are left unsold. He ascribes this to a rule that people in the same stable cannot fight each other, and all the strong ones are now in one stable. I ascribe it to the essential idiocy of sumo. "But it has been popular until now," he says. "'You cannot fool all of the people all of the time,'" I quote.

Then he kindly helps me with my introduction to *Asakusa Kurenaidan*, the book I have been working on for fifty years now. I am beginning to believe that, at last, my half-century-old promise to Kawabata will be honored. "Of course," says Ed, "you got all of your information from me." I agree and add, "That is why in my letter I was wondering how to handle this matter." "What letter?" "The letter I enclosed with the manuscript." "There was no letter." "There was." "Well," he said, "it is but a small matter—still when one has done scholarly work, one would wish for at least some recognition." "That, Ed, is just what I said in my letter." "What letter?" Etc. . . .

Later on we speak of death and dissolution. He tells me that when a person dies, his or her sphincter relaxes and he or she shits him or herself. I tell him that all men die with erections, such being the meaning of stiff. This reminds me of the *conte drôle* of Balzac, where the old maid plucks the corpse of the freshly hung thief from the scaffold and so avails herself that he regains consciousness.

We are into our desserts at this point and agree that it is a droll *conte* indeed.

15 MAY 1997. I take a long walk and, as I have for half a century, revel in the city, in Tokyo, the largest of all cities. When I am in the country I am enchanted for an hour or so, but then become uneasy. In a small town I walk the few streets and then begin to feel closed in upon. But in a city there are always further reaches, places one has never seen, those one never will.

I remember Baudelaire walking with spleenish content the streets of Paris. He said that the pleasure of being in crowds is a mysterious expression of sensual joy. So it is. He said it was because the multiplication of number. I, agree, adding that it is because of the multiplicity of seeming opportunity. In a city anything can happen, in the country little, and in the grave nothing.

19 MAY 1997. Am reading the admirable Umberto Saba: "A poem is an erection; a novel is a birth."

22 MAY 1997. Ran into Ed and we went and had a drink at an *izakaya*, the kind of place I almost never go—first because I don't drink and second because I feel I am ruining the atmosphere (very Japanese) for everyone else. Ed drinks, however, and ruining atmospheres was never a concern of his. Rightly so. They ruin ours (all that smoking) much more than we with our foreignness ruin theirs.

We talked about food dislikes. He does not like *unagi,* my favorite. And I do not like *natto,* his favorite. So he orders *natto* wrapped in *shiso* leaf and deep-fried and, sure enough, it is delicious. We both agree about *oden.* I cannot abide it. He holds his nose when he eats it.

Then in a kindly and concerned manner he asks me about money. Do I have enough? This I take as friendship, because how many people would risk misunderstanding to so inquire. No, he does not want any nor does he intend to give me any. Like a true friend, he worries about my future. I reassure him as best I can.

25 MAY 1997. A review of my *Public People, Private People* says that, ". . . the present reader may feel a little envious of Richie for getting to meet people of a kind that no longer exist in an era that will never come back." Is that true? About the era, of course, but about the people? Yet it was certainly easier to meet people back then. And not just because foreigners were perhaps helpful. Japanese acquaintances tell me that they now have the same problem. Strangers are not so open to experience as they were. Also, solitary people are rare now, though they were once common. People come either pairs or groups now—or, if single, they are accompanied and preoccupied with their cell phones. In all events they come self-sufficient. They do not need anyone. Now the only way to meet people in Japan is the same as everywhere else. Be introduced. One can no longer profitably cruise for acquaintance (nor for anything else), and this is certainly a change from the good old days.

And yet—walking in Ameyokocho I see a palanquin coming toward me, an ornate, phoenix-crowned, and very heavy float carried by a number of men and some women, all gotten up in some kind of Edo costume, the men showing their bare torsos, the *hayashi* of the drums and flute keeping everyone in step. The Ueno summer festival, or part of it.

Walking past it I notice that one of the men, loin-clothed, with an incongruous permanent wave, is looking at me. I look in return and he smiles, and with a free hand waves. It is my barber. Behind his chair at the shop he is the last word in modern: the perm, the dispatch, the cool way of today's youth, the radio blaring American rock, and the shelves stocked with contemporary mousses. Yet here he is—a friendly young man straight from Edo.

26 MAY 1997. Am reading some modern "gay" diaries. They share a remarkable degree of disingenuousness. I suppose I share it as well, or else I would not so much mind it. But I have another reason for disliking it. And this is that those who write in this hypocritical manner are always pleading guilty to the lesser crime. Is this something that afflicts the tribe? My impatience is caused by my not wanting to be a tribe, but an individual.

Maybe this is the reason I so dislike the term "gay"—it has tribal connotations. It means, as we are often told, an alternate "lifestyle," which is plainly familial. Gays do this, gays do that, they also shop at gay stores and employ gay lawyers; there is, I understand, a chain of gay undertakers—a profitable line. The term so stresses the collective that it can only reinforce a stereotype. This is why I would prefer a pejorative, like "queer." Here the stereotype is much less focused because no one wants to focus it.

A useful distinction is made by Robert Aldrich [in *The Seduction of the Mediterranean*, 1993]. He says that there are old and new models of homosexuality: The old was an aesthetic model, but the 1970s gay model promoted hedonism rather than intellectualism. The earlier idealized and spiritualized; the new put a premium on physical expression and espoused a happy promiscuity.

The old destinations were Rome and Venice, Capri and Sicily, the new ones San Francisco and New York, or the gay ghettos of any large city. The old was proudly elitist and rather apologetic; the new view is militantly political, sometimes radical, espousing the idea that gay is good, exalting gay pride, and an egalitarian demand for the right to be different. Another difference: the older style, mine, was attached to the world as it is, the straight world. The new style turns in upon itself and invents a world that has few links with the real one.

In this way it is a bit like Japan, also an exclusive club, also a commercial venture with its own Japanese services for Japanese only. Why do I like one (Japan) and have difficulty tolerating the other (Gayville)?

28 MAY 1997. Reading Boswell. On 1 April, 1776, having heard of a pretty, fair girl on call, "... I sent for her and enjoyed her, and ... a kind of license I have had ... I thought this should be the last act of this fit of debauchery." The ellipses are not his; they are those of his anonymous censors who sliced up the journal. He had had the bravery to put things in. I will too, and will here put in something I was going to leave out.

Tonight I was walking in Sumida Park and a *tobishoku* [scaffolding workman], still in his work uniform, spoke to me. He was in his late twenties or so, and had a pleasant manner. As we talked he said he had once had a foreign friend, met him several times, right here in this park. "Bet you played around (*yappari itazura shita*)," I said. He nodded and held up two fingers. "Twice?" "No, he gave me two thousand yen." "That's a coincidence," I said, "I have two thousand yen right here in my pocket." He smiled and asked, "You want to do it?" I said I sure did and we retired. He took his time but seemed to enjoy it.

Afterward I asked where he was from. From Miyazaki, in Kyushu. Then he asked where I was from. I said Canada, as I often do. He turned and looked at me. "My foreign friend from before was from Canada."

We looked more closely at each other. "How long ago was it?" I asked. "Eight years ago." "Was he wearing bifocals, like me?" "No." "I started wearing them five years ago," I said.

We sat on a bench and tried to remember. Couldn't. Then he asked if I knew how he knew it was eight years ago. He said it was because just after that that he went to "school." School, I wondered? This is what they call jail, he explained. What was he in for, I wondered?

"I killed a man. I didn't mean to. I was drunk. He was drunk too and he kept picking on me, and I had this knife and I took it and wanted to frighten him and hit him in the leg with it. Hey, that hurt, he said. It is supposed to, I said. Then, I don't know why, I stabbed him in the chest. I took him to the hospital. He died on the way. They gave me eight years."

After that we sat on the bench and watched darkness settle in for the night, love having somehow once again joined death.

31 MAY 1997. On the way home I bought a Big Mac Juicy Double Burger and sat in the park to consume it. As I did so I was aware of being looked at. Glancing around I could see no one, and then noticed near me an inhabited cardboard box. In it was a man regarding me. He did nothing but look, did not lick his lips or hold out his hand. The homeless here never beg; they simply sit and slowly die. So I handed him my Big Mac Juicy Double Burger, one bite taken out of it, and he took it and retired into his box.

And I suddenly remembered fifty years ago, in front of the Ginza Hattori Building, now Wako, then the PX, making an identical gesture with a bitten hot dog. I was then twenty-something and he was about five. Now I am seventy something and he is in his fifties. Nothing has changed, except everything.

1 JUNE 1997. To Fumio's bar, the Zakone. He is having a week-long twentieth anniversary party, which opens tonight. The place is full—just like two decades ago. He gets out a new guest book so that I can be the first to sign it, then I am found a seat and given something to eat and drink. The place looks the same, still the same silver pinstripe wallpaper we chose to make it look bigger, still the same round bar he wanted so that everyone could see everyone. On the door and on the place mats—and now on the telephone card he gives to each who comes to the event—the drawing of people lying about in just any which way (*zakone ni*) that I drew twenty years ago.

But we are much changed. An older crowd now. Some, like me, having difficulty with the four-floor walk-up. And Fumio, now heavier, grayer—but inside just the same.

4 JUNE 1997. Something seen fifty years ago and then missing for forty, are people squatting. This is the Asian position for resting—sitting on the heels. In postwar Japan, however, the posture became provincial, and dressed up women could no longer do it in high heels. Yet, it never entirely died out. One saw it in the country and in the country-like sections of the city—Asakusa or Ueno.

But now it is back, and the squatters are young people. There they squat in their nose rings, their low-slung pants, and their dyed hair. This, the traditional Tokugawa position for rest, has become the young's position for hanging out.

6 JUNE 1997. Late, going home, I pass a group of squatting high schoolers. One of the boys, obviously seeking to impress the girls, says that foreigners are funny (*okashii no yo*). The sight of me has prompted the remark and he is, like everyone else, unaware that some foreigners speak Japanese. It is thus not a provocative remark, but an observation he might have made of a passing dog, in reference to dogs in general.

I am not offended by the remark (it is scarcely personal), but I am interested that the remark was made at all. He made it because he wanted to assert their feeling of being in a group. By defining those outside this group as funny, he strengthened their group feeling of not being funny. This made everyone feel good. And for so long as a feel-good grouping is necessary, we will have xenophobia, racism, and all the rest. The only solution is to dissolve the pleasures of groupery.

Had I become angry, felt slighted, outraged, etc., I would have become as culpable as they, for I would have brought my own feelings of group (as a foreigner) to strive against theirs.

7 JUNE 1997. At International House Mr. [Tatsuya] Tanami told me that at the Japan Society recently they were speaking of intellectual exchange—country to country. Then they realized that there were no Japanese they could exchange, because there are no intellectuals.

We tried to decide why and agreed that there are none, because to be an intellectual you must espouse your own independence and your own probity, unswayed by political affiliations. This is an impossibility everywhere, true. There ought not to be Catholic or Communist intellectuals, yet it is said that they exist. If so, however, then they might be, like Sartre, intellectuals first, Communists second.

In Japan, however, everyone is, whether they like it or not, Japanese first. Intellectuals, like everyone else here, are spokesmen for their political (Japanese) identification. Even if they are anti-establishment, or what passes for dissident here, they are still oriented by their nationality and its demands.

Until there are real individuals, there can be no real intellectuals.

Those given to an exercise of the intellect, inclined toward abstract thinking about aesthetic or philosophical subjects, seem to thrive best when words are not used: painters, composers, and filmmakers. Mr. Tanami and I try to think of a proper Japanese intellectual. He can come up only with a dissident manga artist.

14 JUNE 1997. I hear that the old Weatherby plot, house now gone, holds a brand-new parking lot. The Japanese-style garden has thus been razed; the beautiful *sarusuberi* tree has been carted off or destroyed. I know why—the land will now be a place for autos until a certain time and then, in a different tax bracket, the land will accommodate, finally, the desired, massive new building.

3 JULY 1997. I learn that Meredith [Weatherby] has died. He left Japan well over a decade ago, took his friend, Mizuno Fumio, with him, and then dropped all of his friends. Last Friday he was eating and something went the wrong way, and by the time he reached the hospital he was dead.

I owe him much. He taught me how to write; he first published me. At the same time, he later neglected me as he finally neglected everyone, and so I neglected him. At the same time, I wonder that I should have so little feeling for the death of a man with whom I lived, who in many ways formed me, and who was for a time generous with me.

But I do not feel culpable. Meredith so changed. From a man who loved good writing, who liked stylistic experiment, who gave me *Arabia Deserta*, who encouraged and then published my *Companions of the Holiday*, even though (or because) it was about him and his household, he turned into a person who turned on the TV in the morning and left it on until late at night, who stopped reading Japanese, then stopped speaking Japanese, to whom everything was too much trouble, eventually even living here, finally living at all.

4 JULY 1997. Both of us dressed up, Seidensticker Sensei and I accompanied each other to the American Embassy. They had two seatings (though no one sat down), and no ambassador as yet. I discovered the green tea and the food, and Ed discovered the gin and the tonic.

I am doing a panel on Japanese literature for International House, and the idea is that the best translator talks about his specialty. Donald Keene I will ask to do Mishima, and Ed I will ask to do Kafu or, if he wants, Kawabata, and Howard [Hibbett] I will ask to do Tanizaki and . . .

"I want to do Tanizaki," said Ed. "I did him first, and I do think best."

"But if you do Tanizaki, then Howard will have no one to talk about."

"So?"

7 JULY 1997. I went to see Hani Susumu, whose retrospective I want to do at Telluride next year. His films have never received their critical due, and that it was he who created the *nouvelle vague Japonaise* has been forgotten, though he is now locally very popular as the creator of African animal TV shows. We speak of this.

"You remember, when we were young and I was working at Iwanami, doing pictures like *Children Who Draw*. What I admired, no, loved in those children was their innocence, their enthusiasm, their vigor, and their naturalness. Well, we do not find children like that any more. We haven't for decades now. And that is why I turned to animals—to try to find the same thing. And I have."

"It's society's fault. I do not admire people, though I admire many persons. But I don't like what society does to persons. It perverts them. Yet, I don't want to attack society. I am not that kind of person. What I would like to do is to ignore it. Or, better, show something else. This is what I have done in my pictures—all of them, including the animal ones.

His wife, Kimiko, helps him, accompanies him. When she is out of the room he says, "There was another reason. When I was divorcing Sachiko [Hidari, Kimiko's sister], I wanted to cause my wife the least possible trouble—and there was, you remember, a big uproar in the press—and so I just left. I went to Africa and I discovered the animals, and myself."

22 JULY 1997. I read about the bonobo ape, which behaves in a way curiously familiar to me. Whenever it runs into difficulties—experiences stress as it were—it starts to rub its genitals, and those of anyone else around. The behavior is so unselective, so gregarious, that reproduction cannot be its aim. Its aim is successfully using sex as a substitute for aggression.

Looking at myself and making a comparison with the ape, I wonder if I am so filled with aggressions that I too am attempting to use sex as substitute. That is, when I am successful and can find the kind of sex I find appropriate.

When I cannot, however, as in this changing demography, and when I do not redefine what is appropriate, then aggression turns against me. I do not work; I do not really socialize; I take it out on the weaker, and experience that immovable-object, irresistible-force syndrome that is neurosis if I can cope with it, and psychosis if I cannot.

25 JULY 1997. The Kawakita Prize ceremony, the fifteenth. This year it is Imamura Shohei, who now walks with a cane, unsmiling as always, unconcerned with all social niceties, and when he speaks he does so with the unconsidered candor of a farmer. At the same time, he is capable of capturing on film the most delicate of nuances, the most excruciating of social patterns. I remember his calling himself a farmer once. This was when he said, by way of comparison, that Oshima was a samurai.

Oshima not there, but [Tomiyama] Katsue and I talk about him. Still in his wheelchair. She says the trouble now is psychological—he will no longer try. His wife is in worse trouble—psychiatric.

With Okajima Hisashi I talk about the sorrows of the Film Center. With his superior, Mr. Oba (they always move to different rooms at parties), I talk about smoking. Which he still does. "*Warui yatsu,*" (Bad man)," I say. "*Warui yatsu hodo yoku nomu* (The bad smoke well)," says he.

29 AUGUST 1997. "We saw you yesterday," I said to Ed. "And what was I doing when you spied upon me?" he asked, "And, who is we?" "You were wearing your orthopedic shoes and carrying your cane and off to goodness knows where. We saw you from my balcony. Gwen and myself." "How often do you see her?" he wondered. "About once a week." "Well," he said, "that is much more often than I get to see her."

We were lunching with Karel and Ed was an hour late, having broken his glasses, gone to the optometrist, and then taken a taxi, which took over half an hour to accomplish what the subway could have in ten minutes. He was consequently a bit surly.

"Now, now," said Karel. "Now that you are here, let us least have a civilized conversation." This he began by asking the state of Ed's memoirs ("tolerable") and my memoir block ("permanent.") "Oh," said Ed, upon hearing this, "Why ever? It is so easy, and so interesting. I am already almost an adult." "Almost," I said.

We then talked about great memoirs. I said the finest was Nabokov's [*Speak, Memory*] of which, oddly, neither of these cultivated men had heard, and the second was Sartre's [*The Words*], which they had heard of but not read.

Gwen appeared from another table. "Oh, Ed, we saw you yesterday . . ." she began.

"I have heard all about it," he said.

6 SEPTEMBER 1997. I had the Hanis, Susumu and Kimiko, over for dinner. After dessert, Susumu tells me how much he loves Kimiko, how this love grows. All of this in front of her. He says he first met her when she was fifteen, and he was thirty, twice her age. Fifteen, a child, and he knew he loved her at once.

This is not like most Japanese conversations, but then Susumu is not like most Japanese. While warm and compassionate, he has no patience with empty etiquette—what you talk about and what you don't. In this he is like his father, Hani Goro, who was famous for his shortness with the conventional and his warmth to others.

Reminded, I asked something I had always wanted to know: How did his father die? He looked up and then said, "I think he willed himself to. He decided he had had enough. He thought he would die, and so he did. He wasn't sick, you know." Then, "And how will you die?"

We talked heart for a bit, and then he reverted to Kimiko. "Fifteen, imagine. I wanted to be a child molester." He did not mention the other taboo, the fact that the fifteen year-old was his wife's sister. That they did not talk about [Hidari] Sachiko meant, I thought, that I couldn't.

But then I realized that I was behaving in a manner much more Japanese than they were, so I talked about her. Both were mildly interested, as though in some distant relative, while Kimiko sat there looking just like a younger Sachiko.

"But I did the right thing," said Susumu smiling just as he used to smile when he was twenty. "I left Japan because of all the media harassing. And I discovered Africa. And Kimiko came with me. We discovered it together. I changed my life."

9 SEPTEMBER 1997. Lunch with Karel and Ed—our last for a time: Ed to Honolulu, Karel to Amsterdam, and me to New York in just two weeks. "This is our Last Supper," said Ed solemnly. "Actually, our Last Lunch," said Karel. I then wondered if Christ had had a Last Breakfast as well. We agreed it was probably something light—just coffee and toast.

When we got around to literature, Karel wondered what the great American novel was. Ed and I told him that it was *Huckleberry Finn*, botched though the ending is. *Moby Dick* was too pedantic. Ed suggested some James, ". . . but not late—middle." Hemingway? Wondered Karel. No Hemingway, we agreed.

Got around to Irish women. I hoping to goad Karel into marriage, but Ed thought we were talking about the president of Ireland, and so that got us nowhere. Then Ed announced that he had probably just been to the sumo for the last time. It was the pain of getting there—he and his bad legs, his cane, and all those stairs. "And I sat there and I thought, well, this is probably the last time I will sit here." Small, sincere tears appeared, and I, in deference to his feelings, did not ask, as I usually do, what is so attractive in the sight of two fat men pushing each other around.

Dinner with Ed as well, this time in company with Howard Hibbet, John Nathan, and Kato Mikio of the International House, our host, and sponsor of the translators' seminar over which I am to preside next spring. There was some talk of translation difficulties. One then occurred.

The waiter announced that the fish that night was *kanpachi*—and none of us, including him, knew the English name. This sent him upstairs for the dictionary while we waited hungry, and brought him eventually back with the desired entry—amberjack. After all of this, none of us ordered it.

10 SEPTEMBER 1997. I see that an earthquake machine has been temporarily installed in front of Ueno Station. It consists of a kitchen (sink, gas ring, table, and chairs) set on a platform attached to a motor. The public is invited

to enter (taking off shoes first) and sit on the chairs. The motor is turned on. The kitchen shakes. One is supposed to turn off the gas, then crouch under the table. This a number of people do, cheered on by a man in a panda suit.

11 SEPTEMBER 1997. The Kudara Kannon stares back at me as she has so often. This time, from the front page of a newspaper. She is no longer at Horyuji. She is in Paris. Always stylish in that elongated fashion-mannikin kind of way, she now looks positively chic. Made in the seventh century and seeming her age, she nonetheless exudes that assurance and poise we associate with beauty. She could be a modern anorexic model with acne.

24 NOVEMBER 1997. It has begun once again—the rash of performances of Beethoven's Ninth Symphony that so disfigure the year's end in this country. There will be, it is estimated, two hundred renditions in Tokyo alone. Why? I wonder. One understands the Christmas invasion of the *Messiah* in England. After all they like oratorios and it is, after all, a Christian land. But why Beethoven's difficult and vulgar score in a non-Christian country, which does not have the resources or the disposition to create proper performances.

Reasons are offered: It was first performed by a German POW band (a large one apparently) in 1918, and this began a trend. Another reason is that the end of the year is otherwise a time of financial depression—one needs an ode to joy. Another says it is a strategy to generate much-needed New Year's cash, since all the family and friends of chorus members must buy tickets. Yet another says it is an excuse for large numbers of Japanese to get together without having to talk—a kind of a big karaoke.

3 DECEMBER 1997. Walking, I notice a young man, fashionable, long brown-bleached hair, artificial tan, and an earring, stopping young girls and trying to start a conversation, often failing as they brush by him. Nonetheless, all smiles and confidence, he is always ready to begin again. What perseverance, I think, and all just to pick up a girl.

From today's newspaper, however, I now learn what was going on: He was engaged in what such young men (hundreds, says the account) call "scouting." They themselves are called "catchers." Trying to talk girls into work in bars or massage parlors—in other words, pimping.

He gets a thousand yen an introduction plus a thousand yen an hour for his time. They work in teams of six, usually at stations or in the subway. Most can make about ¥150,00 a month. The girls make considerably more.

One of the scouts is quoted: "When you start your pitch never block her path; it puts her on guard. Instead, just walk alongside and gradually you reduce your speed, and then they'll slow down too. If you get them to come to a complete stop, then you've got them."

6 DECEMBER 1997. Went with Stephen Barber and Catherine Lupton to see the Kudara Kannon, just now back from Paris and stopping a few days at the National Museum before returning to Horyuji.

There she was, all seven feet of her, standing slightly sway-backed, a pose perhaps fashionable in the Asuka period. One hand lightly swings an oil flask, and the other is bent at the elbow (a very art deco pose) with the hand held out more as though to receive than give. I decide she looks *parisienne*.

But she is like that, always changing as you yourself change. I first saw her when I was twenty-three and she had not been dusted for decades. The fine powdery finish made her look human. Then I went to see her whenever I went to Horyuji, and each time both she and I had changed. The dust gone, her skin condition got better and, as the fashions changed, her Korean hat came back into vogue.

23 DECEMBER 1997. Yesterday Itami Juzo killed himself, jumped off his balcony. Or fell. I've been on that balcony; the ledge is very low. Maybe he was drunk and toppled. Or was pushed—this last is the contribution of one of the dailies. Lots of other attempts at accounting. There was this girl, or there was the fact that his later movies were not very successful, or there was the mob. I tend to favor the last. The local mafia was furious about a 1992 film he directed, *Minbo no Onna* [*A Taxing Woman*], cornered him in his apartment garage, and slashed his face. The movie says that *yakuza* never actually attack non-*yakuza*, but Itami's experience proved it wrong. Did they drive him to dive off the balcony as well?

28 DECEMBER 1997. Eithne [Jones] has a friend in the Imperial Household. Telling her about the speakers she is representing, she mentioned my name. "Oh, not that dreadful man," said the friend. The reason was what I had written about the Emperor or Empress in *Public People, Private People*. Taken aback, Eithne wondered what in my sympathetic and feeling account could have been taken such exception to. Turns out it was not what I wrote about them, but what I implied about the Imperial Household. She asked if their Imperial Highnesses were equally upset. "Oh, we would never show anything like that to them," was the retort. Eithne told me that the Household reads just everything and holds grudges for centuries.

Ah, there goes my decoration, my imperial *kunsho*. I was in line for one, and had even toyed with the idea of refusing it. It is all right to get awards from the Japan Foundation, but I do not want to be this much Japan's creature, have never joined the chrysanthemum club, and do not want to. My ancient aversion to joining anything raises its hoary head. Now I will be relieved of the decision, since I will never be offered the choice. [Richie, to his astonishment, was awarded an imperial *kunsho* (medal of honor) in late 2004.]

30 DECEMBER 1997. The end of the year—cold, raining. I look from my balcony high over Ueno Park and see that one of the homeless has built himself a cardboard house. As I look down, he emerges with a broom in his hand. He carefully sweeps away in the rain, cleaning up what is his front yard.

I remember another homeless man. This one lived under a bridge in Nihonbashi. It is to him that I owe my present eminence, since it was he whom I interviewed for a story, which got me my first job at *Stars and Stripes,* which led to others, during which I learned how to write. That was fifty years ago, and he was about the age of the man sweeping away in the rain. What was his name? Kiyoshi—Kiyoshi something. He had been put under the bridge by the war. This man has been put in the park by the peace. I remain, above it all, high on my eighth floor, looking down, wondering.

Richie's close friend, the journalist Gwen Robinson, in reading to this date, suggested that his entries were disproportionate—too much sex. It was not that Richie had had too much sex, but that what sex he had he wrote about, neglecting other aspects of his life. So, just as he had pruned the journals, putting things not directly pertaining to Japan in a separate annex, he now grouped together the entries about sex, some of them at least, and removed these from the main manuscript. This new entity he named after the Mori Ogai collection *Vita Sexualis*, and apparently based his decision—what to include, what not to—upon an observation of John Stevens, author of *The Cosmic Embrace*, that the erotic cherishes, celebrates, and elevates sex, but that pornography cheapens, degrades, and negates it; further, that erotic art presents the sexual experience in a bright, positive, and sympathetic manner, but that pornography relishes violence, violation, and perversion. Despite the fact that all of Richie's promiscuous encounters seem to have been both bright and positive, he apparently wanted to make a distinction.

8 MAY 1998. Ed Seidensticker has written a new book and there is a party for it. The volume is called *Lovable Japan, Less Lovable Japan*, but the title is the only part in English, all the rest is in Japanese. Indeed, it is Ed dictating to Shirai Maki (Herb Passin's friend), and her taking it down and then editing it. There is no manuscript and so I must guess as to what it is about. The Japanese title is more explicit—translated it would read: The Japan I Like/The Japan I Don't Like.

Ed has dressed for the occasion and wears a tie filled with large question marks all over it. Though he told me that he thinks the publication a "grave error" and that he hates such gatherings, nonetheless, he seems to be enjoying himself. In an expansive mood, he tells me something he remembers Gene Langston's saying to him: "You go up the hill or, if facing the other direction, you go down the hill." He admires this.

The party is held at the Kojimachi residence of Kase Hideaki, a political figure who has put money into the new film version of the life of Tojo, an effort called *Pride*. The man from the *London Times* keeps talking in scandalized tones about our being there at all, but journalist Sam Jameson says that is perfectly all right to be entertained in the homes of those of whom you disapprove—does it all the time.

Back in Ueno, I am stopped on the street by a young girl carrying an electric guitar and wearing just a slip, underwear, and a large childish hat—this being the fashion of the week. She asks me to go sing karaoke with her—asks in English. It will only cost me six thousand yen. Since this is one thousand less than I paid in order to attend Ed's party, I am tempted.

"You like me?" she asks. I diplomatically tell her she is very pretty. OK, she says, let's go. I tell her I am waiting for a friend. OK, he come, we all go. No, I say, not he, she. Her face falls. Oh, not OK then. But she gives instruction on how to get to this expensive bar for which she is shilling. I, waiting for no one, go home.

This is sign of the new poverty, grown considerably this year. Bar people are hard hit and throng the streets every night, showing off what charms they possess, and trying to entice the public. The homeless swarm, and there are lines at the garbage cans when the restaurants throw away their food for the day. Bankruptcies are daily, and suicides by disgraced Bank of Japan and Ministry of Finance underlings are weekly.

They always hang themselves, though why this is method of choice I don't know. Last month three such officials went together to the same hotel; each booked a room and each hung himself, using sections of the same rope—jointly purchased and cut into three identical lengths. They could have saved money if they had used but one room, but many people here like their togetherness separately.

9 MAY 1998. I go to Yokohama to see Kajima Shozo's new exhibition of poems and sketches. He is there in gray *monpei* with a dove-colored obi and lemon-yellow straw zori. Long hair, beard, the very picture of a *bunjin*, one of those literati so much a part of old Japan. When I first knew him fifty years ago, he was young, round-faced, all eyes, and looking toward the West. Then he was translating Yeats and Sherwood Anderson; now he is writing his own *tanka* and brushing *nihonga*. "You are so Japanese now," I say to him.

"Oh," he says, "but being 'Japanese' is very Japanese of me. First we look West, then we grow up and look East. Think of Tanizaki and his Bunraku, think of Kawabata and bonsai. We can't help it. It is part of our national character."

"I don't believe in national character," I said.

"You ought to. You are the most American person I have ever met."

This is in English. We have never spoken anything else. When we first met I could speak no Japanese, and we called each other Sho and Don. We still do.

"Don," he said. "You are my oldest friend. All the others are dead."

We have gone to a coffee shop and begun to reminisce. He is just back from Australia. The reason he went was that half a year ago he met a woman in the train on the way back to the mountains where he lives. She was fifty-something and they were much taken with each other—went to his place and made love. Then she invited him to Brisbane and he is just back.

"At seventy-four you still get it up?"

"She made me. She was my first foreign woman. I was so surprised. And every night too."

Then he went on to say that this nice foreign woman was not really the first foreigner. "Oh? Who was it?" I ask. Didn't I know? Sho wondered. Holloway. Some fifty years ago. In the back of a jeep. Sho had been shocked. Not sufficiently to escape, however.

"Holloway never told me," I said. Sho nodded, looking back half a century. "That was because it was not a success," he said. "I had to let him know I didn't want any more of it."

We nodded over our coffee, then he asked, "Why didn't you ever try anything like that with me back then? You did with others. I knew about it." I told him that back then I made a distinction between head and heart, and that Sho and I were all head—poetry, literature. My heart was given over to those with whom I had less in common. Those who were into sports, for example.

"Oh, I can understand that," he said.

Then we talked about whether he should marry the Australian. I advised him not to, since neither of them wanted this and also that this particular piece of paper, the marriage license, could ruin a relationship. "Besides," I said, "you are thinking of it only as a kind of insurance. Neither of us has anyone to take care of us, and we're both old, and anyone who might is already gone."

He sipped his coffee and nodded. "Yes," he said, "you're right. You see how American you are. No Japanese would have said that."

And so we sat, quietly, happily, friends for fifty years, until he had to go back to the gallery and I had to go back to Tokyo.

12 MAY 1998. The International House found the funds, and tonight we opened the symposium on translation—experts on Japanese into English. I remind the audience of what Shelley said about translation (. . . it must again germinate from the seed or there is no flower . . .), and then introduce Edwin McClellan who talks on Soseki [Natsume] and Shiga [Naoya]. The speech is elegant, and the answers to later questions are filled with charm. ("I don't know. Perhaps I just don't like some authors," he says.) Later at dinner I talk with his wife, Rachel, who is an expert on James Boswell. "Oh, yes," she tells me, "there are whole passages of the *Life of Johnson* that have never been published. There are two volumes of a complete edition out, but it is rather stuck now. There will be no end." Later yet, in the car going home, Ed Seidensticker says of the presentation, "Yes, charming, but I had expected more nuts and bolts. Mine is going to be more nuts than bolts."

13 MAY 1998. Fumio came over to show me the pictures he took in India. There he was on the steps of the Ganges at Benares just opening his trousers. He then removed them and in his shorts descended until he was crouched in the holy river. Around him people were bathing and brushing their teeth, upstream they were burning corpses, and the bits left over floated past. Then he poured the water over his head and did seven salutations and felt, he told me, a great peace. His tour party, waiting in safety on the boat, were scandalized and prophesied illness. Nothing, however, happened. He remains healthy.

I admire this. He wanted something so badly he went and did it. He is now very glad he did, even brought back some of the water in a little brass vase. Brought me some too, but then, since he was bringing it to me in hospital, he threw it out and just gave me the thoroughly washed vase.

After the Korean vegetable dinner Fumio produced an envelope. It contains money, which he is giving me so that Dae-Yung and I can have a really good Kaga *ryori* meal when we go to the Noto Peninsula week after next.

28 AUGUST 1998. Things looking bad for Japan—politically paralyzed, economically in recession, edging its way closer to a depression. Money fleeing, jobs disappearing, poverty growing. Japan gross domestic product has fallen four percent this year and eight percent since 1989. Public and private sector debts are estimated at around fifteen trillion dollars, which in proportion to the GDP, is much larger than the American debt during the "Great Depression."

I remember that. Canned tomatoes every day. Weevils in the flour. My grandfather appearing on Sundays with bags of groceries for the impoverished family. One early Christmas with no presents, as well—though that was later explained by my parents no longer speaking to each other and hence failing to prepare for the little lad's holiday, each thinking the other had probably done something. I remember lines of unemployed and hands held out. Maybe I will go out as I came in, surrounded by other people's poverty.

I am already. As I was walking back from the subway a wild-eyed, frantic old man busy running along the pavement and eying the people, fixed on me as likely quarrie. *Haro, haro*, he croaked. Had I stopped he would then have somehow tried to communicate his need, thrown himself upon my foreign mercy. But I did not stop. Like everyone else I did not hear; I brushed by.

30 AUGUST 1998. Am reading a new book on Chekhov and find a surprising entry in an 1890 letter to his editor. He had met some Japanese women ". . . with big complicated hairdos, beautifully dressed. . . . When, out of curiosity, you use a Japanese . . . she shows an amazing skill in this business, so that it seemed to you that you do not actually use her but participate in a top-class horse-riding event."

I SEPTEMBER 1998. A morning call from Tani [Hiroaki], wondering about my health. When I called him last year to say I was going into hospital he was a bit distant. In his business (construction) you have to be—politicians on one hand, gangsters on the other, both wanting money. Maybe he thought I wanted some, too. I did not, but I also did not call him again. He has been thinking it over, hence the call this morning—we have been friends for too long now to just drift apart.

Satisfied with my health, he spoke of other things. No, he does not need Viagra. He is only sixty-five and twice a week is quite possible. And who with? The youngest of his collection, though she is already thirty-nine. He must go out and shop for another. That is the problem. Once the purchase is made it is all right, but the acquiring of it takes time and energy. I tell him I know just what he means.

4 SEPTEMBER 1998. Walking in a park, a familiar figure—Ed. He says, "As you are perhaps unaware, I often spend an evening in Asakusa." I accompany him to the bus stop. On the way I see a young scaffolding worker to whom I had recently spoken. On his own in the park, he had also worked at a Shinjuku host bar. So I now ask him, "Going to climb higher or dive lower?" He smiles and says he will stay at sea level. Ed understands the words but not the context. "Well," he says, "You certainly have a way with the wildlife."

5 SEPTEMBER 1998. Lunch with Gwen, here for a few days to close up the place where she and Tim lived. Says she sat at the kitchen table and cried. Had no idea she would take it so hard. I ask if it was love. "Oh, I don't know. I don't even know what love is. Some combination of respect and wild sex—if that's love then this was it." I say consoling things about eggs in baskets and the need to move on. But she, so admirable, has herself under control and is outlining what she plans: go to London for the job, then to a friend's wedding, then back to Australia. She blows her nose and shakes her head. She is herself again.

6 SEPTEMBER 1998. Tonight I learn that Kurosawa is dead. The *Asahi* calls up for a statement. I say what I believe. Then add that I most admired his bravery, his making *The Bad Sleep Well*. The girl interviewing me on the phone asks if I knew that when the Kurosawa Retrospective was held at the Chanter Theater a few years ago, the Toho film company vetoed its being included and so it wasn't. I said I was not surprised, and as I was saying it I realized that there is now no one in all of Japan who would be brave enough to make *The Bad Sleep Well*. After I have hung up, I think about him lying there, in his house. That tall, big-boned, large-handed body that I never once saw in repose is now motionless.

23 SEPTEMBER 1998. Back from the U.S.A.—taught once more how young Japan has kept me. Over there I am suddenly Urashima Taro, gray, ancient, friends and family dead—a Rip Van Winkle. I am old, damaged, withered, and all things have changed.

However, this is also cause for rejoicing as well. I am still young, at least while I am in here in Japan, sheltered from the great, racing wing of time.

Things change here too, though, and I can enjoy the metamorphosis, but since I only came in the middle of the performance, as it were, the change is not great and, in any event, Japan has always incorporated change into its structure, so there it is nothing to explain.

The country where I was born makes no such allowance. So I am there a child of the fifties instead of, as here, a part of the late nineties. And here people can see me, and there, being a ghost, I am invisible.

26 SEPTEMBER 1998. How do you write after you know that what you are writing will be read after you are dead? Since you can no longer defend yourself, you begin early by protecting against any and all possible allegations. It is like planning the perfect suicide. You must think of just everything. Also, the need to make a pattern, any pattern, since it is the unpatterned that is to be avoided. And the drive for vindication, as if you had to prove your right to have lived. I think of all this while reading [Stephen] Spender's journals, and I think of it after looking over this one of my own.

Adrienne [Mancia] has told me that I always want everyone to like me and that this is a defect. She's right. If you want everyone to like you it means that you change yourself to fit everyone. You acquiesce, and this I certainly do. But only to a point. I will bend, but not break.

27 SEPTEMBER 1998. But I am also a descriptive journalist, and this I think more highly of. I want to be the person who penned the best likeness. This is a possible ambition, because for the last half century I have been in the best position to do so. Smilingly excluded here in Japan, politely stigmatized, I can from my angle attempt only objectivity, since my subjective self will not fit the space I am allotted. I am still complimented after fifty years on how well I use chopsticks, and so I become aware of using them—as I never am of using knife and fork, a feat upon which I have never once been complimented.

The person complimenting is, of course, being merely polite. The exclusivity he is implying does not occur to him. For him the word *gaijin* is neutral, a descriptive term—something we cannot claim for, say, "Jap," but one which moves just as readily off the tongue. We may interpret racist overtones in *gaijin*, but that is our problem, not his. Knowing this, I am aware of all words. I know that *okashii* does not primarily mean "funny" (dictionary definition), and that if I use it about him I am saying that he is singular, odd, and—in Japanese parlance—limited. I know that *omoshiroi* does not only mean "interesting," but can also imply the lightweight, the negligible, and the unimportant.

So, how fortunate I am to occupy this niche with its lateral view. In America I would be denied this place. I would live on the flat surface of a plain. In Japan, from where I am sitting, the light falls just right—I can see the peaks and valleys, the crags and crevasses.

30 SEPTEMBER 1998. Wandering in the park under the harvest moon, finding no harvest myself, I realize that I have become like those pandas that will eat only one kind of bamboo, a commodity that they have now eaten all up. Soon they will be extinct, done in by specialization. Concerned friends counsel me to the jungle-like swamps of the sauna, or the conversation pits of the bars, or the strict and narrow confines of the public conveniences, but this is not for me. Only the street, the corner, the park is authentic to me. Only that which is fortuitously found is real.

28 OCTOBER 1998. Loud chanting: "Long poles, we have long poles, poles for just everything, bamboo, bamboo, bamboo." This is an ancient street call, but now it is bellowed from a small truck with a big loud speaker. And he is selling plastic poles at that.

29 OCTOBER 1998. Walking back home through the park I meet one of the local transvestite prostitutes, the quiet one—round face, long hair, fat legs, the one with whom I usually pass remarks on the weather. I say that it looks like more rain and she turns to me, face serious and says: "I have cancer." I stop and ask where. She names the hospital. "No," I say, "where on your body."

"Oh, my lungs, it's my lungs." And as she speaks I see that her normally placid eyes are now disturbed, a small twitch at the corner of one of them. "Just today," she says, "just now, just got the test back, just have to tell someone. Sorry."

I ask if she smokes. If she does I can tell her to stop and she may get better. But she doesn't. "No, I drink too much," she says. I then tell her what little I know about modern medicine, but neither of us are convinced. Advanced lung cancer is fatal. "It makes you frightened," she says, standing there in her heels, her long hair held back with a ribbon, her eyes twitching.

17 NOVEMBER 1998. I ponder a new fashion: perilously high-soled shoes for young women. They teeter on something like six inches of superfluous shoe—boot, really. They lurch and spill on the pavement and in a group sound like a herd of elephants.

This footwear I compare to the high-soled *geta* of the Tokugawa *oiran*, the highest rank of entertainer/prostitute. They teetered on the pavements of the Yoshiwara and had grand parades where one could view them negotiating their way about—and still can in the Kabuki.

There and then, the reason was somewhat like that for foot binding in China. The women were expensive chattel, and were maimed in the same way that cows have ears nicked, brands imposed, and rings put through noses. The results were less instantly utilitarian, but the effect was the same: this is property.

Labor intensive property, and hence the more valuable. The patron of an *oiran* must have felt like the owner of a thoroughbred. And from this came the allure. Rich Chinese merchants, having crippled women so they could not run away, soon learned to savor the various fragrances emitted from the unwashed, curled under, slowly putrefying feet.

But how does one read these equally crippling new Japanese boots? From the woman's point of view the new fashion might be seen as enabling. Now she can be as tall as he, now she can have a military strut, if she doesn't topple over. Now she can also attract a bit of foot fetishism, and—of course, the clincher—she is in the height of fashion.

Are these fetters chosen? Is it a new way to balance femininity (which is all imbalance, the need for a male shoulder on which to lean), with masculinity (taking charge of one's life, forging ahead, jack-booted)? Men read it only as yet another new fashion, and none seem either to resent it or take advantage of it.

12 DECEMBER 1998. Another word everyone has forgotten. I go to the Little Mermaid Bakery and ask for *tomorokoshi pan* [corn bread], as I have for decades. The girl says she can't speak English. I tell her it is Japanese. She says she never heard of it. I point to what I want. Oh, *kon buredo*, she says.

On the way home I hear that Yodogawa Nagaharu, the popular film appreciator, has died. Lots of nostalgic talk about him. He never saw a movie he didn't like. Actually, in private, he was often critical, but never on television. No matter what, it was, oh, what a swell (*sugoi*) movie, wasn't it swell though? I wonder how it feels to live such a mendacious public life. He probably felt nothing at all. He was a performer.

17 DECEMBER 1998. When I look at others it seems I lead a much more conscious life. I am more aware, I notice more. Not that this is desirable. I notice to no point, to no end. It is difficult for me to be unconscious, just as it is difficult to go to sleep. This is nothing to brag about. It doesn't mean whatever Socrates meant when he said that an unexamined life was a life not worth living. Being conscious does not mean that you examine anything. It just means that you've left the motor running. You can't find the switch to turn it off, probably because your kind of consciousness is self-consciousness. I am always aware of self.

I wonder why I am not an addict of some kind. A druggie, or a drunk. I was recently called a sexoholic. Certainly I am as addicted to that as was ever boozer to bottle or gambler to game. It is like shopping, which can well become a substitute for living, something that preoccupies you and hides you from yourself. Other things work too, though not for me. Religion, fast driving, compulsive work. Or—and this *does* work for me—love.

In addition to the journals, Richie was writing *Tokyo: A View of the City* and doing a final editing of *Kumagai* (*Memoirs of the Warrior Kumagai*), to be published in 1999. He was no longer mining his journals for material for other works. At the same time, he was now editing them as he wrote them. Thus, only Richie knows what originally filled the chronological blanks.

7 JANUARY 1999. Kinoshita [Keisuke, film director] died on the last day of the old year. I did not go to the wake or the funeral, but I did sit down and think about him. A smallish, dapper man, demanding and sentimental at the same time. An air of undefined unhappiness about him, which made it easier to understand why he so threw himself into work. No family except that which he created on the set—his unit. Takamine Hideko, Matsuyama Zenzo. He married them to each other as though they were his children. Sada Keiji, Okada Mariko, other Shochiku actors—the family, the only family. All of those placid films about adolescents, usually boys, and then, like mountaintops, the peaks of a few films—*Twenty-four Eyes*, and others.

I remember once showing him a film of mine. Perhaps it was *Dead Youth*. He watched it almost greedily, but by the time the lights were turned on he had already pursed his lips and was shaking his head. Later he told someone (who told me) that he had been shocked, so shocked. Such a vulnerable man he was. And such a long death, well over a decade in that apartment in Aoyama. Today a card from Max [Tessier] about this death, and wondering who might be next.

13 JANUARY 1999. I am reading the journals of Ozu. They have been translated and Catherine Lupton sent me a copy. Translated into French, which makes for a certain oddness—Ozu's expostulating: "Zut alors!" They are curious in other ways as well. I cannot imagine why he kept them. Each entry reads like a social calendar, though it may also include the weather, how he felt, and what he ate. Certainly what he saw—he went to the films every other day. Rarely did he indicate how they struck him. Only occasionally—nothing extraordinary about *La Kermesse Heroïque*, not too impressed by *All About Eve*.

But he knew everyone, and saw everyone all the time. Many entries about being with Shiga Naoya, being with Takamine Hideko. Among the directors he apparently socialized most with were Shimizu Hiroshi and Uchida Tomu. And every night a dinner or a party or a bar. Bars with names like Florida and Candy, geisha houses, hotels. And lots of drinking. "Tonight, again, I overdid it. Upset stomach."

31 JANUARY 1999. I went to a memorial concert for Hayasaka Fumio, through whom I first entered the Japanese film world. They played first an early work, the 1937 *Ancient Dance*, a bit like Gagaku, something like the later score for *Rashomon*. At the end they played his last work, the 1955 *Yukara*, a suite based on Ainu folklore: strong, personal, dissonant, raw—a kind of *Sacre* from the far north. Takemitsu told me once how he cried when he first heard it—for the music but also for his dead teacher, Hayasaka.

In between, the 1948 *Piano Concerto*. I had heard it at its premiere. I was sitting in Hibiya Hall, and there was my friend smiling and bowing from the stage. I now wondered what I would remember of it, as I had not heard it since. Nothing of the rhapsodic opening lento was familiar, but when the rondo started—oh, of course, how could I have ever forgotten it? An engaging pentatonic tune that went through its possible permutations with assurance and charm, and always landed on its feet. And as I listened I relived my five-decade-old delight. It was like meeting Hayasaka again.

1 FEBRUARY 1999. I talk about the Occupation, a panel with only me and Nishiyama Sen on it, a "Luncheon Discussion," as the Press Club calls these things. Afterward, questions. I am asked to account for films, and Sen is asked to account for Reischauer. "Was it not true," asked Sam Jameson, "that you were to make a mistake or two in translation so that Reischauer could publicly correct you and hence know more Japanese than even a Japanese?" Sen denies this.

2 FEBRUARY 1999. I buy a plastic shopping bag to carry home groceries and on it is written: "Knowing—where you're blowing getting to where—you should be going—Golden rain—bring you riches all the good things—you deserve now. Find your way out of Silent Forest."

Opening up a Lotte Choco Bouchée, I read: "Confidence of creating deliciousness. This tastiness can not be carried even by both hands." Slowly chewing, I meditate upon this strange culture that makes so free with mine. Such English as this affects them only as something pleasantly modern, but it makes me believe that I am living in a world where behind every object— a shopping bag, a chocolate cookie—lies paranoia, madness, violence, and death.

12 FEBRUARY 1999. Took Karel to lunch. He says that Japan's only way out of its dilemma is through some kind of revolt that would stop the machine, overturn the bureaucracy, but that he could not imagine it happening. I told him that Nagisa Oshima had said that this had occurred only three times in Japan's history: the Tempo Reforms, the beginning of Meiji, and in 1945. And each time the structure re-crystallized, and petrified. We agree that there are no villains, no tyrants; the problem is structural: this model no longer works in 1999.

17 FEBRUARY 1999. The Hanis, Susumu and Kimiko, take me out to lunch, a new French restaurant specializing in fish. This is in return for my having designed his retrospective and gotten it on the road—where it still is, showing in Toronto this week. I am satisfied that I made this happen, and he is satisfied that it did.

Miho, his daughter is there too. How much she is like Sachiko [Hani's first wife], and she is just now about the same age Sachiko was when I first met her. The same slightly shy way of looking at you, the same modesty. This is now all lost in the mother, but it lives on in the daughter.

21 FEBRUARY 1999. How much greater the display of public anger now that portable phones are everywhere. Never have I heard so many voices raised in ire. A boy with gelled hair shouting into his receiver, adopting that abusive yet whining tone of the wronged young. Seeing that he is observed he begins to gesture as well (though with only one hand)—the clenched fist, then fingers splayed in displeasure.

Very shortly, a fat *yakuza* with a permanent, pinkie in the air, rolling his consonants and calling the other party *omae* and *temae*. Seeing me watching he scowls and turns away. Later, a young man in a gabardine suit shouting into his phone and at the same time pissing on the seats of the parked bikes in the small shelter where he is standing. Noticing that he is observed, he just stares back and then starts to shout again.

I think this kind of behavior (except for the pissing) is only possible because of the portable phone. It is not anonymity that it offers, but distance. The other party cannot get back at the caller, cannot reach out and rebut.

11 MARCH 1999. In my readings I find that in the Edo period, incense was thought of so highly that the term *kyara*—meaning highest-quality incense—became one of general approbation. *Kyara* clogs meant high-quality clogs, kyara women meant beautiful women. Also, find out that there was an Edo term indicating dangerous extravagance. *Kuidaore* meant an overweening taste for fine food, *kidaore* for expensive dress, *hakidaore* for lavish footwear. The implication was that this was a weak point, a source of ruination—particularly for those from Kyoto and Osaka who had come to fashionable Edo.

18 MARCH 1999. [Numata] Makiyo took me out for a birthday dinner and brought along his daughter, Maki, now five. She is beautiful, a little girl version of him. They are very close, she and her father. He no longer speaks baby talk to her because she is no longer a baby, but he still dotes on her, and she on him. There is also a younger child, and I hear yet another one due next month—all girls. He says he wants a son, too. I ask if he is using the lottery method—try and try again.

We talk about what we have in common. Our travels together, his family, but we do not talk about the fact that I at one time loved him almost as much as he now loves his daughter. This always baffled him but, being a good person, he went along with it so far as he was able.

I look at Maki, much as her father must have been as a child, and wonder why I felt so strongly. Then, turning to look at him, late thirties now, my friend for fifteen years, I realize why—he is like a son to me.

25 MARCH 1999. Tani calls. Also he wanted to tell me that he has become a grandfather. "That daughter of mine," he said, "thirty-four, now. Always was lazy. Just slid under the wire, got the baby out. Nice little boy. They named him Kohei. Two months old now. I went to the big shrine here with them today. First time I ever went there. Nice place. Then we all had dinner." About India: "Did you see any crocodiles?"

Consistency . . . Tani does not change, no matter what happens. This is, in the flux we live in, reassuring. Tani was interested in crocodiles at twenty-five, and he is equally interested at sixty-five.

27 MARCH 1999. Re-reading Kawabata, *The Sound of the Mountain*. Can anyone now understand him? I wonder. All those flowers, all those trees, all that regard that is now so un-Japanese that it looks sentimental. Young people, with their Walkmen and manga, their portable phones—not only do they not know one flower from another, they do not even see them.

17 APRIL 1999. My seventy-fifth birthday—diamond jubilee—lunch at the New Sanno Hotel, where University of Maryland was holding its graduation ceremonies, where I was speaker, and where I was awarded the degree of Doctor of Humanities. Wore a cap and gown, and was given a hood, with a white velvet lining.

Maryland has strong military connections here, and the hotel is a small bit of the Occupation, still working fifty years later. The prices are in dollars and there are other indications of transplanted America, all of which I found pleasing. There is a kind of symmetry. This is where I began, in Occupied Japan, and this, for one afternoon, is where I am ending—all that is left of Occupied Japan.

More, I liked the easy American good manners of the occasion. There was none of the solemn reserve, none of the inadvertent coldness with which many Japanese would invest such an gathering. People, the military (particularly the military) relaxed, out to put you at your ease. My dinner companion was a wing commander, and we talked about some existential touches he had noted in my speech and then went on to Camus.

2 JUNE 1999. With Michael Rayns to the National Film Center to see the Gosho [Heinosuke] *Where Chimneys Are Seen*. Since it was shot largely on location, there unreels 1953 Tokyo. The plaza with its statue of Saigo where I now walk almost every Sunday, how small the trees were, and how empty the view. I see the old Nikkatsu Theater down below, long gone, long forgotten. One of the scenes is right in front of where I now live. It is filled with construction and the lake seems smaller. Also there seems to be no Benten Temple, now the principal ornament of my view. The structure was the postwar I knew, but more than eight years postwar . . . ? What moves me most are the people—that friendly, ragged, wily, beautiful, and hopeful crew that I can never forget, even now that they are extinct.

4 JUNE 1999. Went to Maruzen for a photography exhibition—Meiji-period photos taken by early photographers including Shimoka Renjo. Scenes of the Fujiya Hotel, of Nikko, of all the other places early travelers liked. Also scenes of the various "professions"—naked palanquin bearers, a tattooed man, and a village girl, nude, standing, her hands crossed in front of her, all taken over a hundred years ago, everyone peering out from the sepia past. And all for sale. Meiji *meishi* prints, which even ten years ago might have cost a hundred yen in an antique store, are now half a million. Big prints are the equivalent of ten thousand dollars, twenty, and thirty. Such inflation is due to the snobbery that keeps things high here but, I suppose, such things are now rare. I saw no one buying. I wonder how much my modest fifty-year-old monochromes of Ueno are now worth.

9 JUNE 1999. A bill is passed today that specifies the Hinomaru the national flag and "Kimigayo" the national anthem. This will be followed in a few years by a bill that will make them, once again, mandatory. Already, last month, a school principal was knifed because he refused both at graduation ceremonies.

14 JUNE 1999. Early, a uniformed policeman comes to my door and salutes. He wonders if I would be so kind as to close my balcony doors from 10:30 to 10:45 A.M. and again from 12:30 to 12:45 P.M. The Emperor will be passing in the street below. I ask if I should draw the curtains as well—thinking of prewar customs when no one was allowed to look down on the Emperor. No, that would be fine.

I mention that his Imperial Highness has been driven back and forth under my window many times before without my having to close my balcony doors. He sighs, says he realizes this, and then tells me about the threat. He used the term *kyohaku,* which means blackmail. Since neither the Emperor nor the police force is blackmailable, I gather he refers to a bomb or something. I assure him that I will do as he bids, and receive again a smart salute. At 10:35 I peek from behind the curtains of my closed balcony doors, and there below progresses the modest imperial cavalcade—slowly and safely.

21 JULY 1999. [Oda] Mayumi came over for lunch, bringing me a new print—a green Kannon, very cool, reserved—quite unlike this ordinarily ebullient goddess. It reminds me of the Kudara Kannon, so quiet, so filled with dignity. We talk about goddesses in general and why they are so strong. She knows all about this, being a goddess herself. And strong. She and her lawyers stopped a plutonium shipment, turned it around in mid-stream, and sent it back.

Now she is here to show newer goddesses, one of which I have just been given. We talk about her fellow-goddess, Utako, who until age fifty sometimes had a twenty year-old surfing consort. Not now though, too much trouble. She uses some kind of jade implement. Showed it to Mayumi.

This again reminds of us of another goddess, and after lunch we go to the Benten temple, in the middle of a pond now covered with opulent leaves and bright pink clitoris-like budding lotuses, and Mayumi gives a copy of her goddess book to the gently surprised young priest on duty.

"If we were a couple on a date," says Mayumi, "Benten would break us up." "Lucky we are not a couple on a date," say I. But we are—I love Mayumi for her strength, her beauty, her acceptance of life, and her fight for what would hurt it. She is fifty-something now, and her fine, strong-boned face is lined with use, but inside she is still vibrating, the same woman I knew thirty years ago.

22 JULY 1999. I went with a new student, Karim [Yassar], to see a Kawashima Yuzo film at the film center. It—*Ginza Nijuyon-cho*—was just a program filler of the fifties, but it was filmed around the Ginza, and so I see again—living—the buildings, the streets, and the people of over forty years ago. There was the Olympia bread shop, where I used to find French bread, the only place in the city; there was the roof of the Matsuya Department Store that used to have plants for sale; there was the Sukiyabashi canal, with boats for hire.

Karim, fifty years younger than I, noticed differences in the people then and now, and wondered if they were always this friendly with each other, or whether this is just the movies. No, they really were. And I, too, noticed the difference. Now the young are closed, blank-faced, unsmiling, and hiding behind their portable phones or their Walkman or their held-up manga. They do not know how to look at each other, so they hide.

What catastrophe caused this? We wonder. Well, this generation was taught nothing. It had to infer everything, and did not do it well. Also, it demands nothing of itself—the latest gadget satisfies it; it goes to see *Star Wars*. What do they want, I wonder—other than a Sega game, a Prada bag? They can't all be as empty as they appear.

Karim says they are not. He goes to school with some of them at Gei-dai, and he finds pockets of spontaneity, particularly among young people who come to the city from the country. He finds the nadir in "Young Town," the land of the juvenile robots—Shibuya. There these youthful herds await a deliverer, someone to organize them, and a country to give up everything for. Someone like Mussolini or the Emperor Hirohito. Then we discuss the bill making both flag and anthem compulsory now being openly rammed through the Diet.

29 AUGUST 1999. More and more, girls are going out together. The streets are filled with their groups—sometimes in twos, more often in fours or fives. One notices because they are so noisy. They are always laughing. Hard laughter, as though it hurt, interrupted by squeals of simulated delight or surprise.

Boys do not act this way with each other. This is because boys are not trying to reassure each other. Also, perhaps, because boys do not have feelings for each other—usually. Girls, however, empathize. Each knows what the other has gone through. At the same time, each also knows that the other is a kind of rival for what those around her regard as desirable: a job, a husband, a child. So the empathy is wary and takes the form of continual reassurances and much noisy laughter to indicate what a good time we are having, just us girls together.

30 AUGUST 1999. The summer half gone. I walk in the evening in Sumida Park, maybe my first time there this year. It is still as beautiful as ever, though many more high-rises block the sky and there are no bats. The barricades for the fireworks tomorrow are up, and there are fewer people. I sit on a familiar bench, remember others with whom I sat there, and wonder where the summer went.

Ed and I were talking about the increasingly rapid flight of time. When one is older, he says, and he is three years older, time accelerates. Young, time is timeless, and a summer afternoon lasts a week. Old, it races, in a minute or two it is over. This is a blessing he says. Just imagine, he says, the other way around!

I sit and think about Nagai Kafu, who would this year be one hundred and twenty years old and whose big memorial exhibition I have just been to see at the Edo-Tokyo Museum in Ryogoku. There were not only the books and manuscripts, but also his glasses, his seal, his famous greasy hat, and his brown mohair suit with one of the buttons broken. *The River Sumida, Peonies, A Strange Tale from East of the River,* they were all written around here, though I do not remember this park being mentioned. (Others mention it, however—Saikaku for one.) But his spirit is here, the crumbling past, the passing time. He who regretted vanished Taisho would now regret vanishing Showa. Me too—and if I feel like that now, what will I feel like when I am dead?

1 SEPTEMBER 1999. Burt Watson came to lunch and we, two of the last survivors, talked about all the dead we shared: Herschel Webb, Gene Langston, Charles Terry, Meredith Weatherby, and Holloway Brown. Burt himself is holding up well. If I just glance, I see an old codger in a baseball cap. If I look closely, I see my old friend Burt there, owlish, and the finest translator into English of Chinese and Japanese poetry.

We talk of the strange way people have of regarding our companions. Ted de Bary drops in at Burt's place in Kyoto. Burt says, "I believe you've already met my friend, Noboru." Which he had. To which Ted says, "Well, I can't be expected to remember if that's the same young man you were living with before or not." To which Burt now adds, "Imagine someone saying, 'I think you know my wife already,' and you say, 'Well, I can't be expected to remember if that's the same woman you were living with before or not.'"

Then we went on to talk about the strange prevalence of people of like preferences among foreign Japanese specialists. I mention that someone is writing a book about this. "Oh, must read it," says Burt.

3 SEPTEMBER 1999. Watching some young people at the Fantasia [game center], I observe their satisfaction with all the virtual reality. There are games where you zap dinosaurs and the walking dead, others where you pilot fast planes, drive fast cars, others where you don helmet and glove and have adventures that I, standing on the outside of this reality, cannot see. And I wonder at such popularity.

Then suddenly, without trying at all, I understand. Virtual reality is never threatening. This is because it is always virtual and never real. And the reason for the preference is that reality is read as dangerous.

This is, come to think of it, what one would expect in a land where every mother tells every child that something or other is menacing (*Abunai da yo!*), where teenagers are continually advising each other about dangers, real, imagined, or hoped for (*Yabai da yo!*), and where a populace is careful, measured, and suspicious. One never knows where looking at strangers, much less talking with them, might lead.

Much better the manga comic book so you will not have to look at reality, even better the Walkman earphones so you will not have to listen to it, and best of all, the various virtual reality machines where you no longer have to be, strictly speaking, really alive any more.

It is possible to live a life of nothing but special effects. These are always virtual, in that they have no other reality. Fashion offers a beginning—hence its extremes: at present carefully grayed hair on the very young, chestnut faces stained deep with something that comes from a tube, lipstick (for the girls) that is corpse-like, and (for both boys and girls) carefully plucked eyebrows and sparkles that stick to the skin and glitter.

But fashion is still somehow too natural. It is attached to something that is real. Therefore, it is safer, to deny the real entirely and enter into a state (drinks, drugs, virtual reality) where nothing is real any more, and therefore nothing is threatening.

But what a world have we made for ourselves (for Japan is not the only place preferring the virtual) where we spurn the real? Japan traditionally has preferred something other than rank reality, to be sure, hence the classical Japanese garden, ikebana, bonsai, etc. But virtual reality was invented for those who are afraid. Therefore the world had to be fearful before it is invented and (in Japan more than elsewhere) perfected.

The couple I have been looking at laughs as they manipulate their buttons and it is impossible to say that this laughter hides fear. But then you do not have to know to be afraid.

4 SEPTEMBER 1999. Recently fewer homeless in the park below me. Could times be getting better; could the authorities be finally doing something? I wondered. There were now just a few, one or two of the more seasoned, including the homeless prostitute and two younger crew-cut types, always drunk, always abusive.

I saw them several nights ago, squatted in their hoodlum manner in front of a peaceable old man who had been a part of the scenery all summer. One was saying to come on, cough-up, and the other was saying that he knew he had two hundred yen hidden on him. I thought they were marauding high school boys, notorious for picking on the weak, and that they would tire and leave.

Today, however, at a train station down the line I saw the same peaceable old man, sitting in the midst of the commuters. I asked him what he was doing. He said that they had been run out of the park, all of them. It was now too dangerous. There were a lot of homeless *yakuza* (his term), and they took it over.

I then understood why there were so many fewer homeless, and I wondered that the jungle should be so near the surface of our ordinary lives, and that we should be so blind to it. I gave the peaceable old man some money, but felt none the better for it.

5 SEPTEMBER 1999. Talked with Philippe Pons on the phone, and he asked if I was still entertaining my *goût de la boue*. I had not thought of that term for a long time, but as I this time heard it I realized that indeed I was. Why else am I roaming the park? It is because of this "taste for mud" (the term does not translate too well)—but, I wonder, why then do I have this taste?

It is because I, like many another, confuse the "low" with the "real." Somewhere Bernard Shaw spoke of the sentimentality of linking the poor with the virtuous and making the monstrous assertion that to be penniless was to be good. I do something of the same. To me, the poor are more real, more "themselves" than the well to do. It is true that they live in a fashion more elemental—but more "real"? Or, is it because I am intimidated by the moneyed? They also have power. I prefer the powerless, because I am not intimidated by them. There is nothing intentionally sinister in this, but I must think more deeply about the origins of such inclinations as the *goût de la boue*.

4 OCTOBER 1999. To the Korean restaurant with Ed. We talk of various kinds of food, and he asks me if I knew that when cannibals eat humans they must be careful to also consume lots of vegetables, because otherwise human meat is difficult to digest. He says that there may be innate enzymes that prevent digestion. I say that this is unlikely; that the prohibitions against cannibalism are cultural. He is not certain, and then suggests that perhaps the genes could be trained, through careful cannibalism, to remedy indigestion.

This leads to talk of other kinds of odd habits. I tell him that the Goncourt journals speak of Napoleon's habit of rolling small pellets of his excrement while talking. Ed wants to know where it came from. Did he bring a bowl of it to table?

This somehow led to a discussion of the stilt shoes now worn by young women. What could it mean? He wonders. I say it means they want their legs to look longer. He wonders at the possible high incidence of broken ankles. Then he says that the country is truly changing. For years he thought that there was change on the surface, but the core was holding. Now he does not think so: the family system in ruins, the Confucian ethic dead, employment a shambles, and no one making children anymore. I say that these are late Hellenistic times. He says that shortly the last Japanese will go on display, like the last Tasmanian.

12 OCTOBER 1999. Dae-Yung and I went to Nagatoro, a place I had not been for over forty years—back in 1958 when Tani got married for the first time. I somehow remembered the cliffs higher, the boat ride bumpier. But this time it was fall and back then it was spring, and the water then was all mud and now it is green as jade.

Nor did the boat stop at the lair of giant carp, and no one jumped naked off the craft. We were sitting with families and their squirming children, and the water was so low there was no great pool for the giant carp anyway. I found myself remembering an even earlier time there, maybe 1951 or so. This time it was Meredith and [Yato] Tamotsu and Tani. He was wearing a suit for some reason, and Tamotsu was being very funny telling stories, and no one knew he would be dead ten years later.

I tell Dae-Yung about these memories, about this being my third time at Nagato. He never met Meredith nor, of course, Tamotsu, but he has met Tani. How old was he? He wants to know, knowing him only an elderly man. About thirty, I guess. So young, he says, now thirty himself, shaking his head at time, at life, as we drift down the deep green river.

Later, as so often, his thoughts turn to death—mine. He has prepared himself with various contingents. Until recently he was going to carry me up to some mountaintop and we would both live in a temple and bang drums until my demise. Now, however, he has given it up. Either he will come here or I will go there. In either event, he will take care of me.

I hope to die in hospital. It is the best among bad choices. They insure a more or less painless departure and clean up the mess afterward. The ashes will be taken by Dae-Yung and Fumio and dumped into the Inland Sea. They have agreed, and the lawyer has been notified, and dumping ashes is no longer considered by Japanese law to constitute the abandoning of a corpse.

We talk over all this while enjoying the flowing river from a restaurant window, looking in the late afternoon sun at all the fruits of the earth as we slowly spoon our persimmon sherbet.

8 NOVEMBER 1999. I go to the premiere of Oshima's new film, *Gohatto*. It is sober, serious, and beautiful. The style is recognizably his, but it is now autumnal, contemplative. He comes onto the stage, walking haltingly, his hand on his thigh as though pushing himself forward. After his stroke he created this film through will power alone, and now appears before its screening, standing there, upright, victorious.

In the audience is his wife [Koyama Akiko]—we bow. I would not have recognized her, so altered has she been by this illness and its cost. It is as though she herself somehow absorbed all that pain and despair.

9 NOVEMBER 1999. I go to the National Film Center to see *Umi no Seimei-*

sen, the first feature-length propaganda film, a documentary edited by Aochi Chuzo in 1933. It is about the Marianas and the Carolinas, and opens like a travelogue, with all the strange animals and fruits, with bare-breasted beauties and Yap warriors in loincloths. Then, bit-by-bit, its annexation by Japan is touched upon. The natives happily assemble to greet them—they are naked, but the Japanese are in full uniform. Eventually we have the natives in clothes and singing the Japanese national anthem and doing *banzai* for the Emperor. Then, with maps and martial music, we are shown why these islands are important and what would happen if they were threatened. It is like propaganda from any country, except for those animals and fruits and the long lyrical sequences of palm trees. Back then, Japan found nature just everywhere.

I then go to Ueno Station and eat in the station buffet—have a typical Japanese buffet meal: salted fish, seaweed, miso soup, and tofu—the sort of thing one used to eat all the time and rarely does now. And as I am eating the fish, I look around and remember these Ueno Station corridors fifty years ago when the natives lived in them among strange animals, like rats, and ate strange vegetables, like American rice. And they would have sung the American national anthem if America had insisted, and would have cried three cheers for MacArthur if required.

13 NOVEMBER 1999. Last night in front of the park three rental busses stopped and a number of people, all carrying shopping bags, rushed out and, encouraged by numbers of cropped youths in Puma sweat suits, began running through the park. This morning I heard loud chants and cheers that went on for a long time, and when I went out I saw the Puma boys, each a group of three, earnestly instructing them. One girl had to get down on the pavement and pretend to scrub it, in the meantime saying she was sorry and would never do it again. Another was instructed to approach all strangers.

Interested, I asked a cropped youth what they were doing. "We are a part of the Try to Be More Happy Group." I said I had seen them last night and wondered where they slept. "Oh, no one slept; we stayed up all night to prepare for being happy today." I asked how one managed to be happy. He explained: First, one signed one's name and address on these forms and then gave five hundred yen to join. Join what? I asked. "Oh, Nakamura Genpei's Happiness Group. You have probably heard of it." I admitted ignorance. The girl was pushing against me, pencil in hand.

"What is that woman doing scrubbing the pavement? Is that being happy?" "No," said the boy, "But our Teacher thinks we have to show some ex-

amples of unhappiness before people will join us in our mission to be happy."
I thanked him and walked away.

And this is going on at the very time when the Aum trial is announcing
some of its results. Today the driver of the subway poisoners is given life. One
poisoner has been sent to death row. And tonight coming home I see Puma-
suited youths in the park stopping just everyone. Getting nowhere, but stopping just everyone. Much later I hear them in park, exhausted but chanting
away, their calls now hysterical. Terrifying.

24 NOVEMBER 1999. I take Edwin and Rachel McClellan to lunch at Spago.
We talk about the suicide of his friend Eto Jun. "Sat in the bath, he did,"
said Edwin. "Slit both wrists. Very Roman." "Like Seneca," I said. "But by no
means instantaneous," said Rachel. McClellan is giving the memorial talk on
Eto at International House. I had earlier asked Seidensticker if he wanted to
come with me. "Not on your life," he said, "A perfectly dreadful man."

"His wife had died, you know," said Rachel. "A perfectly lovely woman,
and he was lost without her." I looked at them. She is lame and her husband
pushes her wheelchair everywhere, and they both handle this permanent impediment with patience and bravery. If he were to die where would Rachel
be?—or the other way around.

25 NOVEMBER 1999. Finishing the Alan Sheridan biography of André Gide,
I am filled with admiration. For the book itself, to be sure, but also for Gide
himself. In his eighties and still out on the street, as promiscuous as ever.
What an inspiration, what a model to emulate.

27 NOVEMBER 1999. As the economy collapses prices remain high. This is, I
guess, very Japanese. In some other countries there would be at least a few
merchants who would lower their expectations. Not here, however. There are
new alternatives (the hundred-yen malls), but nothing established lowers anything. Perhaps it is because quality is judged by price. If you lower the price
you lessen the quality. There is thus really no such thing as a bargain. Indeed,
some raise their prices as though to tempt through exceptional quality—this
is the way Wako Department Store works. The goods are in no way exceptional, but the prices are. Consequently anything merely wrapped in Wako
paper is first-rate. I remember tales that in the far hinterlands people used to
paper their walls with Tokyo department store paper, simply to give tone.

1 DECEMBER 1999. Karel [van Wolferen] back in Tokyo and over for lunch.
He is enthused about some new ideas he has been having: One of the reasons

that the description of the Japanese economic system has been so inaccurate is that all the wrong questions are being asked. When foreigners (particularly Americans) ask a question, their premises determine what it is—that and their agenda. This is not the way to approach it, he says, as indeed it is not. I mention that in the literary field, reforms have been going on for some time, to say nothing of anthropology, where it is has been determined that the very presence of the anthropologist determines what kind of information he receives. Karel is quite right, however. Such an idea is radical in economic circles. If you so rigidly depend on your own system of public and private sectors, you will not notice that Japan has none.

2 DECEMBER 1999. To International House to hear Edwin McClellan talk about Eto Jun. Spoke of him as a teacher and as a friend. The political persona was not there, since Ed, as he told us, never saw it. And so he heard others denounce Jun (who once left a dinner party because some American was there), but never understood why. He still doesn't—but gave us some indications. Those who hated him did so because he was one of "them" and not one of "us." The divide was political—after Princeton had provided for him, he then went and said that Marius Jansen waddled like a duck. Ed deplores this, but only on grounds of manners. He remembers his friend with warmth and sorrow.

5 DECEMBER 1999. "We are born, so to speak, provisionally, it doesn't matter where; it is only gradually that we compose, within ourselves, our true place of origin, so that we may be born there retrospectively." This is Rilke, as quoted by Coetzee. The poet, hating Austria (where he was born) and spurning Czech (his citizenship), decided to be French. I may have rejected the U.S.A. where I was born, but I did not decide to be Japanese. That is an impossible decision, since the Japanese prevent it. Rather, I decided to decorate Limbo and become a citizen of this most attractive, intensely democratic republic.

15 DECEMBER 1999. End of year, end of millennium. This one especially dramatic because of the computer chip crisis—the Y2K affliction: the fear that our machines cannot read past ninety-nine. This well fits the apocalyptic end of this most brutal of centuries, the one where it was discovered that violence was prime entertainment. People are afraid of the Y2K the way that children are afraid of deserved punishment. Made all the more delectable because we do not know what will happen. Imagine—trusting our lives to machines we do not even understand.

16 DECEMBER 1999. Still, for the other millennia people trusted gods and they didn't understand them, either. The difference is that the machines are ours. We made them. But, come to think of it, that is not a difference. We made our gods too. Since I early learned to get along without gods, have lived with a minimum of machines, spurned portable phones, e-mail, and Internet because I do not think much of promiscuous communication, I feel not superior but curiously out of it. As though there had been a party to which I was invited but did not attend.

17 DECEMBER 1999. Glenn Miller—the last popular music I remember listening to. Of everything after that I know nothing. Rock is noise to me. I missed most of American pop culture by not being there. I asked just recently who the Who was. This is not, I know, a loss—particularly in that I had other music. But I find it curious that, like Briar Rose, I managed to sleep through my generation.

I did so by coming to this magical land where everything looks much the same but acts sometimes otherwise, and where I was forced to share nothing—much less pop music. But, since I escaped all this, I can also know what Rip Van Winkle and Urashima Taro both felt. But they interpreted loss. I feel gain.

30 DECEMBER 1999. Japan shuts down earlier than usual this year. There is such poverty (recession they still call it) that every day's wage saved is a gain for the employers. Even the banks and post offices are closed. Yet there is little of the accustomed New Year emptiness. Most people have no money to travel, and besides they are afraid to—on the first day of the new millennium planes will fall from the sky. Against further threats people today crowd into stores—which will close tomorrow—to buy food, water, flashlights, and oil heaters. Electricity, that force that shaped our century, is no longer to be trusted. In a few days they will feel strange, facing their useless hoardings, but right now they fearfully buy. Me too. I go to the bank and take out enough money that I can live a week or two in case the cash machines fail.

Amid all of this, a rare public rudeness—people shoving each other out of lines, spiteful remarks at others fumbling at the cash machines. Just today the wife of a former prime minister was mugged—a man on a motorbike grabbed her purse and knocked her down to get it. This would not make the news in some other countries, something this common. Nor did it make the news here, but the reason was different. No one in the media wants to admit what is happening.

31 DECEMBER 1999. I go with Chris [Blasdel] and Mika [Kimula] to see in the New Year at the Benten Shrine in Inogashira Park, outside Tokyo. It is cold but clear, and the stars stare down as we walk through the chill to the distant shrine, the fire of which we can see through the bare groves. It is near midnight.

Then we hear cries and shouts and turn to look. There, on a bridge spanning the large pond, are a group of high school children. The girls are screaming with excitement and the boys have taken off their clothes and are standing on the railing of the bridge, one of them with his portable phone to his ear.

He is counting down, timing himself with the telephone company's exact-time service. His hand is in the air, fingers extended. All five, then four, then three, then two, then one. Then all the boys, five or so, jump off the bridge and into the pond.

The girls shout, the boys cry, out thrashing in the pond, the dark water now white with waves. Then, like otters, the boys clamber up the banks and dance around in the cold; one of them lost his underwear, holds his hands over himself and laughs.

Seeing us there the wet boys race forward and throw their arms around us shouting New Year's greetings. I put my arms around a student wet as a seal and we kiss each other's ears, then he races off as the girls squeal and again he jumps into the pond followed by all the others.

A temple bell is booming, the girls are dancing, the boys are clambering up the banks to join them, my ear is wet, and the fires of Benten burn, warm in the distance. For this one moment everything returns—it is the new millennium, but my fifty years have not passed. They have been for this time returned to me. "Happy New Year," sing the jumping girls and the leaping boys.

> **Originally Richie intended to permanently close the *Journals* with the above entry. And indeed, he wrote no more for several years. But, as he said at the time, he came to miss the daily record and, more important, living seemed to have less meaning when it went un-chronicled. Other writings for the year included his final book on cinema, *A Hundred Years of Japanese Film*. Also, in the following year (2001), Arturo Silva's *The Donald Richie Reader* appeared.**

20 JANUARY 2002. Ate lunch at the cafeteria at Ueno Station. Walked in, sat down, waiter appeared. "What's for lunch? I asked. "Mother and child over rice," he said. "Sounds good," I said. Ordered and ate *oyako donburi*, mother chicken covered with child egg. No one thinks this strange, and it is not strange in Japanese, only in English.

15 MARCH 2002. Lunch with Chizuko [Korn], the first time I have seen her since Frank's death last fall. Cancer of the brain, and I sat with him, my oldest friend, as he napped. And now, half a year later, she has been through the awful final days: the cremation, the scattering of the ashes, and the trouble with the daughters. She picks at her salad and says she has no idea what to do with herself—she is no longer Japanese (he made her an American citizen for tax purposes), and she no longer belongs here anyway. Still she is tough and brave and, somehow, smiling.

1 APRIL 2002. Last week, a day a two after his eightieth birthday bash, Ed [Seidensticker], finishing his morning shower, was drying his toes. The bending threw his artificial hip out of its joint and there he was, on the floor in enormous pain, and all alone. It took him an agonizing hour to get to the phone and then, when help came, it could not get in because he still had the safety chain on the door. The janitor had no cutting tools, nor did the ambulance. Finally, the firemen were called, and one leaped from an adjoining balcony to his; the door was not locked, and he got into the apartment, and when he told me about the fireman coming right in the window he again wept with relief. Now he is much his old self, though much muted about the inconvenience he must endure. He is in a wheelchair and will be in hospital for at least another three weeks. Then he will have to wear some kind of wrap-around spandex affair to keep his hip in place.

14 APRIL 2002. Ian [Buruma] interviewed me on the Occupation for his BBC radio documentary, and we then met Philippe [Pons] and went to a Korean restaurant. He, author of a book on the *bas-fonds* of Japan, has found a new *dohan kisa*, right around the corner from me. He has been twice, and says the clientele is younger than at the Shiro but it is also more expensive—and, of course, you still have to have a girl to get in. In Shinjuku, on the other hand, is one where you can go in by yourself and look away to your heart's content. Shows me where the Ueno one is. I walk by it every day and never knew. We discuss the *goût de la boue* that we both share. "I share it too, you know," said Ian, slightly put out by our exclusivity. No, you don't, not at all, we reply. You are married with a child. "That makes no difference," said Ian, defending himself, "I can still appreciate the *goût de la boue*." It had become a point of honor, I saw, so allowed that perhaps, just maybe, he could. We then went into a definition of terms.

15 APRIL 2002. Thinking about writing and how difficult it is to capture anything like the reality of what you are writing about, I remember what Kurosawa once said when I asked him the meaning of some scene or other: "If I could have put it into words I wouldn't have had to film it."

There is something then in the nature of words, of language, that prevents this apprehension. Perhaps it is because words must put things into code before they can communicate. The writer writes his encoding, which the reader, if he can understand it, decodes as he reads.

"She drew her dagger and stabbed him." Not at all realistic. Our minds trip over the words. They are too familiar and leave out all of the details that individualize reality. Already, what we wrote is a genre scene, resembling all others, lifeless.

"The glint of her silver blade, the dripping of his scarlet blood . . ." Also bad, but at least this kind of writing attempts to convey an impression, something like what we might have felt had we been there. A stab at uniqueness, but no bull's-eye.

In fact, try as we may, words hit no bull's-eyes. They are not made for that. They are made for general description, for describing genre scenes. But if you made this sentence into a film, then you would have a unique moment, done once for all time and packed with real detail, no matter how phony the event.

This too is encoding, but how different. This is because the encoding process is special. Read the above sentence, then see this scene (in *Rashomon*, except for the blood), and note the differences. One is more real than the other; one communicates (on one level) more than the other.

25 APRIL 2002. Though it is a bright spring day I suddenly, definitely, feel autumn. Why would that be? I wondered. Then I smelled it. Smoky, pleasantly unpleasant, reeking of the fall. I looked around. An unseasonal chestnut seller, his smoking cart (the nuts baking in hot gravel) sending this strange smell, which is to me completely autumn.

At first whiff I saw not the pleasantly, placid streets of springtime Ueno, but the dappled horse chestnuts of the Rue Canebière in wartime Marseilles, and the dusky streets of Brindisi after dark, the flares making holes in the night, and the dock at Bari, when the sellers came out after the sun went down and it was cold enough that the chestnuts warmed the hands. This was when I first knew this smell (none in Ohio), and it is to these images that the odor returns me.

Strange, the reality of this illusion. Proust says taste, but he could have said smell. They are the same. I stand there and see the past still faintly stenciled on the present, but fading as familiarity follows.

30 APRIL 2002. Out with Susan [Sontag]—had not seen her since last fall when she came to my Japan Society dinner right after she had been attacked on TV for writing her courageous assessment of the World Trade Center attack. In the short *New Yorker* piece she reminded the U.S.A. that there were reasons for its being so hated—that is all. "Oh, it got worse," she says in that fine way she has, as though speaking of someone else. "Death threats, midnight calls." I say that if that happened to me I would have folded up. "No you wouldn't, you just think you would. Anyway, you just wait till they stop." I ask what kind of people. "Oh, professional people, intellectuals, no low life." She tells me that *The New Republic* had an article that began by rhetorically asking: What do Saddam Hussein, Osama Bin Laden, and Susan Sontag have in common? Then answering it with: They all wish the destruction of America.

It is holiday season, Golden Week, and she remarks that there are no Japanese flags. We compare this with the U.S.A., where the American flag is now the most commonly found decoration—Stars and Stripes just everywhere, a country swathed in bunting. We discuss the implications of this triumphalism. "Well," she says, "this is the first time in history that one country has had this much power."

3 MAY 2002. Susan and I go to Asakusa, where we went during her first trip, more than a decade ago. "How clean it all is," she says. "I remember it being much more scruffy." Asakusa has been gentrified, turned into taxidermy, I say. We tour the neat little clutch of Edo temples, and she notices that they all now look plastic, even the real ones.

What will happen to Japan, she wonders, and guesses that the first thing to really go will be the banks. I tell her that everyone is now living on his or her fat, and since Japan was financially obese there is a lot of that. She tells me a "joke" that her son, David, told her: What is the difference between Japan and Argentina? Answer: Three years.

She finds much else different and at the same time now sees things she formerly did not. "These people do not know how to have discourse." Invited here for one of these expensive "conferences" among intellectuals, she tells me what it is like, and gives a very funny impersonation of a famous Japanese architect making a presentation. "And I saw this building. And it was very big. And I thought, this is big, very big."

I mention that the language does not really accommodate discourse, but it does encourage analogical talk, one thing leading to another, and I mention that in Japan it is *suji* instead of plot. At once Susan is interested. With her it is a way of learning.

Out comes the notebook and *suji* is spelled out. I tell her about that favored form, which looks no better written than it seems spoken: "following the brush" (*zuihitsu*), spontaneous nattering. I suggest that this is what the other people in the conference were up to. She writes all this down, and at once agrees that there are, certainly, different modes of thought, then she stops.

"Still, everyone is so corrupt—intellectually, morally." We cast about for reasons why this should be so, and she, only here a couple of times, hits upon the one real answer: "It is because everyone is afraid. They do not want to be punished. And this country is so crony-prone, so given to authority, that if you do speak out, if you are intellectually honest, you will certainly be punished. If the people on my panel spoke out they would not get invited to the next panel, architects would not get commissions. That is what I mean by corrupt."

Corrupt Susan is certainly not. Have I ever known anyone more honest, more forthright, more brave? I think not—nor anyone more moral. She can cut through cant; can see through any amount of bad faith. Just to be with her is to think more clearly, to become more courageous.

4 MAY 2002. I look from my balcony and see that two plainclothes cops are making a derelict woman move her belongings—a set of wheels piled with cardboard boxes, many shopping bags filled with newspapers—the kind of things these people cart about with them.

I used to wonder why, but I really knew. Why do I have books in my bookshelves and clothes in my drawers? It is because I am defined by what I have. My belongings are proof of me. If I had nothing, then I would be nothing. Me in a foreign city, me in the train, me in the airport—I always have my bags about me just as she does. And I imagine the panic I would feel if these worthless things were taken from me.

From high above I watch as she tries to wheel away her cart but no, they want her to go far away, not just a bit. They gesticulate. Far, far, far. So, as though reluctantly, she pushes her cart and tries to gather her bags. But, like all of us, she has too much.

Her further adventures I decline to watch, though I wonder why they are doing this to her. When I descend the street to go out she is gone, but they are there, radios in their ears. They are waiting for a royal—probably the Crown Prince or the Emperor is coming from Ueno, and these two have been given the task of clearing the roads.

5 MAY 2002. To the hospital to see Ed—a precise reprise of last year: in the shower, washing the feet, hip gets dislocated, finally reaches the phone, help comes, to the hospital, knocked out, hip manually reinserted. All this happened three weeks ago. He is sitting in a wheelchair, looks up, and smiles. "It seems the only solution will be for me never again to wash my feet."

I bring him the paper in which I review his memoir. This pleases him. And we speak of banks and the coming collapse, and he is of the opinion that it is richly deserved. Mentions that further injury was that he had planned to finally take out state insurance the very week the accident occurred. So he has to pay the enormous medical bills that Japan insists upon.

19 MAY 2002. The Sanja Matsuri in Asakusa, the greatest of festivals—thousands in the streets, over a hundred floats on the shoulders of naked young men (and some clothed young women, too these days), all noise and sweat and violence. And it went unseen by me, once again.

I used to be excited by it, used to go every spring, often with [Yato] Tamotsu, and I would ogle and he would snap away. He died (on this very day, the day we were to meet by the big Asakusa gate), but that is not why I no longer go to see the spectacle.

I don't go because I am not satisfied merely to watch. I am excited by it, and I want to touch it. Several times I succeeded, but now I find that the kind of exclusion I thought I was used to is still painful. It is so dramatic, this exclusion. But at least it is natural and understandable. What is less so is my ambition to be a part when I know that I cannot.

15 OCTOBER 2002. Rereading, after all these years, André Gide's *Si le grain ne meurt*, I find a compelling sentence. Of some incident he writes: "And if it is indecent to relate it, it would be still more dishonest to pass over it." Though I have nothing to relate that I consider indecent, it is Gide's constant attempts at honesty that continue to impress me. So this sentence is enough to push me to again begin some accounting for my days.

16 OCTOBER 2002. Most of my life has been spent regarding Japan—observing it, considering it, comparing it. And I have been happily occupied; have learned much I would not otherwise have known. It could have been any-place—even places I like better: Greece, Morocco. The results would have been much the same, since I did not remain where I was born.

But now I can see that I am getting older because there are waves of memory, a tide that wants to sweep me back to where I came from. This will not occur, but I must experience its effects.

I, who have spent my time meditating on difference, am now presented with "similarity"—what I experienced then and what I remember now. Forty-five years ago Igor Stravinsky told me that at his age (which is what mine is now), he could for the first time remember the *smell* of the St. Petersburg snow of his childhood. Now, just today, out of nowhere, comes to me the sweet, watery, taste of mulberries.

There was a tree in my aunt's garden, and I used to climb it to pick the white and purple fruit, to get it before the birds got it since, even back then, people did not much eat mulberries.

I remember the reason offered. The birds are fond of them, you see, I was told, and the seeds go right through them and so every tree is born from ex-crement and you don't want to eat that, do you?

I did not then know that many plants and trees thus grow, but I do remember seeing that this made a kind of dim bond between me and the mulberry tree, and that I ate more berries than ever. And now, suddenly, this remembered taste.

17 OCTOBER 2002. My balcony overlooks the great lotus lake. I am often on the shore, sitting there, enjoying my *goût*, nay my *nostalgie de la boue*. Why is mud so comforting? We have mud baths, along with sand baths and seaweed baths, where you are covered with the stuff. Medicinal claims are made, but I think it is the comfort of being thus lathered that attracts.

The only other time this will occur is after we are dead. Whether cremated or not, the remains are covered with earth. "When I am laid in earth . . . ," sings Dido, and Purcell sets these words to a descending melody of grave beauty, both accepting and celebrating.

The *nostalgie* extends to other kinds of *boue* as well. The other day, in the park, I smelled something I could not place. It was pungent and meaty, but at the same time it was rich, even opulent. And familiar, so familiar.

Tovey writes of a similar experience with a melody he knew well but could not place. It was ambiguous, beautiful, and difficult. And when he did recollect, it turned out to be one of Brahms' most famous tunes, but for a time rendered innocent again, luxuriating in its originality, freed of all those hearings that had made it famous.

So this smell, which I eventually identified as shit. Someone had shat in the bushes. The odor at once lost all of its interesting qualities. These were instantly replaced with thoughts of dirt, filth, etc. It was no longer a fragrance but a stench.

I stopped and considered. It was the same smell. It had not changed. What had changed was merely what I chose to think about it. Or had been made to think about it. My initial reaction had been the authentic one.

Walking slowly homeward through the park, the sun setting, the pond slowly disappearing into the dusk, I thought about my liking for mud, fecund mud. My equally strong attraction as well toward a different kind of mud—the smell of humans, their armpits, their crotches—even their smegma, which as a child I thought was a Greek island.

In the growing dark it seemed natural that I next consider the dead, these now useless bodies slowly disintegrating, and the sweet smell of death. All of this seemed a part now of the mud that nurtured the lotus, which I could come and see tomorrow morning blooming pink and glorious for just one day.

18 OCTOBER 2002. In Japan, the incessant urge to aestheticize—everything, from tea ceremony to capital punishment. What this means is bringing everything to an extreme order, which is then presented balanced, and regularized.

In the park I look at the homes of the homeless. Cardboard boxes precisely placed, a blue tarpaulin exactly draped. Inside, the found blanket folded as neatly as it would be at the Imperial Hotel. At one side a smaller box—this is for the shoes. The effect is not only utilitarian; it is also "beautiful," that is, in accordance with the principles of good taste. And this from some anonymous builder who is completely severed from the common opinion he still represents.

23 OCTOBER 2002. What phrase is most overheard in today's Tokyo? It used to be *sumimasen* (excuse me). Now it's *ima doko?* (where you at now?). But, apart from such portable phone use, the one I am hearing more and more these days is *hazukashii*. It is used in a very open fashion by men and women alike, and it describes self in an apparently attractive stance: being ashamed or embarrassed. I wonder why.

I cannot imagine an English-speaking nation where every other phrase is: "Oh, I was so embarrassed." Yet I have heard Japanese footballers thus sugar their remarks. Is this, too, a legacy from the police-state days of 1604–1858, where you were required to show yourself in disarray, to apologize for simply being, the shogun's power so internalized that being craven was good manners?

26 OCTOBER 2002. Coming back through the rain I am stopped by a young woman who asks me if I am Japanese. I ask if I look Japanese. She says not at all, but that sometimes foreigners just don't know where to go of an evening—she has a nice place and perhaps I would like to come. I decline, and she thanks me and proceeds. Hopeless to attempt to connect my perhaps appearing Japanese with her further request. I am like borrowed scenery, and her query was merely to find out if I could speak the language or not. If I could, I was potential. And the rain continues to fall.

28 OCTOBER 2002. Big moon out tonight, but small signs that all is not economically well. We have the newspapers to assure us of coming prosperity, but we have long ago learned to distrust the papers almost as much as we doubt the tube. The smaller the sign, the louder it speaks.

Usually I am ignored when I walk along the Nakamichi, that frantic little street in back of my apartment where every evening touts gather to cajole customers. The boys carry menu cards with pictures of girls on them. The girls themselves display their charms (bunny outfits and the like), and attempt to lure the *sarariiman* into their basement lairs.

Now, however, business is so bad that the passing foreigner is also accosted. You come my house? asks a hesitant lad in English. Why? I ask. Drink, he says. I shake my head. Fuck? He says, but so tentatively that it sounds like a conjuration, a spell, or a hex.

Earlier, Ginza, too. Business so bad that outside the pretentious Sony Building there stands a small girl dressed as an "English" maid with lace cap and frilly apron, and she is passing out flyers for the Briar Rose Pub. And over it all—the moon, now looking like an advertisement for something.

29 OCTOBER 2002. There are cats in Ueno Park, quite a number of them now. They take the bread from the pigeons and steal bits of dried squid and rice crackers from the sleeping homeless. In so doing they have become quite tame—once turned feral, they are now again domesticated. One of them is rubbing itself again the thin shins of the smallest of the resident transvestite prostitutes.

"Looks like you have a friend," I say.

"Only one so far," he replies, ruefully. "Really bad tonight. No customers."

"And you with a family," I say, sympathetically. I have seen him with two of his children and once with his wife. It is her clothes he wears.

"Well, there's always death," he observes.

"But you wouldn't make your family . . ."

"Oh, no, just me."

The cat purrs, rubbing itself on the man's wife's stockings. Then he adds, "We are all in Buddha's hands."

"Buddha's lap," I correct.

He smiles, "I wonder if Buddha's got a big one."

And the cat rubs and purrs.

30 OCTOBER 2002. Smells—they change too with the years, just like sights and sounds. On these very streets the odors were those of roast squid and broiled eel, of pickled radish, and above it the brazen scent of beer, and above that, like a piccolo, the schnapps-like whiff of *shochu*.

Now, though these foods and drinks are still available, the smells are the sweetish reek of the hamburger, the oily stench of the French-fry, and the costly scents of the young.

1 NOVEMBER 2002. All these homeless, all these liveried people trying to get you into their establishments, all the talk in papers and magazines about the new poverty—and yet . . . The new Hermes store is packed; so is the new Vuitton "Centre." So are the fanciest restaurants. People may be living off their fat, but how much fat can you carry around?

I also hear that this recession is really an engineered event, intended to fool the world, particularly the U.S.A., and excuse the criminal banks and the idiot government. I do not believe this, but it would help explain.

4 NOVEMBER 2002. Showing at the Press Club of that film about me, *Sneaking In*. I'd seen it several times before and was hence mostly over the shock of viewing myself as I actually appear rather than as I remember myself, or as I currently like to remember.

And again I am struck by how much I am like my relatives. The way I purse my lips, the narrow look—that is my mother. The measured gravity, the specious reasoning—that is my paternal uncle.

Have not before seen the film with my peers, however. They behave well enough. During the questions afterward nothing much except for one Japanese man, who is confused by the parade of personae, and asks, "Who is this? Critic, filmmaker, s/m addict?" (This latter inspired by a clip from my *Cybele*, a film made with the Zero Jikken, a group that would do anything.) "Who are you?"

This was a pertinent question—indeed, what the film had been about. I asked the audience what it thought. No answers.

10 NOVEMBER 2002. Leo Rubinfein over to ask questions for his book. He asked me what I most regretted having lived half a century here, and witnessed all the change. I said that I most regretted the loss of a kind of symbiosis between people and where they lived, a kind of agreement to respect each other. I again mention the paradigm—the builders make a hole in their wall to accommodate the limb of a tree. No more now. It is more expensive to make a hole than it is cut down the tree, just as it is cheaper to raze than to restore. And since the environment is now so different, the people are different. This is symbiotic, too, degraded environment makes degraded people who make more degraded environment.

And with it I regret the loss of a kind of curiosity. People used to be curious about each other. Now they have their hands full with their convenient and portable environment—Walkman in the ears, manga for the eyes, and the portable phone (which now contains their lives) in the palm of their hands. Many Japanese no longer look at each other, or those they talk to—those on that select menu of known voices on their phones they cannot see. These robots, I regret.

11 NOVEMBER 2002. Rainy Tokyo—and from my elevated seat on the Yamanote Line I look out at the thousands of revolving rooftops, glimpse the hundreds of streets stretching away from every vista, stare at the improbable complexity of this tangle of a city, and suddenly understand the affection of the Japanese for M. C. Escher. He with his thwarted perspectives, his people going up and down, over and under at the same time, his lunarscapes shown from left, right, above and under, simultaneously. This impossible sight from the Piranesi of our times is an accurate rendering of the experience of the Japanese capital.

13 NOVEMBER 2002. I read that it was Rousseau in his *Confessions* who invented the notion of the self as an "inner" reality, unknown to those around us. It is now so ingrained, and used to create such bad faith, that I thought it had occurred much earlier.

There is a quote, too. If he did not hide this real self, then he would have to show himself "not just at a disadvantage but as completely different from what I am." It was the disadvantage he was thinking of, hence his deciding that he was something else.

The Japanese (and many other Asian folk) have escaped this. There is no hidden and real self. Rather, the social self and the individual self are twins, living happily side-by-side, though occasionally quarreling. When getting along together, the social self is called *tatemae* and the personal is called *honne* and the combination is in the West called hypocrisy. When not getting along the social self is called *giri* (obligation) and the individual is called *ninjo* (inclination), and all of Japan's drama is made up of the consequences.

14 NOVEMBER 2002. Walking down the street with Paul [McCarthy] and Ed [Seidensticker], Japan specialists both, we see a youth approaching us." Oh," says Paul, admiringly, "Now that's attitude!"

What he is approving in the slovenly young is the way this schoolboy has altered his uniform. His shirt is open, the coat buttoned wrong, his pants pulled down so that the belt is far below the navel, and the crotch sways.

"No," says Ed, "That's fashion."

16 NOVEMBER 2002. What do I want to be when I grow up? An attractive role would be that of the *bunjin*. He is the Japanese scholar who wrote and painted in the Chinese style, a literatus, something of a poetaster—a pose popular in the eighteenth century and typified by Yosa Buson, and right now by my friend Kajima Shozo. I, however, would be a later version, someone out of the end of Meiji, who would pen elegant prose and work up flower arrangements from dried grasses and then encourage spiders to make webs and render it all natural.

The *bunjin* is useless, knows nothing of commerce and politics, tends to be something of a dandy, and yet in his own way strives after truth. Art is for its own sake, but it also has a moral purpose. It makes one a better person. Privately he is heterodox, and here history is mostly silent.

This budding *bunjin*, myself, writes in English rather than Chinese, is a talented dilettante in almost everything, but a scholar in his field nonetheless. For him, art is a moral force and he cannot imagine a life without it—but art does not mean pictures (though he paints) but, rather, everything—fiction, poetry, drama, music, and films. He is also the kind of casual artist who, after the day's work is done, descends into his pleasure park and dallies.

18 NOVEMBER 2002. I look out at the band shell. Only seven in the morning, but a long and ragged line. The jobless, homeless, waiting. In a few hours the evangelists will come and open the gates. In they will go, all of them, hundreds by then, and then the gates will be shut and locked. The seventh-day people will evangelize them with hallelujahs for an hour or two and then, having saved their souls, will hand out the rice-balls that are the reason the congregation gathered. And no one complains. The reason I know this is that one of the congregation told me. And this was not in complaint.

24 NOVEMBER 2002. Overnight, frigid autumn. North wind—that harsh edge remembered from winter—and shadows fading as cold clouds cover the sun. Why then, as I look out over the ruins of the great lotus pond, this sudden feeling of pleasure, of contentment?

It is because I am observing a great seasonal change, because I am here to do so, and to do so in comfort. It is because I am old and have many of the advantages of age.

I no longer care what people I don't know think of me. And I take the opinion of those whom I do know lightly. I am no longer afraid of empty surmises. I am freed of the tyranny of my loins, if not yet from that of the loins of others. I am no longer afraid of my future since my future is already here, and my seventy-eighth year is my happiest yet.

25 NOVEMBER 2002. Ginza. I look about me. Not a sign of traditional Japaneseness. And to expect it would be like expecting powdered wigs in Philadelphia. Yet search we do, we foreigners. But since no one looks for colonial attributes in the U.S.A. why look for kimono in Japan?

One reason is that we occasionally see them. Another is that the Japanese make a big fuss about their traditional "heritage." Yet another is that the past is centuries deep in Japan, and though erosion is swift and the water is rising, islets of tradition still float by.

Japan started late in the business of being modern. Before that it was timeless, a flat expanse with occasional eddies of modification. Consequently there is a backlog of tradition. But being traditional is nothing that inspires a contemporary young Japanese. Indeed no distinction is made between now and then, and if something old is useful it will be incorporated with no consideration, and if not it will be tossed out.

What I had thought a wall between the Japanese and the foreign no longer exists. And any barrier between then and now has been destroyed as well. And why not? This has gone on for centuries, and the destruction of tradition is a part of tradition itself. We do not remark on this in countries with shallow histories, only those with deep ones.

26 NOVEMBER 2002. In this signaling system that is life we must examine our own earpieces before we use our mouthpieces. We must learn to distrust ourselves, our own apparatus. Instead of assuming that the other made a mistake, we should at least admit the possibility that we did. This is particularly necessary in ascribing motives. How many times have I erred—allowing my agenda or my paranoia to garble the message?

Since my life has been spent in translating, in comparing and judging, my opportunities for error have been more than for many. Years ago, I was attempting to bend a younger person to my ends and he used a word I did not know that ended in *kusai*, a word I only knew as "stinking," "putrid," and so on. I at once took this as an insult and stalked off. Later, I heard the word again and this time recognized it as *terukusai*, a simple phrase meaning, "I'm embarrassed."

28 NOVEMBER 2002. Student eating sandwich on the subway. Egg salad, I think. Big Adam's apple bobbing above a celluloid collar. Very intent on delicate task, egg salad being what it is, and not a glance for those around him, no indication that he is not at home alone.

That is the difference. Even five years ago there would have been some concern at being thus seen consuming. A lapse of decorum—that is how it would be viewed. And still is sometimes. An older woman across from the youth is regarding the spectacle (some egg salad has just dropped onto that black gabardined lap) with a cold gaze. But she will die, this old woman, and the youth will grow to manhood and middle age.

The young may still talk about being ashamed or embarrassed, but this is merely a conversational ploy. No one under twenty feels the kind of social restraint once standard. Now not only does youth eat and drink in full view, but they also (boys and girls alike) pluck eyebrows and pop pimples. Also (just girls this time) put on full make-up in public—lipstick, rouge, and mascara.

Is this a Good Thing? I find it difficult to become as indignant as does the old lady, because it argues for a certain freedom which the young did not before express. Also I remember that the old lady's generation (the men at any rate) pissed freely in the street, something today's youth would not think of doing.

30 NOVEMBER 2002. Fumio for dinner. His birthday, his fifty-third. We met when he was twenty. Now, passion long spent, we are good friends, meet every week or so, and take a selfless interest in each other. I ask about his daughter, Haruka, and he asks about Dae-Yung, the son who took his place.

Over our tandoori chicken he asks me if I was ever interested in someone my equal. Since this was in Japanese he could ask it, no matter how strange it now sounds in English. I suppose it could be translated to mean had I ever "fallen in love" with anyone with the same "general interests," that is, caste/class. In any event the answer is no.

My interests are entirely in differences. The beloved other has to be all things I am not, though I might wish to have been. Dae-Yung, a soccer champ, not interested in books or movies, straight, much more interested in action than in cogitation.

I ask Fumio about himself. Oh, no, for him it is similarities that attract. His wife, for example. Or me. Now wait just a minute, I thought. How come his difference attracted me, and my similarity attracted him?

As though I had said it aloud, he smiled, put down his fork and said, "Maybe I was not much like you at first, but I became like you. You had more influence on me than anyone else. You didn't see how much I had grown like you, and when you did we stopped making love and became friends instead."

I had not known that before.

3 DECEMBER 2002. On the plane coming back from Korea I sit across the aisle from Kitano Takeshi. We are both returning from the Pusan Film Festival. Now he has opened a large, blank-paged notebook, the kind used in primary school, and is scribbling in it, the writing large, unformed. He is creating his new film script.

This is the way he always works. He fills notebook after notebook, and these he presents to his associates. They all sit down and read them and then cobble together a scenario. After Kitano approves it, production begins. Filming is accomplished in an analogous manner. Something shot is inspected. If everyone agrees, it is used. If not it is discarded and the scene is rarely re-shot.

He nods as he writes, apparently agreeing with what his hand is doing, and then starts on a new page. There are many ways to create and this is one of them. Not perhaps the best, but one that fits Japan, where corporate accomplishment is so common. But as I watch his studious profile, observe his careful avoidance of all those staring (me included) at one of the most famous men in Japan, I recognize what he reminds me of—a diligent student doing his homework.

4 DECEMBER 2002. Ian [Buruma] calls from London. He is writing about me for the *New York Review of Books* and wonders how to handle the subject of homosexuality. Cannot leave it out, wonders how to put it in. So do I—I remember Auden: "A capacity for self-disclosure implies an equal capacity for self-concealment."

Possibilities: Not "gay"—gay is a lifestyle now, not a sex style. And not "queer," which I otherwise like, since it has now been taken over by academe. "Faggot" might be misunderstood, and "homosexual" is just too solemn, a po-faced word bristling with medical associations.

Ian does not want to use terms like "preferences," "life-styles," etc., because they are euphemisms. Perhaps no word then. Words are half the trouble anyway. Instead, dramatize. He will think about how to do this, and I add that he might mention the *advantages* of homosexuality.

There is John Updike: "Perhaps the male homosexual, uncushioned as he is by society's circumambient encouragements, feels the isolated, disquieted human condition with special bleakness: he must take it straight." A quote that means several things. Many men finally settle for the fact that they had children and this becomes why they are here—this is something that many women do, too. There is family life to sustain everyone except those who have never made families. In the end, the human condition wins out, to be sure. Maybe this is something that people with specialized roles know.

Later I look up another reference and fax it to Ian. It is from A. M. Cioran's *A Short History of Decay*. "Vice—bestower of solitude—offers the man marked out by it the excellence of a separate condition. Consider the invert . . . he does not accept himself, constantly justifies himself, invents reasons, torn between shame and pride; yet—enthusiasts of the fatuities of procreation—we go with the herd."

5 DECEMBER 2002. At the FilmEx festival a large, sturdy, bald, man comes up to me. It is Amir Naderi, the Iranian film director. We had met some twenty years ago, after he had first gone to the United States, and he had after that made a point of reading me and wondering about me.

Why? Because we are the same. We are both expatriates. He had left his troubled country in order to have the freedom of being himself and so—half a century before him—did I. He went to my former country, and I came to this one.

Now he is, for the first time, here and wants to talk about our condition. He thinks mine was perhaps the more difficult of the two experiences—language and all. Perhaps, I say, but his was the more difficult in another way. After all, there was a period when my adopted country maintained a certain interest in the country I abandoned. He, however, had to cope, still has to, in a country which despises the country that he abandoned.

Does he ever go back? No, never. Could he? Oh, probably—then, do I go back? Yes, I go back, but only if I am invited and only if I have some work to do—about once a year. What do I feel? He asks. Culture shock, I answer.

6 DECEMBER 2002. [Tomiyama] Katsue has been to see Oshima Nagisa. He was dressed and put in a wheelchair for the occasion. She shows me a snapshot taken. He is wearing a red shirt and looks very thin, smiling away.

But he is not well, she tells me. I ask if he remembered me and he giggled and said in a very high voice that yes he did. But he didn't.

It has been six years since he had his stroke. I remember the doctor telling me after Eric [Klestadt] had his that patients usually live five or six years. Eric lived five terrible years.

Oshima's five years have been terrible too, but he somehow found the strength to make one final film, *Gohatto*. After that, the hospital again, then the nursing home, and now a room in his own house.

Does he want some beer? Oh, beer, beer, he says, his voice high. The sister shakes her head, no. The wife, seeing this, says yes; today is an exception.

I look out of the window at anonymous Tokyo in the rain, growing colder, winter here.

11 DECEMBER 2002. Being old is like being convalescent. People tell you how good you look, as though they are pleasantly surprised, had not expected you to look good at all. They also give you their seats and open doors for you. There is tendency to pat as well, as though you are not only convalescent but also a child, or a dog.

One of the best things about being old is that you are no longer expected to do your share. You may now drift down life's stream and not wield the oar. Also, you are asked questions about the course of the river, the coming scenery, just as though you have taken the trip before. You are not, however, asked about the maelstrom at the end.

24 JANUARY 2003. A memorial meeting—ten years since Alan Booth died. His wife and daughter have arranged it. The friends gather—Tim [Harris],

Stephen [Shaw], and others. It has been a decade—some of those I met at the funeral are now unrecognizable.

Since the daughter, still very young though no longer a child, does not remember much, the meeting is to tell her about her father. I talk about the trip to Yufujin and the hot spring jaunt, leaving out his lusting after a local movie star, and instead remember that he told me that one of his ways out of an unhappy childhood was to go and take a long, hot bath.

Most of the others are not so temperate, and when people started talking about his arrogance and his bad manners, the memorial became somewhat like the second half of *Ikiru*. A kind of climax was reached when someone remembered Alan in a coma being visited by Karel, who murmured that they would meet again in a better place. At which point the body opened an eye and said, "I certainly hope not."

If I had stayed I would have seen it turn more accepting, and at the end quite sentimental. What the daughter made of this, what kind of impression she gained of her father, I don't know, but whatever it was, she impressed me as being quite able to take it.

1 FEBRUARY 2003. Cold on Chuo-dori as I walk from the subway to the corner where I turn for home. Many girls, as usual, out on the street, hanging around, their coats open in this cold to show their short skirts and long legs.

Hello, hello. Usually I am ignored as a bad business bet, an elderly white gentleman who most certainly knows no Japanese. This girl accosts me, however, and when I am about to plead being tired and sleepy, she says, in Japanese, "No, no, no. English, English."

She wants to study. So I tell her how to say "I give massages," and "I am cheap." Then she asks how to say ¥15,000. I say that that is not cheap. That is true, she says, but she might as well start high.

Her Japanese is quite bad and I ask where she is from. Shanghai, she says, with a large smile. Since she is so forthcoming I learn more. Her keeper does not like her to fuck in the massage room, so she and her client have to go elsewhere, which is a bother. She has never had a client who merely wanted a massage, though that would be less expensive for him. Usually she begins at ten thousand yen, but will bargain. What else can she do? she asks. Then, suddenly, "I have a very bad accent in Japanese don't I?"

This I tell her can be part of her charm, that Japanese don't like it when we can speak all that well. She nods in a matter of fact fashion, and then we part. Actually she only wanted an English lesson, and this she has had.

5 FEBRUARY 2003. Economy worse, the cracked bottom showing as the money recedes, visible even to me. Today I lost the second of two jobs. The first was last month when Sogetsu, the flower school whose copy I had been doing for years, called and said they would do it themselves, that they could no longer afford even my pittance. Today I called UniJapan Film, that consortium whose yearbook I have done for decades, and they said that they, too, would be doing it in-house. I say that they might at least have told me. Mumbled apologies, indicating that they were afraid to. Many make livings as I do, various jobs here and there, retainers, editing this or that. This is where my money comes from, certainly not from the books I write. And now the convenience of a native English-speaking person on the premises is no longer affordable.

9 FEBRUARY 2003. A hard and sunny winter Sunday and I go to the Furushiba Bunka Senta to see the Ozu Yasujiro exhibition. But first I have to find it—it is on the other side of the river in a section of this enormous city that I do not know.

However, if you ask you will be helped. A druggist got me from the Monzen-nakacho subway station to the Koishifuru district, and a woman at a tobacco counter got me to the Kachidochi Yakuin, and there a florist pointed out the Bunka Senta—people all just as friendly as they are in Ozu's films.

A small exhibition, but it held his favorite tea cup, his reading glasses, a fan he was fond of, some of his art work, gouaches, and a number of school exercise books, including one used for English study. I looked at it and remembered the English lessons in *What Did the Lady Forget, Record of a Tenament Gentleman, Tokyo Story,* and doubtless others films as well.

Ozu was born in Fukagawa, which is near here and in prewar Tokyo was even nearer. There is a map that shows the location of his house back then, his school, even the sites themselves—long gone, since Fukagawa was one of the places destroyed during the fire-bombing of Tokyo.

There are pictures of him, a young man just back from the provinces, now making his way in the big city, working in the movies. A kind of quizzical optimism showed in his blunt and honest features, his hands folded as though they have just completed some big job. There is also a photo of a new bridge—Ozu Bashi—but I do not know where it is.

10 FEBRUARY 2003. Older women on the street, standing by a certain corner, smoking, talking, a bit too made up. A flower arrangement group, a gaggle of prostitutes? No, something even more specialized. These older women are companions. At least that is what they might call themselves. They gather here of an early evening because just down this alley is the Cat's Eye, that new establishment that requires men to have women before they may descend the stairs into those darkened rooms where they sit and drink expensive coffee as they watch other men and their wives or friends screw. These older women rent themselves out so that the single men can go and sit in the dark with them. So far as I can ascertain there is no screwing—they simply sit and sip their coffee and get paid for it.

What a curious profession, I think. And an attractive older woman catches my eye and makes an unmistakable motion with her hand. She is willing to do more for her fee. I smile and she approaches. More pregnant hand motions. She is deaf, and it is her words that I am watching as her nimble fingers spell out messages I am unable to read.

11 FEBRUARY 2003. Standing by the pond is a good-looking young student, in his twenties, probably ready to graduate, already searching perhaps for the means to make a life of his own. I look at him and begin, as always, to make up a life for him—inventing stories to explain where he is from and where he wants to go; fleshing out an emotional life—who he likes, who he doesn't; descending to the hobbies—pachinko? Proust?

I know he is a student because he is wearing a uniform—one I know well: black serge, celluloid collar, and brass buttons with school insignia, a late-nineteenth-century Austrian model miraculously unchanged after more than a hundred years of use.

And as I gaze I remember what that serge smelled like when wet with sweat, and I recall the slippery feel of the collar when I unbuttoned the hooks that held it closed. And under the uniform, perhaps no longer the loincloth, now probably Calvin Klein, but still redolent of dank boy.

Such thoughts, shreds of memory, froth on the surface of my curiosity, but beneath these is a more serious inquiry. What identity has he chosen? Who does he think he is? I regard the eyebrows—maybe he is from Ibaraki. I notice the stance—maybe Kyushu. These are his givens but he is now in the largest city in the world and far from where he was born. He is offered here a freedom he never had back in the paddy. How will he take advantage of this? Did the boy from Lima?

Manhood (or womanhood) in formation is always fascinating. I stand and stare, ever watchful, wondering at an outcome I will never know. Occasionally I strip the subject naked in my mind and find holes in the socks, but at the same time I think about what he himself wants.

I could do this anyplace in the world, including the United States of America, and often have. But how much more interesting to cast about in the future of an inhabitant of another land, an admitted exotic, someone supposedly not of my race, certainly not of my place. To this is added the allure of learning.

Flaubert lends a hand—something read last night: "If it is true that love is a pursuit in others of qualities we lack in ourselves, then in our love of someone from another country, one ambition may be to weld ourselves more closely to values missing from our own culture."

Perhaps that is why I now stood for a long time and imagined a life for the good-looking young student in his twenties. That I did nothing further, made no overtures, did not attempt to mine him, was because I am near eighty to his twenty, and am not unmindful of the ludicrous, but also because I now know the proper rejoinder to the great riddle of life—there is no answer.

12 MARCH 2003. Everyday I pass a hip-hop clothing store. In front of it is standing a black man, his hair attention-getting—corn-row braids—wearing the latest in imported hip-hop wear: oversized jumpers and snow pants, the crotch to the knees. Though there are actually various black men (just one would get pneumonia standing there all day long in the cold), they seem all the same. They are supposed to. Not only are they models, they are also emblems. I am reminded of the blackamoors of eighteenth century, and little picaninnies, all togged up and advertising the colonial empire and, unintentionally, slavery. Red, gold, their livery advertising the Brighton Pavilion, they have now passed their profession down the ages to these Tokyo hip-hoppers.

The standing young men are surrounded by other evidences of their culture. The sound of rap rends the air. I stop to listen to the strains. The voice is always black, and always deliberately cultured as though it is the answer to false charges that blacks do not enunciate well. I think back to that ur-rapper Edith Sitwell and her pre-rap piece, *Façade:* "Though I am black and not comely . . . ," she sang, but these rapping blackamoors are comely indeed.

20 MARCH 2003. Today the U.S.A. invaded Iraq. I think of carnage but cannot see any since I do not have a TV. The newspaper has an Arab scene with somewhere in the back a red blast, like a sunset. America strikes. Lots of public protest, here and elsewhere, people marching and the like. It can mean nothing. People protest, then, having vented their discontent, get on with their lives.

I look for signs about me. None on the street. In the post office, one. I mail a package to the U.S.A. and the clerk says that it might take some time to reach its destination depending upon how the war goes. How the war goes—already it is a part of parlance.

21 MARCH 2003. Today is a holiday, and down in the park, in the band shell below, much yelping. It is a punk rock concert, deafening. It is like having them here in my room, since sound amplifies as it rises. Nothing for me to do but live with it—no one ever complains. And so, knowing my neurosis about noise, my claustrophobia about immobilized suffering, I determine to do something—not about it, but about myself.

Consequently, I put my computer to sleep and descend. Wading through the racket, I approach the gates and ascertain that a group named Basilic Glance is in there with another group named Enemy Zero. ("Can You Feel Me?" is its motto.) They are presenting an entertainment called *Misanthropy*, featuring an all-boy band called Finsternis, the members of which have names like Dr. Sinky, Narciss, Sin, and Ba-C'la.

I go past two orange-headed young ladies guarding the gate (the entertainment is free but you are supposed to buy tapes and DVDs made by the boys), and glimpse a blondined young man in a ripped panda suit raving on the stage. Booming away behind him is a synthesizer and a man battering a drum kit. The man himself (surely this is Narciss) exposes his narrow chest, groans, screams, and drools.

Reacting to this is a clutch of girls who have crowded down to the front. They are all wearing manes and have kohl-blackened eyes. Shaking their shaggy heads they scream and press their thighs together. Narciss drools some more, and opens a safety pin on his slashed panda suit.

They all cavort for a time and then this "set" is over and the happy crowd is verbally cajoled for a bit before the cacophony again commences. It started at 1:30 says the posting and warns that it will go on until 7:30. The girls look ready to stay to the end.

Not me. I go home, but what a difference my immersion has made. Having seen what the poor things look like, petting their paltry selves, screaming away to no possible avail, I find that they are no long intruders. By experiencing, I do not have to imagine. Whatever I may have feared is no longer there. I can shake my head and get on with my work.

A part of this might be to inquire just what the cultural manifestations of this might mean, why something this helpless should be commonly thought of as dissident. Do these bleary little girls and boys really think they are rebelling against anything? Or has punk, like everything else, aestheticized itself out of existence?

22 MARCH 2003. The first warm day. I walk in the park without my topcoat on and feel the spring warmth draped over my shoulders. Pad and pencil in hand I look for things to sketch, and settle on a leaf left over from last year.

In so doing I again notice that attractively odd memorial stone surmounted by a large granite *fugu* [blowfish]. I had thought that it was for the victims of this sometimes-fatal comestible. Today, however, having trained my eye, I paid attention. It is actually for all those victims of the fishmonger's knife, for the departed *fugu* themselves. It is their memorial stone. And having learned this, I am struck once more by the acute difference of this land in which I live.

30 MARCH 2003. Sunday, the blossoms out, the park full—as many faces as there are petals. I shuffle around the lake with them, wondering as always at the sadness of Japanese on an outing. While ruminating, I had a vision.

It took the form of a possible film. All one would need would be a degree of underexposure to whiten the image, and some slow motion to slow it down. The clothes were all right as they were—scruffy, between seasons, layered, as though just grabbed before the catastrophe. Those who sit cramped under a cold tree are those who do not quite understand the seriousness of their situation. Those walking do; they are looking for a way out, but there is none. The waters of the pond glisten, ruffled—a river, something like the Styx. I pass a public toilet with its line of patient women waiting to get in. Here are those who know the worst and prefer the gas chamber. These we will not see again. Equally poignant are the children turning their petal-like faces to the blossoms, all unmindful . . . etc.

These are the dead, and they are proceeding to they know not where. To make this completely believable one would need nothing else—maybe a serious close-up here and there of someone thinking. All else would be in our interpretation, how we see it, as I am seeing it now.

I think of the triumph of Tarkovsky's *Stalker,* where suggestion alone made ordinary scenes (vacant lots) vibrant with danger. And I think of Sokurov's *Russian Ark,* that final dignified waterfall of contented middle-class persons descending the Hermitage staircases, never dreaming of the coming revolution—just hundreds going home on the one hand, an entire class going to extinction on the other. My walking dead still smile, but that is only because they, too, do not know where they are going.

Much satisfied and oddly cheered I return home, glance at the hordes beneath my balcony, and write up the vision.

Around this time Richie was writing *The Image Factory* and collecting the previously published reviews that were eventually comprised in *Japanese Literature Reviewed*. He was also preparing for the new edition of the translation that he and Eric Klestadt had previously published of Ozu's *Tokyo Story*. During a lecture tour of the U.S.A. he suffered a heart attack, his second (the first was in 1983), which resulted in open-heart surgery and a quintuple bypass. He was not well enough to continue these journals until nearly six months later.

21 SEPTEMBER 2003. I go to the show billed as *Jintai no Fushigi* [Mysteries of the Human Body], a very large assemblage of body parts from China. All liquids are pressed out of the cadaver, which is then re-moisturized with plastics and epoxies. The resulting figure, part flesh, part plastic, can then be sliced into CAT-like sections. One display is a body sliced like bread, crosswise, from head to feet, the results spaced out like dominos; another is a standing man with all the implements of surgery left in. Nothing sinister in all this. We are told that these were all volunteers who were dying of illness anyway—and they certainly all look very ill.

Interesting as this is, however, what truly compels my attention is the crowd I see the show with. Though it is Sunday and raining the place is packed, hundreds of people, and all of them behaving in a way distinct, I think, from like crowds elsewhere.

The crowd is, of course, curious, but this is expressed in such a different way. Quiet, serious, intent, and with no laughter—that defense in the face of death. And no mock indignation (Well, really!) in hopes of returning to restrictive normality. Also no blasé assumptions. To be sure, not much fellow feeling for the posed and manipulated corpses, but then I would not expect that any place. What I admire in this crowd is its seriousness, and its inquiring and interested behavior.

22 SEPTEMBER 2003. To lunch with Paul [McCarthy] at Benkei, a Japanese restaurant in Ameyokocho, that section of old Tokyo that remains—pedestrian streets, no cars, shops spilling onto the pavement. We are attended by an elderly woman, a waitress, who in the most natural way talks with us, says the eel looks good today, that it doesn't always, and she wonders about the typhoon said to be on its way. When she goes, Paul tells me what a wonderful neighborhood I live in. "Fat chance," he says, "of our being included in the conversation in Shinjuku or Shibuya."

30 SEPTEMBER 2003. Peter Grilli tells me that in this new age of poverty; the meager is fashionable. He attended an elegant wedding, an event

With Peter Grilli, Nogami Teruyo, 2003.

where in the bubble days hundreds were invited and millions spent. Now there were just six people and one bottle of champagne. It was, he was told, the latest thing, a *jimikon.* The *kon* is from *kekkon,* wedding. And *jimi* is an aesthetic term meaning "plain, simple, in good taste."

17 OCTOBER 2003. People define themselves by their appurtenances. They once always had handkerchiefs, beauty spots, and smart pumps. Now, however, defining accessories are mostly electrical. In Tokyo Station I watch a man carefully put on his Walkman, then deposit his portable CD player in his cargo pocket and his digital camera in his backpack. Then he stops, looks like a man who had forgotten something, pats his pockets, and then locates what he missed. His cell phone. This he takes out and opens and stares at. It contains his address book, his e-mail, TV, the Internet, and much else. And he starts waving it in a strange but familiar fashion.

I identified the movement: He was fanning himself with his gadget. And I understood. All of this equipment was really but to satisfy a primitive social urge to keep the hands occupied, to appear busy. How many times upon enduring public or private scrutiny have we flourished our fingers? This not only accounts for the centuries-old Japanese cult of the fan, but also the ready acceptance of cigarettes, lighter, etc. Anything to keep the hands moving and to appear busy, distracted, already taken—no longer victim to the random gazes of others.

Thus all strangeness disappeared from the cluttered man in front of me. He as simply doing in the twenty-first century what his ancestors had in the eighteenth. Then it was the fan and tobacco pipe, now it was the Walkman and palm phone.

18 OCTOBER 2003. Non-chan [Nogami Teruyo] takes Peter [Grilli] and me out to lunch—the Kurosawa restaurant. I had heard of this place, a kind of theme park based on the director and his work.

It is a large structure done in early Meiji style. It looks like the hospital in *Red Beard* but is much cleaner. You leave your shoes on too, and the muzak, when we went in, was the sound track for *Seven Samurai*, but later on in the meal we were treated to *Dodesukaden* and gems from *Dreams*. The food is divided among courses arranged around a main dish, entitled with a famous cinematic name. *Ikiru* is pork, *Yojimbo* is gamecock, and *Kagemusha* is turtle. The most expensive of these is *The Hidden Fortress*, but I never learned of what it consisted. We have the *soba* course which is not, apparently, cinematically oriented. So we sat there in this ersatz film studio amid all the art (Kurosawa paintings) and kitsch (stuff in the "store" all clamoring for customers), and ate the mediocre food, unembarrassed. Upon my asking, Non-chan tells me that this restaurant is the idea of Kurosawa's son, but that the money came from elsewhere. It is also apparently a big success; all rooms booked every night, despite the prices. What would Kurosawa have thought of it? I wonder. Well, earlier he would have torched the place, but he so mellowed in later years that he might well have enjoyed it.

31 OCTOBER 2003. Motofuji [Akio], the widow of Hijikata Tatsumi [one of the founders of Butoh], died suddenly last week. Heart attack. And, I think, grief. Not at the death of her husband, that was years ago, but at the way she had failed to keep his estate. Overexpanding her theater, she eventually lost everything. Bankrupt, she had to entrust the Hijikata archives to Keio University, which, understandably, did not want her in charge. She devoted herself to Hijikata and his dancing. If she occasionally allowed herself to become a bit vainglorious, still she was sincere in keeping his legacy. And then to have it taken from her, and all her own fault—no wonder she died. She had no more reason to live.

1 NOVEMBER 2003. Strains of the *koto*, swarming cherry blossoms falling, Prince Genji as a large, stuffed doll, music by Tomita imitating ancient court music. This was the opening of the Tokyo Film Festival today. It was so kitschy that I began to think about what it could mean. Was this what foreign guests were being invited to think old Japan was like? Or was this kind of exoticism intended mainly for the home audience, the young sitting open-mouthed around me? If the Philadelphia Film Festival (if there is one) opened with powered wigs and panniers and Betsy Ross embroidering the first flag, whom would the spectacle be for?

5 NOVEMBER 2003. How handsome the autumn foliage. Not so much is made of it compared to the cherry blossom celebrations, but the beauty is even more spectacular. Tawny yellows, russet browns, deep crimsons—these colors I see outside my window. If I were strong enough to go to Nikko, I would see whole panoramas of these autumnal colors. They remind me of the color of a cello, burnished browns with orange shining through. But no promise of anything more glorious to come. Maybe that is why the cherry blossoms get all the attention—they herald summer. These fall colors mean wilting, drying, withering. They announce only deadly winter.

18 NOVEMBER 2003. At Roppongi, trendy nocturnal home of the carousing young, I am buying a subway ticket and suddenly standing in front of me is a young Japanese woman mumbling something. It turns out that she is asking for one hundred yen. Surprised, I ask why. "Shibuya," she answers with an impatient frown, as though I should have known her intended destination. Surprised though I am to encounter begging in affluent High Town Roppongi, I would be inclined to give were it not for her manner. But she is so sullen, so unfriendly, and at the same time so expectant, that I smile and politely observe that she should be out on the street earning her hundred yen. Later, on the escalator, I think about my retort and remind myself that some of her hostility might have been embarrassment. Even so, however, common as this incident might be in, say, New York, where you are asked for handouts everywhere, in Tokyo it rare enough that it ought be discouraged, nay, stamped out.

27 NOVEMBER 2003. During the FilmEx Festival screening of *Father and Son*, just at one of the most intense moments, the projector breaks down. Lights come up; loudspeaker apologizes and says it will be a few minutes. Eventually thirty of these accumulated and still the audience sat. And no one complained. No shouting, not even raised voices, and no demands for funds returned. I wonder in what other country this would have occurred. And, indeed, in less than an hour a new machine was installed and the projection continued.

30 NOVEMBER 2003. Winter slowly comes. The sky is gray and the leaves are black. The lotus petals yellow and fall away, leaving brown stems standing in the dark water.

It is cold. The crows are hungry and begin their calls at dawn as they swoop to savage the garbage bags. The homeless are hungry as well. As the sky slowly brightens they get up from their cardboard or come out of their boxes. A few exercise to warm themselves, but most don't.

The crow problem has been addressed for ten years now but various plans have come to nothing. The homeless problem has been less publicly probed, but here also the result is the same. Still, a kind of solution is evident—solve the problem by getting used to it.

1 DECEMBER 2003. I read that Nagare [Masayuki] is going to rebuild his sculpture that stood at the base of the World Trade Center. There will also be a new building to go with it, a soaring but seeming insubstantial structure that "echoes" the shape of the nearby Statue of Liberty. Nagare's work will be smaller than the original, which was destroyed not by the collapse of the buildings but by the later clearing of the area.

3 DECEMBER 2003. Reading Nagai Kafu's diaries (in Donald Keene's adaptation), and find that he wanted to stay abroad and only returned home upon parental orders. "I feel as if my life first began the day I set foot on the soil of the American continent, and I would like to forget memories of the past in Japan as if they were nothing more than a dream." I know that feeling well, and I had no parental orders to go back, so I stayed.

Here, Kafu disliked Japan until the country had so changed that it was no longer what he had disliked. The Taisho period was very different from the Meiji. Consequently, he could come to miss Meiji because he had this new dislike of Taisho. Ditto for Taisho to Showa, and it would have been the same for Showa to the present Heisei if he had lived.

Have I escaped this? I wonder—not in regards the U.S.A. but in regards Japan. I, too, tend to romanticize the past and to excoriate the present. I do not want to be an old fogy, but I am one. So was Kafu. All romantics turn into them given time. So, I wonder if escape is enough. Apparently not.

20 DECEMBER 2003. The Aum trial is slowly ending. Death sentences have been issued and Asahara sits and mutters, perhaps now truly mad. The courts have been criticized for taking so long—years. But due process usually takes this long in Japan and, in this instance, the prosecution wanted to make certain that all evidence—mountains of it—was in place.

Now the headquarters of the sect have been attacked by a group of right-minded men with swords. They are members of a right-wing sword collectors club. Newspapers are careful not to heroize such local efforts. To have such a questionable group assume such retributive power is something like Baragon coming to help during a Godzilla attack.

23 DECEMBER 2003. I take Paul [Waley] with me to see a preview of Sakamoto Junji's new film, *Out of This World (Kono Yo no Soto e)*, set in the spring of 1947, just a few months after I first came here. The lights go down, and there is the Tokyo of fifty-six years ago: people live in shacks; they wear old army uniforms or, the women, *monpe* or kimono; the kids are often ragged and sometimes feral. GIs on the street in summer khaki with Eighth Army or Seventh Cavalry patches, looking at dressed-up pompom girls. A general air of benevolent business. Sakamoto has got the atmosphere more or less right, but I do not believe a frame of the picture.

I wonder why. Perhaps because it is in color, and movies in color are, if they attempt to look real, artificial. Black and white are, like it or not, the tints of reality. Or, another reason, perhaps because the story is mere melodrama—but then life, particularly life for the Japanese in 1947, was also melodrama.

A more important reason was suggested by Paul. It is strange about generations, he said. No matter what, people change. Those faces, the body language, the very walk of these actors are those of today. They tell us it is 2003 even as they insist it is 1947.

Mr. Koga [Masaki], of Shochiku, distributing the film, tells me that no one will notice anything like this. Young people of today were not there then, and indeed, he says, not all of them are aware that Japan and American had a war that ended in an Occupation. And these young, although he does not say so, are the only audience for this film.

But in the meantime I have had two hours back there—sort of.

24 DECEMBER 2003. Christmas Eve, and the U.S.A. has been successful in cajoling and threatening Japan into sending troops into Iraq. I feel I have come full circle. When I was first here the U.S.A. was criminalizing all war efforts. Now it is applauding them. The Japanese army was being disbanded. Now it is being built up. It is not, to be sure, yet called an army. It consists of a large group of young men known as the Self-Defense Forces who are defending Japan by going off to Iraq.

I know why, of course, but from the reasons one learns little about Japan except of its cravenness. After having been a client state of the U.S.A. for over half a century, after having greatly benefited from the "nuclear umbrella" under which it has waxed and grown wealthy, it suddenly finds that, Russia gone, it must pull an international oar or two. The U.S.A. will make it pay for its passage.

One answer would have been to uphold the Constitution, which renounces war, and refused. But this is something that conciliatory Japan feels it cannot afford to do.

25 DECEMBER 2003. There is another way of looking at my years here: An adolescent Roman, early fed up with the Imperial Way, went to help in the pacification of Antioch. He believed in Roman benefits, but also thought that the ways of the East were in many ways better than those of the West. Consequently, when the legionnaires went home, he stayed and watched the reconstruction. And he forgot that he was still the citizen of a major power and enjoyed all the comforts of living in a client state. He hated Roman arrogance, but did not recognize his own brand of it. He took advantage of his status while he at the same time deplored it. It was in a way an ideally balanced life. Rome turned more purely imperial, ruling over further extensive territories, over more colonies and dependencies, assuming supreme authority, turning regal, and majestic. This, the adolescent, now an old man, deplored, but remained a Roman citizen because of its convenience. And as Antioch turned into an imitation of Rome, he deplored the change and turned nostalgic, remembering the distant days of his first coming, now shimmering like a mirage on the distant horizon of his life.

27 DECEMBER 2003. The first box of DVDs in the Shochiku edition of the complete films of Ozu. This sublime home drama may now be seen in the home; and the celebrations of Ozu's centenary are complete.

Being ill and in hospital much of the time I missed all of them, though invited. Could not go to Tsu, where he went to school; could not attend any of the foreign symposia, not even the local meeting of scholars just ended.

I wonder what Ozu himself would have thought of these. He would have been gratified, certainly, and at the same time skeptical. Particularly, I think, at the theoretical claims of the new generation of Ozu scholars—Hasumi Shigehiko, Yoshimoto Mitsuro, and Yoshida Kiju.

It would not do to cast Ozu as the rough craftsman or as the sensible anti-intellectual, or as the homegrown humanist, but at the same time, one cannot see him as the Derrida of his generation.

And I certainly would not have fit well into the recent symposia, where post-structural papers were produced—Yoshida insisted that Ozu's films were anti-cinema. Nor would I have been welcomed. Sato Tadao, certainly an outstanding early Ozu scholar, was not invited. Nor would I have been was I not safely ill.

I wonder what Ozu would have felt about his apotheosis. Nothing at all, I should guess. All of this has nothing to do with him, and he would have known it.

1 JANUARY 2004. Stayed up long enough to observe the end of the Year of the Sheep and the start of the Year of the Monkey. Stood by the big bonfire at the Benten shrine across from my place until the bells began and the doors opened, then went up, tossed my modest offering into the gaping money box, and made my prayer.

It was like New Year's in the countryside, very quiet, the bark of a distant dog near. Few people, since so many have gone abroad for the holidays, and clear skies, since all the factories are turned off. And with this quiet, these few people, a certain simplicity as though complications had been shed.

I seem to remember that life was once made of much less than it now is, but perhaps this is because of a nostalgic self or merely a faulty memory.

10 JANUARY 2004. *Asakusa Kurenaidan* will finally appear. Translated, it will be published this year. It has been fifty-seven years since I stood on the top of the Subway Tower and looked out over ruined Asakusa. Now *The Scarlet Gang of Asakusa* will be read by anyone who wants to.

It is curious. My life is so entwined with this book. Often I have attempted to translate it, to have it translated. This desire was disappointed a good many times, but then Alisa Freedman did it, and I added to her work by creating the tone—that of the persona (the "Kawabata" of the book) with whom I had been living for half a century, the narrator of this strange book.

I used to live on Kototoi-dori in Yanaka because it led to Kototoi Bridge, which is where some of the action takes place. I used to go to Asakusa every month or so, just to be where those people in the book had been. I looked at other cities, searching for the Asakusa in each. Asakusa became Japan for me, the many in the one, the most fruitful kind of partiality—the final fetish.

15 JANUARY 2004. Fumio to dinner. We look at old photos. I turn up one of [Nakano] Yuji at work—part-time laborer, standing there for forty years now.

I wondered why I still think so much about him, now that I have not seen him for decades, now that he is an old man, if even alive. Fumio said, "Because, he was the last Japanese."

It's true. Yuji had all of the old virtues—he saw a connection between himself and nature, the way things are. He believed in authority, though he was sly about evading it; was polite, decent, honest to the extent that he did not get caught; willing to do his best and allow himself to be much imposed on; fond of pleasure, and probably drank himself to death. And, more, he embodied an attitude now extinct—he accepted without bitterness, and made the most of what was left. I don't know if this defines old-fashioned Japaneseness, but it defines Yuji.

20 JANUARY 2004. Listening to a collection of movie music by Takemitsu, I suddenly hear Gagaku—his own version, composed for some forgotten Toho epic. It is cut down, no *sho*, but all of its moving parts are there, though smaller, further away, as if seen through the wrong end of the telescope. And all the more captivating—its irregular regularity, its main "theme" returning over and over. There is something that reminds me of machines, but simple, small ones—like music boxes. When I first heard Gagaku I thought of music of the spheres—I was hearing geometry. Now I again remember the pines against the sky, the helmeted dancers, their grave movements, and the wondrous mechanism of the music.

Later I play it for Chris [Blasdel] and ask what the time signature is. I had tried to figure it out and not been able to. He listens, thinks, and then says it is 4/4 plus 2/4. Oh, 6/4, I say. No, you had to keep them separate—a bar of four followed by a bar of two. That then is what makes for that irregular charm, reoccurring as a water wheel, but always surprising.

25 JANUARY 2004. This week I gave a talk, took part on a panel, wrote an article and several reviews, and appeared on a public television program—all were about Japan.

Almost everything I do, everything that is known about me, is connected to this country. To be a person so intent upon describing a place not his own—isn't this odd?

Can I think of anyone else? No, not really, not even Lafcadio Hearn, with whom I am all too often compared. But he also at length described the West Indies, New Orleans. For a person to so devote himself to another single country . . . I must be unique.

But I never devoted *myself*. What I have done is to describe myself through Japan. People who do not read carefully still ask when I first fell in love with Japan. I never did. I liked the place from the first, but I fell in love with other places—Greece, for example; Morocco, for example.

What I have done is to draw and redraw my portrait in front of the backdrop of Japan. I have exemplified what Helen Mears devoted *Japan, Mirror for Americans* to. You look into this country and find yourself reflected.

It is not a simple process. You can do this only if you describe the place as it is. Only then, through what you emphasize and what you do not, does your own form become visible. I am the empty places in my books.

2 FEBRUARY 2004. Am being interviewed by a very intelligent graduate student who is doing work on national identity and the way some of us have used the concept. I outlined how I began to doubt its efficacy and how I now doubt the very existence of this "national identity," finding people far too various to be described by such a limited if convenient term.

In the course of our conversation she wondered if women, as an identity, did not even more than men distrust such simplifications. I quite agreed. She then said that she had got the idea from my wife's book [*A Romantic Education*, Mary Richie, 1970].

Here the interview turned a corner and we began to discuss personal identity and how it was constructed, how Japan had answered many personal needs among those foreigners who came to study it. She wondered why so many men were emotionally drawn, if that is what it was.

I told her and she, a Japanese herself, said: "I now understand. You discovered the virtues of being an outsider. And you would not have had you not been excluded. It was the benefits of stigma that you discovered here."

14 FEBRUARY 2004. A warm St. Valentine's Day, and I was looking for romance in the ordinary places. Not finding it, I took the bus to Sumida Park, where I had not been for some time. I remembered its winding paths in the growing dusk, the darkening benches on which the resting workmen might be found.

No longer. Blue tarpaulins have been spread, tents erected among the trees, homes for the homeless, homemade. The winding paths are now fully inhabited, the darkening benches are anchors for the transient homes. I look through the openings on this warm evening and there amid their comforts are the perhaps jobless workmen and their families.

The place is now a kind of suburbia, a collection of orderly homes with a good section (near the drinking fountain) and one not so good (next to the toilet) and no one out on the streets at night.

I MARCH 2004. I rent a tape of *Tarzan of the Apes*, the 1932 version, the first with Johnny Weissmuller. I first viewed it when I was eight, and I now, next month eighty, want to discover if anything remains of what it was then. Expectant,

I stared at the tube and remembered nothing at all about the story—except a bit about when the tribe of dwarfs throw the white people to the monster gorilla. What remained, however, what returned instantly recognizable after seventy years was the erotic atmosphere of Johnny and his jungle. The picture was made before the Hayes Office was instituted, and Tarzan was mostly naked and Jane showed a lot of flesh too, and when he took her into his hut there was no doubt at all—even for an eight year old—what they did. What I had remembered and cherished for seven decades turns out not have been elephants and crocodiles or even dwarfs. Rather, it is the loins of Tarzan, the naked hips hid barely by the loincloth. To be moved so at mere eight!

10 MARCH 2004. Taking a leak at the Ginza subway station toilet, I see a flickering before my eyes. It is an electronic box installed at eye level, one in front of each urinal, and it advertises various health drinks as well as loan organizations, and has perhaps more sponsors if you loiter to view them.

I had noticed merchants renting space in Ueno Station and, of course, Tokyo Station now rivals the grand bazaar of Tehran. This co-opting of private corporate space into public merchandising is due to the economy—people rent or sell whatever they have. How deep the distress is indicated by now being unable to take a peaceful pee.

11 MARCH 2004. Ed is back, just in time for the cherry blossoms. This I tell him as we settle down for supper. No, not at all, he says.

Over our meal we talk of many other things, having a whole half-year to catch up on. President Bush is execrated; we wonder what the country is coming to; Hello Kitty is attacked, as is the general fecklessness of the young; and then we turn to other things—the Vatican show of Roman statuary, which I have seen but he not yet.

In mentioning a sarcophagus picturing the death of Adonis, I note the customary small penis of the gored hero. Then we wonder, why "customary," why did the Greeks and Romans make so tiny what the Japanese in their *shunga* make so huge? I quote a twelfth-century Buddhist monk who said that it had to be, that the only way to make such a dull organ interesting was to enlarge it.

This we do not accept, and I then remember Truman Capote's leaving the country in chagrin at finding no "ten-pennies." "Ten what?" asks Ed. I give Truman's explanation of long ago. Lay it out on the table, and if you can put ten pennies in a row on it then it is a "tenpenny." "Let me see," says Ed, "just how large would that be?" Only one way to find out. We do not have pennies, but we do have ten yen coins. We empty our pockets and pool the contents, lining the coins on the table, and then observing the results. "Oh!" says Ed, and then the conversation turns to other things.

18 MARCH 2004. Again I take the train to Kita-Kamakura, first time in years. This time I recognize nothing. Malls, department stores, apartment complexes, all crowded so near the tracks that it is like traveling through a gorge. What was once open country with paddies and groves is now densely urban, and all in that industrial blue-gray color that civic Japan is so fond of.

Once at Engakuji, I again stand before the great gate. But this time it is early spring, fifty-seven years later. The carved eaves still stretch above me, the roof still soars and touches the pines, and I am still about to enter the land of Zen. But now there are lights, mikes, and cameras. I am being interviewed for a documentary on Dr. Suzuki.

Since his little house is gone, I am taken to a room in the main temple where the acolytes gather before their interviews with the *roshi*. This teacher estimates their progress and attempts to ascertain whether it was really enlightenment that was experienced. The place is thus appropriate for me, though I had experienced little progress, much less enlightenment.

This is what I now talked about, and Dr. Suzuki's attentive guidance out of the maze I had walked into. I tried to remember what he looked like, what he said, how he thought. At the end, asked to describe him in one sentence, I said that he knew how to think in ways other than what I had known.

At least that is what he taught me, what I gathered. And as I sat there remembering for the camera, conjuring up the ghost of my teacher, I also called up my own early twenties—me with my mouth open, somehow learning. And between sentences I thought of this young man I had invoked, and thought how surprised he would have been to learn that nearly sixty years later he would be again sitting, again with Dr. Suzuki.

20 MARCH 2004. Lunch with Karel and Ed. We discuss the fact that no one will publish us. Karel's new book, *George W. Bush and the Destruction of World Order,* cannot be published in America. Publishers already each have one book critical of the Bush policy and want no more, one is enough. Also, since all publishers have now been bought by conglomerates, only those books that will sell well are published. Also, the media has a plot to dominate the world. Ed's book, apparently about *yakuza,* but a novel, cannot be published because, he says, no one takes it seriously. My book of short stories has been the round, but, I am told, short stories do not sell. Only I am doing something about

this. Next week I take my orphan manuscript to a self-publisher. Whether by he himself or me myself, it will at least be properly printed, if not perhaps properly published.

25 MARCH 2004. Shulamith on the telephone. How much better she sounds. Before, enfeebled by her stroke, she seemed an echo at the end of the line stretching from distant California. Today she holds that line in a firm grip and sounds like herself again, pulling California nearer.

31 MARCH 2004. Reading the Isherwood diaries in bed last night I find this passage: Christopher is writing about the United States and says, "I love this country. I love it just because I don't belong. Because I'm not involved in its traditions, not born under the curse of its history. I feel free here. I'm on my own. My life will be what I make of it."

Christopher wrote that March 31, 1940, in Los Angeles. He experienced early what I would later. Much later—it is only recently that I can see what Japan has meant to me. He was about thirty-six when he knew this about America. Took me twice as long.

When I knew him he was past fifty, and naturally did not see here what he saw there. We sat on the bench at the statue of Saigo, and he wondered if I would not find it too narrow, too deep, this valley of an archipelago. And I said, well, yes, compared to wide and shallow America. Then we both laughed.

3 APRIL 2004. Tonight I go to Image Forum and talk about Hijikata Tatsumi. They are showing a long documentary of his last performance, and each Saturday someone involved comes and talks. Tonight it is me, and I show *War Games* and talk about him.

He had said I would need help making this film, and that he would assist. He was right, without him I could not have made it. I needed a dozen little boys, and it was he who found them, picked them right off the streets of the little port we chose to film in. He, so like a child himself, approached them with a smile and they, recognizing another child, I suppose, came with us. He also found the goat I needed.

The idea was that the goat would be accidentally killed by the children and they would be sorry for this, would have a kind of funeral, but would then forget, would become children again, and would run off down the beach, death forgotten.

Hijikata knew what I wanted, and after the funeral, and the boys were standing solemnly around, he slowly pulled down his trunks and showed

DON BACHARDY

With Christopher Isherwood. Tokyo, 1957.

them his navel. He pointed at it and gave them a big smile. The boys smiled a little and one nudged another.

I was photographing the boys, and on the screen it seemed as though they were still looking at the dead goat and had just realized that it was only a dead animal.

He then began dancing about, outside the range of the camera, and pointing to his navel. The boys began laughing, one pointing to another. On the screen it appears that the children are no longer seeing that death lies at their feet.

As his dancing became more extravagant, the children began jumping about as well. And on the screen it appeared that they were happy about being able to forget about death, able to deny it. Then he suddenly started running, and the children, a flock of boys, followed. He ran in back of the camera and the boys took off down the beach.

There they go—death, guilt, and remorse all forgotten. It is a lovely shot, the boys running into the distance; the surf rolling in, each wave seemingly higher, for a typhoon is coming, the sea spray blowing across the sand as the boys run further and further.

I watched it again this evening: that beach of forty years ago, those children now maybe grandfathers, Hijikata long dead, and me soon to be eighty.

10 APRIL 2004. Gwen here on her way from London to Sydney. We talk about Crown Princess Masako. She is at the villa in Nagano and refuses to return to the palace. Her constricted life has given her shingles—that answer to constant stress.

We also speculate on the father of her child. For some years, no children. The inbred Crown Prince was suspected of infertility. Then the child. Whose? Gwen says that the customary procedure would have been his brother, in a test tube. But then he is inbred as well, so who could have been called in?

We sympathize, and congratulate ourselves on our own stress-free lives. But shortly we are bemoaning that we have no one with whom to share them. We disguise the need by restricting it to sexuality, but that is not all that we mean.

12 APRIL 2004. Tani calls from Osaka. Remembers that my birthday is some time around now. Knows that I will be eighty. Knows this because he is near seventy and there is a decade between our ages. We talk about this. Half a century since I first met him but his voice hasn't changed. No, he says, but lots else has. Had third of his stomach removed—ulcers. Still smokes, but stopped drinking. And *hame hame*? I use that old-fashioned Osaka term which I learned first from him. Not much, he says, can't get it up much any more. We laugh genially at this, two elderly gents sharing a joke, but I know we are both thinking back at the time when he could always get it up.

So what does he do now? He has all the money he will ever need, yet still keeps working; his new hobby is farming. He owns this house and garden in Nara and he grows vegetables—radishes, pumpkins, potatoes, and tomatoes, just everything. I think of him tilling the soil, encouraging a sprout, and feel a wave of affection for him—handsome Tani, his youngest now twenty-four, older than when I first met his father, who now spade in hand, encourages an onion.

He also feels something, because he says he wants to come to Tokyo to see me again. Says we can go to the cabarets and watch the girls. I tell him that there are no more cabarets and those girls are as old as we are, but come anyway, even if he can't get it up.

We have never talked about ourselves, how we feel about each other. Always we have spoken through the medium of the expected—two guys who have known each other for a long time, which we also are. Lots of jokes, never a word of affection, yet behind this stands what we have been for each other.

He will come to Tokyo this summer, my oldest friend.

14 APRIL 2004. My Kodansha editor Stephen Shaw gives me a birthday party at a Japanese restaurant in Ueno Park, a beautiful boat-shaped room that looks out over the illuminated trees of the park as the soft spring rain falls and we drink champagne and eat *kaiseki* food. The others are Chris [Blasdel], Paul [McCarthy], Ed [Seidensticker], and Tim [Harris], and we discuss languages and their relative difficulty and beauty.

Ed thinks that Chinese is the ugliest of tongues. Someone quotes Tolkien as saying the most beautiful word in the English language is "cellar door." I remember that Truman Capote said the most beautiful was "cistern."

We then turn to belief, Easter being just over. Paul smiles and says that he gave me up for Lent. Ed, a more reluctant Catholic, says he had nothing to give up, he had already given up everything. "No," says Stephen, "you have given up *on* everything." Ed complains that he is still writing, just not being published. This is a pointed rejoinder, since Stephen is with Kodansha, one of his publishers.

Fine food, all of it unrecognizable in the *kaiseki* manner, and no one gets drunk.

16 APRIL 2004. With Dae-Yung and [Numata] Makiyo to see Fumio in *Three Sisters* at Kinokuniya Hall. He is the ancient Ferapont and does not have much to do. The others make up for it. Hysteria, the three sisters throwing themselves around, great towering rages among the visiting military. All of the melodrama that Chekhov so carefully hid is dug up in Japanese productions such as this, and flung raw onto the stage. Why? I wonder. Perhaps it is because the Japanese usually hide their melodramatic lives as carefully as did ever Chekhov. The stage offers an opportunity to let everything out. For the same reason stage actors gabble and care little for audibility—they are forced to speak slowly and carefully in real life.

As I watch I remember that it was upon this very stage that Fumio appeared in the four verse dramas I directed here in 1975. He was the young boy in the Yeats, and he lost his trousers in the Gertrude Stein. Thirty years ago, he was about twenty then.

Afterward, at Zakone where we all went for drinks and something to eat, I ask if he had thought of that early appearance during this later one. He smiles and says that maybe he once did, but that he has now appeared at Kinokuniya so often that he no longer does.

17 APRIL 2004. My eightieth birthday. Dae-Yung is here, and after breakfast we go to Harajuku and see an exhibition of Kobayashi Kiyochika prints of nineteenth-century Tokyo. There are a number of Ueno, and one sketched from just about where I now live. Unrecognizable. The original Benten Shrine was not as pretty as the postwar concrete version, and the trees are different. But, since it is a print, the view seems pristine—as though it is the original and what I see every day is a copy.

Then, buffeted by the fashionable young, we push our way up Omote-sando and into the grounds of Meiji Shrine. The contrast—in one step from noise to silence, from fabrication to nature. Here we are surrounded by old trees, whole stands of them, a forest, and a wide gravel path leading to the old gods. This is the way to see Tokyo. It was not called a city of contrasts for nothing.

The late afternoon sun slides down, the shadows lengthen, and we go to the restaurant in Nakano where Chris and Leza are giving me a birthday party. Tunisian food, wine, friends, and a cake.

18 APRIL 2004. I wander into the future—Roppongi Hills, an enormous complex of high-rise buildings, including a mighty tower near where I used to live. This is the new Japan—gargantuan, expensive, and wasteful. There are, to be sure, concessions to tradition (trad but mod) in the transplantations of zelkova and gingko trees, all of them expensively mature, and in such touches of the Japanesque as a pocket garden here and a teahouse there. But Keyakizaka Street is lined with Louis Vuitton, Hermès, Gucci, Bulgari, and other high-priced merchants. These are matched by the kind of restaurants now called cutting-edge, which are far too expensive to eat in. People who work in the tower complain that they have to leave the Hills and walk far away to find a place to have an affordable lunch.

I am reminded of other places with captive audiences and high prices. It is said that since opening, Roppongi Hills has attracted twenty-six million visitors, double the draw of Disneyland. Yet it *is* Disneyland, a new model. It is built like one, with all sorts of blandishments and temptations, little byways lined with tourist traps. Again I marvel at the Japanese genius for making space cozy, for anthropomorphizing emptiness. I am also reminded of an airport—this one turned inside out, and open to the friendly skies.

Though there are a lot of cute manga folk around on walls or pavements (standing in for Mickey and Minnie), the real icon is an enormous, nine-meter-high bronze sculpture by Louise Bourgeois. It is in the shape of a spider, some kind of tarantula, and this is somehow fitting.

Roppongi Hills (every hill of which is artificial) cost, it is said, the equivalent of four billion dollars, which might account for the prices now charged there. It costs nearly fifteen dollars to go to the top of the tower for a look around. Mori Minoru, whose company made the place, must somehow manage a return.

I have taken the subway from poor, proletarian Ueno, with its homeless, its bag ladies, its suicides, to this land of the future, futile luxury, and impossible prices. What does it mean? I wonder. Well, it means that Tokyo can, like Calcutta, contain great wealth and great poverty, that there is still fat enough on the old Japanese bones to patronize such an enormous folly as this.

Like all classical follies this one has its tower, and so I go fifty-four stories up to view the city from the height. Out of the great windows I gaze. Here one may look *down* on high-rise Shinjuku, trace the alleys of pulsing Shibuya, take in Tokyo Tower at eye level, and Mount Fuji, low on the horizon.

I can also look straight down at International House, resting near the base of the tower like a mushroom at the foot of a mighty oak. And I can look at pulsating Roppongi crossing, near which I once had a house, the plot now firmly sat upon by the IBM Tower. And, on the other side of the crossing I can trace, through a maze of alleys I only now see and understand, old Ryudo-cho, a street that long ago lost its venerable name (Dragon's Way) and is now called Roppongi something-or-other, and there to one side the single, pointillist dot that is the car park where Meredith's beautiful old farm house used to stand.

But eventually I tire of my tiresome nostalgia. It is all very well to regret the past, but it is not very practical because it fails to account for the present, and what *is* is always more consequential than what *was*. The present is substantial. It is not there, it is here, and it must be encountered.

This then, Roppongi Hills, is the new Japan, just as Las Vegas is the new U.S.A. In just a number of years every place will look like it, and this kind of economic expediency will be the rule, as will those cute nods in the direction of retro and trad, that comedy team of contemporary design. Here, under the spider, I look into the future which is already here.

Uncollected Journals

These *Japan Journals*—plus their appendices, *Excluded Pages*, *Vita Sexualis*, and *The Persian Journals*—are the only edited journals of Donald Richie, but there are many journal collections. Below is a listing, with some indication of mss. and contents. They are in the Donald Richie Archives, Howard Gotlieb Archival Research Center, Boston University, 771 Commonwealth Avenue, Boston, Massachusetts, U.S.A. 02215

A. 1943–44: paperbound booklet containing mainly thoughts, handwritten.

B. 1945: journal, full-year, wartime travels, bound, leather diary, handwritten.

C. 1945–46: black leather-bound notebook, containing mainly thoughts, dated, handwritten.

D. 1946: paperbound booklet, journal, 1 January–24 March, dated, handwritten.

E. 1953: loose sheets, held by clip, unpaginated, a collection of remembered vignettes from the late 1920s to 1953, titled "A Work in Progress," typed ms.

F. Blue folder containing uncollected travel diaries from 1955 to 1965, typed ms.

G. 1960: brown cloth notebook, mainly travels, handwritten.

H. 1962: two red spiral notebooks containing all the notes that eventually became *The Inland Sea*, handwritten.

I. 1963-64: loose sheets, held by clip, unpaginated, notes to analyst, plus "A Report on Transcopal," typed.

J. 1967: olive cloth-bound notebook containing notes on travels in India, handwritten.

K. *New York Journals*. 1950–52, computerized print-out, manila envelope.

L. *The Persian Journals*. 1992–96, computerized print-out, manila envelope.

M. *Japan Journals*, 1947-96, earlier incomplete version, computerized print-out, manila envelope.

N. *Japan Journals*, 1947–2004, the complete edited journals, some 1,000 pages.

O. There is also a pseudo-journal, a "novel" called *Seventh Voyage*, written 1945–46, paper binder, typewritten. There was another journal-novel called *Fifth Voyage*, which appears to be lost.

Memoir Fragments

Though there are a number of attempts at a memoir, none are completed. These fragments are also now in the Donald Richie Archives, Howard Gotlieb Archival Research Center, Boston University.

A. Family History

B. First Memoirs

C. In-Between

D. Sections of a Child

E. Watching Myself

Index of Names

Includes names of principal people mentioned, as well as historical and literary figures commented upon.

Other books by Donald Richie from Stone Bridge Press

The Inland Sea
ISBN 1-880656-69-8

A Lateral View: Essays on Culture and Style in Contemporary Japan
ISBN 0-9628137-4-5

The Donald Richie Reader: 50 Years of Writing on Japan
edited and with an Introduction by Arturo Silva
ISBN 1-880656-61-2

Tokyo Story: The Ozu/Noda Screenplay by Yasujiro Ozu and Kogo Noda
translated by Donald Richie and Eric Klestadt;
introduction by Donald Richie
ISBN 1-880656-80-9

The Broken Bridge: Fiction from Expatriates in Literary Japan
edited by Suzanne Kamata, introduction by Donald Richie
ISBN 1-880656-31-0